DATE DUE

AGENDA
FOR THE
NATION

AGENDA
FOR THE
NATION

HENRY J. AARON

JAMES M. LINDSAY

PIETRO S. NIVOLA

EDITORS

BROOKINGS INSTITUTION PRESS
Washington, D.C.

Library of Congress Cataloging-in-Publication data
Agenda for the nation / Henry J. Aaron, James M. Lindsay, and
Pietro S. Nivola, eds.
   p.   cm.
Includes bibliographical references and index.
  ISBN 0-8157-0126-8 (cloth : alk. paper)—
  ISBN 0-8157-0127-6 (pbk. : alk. paper)
  1. United States—Economic policy—2001– 2. United States—Economic
conditions—2001– 3. Economic forecasting—United States. 4. United
States—Foreign economic relations. 5. United States—Politics and
government—2001– 6. Pluralism (Social sciences)—United States.
7. Social prediction—United States. 8. Terrorism—United States.
9. Globalization. I. Aaron, Henry J. II. Lindsay, James M., 1959–
III. Nivola, Pietro S.
  HC106.83.A34 2003
  320'.6'0973—dc21   2003011352

9 8 7 6 5 4 3 2 1

The paper used in this publication meets minimum requirements of the
American National Standard for Information Sciences—Permanence of Paper
for Printed Library Materials: ANSI Z39.48-1992.

Typeset in Adobe Garamond

Composition by Cynthia Stock
Silver Spring, Maryland

Printed by R. R. Donnelley
Harrisonburg, Virginia

Contents

Foreword

THIS BOOK IS a quintessential Brookings product. It is, like so much of what we do here, collaborative; it is rooted in work that our scholars have been doing for years, yet it also provides thoughtful, constructive answers to the questions most on the minds of Americans today. It also continues a tradition as old as the institution itself. For more than eighty-five years, Brookings scholars have been thinking and writing about the major public-policy challenges facing the United States—in short, the "agenda for the nation."

Once before, that phrase served as the title of a Brookings volume. It appeared a generation ago, in 1968, when Americans were coping with racial tensions and urban disorders at home and an increasingly unpopular war abroad. Two years later, in 1970, one of my predecessors as president of Brookings, Kermit Gordon, launched an annual publication, *Setting National Priorities*. That series of books was devoted to objective, timely, and lucid analysis of the federal budget. The purpose was to subject the federal budget to closer scrutiny by the citizenry. The project capitalized on Brookings's unique standing as a source of advice on fiscal policy. Our researchers had been instrumental in developing the core ideas that resulted in the Budget and Accounting Act of 1921. From 1962 to 1965, Gordon headed the Bureau of the Budget, and two other Brookings scholars,

Charles Schultze and Alice Rivlin, later served as directors of the bureau and its successor, the Office of Management and Budget. The analysis in *Setting National Priorities* served as an inspiration for the creation of the Congressional Budget Office, of which Alice and another Brookings scholar, Robert Reischauer, were subsequently directors (Bob has gone on to head the Urban Institute).

Setting National Priorities ran for fourteen consecutive years and has been published periodically since then. Brookings experts on governance and foreign policy joined our economists in broadening the scope of the project to look at other national issues. To name just a few: the case for deregulation, increased energy efficiency, health-care rationing, the importance of conventional forces in the nuclear age, and the danger of instability in the Persian Gulf, long before that region was attracting much attention from strategists.

While the focus shifted from year to year, the approach was always anchored in the Brookings commitment to independent, nonpartisan research and, accordingly, a wariness of conventional wisdom, ideology, and party preferences. Looking back over past volumes, I was struck by this sentence from the introduction by Henry Owen and Charles Schultze to the 1976 edition of *Setting National Priorities:* "There is no single truth about the performance, the capacity, and the limitations of government."

This latest version of *Agenda for the Nation* is one of our most comprehensive efforts yet. Planning began almost two years ago, and the book went to press just after Congress had passed a huge tax cut and just as the Bush administration was following up on the war in Iraq with an attempt to re-engage the Israelis and the Palestinians in the peace process. This volume harks back to that original one of 1968 in that it takes a longer perspective. Instead of focusing on immediate national problems facing the nation over a one- or two-year period, it addresses challenges that the country must deal with over the next decade.

This latest collaborative endeavor will, we hope, help citizens and policymakers think their way through the problems and opportunities facing our nation and our increasingly globalized world.

STROBE TALBOTT
President

June 2003
Washington, D.C.

AGENDA
FOR THE
NATION

HENRY J. AARON
JAMES M. LINDSAY
PIETRO S. NIVOLA

1

An Agenda
for the Nation

THE UNITED STATES has entered the twenty-first century in a unique position. The U.S. economy is more than twice the size of that of its nearest competitor. America's armed forces have no rivals. Our scientists are preeminent in most fields. The rest of the world thirsts for U.S. goods and services—from pharmaceutical products, computer software, and the bounty of U.S. farms to blue jeans, fast food, motion pictures, television programs, and popular music—even as it sometimes frets about American cultural and economic domination.

America's unequaled power presents new opportunities to influence the course of history. Whether we make the most of them will depend on how well the nation copes with novel perils and obligations. Brookings first published a collection of essays entitled *Agenda for the Nation* thirty-five years ago. The difficulties the nation faced then differed from those before it today. At home, the efforts to provide equal rights to African Americans, provide a safety net for the poor, and reverse urban decay dominated the agenda. Overseas, the United States sought to contain the Soviet Union, fight an increasingly unpopular war in Vietnam, and salvage the international system of fixed exchange rates.

Many of these troubles have passed or diminished. The Soviet Union is gone. The Vietnam War is a distant memory. International currency exchanges rates fluctuate more or less freely now in response to market forces. African Americans have made substantial economic and social gains. Even if equality remains elusive, race is a less tortured and combustible issue than it once was. Many major cities have revived.

The domestic challenges the United States faces today include encouraging strong sustained economic growth, ensuring fair but affordable access to health care, shoring up retirement income for an aging population, and reconciling energy policies with environmental concerns. In foreign affairs the central task is to use America's unprecedented power wisely and to protect a homeland that has been revealed as shockingly vulnerable.

Such challenges are formidable. Spending on health care, for example, has more than doubled as a share of national output in this country since *Agenda for the Nation* first appeared. Health care now accounts for one dollar in every seven of gross domestic product. At the same time, more than 40 million Americans lack any health insurance at all, and their number is growing. Projections indicate that health care will claim an ever-increasing share of national income as the population ages and as science generates costly revolutionary medical advances. No nation, however prosperous, can afford the staggering cost of adopting every beneficial diagnostic and therapeutic procedure that modern medical science conceives. Even the richest of nations will be burdened by the great expense of servicing an elderly population that is likely to expect not only high-quality medical services, but also adequate public and private pension benefits.

September 11 profoundly sobered the national mood. Whether America prudently confronts the problems it faces or fritters its energies on lesser preoccupations will depend in no small part on the fortitude of American political institutions. Future generations, here and abroad, will look back on the first decades of the twenty-first century and judge whether we Americans properly balanced boldness and wisdom, modesty and self-confidence, patience and daring—whether, that is, we met seriously the demands of the American Age.

Health and Well-Being

The Constitution calls on the government to "promote the general Welfare." How well this responsibility is discharged will determine in no small part the quality of our lives and that of our children's and whether the United States will grow stronger or weaker as a nation.

Economic Growth

America's fortunes both at home and abroad rest on a foundation of strong economic growth. Growth results from improvements in human capital as embodied in the skills and experience of the labor force, from expansion of physical capital in the form of plant and equipment, and from progress in science, engineering, and management. Improvements in the education, experience, and health of American workers were major contributors to America's great economic success in the twentieth century. But, as Bradford DeLong, Claudia Goldin, and Lawrence Katz argue in chapter 2, the prospects for continued improvement of human capital are cloudy. Younger cohorts now are only marginally better educated than baby-boomers. The share of experienced workers in the labor force will diminish as the highly experienced and productive baby boom generation ages and retires. Government assistance can help expand opportunities for education, especially for children from disadvantaged socioeconomic groups.

Increases in physical capital require investment, but a country cannot invest more than it saves or borrows abroad. Relying on borrowing, however, implies that much of the direct return from investment will flow to foreign owners. During the 1990s, U.S. private saving remained low compared with domestic saving in previous decades and with saving in foreign countries. Various public policies have sought to increase private saving in the United States. Unfortunately, they have not succeeded. Large government deficits subtracted from saving in the 1980s and early 1990s. By the mid-1990s, a combination of spending cuts, tax increases, and resurgent productivity growth had converted deficits to surpluses. Domestically financed investment boomed. Then the 2001 tax cut, a recession, and increased defense spending following September 11, 2001, halted the brief interlude of budget surpluses. Heavy borrowing to finance the government's budgetary shortfalls and the erosion of national saving resumed. Prospects for continued large additions to the U.S.-owned stock of physical capital are thus unclear.

Additions to the stock of knowledge probably provide the best hope for long-range economic expansion. The revolutions in computers and communications at first seemed to do little to boost productivity, but they sharply increased it in the late 1990s. The biomedical revolution based on molecular biology is emerging as a major potential force for economic growth and human welfare. No recipe for promoting economic growth is foolproof, but low saving and failure to improve human resources can assuredly discourage it. DeLong, Goldin, and Katz argue that our best shot is to make sure that Americans from all backgrounds are well educated, that fiscal policy does not divert private saving from productive investments, and that public and private support for science is sustained.

Inequality

The U.S. economy is growing, but unevenly. Some Americans are enjoying enormous increases in their incomes, others almost none. What are the likely consequences of the nation's increased economic inequality? Gary Burtless and Christopher Jencks tackle this question in chapter 3. In the year 2000, they report, inequality was higher than it had been for sixty years. Virtually all income growth during the boom times of the 1990s was concentrated among the fortunate top 10 percent of the income distribution, particularly among the top 1 percent. The main reason for rising *income* inequality is increasing *earnings* inequality. Technological change has increased the relative compensation of the well educated, who were already at the top of the earnings distribution. Immigration has also swelled the ranks of the poorly educated and poorly paid.

How much inequality matters, and what, if anything, government should do about it, remain perplexing questions. Burtless and Jencks observe that inequality does not appear to be correlated with the growth rates of economies. The evidence is unclear whether inequality diminishes the chances of low-income children to climb the economic ladder. The impact inequality may have on health and longevity is at best small. Nonetheless, economic inequality probably helps tilt political influence in favor of the wealthy.

Government Spending and Taxes

America's continuing ability to sustain its public commitments—domestic and foreign—requires sound management of public finances. As Alan Auerbach and his coauthors show in chapter 4, current public policy is failing this test. In January 2001 the Congressional Budget Office had projected a $5.6 trillion budget surplus over the decade from 2002 to 2011. Two years later that projected surplus had turned into a projected deficit of almost $400 billion. The sources of the deterioration are clear—a mixture of recession, increased spending (in part owing to security-related exigencies following September 11, 2001), and reduced revenues resulting from large tax cuts. Even the official projections understate the probable shortfall because they are based on questionable assumptions and methods. In particular, they assume unrealistically low rates of growth in government spending and unrealistically high revenue.

Under more plausible assumptions, the projected budget deficits would cumulate to approximately $1.1 trillion over the period from 2004 to 2013. Auerbach and his associates argue that immediate measures should be taken to reverse the medium- and long-term deficits. Failure to do so will impede economic growth over the long run. Thriftier fiscal policy now is important also because the first baby boomers will become eligible for Social Security benefits beginning in 2008 and for Medicare in 2011. Federal budget obligations for the elderly and disabled will climb steadily for three decades thereafter.

Health

As Victor Fuchs and Alan Garber explain in chapter 5, the health of U.S. residents is better now than it has ever been, but worse on average than that of residents of many other developed nations. The reason the health of Americans lags behind that of residents of several other rich nations is not that Americans spend too little on health care. Indeed, *per capita* health care spending in the United States in 1999 was 77 percent greater than it was in Canada, the second-biggest spender in the world. Moreover, expenditures are certain to grow. Technological advances promise to continue extending the already lavish menu of medical interventions. A confusing multiplicity of payment mechanisms, public and private, means that payers lack sufficient leverage over how much is spent on health care. The largest public programs—Medicare (for the aged and disabled) and Medicaid (for the indigent)—face sharply rising costs that will strain or outrun current revenue sources.

Further complicating matters, more than 40 million people were uninsured in 2001, and the ranks of the uninsured are growing. The lack of insurance, long a serious problem, has been tolerable only because physicians and hospitals have been willing and able to provide uncompensated care to the uninsured. The continuing availability of uncompensated care is now in jeopardy. Public and private payers are trying to limit payments for patients to no more than the actual cost of care. Such hard bargaining is to be expected in the context of sharp medical cost increases. However, the decline in uncompensated care could leave the uninsured bereft of care.

Fuchs and Garber stress the vast potential for medical innovation to improve the quality and availability of care. Progress in basic science means that the prospects for medical breakthroughs have never been better. A possible dark side of the flood of highly beneficial but pricey advances is that costs could increase so much that access to the latest treatments would be limited to the wealthy and to the well insured. Should this risk become reality, Fuchs and Garber warn, the United States and other rich nations would confront moral and political choices of extraordinary complexity. Because not everyone will have access to all beneficial care, the authors suggest, ethically troubling choices will be inescapable in the future. Fuchs and Garber recommend a major national commitment to a center that would systematically assess the gains and costs from new technologies.

Pensions

The federal government's deteriorating budgetary picture and the aging of the baby boom generation raise important questions about what kind of financial security Americans can expect in their retirement years. Social Security and its well-known projected long-term deficit have been the object of much study and debate. As William Gale and Peter Orszag note in chapter 6, the other two pillars of retirement income—private saving and pensions—have received far less attention but also face severe stresses. The private saving rate has plummeted over the past two decades. Half of all workers—and most low-income workers—have no pension at all. The shift from defined benefit plans, which guarantee retirees a percentage of past average earnings, raises additional concerns about the security of the pensions that workers are now accruing.

Workers are increasingly covered entirely or predominantly by defined contribution plans, under which employers deposit a percentage of workers' earnings in individually owned accounts that workers may invest subject to certain guidelines. How much workers with defined contribution plans have at retirement depends not only on what they earned during their working years, but also on how skillfully they invested and how well financial markets performed. Even sophisticated investors make mistakes or suffer bad luck. Inexperienced workers, especially those with few assets other than their pensions, are particularly vulnerable to financial devastation from such error or bad luck.

The prospects for constructive near-term action to shore up the Social Security system for the long term are not promising. Gale and Orszag hold out somewhat greater hopes for reform of private pensions. They review leading proposals for sweeping overhauls, but suggest that more modest incremental changes might achieve more. These changes would enable workers to allocate part of *future* pay raises to saving plans, discourage workers from withdrawing money from retirement accounts before they retire, and improve financial education and investment advice for workers. Such actions might raise the chances that workers would reach retirement with sufficient assets to sustain their preretirement standards of living.

Diversity

Three decades of increased immigration are remaking America's racial and ethnic mix. A country conditioned to think of diversity in terms of black and white continues to be enriched by other hues, as James Lindsay and Audrey Singer explain in chapter 7. The percentage of Americans who identify themselves as "Hispanic" nearly doubled between 1980 and 2000, while the percentage who identify themselves as "Asian" more than doubled. Meanwhile, the percentage of Americans who identify themselves as multiracial also continues to grow.

The rapidity of America's demographic changes has heightened fears that immigration might undermine America's social cohesion. Some fear that newcomers will not integrate into mainstream society as readily as past immigrants did, and they fear that national unity will suffer as a result. Yet Lindsay and Singer foresee no looming immigration crisis. Although today's immigrants mostly hail from outside of Europe and Americans seem to have become more tolerant of cultural differences, the forces of assimilation are nearly as strong today as they were early in the twentieth century, the time of America's last great influx of newcomers. Lindsay and Singer acknowledge that immigration creates stresses, but suggest that the remedy is to assist immigrants once they arrive, not to keep them out. Government and civil society can do much to encourage immigrants to become citizens, help their economic advancement, and defuse the social tensions that may arise when newcomers rapidly reshape existing communities.

Energy and the Environment

Energy and environmental policies are inextricably linked, as Howard Gruenspecht and Paul Portney point out in chapter 8. Yet the federal government is not organized to reflect this interdependence. Instead, authority is spread across many poorly coordinated agencies: the Department of Transportation handles fuel economy standards; the Environmental Protection Agency has responsibility for vehicle emissions standards; the

Treasury Department has the lead in setting any energy tax policy. All these bureaus have more say about the nation's consumption of oil than does the Department of Energy (DOE).

Gruenspecht and Portney argue that the diffusion of authority for energy and environmental management across multiple agencies imposes substantial penalties. It prevents government from identifying and resolving policy conflicts, and it hampers efforts to design strategies that would harmonize energy and environmental objectives.

While a wholesale government reorganization might improve the situation, Gruenspecht and Portney dismiss that idea as politically unrealistic and excessively disruptive. They focus instead on more modest organizational reforms that would improve interagency coordination and the effectiveness of DOE. The authors would reorganize the department's own programs, move some programs currently located elsewhere into DOE, and require policy and regulatory shops in different cabinet departments to assess how their proposed actions would affect energy and environmental goals. Gruenspecht and Portney believe that such organizational changes, although comparatively modest, would improve the policymaking process.

America's Security and Global Role

Americans felt relieved and triumphant at the end of the cold war. But the euphoria ceased on September 11, 2001. The United States is now engaged in another war, confronting the twin threats of tyrannical states and stateless terrorists, plus a host of other destabilizing global forces.

Foreign Policy

Charting a wise course for U.S. foreign policy in the twenty-first century must begin with a sophisticated understanding of the nature of the modern world. Ivo Daalder and James Lindsay explain in chapter 9 that America has entered a new age of global politics. This new age has two defining and often conflicting features. One is America's dominance. Without U.S. leadership or active participation, many, perhaps most, international endeavors—from trade liberalization to suppressing local aggression—are likely to falter. The other distinctive feature is globalization. The increasingly close linkage of all parts of the world has unleashed economic, political, and social forces beyond the capacity of any one country, including the United States, to control.

Daalder and Lindsay note that the foreign policy debate in the United States does not turn on whether the United States should be actively engaged abroad. Most Americans, regardless of their political affiliation, recognize that U.S. well-being is enhanced by the spread of economic freedom and political democracy—and that America has a large role to play in furthering these ends. Instead, the foreign policy debate is over the means. And that in turn is primarily a debate over the relative importance of the two defining features of global politics.

One viewpoint, which Daalder and Lindsay label *Hegemonist*, sees the primacy of military and economic power as the key to securing U.S. interests. Hegemonists believe the United States should unabashedly exercise its power to protect or promote those interests. Hegemonists see formal international arrangements as complicating rather than enabling this effort. Another view, which Daalder and Lindsay label *Globalist*, contends that globalization both expands the list of foreign policy problems and limits the effectiveness of American power to deal with them unilaterally. Globalists reject the unilateralism of Hegemonists and emphasize working through international institutions and adherence to international law. This conflict was transparent in the dispute within the Bush administration and in the larger foreign policy community over whether it was important to secure the approval of the UN Security Council to use force against the Iraqi regime of Saddam Hussein. Hegemonists saw such approval as unnecessary. Globalists believed it to be crucial for the legitimacy of any military action.

What both Hegemonists and Globalists miss, Daalder and Lindsay argue, is that any successful foreign policy in the age of global politics must combine elements of both power *and* cooperation. Power helps the United States achieve its goals abroad. Washington must be willing to assert its primacy in defense of core interests, even if it sometimes angers friends and allies. Yet a policy based on indiscriminate muscle flexing will not work. The U.S. military was fully capable of winning the military war in Iraq without aid from other nations, but winning the subsequent peace will require broad international involvement. The solution of this and other problems requires mutual cooperation, which will become increasingly difficult to secure if other countries perceive Washington as indifferent to their interests. Preventing such perceptions from spreading requires America to use its power in concert with friends and allies, to strive to increase the efficacy of international rules and institutions, to forge new structures of cooperation to deal with emerging difficulties and opportunities, and to ensure that agreed rules and norms are effectively enforced.

Foreign Economic Policy

America's prosperity is inextricably tied to that of other nations. This reality, as Lael Brainard and Robert Litan stress in chapter 10, creates for the United States an interest in improving the economic prospects of poorer countries, in expanding trade, and in reforming the rules that regulate the flows of capital across national borders. Brainard and Litan acknowledge that reversing the decades-long decline in U.S. spending on foreign aid will not necessarily buy much relief from terrorist threats, but the authors make a strong case for greater generosity toward poor countries on humanitarian grounds. No amount of aid will help lift countries out of poverty, however, if funds are misused. The return on investment is reasonably dependable in areas such as public health, sanitation, and education. Tossing money at projects with a glamorous profile—dams, highways, and factories—is too often wasteful.

Furthermore, no amount of foreign aid, no matter how skillfully distributed, can do as much for poor countries as could a U.S. willingness to open world markets to their exports. Nevertheless, continued liberalization of multilateral trade is a contentious issue everywhere, as attested by the shaky start to the current round of multilateral trade talks organized under the banner of the World Trade Organization. Given the friction among major trading partners, the United States often has turned toward bilateral deals in which U.S. negotiators can maximize their leverage. Brainard and Litan warn that Washington should mostly resist this temptation. Bilateral accords may divert trade from third parties, reduce international specialization, and retard rather than encourage global economic growth. The United States would be wiser to make broad multilateral agreements its top priority and take steps to reduce trade barriers in sectors such as agriculture, services, and labor-intensive manufactures that traditionally have been shielded from foreign competition.

A smoothly functioning international trading regime also requires stable financial markets. International financial crises have repeatedly rattled world markets in recent years. The pattern is familiar. A nation borrows heavily abroad. It accumulates an unsustainable debt. Its currency collapses. Severe economic disruption ensues. Globalization has increased the risk that such crises will damage the global financial system. The United States and other rich nations have responded to these crises by insisting that troubled countries curb their unsound practices and offering assistance if they do. Brainard and Litan propose that these policies be supplemented by enlisting the cooperation of private investors in efforts to avert emergencies. The authors also warn that America's large and persistent trade deficits are coming to threaten international economic stability. Correcting the U.S. trade imbalance will probably require a considerable decline in the value of the dollar relative to other major currencies. If that adjustment is not managed well, widespread global economic dislocations could ensue.

Defense

Does the United States have the right defense orientation and force structure at this critical stage in history? In the main it does, concludes Michael O'Hanlon in chapter 11. American military power dwarfs that of its nearest competitors. Some other militaries are larger, but none can match U.S. forces in technology, equipment, and training. U.S. military supremacy serves not only American interests, O'Hanlon argues, but also those of most other countries. The U.S. military provides the glue that holds alliances together and the stability necessary for the world's major economies to flourish. No other country or coalition of countries is prepared to share much of this burden. Proposals to reduce U.S. defense capabilities substantially may seem attractive in a time of growing federal budget deficits. However, O'Hanlon argues, they would do more harm than good. Instead, prudence calls for modest increases in defense spending. Equipment bought during the 1980s needs to be replaced or refurbished, and the war against terrorism, among other contingencies, is placing greater demands on the military.

While some additional U.S. defense spending is justified, O'Hanlon argues that large increases are not. The United States spent roughly $350 billion on defense in 2002. The Bush administration projects increasing that amount until real defense spending reaches about $500 billion in 2009. O'Hanlon maintains that spending of such magnitude is unnecessary. In his view, it is possible to hold the line on defense spending at roughly $400 billion a year in real terms, excluding the immediate costs of the Iraq war and the costs of stabilization operations in Iraq and Afghanistan.

O'Hanlon offers several suggestions for how the Bush administration could moderate its proposed boost in defense spending. One is to further exploit technological advances in electronics, sensors, and munitions to modernize existing systems. That approach allows for economical and effective innovations—as seen in the war in Afghanistan, where aging B-52 bombers dropped smart bombs that were guided to their targets by state-of-the-art targeting and communications systems in the hands of soldiers on the ground. Second, the Bush administration should be more selective in acquiring new generations of weapons systems. O'Hanlon criticizes the Bush administration for relying too heavily on replacing major combat systems with new ones that are unnecessarily costly. A third suggestion has to do with military compensation, which has never been higher in inflation-adjusted dollars than it is today. That means that in most instances the growth rate in military compensation does not need to be much higher than the inflation rate. Finally, O'Hanlon recommends that the growth of spending on operations and maintenance be reduced by, among other things, closing unneeded military bases and reforming military health-care services.

None of these changes would dramatically change U.S. defense policy. However, in O'Hanlon's view, the decisive victory of American-led forces in the Iraq war demonstrates that radical changes in the size or composition of the U.S. military are unnecessary. The fact that U.S. troops were highly trained and well equipped enabled them to oust Saddam Hussein from power in less than a month and with fewer allied casualties than were incurred during the Persian Gulf war. What is needed in place of a major restructuring is prudent action to reduce defense costs. Smart cost-cutting in the defense budget has considerable virtue given the huge fiscal deficits looming in the years ahead.

Terrorism

September 11 introduced Americans to what Steven Simon in chapter 12 calls the "new" terrorism. Secular concerns motivated "old'" terrorist groups, such as the Irish Republican Army and the Palestinian Liberation Organization. In contrast, religious zealotry drives members of al Qaeda and other similar groups. They see apocalyptic conflict with nonbelievers as a route to redemption. Al Qaeda's extreme and violent militancy draws on a messianic strand in Islamic thinking that dates back nearly a millennium but that is not shared by most Muslims. This dimension is what makes al Qaeda more dangerous than most other terrorist organizations.

Attempts to blunt al Qaeda's appeal by addressing supposed "root causes" such as economic stagnation, illiteracy, and political repression may be desirable, Simon argues, but they are unlikely to help much in the near term. The United States, for now, should concentrate on reducing its vulnerability to terrorism through actions. These actions combine offensive strategies abroad and defensive ones at home. We need improved intelligence and covert capabilities. We also need to improve our law enforcement capabilities, prevent terrorists from obtaining weapons of mass destruction, better protect high-value targets, and increase the capacity to mitigate the effects of terrorist attacks when they do occur. Technology offers some promise for making this tall order easier to accomplish.

Simon observes, however, that the United States will also need to pursue broader strategies for dealing with the new terrorism. Cooperation with other countries is and will remain essential to tracking and disrupting terrorist operations: it may even be necessary to sacrifice some U.S. interests to help preserve that cooperation. The Israeli-Palestinian peace process should be revived and gradual democratization encouraged in the Arab world. Pushing for rapid political change in the Arab world would be unwise, in Simon's view, but so too is indefinite support of prowestern autocrats.

Security and Civil Liberties

Among the troubling questions raised by the catastrophic terrorist attacks launched against the United States is this: Do some of the traditional personal freedoms that Americans enjoy conflict with the measures to promote domestic security? In chapter 13 Stuart Taylor grapples with this dilemma. He suggests that the pre-September 11 balance between civil liberties and personal security warrants considerable revision. The American people now have legitimate reason to grant government expanded investigative powers. Critics often exaggerate the dangers that such powers pose to our core freedoms. Security, after all, is a *precondition* for liberty.

Taylor suggests that investigative powers ought to be extended to include additional electronic surveillance, aggressive interrogation (but not torture), and even preventive detention under well-defined circumstances. He also doubts that law enforcement authorities can entirely forgo some forms of "profiling" if, for example, the screening of airline passengers is to be effective.

Taylor acknowledges that the steps he is proposing require safeguards to minimize abuse. He deplores the continued detention of hundreds of foreign-born residents arrested in the United States since September 11 on suspicion of having ties to al Qaeda. To limit the government's misuse of its new security powers, he recommends that Congress write legislation carefully spelling out allowable procedures. Taylor emphasizes that even if all the changes he outlines were adopted, Americans would continue to enjoy more civil liberties than are available to the people of almost any other nation.

Politics and Governance

The contributors to this book put forward an extensive set of tasks for the government to perform in coming years. Will our political institutions rise to the occasion? The authors of the last two chapters ponder this question.

Toward Political Sobriety

In chapter 14, Pietro Nivola finds that an introspective public mood following America's triumph in the cold war, intensified party competition, and the news media's emphasis on petty or parochial subjects contributed to a trivialization of the nation's political dialogue over the past decade. Palace intrigue, arcane legal inquests, and bitter disputes over mundane domestic matters became routine. Civility in public life became a casualty. The federal government increasingly became immersed in quotidian matters that typically occupy local authorities. Partisan wrangling, frequently over questions of symbolic rather than substantive significance, became more pronounced. The result was a distracted and overextended government—one that, Nivola contends, devoted something less than adequate attention to the nation's highest priorities, including the security of its citizens.

Today Nivola sees heartening signs that the nation is moving away from "small matters" and reengaging "great causes," as President George W. Bush remarked in his January 2002 State of the Union address. The continuing aftershock of September 11, 2001, and Saddam Hussein's dangerous defiance of United Nations resolutions over the past dozen years led the United States to insist on Iraq's disarmament. How the U.S. government will contend simultaneously with the latest lethal threat from North Korea is less clear as this book goes to press. More generally, the durability of whatever transformation has occurred in American politics remains to be tested. Certainly, the merits of more tax cuts even as projected deficits soar, terrorist activity persists, and military commitments proliferate are debatable.

Further corrections in the U.S. political process may be desirable to fortify the capacity of the federal government to meet the responsibilities this nation must confront over the long haul. The correctives, Nivola writes, probably have to include additional adjustments in the party system and the nature of electoral campaigns, the uses of opinion polling, the process of recruitment for the public service, and, perhaps most important, the division of labor between national and local levels of government. In the absence of such improvements, Nivola worries that the United States gradually might lapse back into what he calls "low politics"—where the energies of national policymakers are diverted to narrow expediencies, new rounds of partisan squabbling, and ventures not befitting a serious central government.

Looking Backward, Looking Forward

Alone among the authors in this volume, James Q. Wilson also contributed to the first edition of *Agenda for the Nation*. In chapter 15, he surveys developments over the intervening thirty-five years. He notes that much has changed and, in his view, not always for the better. The federal government has delved into so many of society's supposed "problems" that arguably its agenda now is overloaded. The rise of divided government and growing distrust between Democrats and Republicans have polarized Congress, hindered efforts to reach sensible compromises, and often produced an excess of detailed, prescriptive legislation. Federal courts have taken on an increasingly prominent policymaking role, deciding issues once left to the political branches and sometimes assuming effective control of local-government agencies. Voters show less confidence in government officials, in part because the officials appear to dissipate resources on countless secondary undertakings rather than focusing effectively on society's central needs.

Despite this unsettling assessment, Wilson regards the American political system as generally resilient. The problem is not, as some would have it, that we are saddled with an eighteenth century constitution ill-suited to the demands of the twenty-first century. Through the history of the republic, our government has usually managed to act decisively in times of major crisis. Wilson—and the editors of this book—are cautiously optimistic that now will be no exception.

No book, even one presumptuous enough to propose an agenda for the nation, can speak to every important issue government must address. Many readers no doubt would add to our list of priorities, though we think few would casually subtract from it. Many readers no doubt also would disagree with the arguments some of our contributors make in the following essays. Indeed, not all of the views expressed here are congenial even to all of this volume's editors. Our hope, nonetheless, is that the essays in this book will help inform debates on how the United States government can effectively serve its citizens and meet its global responsibilities.

J. BRADFORD DELONG
CLAUDIA GOLDIN
LAWRENCE F. KATZ

2

Sustaining U.S. Economic Growth

AFTER TWO DECADES in the economic doldrums, the U.S. economy revived strongly in the late 1990s, as the rate of productivity growth doubled. Although continued rapid growth during the next several decades is certainly possible, it is not assured—and the stakes are enormous. This chapter outlines what is known about the sources of U.S. economic growth and describes steps that policymakers—public and private—can take to realize the potential for growth.[1]

Economic Growth: Benefits, Costs, and Uncertainties

Rapid economic growth boosts private incomes and government revenues, and thereby expands options for both private and collective action. Increased output permits people—through their private, individual decisions and through government action—to boost consumption, lower tax rates, extend or enrich schooling, clean up the environment, strengthen national defense, or tackle other goals. In contrast, slow economic growth appears to foster diminished national expectations and political gridlock.[2] From 1973 through the mid-1990s, for example, a lower growth rate in private incomes—and the resulting decrease in the growth rate of tax revenues—constrained the federal government's capacity to undertake costly projects. Advocates of small government may regard such constraints as benign, but it was the relatively conservative president George H. W. Bush who lamented at his inauguration, in 1989, that Americans "have more will than wallet."[3] And it was during his administration and that of his predecessor, Ronald Reagan, that large government deficits diverted private savings from growth-enhancing investments to finance government consumption. Indeed, sluggish revenue growth was among the factors that prevented the Bush administration from constructive responses to the end of the cold war and the fall of communism in Eastern Europe. Whether or not the administration had the will, it did not have the wallet to fund government actions that could have expanded opportunity in America.

Policies to improve economic growth prospects typically involve a trade-off between known present costs and uncertain future benefits. The investments that contribute to growth come at the price of resources diverted from current consumption. To add to the complexity of the undertaking, contemporary understanding of economic growth—what makes it vary over time and how it is affected by public policy—is quite incomplete.

Beginning in the early 1970s, for example, the growth of U.S. productivity (as measured by output per person-hour worked in nonfarm business) fell by more than half, from an average of 2.8 percent a year between 1947 and 1973 to 1.3 percent a year from 1973 to 1995. If productivity had continued growing from 1973 to 1995 at its previous trend rate, output per worker would have been 38 percent higher in 1995 than it actually was. Although the drop in the productivity growth rate was a watershed event, its causes remain somewhat mysterious and are the subject of continuing dispute.[4] Many analysts believe they have a better fix on why growth rebounded in the second half of the 1990s and resumed its pre-1973 pace. They believe that the cause of speed-up in productivity growth was the technological revolution in data processing and data communications, yet few if any had forecast such a speed-up.[5]

What is fairly certain, however, is that three broad factors have played major roles in long-run American economic growth. Human capital—the combination of the formal knowledge and practical skills acquired by the labor force—is the first. Physical capital—the machines, buildings, and infrastructure that increase productivity and embody much of our collective technological knowledge—is the second. The third is the body of ideas that encompasses modern technology and management techniques. This body of ideas is the principal reason we are so much more affluent than our forebears were. Ideas—and the technology that derives from them—are the primary long-term cause of economic growth. Nevertheless, beyond maintaining secure property rights, government policy may have its largest effect on economic growth by facilitating additions to human capital—that is, to education and skills.

Human-capital policy represents a crucial lever on growth for three reasons. First, increases in educational investment have been a major source of American economic growth for at least the past century and a principal cause of America's economic edge over other industrial nations in the twentieth century. Second, more is known about the effects of human-capital policies than about the effects of policies intended to increase physical capital investment or the stock of ideas. Third, and probably most important, efforts to upgrade the knowledge and skills of America's workers promise not only to increase output but to lower income inequality. The ultimate goal of economic growth should be not only to expand output but to distribute that output so that as many Americans as possible can lead better lives.

This chapter examines trends for each of the three major drivers of U.S. economic growth—human-capital formation, investment in physical capital, and technological progress—and offers recommendations for encouraging growth in each area.

Investment in Human Capital

Ever since the industrial revolution, "capital" has been central to a nation's economic growth. In the preindustrial age, land and other natural resources largely determined a nation's economic capacity; sometime in the nineteenth century, this role was usurped by physical capital. During the twentieth century, human capital accumulated through formal schooling became a key to economic growth. In determining a nation's success in the increasingly knowledge-driven economy of the twenty-first century, human capital is likely to remain crucial.

Investments in human capital—including formal schooling, on-the-job training, and opportunities for informal learning—directly contribute to economic growth by increasing the productivity, or "quality," of a nation's work force. (We caution that *quality* used in this sense implies nothing about people's innate characteristics; it refers only to their economic contributions as valued in the marketplace.) Education and training also contribute to technological advance, because scientists, managers, and other highly trained and experienced workers are instrumental to the creation and application of new ideas. A better educated work force, furthermore, facilitates the adoption and diffusion of new technologies.[6]

Although almost all modern governments maintain schools, subsidize educational investments, and mandate some minimum level of education, not all governments have always viewed investments in schooling alike. For example, most of the early twentieth century industrial powerhouses were not favorably disposed to mass education beyond primary schooling. In Europe during the first half of the twentieth century, secondary and postsecondary schooling were either for the elite, as in France and England, or bifurcated, as in Germany, where those who did well or had resources could attend the upper grades and others did apprenticeships.

Not so in America. With few exceptions, schooling in America was for the masses throughout the twentieth century. It was publicly funded by large numbers of fiscally independent districts. In constrast to schooling in other industrialized nations, American public education has historically been open, sex-neutral, primarily academic rather than industrial and vocational, and subject to secular control.[7]

America in the Human-Capital Century

The United States led the world in mass education during the nineteenth century and substantially widened its lead over much of the twentieth century. It forged ahead by instituting mass secondary schooling early in the twentieth century and by establishing a flexible and multifaceted higher education system.[8] And early in the twentieth century, the United States achieved the world's highest per capita income—a position that it maintained for the remainder of that century.[9] The twentieth century can thus be thought of not only as the "American century" but as the "human-capital century."

The twentieth century became the human-capital century because of wide-ranging changes in business, industry, and technology that increased the demand for particular cognitive skills.[10] The early twentieth century rise of big business and of large retail, insurance, and banking operations, for example, generated increased demand for literate and numerate office workers. As technological changes—in industries ranging from petroleum refining to food processing—intensified the use of science in industry, demand increased not only for professionals and office workers but for educated blue-collar workers. The relative value of workers who could read blueprints and knew algebra, geometry, chemistry, and some physics increased enormously with electrification, with the spread of the internal combustion engine, and with the increased use of complex chemical processes. Farmers who understood chemistry, botany, and accounting had a competitive edge over their less educated neighbors. Education beyond the elementary grades was no longer just for the professionals. It was for all.

Secondary education paid high returns, and youths responded by continuing on to the upper grades. In 1915, the earliest year for which estimates have been made, each additional year of high school increased earnings by about 12 percent.[11] These high returns and the rising need for more educated workers greatly increased the demand for education. But until World War I, more than 50 percent of Americans lived in rural areas. Meeting the increased demand for education required costly investments to build schools and hire teachers—and local governments and school districts, many of them quite small, made these investments. Thus in the United States the highly decentralized system of financing education permitted the diffusion of mass secondary schooling, whereas in Europe centralized school systems were less responsive to local demands for further schooling and hampered the initial spread of mass secondary education.

Greater secondary school completion rates increased attendance at colleges and universities. Higher education in the United States had been a patchwork quilt of public, private, secular, religious, coed, and single-sex institutions from its beginnings in the seventeenth century. But as the demand for higher education increased, the role of the public sector in tertiary schooling expanded: over the course of the twentieth century, the proportion of students enrolled in public four-year schools soared from 20 to 70 percent.[12]

Toward the end of the twentieth century, however, the rate of increase in years of schooling declined substantially in the United States. Beginning with the cohorts born around 1950, the growth in educational attainment for native-born Americans slowed perceptibly (see figure 2-1). By the 1980s, this slowdown had translated into a reduced rate of increase in the educational attainment of the American labor force. Because the increasing quality of the labor force contributed significantly to economic growth in the United States throughout most of the twentieth century, the slowdown in the growth of educational attainment threatens to retard future economic growth. Moreover, because the slowdown has been concentrated among youth from minority and lower-income households, it also threatens to increase economic inequality. The deceleration of growth in educational attainment has occurred despite rising economic returns to education during the past twenty years. Meanwhile, progress in educational attainment elsewhere has continued apace. Among the advanced member nations of the Organization for Economic Cooperation and Development, the level of educational attainment is now increasing more rapidly in nations other than the United States, and the educational attainment of young American adults now lags that of young adults in some other countries.[13]

Educational Advance in the Twentieth Century

An ideal measure of human capital would not be limited to formal schooling. It would also include parental and other child care during the preschool years, training in commercial and vocational institutions, on-the-job training, and learning in informal settings. But because such an ideal measure does not exist, we measure human capital by the number of years of formal schooling or the highest grade attained.[14]

Americans born in 1975 spent nearly twice as many years in school— 14.1 years versus 7.4 years, an increase of 6.7 years—as did Americans born a century earlier (see figure 2-1).[15] For cohorts born between 1876 and 1951, the increase was 6.2 years, or 0.82 years a decade. Educational attainment was then roughly constant for cohorts born between 1951 and 1961, and it increased by only 0.5 years for cohorts born between 1961 and 1975.

About one-half of the overall increase in educational attainment over the twentieth century is attributable to the increase in high school attendance and graduation, and about one-quarter is attributable to the increase in college and postcollege education. Thus the spread of mass secondary schooling, a movement that began in earnest around 1910, was responsible for much of the increase in the educational attainment of native-born Americans in the twentieth century.

At the start of the period for cohorts born in the late 1870s, the gap in educational attainment between whites and African Americans was 3.6 years; and on average white students spent nearly twice as long in school as did black students. Beginning with the cohorts born around 1910, the gap began to close (figure 2-1). The convergence slowed for cohorts born between 1940 and 1960 and slowed further for those born since 1960. The black-white schooling gap for recent cohorts (those born in the 1970s) is 0.6 years—one-sixth of what it was a century ago. The current gap in educational attainment between non-Hispanic whites and Hispanics—2.3 years for those born 1970 to 1975—is nearly four times larger than that between whites and blacks.[16] Because Hispanics are a large and

Figure 2-1. *Years of Schooling by Birth Cohort, U.S. Natives by Race, 1876–1975*[a]

Years of schooling at age 35

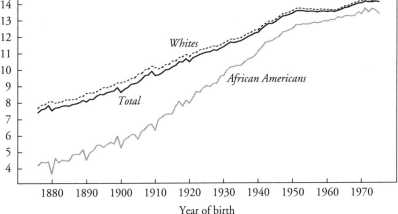

Year of birth

Sources: 1940–90 Integrated Public Use Microsamples (IPUMS) of the U.S. federal population censuses; 1999 and 2000 Current Population Survey (CPS) Merged Outgoing Rotation Group (MORG) samples.

a. Figure plots mean years of completed schooling for native-born residents by birth cohort at thirty-five years of age (data for cohorts not observed at exactly this age were adjusted to age thirty-five). For the 1940–80 samples, years of schooling are given by the highest grade completed, top coded at eighteen years. Those with seventeen years of schooling in 1940 and 1950 (the highest category in those years) were assigned 17.6 years of schooling (the mean for those with seventeen or eighteen years of schooling in 1960). The categorical education variable for the 1990, 1999, and 2000 samples was converted to years of completed schooling. Categories covering more than a single grade were translated as follows: 2.5 years for those in the first through fourth grade category; 6.5 years for those in the fifth through eighth grade categories; twelve years for those with twelve years of schooling, a general equivalency diploma, or a high school diploma; fourteen years for those with some college or an associate's degree; sixteen years for those with a bachelor's degree; 17.6 years for those with a master's degree; and eighteen years for those with a professional or doctoral degree.

To age-adjust reported years of schooling, we used the proportional life-cycle change in reported years of schooling for U.S. birth cohorts from 1876 to 1975. Specifically, we collapsed the data into birth cohort-year cells. We then ran a regression of log mean years of schooling on a full set of birth cohort dummies and a quartic in age, pooling all the samples from 1940 to 2000 for native-born residents aged twenty-five to sixty-four (covering birth cohorts from 1876 to 1975). The age coefficients from this regression were used to create age-adjusted measures of schooling evaluated at age thirty-five. For birth cohorts observed at age thirty-five in one of our sample years, we used actual mean years of schooling at that age. For cohorts not observed in our samples at exactly age thirty-five, we adjusted to that age the mean years of schooling for the observed year closest to age thirty-five (or to the average of the closest pair of years in the case of a tie). The results are quite similar if we average the age-adjusted years of schooling of a birth cohort across all the years we observe the cohort.

Figure 2-2. *Years of Schooling by Birth Cohort, U.S. Natives by Sex, 1876–1975*[a]

Years of schooling at age 35

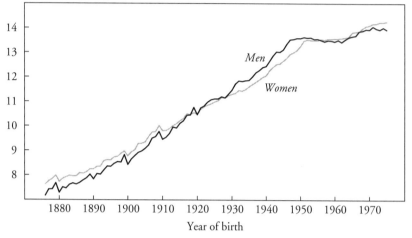

Year of birth

Sources: 1940 to 1990 IPUMS of the U.S. population censuses; 1999 and 2000 CPS MORG samples.

a. Using the approach described in the notes to figure 2-1, the figure plots the mean years of completed schooling for native-born residents by birth cohort and sex, adjusted to age thirty-five.

rapidly growing share of the U.S. labor force, their level of educational attainment is critically important for future American productivity.[17]

Men and women spent similar amounts of time in school *on average* over the twentieth century (figure 2-2), but men born before about 1955 were more likely to graduate from college (figure 2-3). Male college graduation rates surged for the peak World War II draft cohorts, born from the early 1920s, and continued to grow rapidly for the Korean War draft cohorts. The expansion in college graduation rates reflects, in part, the educational benefits provided by the G.I. Bill, which were available to the (mostly) male veterans of World War II and the Korean War.[18] College graduation rates for men again soared during the Vietnam War, as young men sought to avoid the draft through student deferments. When the draft ended, in 1973, the rate at which men graduated from college plummeted, only to rise again in the face of rising labor market returns to education in

Figure 2-3. *Graduation from College by Birth Cohort, U.S. Natives by Sex, 1876–1975*[a]

Fraction college graduate at age thirty-five

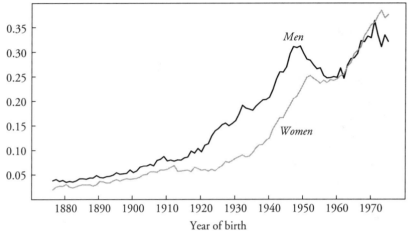

Year of birth

Sources: 1940 to 1990 IPUMS of the U.S. population censuses; 1999 and 2000 CPS MORG samples.

a. The figure plots the fraction of native-born college graduates by birth cohort and sex adjusted to age thirty-five. For the 1940–80 samples, college graduates were defined as those who had completed sixteen or more years of schooling; for the 1990–2000 samples, college graduates were defined as those who had a bachelor's degree or higher. The log of the college graduation rate for a birth cohort-year cell is the dependent variable in the age-adjustment regressions. The adjustment approach was the same as that described in the notes to figure 2-1.

the 1980s (which were apparent for cohorts who had been born in the early 1960s). Women's rates of graduation closely follow those of men, with some exceptions, such as for the World War II and Korean War cohorts. For cohorts born since the early 1960s, the women's college graduation rate exceeds that of men.

Differences in educational attainment by race and socioeconomic status have persisted and in some cases increased over the past two decades. For cohorts born since 1960, the rate at which African Americans graduated from college increased less rapidly than the rate at which whites did. Moreover, during the period of sharply rising educational wage differentials in the 1980s, differences in the rate of college attendance and graduation by family income increased.[19]

Figure 2-4. *Educational Attainment of the Work Force, 1940–2000*

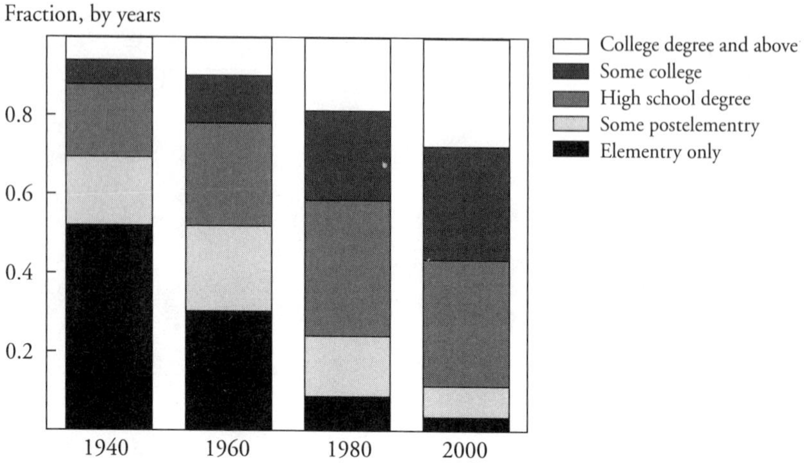

Fraction, by years

Source: Table 2A-1.

Educational Attainment of the Work Force and Educational Wage Differentials

To measure the impact of human-capital accumulation on economic growth, we must measure the educational attainment of the work force and the economic returns to educational investments. Behind the large contribution made by human capital to U.S. economic growth in the twentieth century lies a spectacular increase in the educational attainment of American workers (see figure 2-4; for more detailed information, see appendix 2A).[20]

Between 1940 and 2000, the average number of years of schooling for members of the work force increased by 4.4 years: from 9 to 13.4 years. In 1940, only 30 percent of U.S. workers had graduated from high school and fewer than 6 percent had a college degree. By 2000, 89 percent had graduated from high school and 28 percent had a college degree. During the first half of the twentieth century, the major change in educational attainment in the labor force was the replacement of workers who had less than a high school education by workers who had completed high school. Late in the twentieth century, the major change was the influx of workers with at least some college education. The educational attainment of the

American work force increased particularly rapidly from 1940 to 1980, as better educated young people replaced less educated older cohorts in the work force.[21] Progress slowed thereafter.

How have the private economic returns to education, as measured by educational wage differentials, evolved? Even as early as 1915, the private economic return to a year of either high school or college was substantial. Those returns likely helped to spur the rapid increases in educational attainment that characterized the era of the high school movement, from around 1910 to 1940. Educational wage differentials narrowed substantially from 1915 to 1950, then expanded modestly for several decades before narrowing again in the 1970s. Significant increases occurred again in the 1980s, and some modest advances continued in the 1990s (figure 2-5).

Changes in the wage structure are largely shaped by a race between the rising demand for skills, which is driven by technological changes and industrial shifts in employment, and the increasing supply of skills, which is driven by immigration, demographic shifts, and changes in educational investment across cohorts.[22] Throughout the twentieth century, demand shifted toward industries and occupations that employed workers with higher than average levels of education. At the same time, technological change also increased the demand for well-educated workers, both within industries and within occupations.[23] From 1915 to the 1970s, when increasing supply more than offset the added demand for skilled workers, educational wage differentials narrowed. Since 1980, demand for well-educated workers has outpaced supply, and educational wage differentials have been rising in consequence.

Countries in which increases in educational attainment have recently slowed—including the United States, the United Kingdom, and Canada—have experienced greater increases in educational wage differentials, especially for younger cohorts, than have countries where educational attainment has continued to expand rapidly, such as France, Germany, and the Netherlands.[24] Since about 1980, several factors have boosted education returns and wage inequality in the United States. The growth in the supply of college-educated workers has slowed, and the demand for better educated workers has risen—a change that has been driven, in part, by technological and organizational changes. Unions have lost membership. Compensation for the top achievers in many fields, including business, sports, and entertainment, has greatly increased. The real value of the minimum wage has fallen. Beginning in 1995, tight labor markets, an increase in the real minimum wage, and rapid growth in productivity helped spur

Figure 2-5. *Educational Wage Differentials for All Workers and Young Male Workers, 1915–2000*

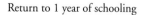
Return to 1 year of schooling

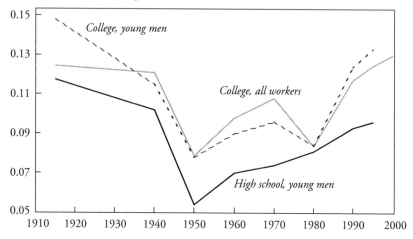

Sources: Returns to a year of high school and a year of college for young men are from Claudia Goldin and Lawrence F. Katz, "Decreasing (and Then Increasing) Inequality in America: A Tale of Two Half-Centuries," in F. Welch, ed., *The Causes and Consequences of Increasing Income Inequality* (University of Chicago Press, 2001), table 2.4 and figure 2.6, and are based on data from the 1915 Iowa State Census, the 1940–70 IPUMS of the U.S. population censuses, and the 1970 to March 1996 CPSs. The samples include full-year nonfarm workers with zero to nineteen years of potential experience. Returns to a year of college for all workers are based on data from the 1915 Iowa State Census, the 1940–80 IPUMS of the U.S. population censuses, and 1980–2000 CPS MORG samples. The return to a year of college equals the regression-adjusted wage differential between a worker with exactly sixteen years of schooling (or a bachelor's degree) and with exactly twelve years of schooling (or a high school degree), divided by 4. The college returns for 1940 to 2000 were derived from log hourly wage regressions for samples of all workers (men and woman) aged eighteen to sixty-five, using the same specifications and data-processing procedures as David H. Autor, Lawrence F. Katz, and Alan B. Krueger, "Computing Inequality: Have Computers Changed the Labor Market?" *Quarterly Journal of Economics*, vol. 113, no. 4 (1998), table 1. The 1915 to 1940 change in the college wage premium uses samples of full-year workers from Iowa and the methods of Claudia Goldin and Lawrence F. Katz, "Education and Income in the Early Twentieth Century: Evidence from the Prairies," *Journal of Economic History*, vol. 60, no. 3 (2000), pp. 782–818.

wage growth among low earners. These developments slowed the trend toward increasing wage inequality—and in the late 1990s even narrowed wage inequality among workers whose earnings were below the median. In the United States, current economic returns to a college education are at least as high as they have been in sixty years. An increase in the ranks of college-educated workers should boost economic growth and reduce wage inequality.

Education, Labor Quality, and Economic Growth

For nearly fifty years, economic analysis has shown that an increase in the quality of the labor force will boost output. The differences in the wages paid to workers with differing characteristics reflect the quality—or market value—of those characteristics.

Analysts disagree on the precise importance of the different channels by which education affects economic growth, but they concur that the overall effect of education on growth is large.[25] Research comparing economic growth among different countries has found that per capita output increases more rapidly in nations that have both a high level of educational attainment and rapid growth in educational attainment.[26]

The direct contribution to economic growth of increases in the educational attainment of the U.S. labor force can be estimated through standard "growth-accounting" methods.[27] The procedures involved are straightforward. The key assumption is each factor of production is paid a price—wages, profits, or rents—that equals the value of its contribution to production. The first step, then, is to measure the change in the quantity of each measurable factor of production. The proportionate change in the quantity of a measurable input, multiplied by its share of national product, measures its contribution to the rate of economic growth. Usually, changes in the directly measurable factors of production do not account for the entire change in output. The residual is referred to as the change in total factor productivity. In the next two sections we measure the contributions of improvements in the education, work experience, and other characteristics of the labor force to U.S. economic growth from 1915 to 2000. We also consider the implication of recent demographic and educational trends for future U.S. economic growth.

EDUCATION. Compensation of labor—wages plus fringe benefits—accounts for approximately 70 percent of production. Assuming labor is paid its marginal contribution to output and that output is proportional to inputs, a 1 percent increase in effective labor, occurring through an increase in the average human capital of the work force, directly boosts output by 0.7 percent.[28]

On average, from 1915 through 2000, increases in educational attainment boosted the effective size of the work force by 0.5 percent a year

Table 2-1. *Educational Growth Accounting, Chain-Weighted Indexes, 1915–2000* [a]

Period	Annual percent change in educational productivity		Change in educational attainment of work force (years)
	Employment	Hours	
1915–40	0.52	0.50	1.38
1940–60	0.50	0.49	1.52
1960–80	0.61	0.59	1.93
1980–2000	0.35	0.35	0.86
1915–2000	0.50	0.48	5.69

Sources: 1915 Iowa State Census sample; 1940, 1960, and 1980 IPUMS of the U.S. federal population censuses; 1980 and 2000 CPS MORG samples.

a. Details of the construction of the educational productivity indexes are given in appendix 2B. The indexes cover the civilian work force (aged sixteen or older) in each year. The reported educational productivity changes are based on chain-weighted prices. (Fixed-weighted prices give similar results.) Changes from 1915 to 1940 are for Iowa; changes for the other periods cover the entire United States. The education groups used are 0–4, 5–6, 7–8, 9–11, 12, 13–15, and 16 or more years of schooling. The chain-weighted index covering years t to t' uses the average educational wage differentials for t and t'. The employment-based indexes weight workers by their sampling weights; the hours-based indexes weight workers by the product of their sampling weight and their hours worked in the survey reference week.

(table 2-1).[29] Thus education contributed an average of 0.35 percentage point a year to economic growth (0.7 x 0.5) over an eighty-five-year span—a contribution that equals 22 percent of the average annual increase in labor productivity of 1.62 percent.[30] (The contribution of education to economic growth depends partly on how the changes are measured. The text box and appendix 2B explain in more detail how the contribution of education to the effective labor force was measured.)

Improvements in educational attainment and the contribution of education to productivity varied during the twentieth century. As shown in table 2-1, in the two decades from 1980 through 2000 the mean educational attainment of the labor force rose by only 0.86 years; by comparison, mean educational attainment increased by 1.93 years from 1960 to 1980, by 1.52 years from 1940 to 1960, and by 1.38 years from 1915 to 1940. Increases in productivity attributable to education accelerated in the two decades from 1960 to 1980, then fell by nearly half from 1980 to 2000— to the lowest levels of the century. The slower growth in the educational attainment of the work force from 1980 to 2000 shaved productivity growth by 0.13 percent a year relative to the average for 1915 to 1980.

Measuring the Contribution of Education to Economic Growth

To measure the contribution of education to economic growth, we compute an education productivity index, E_t, of the U.S. work force for selected years t. The index is given by $E_t = \Sigma_i w_{i\tau} S_{it}$, where $w_{i\tau}$ is the (adjusted) wage of education group i (relative to a reference education group) in a base period τ, and S_{it} is the share of education group i in employment (or total hours) in year t. The wage of each education group is adjusted for differences across the groups in experience and demographic variables. If one assumes that differences in education reflect the impact of schooling on productivity, the growth in this index measures the contribution of educational upgrading to aggregate labor-input growth (through improvements in the average human capital or "quality" of the work force). Although an alternative view holds that education signals inherent differences in the productivity of workers that it *uncovers* but does not cause, the bulk of evidence supports the assumption that education actually contributes to increased economic productivity (see David Card, "The Causal Effect of Education on Earnings," in O. Ashenfelter and D. Card, eds., *Handbook of Labor Economics,* vol. 3A [Elsevier, 1999]). Appendix tables 2A-1 and 2A-2 provide detailed information on the changes in the educational attainment of the U.S. work force over the course of the twentieth century; these changes are summarized in figure 2-4. The relative wages used in the education productivity index can be computed either period by period, with changing weights in each period (a "chain-weighted" index), or with fixed weights. These two approaches produce similar results; the results shown in table 2-1 were obtained using the first approach.

Prospects for a return to rapid increases in educational attainment and high contributions of human capital to economic growth do not appear favorable. Recent projections indicate that during the next two decades, the proportion of the labor force that is college educated will increase by 1.5 to 5 percentage points.[31] By comparison, the college-educated portion of the labor force increased by 8.6 percentage points from 1980 to 2000. We project that the annual rate of productivity growth attributable to education, which was 0.35 percent from 1980 to 2000, will decline to between 0.06 and 0.17 percent from 2000 through 2020.[32]

Although the contribution is difficult to quantify precisely, increases in educational attainment also made a large indirect contribution to economic growth by fueling innovation and the diffusion of new technologies into the work place. Businesses with better-educated workers adopted new technologies sooner and showed greater productivity benefits from investments in information technology.[33] Furthermore, highly educated labor is the primary input into research and development (R&D), and some estimates suggest that the intensity of R&D has been a significant (and possibly the largest measurable) contributor to growth in U.S. labor productivity over the past fifty years.[34]

OTHER ASPECTS OF LABOR QUALITY. Wage rates vary not only with education but also with experience, sex, nativity, and race. If one makes the critical assumption that differences in wage rates reflect differences in worker productivity, it is possible to construct an "augmented" measure of the quality of the labor force that encompasses a broader set of worker characteristics associated with significant wage differentials. To the extent that discrimination on the basis of characteristics such as race, nativity, or sex distorts wages, the assumption that wage differentials measure genuine differences in economic productivity is not warranted.[35] However, the indirect effects of discrimination on wages—those that arise, for example, from being denied access to good schools or to in-service training—do affect productivity and are therefore included.

Labor force quality, measured in this fashion, increased by an average of 0.42 percent annually from 1915 to 2000 (table 2-2)—a contribution that is almost identical to that of increasing educational attainment. In other words, improvements in educational attainment can account for the entire secular increase in the measured quality of the labor force from 1915 through 2000. Factors other than education sometimes added to and sometimes subtracted from improvement in labor quality, but these effects canceled each other out over the period as a whole. The rising proportion of women in the work force slightly lowered measured labor quality. The effects of changes in the age composition of the work force differed by subperiod. As more and more children remained in school until their late teens, the proportion of youth in the labor force declined, which contributed to faster growth in the quality of labor from 1915 to 1940. From 1960 to 1980, the entry of the large baby boom cohorts, who were initially young and inexperienced, decreased the quality of the labor force. The resulting large increase in the proportion of younger, inexperienced workers almost completely offset the coincident rapid improvements in educational attainment. As a result, the period from 1960 to 1980 saw unusually small growth in overall labor quality, despite being a period of an

Table 2-2. *Augmented Labor Quality Index: Annual Percent Changes, Chain-Weighted Prices, 1915–2000*[a]

Period	Employment	Hours
1915–40	0.61	n.a.
1940–60	0.47	0.46
1960–80	0.12	0.14
1980–2000	0.43	0.43
1915–2000	0.42	n.a.

Sources: 1915 Iowa State Census sample; 1910, 1920, 1940, 1960, and 1980 IPUMS of the U.S. federal population censuses; 1980 and 2000 CPS MORG samples.

a. Details of the construction of the labor quality index are given in appendix 2B. The reported labor force quality changes are based on labor force quality indexes using chain-weighted prices. The indexes cover the civilian work force (aged sixteen or older) in each year. The chain-weighted index covering years t to t' uses a predicted wage, based on average wage differentials for t and t'. The employment-based indexes weight workers by their sampling weights; the hours-based indexes weight workers by the product of their sampling weight and their hours worked in the survey reference week.

unusually rapid work force educational advance. From 1980 to 2000, however, as baby boomers acquired experience, the corresponding increase in the quality of the labor force offset the unusually small increase in educational attainment. Thus the increase in the quality of the labor force during these two decades was equal to the average for the twentieth century.

Once again, prospects for the future are not good. During the next twenty years, as the baby boom cohorts move beyond their peak earning years, the gains in labor quality that have stemmed from changes in the age structure of the work force are projected to stop.[36] Because improvement in educational attainment is also projected to slow during the next two decades, improvement in the quality of the labor force is likely to contribute less to increased worker productivity than it did, on average, during the twentieth century.

Human-Capital Policy

Governments mandate and subsidize schooling in part because people, if left to their own devices, may invest less in education than is socially optimal. Many families are too poor to pay for much education directly. Neither children nor their parents can borrow against the future earnings that education will help pupils to earn. Some parents, even those who can afford to pay for education, may not act in the best long-term interests of their children. Nor are children always rational and compliant. Finally, many argue that, in addition to the direct benefits for students and their families, education benefits society at large through peer effects, knowledge spillovers, and reductions in crime.[37] Education can also facilitate the economic advance of those from disadvantaged backgrounds. The credit market imperfections facing many families in financing educational investments, along with the possible broader social benefits of education, help justify substantial government subsidies for investment in human capital.

Increased investments in human capital offer an unusual opportunity to both promote economic growth and reduce economic inequality. The key policy question is whether, given the current level of government support for education in the United States, many families still face large financial and information barriers that may seriously hinder them from making high-return educational investments, ranging from early-childhood education to postsecondary schooling and training. Much evidence suggests that such constraints remain significant for low-income and minority families. For that reason, targeted investments in education and training have the potential to generate social rates of return at least comparable to those of other private investments.[38]

A first area of concern involves the access to and affordability of college for low-income and minority youth. Since 1980, the earnings of college graduates have risen substantially in comparison to the earnings of those with less education. This evidence suggests the existence of large economic returns to expanding college attendance and completion. Although overall college attendance has increased since 1980 (the proportion of high school graduates continuing on to college rose from 49 percent in 1980 to 60 percent in 1990 and to 63 percent in 1999), the gap in college attendance rates by race, ethnicity, and parental income remains large—and appears to have widened over the last twenty-five years.[39] And among students with similar academic grades and scores on achievement tests, family income remains an important factor in explaining differences in college enrollment rates.[40]

Thus financial constraints appear to remain a barrier to college for low- and moderate-income youths.[41] Furthermore, reductions in college costs (lower tuition and increased financial aid) greatly increase college attendance rates for youths from moderate-income families.[42] Recent estimates—using "natural experiments" involving changes in access to college, changes in college costs, and compulsory schooling laws—indicate high rates of return accruing to the marginal (typically low-income) youths affected by such policy interventions.[43] From the early 1980s to the mid-1990s, college attendance costs—tuition and fees minus financial aid—

rose far more rapidly than did income for low- and moderate-income families.[44] These increases in net college costs are likely to have hindered low-income and moderate-income youth from attending college. Improvements in the targeting of private and public financial aid and the creation of a more transparent system for financial aid applications and financial aid information could increase college attendance among disadvantaged youth. Easier access to college may be too late for many low-income youth who do not have sufficient academic preparation. Mentoring programs that combine social and academic support with financial assistance for postsecondary training can substantially improve academic preparation and likelihood of going to college for low-income children.[45] Some "second-chance" job-training programs for disadvantaged youth who have dropped out of high school also appear promising. In particular, the residential-based Job Corps program, which serves mostly poor urban dropouts aged sixteen to twenty-four, has consistently produced high social returns by increasing earnings and reducing criminal activity.[46] Expanding the funding for successful mentoring programs and increasing the number of Job Corps slots are both warranted.

Policies intended to improve human capital should also target early childhood. Most research has found large returns from investment in high-quality early-childhood education programs targeted to low-income families.[47] Increased funding for Head Start, the largest federal preschool program, could strengthen its quality and increase access; with sufficient funding, it might also be possible to include children younger than three years old.

There is less agreement about the effectiveness of specific policies intended to improve the quality of primary and secondary schooling. The impact of increases in school resources within current public school systems remains a controversial issue.[48] For example, evidence from the large-scale random-assignment STAR experiment in Tennessee strongly suggests that, holding teacher quality constant, smaller class sizes in the early grades improve academic performance, particularly for poor and minority children.[49] Research also indicates that the quality of teachers, although difficult to measure, is especially important for pupils from disadvantaged backgrounds. But attempts to reduce class size for all public school students, as mandated under California's recent statewide policy, are likely to make it difficult to hold teacher quality constant: universal reductions in class size are quite likely to require increasing the share of teachers who are less experienced, less qualified, or both (at least for some intermediate-run period). Moreover, the more affluent schools and districts are likely to out-bid their poorer counterparts in efforts to hire the most qualified teachers. Thus reducing class size for all may do little to help students from low-income backgrounds. For schools with low-income students, more targeted attempts to increase the quality of teachers and reduce class size appear to be more promising—and would certainly be less expensive than universal reductions in class size.

In the United States, where schools have traditionally been financed locally, parents have been able to express their educational preferences by choosing where to live. In effect, this exercise of parental choice created competition among schools—which, throughout much of the twentieth century, helped expand and improve schooling in the United States. But such a system may not work well for those from disadvantaged back-grounds when poverty constrains residential choice. Programs that allow low-income families to exercise choice and expand their children's educational options—including public school choice, charter schools, and vouchers—deserve further experimentation.

Since 1970, poverty has become increasingly concentrated in inner cities, and residential segregation by family income has risen sharply.[50] Both factors have lowered the level of investment in human capital for children from low-income families. Recent research on programs that enabled low-income families to move from high-poverty neighborhoods to middle-class communities indicates that concentrated neighborhood poverty greatly harms children and that living in lower-poverty neighborhoods improves children's educational performance, health, and behavior.[51] These studies suggest that policies to promote residential mobility—increasing the availability of housing vouchers, for example—would also improve human capital among children from low-income families.

Investment in Physical Capital

Could shifts in government policy produce large enough changes in rates of investment in physical capital to significantly boost economic growth? In the 1950s, Robert Solow and Moses Abramovitz published theoretical and empirical studies showing that physical capital was not the most important source of the increase in labor productivity and living standards in the twentieth century.[52] Physical capital deepening (increases in the quantity of capital used to produce each unit of output) has played second or even third fiddle. Nearly all research, at least since the pioneering work of Edward Denison, has found that total factor productivity—the "residual" increase in output that cannot be directly accounted for by increases in the quantity or quality of labor or capital—was the primary cause of rising U.S. incomes and productivity in the twentieth century.[53]

Moreover, the capacity for shifts in policy to generate faster growth through higher physical capital investment is lower than one would suppose from a standard growth-accounting analysis dividing growth between labor, capital, and the "residual." With a constant investment (or saving) rate as a share of national product, increases in incomes arising from growth in total factor productivity will induce increases in investment, so that the capital stock will grow roughly as fast as total output. In this case, a standard growth-accounting analysis will attribute perhaps a third of labor productivity growth to this increased physical capital stock. But this higher income–driven increase in the physical capital stock is, in some sense, mechanical. Policies—whether good or bad—that attempt to affect growth by affecting investment and saving must do so by *changing* the economy's capital-output ratio. Significant changes in the economywide capital-output ratio have been rare since the nineteenth century and are difficult to accomplish through economic policy.

Fluctuations in U.S. economic growth have stemmed primarily from changes in total factor productivity. Since World War II, growth in total factor productivity has oscillated from a relatively robust 2 percent a year from 1947 to 1973, to near zero from 1973 to 1995, and back to a healthy 1.5 percent a year since 1995. The ratio of capital to output, in contrast, was relatively steady from before World War I until the past decade. Neither economic policies nor changes in the behavior of the private sector materially changed the rate of investment in physical capital; thus the effect of capital investment on overall economic growth remained relatively constant.[54]

Starting in 1994, however, gross physical investment—much of it in information technology—began to rise sharply as a share of GDP (see figure 2-6). The extraordinary and ongoing revolution in information technology has substantially increased investment in physical capital since the mid-1990s and is likely to continue to increase such investment in the future. Almost all analysts agree that two factors account for much of the mid-1990s acceleration in the rate of American economic growth: the sharp rise in investment in information technology and the increases in total factor productivity in the manufacture of capital goods related to information technology. These two factors combined have boosted the

Figure 2-6. *Real Private Investment Divided by Real GDP*[a]

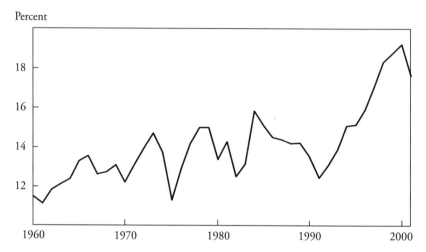

Percent

Source: National Income and Product Accounts, revised as of December 2001, as constructed by the Bureau of Economic Analysis.
a. Gross private domestic investment estimates.

growth rate of gross output by an estimated 1 percentage point a year (see table 2-3).

Government's Role in Physical Capital Investment

Higher rates of investment in physical capital eventually increase economic growth and the ratio of physical capital to output. In the short run, however, increased investment diverts output from current consumption, both public and private.

Although decisions about the allocation of output between investment and consumption are usually best left to the free market, there are some situations in which market allocation produces inferior results. For example, when investment in physical capital has powerful effects—known as spillovers, or externalities—on people and businesses that are not parties to the investment decision, markets may generate too little or too much investment. In the case of research, investment produces knowledge that is useful to people or businesses outside the company that sponsors the research—a positive externality. When, as in this case, the social value of investment exceeds the private gain, free markets produce less investment

Table 2-3. *Components of Acceleration in Productivity Growth, 1996–2000 versus 1991–95*

Component	Percent
Total acceleration in labor productivity 1996–2000 versus 1991–95	1.00
Capital deepening	0.57[a]
Information technology	0.54
Computer hardware	0.36
Computer software	0.13
Telecommunications equipment	0.07
Other capital	0.02
Multifactor productivity	0.62
Semiconductor production	0.30
Computer hardware manufacturing	0.06
All other sectors	0.26
Labor quality	−0.20

Source: Steven D. Oliner and Daniel E. Sichel, *Information Technology and Productivity: Where Are We Now and Where Are We Going?* (Washington: Federal Reserve Board, 2002).

a. Detail may not add to total due to rounding.

than is socially optimal. When investment produces negative externalities, however, as is the case with manufacturing processes that cause pollution, the investment will have a "negative" social value unless producers or consumers pay the true cost of cleanup. Similarly, when taxes reduce the private return to saving below total social returns, markets result in too little saving and investment. Saving and investment will also be too low when people are unable to look ahead—to see the future value of investments made today. In such cases, government policy can, in principle, improve economic welfare by encouraging saving or investment or by fostering a change in the composition of savings or investment. What is possible in principle may be difficult to implement in practice, however—a problem that will be discussed later in this chapter.

As noted earlier, governmental support of education—through mandates, financial assistance, or other policy initiatives—is justified by capital market imperfections that prevent individuals from borrowing in advance against the increased earnings that education will produce and by possible positive external benefits of educational investments. Preventing shortfalls in investment in both human and physical capital is important because each depends on the other: without substantial investment in physical capital, workers will not be able to use their skills effectively, and without the requisite education, workers will not be able to use capital equipment effectively.[55]

Cross-country studies of patterns of economic growth have identified a strong positive correlation between investment in physical capital—especially in machinery and equipment that embody modern technology—and rapid growth in labor productivity. This result is hardly surprising, but the estimated annual rate of social return—20 percent a year or more—exceeds the estimated after-tax private return to investment by 5 to 10 percentage points. Of course, correlation is not causation. Other factors could conceivably be causing both high investment and rapid increases in labor productivity. However, the cross-country correlation holds whether the source of high rates of investment is high national savings or low domestic prices on investment goods.[56]

Industry studies also point to important complementarities between investment in physical capital and the growth of total factor productivity. Successful workplace reorganizations to take advantage of new information technologies require substantial up-front investments in physical capital. But much larger investments are necessary to reorganize business operations to make full use of the new technologies.[57] Once one company has made such investments and figured out how to do business in a new way, other companies can apply these lessons at a lower cost. A historical example can illustrate such complementarities.[58] A century ago, when electric power first became available to U.S. industries, a few companies began to experiment with new ways to organize production. These experiments, which took advantage of the flexibility made possible by electric power, eventually led to the development of what became known as mass production. As other companies imitated these new techniques, they spread throughout the economy, producing vastly larger benefits than those that accrued to the companies that had originally developed them. The social learning and experimentation that produced these efficiencies were not possible, however, until the new technology had diffused sufficiently.

If other companies can save even a small proportion of the costs incurred by the innovating company, the social returns to investment in newly developed technologies are much larger than the private returns. It is because the social returns to investment in physical capital can exceed the private returns that government should concern itself with the level of physical investment. The steady decline of the U.S. private saving rate during the past generation strengthens the case for such involvement. During the 1950s and 1960s household savings were more than 7 percent of household income; by 2001 they had fallen to 2 percent. One possible explanation is that there has been a radical drop in Americans' interest in the future relative to the present, but there is little other evidence that we no longer care about our future well-being or that of our children. Another possible explanation is that there is a sense that we are subject to fewer economic risks (and therefore have less need to build up wealth as a hedge). But risks have not vanished, as household saving very nearly did during the late 1990s. More likely, the drop in saving is not an example of purely rational household optimizing behavior, but stems instead from an somewhat irrational faith that the stock market gains of the 1990s would continue forever (a delusion that ended abruptly in 2001), or from aspects of American life that encourage consumption rather than saving.[59]

Precise estimates of the gap between private and social returns to investment in physical capital are hard to make. Nevertheless, most empirical research suggests that the social benefits of investment greatly exceed the private returns.[60] Thus, provided that effective policies can be designed, enacted, and implemented, government policies to boost saving and investment could produce social benefits that exceed their cost.

Strategies for Boosting Investment in Physical Capital

That it is desirable in principle to influence saving and investment does not mean that it is possible to do so effectively in practice. Nevertheless, there are a number of strategies worth exploring. Government can try to encourage private saving, it can try to make investment more attractive, and it can make a direct contribution to national saving by running budget surpluses.[61]

SAVING INCENTIVES. Traditional tax-based initiatives to provide incentives for household saving have been consistently difficult to design and implement. They also appear to have been relatively ineffective. During the 1980s and 1990s, for example, Congress enacted a welter of tax incentives to promote retirement saving, including two kinds of individual retirement accounts, two types of Keogh plans, simplified employee pensions, and 401k plans. These plans shared certain features: all permitted savers to make deposits in qualified accounts up to some legislatively defined limit; all allowed such deposits to be deducted or excluded from current taxable income; all excluded the investment earnings on such accounts from current tax; and all stipulated that when funds were withdrawn, they would be subject to ordinary income tax—and if withdrawn prematurely, to an additional penalty tax. Deposits in these plans grew rapidly and had reached $5 trillion by 1999.[62] Despite the large flow of funds into such accounts, however, household savings fell from over 7 percent of household income during the 1980s to an average of 2 percent in 2000–01. One of two conclusions is inescapable: that households would actually have been net borrowers but for these incentives or that the incentives substantially failed.

The problem with these saving incentives, and most others, is that they produce two roughly offsetting effects. On the one hand, tax concessions increase savers' real lifetime wealth by lowering their tax payments. Ordinarily, increases in wealth lead to increases in consumption, and increased consumption leads, in turn, to reduced saving—because saving is simply the difference between income and consumption. With tax and other saving incentives in place, however, current saving buys more future consumption—by, in effect, reducing the "price" of future consumption. And when the price of any good falls (holding real income constant), people want more of it. Research to determine whether the "wealth effect" (which decreases saving) or the "price effect" (which increases saving) is dominant has reached conflicting conclusions. The lack of clear findings suggests that whatever effect such saving incentives have, they are almost surely small.[63]

Unconventional saving incentives may prove to be more promising than tax incentives, however.[64] Some studies suggest that people divide their wealth into separate "mental accounts," some of which they regard as available for current consumption, while others are not. If household wealth can be channeled into accounts that are not regarded as available for current consumption, saving could increase. Evidence also suggests that people may be willing to commit a larger part of future wage increases to saving than of current income. Public policies designed to encourage households to make such commitments could gradually increase saving.[65] To the extent that household saving patterns are dominated by such quasi-rational behaviors, public policies that take advantage of such behaviors may prove to have large net effects on saving rates.[66] However, no consensus has emerged on the importance of such quasi-rational behaviors, or on how government economic policy can manipulate such behaviors to increase social welfare.

INVESTMENT INCENTIVES. Direct incentives to investment have considerable intuitive appeal. If the ultimate goal is to increase the positive externalities induced by investment, incentives that directly promote investment are an appropriate strategy.[67] For most of the period from 1962 through 1986, Congress provided a tax credit for investment in equipment but not in structures. The Tax Reform Act of 1986 repealed this credit for several reasons. To begin with, because the government lacks the capacity to reliably distinguish between investments that were induced by the incentives and those that would have been made anyway,[68] most of the credits rewarded firms for having made investments that would have been undertaken in any case. In addition, the credit raised formidable administrative problems and distorted investment decisions. In order to minimize construction costs and maximize equipment costs, for example, office buildings were constructed with movable interior partitions and wiring (which were regarded as equipment and therefore favored under the tax law) rather than with fixed walls (which were regarded as structures and did not qualify for the credit). In addition, like all other tax incentives, the credit narrowed the tax base, which necessitated increased tax rates and brought about associated distortions in incentives on the items that remained taxable. In the end, Congress decided that a tax law that applied lower rates to a broader tax base would distort economic behavior less than would a tax law that applied higher rates to a narrow base.

A tax credit that applied only to incremental investment would have narrowed the tax base less than did the full investment tax credit. But a narrow incremental credit creates even more vexing administrative complexities and unintended incentives: namely, businesses dissipate time, energy, and resources in making a normal investment project seem "incremental." The Internal Revenue Code is far from neutral in its treatment of different forms of investment—in part because, as a practical matter, it is impossible to tax everything in a complex modern economy (agriculture, mining, forestry, manufacturing, and finance, for example) in exactly the same way, and in part because some industry representatives are more successful than others in securing tax breaks from elected officials. But in nearly all cases, impartial analysts agree that taxing different forms of investment at different rates diverts capital from its most productive uses and reduces economic efficiency.

THE GOVERNMENT BUDGET. The most direct and effective means of boosting investment in physical capital through public policy is one that was proposed forty years ago. The 1962 *Economic Report of the President* recommended that over the business cycle as a whole, government should use a "tight," high-surplus fiscal policy to boost national saving, accompanied by a "loose," low–interest rate monetary policy to ensure that the savings are invested and that full employment is maintained. The logic is straightforward. National investment is constrained by national saving. National saving equals saving by the private sector plus the government's budget surplus (or minus the government's budget deficit). If public policy cannot, as a practical matter, increase private saving very much, the only way to boost national saving is for the government to run a budget surplus. Increasing national saving makes it possible to increase national investment.

The experience of the 1990s demonstrates clearly the effect of increased government saving. From 1990 through 1995, government budgets, on average, borrowed 3.9 percent of GDP. In 2000 government budgets were in surplus and added 2.6 percent of GDP to savings, a swing of 6.5 percentage points. Over this period, domestic investment rose by 3.5 percent of GDP, despite a drop in private savings of 4.5 percent of GDP. The events of 2001 and 2002 sharply reversed this situation. As a result of tax cuts, a recession, and increased defense spending, both the federal budget and state budgets swung from surplus to deficit. It now appears that for much of the upcoming decade, the government will once again drain private savings from potentially productive private investments to finance current consumption (for further detail on the prospects for the budget, see chapter 4).

Given the difficulty of accurately focusing incentives to encourage investments in physical capital and the ineffectuality of traditional saving incentives, a budget surplus remains possibly the best way for the federal government to boost physical capital investment.[69] Because of the tax cut of 2001, however, which was implemented in the face of increased federal spending, it now appears that federal policy will discourage, rather than encourage, investment and associated economic growth for much of the current decade.

Investment in Technology

Society invests not only in human capital and in physical capital but in ideas—in science, engineering, and business organization. Ideas have an important advantage over physical assets: they are "nonrival" goods, meaning that many people can use them at the same time without reducing the supply available for others.[70] Thomas Jefferson put it best: "He who receives an idea from me, receives instruction himself without lessening mine; as he who lights his taper at mine, receives light without darkening me."[71]

Because each person can use ideas without diminishing the stock available to others, the most basic of economic principles suggests that technology should be available to everyone free of charge. Once an idea exists, the cost of letting another person use it is zero. But at this point, different economic principles cut in different directions. If the price of using an idea is zero, private companies have no incentive to create it. Profit-oriented businesses, which must cover their costs to keep operating, will not ordinarily invest in something that cannot be sold at a profit. Thus the price that will encourage companies to develop new ideas is higher than the price that will encourage the efficient use of existing ideas.

A government subsidy for the development of new ideas is one way to close this gap. But if the government is to subsidize investment in technology on a large scale, it needs to determine where the subsidies should flow. Unfortunately, government officials lack the incentive—and often the knowledge—to decide how best to allocate subsidies for applied R&D. As noted by the economist Friedrich von Hayek, market competition is a discovery mechanism and the best way to promote innovation. Von Hayek also recognized that there are powerful administrative defects in the top-down control that comes with centralized funding.

Another way to encourage R&D is by granting patents—or in the case of some intellectual property, copyrights—which enable the holders to charge what are essentially monopoly prices. Once again, however, the monopoly prices that encourage the development or discovery of new products discourage the efficient use of products covered by existing patents or copyrights. (This dilemma is particularly important for the burgeoning health technologies examined in chapter 5, and for the issues of international trade examined in chapter 10.) To complicate the matter still further, because both basic and applied research are cumulative enterprises, the benefits of basic research can be realized only if the research is widely disseminated. Isaac Newton said that the only reason he was able to see farther than others was that he stood on the shoulders of giants.[72]

The difficulties associated with creating incentives for research are particularly acute in the case of information technology. No one yet knows enough to design systems that will successfully nurture investment in ideas and technology. New institutions and new kinds of institutions may be required, and it may be necessary as well to revisit some that have been tried before. Some computer software developers, for example, found that they could do better when they removed program components that had prevented users from copying their software (in effect, enabling users to violate the developer's copyright) because increased use promoted sales. In the early nineteenth century, the French government purchased the first photographic patents and placed them in the public domain. Similar steps may again be necessary if the United States is to simultaneously ensure that goods can be sold at marginal production cost—the condition for production efficiency—and elicit entrepreneurial energy, support cumulative research, and promote R&D.[73]

So far, the difficulty of managing the rewards for innovation and the diffusion of knowledge has not prevented the American economy from undergoing a long-term, knowledge-driven productivity boom. Productivity growth normally collapses during recessions. But during the recession of 2001 and 2002 it remained robust, strongly suggesting that the productivity recovery that began in the mid-1990s will persist.

The inventions and innovations that fueled the information technology–driven boom promise a bright future for the growth of labor productivity in America. But the outlook could be brighter still. Estimates of the annual social rate of return to R&D investments often exceed 25 percent—at least twice as high as typical estimates of the private rate of return to R&D.[74] The large gap between social and private returns to investment in R&D suggests that the United States invests too little in R&D—and that even imperfect tax subsidies for private R&D may have substantial payoffs in term of economic growth, as long as decisions about what projects to undertake remain in private hands.

The importance of the system governing intellectual property cannot be exaggerated. Whether or not the United States can sustain rapid economic growth in the twenty-first century may well rest on our ability to devise rules for an economy in which nonrival goods are an increasingly important component. Such "idea products" are likely to be at the core of future economic growth, and it is in the realm of technology that the stakes involved in policies to boost economic growth may well be the largest. It is particularly frustrating, therefore, that little is currently known about how to design economic institutions that will encourage the development of these products and ensure their diffusion.

Conclusion

Rapid economic growth will facilitate solutions to virtually every problem examined in other chapters of this book. It not only directly increases household incomes and living standards but also softens many other policy trade-offs that Americans face. Because so many factors affect economic growth, many different policies can contribute to or inhibit it, including those that are designed to boost the skills of the labor force; those that act as incentives to increase public saving, private saving, or private investment in physical capital or R&D; those that are intended to facilitate public R&D spending; and those that govern intellectual property.

Effective policy requires the solution of two problems: identifying what should be done and enacting and administering initiatives that actually accomplish the intended goals. Effective incentives for private saving and for private investment in physical capital and R&D are difficult to design; and we have much work to do in creating an intellectual property system that may be able accelerate technological progress. One line of policy, however, is both straightforward and effective in boosting capital accumulation and growth: the government should run a budget surplus. Unfortunately, recent policies are taking the United States in just the opposite direction.

In contrast to policies that appear to have less predictable outcomes, those that increase education and training among the young, especially those from minority and low-income families, promise both to spur economic growth and to reduce wage inequality. The enormous rise in educational wage differentials since 1980 has created greater incentives for increased education. Not all groups have invested equally, however. A lack of financial resources continues to deter low-income families from college enrollment, and differences in enrollment rates between blacks and whites and between Hispanic and non-Hispanic whites have actually widened since 1980. Earlier mentoring, improved targeting of financial aid, and a more transparent financial aid system promise large payoffs not only for disadvantaged families but for the United States as a whole. Ensuring wider access to effective second-chance training programs, such as the Job Corps, is also warranted.

Moreover, since "learning begets further learning," human-capital policies must target early childhood. As part of this effort, the United States should be willing to experiment further with policies—including school choice—that offer the potential to improve the quality of primary and secondary schooling. Policies, such as housing vouchers, that may help offset residential segregation by economic status could also prove beneficial.

During the twentieth century, America's investment in education was a principal source of its extraordinary economic performance. Projections indicate, however, that the increase in the educational attainment of the

American labor force is slowing. A renewed commitment to invest in education is probably the most important and fruitful step that federal, state, and local officials can take to sustain American economic growth.

Appendix 2A
Educational Attainment of the Work Force

Table 2A-1 presents summary measures of the educational attainment of the civilian work force (aged sixteen or older) that weight individual workers equally. Table 2A-2 presents summary measures that weight individual workers according to their hours worked. The "person weights" provide a sense of the educational attainment of a typical worker, whereas the "hours-worked weights" are more useful for evaluating the contribution of education to labor productivity (output per hour worked).

We used the federal population censuses for 1940 to 1990 and the Current Population Survey for 2000 to estimate the distribution of the highest grade attained for the U.S. work force. (The 1940 census was the first to ask about educational attainment.) For 1915, the tables include comparable data from the Iowa State Census, the earliest large-scale representative sample with information on educational attainment and earnings.[75] Iowa was a leading state in education early in the century and had a more educated population than did the rest of the United States in 1940. By the end of the twentieth century, however, Iowa was no longer a leading state and was far more like the U.S. average.

Appendix 2B
Constructing the Educational Productivity and Labor Quality Indexes

To construct educational productivity and labor quality indexes for the U.S. work force for selected years from 1915 to 2000, we followed the approaches of Goldin and Katz and Aaronson and Sullivan.[76] We began by assuming that the impact of worker characteristics on productivity equals the impact of worker characteristics on wages. We then used standard regressions of (log) wages on education, experience, sex, and other control variables to identify the impact of worker characteristics on wages (and productivity). These regression coefficients were combined with microdata on the characteristics of the work force to arrive at an average predicted

Table 2A-1. *Educational Attainment of the Work Force, 1915–2000*[a]

| | United States | | | | | Iowa | | | | | |
| | U.S. census | | | CPS | | State census, | U.S. census | | | CPS | |
	1940	1960	1980	1980	2000	1915	1940	1960	1980	1980	2000
Mean years of education	9.01	10.53	12.46	12.54	13.40	8.45	9.83	10.87	12.49	12.51	13.40
Fraction, by years of education											
0–8	0.522	0.303	0.087	0.079	0.034	0.726	0.476	0.289	0.077	0.062	0.021
9–11	0.174	0.218	0.154	0.142	0.080	0.129	0.165	0.184	0.126	0.132	0.074
12	0.185	0.262	0.346	0.368	0.322	0.083	0.229	0.316	0.424	0.461	0.340
13–15	0.061	0.121	0.228	0.219	0.288	0.037	0.076	0.128	0.210	0.188	0.326
16+	0.058	0.096	0.185	0.192	0.275	0.026	0.055	0.083	0.164	0.157	0.240

Sources: 1915 Iowa State Census; 1940, 1960, and 1980 Integrated Public Use Microsamples (IPUMS) of the U.S. federal population censuses; 1980 and 2000 Current Population Survey (CPS) Merged Outgoing Rotation Group (MORG) samples.

a. Samples were restricted to those aged sixteen or older and excluded those who were in the military or institutionalized. The work force in each year from 1940 to 2000 consists of those who were employed during the survey reference week. The work force for Iowa in 1915 consists of those reporting occupational earnings for 1914; each individual is weighted according to the number of months worked in 1915. Years of schooling for 1940 to 2000 were measured using the same approach as that used for figure 2-1. Measures of years of schooling and months worked for Iowa in 1915 were constructed using the methods of Goldin and Katz, "Education and Income in the Early Twentieth Century." For 1960 to 1980, all those who had attained thirteen years of schooling (whether or not they completed the final year) were included in the 13–15 years of schooling category, following the methods of Autor, Katz, and Krueger, "Computing Inequality." Sampling weights were used for all samples.

Table 2A-2. *Educational Attainment of the U.S. Work Force, Weighted by Hours, 1940–2000*[a]

| | United States | | | | | Iowa | | | | |
| | U.S. census | | | CPS | | U.S. census | | | CPS | |
	1940	1960	1980	1980	2000	1940	1960	1980	1980	2000
Mean years education	9.10	10.61	12.58	12.65	13.51	9.81	10.88	12.58	12.62	13.50
Fraction, by years education										
0–8	0.514	0.299	0.084	0.076	0.033	0.484	0.296	0.078	0.059	0.021
9–11	0.173	0.210	0.138	0.126	0.066	0.161	0.168	0.103	0.104	0.052
12	0.191	0.269	0.354	0.375	0.323	0.229	0.332	0.443	0.480	0.352
13–15	0.063	0.119	0.224	0.219	0.285	0.073	0.117	0.201	0.188	0.328
16+	0.060	0.102	0.199	0.204	0.292	0.053	0.086	0.175	0.169	0.247

Sources: 1940, 1960, and 1980 federal population census IPUMS; 1980 and 2000 CPS MORG samples.

a. Methodology is the same as for table 2A-1, except that the summary statistics weight all individuals by the product of hours worked during the reference week and sampling weight.

wage (only the education variables were used for the education productivity index; a wider range of variables was used for the augmented labor quality index). Using the same base-period regression coefficients to predict wages for two different years (t and t'), we measure the change in labor quality from t to t' as the change in the average predicted wage.

We used data from the 1915 Iowa State Census; the 1940, 1960, and 1980 Integrated Public Use Microsamples (IPUMS) of the U.S. federal population censuses; and the 1980 and 2000 Current Population Survey (CPS) Merged Outgoing Rotation Group (MORG) samples. Our first step was to estimate a wage regression in each year of the following form:

$$\log w_{it} = E_{it}\alpha + X_{it}\beta + R_{it}\delta + \varepsilon_{it},$$

where w_{it} is the wage of worker i in year t; E_{it} is a vector of dummy variables for educational attainment levels (0–4, 5–6, 7–8, 9–11, 12, 13–15, and 16 or more years of schooling); X_{it} contains other variables that are potentially related to productivity, including a quartic in potential experience, a female dummy and its interaction with the experience variables, a nonwhite dummy, and a U.S.-born dummy; R_{it} are census-region dummies; and ε_{it} is the error term. The wage regressions were estimated for national samples of civilian, nonagricultural wage and salary workers aged eighteen to sixty-five. The estimates for 1915 cover Iowa only and include the self-employed. Following the approach of Goldin and Katz, we adjusted the 1915 estimates of wage differentials for Iowa to be representative for the entire United States.[77] The educational attainment categories for 1940 to 1980 are based on the highest grade completed, except that all those who completed thirteen years of schooling were placed in the 13–15 group. To compute years of schooling and potential experience for the 2000 CPS, we followed the approach of Autor, Katz, and Krueger.[78] In the wage regressions for the hours-weighted indexes, we used log hourly wages as the dependent variable. Data on hours worked were not available for the 1915 Iowa state sample, so we used a monthly wage measure for 1915. The wage regressions for the employment-weighted indexes were restricted to samples of workers who had worked fifty or more weeks within a year, and log annual earnings were used as the dependent variable (except for the 1980–2000 changes, where hourly wages for full-time workers were used).

The next step was to estimate average predicted wages in each year for the entire civilian work force aged sixteen or older. A chain-weighted index for t to t' used the average of the wage regression coefficients for t and t'. The fixed-weight indexes used the average regression coefficients prevailing for the entire 1915–2000 period. The predicted wage for the education productivity index for i in year t using base-period b regression coefficients is given by

$$W_{it}^e = \exp(E_{it}\alpha^b).$$

The analogous predicted wage for the labor quality index is given by

$$W_{it}^q = \exp(E_{it}\alpha^b + X_{it}\beta^b).$$

The educational productivity index for t (E_t) is the weighted mean of W_{it}^e for all members of the civilian noninstitutional work force aged sixteen or older; person-sampling weights were used for the employment-based indexes, and the product of the sampling weight and hours worked last week were used for the hours-based indexes. Thus

$$E_t = \Sigma_i \omega_{it} W_{it}^e = \Sigma_j W_{jt}^e S_{jt},$$

where ω_{it} is the appropriate sampling weight, j indexes education groups, and S_{jt} equals the share of the work force in education group j in year t. The augmented labor quality index for t is given by the analogous weighted mean of W_{it}^q.

The civilian noninstitutional work force in each year from 1940 to 2000 includes those sixteen or older who were employed during the survey reference week and excludes those who were in the military or institutionalized.

Changes in the educational productivity index from 1915 to 1940, shown in table 2A-1, are based on data on the distribution of education in the Iowa work force for 1915 (from the Iowa State Census) and 1940 (from the U.S. Census). The 1915 Iowa work force includes those aged sixteen or older who reported positive occupational earnings for 1914 and excludes those who were in the military or institutionalized. We assumed that the growth of educational productivity from 1915 to 1940 was the same for Iowa and the United States. The U.S. labor quality index in table 2A-2 uses information on the age, sex, race, and nativity distribution of the U.S. work force from 1915 to 1940 and uses information only from Iowa for changes in the education component. The characteristics of the U.S. work force for 1915 are the average of characteristics for 1910 and 1920, based on the 1910 and 1920 U.S. Census IPUMS data. The work force for 1910 and 1920 excludes students and includes those aged sixteen to sixty-five who were gainfully employed. The 1940 federal census sample used for the 1915–1940 change in augmented labor quality also excludes students and includes labor force participants aged sixteen to sixty-five. In both tables, changes from 1940 to 1960 and from 1960 to 1980 use the U.S. Census IPUMS data, and changes from 1980 to 2000 use the CPS MORG data.

Notes

1. Also see chapter 3, on inequality.

2. Paul Krugman, *The Age of Diminished Expectations: U.S. Economic Policy in the 1990s* (MIT Press, 1994).

3. George H. W. Bush, *Inaugural Address of President George H. W. Bush* (Government Printing Office, 1989).

4. Martin Baily, "The New Economy: Post Mortem or Second Wind?" *Journal of Economic Perspectives,* vol. 16, no. 2 (2002), pp. 3–22, summarizes the growth-accounting literature on the productivity slowdown as "large but inconclusive." No single factor provides a convincing and coherent explanation, and the theory that a large number of growth-retarding factors suddenly happened to hit at once is but the least unlikely of the proposed explanations. Dale Jorgenson, "Productivity and Postwar U.S. Economic Growth," *Journal of Economic Perspectives,* vol. 2, no. 4 (1988), pp. 23–41, convincingly demonstrates that the oil-price shocks can account for slow growth in potential output during the 1970s, but why did potential output growth remain slow after 1986, when real oil prices fell? Zvi Griliches, "Productivity Puzzles and R&D: Another Nonexplanation," *Journal of Economic Perspectives,* vol. 2, no. 4 (1988), pp. 9–21, finds that a slowdown in innovation is an unattractive explanation; Robert Gordon, "Technology and Economic Performance in the American Economy," Working Paper 8771 (Cambridge, Mass.: National Bureau of Economic Research, February 2002), finds the opposite.

5. See, for example, Gordon, "Technology and Economic Performance in the American Economy"; Steven D. Oliner and Daniel E. Sichel, "The Resurgence of Productivity Growth in the Late 1990s: Is Information Technology the Story?" *Journal of Economic Perspectives,* vol. 14, no. 4 (2000), pp. 3–22; Dale Jorgenson, Mun S. Ho, and Kevin J. Stiroh, "Projecting Productivity Growth: Lessons from the U.S. Growth Resurgence," Harvard University, Department of Economics, 2001; and J. Bradford DeLong, "Productivity Growth in the 2000s," in M. Gertler and K. Rogoff, eds., *NBER Macroeconomics Annual,* vol. 17 (National Bureau of Economic Research, 2002).

6. Richard R. Nelson and Edmund S. Phelps, "Investment in Humans, Technological Diffusion, and Economic Growth," *American Economic Review,* vol. 56, no. 2 (1966), pp. 69–75.

7. Claudia Goldin, "The Human Capital Century and American Economic Leadership: Virtues of the Past," *Journal of Economic History,* vol. 61, no. 2 (2001), pp. 263–92. These characteristics persist, although some are now being questioned. The movement to stricter standards, for example, which promises benefits in some directions, threatens to prevent poor performers from recovering later. The proliferation of small, independent school districts led to fiscal inequalities, and the resulting variations in spending for each pupil are now the subject of judicial scrutiny; nevertheless, the very system that created inequalities also fostered educational expansion and allowed parents to express their different educational preferences.

8. Ibid.

9. The text refers to industrial nations. Some oil-rich countries have higher per capita incomes.

10. Claudia Goldin and Lawrence F. Katz, "The Origins of Technology-Skill Complementarity," *Quarterly Journal of Economics,* vol. 113, no. 3 (1998), pp. 693–732; Claudia Goldin and Lawrence F. Katz, "Decreasing (and Then Increasing) Inequality in America: A Tale of Two Half-Centuries," in F. Welch, ed., *The Causes and Consequences of Increasing Income Inequality* (University of Chicago Press, 2001), pp. 37–82.

11. Claudia Goldin and Lawrence F. Katz, "Education and Income in the Early Twentieth Century: Evidence from the Prairies," *Journal of Economic History,* vol. 60, no. 3 (2000), pp. 782–818; Goldin and Katz, "Decreasing (and Then Increasing) Inequality in America."

12. Claudia Goldin and Lawrence F. Katz, "The Shaping of Higher Education: The Formative Years in the United States, 1890–1940," *Journal of Economic Perspectives,* vol. 13, no. 1 (1999), pp. 37–62.

13. Organization for Economic Cooperation and Development, *Education at a Glance 2001* (Paris, 2001).

14. Even these measures, however, inadequately represent formal education because they do not adjust for the quality of "a year of education." The length of the school year increased during the twentieth century, particularly for the elementary grades and in rural schools. Nonetheless, our figures for educational attainment are not adjusted for changes in education days. (Nor are adjustments made for aspects of educational quality, such as teacher certification, school facilities, and curriculum.) Although an adjustment for the length of the school year would be imprecise, it would probably modestly increase estimates of the growth in educational attainment for the first half of the twentieth century.

15. We use the decennial U.S. Censuses of Population for 1940 to 1990 and the Current Population Surveys for 1999 and 2000 to estimate the mean years of schooling and the share of college graduates by birth cohort for native-born Americans, standardized to age 35. Where the data allowed, we used the actual educational attainment of each cohort at age 35. In other cases, we predicted what the cohort's attainment was (or will be) at age 35 using the observed within-cohort historical patterns of changes in (reported) educational attainment over the life cycle, from ages 25 to 64 for birth cohorts born from 1876 to 1975. We know from comparisons with administrative records that census respondents, especially in 1940, occasionally overstated their educational attainment (Claudia Goldin, "America's Graduation from High School: The Evolution and Spread of Secondary Schooling in the Twentieth Century," *Journal of Economic History,* vol. 58, no. 2 [1998], pp. 345–74). We did not adjust the data for the overstatement, which imparts a downward bias to the increase in educational attainment across the twentieth century, just as the quality issue probably does.

16. These calculations are based on the 2000 Current Population Survey.

17. David T. Ellwood, "The Sputtering Labor Force of the Twenty-First Century: Can Social Policy Help?" Working Paper 8321 (Cambridge, Mass.: National Bureau of Economic Research, June 2001).

18. John Bound and Sarah Turner, "Going to War and Going to College: Did World War II and the G.I. Bill Increase Educational Attainment for Returning Veterans?" *Journal of Labor Economics,* vol. 20, no. 4 (2002), pp. 784–815; Marcus Stanley, "College

Education and the Mid-Century GI Bills," *Quarterly Journal of Economics,* vol. 118, no. 2 (2003, forthcoming).

19. Pedro Carneiro, James J. Heckman, and Dayanand Manoli, "Human Capital Policy," in James Heckman and Alan Krueger, eds., *Inequality in America: What Role for Human Capital Policies?* (MIT Press, 2003, forthcoming); David T. Ellwood and Thomas Kane, "Who Is Getting a College Education? Family Background and the Growing Gaps in Enrollment," in S. Danziger and J. Waldfogel, eds., *Securing the Future: Investing in Children from Birth to College* (New York: Russell Sage Foundation, 2000), pp. 283–324.

20. The evolution of the educational attainment of the work force as a whole, shown in figure 2-4, differs from that shown in figures 2-1 through 2-3 because of the inclusion of immigrants, differences in cohort size over the past century, and variation in labor force participation rates by age and sex.

21. Data from Iowa (see appendix 2A) indicate that progress was also rapid from 1915 to 1940.

22. Lawrence F. Katz and David H. Autor, "Changes in the Wage Structure and Earnings Inequality," in Orly Ashenfelter and David Card, eds., *Handbook of Labor Economics,* vol. 3A (Amsterdam: Elsevier, 1999), pp. 1463–555.

23. David H. Autor, Lawrence F. Katz, and Alan B. Krueger, "Computing Inequality: Have Computers Changed the Labor Market?" *Quarterly Journal of Economics,* vol. 113, no. 4 (1998), pp. 1169–213; Claudia Goldin and Lawrence F. Katz, "The Decline of Non-Competing Groups: Changes in the Premium to Education, 1890 to 1940," Working Paper 5202 (Cambridge, Mass.: National Bureau of Economic Research, August 1995); Goldin and Katz, "The Origins of Technology-Skill Complementarity."

24. David Card and Thomas Lemieux, "Can Falling Supply Explain the Rising Return to College for Younger Men? A Cohort-Based Analysis," *Quarterly Journal of Economics,* vol. 116, no. 2 (2001), pp. 705–46; Richard B. Freeman and Lawrence F. Katz, *Differences and Changes in Wage Structures* (University of Chicago Press, 1995).

25. Robert M. Solow, "A Contribution to the Theory of Economic Growth," *Quarterly Journal of Economics,* vol. 70, no. 1 (1956), pp. 65–94, and Robert E. Lucas, "On the Mechanics of Economic Development," *Journal of Monetary Economics,* vol. 22, no. 1 (1988), pp. 3–42, posit that the rate of growth of the human-capital stock (typically measured by the rate of growth in the educational attainment of the work force) affects the rate of economic growth by changing the effective quantity of labor. Paul Romer, "Endogenous Technological Change," *Journal of Political Economy,* vol. 89, no. 5 (1990), pp. S71–102, posits that the level of the educational attainment of the work force affects economic growth by influencing technological progress and the creation of new ideas.

26. Alan B. Krueger and Mikael Lindahl, "Education for Growth: Why and for Whom?" *Journal of Economic Literature,* vol. 39, no. 4 (2001), pp. 1101–36. Issues related to measurement error and to the likely omission of important variables correlated with national schooling levels (and changes in those levels) raise questions concerning the causal interpretation of the estimates from such cross-country growth regressions.

27. Edward F. Denison, *The Sources of Economic Growth in the United States and the Alternatives before Us* (New York: Committee for Economic Development, 1962).

28. Charles I. Jones, "Sources of U.S. Growth in a World of Ideas," *American Economic Review,* vol. 92, no. 1 (2002), pp. 220–39, argues that the standard growth-accounting framework *understates* the contribution of human capital because it does not include the

indirect effect on capital investment of the higher incomes generated by increases in human capital. Jones's alternative framework implies that a 1 percent increase in human capital per worker would boost output by a full 1 percent. Mark Bils and Peter Klenow, "Does Schooling Cause Growth?" *American Economic Review,* vol. 90, no. 5 (2000), pp. 1160–83, argue, in contrast, that to the extent that increased schooling endogenously responds to other sources of improvement in productivity, standard growth accounting *overstates* the causal contribution of human capital to growth.

29. Dale Jorgenson and Mun S. Ho, "The Quality of the U.S. Workforce, 1948–95," Harvard University, Department of Economics, 1999, using a slightly different methodology, provide estimates of the growth in the educational quality of the U.S. work force since 1948, and Daniel Aaronson and Daniel Sullivan, "Growth in Worker Quality," *Economic Perspectives* (4th quarter, 2001), pp. 53–74, using a methodology close to ours, provide estimates for the post-1960 period. Our estimates are quite similar to the findings of these two studies.

30. This estimate from Robert J. Gordon, "Interpreting the 'One Big Wave' in U.S. Long-Term Productivity Growth," Working Paper 7752 (Cambridge, Mass.: National Bureau of Economic Research, June 2000), is for the increase in nonfarm, nonhousing, business GDP per worker. Using the alternative growth-accounting framework of Jones, "Sources of U.S. Growth in a World of Ideas," our estimates imply that the full contribution of education to the growth in labor productivity over the twentieth century was 0.5 percent a year, or 31 percent of the overall increase.

31. Ellwood, "The Sputtering Labor Force of the Twenty-First Century."

32. These projections are based on our estimates from the 2000 Current Population Survey of educational wage differentials and on Ellwood's estimates of the change in the educational attainment of the U.S. labor force (aged twenty-five and over) from 2000 to 2020 (ibid.).

33. See, for example, Mark Doms, Timothy Dunne, and Kenneth R. Troske, "Workers, Wages, and Technology," *Quarterly Journal of Economics,* vol. 112, no. 1 (1997), pp. 253–90; and Timothy F. Bresnahan, Erik Brynjolfsson, and Lorin M. Hitt, "Information Technology, Workplace Organization, and the Demand for Skilled Labor: Firm-Level Evidence," *Quarterly Journal of Economics,* vol. 117, no. 1 (2002), pp. 339–76.

34. Jones, "Sources of U.S. Growth in a World of Ideas," estimates that the increasing intensity of R&D can account for 49 percent of the growth in U.S. output per worker from 1950 to 1993.

35. In practice, the inclusion or exclusion of race and nativity as productivity-related variables makes little difference to the estimates of the labor quality index. But changes in the sex composition of the work force are significant for certain subperiods.

36. Aaronson and Sullivan, "Growth in Worker Quality"; Ellwood, "The Sputtering Labor Force of the Twenty-First Century."

37. Daron Acemoglu and Joshua Angrist, "How Large Are Human Capital Externalities? Evidence from Compulsory Schooling Laws, " in B. Bernanke and K. Rogoff, eds., *NBER Macroeconomics Annual,* vol. 15 (National Bureau of Economic Research, 2000), pp. 9–59.

38. Carneiro, Heckman, and Manoli, "Human Capital Policy," and Alan B. Krueger, "Inequality, Too Much of a Good Thing," Princeton University, Department of Economics, 2002, offer comprehensive evaluations of evidence on the effectiveness of a wide range of targeted education and training policies, including early-childhood interventions,

changes in resources for primary and secondary schools, second-chance programs for youth, and financial aid for college.

39. U.S. Department of Education, National Center for Education Statistics, *The Condition of Education 2001* (Government Printing Office, 2001).

40. Ellwood and Kane, "Who Is Getting a College Education?"

41. Pedro Carneiro and James J. Heckman, "The Evidence on Credit Constraints in Post-Secondary Schooling," Working Paper 9055 (Cambridge, Mass.: National Bureau of Economic Research, 2002), provide a more skeptical interpretation of the evidence on the effect of credit constraints on low-income youths' investments in postsecondary education.

42. Susan Dynarski, "The Behavioral and Distributional Implications of Aid for College," *American Economic Review*, vol. 92, no. 2 (2002), pp. 279–85; Thomas Kane, *The Price of Admission: Rethinking How Americans Pay for College* (Brookings, 1999).

43. David Card, "The Causal Effect of Education on Earnings," in O. Ashenfelter and D. Card, eds., *Handbook of Labor Economics*, vol. 3A (Amsterdam: Elsevier, 1999), pp. 1801–63.

44. Kane, *The Price of Admission*, table 3-1, p. 60, estimates that mean real net tuition for public two-year and four-year colleges increased by 107 percent and 106 percent, respectively, from 1980–81 to 1994–95. Reductions in the share of expenditure on public college from state government subsidies contributed substantially to these rising costs. In contrast, real family incomes were essentially stagnant for the bottom 40 percent of families from 1980 to 1995.

45. James J. Heckman and Lance Lochner, "Rethinking Myths about Education and Training Policy: Understanding the Sources of Skill Formation in a Modern Economy," in S. Danziger and J. Waldfogel, eds., *Securing the Future: Investing in Children from Birth to College* (New York: Russell Sage Foundation, 2000), pp. 47–83.

46. Krueger, "Inequality."

47. Ibid.; Janet Currie, "Early Childhood Intervention Programs: What Do We Know?" *Journal of Economic Perspectives*, vol. 15, no. 2 (2001), pp. 212–38.

48. Larence Mishel and Richard Rothstein, *The Class Size Debate* (Washington: Economic Policy Institute, 2002).

49. Alan B. Krueger, "Experimental Estimates of Educational Production Functions," *Quarterly Journal of Economics*, vol. 114, no. 2 (1999), pp. 497–532; Krueger, "Inequality."

50. Tara Watson, "Inequality and the Rising Income Segregation of American Neighborhoods," Harvard University, Department of Economics, 2002.

51. Lawrence F. Katz, Jeffrey R. Kling, and Jeffrey B. Liebman, "Moving to Opportunity in Boston: Early Results of a Randomized Mobility Experiment," *Quarterly Journal of Economics*, vol. 116, no. 2 (2001), pp. 607–54; James E. Rosenbaum, "Changing the Geography of Opportunity by Expanding Residential Choice: Lessons from the Gautreaux Program," *Housing Policy Debate*, vol. 6, no. 1 (1995), pp. 231–69.

52. Robert M. Solow, "Technical Change and the Aggregate Production Function," *Review of Economics and Statistics*, vol. 39, no. 3 (1957), pp. 312–30; Solow, "A Contribution to the Theory of Economic Growth"; Moses Abramovitz, "Resource and Output Trends in the United States since 1870," *American Economic Review*, vol. 46, no. 2 (1956), pp. 5–23.

53. Denison, *The Sources of Economic Growth in the United States and the Alternatives before Us.*

54. Moses Abramovitz and Paul David, "Reinterpreting Economic Growth: Parables

and Realities," *American Economic Review,* vol. 63, no. 2 (1973), pp. 428–39; Jones, "Sources of U.S. Growth in a World of Ideas."

55. Daron Acemoglu, "A Microfoundation for Social Increasing Returns in Human Capital Accumulation," *Quarterly Journal of Economics,* vol. 111, no. 3 (1996), pp. 779–804; Goldin and Katz, "The Origins of Technology-Skill Complementarity."

56. J. Bradford DeLong and Lawrence H. Summers, "Equipment Investment and Economic Growth," *Quarterly Journal of Economics,* vol. 116, no. 2 (1991), pp. 445–502. Xavier Sala-i-Martin, "I Just Ran Four Million Regressions," Working Paper 6252 (Cambridge, Mass.: National Bureau of Economic Research, November 1997), and others have noted that the association between investment in physical capital and growth is remarkably robust to changes in regression specifications.

57. Erik Brynjolfsson and Lorin Hitt, "Beyond Computation: Information Technology, Organizational Transformation, and Business Performance," *Journal of Economic Perspectives,* vol. 14, no. 4 (2000), pp. 23–48.

58. Paul David, "Computer and Dynamo: The Modern Productivity Paradox in a Not-Too-Distant Mirror," in Organization for Economic Cooperation and Development, *Technology and Productivity: The Challenge for Economic Policy* (Paris, 1991); Warren Devine, "From Shafts to Wires: Historical Perspectives on Electrification," *Explorations in Economic History,* vol. 63, no. 2 (1983), pp. 347–72.

59. Clear evidence that private decisions led to the wrong balance of resources and well-being across generational cohorts would be an additional reason for government action to influence investment. Unfortunately—or perhaps fortunately—economists have reached no consensus on whether the past (and the likely future) cross-generational cohort pattern of consumption is unfairly weighted toward early generations, unfairly weighted toward later generations, or about right. The likelihood that future cohorts will be richer than their forebears, coupled with a simplistic utilitarianism, suggests that current consumption is too low, current saving is too high, and the current rate of American economic growth too fast. On the other hand, the likelihood that an America rich and powerful enough, in relative terms, to be a global superpower confers massive positive external benefits on the rest of the world—the defeat of Germany in World War II, for example—suggests that the current rate of American economic growth is too slow. The behavioral economic literature on "impatience" and "myopia" suggests that Americans devote less attention to the distant future than they "really want to," which implies that the current rate of saving is too low (David Laibson, "Golden Eggs and Hyperbolic Discounting," *Quarterly Journal of Economics,* vol. 112, no. 2 [1997], pp. 443–77). These self-control problems may be the most important of all.

60. Lawrence H. Summers, "What Is the Social Return to Capital Investment?" in Peter Diamond, ed., *Growth, Productivity, Unemployment: Essays to Celebrate Bob Solow's Birthday* (MIT Press, 1990).

61. The fourth option—direct government investment—will not be considered because, apart from investment in public capital goods, such as roads, canals, airports, and other items lumped under the heading of infrastructure, the record of direct government investment, except during national emergencies, has been poor around the world.

62. Investment Company Institute, "Mutual Funds and the U.S. Retirement Market in 2001," *Fundamentals: Investment Company Institute Research in Brief,* vol. 11, no. 2 (2002).

63. See, for example, Eric Engen, William G. Gale, and John Karl Scholz, "The Illusory Effects of Saving Incentives on Saving," *Journal of Economic Perspectives,* vol. 10, no. 4

(1996), pp. 113–38. But recent work in behavioral economics suggests that changes in financial education and in the plan rules (and default options) for private defined-contribution pensions have potentially powerful effects on retirement saving; see James J. Choi and others, "Defined Contribution Pensions: Plan Rules, Participant Choices, and the Path of Least Resistance," *Tax Policy and the Economy,* vol. 16 (2002), pp. 67–113.

64. See David Laibson, "Psychological Perspectives on 401Ks," in David Wise, ed., *Frontiers in the Economics of Aging* (University of Chicago Press, 1998), pp. 106–20; Choi and others, "Defined Contribution Pensions."

65. Shlomo Benartzi and Richard Thaler, "Save More Tomorrow: Using Behavioral Economics to Increase Employee Savings," Anderson School of Business, University of California, Los Angeles, 2001.

66. As Annamaria Lusardi, Jonathan Skinner, and Steven Venti, "Saving Puzzles and Saving Policies in the United States," Working Paper 8237 (Cambridge, Mass.: National Bureau of Economic Research, 2001), have pointed out, such "impatience," or "myopia," can be generated by the interaction between even fully rational and farsighted households and a means-tested social insurance system. For example, if the chances are high that health problems late in life will eat up all accumulated private wealth before Medicaid kicks in, households will regard this eventuality as a powerful disincentive to private saving. A countervailing government focus on saving incentives might well be appropriate to offset the effects of such a distortion.

67. The belief that such incentives can be counterproductive because they encourage foreign investment in the United States—which would mean that a significant part of the returns from the increased capital stock would flow abroad—is simply wrong: the point of the exercise is to capture the positive externalities that arise from increasing capital stock. It is true that when foreigners invest in America, the normal—that is, private—profits flow abroad, but it is also true that foreign investment does not have to be financed through reductions in current American consumption. These two effects balance each other, leaving the positive external benefit from investment as an improvement in social welfare.

68. Alan Auerbach and James Hines, "Investment Tax Incentives and Frequent Tax Reforms," *American Economic Review,* vol. 78, no. 2 (1988), pp. 211–16.

69. That Robert Barro's ("Are Government Bonds Net Wealth?" *Journal of Political Economy,* vol. 82, no. 6 [1974], pp. 1095–117) doctrine of Ricardian equivalence (and of the neutrality of government budget deficits) is likely to be of limited applicability in the contemporary United States appears to be demonstrated by the failure of private saving rates to offset either the rise in the federal deficit in the 1980s or the fall in the federal deficit in the 1990s. B. Douglas Bernheim and Kyle Bagwell, "Is Everything Neutral?" *Journal of Political Economy,* vol. 96, no. 2 (1988), pp. 308–38, argue that the assumptions about altruism and intergenerational linkages needed for such Ricardian equivalence to be effective with respect to government finance carry other powerful unobserved and unrealistic consequences for economic behavior.

70. Romer, "Endogenous Technological Change."

71. Quoted in Summers, "What Is the Social Return to Capital Investment?"

72. Nancy Gallini, "The Economics of Patents: Lessons from Recent U.S. Patent Reform," *Journal of Economic Perspectives,* vol. 16, no. 2 (2002), pp. 131–54.

73. Michael Kremer, "Patent Buyouts: A Mechanism for Encouraging Innovation," *Quarterly Journal of Economics,* vol. 113, no. 4 (1998), pp. 1137–67.

74. Charles I. Jones and John C. Williams, "Measuring the Social Return to R&D," *Quarterly Journal of Economics,* vol. 113, no. 4 (1998), pp. 1119–35.

75. The data from the Iowa 1915 State Census are described and documented in Goldin and Katz, "Education and Income in the Early Twentieth Century: Evidence from the Prairies."

76. Claudia Goldin and Lawrence F. Katz, "The Legacy of U.S. Educational Leadership: Notes on Distribution and Economic Growth in the Twentieth Century," *American Economic Review,* vol. 91, no. 2 (2001), pp. 18–23; Aaronson and Sullivan, "Growth in Worker Quality."

77. Goldin and Katz, "Decreasing (and Then Increasing) Inequality in America: A Tale of Two Half-Centuries," in F. Welch, ed., *The Causes and Consequences of Increasing Income Inequality.*

78. Autor, Katz, and Krueger, "Computing Inequality: Have Computers Changed the Labor Market?"

GARY BURTLESS
CHRISTOPHER JENCKS

3

American Inequality and Its Consequences

INCOME INEQUALITY HAS risen sharply in the United States over the past generation, reaching levels not seen since before World War II. But while almost two-thirds of Americans agree with the statement "income differences in the United States are too large," policies aimed at reducing income differences command relatively little popular support.[1] In most rich countries sizable majorities "agree strongly" that the government ought to guarantee each citizen a minimum standard of living. Only one American in four agrees strongly with this proposition.[2] The same pattern holds in Congress, where legislators show little interest in policies aimed at taxing the rich, raising the wages of the poor, taxing inherited wealth, or guaranteeing shelter and health care to all Americans.

One possible explanation for this apparent paradox is that, while most Americans think income inequality is too high, most also distrust the government and attribute America's economic success to the fact that its economy is lightly regulated. A second possible explanation is that while

We gratefully acknowledge the helpful research assistance of Molly Fifer and Alice Henriques of the Brookings Institution and Andrew Clarkwest of Harvard University. We are also grateful to David Jesuit and Timothy Smeeding for providing tabulations of Luxembourg Income Study data and to Jesuit, Smeeding, the editors, and an anonymous referee for helpful comments on an earlier version of this chapter.

most Americans think income inequality is too high, they worry far more about abortion, crime, immigration, and the environment than about inequality. If those who benefit from inequality give money to candidates who protect their economic interests, while those who think inequality is too high mostly vote on the basis of noneconomic issues, legislators will protect the economic interests of the rich and the noneconomic interests of everyone else.

We begin by describing how the distribution of income has changed in the United States since the 1970s, why it has changed, and why it is more unequal than the distribution in other rich democracies. We then assess the evidence on whether changes in economic inequality affect four other things that Americans care about—economic growth, equality of opportunity for children, longevity, and the distribution of political influence. We conclude that inequality probably does not have a consistent effect, either positive or negative, on economic growth in rich democracies. We show that college attendance became more related to parental income as economic inequality increased in the United States. Nonetheless, evidence does not show that a father's economic status has more influence on his children's economic prospects in the United States than in other rich countries where incomes are more equal. Increases in economic inequality probably slow the rate of improvement in longevity, but the effect is very small, probably only a few months.[3] We also consider the impact of economic inequality on the distribution of political power. We argue that increases in economic inequality tend to increase the political power of the rich, at least in the United States. Overall, we conclude that the effects of inequality on economic growth, health, and equality of opportunity are modest and uncertain in rich countries. Accordingly, citizens of these countries should decide how much economic inequality they are willing to tolerate largely on the basis of what they think is just, not on the basis of its alleged beneficial or adverse effects.

How Has the Distribution of Income Changed in the United States?

The Census Bureau did not begin asking Americans about their incomes until 1940. The best pre-1940 data are based on tax returns. These data indicate that the share of income going to the richest 10 percent of Americans fell dramatically during the first half of the twentieth century, was flat

Figure 3-1. *Trend in Family Income Inequality, 1947–2001*

Income ratio

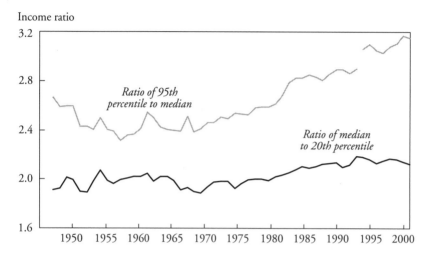

Source: Authors' calculations based on data tabulated by the U.S. Bureau of the Census.

from about 1952 to 1973, and began to rise after 1973, sharply after 1981.[4] Before World War II the richest 10 percent typically got 40 to 45 percent of all income. From 1952 to 1973 their share was about 33 percent. In the late 1990s their share averaged 41 percent of total income.

Census surveys miss much of the income received by people in the top 2 percent of the distribution, but they provide better evidence about the incomes of those in the middle and near the bottom. Figure 3-1 shows the ratios of incomes at the ninety-fifth and the fiftieth percentiles of the family income distribution and the ratio of incomes at the fiftieth and twentieth percentiles. The top line shows that the proportional difference between well-to-do and middle-income American families was lower in the late 1950s than in the late 1940s and that there was no clear trend between the late 1950s and the late 1960s, which is consistent with tax data. After 1969 the proportional gap between the ninety-fifth and fiftieth percentiles began to widen steadily. The apparent jump in inequality between 1992 and 1993 is partly due to a change in the Census Bureau's Current Population Survey that led to better measurement of rich families' incomes. Even if we exclude this jump, however, the gap between the ninety-fifth and fiftieth percentiles rose by about a quarter between 1970 and 2001. That, too, is consistent with tax data on the share of total income going to the top 10 percent.

The lower line in figure 3-1 shows the ratio of family incomes at the fiftieth and twentieth percentiles. There was no clear trend from the late 1940s to the late 1960s. The gap widened from 1969 to 1989, just as it did in the top half of the distribution. But unlike the gap between the top and the middle, the gap between the middle and the bottom showed no clear trend after 1990. Nonetheless, figure 3-1 suggests that the overall increase in inequality since 1969 has not been driven solely by the remarkable gains of the rich. At least in the 1970s and 1980s, disparities widened throughout the income distribution.

Still, the spectacular increase in the incomes of the richest Americans accounts for much of the growth in economic inequality since 1980. The Congressional Budget Office has combined census and tax data to examine trends in the after-tax distribution of income. Its analysis shows that the richest 1 percent of American households raised their share of after-tax income from 7.5 percent in 1979 to 13.6 percent in 1997. Meanwhile, the share going to households between the eightieth and ninety-ninth percentiles only rose from 35.2 to 36.2 percent. This pattern is not obvious in census data, partly because the Census Bureau defines income more narrowly and partly because census respondents seriously underreport their income from assets. The Congressional Budget Office findings confirm the analysis of tax returns, which also showed that most of the rise in the gross income share received by the top 10 percent of Americans actually went to the top 1 percent.[5]

We can use Census Bureau tabulations of family income to estimate changes in purchasing power (income adjusted for inflation). For this purpose, the postwar era falls into two distinct periods: before and after 1973. Figure 3-2 shows the average annual gain in purchasing power among families in different parts of the distribution for each period. Between 1947 and 1973, real incomes rose fastest near the bottom of the distribution and slowest near the top. After 1973, growth slowed in most parts of the income distribution, but it slowed most at the bottom. Only the top 5 percent of families gained as much per year after 1973 as before. Income growth between 1973 and 2001 was six times faster for the top fifth than for the bottom fifth of families.

Like all estimates of the change in people's real income, the estimates in figure 3-2 are sensitive to one's choice of a price index. The goods and services available in 2001 were very different from those available in 1947.

Figure 3-2. *Annual Growth Rate of Real Income across the U.S. Family Income Distrubution, 1947–2001*

Annual rate of growth (percent)

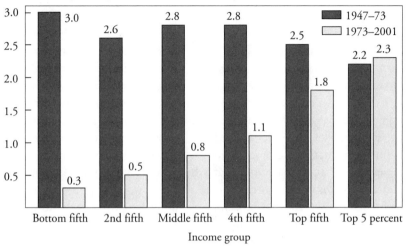

Source: Authors' calculations based on data tabulated by the U.S. Bureau of the Census.

No price index can make 1947 dollars truly equivalent to 2001 dollars. Nor is there any consensus about the best procedures for measuring price changes.[6] Fortunately, however, one's choice of a price index does not affect conclusions about inequality.

A more serious problem for measuring changes in inequality is adjusting for shifts in the size of American families. Figures 3-1 and 3-2 ignore the fact that American families have been getting smaller. The average American family had 3.6 members in 1947, 3.4 members in 1973, and 3.1 members in 2001. Because family size shrank about 0.3 percent a year, income per family member would have increased 0.3 percent a year even if families' average income had not changed at all. In addition, a growing percentage of Americans live alone or with someone who is not a relative. The incomes of these unrelated individuals are excluded from the Census Bureau's tabulations of family income. One reason more Americans live alone is that more of the elderly can afford to maintain their own household instead of living with their children. Another reason is that the young are waiting longer to marry and start families. Of course, living alone carries a price.

Two people who live alone need more kitchens, bathrooms, furniture, and household appliances than two people who live together. It is not surprising that households with high incomes on average also have more members than households with low incomes, so some of the income gap between high- and low-income families disappears if we calculate each family's income per person. On the other hand, household size has declined a bit faster in households with above-average income than it has in households with below-average income, implying a greater trend toward inequality if income is measured on a per person rather than a per family basis.

One way to deal with changes in family size is to estimate the change in expenditure required to hold living standards constant when a family gets larger or smaller. In principle, such an adjustment allows us to calculate "equivalent" incomes for households of different sizes. One popular adjustment, which we use, assumes that a household's spending requirements increase in proportion to the square root of the number of household members.[7] Under this assumption, a family of four needs twice as much income as a single individual living alone to achieve the same standard of living.[8] If this adjustment is valid, the 14 percent decline in family size between 1947 and 2001 implies that families typically needed 7 percent less real income in 2001 than in 1947 to enjoy the same standard of living.

The income data in figure 3-1 are also limited to pretax money income. Ignoring a family's tax liabilities overstates the resources it has available for consumption. Focusing exclusively on money income ignores the fact that some families own their home mortgage-free, while others must make monthly rent payments, as well as the fact that some families receive food stamps, rent subsidies, and other noncash transfers. Because noncash benefits expanded dramatically between 1965 and 1979, ignoring them understates gains near the bottom of the distribution during these years. Since 1979 the Census Bureau has tried to remedy some of these problems by estimating each family's income and payroll taxes and by asking households about noncash income. Unfortunately, such data are unavailable for years before 1979, when noncash income grew fastest.

In figure 3-3 we report income trends in a way that eliminates some of the problems in the official census statistics. The chart shows income growth since 1979 at the tenth, fiftieth, and ninety-fifth percentiles of the "household-size-adjusted" distribution of personal income. Our sample includes all individuals except those who live in institutions. We adjust each person's household income to reflect differences in household size. The top panel shows growth in size-adjusted household income after taxes

Figure 3-3. *Trends in Size-Adjusted Household Incomes before and after Taxes and Transfers at Selected Points in the Distribution, 1979–2000*[a]

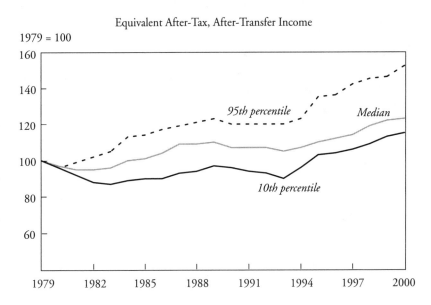

Equivalent After-Tax, After-Transfer Income

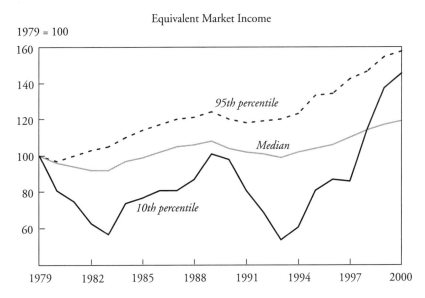

Equivalent Market Income

Source: Authors' tabulations of 1980–2001 March files of the Current Population Survey (CPS).
a. Incomes are deflated using the CPI-U-RS price index.

and transfers, including the value of food stamps and means-tested housing subsidies. (We do not include the value of owner-occupied housing or medical care subsidies, because such imputations are unreliable.) Like figure 3-1, figure 3-3 shows that inequality grew after 1979. But whereas figure 3-1 shows no change in the gap between the bottom and the middle during the 1990s, figure 3-3 shows that, once we replace families with households, adjust for changes in household size, subtract taxes, and add noncash benefits, the gap between the bottom and the middle narrowed significantly during the first half of the 1990s. The gap between those at the top and those in the middle of the distribution continued to widen after 1993, just as it does in figure 3-1.

The lower panel in figure 3-3 shows trends in "market" income, which we define as income before taxes are subtracted and government transfers are added. Market income includes income from self-employment, wages, interest, dividends, rents, and private pensions. It does not include income from public assistance or Social Security. Year-to-year movements in market income are much bigger than those for income after taxes and transfers, especially near the bottom of the distribution. Between 1979 and 1983, when unemployment reached its highest rate since the 1930s, market income at the tenth percentile fell 43 percent, whereas income after taxes and transfers fell only 13 percent.[9] Market incomes at the tenth percentile were no greater in 1989 than they were in 1979. Market income at the tenth percentile rose far more during the 1990s, ending the decade almost 40 percent higher than it had been in 1989.

The top panel of figure 3-3 uses a more comprehensive definition of income than the Census Bureau's traditional measure, but it does not include any adjustment for health insurance or free medical care. Health care spending poses a difficult challenge for measuring changes in American inequality. The national income accounts show that medical care represents 15 percent of personal consumption in the United States, a much larger share than in the 1950s or even the 1970s. Yet despite steep increases in the share of all consumption devoted to medical care, such spending accounts for about the same percentage of households' out-of-pocket spending today as in 1950.[10] The reason is that most Americans are now covered by health insurance, and the cost of insurance is financed largely by employers and the government. The distributional impact of this change is not easy to assess, but we know that public assistance financed $200 billion worth of medical care for the needy in 2000, mostly through the Medicaid program. Indeed, means-tested public assistance finances one-fifth of total health care consumption in the United States. While low-income Americans do not have the same access to medical care as middle- or upper-income families, health care utilization rates have risen more among the poor than among the affluent since Medicaid and Medicare were established in 1965. Figures 3-1 through 3-3 do not capture this change.

Measuring health care consumption and access to medical care highlights a more basic limitation of using money income to assess inequality. Money income inequality captures disparities in those domains where money can be used to purchase improvements in well-being. If two people have identical incomes, they can buy identical amounts of goods and services that are for sale and not rationed. However, if one person has severe arthritis while the other enjoys robust health, the equality of their incomes obscures a major disparity in their circumstances. Money can buy care and medicine that reduces some of the pain and inconvenience caused by arthritis, but it cannot place sufferers and nonsufferers on an equal footing with respect to the enjoyment of life. Their health would not be equal even if they both had insurance that paid for all their medical care.

Innovations in both medical care and the provision of health insurance have changed inequality in both consumption and health itself. Health insurance lessens nonmedical inequality between the healthy and unhealthy, because it reduces the percentage of income that the unhealthy must devote to medical care and allows them to purchase food, clothing, and shelter that are more nearly equal to those available to healthier people who have the same cash income. In addition, insurance probably reduces health inequality, although that is harder to prove. Standard income statistics do not capture the effects of changing insurance coverage *either* in the domain of nonmedical consumption *or* in the domain of health.

Nor do income statistics tell us much about the distribution of educational opportunity. Local governments offer free public education through the twelfth grade to every child in the United States, which almost certainly means that educational opportunity is more equally distributed than income. Nonetheless, low-income students typically attend worse schools than do high-income students. Some people believe that the quality gap in the schooling of rich and poor students has grown since 1970. As we indicate below, differences in access to higher education pose even thornier issues.

In principle, the United States also tries to protect everyone against crime. But not all neighborhoods are equally safe. People with higher incomes can afford to live in safer places. The steep increase in violent crime during the late 1960s and early 1970s accentuated the price difference between safe and unsafe neighborhoods, while the fall in crime during the 1990s probably reduced such differences. These differences, too, are missed by the standard income distribution statistics.

Why Has the U.S. Income Distribution Changed?

Since 1979 the widening income gap between rich and poor households in the United States has been closely connected to widening disparities in the pay of U.S. workers. Among men who worked full time throughout the year, real wages fell near the bottom of the distribution, were essentially flat near the middle, and rose near the top. As a result, the ratio of earnings at the ninetieth percentile to earnings at the tenth percentile rose from 4.0 in 1979 to 5.7 in 2000. The annual increase in real wages was about 1 percent faster for women than for men between 1979 and 2000, but the growth of inequality was very similar. As a result, women's real wages were flat near the bottom of the distribution, rose moderately in the middle, and rose sharply near the top. The ratio of earnings at the ninetieth and the tenth percentiles for women rose from 3.2 to 4.7.

The trend in inequality between families cannot be explained solely by the trend in wage disparities, however. Wage inequality also increased between 1947 and 1969, but family income inequality fell.[11] Earnings inequality rose moderately among men and fell among women during the 1970s, while money income inequality rose.

Wage differentials based on education, job experience, and occupational skill all widened during the 1980s and 1990s. Less well known but even more important, wage differentials among workers in the same occupation with the same amount of education and experience also widened over the same period.[12] Some economists believe that these increases reflect the fact that employers now place more value on job-specific skills that vary independent of education and experience. Others argue that institutional changes, such as the decline in the minimum wage relative to the average wage and the decline of private sector unions, played a significant role.[13] Social norms may also have changed, particularly with regard to whether workers should be rewarded for effort or results, although it is hard to tell whether normative change is a cause or a consequence of changes in firms' actual practices.

Two explanations for rising wage inequality dominate popular discussion—technological change and globalization. Most economists believe that the best explanation for widening inequality was a shift in employers' demand for labor linked to the introduction of new production techniques. Innovative management practices and new technologies, such as personal computers and improved communications, caused a surge in demand for highly skilled workers. Technological innovation put competitive pressure on employers to change their production methods in ways that required a more entrepreneurial and more skilled work force. Throughout the 1980s and 1990s employers persisted in hiring more highly skilled workers even though rising wage differentials made this strategy more expensive than ever. The resulting surge in demand for highly skilled workers pushed up the relative wages of such workers.[14]

Among noneconomists a more popular underlying explanation for rising wage inequality is globalization—the growing importance of international trade, especially trade with developing countries. According to its critics, freer trade with low-wage countries has harmed all but the most skilled workers in the manufacturing sector of the American economy. This argument was forcefully advanced by opponents of the North American Free Trade Agreement and other trade agreements during the 1990s. Labor leaders and editorial writers warned that free trade with Mexico and other poor countries would eliminate middle-income industrial jobs and undermine the wages of semi-skilled U.S. workers. Most economists who have studied the influence of international trade are skeptical of these claims. With few exceptions, economists find little evidence that trade is the main explanation for growing wage disparities in the United States. Most would concede, however, that free trade has added to the downward pressure on the wages of less skilled workers and contributed modestly to their decline.[15]

Increased immigration and the changing characteristics of immigrants have played at least as big a role in depressing the wages of the less skilled. The effect of surging immigration on the wages of native-born workers with limited education has been particularly large, because immigrants represent a large and growing percentage of workers with the lowest levels of education.

As wage inequality rose, women's labor force participation also increased steadily after the 1960s, while men's participation edged down. In many families, a drop in men's real earnings has been offset by an increase in women's earnings, either because of higher wages or increased hours, allowing married couples to maintain or even improve their standard of living. Indeed, some critics of American economic performance think that the increase in women's earnings is the main reason middle-income families have been able to increase their consumption.[16]

But while the anemic growth of male wages may explain why some women in middle-income families have joined the work force, women who are married to highly skilled men have also increased their earnings dramatically, even though their husbands' real earnings have not declined. Among working-age men in the top fifth of the male earnings distribution, the percentage with a working wife increased by one-quarter between 1979 and 1996, and their wives' overall earnings more than doubled. These gains have disproportionately increased the incomes of families in which income would be high even without the wife's earnings, exacerbating household income inequality.[17]

Changes in family composition have also played a role in widening the gap between families at different points in the distribution. Although mortality rates have fallen steeply since the late nineteenth century, reducing the proportion of families headed by a widow or widower, divorce rates jumped dramatically between 1960 and 1980, boosting the fraction of Americans living in households with only one adult. The proportion of children born out of wedlock also rose dramatically between about 1964 and 1994. Many mothers who have a child out of wedlock eventually marry, and many of those who divorce eventually remarry. Nonetheless, more children were living in single-parent families in the 1990s than in earlier decades.[18] These families have much lower market incomes than two-parent families, both because they have only one potential earner instead of two and because the family breadwinner is seldom the parent with the highest earning power.

Family income is also more unequally distributed among one-adult families than among two-adult families. The wages of husbands and wives are not perfectly correlated, and the earnings of families with two earners are somewhat more equal than the earnings of these same husbands and wives examined separately. But even when the husband is the principal breadwinner, his wife can enter the labor force if he loses his job and is either unemployed for a lengthy period or has to take a job with lower pay. This means couples have better insurance against hard times than do single-parent families. (Families with three or four potential earners are even better insured against such risks, which may be one reason why such extended families are more common in poor societies with no government safety net.) The net result is that while improvements in women's labor market position have somewhat reduced the income gap between one- and two-parent families, the spread of single-parent families has still raised overall economic inequality.[19]

Cross-national comparisons show that taxes and transfers also have a major effect on the distribution of disposable income (income after taxes and transfers). But while different countries pursue very different policies in this regard, countries rarely make drastic changes in whatever policy they have adopted. In the United States, Congress and the president never tire of tinkering with the tax code, but the changes enacted since 1980 have not greatly altered the basic shape of the disposable income distribution. Congress lowered the effective tax rate for families with very high incomes in 1981 and 1986.[20] It also reduced taxes for low-income families, and in 1993 it greatly increased the earned income tax credit, which now provides a relatively large refundable credit for low-wage workers with children. According to our estimates, people in the bottom tenth of the size-adjusted income distribution owed taxes equal to 7 percent of their pretax income in 1979. In 2000 these low-income people typically received a tax credit that slightly exceeded their total tax liability, making their after-tax income 1 percent higher than their pretax income.

The redistributive impact of a more generous earned income tax credit was, however, largely offset by a drop in means-tested cash and noncash benefits. Part of this drop was directly attributable to welfare reform in the 1990s, which cut the number of families collecting cash benefits. In addition, the take-up rate for food stamps and Medicaid fell among low-income families who were, in principle, still eligible for such benefits. This change was probably an indirect by-product of welfare reform, as welfare applicants receive these benefits automatically, whereas other low-income families must apply for them directly.

Because the decline in means-tested benefits roughly offset the decline in net taxes, the bottom decile's size-adjusted disposable income remained almost unchanged. The income of some specific families changed substantially, however. Low-income households containing a working breadwinner tended to gain, while households in which no one worked tended to lose. This kind of redistribution was, of course, precisely what legislators sought to achieve when they reformed welfare in the 1990s.

Immigration has also contributed to the growth of economic inequality since 1970. If immigrants were exactly like natives, their arrival would not have much effect on the distribution of income. Even when immigrants are less skilled than natives, as has traditionally been the case during periods of high immigration into the United States, the distribution of income will change only if the ratio of immigrants to natives changes or if the skill gap between the two groups changes. But that is precisely what has happened over the past generation. In 1970 less than 5 percent of the resident population had been born abroad, and recent immigrants earned 17 percent less than natives. By the end of the 1990s, 11 percent of the resident population had been born abroad, and recent immigrants earned 34 percent less than natives.[21]

Poverty statistics provide a simple illustration of how immigration has affected income statistics. The poverty rate for households headed by native-born Americans did not change between 1979 and 1998. But both the number of immigrant households and their poverty rate rose. As a result, the poverty rate for all residents, both native- and foreign-born, rose from 11.7 to 12.7 percent.[22] If competition from immigrants depressed the wages and employment prospects of unskilled natives, which seems likely, the overall effect of immigration on poverty (and inequality) was even larger than this calculation implies.

Immigration raises fundamental questions about how to interpret statistics on poverty and inequality within the United States. Most immigrants come to the United States from countries where the average family's income is below the U.S. poverty line. Most enjoy higher incomes in the United States than they did in their country of origin. Even if their incomes place them near the bottom of the American distribution, they are usually better off than they would have been in their place of birth. (Those for whom this is not true usually go home.) Thus while slowing the flow of new immigrants or increasing the skill requirements for entry would almost surely reduce both inequality and poverty in the United States, the would-be immigrants thus excluded would be worse off.

America's current immigration policy almost certainly reduces global inequality at the same time that it increases inequality within the United States. Indeed, the increase in inequality within the United States is to some extent an illusory by-product of the fact that the Census Bureau tracks income trends for places, not specific people. If census data on trends in inequality between 1970 and 2000 included the 1970 incomes of those who moved to the United States between 1970 and 2000, the 1970 distribution would look far more unequal. This change in perspective would not alter the fact that the income gap between the top and the middle has widened, but inequality for the population as a whole might well show a decline.[23]

How Does the United States Compare with Other Rich Countries?

Many poorer countries, including Brazil, Nigeria, and Russia, have household incomes that are far less equal than those in the United States, but these countries differ from the United States in so many other ways that comparing them to the United States is not very informative. We therefore focus on comparisons among rich countries that collect consistent information on household income. Inequality tables for rich countries invariably show that the United States ranks at the top or near the top.[24] Comparing measures of income inequality across countries raises many of the same issues as does comparing inequality over time within a single country. Differences in national arrangements for financing health care, housing, and education mean that money income is more important in determining overall consumption in some countries than in others. Income differences are likely to produce wider differences in health care, housing, and education in places where families must finance these things out of their own pocket than in places where such costs are financed largely from taxes. In the United States, however, low-income families often receive subsidized health care, food, housing, and higher education, while the more affluent pay higher prices. As a result, it is hard to be sure whether inequality in disposable income overstates inequality in consumption more in the United States or in Europe.

Figure 3-4 shows estimated Gini coefficients for seventeen countries in the Organization for Economic Cooperation and Development (OECD). The Gini coefficient is a standard statistic for measuring economic inequality. It ranges from 0 (when all families or persons have identical incomes) to 1 (when all income is received by a single family or individual). The data come from the Luxembourg Income Study (LIS), which is a cross-national project that assembles and tabulates income distribution statistics using consistent methods for all countries. The estimates use the same measure of after-tax, after-transfer "equivalent income" that we present in figure 3-3. Each person in the national population is ranked from lowest to highest in terms of size-adjusted income, and the coefficient is then calculated. The bars in figure 3-4 show the Gini coefficient of after-tax, after-transfer income (that is, the Gini coefficient of the final income distribution), while the black squares indicate the Gini coefficient of market income (that is, labor and property income before taxes are subtracted).[25]

Figure 3-4. *Inequality of Market Income and Net Disposable Income in OECD Countries, 1990s*

Gini coefficient × 100

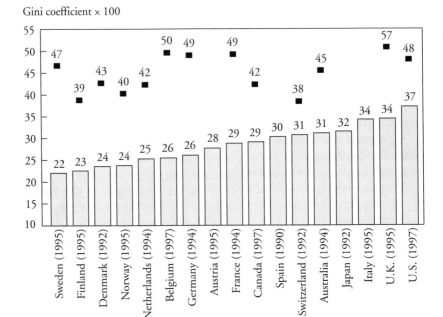

Source: Luxembourg Income Study.

Disposable income inequality is highest in the United States, the United Kingdom, and Italy and lowest in the Scandinavian countries.[26] Inequality as measured by the Gini coefficient is on average one quarter lower in the other OECD countries than it is in the United States. Many people have a hard time interpreting Gini coefficients. They find it easier to understand income ratios, which are highly correlated with Gini coefficients. The LIS estimates suggest that someone at the ninetieth percentile of the Swedish income distribution received an equivalent income only 2.6 times that of someone at the tenth percentile. In the United States, the same income ratio was 5.6 to 1. Thus the proportional distance between the ninetieth and tenth percentiles is more than twice as large in the United States as in Sweden. In France, the ratio was 3.5 to 1. Clearly, income gaps are much wider in the United States than in most other OECD countries.

Figure 3-4 also shows that households' market income is more unequal than their disposable income in all OECD countries. It is hardly surprising that government transfers tend to equalize the distribution of income generated by labor and capital markets. The surprise is that market income inequality in the United States is not especially high by OECD standards. The Gini coefficient for market income is 0.48 in the United States, compared to 0.49 in Germany and France and 0.47 in Sweden. Averaging across the twelve OECD countries for which we have such data, the Gini for market income averages 0.45. The main reason why disposable income is more unequal in the United States than in other rich countries is that the U.S. system of taxes and transfers does less to reduce inequality than do the systems in most other countries. In the United States, taxes and transfers reduce the Gini by 23 percent (from 0.48 to 0.37). In the other twelve countries for which we have data, the reduction averages 39 percent. If the United States redistributed as much income as the average OECD country, the dispersion of disposable incomes would be about the same in the United States as in France or Canada.

Many people may be surprised to learn that households' market incomes are no more unequal in the United States than in France or Germany. To begin with, there is abundant evidence that Americans at the top of the pay distribution receive much higher compensation than do their counterparts elsewhere, both absolutely and relative to the earnings of an average worker. For example, a recent pay survey shows that U.S. chief executives typically receive forty-one times as much compensation as an average employee in manufacturing. Great Britain has the next highest ratio, but British chief executive officers receive only twenty-five times as much as British manufacturing workers. In France the ratio is 16 to 1, and in Japan it is just 12 to 1.[27] Census surveys may miss some of this compensation. But census surveys still find wider pay disparities in the United States than do similar surveys in other countries.

So why is market income inequality so similar in the United States and other OECD countries? The main explanation is that while those with jobs are more unequally compensated in the United States than in other industrial countries, not having a job at all is more common in most other industrial countries. As soon as one includes individuals with zero earnings in the distribution, the Gini coefficient for earnings in the United States looks similar to that of other rich countries.[28] Americans who have retired are also more likely than their counterparts in many other rich countries to receive income from employer-sponsored pensions and retirement savings accounts. Retirees in many other countries are more likely to rely solely on public pensions. Overall, about 95 percent of Americans live in households that derive some part of their income from the market.[29]

Differences in countries' tax and transfer systems help to explain these facts. Almost all working-age American families have some market income because low government transfers make not working very costly. More generous transfer payments, especially for working-age families in which no one has a job, make not working more attractive in other OECD countries, especially in continental Europe, than it is in the United States. Figure 3-5 shows the relationship between the labor utilization rate and government transfers in the seventeen OECD countries in figure 3-4. The labor utilization rate is the average number of hours worked by fifteen- to sixty-four-year-olds as a percentage of the U.S. average.[30] Transfers are defined as government spending on public pensions and nonhealth transfers to the working-age population and are measured as a percentage of a nation's gross domestic product (GDP). Two countries with the same labor force participation rate, unemployment rate, and average workweek would have identical rates of labor utilization. Japan is the only OECD country with a higher labor utilization rate than the United States. Figure 3-5 shows a strong negative association between government transfers and labor force utilization; the correlation is –0.79. Although this correlation is unlikely to be entirely causal, it does suggest that generous transfers to nonworkers affect the employment and hours worked of adults.

Of course, a high labor utilization rate means that the working-age population has less free time for activities other than paid employment. Most of us value such activities, so having less time for them is a cost. On average, Americans have more income than residents of other OECD countries. But Americans, on the average, are also employed during more years of their life and work more hours each year. Some of the U.S. income advantage represents compensation for this sacrifice of leisure time. For Americans who earn low hourly wages, the compensation is not very large. Nor does encouraging such individuals to work add much to the nation's economic output.

Differences between national transfer systems also help to explain why some countries have larger wage disparities than others. More generous transfer payments make it easier for working-age Europeans who have jobs to resist wage cuts when the demand for labor falls. Americans may be more willing than Europeans to accept wage cuts rather than lose employment, because job loss is more costly in the United States than in Europe.

Figure 3-5. *Social Spending and Utilization of Labor in OECD Countries, 1997–98*

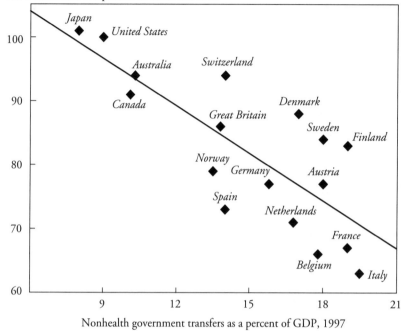

Labor utilization as a percent of U.S. level, 1998

Nonhealth government transfers as a percent of GDP, 1997

Sources: For transfers, Organization for Economic Cooperation and Development, *Society at a Glance: OECD Social Indicators* (Paris, 2001); for labor utilization, Stafano Scarpetta and others, "Economic Growth in the OECD Area: Recent Trends at the Aggregate and Sectoral Level," Economics Department Working Paper 248 (Paris: Organization for Economic Cooperation and Development, 2000).

Finally, differences in transfer systems help to explain why the trend in economic inequality has varied so widely across OECD countries. Inequality in pretax market incomes increased in nearly all of the countries where reliable measurement is possible.[31] As a result, no rich country has made its distribution of disposable income significantly more equal since 1980. But only about half of the rich countries have allowed the distribution of disposable income to become significantly more unequal. Some countries, like Canada and France, modified their transfer or regulatory systems to offset the impact of wider market income inequality. Several U.S. reforms also helped to offset the impact of widening market income disparities, but other reforms reduced the equalizing effects of taxes and transfers. Among the countries listed in figures 3-4 and 3-5, the United Kingdom has probably taken the biggest steps to reorient its transfer and labor regulation environment. Those steps almost certainly have contributed to the widening gap between Britain's rich and poor. Inequality has risen proportionally faster in the United States than in any other rich country except Great Britain.

How Does Inequality Affect Economic Growth?

Economists have proposed a number of possible links between the distribution of income and economic growth. This literature has had three major themes. In the 1950s, Simon Kuznets emphasized the impact of economic growth on inequality. In agricultural societies the distribution of income among those who live off the land is largely determined by the distribution of land and the primitive state of technology.[32] In the initial stages of industrial and commercial development, many workers move into more productive activities that take place in towns and cities. The gap between incomes in the traditional and modern sectors causes overall inequality to rise until a critical percentage of the working population has entered the modern sector. But because inequality is lower within the modern sector than within the traditional agricultural sector, the growth of the modern sector eventually begins to push inequality down again. Kuznets also argued that urbanization leads to political changes that further reduce inequality. As urban workers grow richer and more politically powerful, they press for regulation and social protection, which leads to equalization of both opportunity and income.

But although Kuznets and later investigators have found evidence that some industrialized countries have gone through a cycle in which inequality first grew and then declined, the Kuznets model cannot account for differences in inequality among today's rich countries. The United States is the richest OECD country (aside from Luxembourg), but it has the most inequality. Among the seventeen largest OECD countries, the correlation between per capita GDP and inequality is positive, which is the opposite of what the Kuznets model predicts. It is true that if we eliminate the United States and look at the sixteen remaining big OECD countries, the richer ones have *less* inequality than the poorer ones, as the Kuznets model predicts.[33] Nonetheless, a model that predicts lower inequality in the United States than in Europe is clearly incomplete.

Nor can the Kuznets model explain recent *trends* in inequality within OECD countries. Average income continues to rise in all the rich countries, but income inequality is no longer declining in any of them. Instead, inequality is climbing in some rich countries, while remaining stable in the rest. Even though the Kuznets model was developed partly from information on Britain, Germany, and the United States, it seems to apply only to an earlier stage of their development. It may also remain relevant for less affluent societies today, although several writers have challenged that view.[34]

More recent theories focus on the ways in which economic inequality can affect growth rather than the ways in which growth affects inequality. Arthur Okun provides a succinct summary of such theories in his 1975 book, *Equality and Efficiency*.[35] Okun highlights the ways in which both regulating economic markets and redistributing market incomes could reduce efficiency—themes that have become increasingly popular among economists since 1975. Okun argues that when governments try to equalize incomes, they change the incentives facing firms, workers, and consumers, and that these changes often lower economic output.

Generous unemployment benefits, for example, reduce income disparities between those with jobs and those without jobs, but they also reduce the incentives for unemployed workers to search diligently for a new job. Indeed, if the monetary cost of unemployment is low enough and if the stigma associated with drawing unemployment benefits is also low, workers may not accept any job until their benefits are almost exhausted.

Figure 3-5 clearly supports this part of Okun's theory. Countries that spend more on redistribution have lower rates of labor utilization. If redistribution to those who are not working were cut, people would almost certainly work more hours, which would boost national output and average income. Of course, raising average income would not necessarily raise average well-being. Eliminating all disability benefits, for example, would induce some people with disabilities to find work. Economic output would rise a little, and taxes could fall a little. But eliminating disability benefits would also leave some disabled individuals destitute, substantially reducing their well-being (and that of their relatives). The reason all rich societies have some kind of support system for the disabled is that legislators and voters think the benefits of such a system outweigh the costs.

A skeptic might argue that making causal inferences from cross-national data like that in figure 3-5 is quite likely to be misleading. To begin with, the causal connection between transfer payments and labor supply could run either way. Perhaps France and Italy adopt policies aimed at reducing the cost of not working because they are unwilling or unable to adopt policies that produce a tight labor market. Or perhaps both transfer policies and labor supply have a common cause. Most French and Italian voters may prefer not working very hard and may elect legislators who promise to cut the cost of indulging this preference. Meanwhile, most American and Japanese voters may think work is morally superior to idleness and may elect legislators who promise to keep idleness costly.

One way around some of these uncertainties is to ask whether *changes* in a given policy produce *changes* in the outcome of interest. This strategy makes sense when we expect the full effect to be immediately apparent, but in many cases that is unlikely. Consider early retirement. A large body of research shows that the financial incentives connected with early retirement have relatively modest effects on individual behavior within any given country. Yet in countries where early retirement is more financially advantageous, the average age of retirement is much lower. This too could be a case of reverse causation, in which political parties make early retirement easy because they know that is what people want to do. But it could also mean that changing the incentive to retire does not exert its full effect for many decades. After all, few people understand the full economic consequences of retiring at one age rather than another. Most people therefore take their cues from what they see others doing and from social norms about what constitutes appropriate behavior. A change in economic incentives may therefore produce a small initial change in a few people's behavior, but this change may then affect other people's expectations, gradually altering norms about what is socially appropriate.[36] The only way to estimate the full impact of a policy change is then to compare societies that have had different policies for a long time.

This example leads us to two conclusions. First, it is very dangerous to make strong causal inferences from cross-national correlations. Second, it is often even more dangerous to make strong causal inferences from studies of individual differences within a given country or from studies that focus on the short-term impact of either a specific policy change or the overall level of economic inequality.

Okun also noted that high marginal taxes could lead some people to work fewer hours or choose less arduous occupations. In this case, however, the effect of high taxes can also work in the opposite direction. High tax rates have the same effect as a wage cut. Some people facing higher tax rates will work less, because they value leisure more than the (reduced) net wage they can earn at work, while other people will work more, because that is the only way they can achieve the standard of living to which they aspire. On balance, however, more redistribution—and more equality—is likely to reduce work.

A third and more recent set of theories explores the possibility that inequality can reduce growth through the political system, by reducing citizens' ability to accumulate human, financial, and physical capital and by increasing social conflict.[37] Some economists suggest, for example, that high levels of inequality may slow growth by encouraging the median voter to favor excessive taxes on productive activities. If the distribution of income before taxes and transfers is very unequal, the median income will be far lower than the mean income. Under these circumstances, the median voter may reason that he can gain more from generous redistribution than from more rapid economic growth, which would mainly benefit the rich. If redistributive policies depress economic growth, however, they may benefit the median voter only in the short run, not in the long run. Alternatively, high inequality may reduce the percentage of citizens who feel they can afford to invest in education, training, or a small business or who provide their children with nutritionally adequate food and health care. If returns on these investments are very high, especially for children in poor circumstances, inequality can severely limit growth. Finally, high inequality may create social conflict and political unrest, which in turn discourage productive investments and drive up prices as commerce becomes more dangerous.

Research on the links between inequality and growth has mushroomed over the past decade. Unfortunately, analysts have reached no consensus on the nature of the relationship. Much of the recent evidence pools data on inequality and growth in both rich and poor nations. This may be a mistake. Inequality may well lead to political instability in poor or middle-income countries, for example, but there is little evidence that it has had this effect in rich countries since 1945. Likewise, inequality in poor and middle-income countries may prevent some parents from feeding their children adequately or keeping them in school, but this is not a major problem in rich countries. Even the hypothesis that inequality leads voters to support inefficient redistribution, while plausible in principle, does not seem to describe rich democracies very well. On the contrary, while voters

Figure 3-6. *Income Inequality and Growth Rate of GDP per Capita in OECD Countries*

Annual growth rate (percent)[a]

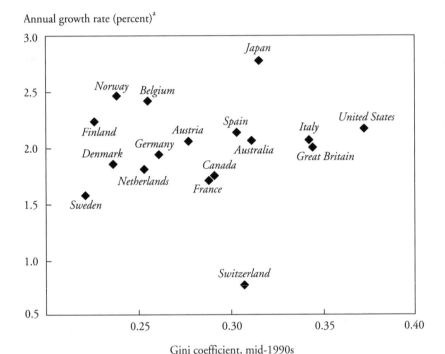

Gini coefficient, mid-1990s

Sources: For Gini coefficient, Luxembourg Income Study (see figure 3-4); for per capita GDP growth rate, International Monetary Fund, World Economic Outlook data file (June 26, 2002).

a. Real per capita GDP, 1980–2000.

in some European countries seem to have become more egalitarian as inequality has risen, voters in English-speaking countries seem to have moved in the opposite direction.

Nor does empirical evidence suggest that inequality has any consistent effect on economic growth in rich countries. Figure 3-6 shows growth rates between 1980 and 2000 in seventeen large industrial countries with differing levels of income inequality. The correlation between inequality and growth is 0.03—that is, almost precisely zero. The fastest and slowest growing nations (Japan and Switzerland) had almost identical inequality. The four Scandinavian nations (Sweden, Finland, Denmark, and Norway) had the lowest income inequality. Norway's growth rate was second only to

Japan's, while Sweden's was lower than that of any country but Switzerland. The most unequal nation, namely the United States, had a growth rate just below that of Finland. We do not interpret figure 3-6 as showing that inequality and growth have no effect on one another. A more sensible interpretation is that the relationship between inequality and growth is complicated and imperfectly understood. Some government policies, such as good public schools and good primary health care, may promote both equality and growth. Others, like generous unemployment benefits and laws restricting businesses from dismissing workers, probably reduce both inequality and growth.

Still, it is worth considering what might happen to incomes in the United States if the United States used government policy to achieve a more equal distribution of final incomes. Suppose that reducing inequality by a quarter lowered average income in the United States by about a quarter, to the average income level of the other OECD countries in figures 3-4 and 3-5. If that happened, the income of an American at the tenth percentile would probably rise slightly, while incomes in the middle and at the top of the income distribution would almost certainly fall.

Although it seems very unlikely that American incomes would fall by a quarter if U.S. institutions were changed so as to achieve levels of inequality now common in the rest of the OECD, we find it equally implausible that inequality could be reduced by a quarter without any reduction at all in output or efficiency. We believe the drop in average income would be closer to zero than to one quarter, but no one can be sure. If voters are worried about *both* high inequality *and* the adverse consequences of policies that reduce inequality, it seems sensible to focus on those equalizing policies that have the largest chance of boosting growth and the smallest chance of retarding it. Programs that improve the health, education, and work readiness of low-income children and young adults seem to have the most promise for success along these lines.

Equal Opportunity

Up to this point we have presented evidence on whether economic inequality affects the ability of rich countries to achieve traditional economic goals, such as full employment and rapid increases in living standards. We now examine the relationship between inequality and three noneconomic goals: equalizing opportunity, improving life expectancy, and keeping the government relatively democratic.

Equal opportunity is an ambiguous and controversial ideal, but its political rationale is clear. All democratic societies need to convince their citizens that the distribution of economic prizes is just. Advocates of "equal opportunity" use the phrase to describe whatever system for distributing rewards they regard as just. Most advocates of equal opportunity also assume that the best way to measure inequality of opportunity is to measure the effect of family background on children's educational attainment or income in adulthood. The smaller is the effect of family background, the more equal they think opportunity is. This approach to equal opportunity poses many conceptual problems, but since it is widely accepted, we adopt it here.[38]

Intuitively, it may seem obvious that as economic inequality between parents rises, poor children will find it harder to compete successfully with rich children. The wider the income gap between the rich and poor, the easier it is for rich parents to buy their children advantages that other parents cannot afford. But although this argument is intuitively compelling, it only holds up if spending large sums of money on your children really gives them a significant advantage. Investigating this question, Susan Mayer finds that while high-income children fared much better than low-income children on almost every measure she examined, there was little evidence that most of the correlation was truly causal. Parental income did seem to have a direct effect on children's chances of attending college. But parental income per se did not appear to be a major influence on children's behavior, how well they did on cognitive tests, whether they finished high school, or whether they became teenage parents. These outcomes were correlated with parental income, but they did not change much when parental income changed.

How can this be? Mayer finds that the kinds of expenditures that are strongly related to parental income—how much parents spend on things like housing, motor vehicles, and eating out—had little influence on their children's prospects. Children's success was associated with certain kinds of expenditure, like books and trips to museums, but expenditures on these things were not strongly related to parental income, presumably because the amounts of money involved were seldom large.[39] These findings suggest that changing the distribution of income might not have a big impact on children's life chances unless other things change at the same time. But changing the distribution of income may, in fact, change all kinds of other things. Mayer finds, for example, that economic segregation increased faster during the 1970s and 1980s in U.S. states where the overall distribution of income became more unequal. Expenditures on kindergarten through twelfth-grade (K–12) schooling also rose faster in these states.[40] Many observers also think that increases in economic inequality erode social solidarity and increase relative deprivation.[41] How all this might affect equality of opportunity is a complex empirical question.

One way to measure equality of opportunity is to calculate the correlation between parents' family incomes and their children's family incomes. If one averages incomes over a number of years, this correlation appears to be about 0.4 in the United States. We do not have such data for other countries, but we do have some data on the correlation between the annual earnings of fathers and sons. The correlations found in the United States, Britain, and Germany do not differ significantly, although that may be because the samples are all quite small. The correlations found in Finland and Canada are significantly lower than those in the United States.[42]

Another way to measure equality of opportunity is to compare the occupations of fathers and sons. Such correlations tend to be highest when we rank both fathers and sons on the basis of their occupation's educational requirements and economic rewards. We have correlations of this kind for reasonably large samples in the United States, Britain, the Netherlands, Germany, and Ireland. The correlations for the United States and Britain are almost identical (0.34 versus 0.35). The correlations for the Netherlands, Germany, and Ireland are all somewhat higher (0.40 to 0.49).[43] Robert Erikson and John Goldthorpe also compare the United States, Britain, and Sweden using somewhat different measures and find little clear evidence of differences.[44] All in all, then, intergenerational economic mobility seems to be about as common in Britain as in the United States, perhaps more common in Finland and Canada than in the United States, and probably less common in Germany, the Netherlands, and Ireland than in the United States. These results do not suggest that the distribution of income has much effect on equality of opportunity, but they should be treated quite cautiously, because the data on parents predate the big increases in economic inequality in the United States and Britain.

Although findings of this kind have been widely available since the early 1960s, most Americans and many Europeans still assume that family background counts less in America than in Europe. This assumption is rooted more in history and culture than in current experience. Most people see America as "the land of opportunity" because they know that millions of poor Europeans came to the United States between 1840 and 1914 and that the descendants of these immigrants are now about as successful as "old stock" Americans.[45] (They often forget that this process took three generations.) In addition, the United States has never had a hereditary aristocracy, and its culture has always emphasized equality rather than deference. Successful American politicians stress their social and cultural similarity to their constituents, even when they are multimillionaires, rather than emphasizing accomplishments that might make them seem unusually competent to lead a complex society. America's dress code, vocabulary, and music are also populist and egalitarian. But although differences of this kind are important to both Americans and Europeans, they do not make family background markedly less important in the United States than in most of Europe.

What we would like to know, however, is not whether opportunity is more equal in the United States than in Europe but whether the *change* in economic inequality in the United States and Britain has changed children's chances of moving up or down the economic ladder. Unfortunately, we cannot answer this question. We know that the effect of family background on the family income of adults fell during the 1960s and was fairly flat after that.[46] But it is still too soon to know how the big increase in economic inequality after 1980 will affect the family incomes of American children in adulthood.

We do, however, know something about changes in the distribution of *educational* opportunity since 1980. Table 3-1, which is taken from work by David Ellwood and Thomas Kane, shows changes between 1980–82 and 1992 in the fraction of high school graduates from each income quartile who entered a four-year college.[47] Among students from the top income group, college entrance rates rose substantially. Among students from the middle two groups, entrance rates rose more modestly. Among students from the poorest group, college entrance rates hardly changed.

Any effort to explain table 3-1 must take account of two facts. First, the growth of economic inequality during the 1980s was linked to an increase in the value of a college degree. Had everything else remained equal, making a bachelor's degree more valuable should have enhanced *all* teenagers' interest in attending college and made all parents more willing to help their children with college bills. The second relevant fact is that as the value of a college degree rose, state legislatures raised tuition. Tuition, room, and board at the average four-year public institution rose from 10.8 percent of the median family's pretax income in 1979–80 to 15.8 percent in 1991–92.[48] If American high school graduates had all been well informed and far-sighted, they would have realized that the monetary value

Table 3-1. *Percent of High-School Graduates Enrolling in Some Form of Postsecondary Education within Twenty Months of Graduation, by Income Quartile, 1980–82 and 1992*
Percent

| Income quartile | High school graduation year | | Change |
	1980–82	1992	
Lowest	29	28	−1
Second	33	38	5
Third	39	48	9
Highest	55	66	11
All	39	45	6

Source: David Ellwood and Thomas Kane, "Who Is Getting a College Education? Family Background and the Growing Gaps in Enrollment," in Sheldon Danziger and Jane Waldfogel, eds., *Securing the Future* (New York: Russell Sage, 2000).

of a college degree was rising even faster than its cost. Students from affluent families would have tried to persuade their parents to pay these costs. Students from poorer families would have borrowed more money, worked more hours, or taken longer to earn a degree.

Table 3-1 suggests that while students from affluent families responded in the predicted way, students from poor families did not. The response of poor students is consistent with other evidence suggesting that they are more sensitive to changes in college tuition than to changes in the long-term value of a college degree.[49] Perhaps a lot of poor students cannot borrow enough money or work enough hours to pay their college bills, while simultaneously maintaining an acceptable grade-point average. Or perhaps they do not apply to college because they do not realize how much financial aid is actually available.

A third hypothesis that could explain the widening disparity in the college prospects of high- and low-income students is that most seventeen-year-olds have relatively short time horizons regardless of how rich or poor their parents are. Left to their own devices, they decide what to do after high school by comparing their picture of life as a college freshman with their picture of life in a low-level job. If they hate schoolwork and think they will have to work nearly full time to pay their college bills, they are unlikely to attend. If they like schoolwork and their parents offer to pay their college bills, they are likely to attend. If they are lukewarm about schoolwork, their decision depends on whether their parents bribe them to attend. When returns to higher education rise, more parents want their children to attend. But while affluent parents can influence their children's decisions by offering to pay, poor parents cannot. As a result, affluent students respond to changes in the long-term benefits of college, while poor students respond mainly to changes in short-term costs.

None of these explanations for the widening gap in college attendance between students from high- and low-income families depends on a change in the actual distribution of parental income. And, indeed, Ellwood and Kane find that changes in the incomes of the top and bottom quartiles do not explain the changes in attendance rates shown in table 3-1. Nonetheless, another recent study by Mayer suggests that the college attendance gap between rich and poor students widened more in states where inequality grew fastest.[50] Increases in economic inequality led to rapid increases in educational attainment among students from the top half of the income distribution, but not much change among students from the bottom half. Like Ellwood and Kane, Mayer finds that the change in attendance patterns was much larger than she would have predicted on the basis of changes in parents' own incomes. This finding supports the notion that increases in economic inequality have important ramifications that go beyond what happens to the income of any given individual.

The evidence currently available suggests two seemingly contradictory conclusions. First, while family background affects children in myriad ways, income per se is seldom the primary force. This finding means that changing the distribution of income is not likely to have a big impact on children's life chances unless other things change at the same time. But our second tentative conclusion is that changes in the distribution of income do, in fact, change other things, ranging from the degree of economic segregation to state spending patterns, and that these changes appear to influence the distribution of educational opportunity. How they influence economic opportunity we do not yet know.

Life Expectancy

The relationship between economic inequality and health has been hotly debated over the past decade.[51] The public health literature mostly argues that inequality is bad for health. Economists mostly hold that the relationship is spurious. Our reading of the evidence is that it suggests some causal connection between income inequality and life expectancy, but that the connection is probably weak.

Figure 3-7. *Expected Age of Death among White Men and Women in the National Longitudinal Mortality Study Who Had Survived to Age 25, by Family Income*

Expected age of death (years)

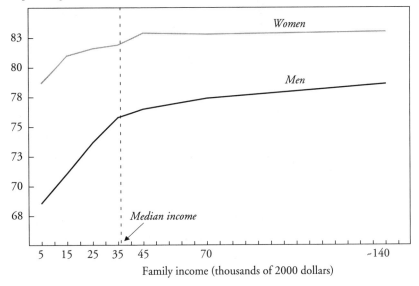

Family income (thousands of 2000 dollars)

Source: Eugene Rogot, Paul Sorlie, and Norman Johnson, "Life Expectancy by Employment Status, Income, and Education in the National Longitudinal Mortality Study," *Public Health Reports,* vol. 107, no. 4 (1992), pp. 457–61.

Economic inequality can influence health in at least three ways. First, if giving an extra $10,000 a year to the rich has less impact on longevity than giving it to the poor, shifting income from the rich to the poor should increase average life expectancy. Second, economic inequality may have political ramifications that affect government policies ranging from pollution and crime control to Medicaid spending and the quality of nursing homes. Third, economic inequality may affect the strength of community ties and the way people treat one another.[52]

Figure 3-7 shows the life expectancy at age twenty-five of white men and women in each of seven income groups.[53] The data span the period 1979–85. The estimates suggest that low-income white men typically die 10.0 years younger than high-income white men, while low-income white women die 4.3 years younger than high-income white women. Figure 3-7 also suggests that the value of additional income is far greater among individuals whose family income is below rather than above the median.[54] If these relationships were truly causal, shifting income from the top to the bottom of the distribution would obviously increase life expectancy. In the most extreme case, dividing incomes equally would have given each of these white families about $42,000 in today's money. If nothing else had changed, average life expectancies of twenty-five-year-old white men and women would have risen 1.3 and 0.6 years, respectively.

Of course, no complex society can afford to distribute income exactly equally. So we need to ask what might happen when income inequality merely fluctuates within the range that we actually observe in rich democracies. According to LIS, the U.S. Gini coefficient for size-adjusted disposable income rose by about a quarter between 1979 and 1997. If the entire relationship between income and life expectancy in figure 3-7 were causal, increasing inequality by a quarter while leaving the shape of that relationship unchanged would have reduced the "normal" increase in American life expectancy at age twenty-five by about one-tenth.[55]

In reality, of course, the relationship between income and life expectancy in figure 3-7 is *not* all causal. (If it were, raising life expectancy would be much easier than it is.) Lottery winners do not automatically take on the life expectancies of the wealthy. Characteristics other than low income affect the life expectancies of the poor. Many are poor because bad health limits their earning power, not the other way round. Good medical treatment would lengthen their lives, but it would not make them live as long as the rich do. The poor disproportionately exhibit life-shortening and income-reducing characteristics or behaviors—alcoholism, obesity, and limited literacy—that no amount of medical care can offset.[56]

The foregoing calculations imply that the longevity payoff from reduced inequality is quite small. But big changes in the distribution of income are also likely to have political and social consequences for society as a whole, independent of their effect on the income of any given individual. Changing the distribution of income may, for example, alter the political environment in ways that affect expenditure on public health or access to medical care, although it is not clear on a priori grounds whether growing inequality is likely to strengthen the hand of those who favor or oppose egalitarian social programs. Changing the distribution of income may also fray social ties and increase stress levels. As a result, the overall impact of economic inequality on health remains unclear.

One way to get more insight into this question is to compare life expectancy in different rich countries. Figure 3-8 shows that life expectancy and income inequality are indeed negatively correlated ($r = -0.30$) in the thirteen rich democracies on which LIS provided data for the mid-1990s.[57] To be sure, the correlation depends entirely on the fact that the United States has unusually low life expectancy and unusually high inequality. Excluding the United States drops the correlation for the twelve remaining countries to -0.04. If we add Japan, which has very high life expectancy and relatively high income inequality, the correlation becomes positive.

The countries in figure 3-8 differ in so many ways that no amount of statistical analysis can take account of them all. One way around this problem is to ask whether *changes* in life expectancy within a given country depend on *changes* in economic inequality. LIS provides income inequality estimates going back to the 1970s for Canada, France, Norway, Sweden, the United Kingdom, and the United States, although the trend estimates for both France and the United States are somewhat problematic.[58] Wherever possible, we compare the mid-1970s to the mid-1990s. Figure 3-9 shows that life expectancy grew a little faster in countries that constrained the growth of income inequality over this period, but the correlation does not come close to being statistically reliable. If we drop France and Norway, for which we have no pre-1979 data, the relationship disappears. Figure 3-9 should not lead those with strong a priori beliefs about the relationship between inequality and health to change their views, but it is consistent with the hypothesis that increases in economic inequality at the national level have a small negative effect on the rate of growth in life expectancy.

In an attempt to sharpen the estimate of how changes in economic inequality relate to changes in life expectancy, Andrew Clarkwest uses all the LIS data on rich democracies. He matches each inequality estimate to a concurrent estimate of life expectancy and to changes in the country's per capita GDP. He also controls for the fact that life expectancy was rising in all rich countries regardless of what happened to their income. In his analysis, a one-point increase in a country's Gini coefficient lowered the expected increase in life expectancy by 0.062 years.[59] After adjusting for changes in the Current Population Survey, the LIS Gini coefficient for U.S. disposable income rose 5.8 points between 1979 and 1997, while U.S. life expectancy rose 3.0 years. The Clarkwest estimate implies that if income inequality had not risen at all, U.S. life expectancy would have risen by 3.4 years rather than 3.0 years, or by an extra five months.

Figure 3-8. *Income Inequality and Life Expectancy in Thirteen Rich Democracies, mid-1990s*

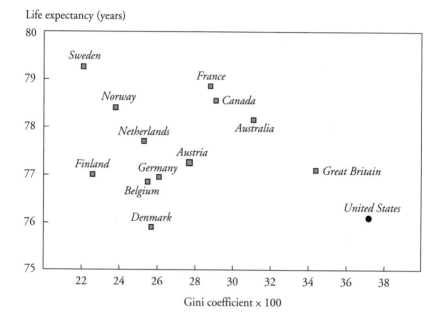

Life expectancy (years)

Source: Authors' calculations from data assembled by the Luxembourg Income Study and the National Center for Health Statistics.

Comparisons among American states suggest an even weaker relationship between income inequality and life expectancy. When Clarkwest used mortality rates to calculate each state's average life expectancy in 1969–71, 1979–81, and 1989–91, a one-point increase in a state's Gini coefficient for pretax household income was associated with a reduction in white life expectancy of about 0.05 years, or roughly one-half of a month.[60] But when he looked at the effect of *changes* in a given state's Gini coefficient, the relationship vanished. Nonetheless, more unequal states do score poorly on federal "quality of health care" measures, so we are inclined to believe that something real is going on.[61]

These findings suggest that the debate over economic inequality and health should be redirected. The debate has focused on whether such a relationship exists. We think that the question should be whether it is large enough to matter. Our conclusion is that a relationship may exist, but that

Figure 3-9. *Average Annual Change in Life Expectancy by Average Annual Change in Income Inequality, Six Rich Countries, 1974–79 to 1994–95*[a]

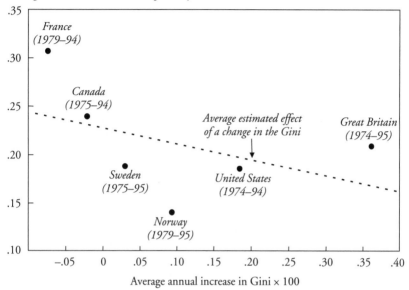

Average annual increase in life expectancy

France (1979–94)

Canada (1975–94)

Average estimated effect of a change in the Gini

Great Britain (1974–95)

Sweden (1975–95)

United States (1974–94)

Norway (1979–95)

Average annual increase in Gini × 100

Source: See figure 3-8.

a. The estimated effect of the average annual within-country change in the Gini (ΔG) on the average annual change in life expectancy is .227 − .165 (ΔG). The standard error of the coefficient on ΔG is .159.

it is small, hard to detect, and not very important compared to more direct and controllable influences on longevity and health. Our cross-national comparisons suggest that economic inequality may slightly lower longevity. Our best guess (and it is only that) is that increases in U.S. income inequality between 1979 and 1997 reduced life expectancy about five months. The average annual increase in U.S. life expectancy during this period was two months, so one can think of the increase in inequality as having offset the effects of two to three years of medical progress. The possibility that holding income inequality at its 1979 level would have added five months to the average American's life is certainly an argument in its favor. But if you oppose income redistribution for other reasons, the somewhat uncertain prospect of a five-month increase in life expectancy is not likely to alter your views.

Given the intense political resistance to egalitarian economic policies in the United States, those who want to improve Americans' health need to ask how the benefits of reduced economic inequality compare to the benefits of other strategies. One obvious alternative is to concentrate on measures to raise incomes near the bottom of the distribution and to ameliorate extreme material hardships, such as homelessness, malnutrition, or lack of access to medical care for the sick. The political shortcoming of this strategy is that it directly aids only a tiny fraction of the total U.S. population. Furthermore, the aided group is politically unorganized and votes at low rates. As a result, programs for this group depend on altruism—a scarce and evanescent virtue. For those who prefer a more inclusive approach to health improvement, it might make sense to concentrate on taxing cigarettes and using the revenue to subsidize clinics or gyms.

Political Influence

Almost everyone who compares rich democracies agrees that the main reason the income distribution is more equal in some of them than in others is political. Some countries have more progressive taxes than others, and some transfer more money to people who are retired, unemployed, sick, disabled, poorly paid, or raising children. Some countries also have high minimum wages, centralized wage bargaining, or laws that make unionization easy, all of which tend to compress the distribution of earnings. In addition, some countries require employers to give all their workers expensive fringe benefits, such as lengthy paid leave and good severance pay. The direct and indirect costs of these policies can be high, but few experts deny that they can and do equalize the distribution of income. The United States does not have centralized wage bargaining, does not make unionization easy, sets its minimum wage low, mandates few fringe benefits, and is not especially generous in its treatment of the unemployed, the sick, the disabled, or families with children. It also ends up with a very unequal distribution of income.

As we note at the beginning of this chapter, support for egalitarian economic policies is not as widespread in the United States as in most other rich democracies, partly because Americans are somewhat more tolerant of income inequality and partly because they are more hostile to government intervention in the economy. Raising the minimum wage is one of the few egalitarian policies that wins overwhelming popular support, perhaps because it seems equitable to most voters and does not require a large public budget for enforcement.

Although attitudinal differences between the United States and other rich democracies have existed for a long time, they do not persist unaided. Every rich democracy has had a long-running ideological war about whether the government should regulate or deregulate markets, raise or lower taxes, and expand or shrink social programs. The outcome of this struggle at any given time depends partly on the views that citizens develop from their everyday experience and partly on the relative influence of propagandists for different views. We have not been able to find data on how much money Americans spend trying to influence one another's political views, but the amount has almost certainly risen over time, both absolutely and as a fraction of GDP.

The rich also provide the bulk of the money that political candidates now need to run for office. Until the 1960s political candidates relied largely on volunteers to staff their campaign offices and contact voters. Now they rely largely on paid staff and advertising. Many attribute this change to technological innovations like television and direct mail. But political candidates can only exploit costly innovations of this kind if someone is willing and able to pay for them. Campaign managers always preferred a professional office staff over volunteers, for example. They relied on volunteers because that was all they could afford. They hire more professionals today because candidates can raise more money. The same logic applies to campaign advertising.

One reason America now spends more money on election campaigns is because government regulates more aspects of our lives, so people with money care more about who controls it. Another reason may be that television is more cost-effective than earlier forms of campaign advertising, making it easier for politicians to convince potential contributors that another $1,000 could make all the difference. But the fact that America's richest families now have a larger share of the nation's income is also likely to be a factor. That change presumably allows politicians with a finite amount of time to raise more money per phone call.

The same logic applies to less direct methods of exercising political influence. The more concentrated is the distribution of income, the easier it is to raise money for nonprofit organizations that seek to influence opinion. If these organizations have some influence, making the distribution of income more unequal is likely to increase the influence of those with money to spend on such activities. In the 1960s elite opinion on many domestic issues had a somewhat liberal cast. Since then, however, the affluent have poured more of their money into conservative organizations that endorse laissez-faire economic policies, low taxes, and cutbacks in social programs. Unlike liberal groups, which spend much of their money trying to help the needy, conservatives spend heavily on think tanks and publications aimed at swaying the views of people with political influence. These efforts have probably played some role in reducing political support for redistributive policies, although we have no way of saying how large their role has been.

The impact of income inequality on the distribution of political influence remains far from certain, but of all the ways in which increases in economic inequality can influence a society, this one worries us most. If all Americans had equal political influence and decided collectively to let everyone's wages depend on an unregulated market, we would find it hard to argue against the legitimacy of that decision, although we might question its wisdom. But if the rich can buy more political influence than other Americans, and if the political process then yields policies that allow the rich to further increase their share of total income, it is hard to reconcile this result with traditional norms about how a democracy should operate.

Of course the political economy theories described earlier predict that if the share of income going to the rich keeps rising, the "have-nots" will eventually decide to tax the "haves" rather than pay taxes themselves. Once that happens, the have-nots may also support policies that use revenue raised from the rich to finance more government services that they currently pay for out of their own income. But although such a populist revolt is theoretically possible, it is far from certain. Nor would such a revolt necessarily serve the long-run interests of the have-nots. Populist revolutionaries may favor policies that yield quick results. Policies that deliver a big, quick change in the distribution of income are likely to be policies that also lower investment and slow growth.

Inequality and Justice

When egalitarians argue in favor of the inheritance tax or a progressive income tax, they seldom stress the economic or social benefits of taxing the rich. They favor taxing the rich because they think the current level of economic inequality is unjust and because they think it is unfair to ask ordinary workers to pay more taxes when their bosses live in unprecedented luxury. Egalitarians who advocate a federally financed health insurance system, low tuition at state colleges, or a higher minimum wage also emphasize moral arguments. It is wrong, they say, to deny people medical care because they cannot pay or to deny qualified youngsters college educations just because their parents cannot afford it. Americans should not be poor if they work hard every day.

Egalitarians sometimes supplement these moral arguments with practical claims: extreme inequality leads to crime and violence; inadequate health care reduces productivity and reduces the proportion of adults who can support themselves; encouraging the young to attend college eventually pays for itself through higher taxes; raising the minimum wage helps to keep families together and reduce welfare dependency. But these are afterthoughts, aimed at winning the support of waverers who cannot see that the current level of inequality—or perhaps any level of inequality—is simply unjust. Egalitarians would still favor redistribution even if crime proved unrelated to inequality. They would also favor free health care even if it had no effect on longevity and a higher minimum wage even if it did not keep families together.

Those who oppose egalitarian proposals also tend to see the struggle in moral terms. They do not argue, of course, that inequality is good in itself. Rather, they argue that the market distributes income more justly than the government. As they see it, the economy rewards people for doing things that others value. People who do nothing that anyone else is willing to pay for have no right to live parasitically off the people who engage in activities that others value. Those who see the market as fundamentally more just than the government often argue that high taxes and generous transfer programs discourage investment, slow growth, raise unemployment, or promote dependency. But their opposition to redistribution seldom derives from considerations of this kind. Like egalitarians, they seldom change their views when empirical evidence suggests that redistribution has fewer costs than they claimed. At bottom, those who oppose redistribution usually believe that virtue should be rewarded and vice punished and that the market is more likely than the government to do this.

People have debated these issues for a long time. John Rawls summarizes the egalitarian case well in his classic, *A Theory of Justice*.[62] Robert Nozick's influential rebuttal, *Anarchy, State, and Utopia*, makes the opposite case.[63] Whether either of these books has changed anyone's mind we do not know. Our own view is that neither the market nor the political process is ever likely to produce a just distribution of income and that the best response to this fact is a series of ad hoc compromises. Compromise, of course, is what all successful democracies do. As we have seen, all rich democracies have quite unequal distributions of market income, they all use taxes and transfers to make the market distribution somewhat more equal, and none of them makes the distribution completely equal. Even though the Gini coefficient for size-adjusted disposable income can range from 0 to 1, all the rich democracies covered by LIS had coefficients between 0.22 and 0.37 in the mid-1990s.

Our review suggests that, for countries that fall within this range, it makes sense to evaluate policies aimed at changing the distribution of income by asking whether they are consistent with widely held norms about justice. This conclusion is not a tautology. If we had found strong evidence that tolerating inequality greatly increased economic growth, dramatically increased the impact of family background on children's economic prospects, or substantially reduced life expectancy, we would have argued for weighing these effects against the uncertain and controversial claims of justice. But as anyone who has read this far will recognize, the evidence for such effects is relatively weak, probably because the effects of inequality are fairly modest compared to the other determinants of economic growth, intergenerational mobility, and longevity.

We worry most about the possibility that changes in the distribution of income lead to changes in the distribution of political power, both because such a change can undermine the legitimacy of the political system and because it can make the increase in economic inequality irreversible. In theory, countries can minimize the political impact of changes in economic inequality, first by designing a political system that minimizes the influence of money and then by mobilizing less affluent voters around distributional issues. But the United States does not have such a political system, and the system it does have seems almost immune to change. Both major political parties have become dependent on large contributions from the affluent. Both major parties want to portray themselves as supporters of campaign finance reform. But both parties also believe that money is absolutely crucial to their electoral success. The major parties' reliance on large contributions might be reduced if less affluent voters could be mobilized around distributional issues, but, as we note earlier, such issues do not seem compelling to many Americans.

Voter turnout has declined slightly as inequality has widened and has declined most among people with low income. If growing economic inequality increases the political influence of the rich, and if the political influence of the rich allows economic inequality to grow even more, legislative support for redistribution in the United States could go into irreversible decline. But although we worry about this risk, we have no way of knowing how great it is. Likewise, although the influence of money obviously reduces the legitimacy of the American political system, we have no way of knowing how serious this threat is.

The other costs and benefits of economic inequality are equally uncertain and considerably less worrisome. During the 1990s, the contrast between the United States and Europe convinced many Americans and some Europeans that tolerating high levels of economic inequality led to faster economic growth and tighter labor markets. But this conclusion does not seem as convincing when we make comparisons among rich democracies other than the United States, and it does not hold before the 1980s. Furthermore, while output per worker is currently higher in the United States than in other rich democracies, that is partly because Americans work more hours—a growth strategy that most European countries have explicitly rejected. Allowing economic inequality to grow probably increases the influence of family background on children's opportunities, but the evidence for this claim is not conclusive. Allowing economic inequality to grow may also reduce life expectancy or at least slow the rate at which it improves. But here again the evidence is not definitive, and the size of the effect is almost certainly modest.

Our conclusion that changes in economic inequality have a modest impact on economic growth, equal opportunity, and life expectancy should not be overgeneralized. We are not arguing that if income in the United States were as unequally distributed as it is in Mexico this change would have no long-term impact on future growth, intergenerational mobility, or longevity. Nor do we believe that if Scandinavian governments were to cut current inequality in half over the next generation, investment, labor force participation, and growth rates would be unaffected. Our argument is that, *within the range currently found in rich democracies*, measured inequality does not have large and obvious effects on growth, mobility, and longevity. By definition, rich countries have relatively similar living standards. They also have surprisingly similar life expectancies and intergenerational mobility. What distinguishes rich democracies is the relative political influence of different economic and ideological groups. Those political differences largely explain why some rich democracies are more equal than others.

This reasoning leads us to two further conclusions. First, if you care mainly about growth, health, or equal opportunity, changing the distribution of income is not the best strategy for promoting these goals. Redistribution is a hard sell politically and normally consumes a lot of government resources. Those who care about growth, health, and equal opportunity are likely to achieve more if they focus on more proximate determinants of these outcomes, such as encouraging public and private investment in innovation, ensuring good health care and early education for children, reducing smoking and obesity, and making public universities affordable for all talented youngsters. Our main caveat is that if economic inequality increases the political influence of the well-to-do, using the government to achieve these goals is likely to become more difficult.

Our second conclusion is that when the practical effects of a policy are both uncertain and modest, legislators should choose the policies that they and their constituents regard as just. That judgment does not resolve the question of what is just in any particular situation. It merely asserts that political legitimacy is a democracy's most precious asset and that a democracy's political legitimacy depends to a great extent on whether its citizens believe it tries to behave justly. Preserving that kind of legitimacy is an essential precondition for almost everything else we care about.

Notes

1. The U.S. data are from the 1996 General Social Survey. Even higher percentages of adults in other rich democracies think income differences are too high (87 percent in France, 82 percent in Germany, and 81 percent in Britain, for example). The most distinctive feature of American opinion is the unusually high percentage of adults who explicitly disagree with the statement that income differences are too large: 20 percent in the United States compared to 16 percent in Canada, 11 to 14 percent in Japan, New Zealand, the Netherlands, Norway, and Sweden, and only 6 or 7 percent in France, Britain, and Germany. Marc Suhrcke, "Preferences for Inequality: East vs. West," Working Paper 89 (Florence: Unesco Innocenti Center, October 2001).

2. On average in five European countries and Japan, 64 percent of adults strongly agree that the government should guarantee a minimum standard of living. Everett C. Ladd and Karlyn H. Bowman, *Attitudes toward Economic Inequality* (Washington: American Enterprise Institute, 1998).

3. See also the contribution by Victor Fuchs and Alan Garber in this volume.

4. Thomas Picketty and Emmanuel Saez, "Income Inequality in the United States, 1913–1998," *Quarterly Journal of Economics*, vol. 118 (February 2003), pp. 1–39, compare information from income tax returns with estimates of national income to calculate the percentage of total income received by Americans in the top ranks of the distribution. Some of the short-term changes appear to be driven by changes in the tax code. Reported income falls when tax rates rise and rises when tax rates fall.

5. See ibid., figs. 3-1 to 3-3, and Congressional Budget Office, *Historical Effective Tax Rates, 1979–1997* (Washington, 2001), table G-1c.

6. Compare Michael Boskin and others, "Toward a More Accurate Measure of the Cost of Living," Final Report to the Senate Finance Committee, December 4, 1996, and

Charles Schultze and Christopher Mackie, *At What Price? Conceptualizing and Measuring Cost-of-Living and Price Indexes* (Washington: National Academy Press, 2002). The Bureau of Labor Statistics, which produces the consumer price index, has made numerous changes over the years. Figure 3-2 uses the CPI-U-RS, which tries to apply today's methods retrospectively. The official CPI-U inflation series shows larger increases in prices and therefore implies smaller increases in purchasing power. Had we used the CPI-U instead of the CPI-U-RS, for example, real income growth for the bottom fifth of the distribution between 1973 and 2001 would have fallen from 0.3 to -0.2 percent a year (that is, average real income would have *declined*).

7. Another popular solution to the size problem is to divide each family's income by the poverty line threshold that corresponds to the family's size and composition. Still another solution is to divide family income by the number of family members, although this adjustment does not seem consistent with the view that people can live more cheaply if they share expenses than if they live separately. The adjustment we have used is the most common in the international literature on income distribution.

8. Applying a standard size adjustment to households of one person ignores the value that many people place on privacy. As incomes rise, living alone has become more common, especially among the elderly, many of whom once lived with their children after they stopped working. Maintaining a separate household can lower an individual's material standard of living, for the reasons mentioned, but for many people the gain in autonomy dominates these costs. Thus while our size adjustment implies that two people with fixed incomes are always worse off when they live separately than when they live together, real people who live alone seldom look hard for roommates unless their incomes fall.

9. The bottom panel ranks individuals according to their market income, so the household at the tenth percentile of the market distribution is not the same as the household at the tenth percentile of the distribution after taxes and transfers.

10. Statistics on aggregate health care and consumption spending are from the U.S. Department of Commerce's national and income product statistics. Statistics on out-of-pocket spending on medical care are from the Bureau of Labor Statistics, Consumer Expenditure Survey, various years (http://stats.bls.gov/cex/home.htm); and Eva Jacobs and Stephanie Shipp, "How Family Spending Has Changed in the U.S.," *Monthly Labor Review*, vol. 113, no. 3 (1990), pp. 20–27.

11. Postwar trends in wage inequality are summarized in Gary Burtless, "Earnings Inequality over the Business and Demographic Cycles," in Burtless, ed., *A Future of Lousy Jobs? The Changing Structure of U.S. Wages* (Brookings, 1990), pp. 77–117.

12. Chinhui Juhn, Kevin Murphy, and Brooks Pierce, "Wage Inequality and the Rise in the Returns to Skill," *Journal of Political Economy*, vol. 101 (June 1993), pp. 410–42; and Burtless, "Earnings Inequality over the Business and Demographic Cycles."

13. On the minimum wage, see David Lee, "Wage Inequality in the United States during the 1980s: Rising Dispersion or Falling Minimum Wage?" *Quarterly Journal of Economics*, vol. 114 (August 1999), pp. 977–1023. On other institutions, see Richard Freeman and Lawrence Katz, "Rising Wage Inequality: The United States vs. Other Advanced Countries," in Freeman, ed., *Working under Different Rules* (New York: Russell Sage, 1994), pp. 29–62.

14. Juhn, Murphy, and Pierce, "Wage Inequality and the Rise in the Returns to Skill."

15. Gary Burtless, "International Trade and the Rise in Earnings Inequality," *Journal of Economic Literature*, vol. 33 (June 1995), pp. 800–16.

16. The contribution of employment growth among women to increased inequality is controversial, partly because one's conclusions depend on the treatment of unmarried men and women. Between 1979 and 1996, there was little change in the probability that men with wages in the middle fifth of the male distribution would have a working spouse. Among those who were married, wives' rates of employment rose. But this increase was just about offset by the fact that such men were also less likely to be married. See Gary Burtless, "Effects of Growing Wage Disparities and Changing Family Composition on the U.S. Income Distribution," *European Economic Review*, vol. 43 (May 1999), pp. 853–65.

17. If one contrasts men in the middle fifth of the wage distribution with men in the top fifth, both the employment rate and earnings of spouses increased faster among men in the top fifth (ibid., table 2).

18. For example, the fraction of American children under eighteen who are currently living with two married parents fell from 88 percent in 1960 to 69 percent in 1994. It has varied only slightly since 1994. See www.census.gov/population/socdemo/hh-fam/tabch-1.xls [July 7, 2002].

19. For details, see Burtless, "Effects of Growing Wage Disparities and Changing Family Composition on the U.S. Income Distribution."

20. Congressional Budget Office, *Historical Effective Tax Rates, 1979–1997* (Washington, 2001), p. 29, figure 1.8.

21. George Borjas, *Heaven's Door: Immigration Policy and the American Economy* (Princeton University Press, 1999), p. 28.

22. Gary Burtless and Timothy M. Smeeding, "The Level, Trend, and Composition of Poverty," in Sheldon Danziger and Robert Haveman, eds., *Understanding Poverty: Progress and Problems* (Harvard University Press, 2001), table 4.

23. For evidence that including the estimated 1979 wages of those who migrated to the United States between 1979 and 1996 reverses the trend in wage inequality, see Robert Lerman, "U.S. Wage-Inequality Trends and Recent Immigration," *American Economic Review, Papers and Proceedings*, vol. 89 (May 1999), pp. 23–28.

24. OECD data suggest that economic inequality among households is about the same in Italy as in the United States. In contrast, the Luxembourg Income Study (LIS) indicates that inequality is lower in Italy than in the United States. See Michael Förster with Michele Pellizzari, "Trends and Driving Factors in Income Distribution and Poverty in the OECD Area," Occasional Paper 42 (Paris: Organization for Economic Cooperation and Development, 2000), p. 70. Since Italians report only about half their income in household surveys, we think estimates of Italian inequality should be treated with skepticism.

25. For sixteen of the seventeen countries, the estimates are based on calculations of the Luxembourg Income Study. The estimates for net disposable income inequality were derived from the LIS "Key Figures" file, www.lisproject.org/keyfigures/ineqtable.htm [July 2, 2002]; the estimates of market income inequality were supplied to the authors by Timothy Smeeding and David Jesuit on July 16, 2002, based on tabulations of the LIS database. The estimate for Japan was calculated from national sources using the LIS methodology and is reported in Timothy M. Smeeding, "Changing Income Inequality in OECD Countries: Updated Results from the Luxembourg Income Study," Working Paper 252 (Luxembourg: Luxembourg Income Study, 2000), figure 1. The LIS estimates of final income inequality are generally similar to those reported by the OECD, although the cross-national pattern of market income inequality differs somewhat. See Förster and Pellizzari, "Trends and

Driving Factors in Income Distribution and Poverty in the OECD Area"; and Roman Arjona, Maxime Ladaique, and Mark Pearson, "Growth, Inequality, and Social Protection," Labor Market and Social Policy Occasional Paper 51 (Paris: Organization for Economic Cooperation and Development, 2001).

26. Like other users of income data, we regard the Italian distributional statistics with skepticism. We include them because suppressing inconvenient data might arouse readers' suspicions and require extensive justification.

27. Towers Perrin, "2001–2002 Worldwide Total Remuneration" (www.towers.com [July 15, 2002]).

28. The Gini coefficient for a population can be written $p + (1 - p)G^*$, where p is the fraction of people with no income and G^* is the Gini coefficient among persons with a positive amount of income. Most studies show that G^* for labor incomes is greater in the United States than it is elsewhere. Because p is smaller, however, the overall inequality of labor income is similar in the United States and other OECD countries. For a comparison of labor income inequality in five OECD countries, see Ignazio Visco, "Commentary: The Distribution of Income in Industrialized Countries," in *Income Inequality Issues and Policy Options* (Kansas City: Federal Reserve Bank of Kansas City, 2000), p. 50. When Visco considered inequality among full-time workers and among all people with positive labor income, the United States had the highest inequality of the five countries considered. However, once working-age people with zero earnings are considered, overall U.S. labor income inequality was approximately the same as inequality in Canada and Germany and lower than inequality in the Netherlands. Only Sweden had less labor income inequality in the late 1980s.

29. Authors' calculations with March Current Population Survey files, 1996–2002. OECD tabulations show that only 6 percent of Americans living in a household with a working-age member have no household income from employment. This percentage is the lowest in the rich OECD countries. In comparison, 12 percent of people in French and German households with a working-age member receive no household income from employment, and in Australia and the Netherlands, the percentage is 14 percent. Förster and Pellizzari, "Trends and Driving Factors in Income Distribution and Poverty in the OECD Area," table 3.4.

30. See Stafano Scarpetta and others, "Economic Growth in the OECD Area: Recent Trends at the Aggregate and Sectoral Level," Economics Department Working Paper 248 (Paris: Organization for Economic Cooperation and Development, 2000), pp. 41–43. The age structure of OECD countries varies. The calculations in figure 3-5 remove this variation and focus solely on differences in the utilization of the working-age population.

31. See Arjona, Ladaique, and Pearson, "Growth, Inequality, and Social Protection."

32. Simon Kuznets, "Economic Growth and Income Inequality," *American Economic Review*, vol. 45, no. 1 (1995), pp. 1–28.

33. The correlation between average income and the Gini coefficient is +0.18 if the United States is included and –0.27 if the United States is excluded. The seventeen countries are the ones shown in figures 3-4 and 3-5. In calculating the correlation of average income and inequality, we use the most recent OECD estimates of GDP per capita in purchasing-power-parity exchange rates for 2000 and the LIS estimates of the Gini coefficient of final income inequality shown in figure 3-4.

34. See Francisco H. G. Ferreira, "Inequality and Economic Performance: A Brief

Overview to Theories of Growth and Distribution," World Bank, 1999 (www.worldbank.org/poverty/inequal/index.htm).

35. Arthur Okun, *Equality and Efficiency: The Big Tradeoff* (Brookings, 1975).

36. The limitations of microeconomic evidence on the effect of pension incentives on the timing of retirement are discussed in Gary Burtless, "An Economic View of Retirement," in Henry J. Aaron, ed., *Behavioral Dimensions of Retirement Economics* (Brookings, 1999), pp. 30–40. Robert Axtell and Joshua Epstein, "Coordination in Transient Social Networks: An Agent-Based Computational Model of the Timing of Retirement," in Aaron, *Behavioral Dimensions of Retirement Economics,* pp. 161–84, argue that the gradual decline in the average U.S. retirement age is appropriately modeled as a shift in social norms through the imitation of peer behavior. Cross-national evidence on the impact of pension incentives on retirement is presented in Jonathan Gruber and David A. Wise, "Introduction," in Gruber and Wise, eds., *Social Security and Retirement around the World* (University of Chicago Press, 1999).

37. For good surveys, see Ferreira, "Inequality and Economic Performance"; and Philippe Aghion, Eve Caroli, and Cecilia Garcìa-Peñalosa, "Inequality and Economic Growth: The Perspective of the New Growth Theories," *Journal of Economic Literature,* vol. 37, no. 4 (1999), pp. 1615–60.

38. For an examination of some of these issues, see John Roemer, *Equality of Opportunity* (Harvard University Press, 1998); or Christopher Jencks, "Whom Must We Treat Equally for Educational Opportunity to Be Equal?" *Ethics,* vol. 98 (April 1988), pp. 518–33.

39. Susan E. Mayer, *What Money Can't Buy: Family Income and Children's Life Chances* (Harvard University Press, 1997).

40. Susan E. Mayer, "How Did the Increase in Economic Inequality between 1970 and 1990 Affect Children's Educational Attainment?" *American Journal of Sociology,* vol. 107 (July 2001), pp. 1–32.

41. See, for example, Richard Wilkinson, *Unhealthy Societies: The Afflictions of Inequality* (London: Routledge, 1996).

42. Anders Björklund and Markus Jantti, "Intergenerational Mobility of Socioeconomic Status in Comparative Perspective," *Nordic Journal of Political Economy,* vol. 26, no. 1 (2000), pp. 3–33.

43. Ibid. The samples for these five countries all exceed 1,500.

44. See Robert Erikson and John Goldthorpe, "Are American Rates of Social Mobility Exceptionally High? New Evidence on an Old Question," *European Sociological Review,* vol. 1 (May 1985), pp. 1–22.

45. See, for example, Christopher Jencks, *Rethinking Social Policy: Race, Poverty, and the Underclass* (Harvard University Press, 1992), table 1.1.

46. For data on changes in the effect of family background on children's family income in adulthood, see David Harding and others, "The Changing Effect of Family Background on the Incomes of American Adults," in Samuel Bowles, Herbert Gintis, and Melissa Osborne, eds., *Unequal Chances: Family Background and Economic Success* (New York: Russell Sage, forthcoming).

47. David Ellwood and Thomas Kane, "Who Is Getting a College Education? Family Background and the Growing Gaps in Enrollment," in Sheldon Danziger and Jane Waldfogel, eds., *Securing the Future: Investing in Children from Birth to College* (New York: Russell Sage, 2000).

48. Average undergraduate tuition, room, and board at a public four-year college rose from $2,327 in the spring of 1980 to $5,693 in the spring of 1992; National Center for Education Statistics, *Digest of Education Statistics, 2000* (Government Printing Office, 2001), table 313. Median pretax family income rose from $19,587 in 1979 to $35,939 in 1991; U.S. Bureau of the Census, *Money Income in the United States, 1999* (GPO, 2000), tables B-1 and B-4.

49. See Thomas Kane, *The Price of Admission: Rethinking How Americans Pay for College* (Brookings, 1999).

50. Mayer, "How Did the Increase in Economic Inequality between 1970 and 1990 Affect Children's Educational Attainment?"

51. The argument that inequality is bad for health goes back to the 1970s. Recent research on the topic was inspired by Richard Wilkinson, "Income Distribution and Life Expectancy," *British Medical Journal,* vol. 304 (January 1992), pp. 165–68. For a recent summary, see Ichiro Kawachi and Bruce P. Kennedy, *The Health of Nations: Why Inequality Is Harmful to Your Health* (New Press, 2002).

52. Both Wilkinson, "Income Distribution and Life Expectancy," and much subsequent work in public health have emphasized the social and psychological effects of economic inequality. For a wide range of papers in this tradition, see Ichiro Kawachi, Bruce Kennedy, and Richard Wilkinson, eds. *The Society and Population Health Reader,* vol. 1, *Income Inequality and Health* (New Press, 1999). Although there is strong evidence that changes in an individual's position within a social or economic hierarchy can have important health consequences, there is little evidence that changes in the economic distance between such positions affect people's health (but see Christine Eibner and William Evans, "Relative Deprivation, Poor Health Habits, and Mortality," Working paper, Department of Economics, University of Maryland, 2001).

53. The National Longitudinal Mortality Survey measured Americans' total family income around 1980 and then used the national death index to identify family members who died over the next few years. Each family was assigned to one of seven income groups. In today's dollars the bottom five intervals correspond to households with incomes below $50,000, each covering a $10,000 interval. The next interval runs from $50,000 to $99,999, and the top interval covers families with incomes of more than $100,000. Like all estimated life expectancies, those shown here assume that mortality rates observed at the time will continue into the indefinite future. The life expectancies are higher than those for the general population because (a) they are estimated for individuals who survived to age twenty-five, and (b) they do not include individuals who were institutionalized at the time of the initial survey. The bottom five intervals are assigned their midpoint. The top two intervals are assigned values based on the estimated distribution for all households at the time. Incomes are converted to 2000 dollars using the CPI-U-RS.

54. Moving from the lowest income interval to the median raised a man's life expectancy 7.2 years. Moving from the median to the highest income interval (the richest 5 percent of the sample) raised a man's life expectancy only 2.8 years. For men below the median, each $10,000 increment in family income lengthened life about 2.4 years. Once a man's family income reached the median, it took another $90,000 to raise his life expectancy 2.4 years. Income matters less for women, but the law of diminishing returns operates in much the same way for women as for men.

55. The reduction in life expectancy would have been about 0.32 years for white men

and 0.15 years for white women. The observed increase in white life expectancy at age twenty-five during these years was 2.7 years for men and 1.2 years for women. The changes in life expectancy at age twenty-five are from National Center for Health Statistics, *National Vital Statistics Report,* vol. 47, no. 28 (1999), pp. 14–16, and vol. 50, no. 6 (2002), pp. 30–31. The estimated effect of letting inequality increase assumes that in the absence of such an increase, life expectancy at age twenty-five would have risen 2.7 + 0.32 = 3.02 years for white men and 1.2 + 0.15 = 1.35 years for white women.

56. See, for example, James P. Smith, "Healthy Bodies and Thick Wallets: The Dual Relation between Health and Economic Status," *Journal of Economic Perspectives,* vol. 13 (Spring 1999), pp. 145–66.

57. As noted above, LIS calculates Gini coefficients after adjusting household income for household size and imposing uniform top codes for all countries, so its estimates are somewhat lower than those found elsewhere in the literature, but the LIS estimates are also more nearly comparable across countries. Figure 3-8 covers countries that supplied LIS with income data for at least one year between 1994 and 1997. Because life expectancy data rise rapidly over time, all life expectancies are for 1996 and come from National Center for Health Statistics, *Health, United States, 2001* (GPO, 2001), table 27.

58. In France, LIS estimates of the Gini coefficient rely on different surveys to measure changes in the income distribution before and after 1984. Since Gini coefficients from both surveys are available for 1984, however, we can correct for the likely impact of this change. In the United States, the LIS always uses data from the March Current Population Survey, but as we noted in our discussion of figure 3-1, procedural improvements in the survey mean that more inequality was detected beginning in 1993. If we made an adjustment for the 1992–93 break in survey methods, the U.S. data point in figure 3-9 would be modestly affected, but this would have little impact on our qualitative interpretation of the underlying relationship.

59. Clarkwest's estimate is less than half that shown in figure 3-9. Because it is based on far more observations, however, there is only one chance in ten that it occurred by chance. Details are available in Andrew Clarkwest, "Notes on Cross-National Analysis of the Relationship between Mortality and Income Inequality," Harvard University, Kennedy School of Government, Malcolm Wiener Center for Social Policy, 2000 (www.ksg.harvard.edu/socpol/MWCstdntresearch.htm). Clarkwest uses a fixed-effects model with sixteen countries, which contribute an average of four years of data each. Such a model will be biased downward if there are lagged effects, but although we expected to find such effects, none were statistically significant in either cross-national comparisons or comparisons among American states.

60. This estimate controls for the effects of a state's racial and ethnic mix and for the percentage of the population in rural areas.

61. The quality of care measures are from Stephen Jencks and others, "Quality of Medical Care Delivered to Medicare Beneficiaries," *Journal of the American Medical Association,* vol. 284 (October 4, 2000), pp. 1670–76. We link these measures to states' economic and demographic characteristics in the 1990 census. The quality of care is assessed by comparing the treatment of Medicare patients recorded in their medical records to guidelines recommended by various professional bodies.

62. John Rawls, *A Theory of Justice* (Harvard University Press, 1971).

63. Robert Nozick, *Anarchy, State, and Utopia* (Basic Books, 1971).

ALAN J. AUERBACH
WILLIAM G. GALE
PETER R. ORSZAG
SAMARA R. POTTER

4

Budget Blues:
The Fiscal Outlook
and Options for Reform

T HE OTHER CHAPTERS in this book focus on a particular area of public
policy. Should society devote more resources to helping unskilled
workers get job training? Should defense spending increase? Should we
provide new tax subsidies for retirement saving? This chapter focuses on a
broader, but in some sense more straightforward, question: once all the
individual components and policies are added together, is the government
living within its means? Are the tax laws that legislators have enacted consistent with the spending programs they have created?

If tax and spending decisions only had implications for the current year,
it would be straightforward to determine whether the government was living within its means: one could simply compare revenue and spending in
that year. But the economic effects of past and current legislation play out
over many years—even decades. As a result, decisionmakers and the public require a clear understanding of the claims that previously enacted laws
and current decisions make on resources not only today but in the future,
and whether laws currently in place commit the government to future taxes

The authors thank Manijeh Azmoodeh and David Gunter for outstanding research assis-
tance; Robert Cumby, Eric Engen, Joel Friedman, Robert Greenstein, and especially
Richard Kogan for helpful discussions and comments; and Sandy Davis, Ben Page, Wendell
Primus, and Jina Yoon for providing data.

that equal, exceed, or fall short of future spending obligations. Indeed, it is difficult to see how intelligent fiscal policy could be made in the absence of such information.

Ideally, the federal budget would provide this information. In practice, it does not, at least partially because of the difficulty of the task itself. But even compared with what is feasible within a timely and understandable budget, current practice falls short of the desirable. First, the budget uses assumptions defining current tax and spending policy that are unrealistic. Second, official budget projections employ a ten-year horizon. Practical considerations make some limit necessary, as projections become more speculative as the horizon lengthens. But such a budget "window" excludes the fiscal effects associated with the aging of the baby boomers, most of which will occur well after the next ten years. Third, even within the ten-year budget window, budget projections are uncertain, in part because the economic events that affect the projections are difficult to predict accurately.

The upshot is that the official budget bears little relation to the underlying financial status of the federal government. A person asking if the government is living within its means would be hard-pressed to find the answer in current official budget projections.

But getting the answer right is important because a government living beyond its means can impose substantial costs on the economy. If revenues are not sufficient to match spending, the government must meet the shortfall by printing money or by borrowing.[1] Sustained reliance on printing money to finance deficits can lead to escalating price inflation, which can have debilitating consequences. Sustained reliance on government borrowing leads to reductions in the domestic capital stock (to the extent that government borrowing draws financing away from private capital in the United States) or increased indebtedness to the rest of the world (to the extent that government borrowing draws financing from other countries). Regardless of how the government borrowing is financed, Americans' claims on future output would be reduced and future living standards harmed. As a result, establishing and maintaining a sustainable fiscal policy is central to the nation's long-term prospects for growth.[2]

The government's ability to run a sustainable fiscal policy, though, depends on the provision of appropriate information. More accurate budget figures would give policymakers and the public the best available information to guide policy choices. For example, when President George W. Bush came into office, the official projected ten-year surplus was $5.6 trillion—more than 4 percent of the economy—over the ensuing ten years. More realistic estimates, however, suggested that, even before considering the president's tax cut, the ten-year surplus was only about $1 trillion and was substantially uncertain, and longer-term projections showed a significant fiscal shortfall.[3] Nevertheless, the public debate that led to the $1.35 trillion tax cut in 2001 ignored the long-term figures and focused on the faulty, official ten-year projections. To be sure, some would argue that the tax cut was the right choice under any budget situation. At the very least, though, a more informative debate and a better-informed decision would have occurred if policymakers and the public had focused on more realistic budget figures.

The difference between the official budget estimates and more reasonable projections are even more striking today, in part because the 2001 tax cut exacerbated the bias in the official numbers. Indeed, the impact of more realistic spending and tax assumptions has become large enough to convert a forecast ten-year surplus of $1.3 trillion into a *deficit* of more than $4.5 trillion. The resulting deficit amounts to more than 3 percent of the economy and about 16 percent of federal revenues during the next ten years.

Using longer time horizons, the budget picture is even bleaker. Although the government provides no regular budget estimates beyond a ten-year horizon, spending on Social Security, Medicare, and Medicaid is almost certain to grow faster than national income or revenues as the baby boom generation retires, life spans lengthen, and per capita health care expenditures rise. We estimate that federal revenues are likely to fall short of federal spending by 4 to 8 percent of GDP in the long run. That is, it would require an increase in federal revenues of about 20–40 percent, a comparable drop in spending, or some combination of the two, to bring the long-term budget into balance. These projections, even more than the ten-year forecasts, are subject to error, but a large shortfall is probably a safe bet even after taking the relevant uncertainties into account.

The resulting budget outlook—bad over the next decade and worse in future years—presents policymakers with difficult choices. There are only three ways to close the fiscal gap: encouraging economic growth, which makes the costs of federal spending more affordable; raising tax revenues; or reducing spending. The first way is easy to embrace but hard to achieve. The second and third are politically difficult: tax increases and spending cuts are not popular, however necessary they may be.

Given the uncertainty inherent in the long-term estimates—which implies the possibility that large long-term deficits might not materialize—

and the daunting economic and political risks associated with large-scale tax increases and spending cuts, elected officials have so far chosen not only to ignore the long-term problems but to make them worse by enacting significant tax cuts and spending increases in recent years.

We believe that increasing the fiscal gap is a significant policy error and that actions to reduce the gap should come sooner rather than later. We present estimates of the extent to which alternative tax and spending policies would close the fiscal gap. Moreover, because the actions needed are politically difficult, we also examine changes in budget rules that could nudge elected officials toward responsible behavior. Although it is possible to make the budget process more conducive to long-term fiscal discipline, in the end there is no substitute for making painful choices.

Building Blocks

Budget experts use a specialized vocabulary as short-hand to represent complex concepts and rules (box 4-1). The most common measure of the federal government activity is the "unified budget," which was adopted in 1967 to implement recommendations of the President's Commission on Budget Concepts. It includes almost all of the activities of the federal government. Expenditures and revenues are measured on a cash-equivalent basis, which means that accrued and accruing assets and liabilities are generally not counted.[4]

The unified budget is useful for several purposes. The unified budget balance essentially equals the change in federal government debt held by the public. Deficits correspond to increases, surpluses to reductions, in debt held by the public. The unified budget balance shows net cash flow between the private sector and the federal government. It is one indicator of the impact of government operations on the private economy.

It is an imperfect indicator, however.[5] The state of the economy affects outlays and revenues, and hence the unified budget surplus or deficit. During a recession, for example, tax revenues tend to fall, and spending through such programs as food stamps, unemployment insurance, and Medicaid tend to expand. As a result, unified budget deficits tend to increase and surpluses tend to fall even if policy is unchanged. Analysts sometimes use a "cyclically adjusted" budget balance to eliminate such transitory economic influences. Such a cyclically adjusted balance is an estimate of what the budget balance would be if economic resources were fully employed. A deficit in the budget as conventionally reported may

Box 4-1. *Keeping Score*

Unified budget. A comprehensive display of the federal government budget, compiled with few exceptions on a cash-flow basis. The unified budget includes all regular federal programs and trust funds (such as those for Social Security and Medicare). The balance on the unified budget equals the sum of the on-budget and off-budget balances. In fiscal year 2002, the unified budget ran a deficit of about $158 billion.

On-budget balance. The on-budget balance reports revenues and expenditures on all operations of government, other than of the Social Security Trust Funds and the Postal Service. It is equal to the unified budget balance minus the off-budget balance. The on-budget accounts ran a deficit in fiscal year 2002 of about $317 billion.

Off-budget balance. The off-budget accounts include only the operations of the Social Security Trust Funds and the Postal Service. It was in surplus—by about $160 billion in fiscal year 2002—but large and growing deficits are forecast after the baby boomers enter retirement.

Cyclically adjusted budget. The cyclically adjusted budget measures what the unified budget balance would be if the economy were fully using available capacity; it removes the effect of the business cycle on the budget. The CBO estimates a cyclically adjusted deficit of $117 billion in fiscal year 2002, about $40 billion lower than the actual deficit of $158 billion because of the recession during 2002.

Debt held by the public. Debt held by the public reflects the government's borrowing from the private sector (that is, from banks, pension plans, private bondholders, foreign investors, and others). Debt held by the public at the end of fiscal year 2002 amounted to $3.5 trillion. (Technically, this figure includes about $600 billion in debt held by the Federal Reserve banks; many economists subtract this portion from the debt held by the public figure.)

Gross federal debt. Gross federal debt is equal to debt held by the public plus debt held by various government trust funds (including, for example, the Social Security Trust Funds). It amounted to $6.2 trillion at the end of fiscal year 2002.

Primary deficit/surplus. The primary budget excludes net interest payments of the federal government. It is equal to the unified budget balance excluding such interest payments. In 2002, net interest payments were $171 billion. The primary budget was therefore in surplus to the tune of $12 billion—the unified budget deficit of $159 billion, less interest payments.

Mandatory spending. Mandatory spending is determined by formula or by statute, rather than by annual appropriations. For example, Social Security benefit payments are determined by a benefit formula specified by law. In 2002, mandatory spending was $1.1 trillion.

(continues on the following page)

Box 4-1 *(continued)*

Discretionary spending. Discretionary spending is governed by thirteen annual appropriations bills. It includes items such as the operating budgets for federal departments and accounts for slightly more than one-third of annual spending. Discretionary spending in 2002 was about $734 billion.

Budget baseline. A budget baseline provides a projection of future spending and revenues if policy is unchanged. The effects of policy changes can then be evaluated by comparing the outcome inclusive of the policy change to the baseline (which excludes the policy change).

Gramm-Rudman-Hollings. In 1985, Congress passed the Balanced Budget and Emergency Deficit Control Act, usually referred to as Gramm-Rudman-Hollings (sometimes as Gramm-Rudman) after the bill's principal sponsors, Phil Gramm (R-Tex.), Warren Rudman (Republican-N. H.), and Ernest Hollings (D-S. C.). It set deficit targets and required "sequestration" (that is, a formulaic reduction in spending) if the targets were not met. The Supreme Court declared the original version of the bill unconstitutional, and Congress passed a revised version.

Budget Enforcement Act. The Budget Enforcement Act of 1990 set caps on discretionary spending, which could not be exceeded except in "emergencies" and defined pay-as-you-go rules for mandatory programs and taxes. The pay-as-you-go rules were intended to ensure that expansions in mandatory spending programs or reductions in taxes were balanced by cutbacks in other mandatory programs or increases in other taxes.

EGTRRA. The Economic Growth and Tax Relief Reconciliation Act of 2001 phased in various income and estate tax reductions between 2001 and 2010. All of the changes officially sunset in 2010 or before, meaning that the tax code in 2011 would revert to its form before passage of the legislation in 2001 if action is not taken before 2011 to modify the sunset in some way.

reflect no more than the transitory effects of an economic slowdown; a deficit in the cyclically adjusted budget suggests a structural imbalance between revenues and expenditures.

Another reason the unified budget is not an accurate indicator of the effect of government policy on the economy is that to the extent that currently legislated policies have effects in future years, they can influence the economy now but not show up in short-term budget projections. In some cases, the lags can be quite long. As a result, cash flow over a few years provides a misleading picture of the long-term budget position of the federal government when current or past policies result in a spending-revenue imbalance after the end of the budget projection period. There are several potential ways to address this problem, each with different strengths and weaknesses.

One approach is to retain the ten-year budget horizon but exclude some or all of these programs from the official budget. In various pieces of legislation between 1983 and 1990, Congress took a step in this direction by classifying Social Security as "off-budget."[6] The Congressional Budget Office and the Office of Management and Budget now report revenues and expenditures not only for the unified budget but also for "off-budget" programs and "on-budget" programs. The exclusion from the on-budget accounts of current cash flow surpluses in Social Security partially offsets the omission of sizable deficits in that program that are expected to occur in years beyond the ten-year budget window. Focusing on the on-budget accounts, rather than the unified budget, gives a somewhat more accurate picture of the current fiscal status of the government. Even so, that emphasis is only an awkward half-step to examining long-term budget issues directly.

An alternative solution is to extend the budget horizon beyond ten years. The Social Security and Medicare actuaries, for example, annually publish seventy-five-year projections of the financial balance under these programs. This approach captures projected shortfalls in Social Security and other programs and generates long-term budget figures. Naturally, however, estimating over a longer horizon means increased uncertainty.

The Ten-Year Budget Outlook

Figure 4-1 shows the Congressional Budget Office's (CBO's) January 2003 budget baseline for the unified budget and the on-budget accounts. The CBO reports that the unified budget deficit was $158 billion in 2002. The baseline projects a unified deficit of $199 billion in 2003, with the deficit then falling and eventually turning to a surplus by 2007. The official projected surplus then rises to more than $500 billion by 2013.[7] As a result, the budget for 2004 through 2009 runs a cumulative deficit, and more than 90 percent of the cumulative $1.3 trillion ten-year surplus for 2004 to 2013 is accounted for by surpluses projected for 2011 to 2013. Outside of Social Security, the ten-year budget now faces a baseline deficit of $1.2 trillion, with deficits in every year through 2011.

Figure 4-1. *CBO Budget Baseline, January 2003*

Surplus or deficit (billions of dollars)

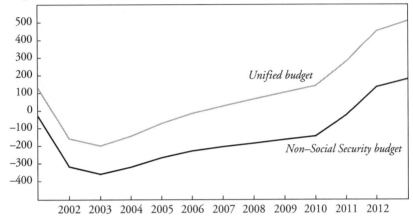

Sources: William Gale and Peter Orszag, "Perspectives on the Budget Outlook," *Tax Notes,* vol. 98 (February 2003), pp. 1005–17.

Adjusting the Baseline for Likely Outcomes

The CBO publishes such revenue and outlay baselines at least twice a year. The CBO describes the budget baseline as a mechanical forecast of current policy that is intended to serve only as a "neutral benchmark. . . . according to rules [that are] set forth in law and long-standing practices."[8] The baseline is used for measuring the costs of proposals that change tax law, spending rules, or spending amounts to ensure that such proposals are consistent with the current rules.

The CBO baseline budget projections dominate public discussions of the fiscal status of the government, but as CBO itself emphasizes, the baseline is not intended to predict likely budget outcomes, for at least three reasons. First, major new initiatives may be enacted. Second, the economy—and with it revenue and spending totals—may evolve differently than the baseline projections assume. Third, the assumptions about spending and tax policy options used to develop the baseline are often unrealistic.

To obtain a better understanding of whether the government is living within its means under current policies, we adjust the baseline budget figures. To do this, we maintain the assumption that no major new initiatives are enacted and that the economy evolves according to CBO's projection. But we make what we believe are more realistic assumptions than the baseline about what constitutes current policy for spending and taxes. This clearly involves judgment calls, so we also explain the adjustments and their justifications.

The CBO baseline assumptions do not appear to be good predictors of likely outcomes for discretionary spending, which represents slightly more than a third of total outlays and requires new appropriations by Congress every year. That is, in any given year, there are no laws explaining what discretionary spending will be in future years. This raises the issue of what levels should be assumed in the budget projections for such spending. The CBO routinely assumes that *real* discretionary spending (that is, spending adjusted for inflation) will remain constant at the level prevailing in the first year of the ten-year budget period. Because population and income grow over time, this assumption implies that by 2013 discretionary spending will fall by about 20 percent relative to gross domestic product (GDP) and by about 8 percent in real per capita terms.

Although judgments may reasonably differ about future spending choices, CBO's assumption is unrealistic—either as a measure that holds current policy constant or as a prediction of likely spending outcomes.[9] In order to maintain current policy, we believe that a baseline computed on the assumption that real discretionary spending grows at the same rate as the population would be appropriate.[10] This is the same criterion endorsed by George W. Bush as a presidential candidate.[11]

The second area where the baseline makes unrealistic assumptions involves expiring tax provisions. The CBO assumes that Congress will extend expiring spending programs but is legally required to assume that all temporary tax provisions (other than excise taxes dedicated to trust funds) expire as scheduled, even if Congress has repeatedly renewed them. The assumption about spending is reasonable, since spending programs with expiration dates are normally renewed. But the assumption about taxes is not reasonable in most cases. The Internal Revenue Code currently contains three sorts of expiring tax provisions. The first includes provisions of the 2001 tax cut, the Economic Growth and Tax Relief Reconciliation Act (EGTRRA). All of these provisions "sunset" or end automatically in the next ten years. The second category includes the elements of the 2002 economic stimulus package. Third, other tax provisions have statutory expiration dates but are routinely extended for a few years at a time as their expiration date approaches. We believe that the most accurate assumption of current policy, on balance, would be that these various provisions will be extended (box 4-2).

The individual alternative minimum tax (AMT) is a dramatic example of how following current law generates unlikely outcomes. The individual AMT was designed in the late 1960s, and then strengthened in 1986, to curb excessive use of tax shelters and other means of tax avoidance (box 4-3). The AMT runs parallel to the regular income tax system. It uses a somewhat different measure of income, permits fewer deductions, and applies flatter rates than the regular income tax. Taxpayers must compute tax liability under both the conventional income tax and the AMT and pay the larger liability. In practice, the AMT currently generates larger liability for so few taxpayers—about 3 percent—that few filers, other than the tiny minority who might be affected, bother with it.

Because the AMT is not adjusted for inflation, while the ordinary income tax is, the AMT applies to ever more taxpayers as prices rise. In addition, EGTRRA, which cut the ordinary income tax but not the AMT, will greatly increase the number of people subject to the AMT. All told, by 2010 an estimated 36 million filers will become subject to the AMT under current law. This result is troubling in large part because the AMT is significantly more complex than the regular tax. Policymakers will therefore be under powerful pressure to modify the AMT.

Our budget estimates reflect current policy toward the AMT in two ways. First, we assume that provisions of the AMT that are slated to expire before the end of the budget window are granted a continuance. Under current law, the AMT exemption is increased for 2001 to 2004, but after 2004 it reverts to its 2000 level. We assume that the temporary increase in the exemption is made permanent. Also, under current law, the use of non-refundable personal credits against the AMT is allowed through 2003. We assume that this provision is made permanent as well. Our second adjustment is to index the AMT exemption, brackets, and phase-outs for inflation starting in 2004 and to allow dependent exemptions in the AMT.[12]

In table 4-1, these costs are distributed in two places. The cost of extending the exemption and use of nonrefundable credits is shown as an "adjustment for expiring tax provisions" and based on CBO estimates. The additional costs of indexing and adding a dependent exemption are shown separately and are based on estimates using the Tax Policy Center

Box 4-2. *Expiring Provisions in the Tax Law*

Under current law, all of the provisions of EGTRRA terminate at the end of 2010 if they have not already been terminated by then. As of the end of 2010, the tax code reverts to what it would have been had EGTRRA never existed. Perhaps the oddest of these rules concerns the estate tax. The act repeals it at the start of 2010 and restores it at the end of 2010. Forecasters, who try to understand what "current policy" is and to forecast its budgetary implications, are hard pressed to carry out their instructions under these circumstances. In the case of the estate tax, although CBO must follow current law, virtually no one believes that current law will be implemented in full. More generally, it is unlikely that the tax provisions will sunset completely as stipulated by EGTRRA. In 2002, the Bush administration clearly stated its desire that the tax cuts be made permanent. After the 2002 elections, few doubted that many elements of EGTRRA would be made permanent.[1] But how much of it would become permanent, or when, remained obscure. Our projections assume that all tax cut provisions of EGTRRA will be made permanent.[2]

We also assume that the traditional package of expiring tax provisions will be extended.[3] In the past, these provisions have been temporarily extended each time the expiration dates approached. Indeed, CBO calls the extensions a "matter of course."[4]

How projections should handle the 2002 stimulus package—whose most important tax provision allows partial expensing for business investments—is less clear. Measures to combat recession are customarily temporary. On the other hand, the package expires just before the 2004 election, which will create political pressure to extend it. Proponents of the bill wanted the provisions of the stimulus package permanent in the first place. For simplicity and consistency with the other expiring provisions, we treat the stimulus package as a permanent tax cut. Altering this assumption would not materially affect our conclusions.

1. President Bush called for making the tax cuts permanent in his January 2002 State of the Union address, and the administration's 2003 and 2004 budgets include such a proposal. But even before the tax cut was signed, Treasury Secretary Paul O'Neill indicated that "All these things are going to become permanent. They'll all be fixed." "Tax-Cut Gimmicks Portend Return to Deficit Spending," *USA Today,* June 6, 2001, p. 14A. Lawrence B. Lindsey refers to the tax cuts as "permanent." See Lindsey, "Why We Must Keep the Tax Cut," *Washington Post,* January 18, 2002, p. A25.

2. Donald Kiefer and others, "The Economic Growth and Tax Relief Reconciliation Act of 2001: Overview and Assessment of Effects on Taxpayers," *National Tax Journal,* vol. 55 (March 2002), pp. 89–117, make a similar assumption. Congressional Budget Office, "The Budget and Economic Update: An Outlook" (August 2001), makes the same assumption when it analyzes the economic effects of the tax cut, even though it cannot make that assumption when analyzing the budget projections themselves.

3. These include, for example, the research and experimentation tax credit, which is to expire on June 30, 2004, the Work Opportunity Tax Credit, the Welfare-to-Work Tax Credit, and several other items.

4. Congressional Budget Office, "The Budget and Economic Outlook: Fiscal Years 2002–2012 (January 2002).

Box 4-3. *The Alternative Minimum Tax*

In 1969, public outrage following a Treasury report that 155 high-income tax filers had paid no income tax goaded Congress to enact a "minimum tax." Today's version, introduced in 1978, parallels the income tax but defines income differently, allows different deductions, and applies flatter tax rates. Taxpayers must pay the alternative minimum tax when it exceeds their regular income tax.

About 1 million households paid the AMT in 1999. By 2010, an estimated 36 million taxpayers will face it, including virtually all upper-middle-class families with two or more children. The AMT raises little revenue today. By 2008, however, it would cost more to repeal the AMT than the regular income tax.

The projected expansion can be tied directly to the last two major tax cuts. The regular income tax was indexed for inflation beginning in 1985, but the AMT was not. As a result, AMT liabilities rise every year even if income just keeps up with inflation. The 2001 tax cut reduces regular income-tax liabilities during the next decade. With AMT liability rising and regular taxes falling, ever more taxpayers find that AMT liability exceeds ordinary income taxes.

These trends are alarming because the AMT is bad tax policy. It is notoriously complex. Most taxpayers who are required to plod through the forms do not end up owing any additional tax. Those who do pay are often subjected to higher marginal tax rates than under the regular tax.

The complexity is also increasingly pointless. The AMT was originally intended to deter tax shelters but now raises less than 10 percent of its revenue from its anti-shelter provisions. Instead, the tax increasingly burdens married filers earning under $100,000 with several children.[1]

1. See Leonard E. Burman, William G. Gale, Jeffrey Rohaly, and Benjamin H. Harris, "The Individual AMT: Problems and Potential Solutions," Urban-Brookings Tax Policy Center Discussion Paper 5 (Brookings, September 2002).

microsimulation model. Taken together, the adjustments would reduce revenues by $638 billion and add $114 billion to debt service costs, for a total budgetary cost of $752 billion. Even so, they would leave 8.5 million taxpayers on the AMT in 2013 assuming that EGTRRA is extended— well above current numbers but well below the 43.5 million slated to face the AMT without such changes.

Table 4-1. *CBO Baseline and Adjusted Budget Projections, 2004–13*[a]
Billions of dollars

CBO unified budget (+surplus, –deficit)	+1,336
Adjustments for current policy	
For expiring tax provisions[b]	–1,425
For AMT[b, c]	–517
To hold real per capita discretionary spending constant[b]	–525
Adjusted unified budget	–1,131
Adjustments for retirement funds	
For Social Security	–2,567
For Medicare	–349
For government retirement funds	–484
Adjusted nonretirement budget	–4,531
If discretionary spending is a constant share of GDP[d]	
Further adjustment[b, d]	–951
Adjusted unified budget	–2,082
Adjusted nonretirement budget	–5,481

Source: William Gale and Peter R. Orszag, "Perspectives on the Budget Outlook," *Tax Notes*, vol. 98 (February 2003), pp. 1005–17.
a. Fiscal years.
b. Includes effects on debt service costs.
c. As described in the text.
d. Rather than being held constant in real per capita terms.

Retirement Funds

The unified budget baseline generally uses cash-flow accounting to measure outlays and revenues over a fixed period, currently ten years. For programs under which future liabilities are accruing, this practice is misleading. Currently, taxes earmarked to pay for Social Security and Medicare Hospital Insurance exceed outlays on those programs. But in the long run, the programs face significant deficits. Yet the current cash-flow surpluses in Medicare and Social Security, and general revenues allocated to trust funds for future federal military and civilian employee pension programs, are counted as part of the unified budget. As noted, one approach to dealing with this kind of program is to move the programs off budget, and that is the approach we follow in this section.[13]

Implications of the Adjustments

Table 4-1 and figure 4-2 show the sizable effects of adjusting the surplus for current policy assumptions and retirement trust funds. The CBO unified budget baseline projects a ten-year surplus of $1.3 trillion, with surpluses rising sharply over time. Adjusting the CBO baseline for our assumptions regarding current policy implies that the unified budget will be in *deficit* to the tune of $1.1 trillion over the next decade. Notably, the adjusted unified budget would be in deficit every year through 2013. Adjusting further by taking the retirement funds off budget would generate a ten-year deficit of $4.5 trillion. If discretionary spending were held constant as a share of GDP, rather than on a real, per capita basis, each of the ten-year deficits would be about $1 trillion larger.

Although the precise figures should not be taken literally because of uncertainty and other factors, the basic trends in the data are clear. First, the CBO baseline suggests that the budgetary future contains rising surpluses over time, at least within the ten-year window. Our adjusted baseline suggests rising deficits over time. Second, the differences grow over time. By 2013, the annual difference between the official projected unified budget and our alternative unified deficit is more than $600 billion. Third, acknowledging that the retirement trust funds are running current surpluses but will run deficits in the future makes the budget outlook far worse. The adjusted budget outcome outside of the retirement trust funds—$4.5 trillion—is almost $6 trillion less than the baseline budget outcome over the next decade, and the difference between the official unified projection and our adjusted nonretirement trust fund budget exceeds $1 trillion in 2013 alone.

The Long-Term Fiscal Gap

The adjusted budget measures in table 4-1 and figure 4-2 depict more accurately than does the CBO unified budget baseline the cash-flow budget prospects over the next decade. Yet any budget measure that is limited to developments over the next decade is inherently imperfect. As noted, although Social Security and Medicare are currently running cash-flow surpluses, each program faces large and growing projected cash-flow deficits under current law. In the context of an aging population and rapidly rising medical care expenditures, an accurate picture of the government's long-term fiscal status is impossible without inclusion of these deficits.

Figure 4-2. *Baseline and Adjusted Budget Outcomes, 2003–13*

Surplus or deficit (billions of dollars)

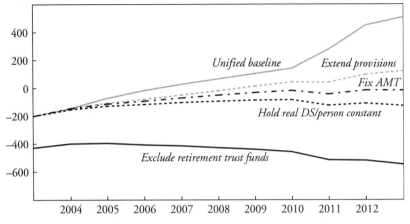

Source: Gale and Orszag, "Perspectives on the Budget Outlook."

We present estimates of the "fiscal gap," the increase in taxes or reductions in noninterest expenditures, measured as a share of GDP, that would be required if implemented immediately to hold constant the ratio of government debt to GDP.[14] This measure of the fiscal gap describes the current long-term budgetary status of the government.

We present several measures of the gap. One set uses the CBO baseline for spending and taxes over the next decade. After the first decade, we assume that all taxes (including those earmarked to pay for Social Security and Medicare) and discretionary spending remain the same share of GDP as they were in 2012.[15] We assume that Social Security and Medicare expenditures follow the 2002 intermediate projections of the Social Security and Medicare actuaries. We also assume that Medicaid spending grows at a rate determined by the growth of the population and per capita health care spending. Interest payments are determined by debt accrual and interest rates. We present estimates through 2075 and for the indefinite future.

The least pessimistic projection uses CBO's baseline revenue and spending figures for the next decade and then the long-term assumptions for the rest of the period ending in 2075. Under these assumptions, the fiscal gap is 1.6 percent of GDP (table 4-2).[16] An immediate tax increase or spending

Table 4-2. *The Long-term Fiscal Gap*
Percent of GDP

Period	CBO assumptions[a]	Adjusted budget[b]
2002–75	1.6	4.9
Permanent	4.4	7.8

Source: Authors' calculations as described in text.

a. The CBO spending baseline holds discretionary spending authority constant in real terms from 2004 to 2013 at the level prevailing in 2003. The CBO revenue baseline assumes current law: EGTRRA and the stimulus bill sunset as legislated, other temporary tax provisions expire as scheduled, and no AMT adjustments are made.

b. The adjusted spending baseline holds discretionary spending outlays constant as a share of GDP from 2004 to 2013 at the level prevailing in 2003. The adjusted revenue baseline assumes that the phase-out and sunset provisions of EGTRRA are repealed, other temporary tax provisions are made permanent, and the AMT is changed as described in the text.

cut of 1.6 percent of GDP in each year from 2003 through 2075 would maintain fiscal balance over this period. That shift translates into a current tax increase or spending cut of about $170 billion a year—approximately 8 percent of the budget.

These fiscal gap figures reflect a sharp projected rise in spending on Social Security, Medicare, and Medicaid—from about 9 percent of GDP in 2012 to 15 percent by 2040 and 21 percent by 2075, the last year of this projection. Under this projection, these three programs would ultimately absorb a larger share of GDP than does all of the federal government today. To be sure, these programs have been amended frequently in the past, and virtually no one expects them to persist unchanged for the next seven decades. The projections, however, indicate what will happen if action is not taken, thereby serving as a benchmark that indicates the size of the changes in spending and revenues that are needed.

Because these programs grow much faster than GDP, extending the horizon increases the fiscal gap. To maintain the ratio of debt to GDP indefinitely requires that taxes be increased or spending cut by 4.4 percent of GDP. The gap increases with the projection period because the budget is projected to be substantially in deficit after 2075. This result, like the earlier one, is explained mainly by population aging and attendant increases in pension and health care costs.

The fiscal gap is sensitive to revenue and spending assumptions over the next decade. Using our adjusted revenue and spending figures for the next ten years, and assuming those changes persist over time, raises the fiscal gap through 2075 from 1.4 to 4.9 percent of GDP. Using our adjusted baseline implies that it would take spending cuts or tax increases equal to 7.8 percent of GDP to close the *permanent* fiscal gap, rather than 4.4 percent of GDP under the CBO baseline. These comparisons underscore the fact that changes within the current budget window can have a large effect on the long-term gap if they persist.

Uncertainty

Substantial uncertainty surrounds the short- and long-term budget projections. Much of the problem stems from the fact that the surplus or deficit is the difference between two large quantities, taxes and spending. Small percentage errors in either one can cause large percentage changes in the difference between them. For example, if annual economic growth exceeded forecasts by 0.5 percentage point, the economy would be about 5 percent larger than forecast after a decade. Revenues would increase above and spending would decline below forecasts. The resulting budget surplus would be $1 trillion dollars larger or the deficit $1 trillion smaller than forecast. Such a shift would be sufficient to double the CBO baseline surplus shown in table 4-1. Conversely, annual growth about 0.5 percentage point below forecast would be sufficient to eliminate almost the entire projected ten-year surplus.[17] In addition, revenues significantly exceeded what revenue estimators had expected in the late 1990s and fell significantly short in 2001–02, even controlling for the size of the economy.

As a result, budget projections can change significantly on a year-to-year basis. For example, in January 2001, CBO forecast a unified budget surplus for 2002 to 2011 of $5.6 trillion. Shortly thereafter, Congress and the administration agreed to cut taxes over the next decade. The economy weakened, and the nation fell victim to terrorist attack. A scant eighteen months later, the overall surplus for the 2002 to 2011 time period had fallen to $336 billion. Of this $5.3 trillion shift, the 2001 tax cut and the associated increases in interest payments accounted for about $1.7 trillion. The economy, stock market, and other factors accounted for the rest.

The Congressional Budget Office is unusually candid in acknowledging these projection surprises. Recent CBO publications have included a "fan graph," based on CBO's past forecasts, which shows the likelihood of different budget outcomes (figure 4-3 reproduces the fan graph for 2002). The graph shows the wide range of possible short- and medium-term outcomes.

Figure 4-3. *Uncertainty in CBO's Projection of the United Budget Surplus*

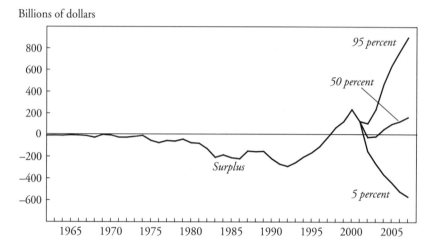

Source: Congressional Budget Office, "The Budget and Economic Outlook: Fiscal Years 2003–2012" (January 2002).

Not only are forecasts often far off the mark, but errors in one direction tend to be followed by errors in the same direction the next year. It is particularly difficult to predict and understand turning points. Nonetheless, CBO's forecasts appear to be unbiased, in the sense that positive and negative errors have roughly offset one another over time, and are at least as good as those provided by the Office of Management and Budget (OMB), the major macroeconometric models, and the Blue Chip forecasters.[18]

Long-term projections are subject to these and other uncertainties. Small differences in growth rates sustained for extended periods can have surprisingly large economic effects. For example, if the United States were to grow by 3 percent per year it would be about twice as large by 2075 as it would be if it grew 2 percent annually. Holding the tax system fixed, government revenues would be much higher with 3 percent growth than with 2 percent growth. Whatever a rapidly growing economy chooses to do with the extra revenues—cut tax rates, boost government spending, or pay down public debt—it has vastly larger options than does a slow-growth economy. A 1 percentage point difference in annual economic growth is within the variation found among responsible forecasts.

A second source of uncertainty is the characterization of "current policy." For example, in 2000, CBO raised its assumption about the growth of Medicare and Medicaid spending by 1 percentage point per year starting in 2020. This change alone raised the fiscal gap for the 2000–2070 period by 1.7 percent of GDP and the permanent fiscal gap by 3.4 percent of GDP.[19] The long-term projections we report also incorporate the assumption that effective income tax rates do not increase as GDP rises. But that assumption implies that bracket widths, personal exemptions, the standard deduction, and other nominal quantities increase faster than they do under current law. Otherwise, real economic growth will push households into higher marginal tax rates and raise the tax share. In this case, our "current policy" projections rest on the tacit assumption that Congress continually lowers statutory tax rates or reduces the statutory base of taxable income. In the case of Social Security and Medicare, we assume that benefits rise with average real earnings, as called for under current law. If we instead assumed constant real per capita Social Security and Medicare costs, the fiscal gap would shrink or vanish.[20] This would mean, however, that retirement benefits were falling on a continual basis relative to wages.

Changes in demographic factors and economic behavior generate a third source of uncertainty.[21] In the short run, variations in birth rates and life expectancy cannot have much effect on the labor force, the number of children who need education, or the number of elderly who are disproportionately likely to be dependent on public services. But over extended periods, plausible variations in demographic variables can have large effects on economic growth, which influences revenues, and on the demand for public services, which affects outlays.

The imminent retirement of the baby-boom generation, the leading edge of which turns sixty-two in 2008, underscores the importance of changes in retirement age in affecting federal revenues and outlays. From 1950 to the mid-1980s, American men were retiring at ever earlier ages. Labor force participation rates may now be rising a bit among men in their sixties. Whether men (and women) have begun to extend their working lives or they resume the trend toward early retirement will profoundly affect the overall labor force and hence total production and tax collections. It will also influence public spending because it will affect the number of people who are dependent on Medicare and Medicaid. (The age at which people first claim Social Security benefits has little effect on overall program costs because older first-time claimants receive actuarially increased annual benefits.)

Other behaviors can have important effects on government revenues and expenditures—for example, how long young people stay in school, how many nonaged adults drop out of the labor force, how many immigrants enter the country, how much people voluntarily save (which affects investment, economic growth, and interest rates), and what happens to workplace safety and other environmental hazards and, hence, to disability rates. Many of these behaviors depend sensitively on public policies, as well as on autonomous changes in individual preferences.

Demographic and behavioral change can interact in complex ways in their effect on the fiscal outlook. If longevity increases, retirement ages remain about where they are, and the advent of physical and mental frailty is not delayed, the aging of the baby-boom generation may impose enormous costs on the working population. However, if retirement ages increase and medical advances delay physical and mental decline, a growing population of people of advanced years would cause less severe fiscal problems or none at all.[22]

Uncertainty makes long-term projections imprecise. Nonetheless, almost all studies that have examined the issue suggest that even if major sources of uncertainty are accounted for, serious long-term fiscal problems will remain.[23]

Policy Responses

The budget outlook presents policymakers with a complex and difficult set of problems. First, a medium-term deficit is highly likely, and a significantly larger long-term fiscal gap seems probable. Second, the sources of the two problems are quite different. The ten-year deficits entirely reflect deficits in operations of government other than Social Security or Medicare, both of which are currently running cash-flow surpluses and are expected to continue doing so for many years. Over the longer term, both Social Security and Medicare costs are likely to rise more than either taxes earmarked to them or revenues in general. Third, raising taxes or cutting spending enough to close the fiscal gap will be painful, both for the elected officials who must enact them and for the citizens who will pay higher taxes and receive fewer public services than current policy indicates.

Addressing the Long-Term Fiscal Gap

Some have argued that the correct policy response to the fiscal gap is to ignore it, for any of four reasons. For example, the significant uncertainty surrounding future events means that fiscal prospects might improve markedly even without significant policy change. If so, avoiding the painful tax increases or spending cuts that would be required to close the gap is desirable. Others say that steady economic growth means that future generations will be better off than the current generation, and over long periods, much better off. If future generations are richer, they will be better able to afford the fiscal burdens. Some claim that fiscal deficits are desirable because they make it difficult to raise public spending and thus serve to constrain the size of government. Adherents of this view believe that the prospect of a smaller government provides economic (and perhaps political or ideological) benefits that outweigh the costs of worsening fiscal prospects. Finally, some analysts claim that budget deficits do not have deleterious economic effects.

We believe it would be a mistake to ignore the fiscal gap, and that all of the preceding claims are flawed. First, although fiscal prospects are uncertain, most studies show that a sizable fiscal gap will probably remain even after adjusting for a plausible range of uncertainty. Simply put, population aging and health care technologies will create budgeting problems under almost any scenario. The likelihood of a long-term fiscal gap should spur a precautionary response from policymakers now.[24]

Although future generations will in all likelihood receive higher wages than current generations, the fiscal gap is so large under current policies that it would be prudent and fair for the current generation to bear a nontrivial portion of the costs. Doing so would still leave a sizable burden for future generations to shoulder. Moreover, one must also account for the distortionary effects of taxation in comparing the welfare of current and future generations. The welfare costs of tax distortions rise roughly with the *square* of revenues as a share of GDP, so the higher revenues required of future generations would have a much larger negative effect on welfare than is directly attributable to the increase in revenue.

Although it may make sense to constrain government, choosing to ignore the fiscal gap is a serious gamble. It may not work—or at least may not work for a long time. When taxes were cut in the 1980s, for example, federal spending rose as a share of GDP. It was not until budget rules were imposed in 1990 and reauthorized subsequently that federal spending came under control. In the meantime, the ratio of public debt to GDP doubled. If reporting a larger budget deficit does constrain spending, that goal can be achieved by emphasizing the long-term fiscal gap figures just reported or some of the other measures we consider, rather than the official budget projections. The use of alternative budget measures would raise the reported deficit, but it does not create a fiscal gamble. Better budgetary rules could also help constrain federal spending. For all of these reasons, if the goal is to constrain spending, ignoring (or increasing) the fiscal gap is not the best way to achieve that goal. Moreover, under current circumstances, with a fiscal gap that is large and concentrated in politically popular programs, ignoring the fiscal gap now may create the need for massive, last-minute future policy changes.

Finally, the claim that budget deficits do not have deleterious long-term effects is based on the notion—holding spending constant—that when the government increases its borrowing, private citizens increase their saving by the same amount. The overwhelming majority of economic evidence firmly rejects this view.[25] Sustained budget deficits result in more government borrowing, less national saving, a smaller capital stock owned by Americans, and lower future incomes than if deficits were eliminated. This implies that future living standards of Americans would be significantly higher if we act now to close the fiscal gap (box 4-4).

Acting sooner also gives people time to adjust their own plans based on changes in public programs. Because any solution to the Social Security and Medicare financing problem will likely involve benefit cuts, tax increases, or both, acting now would give people more advance notice and a chance to modify their plans. If the fiscal gap widens with time, as current projections indicate, gradual change now may spare the nation serious dislocations from abrupt and massive change later.

Finally, if the long-term budget outlook is not kept front and center in the policy debate, elected officials can all too easily succumb to the temptation to use any temporary surpluses that emerge not to address looming problems but to finance tax cuts or spending increases that will aggravate the long-term problem. Precisely such shortsightedness seems to have contributed to the size of the tax cuts enacted in 2001.

Policies to Close the Long-Term Fiscal Gap

A variety of policies are available to help close the gap. If the tax cuts enacted in 2001 that took effect before the end of 2003 were to remain in place and were made permanent, but all cuts scheduled to take effect beyond 2003 were suspended, the fiscal gap between now and 2075, relative to our adjusted budget baseline, would be cut by 0.8–0.9 percent of GDP.[26] By way of comparison, the estimated actuarial deficit in Social Security in the same period is 0.7 percent of GDP.[27]

Box 4-4. *Budget Deficits, National Income, and Interest Rates*

The link between the government's budget and economic performance contains several steps. First, national saving is the sum of private saving (which occurs when the private sector spends less than its after-tax income) and public saving (which occurs when the public sector runs budget surpluses). Second, national saving is used to finance domestic investment or net foreign investment—the difference between Americans' investments overseas less foreigners' investments here. That is, national saving finances the accumulation by Americans of assets at home (domestic investment) or it finances the accumulation by Americans of assets abroad (net foreign investment). Either way, the accumulation of assets due to higher national saving means that the capital stock owned by Americans is increased. Third, the returns to that additional capital—whether domestic or foreign—raise the income of Americans in the future.

Given these links, it is staightforward to see why sustained budget deficits reduce future national income. The empirical evidence suggests that private saving only offsets about 20 to 50 percent of declines in public saving due to increased deficits.[1] As a result, increases in budget deficits (declines in public saving) reduce national saving. The decline in national saving must reduce the sum of domestic and net foreign investment and hence reduce future national income.

A back-of-the-envelope calculation may help to illustrate the sizable effects of dissipating future budget surpluses. The projected ten-year budget surplus for 2002–2011 fell by $5.6 trillion between January 2001 and August 2002 according to Congressional Budget Office projections. That increase reflects the cumulative deterioration in government saving between 2002 and 2011 under the official forecasts. If 25 percent of the deterioration in government saving is offset by increased private saving, the budget shift reduces the stock of net assets owned by Americans at the end of 2011 by about $4.2 trillion. Assuming conservatively that capital earns a return of 6 percent on the margin, the deterioration in the budget balance over the next ten years reduces real gross national product (which includes income received by Americans on their foreign investments) in 2012 by $252 billion or by about 1.5 percent. This translates into about $2,100 per year for each household in the United States.[2]

When budget deficits increase and national saving falls, a related question is how national saving and investment are brought back into equality. One possible channel is that interest rates rise. At a given interest rate, a reduction in national saving relative to current domestic and net foreign investment implies a shortage of funds to finance such investments. That imbalance puts upward pressure on interest rates as firms compete for the limited pool of funds to finance their investment projects.

(continues on the following page)

Box 4-4 *(continued)*

The increase in interest rates then serves to reduce domestic and net foreign investment and bring national saving and investment back into equality. A second possibility is that the entire decline in national saving is financed by increased capital
inflows from abroad. These capital inflows would dampen and perhaps eliminate the
increase in domestic interest rates.

   Although the potential effect of deficits on interest rates has received much attention in the policy debate, the reduction in national saving entails an economic cost
regardless of whether interest rates rise. In particular, the capital inflows represent a
reduction in net foreign investment and thus a reduction in future national income.
The equality between national saving and domestic plus net foreign investment
holds even if interest rates are unaffected, so that a reduction in national saving must
therefore reduce the capital owned by Americans and future national income.

   1. See Douglas Bernheim, "A Neoclassical Perspective on Budget Deficits," *Journal of Economic Perspectives,* vol. 3 (Spring 1989), pp. 55–72; Congressional Budget Office, "Description
of Economic Models" (1998); Douglas W. Elmendorf and Jeffrey B. Liebman, "Social Security
Reform and National Saving in an Era of Budget Surpluses," *Brookings Papers on Economic
Activity 2:2000,* 1–71; and William G. Gale and Samara R. Potter, "An Economic Evaluation
of the Economic Growth and Tax Relief Reconciliation Act of 2001," *National Tax Journal,* vol.
55 (March 2002), pp. 133–86.
   2. For details of this calculation see William Gale and Peter Orszag, "The Economic Effects
of Long-Term Fiscal Discipline," Urban-Brookings Tax Policy Center Discussion Paper
(Brookings, December 2002).

An even more aggressive policy would be to take seriously the expiration
dates in EGTRRA and allow the tax cut to expire as scheduled at the end
of 2010. This policy would have no effect on the CBO baseline, which is
based on the assumption that EGTRRA will indeed expire. But relative to
our adjusted baseline, which treats EGTRRA as permanent, allowing the
tax cut to expire would affect the final three years of the ten-year forecast,
reducing the projected ten-year deficit by more than half a trillion dollars.
Allowing the tax cuts to expire would reduce the fiscal gap measured to
2075 by 35 percent—from 4.9 percent to about 3.2 percent of GDP.

   Suspending those elements of the tax cut that have not yet been implemented or allowing the entire tax cut to expire on its legislated schedule
would be clear steps toward fiscal responsibility, but a large fiscal gap would
still remain. Because Medicare, Medicaid, and Social Security will constitute the bulk of the federal budget, the solution to the fiscal gap must

involve these three programs. Eliminating the Social Security actuarial deficit through 2075, as just noted, would reduce the fiscal gap through 2075 by 0.7 percent of GDP.[28]

Medicare poses even more serious challenges, as health spending will be driven not only by the demographic trends that affect Social Security, but also by the revolutionary—and to date largely expenditure-increasing—technological advances emerging from biomedical research. These costs also depend sensitively on which services Medicare covers and how much of the rising total cost of care Medicare pays. Currently, Medicare coverage omits major services, such as outpatient prescription drugs and ordinary nursing home care, and patients' share of medical costs is higher than under most private insurance plans. The elderly and disabled will almost certainly have to bear increasing costs for health care. But it is also clear that higher taxes—payroll or other taxes earmarked to Medicare or general revenues—will be necessary to close the current projected deficit, finance benefits promised under current law, and modernize the Medicare benefit package.[29] Medicaid poses similar problems.

Thus, some combination of benefit reductions in Social Security and higher payments by Medicare beneficiaries seem inescapable. But so also do increased taxes to meet the costs of an expanding elderly and disabled population, modernize Medicare, and assure the elderly of adequate basic income during retirement.

Addressing the Near-Term Budget Deficit

Addressing the near-term budget deficit is less important than addressing the long-term fiscal gap. In the near term, as long as economic growth is sluggish and capacity is underutilized, budget deficits can help stimulate aggregate demand and return the nation to its full-employment growth path. In fact, having a near-term deficit may prove useful in helping poli- cymakers to focus on fiscal restraint that will pay off in the long run.

Nevertheless, the near-term deficit may be of concern. If long-term fis- cal prospects were rosy, current deficits would raise little concern. If private saving were high, the fact that government is now in deficit and absorbing some private saving to cover the gap would not prevent the nation from using the rest of private saving to augment its capital stock. Unfortunately, neither condition is satisfied. Long-term budget prospects are poor, and private saving is low, compared either with historic averages or interna- tional standards. Thus, reducing the deficit as soon as the current recession has ended is important because continued deficits will have a significant negative effect on the nation's economic growth. Policies that increase the deficit now but reduce it in future years could be used to help stimulate the economy in the short term and provide fiscal discipline in the long term.

Improving Budgetary Governance

The political hurdles that any changes to close the fiscal gap will face heighten the importance of budget rules that might facilitate responsible decisionmaking by elected officials. Budget rules by themselves cannot pro duce fiscal discipline. Without a consensus that fiscal discipline is impoi tant, the rules will simply be ignored or evaded. But the rules for evaluat- ing proposals can affect budget outcomes. We suggest that impending deficits and the political impediments to dealing responsibly with them jus- tify placing larger procedural obstacles before spending increases or tax cu' than before spending cuts or tax increases. They also justify the preparati and dissemination of information that reveals the long-term fiscal gap.

BUDGET REQUIREMENTS. If the goal is to control the deficit, why no simply mandate declining deficits or balanced budgets? One answer is that no single budget total adequately describes the government's fiscal status. Any requirement for balance or declining deficits would necessitate focus on a single such measure, which would bias decisions in favor of actions that met the standards of that measure, even if those same decisions dam- aged budget prospects as indicated by other measures. More fundamen- tally, policymakers have proved capable of evading all deficit targets yet devised, including the Gramm-Rudman-Hollings requirements under which Congress operated in the 1980s. In addition, since deficits tend to emerge when the economy weakens, balanced budget rules tend to require tax increases or spending cuts at the wrong time in the business cycle. When unemployment is rising, the best short-term policy is to let taxes fall and spending rise, through unemployment insurance, aid to the poor, and other so-called automatic stabilizers—programs under which spending increases when the economy weakens and without new legislation.

PAYGO RULES. The Budget Enforcement Act of 1990 (BEA) introduced rules establishing caps on discretionary spending and pay-as-you-go (PayGo) rules governing changes in taxes and entitlement spending. Although these rules were inflexible and had shortcomings (for example, they encouraged trade-offs between changes in entitlements and taxes, but not between entitlements and discretionary spending), they contributed to fiscal discipline that led in the late 1990s to the emergence of substantial cash-flow surpluses. Unfortunately, when surpluses emerged in the late 1990s Congress began to waive or circumvent the rules. Some of the evasions were extreme. For example, some expenses associated with the 2000 decennial Census were classified as "emergency" spending, although the decennial censuses have been fielded for more than 200 years and are mandated in the Constitution. The motivation for this ludicrous misclassification was transparent—emergency spending was excluded from the discretionary spending caps.

It should be emphasized, though, that these spending transgressions were smaller than the size of the 2001 tax cut. That is, to the extent that the disappearance of the surplus was because of policy, it was more the tax cut, rather than spending increases, that undermined fiscal discipline.

The PayGo and other budgetary rules matter more in the Senate than in the House of Representatives, because the House can waive rules by majority vote, but waivers require sixty votes in the Senate. The BEA PayGo rules and spending caps expired in September 2002; other Senate rules expired in the spring of 2003. Failure to restore these or similar rules and make them permanent congressional procedure would be a serious mistake.

UNCERTAINTY. Budget rules should reflect the fact that projections are subject to error. Former CBO director Robert Reischauer suggested rules under which Congress could take formal cognizance of this uncertainty. Only a part of any projected budget surpluses would be available for tax cuts or spending increases. The more distant the projection, the smaller the part of the projected surplus that would be available. Such a rule would enable Congress to engage in long-term planning that uses a part of projected surpluses for spending increases or tax cuts but would reduce the likelihood that decisions made during a temporary period of excessive optimism would result in large deficits.[30]

THE BUDGET HORIZON. Because the House and Senate budget committees use projections of the Congressional Budget Office to develop funding allocations for various oversight and appropriation committees, deciding how far into the future to make such projections is significant. Projections over one or a few years create powerful biases to enact bills whose costs are small in the near term but balloon in years beyond the budget horizon. The longer the projection period, the smaller the bias. But as the projection period lengthens, uncertainties multiply. Choosing how far into the future to project expenditures and revenues is therefore a matter of judgment and requires a balance between distorted legislative incentives and the imponderables of the future. We believe that the damage to responsible legislation from any shortening of the ten-year projection period would be significant. Even with the current horizon, Congress frequently delays implementation of spending increases or tax cuts to hold down the estimated ten-year cost of their actions. For the 2001 tax cut, for example, delays in implementation, the deepening of the AMT problem, and the sunset provisions and phaseouts held down the estimated reduction in revenues (measured as a fraction of GDP) for 2001 to 2011 to about half the cost of the fully implemented tax cuts in 2011 (assuming that the provisions are made permanent).[31] Shortening the budget horizon to fewer than ten years would exacerbate this problem.

DYNAMIC SCORING. Under current budgetary procedures, the congressional Joint Committee on Taxation (JCT) scores—that is, measures the costs of—new tax legislation, allowing for a variety of behavioral responses that affect the timing and composition of economic activity but not for changes that alter the real level of macroeconomic activity. For example, the impact of tax cuts on aggregate labor supply and investment is presumed to be zero in determining the revenue estimates. This is often referred to as static scoring.

Critics argue that static scoring biases outcomes against proposals that generate economic growth and advocate that the JCT include the macroeconomic impact of proposals on revenues—which is called dynamic scoring. While no economist doubts that tax policies can affect the macroeconomy, there are nevertheless some real concerns about estimating macroeconomic feedback effects on revenues.

The macroeconomic effects of a proposal depend sensitively on a number of complicated issues. Individuals and businesses can respond in various ways to tax policy. The extent, timing, and nature of these reactions are subject to debate. The federal government itself will have to respond to a tax cut or spending increase, since it has to finance such changes over time, but little is known about the details of these changes. Other governmental entities—including the Federal Reserve Board, state governments, and foreign governments—may also respond to the tax policy. Reasonable variation in assumptions about each of these responses can generate a very wide range of effects of the proposals on economic growth, often including positive and negative responses.

This complexity and uncertainty does not mean that policymakers should be deprived of information on the growth effects of policies, but it does mean that any single figure for the macroeconomic impact of growth proposals is subject to substantial uncertainty, and that even the sign of the effect for many proposals will prove uncertain. As a result, we believe it would be appropriate for the JCT or the CBO to provide information on the macroeconomic effects of major policy initiatives, but that trying to provide a single number to use as part of the official scoring process would be subject to too much uncertainty to be accepted as reliable.[32]

ALTERNATIVE PERSPECTIVES. For legislative purposes, Congress must rely on a single set of projections. But projections using alternative methods can enrich the understanding of Congress and the public about budget prospects. In tables 4-1 and 4-2 we illustrate alternative projections that apply different assumptions from those in official projections. Two additional kinds of projections could also be useful.

For many purposes, accrual accounting is more informative than cash-flow accounting. Under accrual accounting, one values accrued assets and liabilities and computes the present discounted value of future spending and revenues under certain programs—namely, those that entail long-term commitments—rather than the cash flow over a limited period or present discounted value of all government activities, as in fiscal gap calculations. Accrual accounting generally affects only programs with multi-year spending or revenue provisions that are based on program eligibility—such as Social Security and Medicare—rather than discretionary appropriations. Accrual accounting has already been implemented for certain isolated government programs, including the Federal Employees Retirement System pension for federal employees, and (as of 2003) military retiree health benefits. The administration has proposed that it be extended to all federal employees' pension and health care expenses.[33] The General Accounting Office recommends adoption of accrual budgeting for insurance programs, pension and retiree health programs, and environmental cleanup costs.[34] Other countries have employed accrual accounting to varying degrees.[35] The main disadvantage of accrual accounting is that future costs are less certain than current cash flow. Nevertheless, accrual accounting is appealing because in some senses it presents a truer picture of government's assets and obligations than does cash-flow accounting over a short horizon.[36] Although full accrual accounting may require too many assumptions to be appropriate for the budget itself, publications of studies based on accrual accounting would offer legislators and the public useful information.

Generational accounting constitutes yet another way to measure the government's fiscal position.[37] Generational accounting attempts to measure how the net burden of government is distributed across birth cohorts. Generational accounting allocates taxes and transfer payments under current policy to members of different generations and does the same for changes in taxes that may be needed to close the fiscal gap. The initial assignment of tax liabilities and the resulting generational accounts indicate how large the net present value of tax liabilities is for members of each generation.[38] The allocation of additional burdens needed to close the long-run fiscal gap indicates how different generations will be affected by the policy change.[39] Generational accounting provides insight into how different policies will affect people of different ages; with the advantage of more information, though, comes the need for more assumptions and data. As with accrual accounting, generational accounting estimates provide useful supplements to the cash-flow budget figures.

Conclusion

The United States faces significant fiscal challenges. Official projections from January 2003 celebrated a projected budget surplus exceeding $1 trillion over the next decade. Under realistic assumptions, however, the budget will run deficits of several trillion dollars in the next ten years, even without major new initiatives, and much larger deficits loom over the longer term as aging of the population and expanding medical technology drive up pension and health care outlays. The focus on the ten-year window and other current budget rules obscures our long-term challenge. Preparing for the fiscal challenges ahead is America's responsibility now. Failure to make the difficult and painful choices necessary to fulfill that responsibility will imply a long-term weakening of the economy and slowing growth of living standards well into the future.

Notes

1. Theoretically, the government could also sell some of its assets to finance an imbalance between revenue and expenditure. (In the federal budget, asset sales are misleadingly classified as spending reductions rather than as a source of financing for a deficit, so they reduce the measured deficit rather than provide a means of financing it.)

2. It can also have an effect on the economy's short-run performance, if increased government borrowing raises interest rates, and hence make investment more costly. See William Gale and Peter Orszag, "The Economic Effects of Long-Term Fiscal Discipline," Urban-Brookings Tax Policy Center Discussion Paper (Brookings, December 2002).

3. Alan J. Auerbach and William G. Gale, "Tax Cuts and the Budget," *Tax Notes*, vol. 90 (March 2001), pp. 1869–82.

4. Under the Federal Credit Reform Act of 1990, only the subsidy cost of a government loan or loan guarantee is recorded in the unified budget. Interest on the public debt is also recorded on an accrual basis. For example, implicit interest on a zero-coupon bond is recorded as an outlay while it accrues. Other minor divergences from pure cash-flow accounting also exist.

5. Other actions of the government, such as regulations, can affect the private economy without affecting federal spending or revenues.

6. At the same time, Congress also designated the U.S. Postal Service as an off-budget entity. The Postal Service's budgetary impact, though, is a tiny fraction of Social Security's.

7. All years reported are fiscal years. Fiscal year *x* ends on September 30 of calendar year *x*.

8. Congressional Budget Office, "The Budget and Economic Outlook: Fiscal Years 2003–2012" (January 2002), p. xiii.

9. As a measure of likely budget outcomes, we believe that holding discretionary spending constant as a share of GDP would be appropriate. As CBO notes, nondefense discretionary spending has been roughly constant as a share of GDP since the early 1980s. Congressional Budget Office, "The Budget and Economic Outlook: Fiscal Years 2004–2013" (January 2003). Defense and homeland security spending will likely rise as a share of GDP over the next decade. For convenience, we also report budget measures below with discretionary spending held constant as a share of GDP.

10. In recent years, CBO has presented sensitivity analysis with a variety of alternative discretionary spending paths. Theoretically, one would prefer the measure that best reflects the cost of maintaining a given level of government services. The problem arises because some types of discretionary spending (like FBI staffing) likely require real increases that at least keep pace with population growth in order to maintain a given level of services, whereas others (like administrative expenses for government departments) may be largely fixed in real terms and therefore not need to keep pace with population growth. Still other types of spending (like the costs of inspecting imports, which may be proportionate to the volume of imports) may require a constant or rising share of output in order to maintain a constant level of services. In any case, both casual inspection of the fixed cost component of various categories of spending and historical analysis of spending trends suggest that real discretionary spending is unlikely to decline sharply on a per capita basis.

11. Bush argued that an "honest comparison" of spending growth should take inflation and population growth into account. Wayne Slater, "Bush Defends Fiscal Record, Scolds Forbes: His Ads on Spending Challenged," *Dallas Morning News*, October 28, 1999, p. 14A; and Jackie Calmes, "In Debate on Spending, Forbes vs. Bush Resemble Bush vs. Richards, and Both Sides May Be Right," *New York Times*, November 5, 1999, p. A20.

12. This is "plan 2" in Leonard E. Burman and coauthors and is designed to reduce the effects of the AMT on households with income below $100,000. Leonard E. Burman, William G. Gale, Jeffrey Rohaly, and Benjamin H. Harris, "The Individual AMT: Problems

and Potential Solutions," Urban-Brookings Tax Policy Center Discussion Paper 5 (Brookings, September 2002).

13. This economic logic may help explain the significant, bipartisan political support for the notion that retirement trust funds ought to be kept separate from the rest of the budget. Both Houses of Congress voted overwhelmingly in 2000 to support measures that protected the Medicare Hospital Insurance trust fund from being used to finance other programs or tax cuts. See Patti Mohr, "House Passes Social Security and Medicare Lockbox Legislation," *Tax Notes*, vol. 90 (February 2001), pp. 981–83. A recent legislative proposal would provide similar protection to military pensions. U.S. House of Representatives, 107 Cong. 1 sess., H. RES. 23, January 30, 2001. Almost all states already separate pension reserves from their operating budgets.

14. If underlying rates of growth of spending and taxes are stable, any small increase in the ratio of debt to GDP would lead to further increases, with attendant jumps in interest costs, leading to an explosive increase in the debt-GDP ratio. See Alan J. Auerbach, "The U.S. Fiscal Problem: Where We Are, How We Got Here, and Where We're Going," in Stanley Fischer and Julio Rotemberg, eds., *NBER Macroeconomics Annual* (Cambridge, Mass.: National Bureau of Economic Research, 1994); Alan J. Auerbach, "Quantifying the Current U.S. Fiscal Imbalance," *National Tax Journal*, vol. 50 (September 1997), pp. 387–98; Alan J. Auerbach and William G. Gale, "Does the Budget Surplus Justify a Large-Scale Tax Cut?" *Tax Notes*, vol. 82 (March 1999), pp. 1827–50; Alan J. Auerbach and William G. Gale, "Perspectives on the Budget Surplus," *National Tax Journal*, vol. 53 (September 2000), pp. 459–73; Alan J. Auerbach and William G. Gale, "Tax Cuts and the Budget," *Tax Notes*, vol. 90 (March 2001), pp. 1869–82; and Congressional Budget Office, "The Long-Term Budget Outlook" (October 2000).

15. In fact, under current law payroll taxes would decline and income taxes would increase as a fraction of GDP. Payroll taxes are levied on cash wages; because fringe benefits, which are not subject to payroll tax, are expected to increase as a share of GDP, while total labor compensation is projected to be roughly constant, the share of GDP taking the form of taxable wages is projected to fall. Income taxes would claim an ever larger share of GDP, as bracket widths, personal exemptions, and the standard deduction are not indexed for increases in real incomes.

16. This figure is lower than the comparable estimate presented in Alan J. Auerbach, William G. Gale, and Peter Orszag, "The Budget Outlook and Options for Fiscal Policy," *Tax Notes*, vol. 95 (June 2002). Three factors explain the change. Our previous estimate (and all other long-term estimates in that paper) was too high by nearly 2 percent of GDP as a result of our misinterpretation of unpublished projections obtained from CBO. In addition, the short-term outlook has worsened in the intervening months, while the long-term projections for entitlement spending have improved somewhat, roughly offsetting each other in effect over the seventy-five-year horizon.

17. Congressional Budget Office, "The Budget and Economic Outlook: Fiscal Years 2004–2013" (January 2003).

18. See, for example, Alan J. Auerbach, "On the Performance and Use of Government Revenue Forecasts," *National Tax Journal*, vol. 52 (December 1999), pp. 767–82; Congressional Budget Office, "The Economic and Budget Outlook: Fiscal Years 2003–2012" (January 2002); and Rudolph G. Penner, "Errors in Budget Forecasting" (Washington:

Urban Institute, 2001). Although the *economic* assumptions used in the CBO budget projections may be unbiased predictions of future events, the *policy* assumptions are not.

19. Auerbach and Gale, "Tax Cuts and the Budget," pp. 1869–82.

20. Martin A. Sullivan, "The Federal Budget: Is It Going to Hell?" *Tax Notes*, vol.16 (September 2002), pp. 1303–07.

21. Henry J. Aaron and William B. Schwartz, *Creating Methuselah: Molecular Medicine and the Problems of an Aging Society* (Brookings, 2003, forthcoming).

22. John B. Shoven, "The Impact of Major Life Expectancy Improvements on the Financing of Social Security, Medicare, and Medicaid," in Henry J. Aaron and William B. Schwartz, eds., *Creating Methuselah: Molecular Medicine and the Problems of an Aging Society* (Brookings, 2003, forthcoming).

23. Ronald Lee and Ryan Edwards, "The Fiscal Impact of Population Aging in the U.S.: Assessing the Uncertainties," mimeo, University of California-Berkeley, 2001; Shoven, "The Impact of Major Life Expectancy Improvements on the Financing of Social Security, Medicare and Medicaid"; and Congressional Budget Office, "The Budget and Economic Outlook: An Update" (August 2001).

24. Alan J. Auerbach and Kevin A. Hassett, "Uncertainty and Design of Long-Run Fiscal Policy," in Alan J. Auerbach and Ronald D. Lee, eds., *Demographic Change and Fiscal Policy* (Cambridge, UK: Cambridge University Press, 2001), pp. 73–100, and Alan J. Auerbach and Kevin A. Hassett. "Optimal Long-Run Fiscal Policy: Constraints, Preferences and the Resolution of Uncertainty," Working Paper 9132 (Cambridge, Mass.: National Bureau of Economic Research, 2002) address the optimal policy response to uncertainty in long-term forecasts.

25. See B. Douglas Bernheim, "Ricardian Equivalence: An Evaluation of Theory and Evidence," NBER Working Paper 2330 (Cambridge, Mass.: National Bureau of Economic Research, July 1987); Douglas W. Elmendorf and N. Gregory Mankiw, "Government Debt," in John B. Taylor and Michael Woodford, eds., *Handbook of Macroeconomics,* vol. 1C (Amsterdam: Elsevier Science B.V., 1999), pp. 1615–69; and John Seater, "Ricardian Equivalence," *Journal of Economic Literature*, vol. 31 (March 1993), pp. 142–90.

26. An expiration or freeze would impose the costs of the government's fiscal imbalance primarily on high-income households, as the tax cuts scheduled to take place in future years are even more heavily skewed in favor of higher-income households than was the tax cut as a whole. William G. Gale and Samara R. Potter, "An Economic Evaluation of the Economic Growth and Tax Relief Reconciliation Act of 2001," *National Tax Journal,* vol. 55 (March 2002), pp. 133–86.

27. Board of Trustees, Federal Old Age and Survivors Insurance and Disability Insurance Trust Funds, *The 2002 Annual Report of the Board of Trustees of the Federal Old-Age and Survivors Insurance and Disability Insurance Trust Funds* (2002), table VI.E5, p. 150; and Richard Kogan, Robert Greenstein, and Peter Orszag, "Social Security and the Tax Cut" (Washington: Center for Budget and Policy Priorities, April 2002). Note that the actuarial imbalance figure is lower than the present value of the additional future cash flow required to finance scheduled benefits because of the current value of the Trust Fund.

28. Technical differences in how the fiscal gap and the actuarial imbalance within Social Security are computed mean that the figures in the text are necessarily approximations.

29. National Academy of Social Insurance, "Financing Medicare's Future" (Washington, September 2000).

30. A related approach to uncertainty involves "trigger rules," which would cancel revenue reductions or spending increases if projected surpluses failed to materialize. Richard Kogan, "How to Avoid Over-Committing the Available Surplus: Would a Tax-Cut 'Trigger' Be Effective Or Is There a Better Way?" (Washington: Center on Budget and Policy Priorities, March 2001), describes several reasons why triggers may work poorly. If they are tied to surplus or deficit projections, they would create incentives for rosy forecasts. If the triggers instead depend on actual budget results, they would create incentives for timing tricks and budget gimmicks to avoid the triggers, and hence would require additional budget rules. Moreover, policy changes induced by the triggers would be procyclical: in a recession, the trigger would force spending cuts or tax increases, exactly the wrong response at the wrong time. Also, triggers attempt to determine whether future tax cuts are affordable by looking at current or previous years'–rather than projected–surpluses. Finally, triggers may simply be politically untenable: they would require Congress to cancel already passed tax cuts or spending programs.

31. William G. Gale and Samara R. Potter, "An Economic Evaluation of the Economic Growth and Tax Relief Reconciliation Act of 2001," *National Tax Journal*, vol. 55 (March 2002), table 2.

32. For further discussion, see Alan J. Auerbach, "Dynamic Revenue Estimation," *Journal of Economic Perspectives*, vol. 10 (Winter 1996), pp. 141–57; William Gale, "Taxes, Growth, and Dynamic Analysis of New Legislation," *Tax Notes*, thirtieth anniversary issue (December 2002), pp. 29–44; and Peter R. Orszag, "Macroecomonic Implications of Federal Budget Proposals and the Saving Process," testimony before the Subcommittee on Legislative and Budget Process of the House Rules Committee, 107 Cong. 2 sess. (May 2, 2002).

33. Congressional Budget Office, "The President's Proposal to Accrue Retirement Costs for Federal Employees" (June 2002).

34.General Accounting Office, "Budget Issues: Budget Enforcement Compliance Report," GAO-01-777 (June 2001).

35. Australia, New Zealand, and the United Kingdom have implemented full accrual accounting systems. Germany plans to supplement its cash-flow accounts with accrual accounting information, and Korea, the Netherlands, Sweden, and Switzerland are moving toward full accrual systems. Organization for Economic Cooperation and Development, "A Brief Comparison of the Budgeting Systems in the G7 Countries" (Paris, April 2002).

36. Capital budgeting is often mentioned as an alternative reform. Under capital budgeting, borrowing finances capital purchases, and the budget records only the annual usage cost of capital investment. A transition to capital budgeting, however, would face several problems. The definition of capital is ambiguous, would be subject to abuse, and may turn out to encourage spending rather than discourage it. President's Commission on Budget Concepts, "Report of the President's Commission on Budget Concepts" (Washington, October 1967) and the President's Commission to Study Capital Budgeting, "Report of the President's Commission to Study Capital Budgeting" (Washington, February 1999) recommend against adopting capital budgets.

37. The original formulation of generational accounting is in Alan J. Auerbach, Jagadeesh Gokhale, and Laurence J. Kotlikoff, "Generational Accounts: A Meaningful Alternative to Deficit Accounting," in David Bradford, ed., *Tax Policy and the Economy* (Cambridge, Mass.: National Bureau of Economic Research, 1991), pp. 55–110.

38. In practice, generational accounts reflect only taxes paid less transfers received. With the occasional exception of government expenditures on education, the accounts presented in past research typically have not imputed to particular generations the value of the government's purchases of goods and services. Therefore, the accounts do not show the full net benefit or burden that any generation receives from government policy as a whole, although they can show a generation's net benefit or burden from a particular policy change that affects only taxes and transfers. Thus generational accounting tells us which generations will pay for government spending rather than telling us which generations will benefit from that spending.

39. Generational accounting, traditional deficit accounting, and estimates of the long-run fiscal gap all exclude the effects of induced behavioral effects or macroeconomic responses of policy changes. For further discussion, see Hans Fehr and Laurence J. Kotlikoff, "Generational Accounting in General Equilibrium," in Alan Auerbach and others, eds. *Generational Accounting Around the World* (University of Chicago Press, 1999), pp. 43–71. They use the simulation model in Alan J. Auerbach and Laurence J. Kotlikoff, *Dynamic Fiscal Policy* (Cambridge, England: Cambridge University Press, 1987) to assess the impact of general equilibrium effects on generational accounts. They find that the accounts typically provide a good approximation of the full general equilibrium impact. Also see Volker Börstinghaus and Georg Hirte, "Generational Accounting versus Computable General Equilibrium," *FinanzArchiv,* vol. 58, no. 3 (July 2002), pp. 227–43.

VICTOR R. FUCHS
ALAN M. GARBER

5

Health and Medical Care

Few economic predictions can be made as confidently as that the coming decade will be tempestuous for the one-seventh of the economy devoted to medical care. New, more costly—and more effective—diagnostic and therapeutic technology will emerge. The ratio of retirees to workers will begin a three-decade-long climb. Concern about the quality of care will increase. And pressure to distribute services more widely will intensify. These developments guarantee that the "crisis in health care" will be a political perennial.

The American health system is quick to embrace technological innovation. Access to care is often uneven, but usually the most important and valuable innovations diffuse quickly. Recent scientific advances promise that the United States may soon enter an era of dramatically accelerated innovation. The challenge to the health care system is to find the right balance among three goals:

—To translate recent scientific advances into improvements in the prevention, diagnosis, and treatment of disease,

—To distribute the fruits of that research to all Americans,

—To prevent health care expenditures from rising so rapidly that they compromise the nation's ability to respond to other pressing social and private needs.

The dissemination of technological advances in such dynamic industries as telecommunications, information technology, and consumer electronics rarely provokes the excitement or angst that accompanies medical advances. The greater concern about access to medical care undoubtedly springs from a view that medical care is special. To many, it is a basic right; to some, it is a service that should be publicly financed and delivered.

Concern may also arise from the veiled, yet crucial, role that costs play in decisions about medical care in the United States. Every system of financing operates with a budget, whether the payer is the Medicare program or a small health maintenance organization (HMO). Expenditures for a new drug or medical procedure may mean less money, at least in the short term, for other medical products and services. In the longer term, the added health care expenditures mean less of something else. They may necessitate higher premiums or taxes, reducing the funds available for other purposes—education, housing, transportation, or personal consumption. When individuals or businesses buy most goods and services, they implicitly weigh their cost and value against those of alternative uses of the funds. When they purchase medical care, however, most patients bear only a fraction of the costs directly.

Costs therefore play a circumscribed role in patients' decisions to buy health care. In principle, payers who conclude that a new technology offers little benefit for a very high cost could set a low reimbursement rate and force patients to bear the costs. But payers are not free to set reimbursement rates arbitrarily. Guidelines for reimbursement are often constrained by habit, tradition, statute, or contract or are linked to payments for a similar existing service. Even as large a payer as Medicare has limited flexibility in setting reimbursement amounts. Furthermore, new products (as opposed to clinical practices) are often patented or depend on proprietary technology. As a result, sellers often face little competition and have substantial discretion about how much to charge. And, of course, if reimbursements do not at least cover the costs of production, producers decide not to offer the service.

Buyers of most goods and services can simply decline to purchase any product or service that is too expensive. But health plans often cannot do so. State and federal regulations mandate the inclusion of many products and services in health insurance. The language in insurance contracts itself is often interpreted to mean that coverage exclusions cannot be based on cost. When public or private payers suggest that cost might be used in deciding coverage, the reaction is often loud and negative. Consequently, neither public programs like Medicare nor private health plans have routinely used cost considerations to deny or offer coverage.

Public discomfort with the idea that a payer might deny an effective treatment or diagnostic test because it is too expensive doubtless explains the reluctance of payers to base coverage decisions on cost. But proscribing explicit consideration of costs often results in inefficient use of resources and confusion about coverage decisions. Costly but effective new technologies will intensify pressure to break the taboo against explicit discussion of cost. Nothing can spare Americans from the need to balance the benefits of these innovations against reductions in other public services or higher taxes that reduce private consumption and investments. More appropriate incentives, coupled with better information, would help the health care system cope with these issues. Two changes are most important: (1) a greatly expanded flow of reliable information about the cost-effectiveness of drugs, screening programs, and other medical technologies; and (2) a financing system that induces individuals, organizations, and the government to consider the value of health services rather than encouraging them to pursue quality alone.

This chapter does not pretend to solve these problems. Indeed, *improvement* in and *amelioration* of health and medical care are more realistic goals than are comprehensive solutions. Our objective is more modest—to provide concepts, facts, and analyses that can guide thinking about these problems.

Some Simple Concepts

Our starting point is the distinction between *health* and *medical care*. Health, whether measured by mortality, morbidity, or anything else, depends in part on medical care. But it depends also on genetic endowment, physical and psychosocial environments, socioeconomic factors, and individual behaviors. Better health is probably the most important contribution of medical care. But people value medical care also for the sympathy, information, explanation, and validation that physicians, nurses, and other medical care personnel provide.

Most measures to improve health are costly, and they compete with other social and individual goals. Discussions about initiatives to improve health and medical care often neglect these trade-offs. Moreover, given health as a goal, choices must be made between more medical care and other ways to enhance health, such as reductions in air pollution, cigarette smoking, and alcohol abuse. These choices are usually "more-or-less," not "all-or-nothing," and the changes in question are a small fraction of expenditures. But in a nation as large as the United States even changes involving 1–2 percent of health expenditures amount to tens of billions of dollars. The challenge to those who seek to improve policymaking is to determine the relationships between "inputs" and "outputs" *at the margin*.

We also stress the distinction between factors responsible for changes in health *over time* and those that explain differences in health *at a given point in time*. The decline in mortality in the United States between 1950 and 2000 was primarily the result of advances in knowledge, some of which were embodied in new medical technologies and some of which were simply new understandings of the causes of disease. In contrast, differences in mortality rates across areas of the United States at any given time during that period are mostly explained by differences in cigarette smoking, obesity, air pollution, and other nonmedical determinants of health.

In the following sections, we address a selective list of issues. Our choices are based on the current state of health and medical care and on trends known today. Some changes, such as the demographic shifts, are predictable. Others, such as the rate of introduction and specific characteristics of new medical interventions, are highly speculative. Some health-relevant events, such as the effects of war, economic upheaval, and unforeseen outbreaks of new infectious disease, are even harder to predict and are outside the purview of this chapter.

Health

"The health of the people," said British prime minister Benjamin Disraeli, "is really the foundation upon which all their happiness and all their powers as a State depend."[1] The good news is that the health of the American people has never been better. Age-specific death rates are the lowest in the nation's history. Mortality rates are now 22 percent lower than they were twenty-five years ago and 40 percent lower than they were fifty years ago, after adjusting for changes in the age distribution of the population. Among the elderly, disability has also been declining in recent decades.[2] Americans reaching the age of sixty-five in 2002 can expect many more years of healthy life than could their counterparts a generation ago.

These favorable assessments must be tempered in three ways. First, people in many other developed nations are healthier than Americans are. In a score of countries, including Japan, most of Western Europe, Australia,

Canada, and New Zealand, life expectancy at birth is greater than in the United States. The advantage over the United States ranges from just a few months to more than four years. Second, large disparities in health persist within the United States—across geographic areas, ethnic groups, and socioeconomic categories. The reasons for the international and intranational differences are poorly understood, despite numerous theories. They include access to medical care, income inequality, and differences in "life styles." Third, improvements in health have been accompanied by huge increases in health care expenditures that divert public and private funds from other goods and services. The affluent and the middle class may welcome the shift, but for low-income households health care may come at the expense of an adequate diet or a decent place to live.

The Choices Ahead

In the next decade, the United States will face several difficult choices regarding health and medical care. First, how aggressively should the nation pursue the goals of longer life and higher level of function? These goals command wide support, but some worry about the economic, social, and moral problems that follow in an aging society from the introduction of major advances, such as innovations in biotechnology. Bioethicist Daniel Callahan believes that death is "an inescapable reality of human life and always will be" and asks medicine not to "lure people on to higher and higher expectations" regarding the ability of new technology to change that reality.[3] Francis Fukuyama fears that new biotechnology—cloning, genetic manipulation, cross-species organ transplants, and other medical innovations—will be dehumanizing.[4]

Second, should health policy aim to reduce disparities? Many say yes, of course. But David Mechanic, a medical sociologist, notes that efforts to improve health outcomes in general "might improve the absolute health of disadvantaged groups more than would initiatives directed specifically at reducing health disparities."[5] And Angus Deaton, a Princeton economist who has done extensive research on inequality in income and health, concludes that the reduction of health inequalities is "an inappropriate target for health policy."[6] He therefore would oppose a policy barring a cost-effective innovation that potentially would help everyone but that also would increase health inequalities.

Other questions concern means rather than ends. Even if one accepts that improving health is important, one must decide which tools are most effective. How effective, for example, are expenditures to increase the supply of medical care (more physicians, nurses, hospital beds, and the like) relative to expenditures to reduce cigarette smoking, alcohol abuse, obesity, or air pollution? How does either strategy compare with further investments in physical, biomedical, behavioral, and social research, or in a large-scale effort to assess the value of new and existing medical technologies?

To provide background for discussion of these questions, we briefly review data on trends and disparities in health, consider the major determinants of health, and examine the relative importance of different causes of death.

Trends in Health

Age-adjusted death rates have been falling for decades. Since 1950, the rate of decline has averaged 1 percent a year but has varied widely over time (see figure 5-1). The uneven pace of advances in medicine may explain these fluctuations, but their causes merit more investigation. The rate of decline has been approximately the same for blacks and whites and for women and men. For the sexes, however, the timing of the decrease has been different. From 1950 to the mid-1970s mortality rates fell faster for women than for men. Since then, mortality rates have fallen faster for men than for women.

One important consequence of the fall in mortality is a dramatic change in the age distribution of deaths. Figure 5-2 shows the percentage of a cohort born in three different years who would die at each age if the cohort experienced the age-specific death rates of that year. (The actual age distribution of deaths might differ because it also depends on the age distribution of the population as determined by previous trends in fertility, mortality, and immigration.) Deaths of people younger than age forty-five fell from 10.4 percent of all deaths in 1950 to 4.8 percent in 1999. The percentage of deaths at ages forty-five to sixty-four fell by almost half. At the other end of the life cycle, deaths at ages eighty-five or above more than doubled from 15.8 to 34.5 percent of all deaths. These numbers tell a simple story—chronic disease precedes death far more frequently now than in the past.

Disparities in Health

Two disparities in health outcomes have attracted much discussion: whites live longer than blacks, and the rich and well educated live longer than those with low incomes and little education. The age-adjusted death rate for blacks is 33 percent higher than the rate for whites. The mortality rate for blacks in 1999 was the same as that for whites in 1974. This statistic

Figure 5-1. *Annual Rate of Change of U.S. Age-Adjusted Death Rate,*
1950–95[a]

Annual percentage change

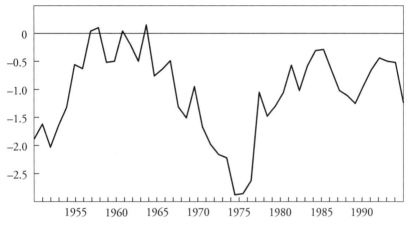

Source: Authors' calculations based on data from National Center for Health Statistics (NCHS), Centers for Disease Control and Prevention (CDC), *Vital Statistics, Mortality Tables, Historical Data, Age-Adjusted Death Rates,* table HIST293, "Age-Adjusted Death Rates for Selected Causes, Death Registration States, 1900–32, and United States, 1933–98."
a. Five-year moving average centered on middle year.

is a grim reminder of the legacy of centuries of slavery, segregation, and discrimination.

The wealth and education gradient in health is as great as the black-white difference, but it cannot be summarized in a single number. Furthermore, the clear correlation of health with income and education is open to alternative interpretations. Poor health may cause or may be caused by low income. The most popular explanation for the correlation between years of schooling and health is that education makes individuals more efficient "producers" of health. But both education and good health may also result from one or more "third" variables such as differences in people's ability to defer gratification and hence in their willingness to invest money or time now to provide benefits in the distant future. The black-white difference and the income-education gradient are related, but whites live longer than blacks even when one controls for differences in income and education.

Figure 5-2. *Age Distribution of Deaths Based on U.S. Life Tables,*
1950, 1975, and 1999[a]

Percent of deaths

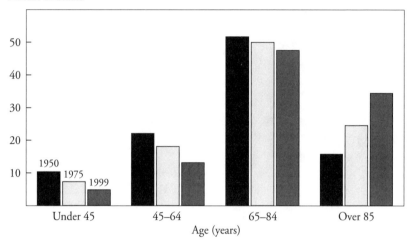

Age (years)

Source: Authors' calculations based on data from NCHS, CDC, *Vital Statistics, Mortality Tables,*
Historical Data, Life Expectancy, "Abridged Life Tables by Color and Sex: United States (1950,
1975)" and "Life Table for the Total Population: United States, 1999."
a. Assuming a stationary population.

Nonmedical Determinants of Health

Nonmedical determinants of health can be grouped into five major categories: genes, physical environment, psychosocial environment, socioeconomic factors, and individual behaviors. Potential interactions among
the determinants are also important.

GENES. Most diseases do not occur randomly. They are more likely to
strike some families and ethnic groups than others. Recent advances in
genetic research, combined with epidemiological studies, suggest that
genetic factors play a role in most diseases. No ethnic group, however, is
distinguished by "good" or "bad" genes. Moreover, the same gene may
favoraby affect health in one environment and harm it in another. A few
diseases have been linked directly to mutations of a single gene. Major diseases such as cancer, heart disease, and stroke are now thought to reflect the

combined influence of many genes and the environment. Genetic therapies are not likely to cure these diseases in the near future. However, a more complete understanding of the role of genes in disease should create opportunities for more effective interventions through prevention, screening, and treatment.

THE PHYSICAL ENVIRONMENT. The physical environment can profoundly affect health, even before birth. Cigarette smoking by a pregnant woman increases the probability of a low-weight birth (under 2,500 grams or about five pounds) by more than 50 percent. Pregnancy at high altitudes also adversely affects birthweight. White, non-Hispanic women in the high-altitude states of Colorado, New Mexico, and Wyoming are 20 to 25 percent more likely to deliver a low-birthweight baby than are their counterparts in the nation as a whole.

The home poses substantial health hazards, including physical abuse, falls, fires, and the ingestion of poisons by small children. Thousands die in workplace accidents each year. Millions more are exposed at work to hazards that will adversely affect their health later in life. Air pollution, especially in the form of inhalable particles, is a significant cause of mortality and morbidity. The streets and highways pose a particularly grave threat to health, primarily through motor vehicle accidents. Accidents are the leading cause of death for children and for adults through age forty-four. Between the ages of five and twenty-four, accidents plus homicide account for six out of every ten deaths. Accidents also shorten the lives of many elderly persons, even when the death certificate indicates some other cause. It is not unusual for an elderly person to break a hip, undergo apparently successful surgery, and then die of complications soon afterward.

THE PSYCHOSOCIAL ENVIRONMENT AND SOCIOECONOMIC FACTORS. Social interaction—in the home, school, and workplace—can strongly affect health. These interactions influence whether a teenager will smoke or drink, eat a poor diet, or be physically inactive. So do television, movies, and the radio. The average child spends more hours watching television than attending school. Geographic, religious, and ethnic communities also contribute, positively and negatively, to health. Many of the harmful effects of the psychosocial environments become evident only in middle age or older. Even at ages fifteen to twenty-four, however, suicide is the third leading cause of death, exceeded only by accidents and homicides.

The correlations among income, education, and ethnicity are all strong, but the causal connections are not firmly established. Some health analysts believe that *relative* income influences health more than *absolute* income does, but evidence remains inconclusive. Several empirical studies find a significant negative relation between income inequality and health, but more recent studies, using more rigorous methods, find no support for this hypothesis.[7] (Burtless and Jencks reach a somewhat different conclusion in chapter 3.)

INDIVIDUAL BEHAVIORS. Individual behaviors—such as cigarette smoking, alcohol abuse, unhealthy diets, insufficient exercise, illegal drug use, and unsafe sexual practices—are the best-studied nonmedical determinants of health. While all can cause poor health, little is known about the reasons why people adopt these behaviors. Do they reflect the influence of genes, the physical or psychosocial environment, or socioeconomic factors, or some combination of genes and environment? Despite major efforts—and scattered successes—to reduce these known risk factors, most persist. A better understanding of their origins could make a major contribution to health.

Context and Policy

One of the most important tasks for policymakers—public and private—is to decide which are the most important health goals for the nation. The choice of goals is a political act. It reflects values, material interests, costs, and probabilities of success. A national health policy that promises everything for everyone is bound to fail. An informed choice of priorities is essential. Because health risks vary widely by age, sex, race, and geography, a single national policy is unlikely to address efficiently the particular health problems confronting various groups.

In setting those priorities, policymakers should recognize that improvements in health *over time* arise from factors different from those that explain differences in health *at a given time* among regions, ethnic groups, or sexes. Genes, for example, help to explain health differences among individuals. But genes change much too slowly to explain the large decline in age-adjusted mortality rates over the last fifty years. Also nonmedical determinants of health probably explain little of this improvement. Some trends—a reduction in cigarette smoking, for example—have improved health, but they have been wholly or partly offset by unfavorable trends in obesity, the use of illegal drugs, and changes in sexual practices. Advances in medicine, such as antibiotics and control of hypertension, were major

Table 5-1. *Death Rate, by Race, Gender, and Age*
Deaths per 100,000

Race and gender	1–44 years of age	45–64 years of age	65–84 years of age
White men	119	772	4,528
Black men	215	1,503	5,518
White women	60	467	3,184
Black women	116	839	3,923

Source: Authors' calculations based on data from the National Center for Health Statistics (NCHS), Centers for Disease Control and Prevention (CDC), *Vital Statistics, Mortality Tables, Leading Causes of Death,* table LCWK2, "Deaths, Percent of Total Deaths, and Death Rates for the Fifteen Leading Causes of Death in Ten-Year Age Groups, by Race and Sex: United States, 1999."

contributors to lengthening life expectancy. At any point in time, however, differences in medical care explain little of the variation in health among population groups, while differences in smoking, obesity, air pollution, and sexual practices are highly significant.

The importance of these problems varies widely among population groups. Consider, for example, air pollution, cigarette smoking, and obesity. Residents of metropolitan areas with bad air—in California, for example—tend to smoke less and to be less obese than are residents of cities with cleaner air. In some states—Virginia and Florida, for example—smoking is a major problem, but obesity is not. In others—like Iowa and Nebraska—obesity is common, but smoking is not.

The rates and causes of death differ markedly by age, race, and sex (see tables 5-1 and 5-2). Among young men, accidents and violence are the principal causes of death. Cancer is the leading cause of death for young black women. It is the second leading cause for young white women. AIDS is a major cause of death for blacks, but not for whites. Among middle-aged women and white men, cancer is the leading cause of death. Heart disease is the principal killer of middle-aged black men and of older people of both races and sexes. Diabetes, a disease that has an important genetic component but is also influenced by diet and obesity, is a major cause of death for middle-aged and older black women.

The economic and human loss from illness depends not only on the proportion of deaths each disease causes—after all, everyone eventually dies from some cause—but also on the number of years of life lost because of disease. Table 5-3 presents three measures of the relative importance of eight causes of death. The first measure is the proportion of total deaths

Table 5-2. *Four Leading Causes of Death, by Race, Gender, and Age Group, 1999*

Race and gender	1–44 years of age		45–64 years of age		65–84 years of age	
	Leading cause of death	Percent of all deaths	Leading cause of death	Percent of all deaths	Leading cause of death	Percent of all deaths
White men	Accidents	32.1	Malignant neoplasms	31.3	Heart disease	32.3
	Suicide	13.0	Heart disease	29.3	Malignant neoplasms	28.4
	Heart disease	10.8	Accidents	5.8	Chronic lower respiratory diseases	7.4
	Malignant neoplasms	10.5	Chronic liver disease and cirrhosis	3.9	Cerebrovascular diseases	6.0
Black men	Assault	20.4	Heart disease	28.0	Heart disease	30.8
	Accidents	19.0	Malignant neoplasms	26.5	Malignant neoplasms	29.6
	HIV	12.4	Accidents	5.3	Cerebrovascular diseases	6.9
	Heart disease	11.4	Cerebrovascular diseases	5.1	Chronic lower respiratory diseases	4.6
White women	Accidents	23.7	Malignant neoplasms	43.7	Heart disease	29.2
	Malignant neoplasms	23.5	Heart disease	18.4	Malignant neoplasms	26.5
	Heart disease	8.7	Chronic lower respiratory diseases	5.1	Cerebrovascular diseases	8.0
	Suicide	6.2	Cerebrovascular diseases	4.0	Chronic lower respiratory diseases	7.6
Black women	Malignant neoplasms	16.4	Malignant neoplasms	31.3	Heart disease	32.7
	Heart disease	12.8	Heart disease	24.8	Malignant neoplasms	23.5
	Accidents	12.7	Cerebrovascular diseases	6.2	Cerebrovascular diseases	8.6
	HIV	11.3	Diabetes	6.0	Diabetes	6.5

Source: See table 5-1.

Table 5-3. *Relative Importance of Different Causes of Death in the United States by Three Measures: Number of Deaths, Years Lost, and Work Years Lost, 1999*

Percent

Cause of death	All			Men			Women		
	Deaths[a]	Years lost[b]	Work years lost[c]	Deaths[a]	Years lost[b]	Work years lost[c]	Deaths[a]	Years lost[b]	Work years lost[c]
Heart disease	30.3	23.1	9.9	29.9	23.1	10.9	30.7	22.7	8.4
Malignant neoplasms	23.0	23.4	13.1	24.3	21.4	10.4	21.7	25.8	17.9
Cerebrovascular	7.0	4.7	1.8	5.5	3.7	1.5	8.5	6.0	2.3
Chronic lower respiratory disease	5.2	4.0	1.0	5.3	3.6	0.9	5.1	4.5	1.3
Accidents	4.1	8.9	21.7	5.4	11.4	24.1	2.8	6.0	17.0
Suicide	1.2	2.9	6.7	2.0	4.2	8.5	0.5	1.3	3.5
Assault	0.7	2.2	6.4	1.1	3.1	7.6	0.3	1.2	4.1
HIV	0.6	1.5	3.3	1.0	2.1	3.7	0.3	0.9	2.5
All other	28.5	30.8	36.2	26.5	29.7	32.5	30.4	32.5	43.0

Source: Authors' calculations based on data from NCHS, CDC, *Vital Statistics, Mortality Tables, Leading Causes of Death*, table GMWK293, "Age-Adjusted Death Rates for 113 Selected Causes, United States, 1999," and "Life Table for the Total Population: United States, 1999."

a. Proportion of total deaths caused by the disease.

b. Proportion of years of life lost that is attributable to deaths from a particular illness. Based on life tables.

c. Proportion of all years of work lost because of deaths attributable to a particular illness. Based on life tables and age- and sex-specific annual hours of work.

caused by the disease. The second is the proportion of years of life lost that is attributable to deaths from a particular illness. The third measure is the proportion of all years of work lost because of deaths attributable to a particular illness.[8]

Differences among the three measures are striking. Accidents, which disproportionately affect the young, account for only 4 percent of all deaths, but 9 percent of years of life lost and 22 percent of work years lost. Suicides, assaults, and AIDS exhibit a similar pattern. Combined, they exceed cancer and heart disease as causes of lost work years. The percentage of deaths from heart disease is almost one-third larger than that from cancer, but cancer costs one-third more lost work years, because it strikes young and middle-aged women. Heart disease, in contrast, largely strikes older men and women. Accidents, assault, and suicide are of much greater importance for men than for women.

In setting priorities, policymakers should avoid "fighting the last war." The nation needs to make sure that legislation, funding, and institutions adapt to changes in the relative importance of health problems. For example, the number of infant deaths in 1960 approximately equaled the number of deaths at all ages from accidents. By 2000, thanks to medical advances in the treatment of low-birthweight and other impaired infants and a lower birthrate, infant deaths were only one-fourth as numerous as deaths from accidents. Obesity is emerging as one of the most important causes of ill health and premature death in the United States. Obesity is associated with diabetes, hypertension, and high cholesterol. It is implicated in strokes, heart disease, and circulatory, vision, and other health problems. It probably plays a major role in black-white differences in mortality, as black obesity rates are almost 50 percent higher than white rates. Unhealthful diet, lack of exercise, and genetic endowment all contribute to the development of obesity. Cigarette smoking remains a major health hazard, particularly because many of the illnesses it causes cannot be treated effectively. Because of tobacco's addictive properties, primary emphasis should be given to discouraging young people from becoming smokers.

Other areas that we believe deserve high priority include prevention of accidents and reduction in air pollution. Publicly supported research should also focus on interactions between genes and nonmedical determinants of health such as diet, alcohol, exercise, and cigarette smoking. Strong commercial interests stand ready to explore the interaction between prescription drugs and genes. But research on the nonmedical interactions is unlikely to receive substantial commercial support, because the private payoff to such an investment is small. The pursuit of better health also must be tempered with consideration of other values such as privacy, autonomy, and civil liberties. In a free society the state can provide accurate information, subsidize research, and use taxes and subsidies judiciously to help its citizens achieve their health goals. It can use taxes or mandates to reduce air pollution, and it can use subsidies or mandates to increase immunizations. But it cannot command healthy behaviors or guarantee good health outcomes.

Medical Care

America's health care system is technologically sophisticated and innovative and has had spectacular successes. But its size and rate of growth continue to provoke questions about its efficiency and overall cost.

After a mid-1990s pause in the growth of health expenditures, at the beginning of the new century the United States faced resurgent growth in per capita expenditures and double-digit growth in commercial health insurance premiums. Americans spent far more for health care than did others—$4,358 in 1999 compared to second-ranked Canada's $2,463[9]—but growth in health care spending was not unique to the United States. During the 1990s, real per capita health expenditures grew at an annual rate of 3 percent not only in the United States but also in other wealthy nations, including Austria, Belgium, Japan, Norway, Switzerland, and the United Kingdom.[10]

The recent resumption in the growth of health expenditures in the United States came at a time of modest demographic change, when the much-heralded biotechnology and genomics revolution had scarcely begun. The nation will soon face larger challenges. The aging of the baby boom generation will promote much greater use of health care. The pace of innovation is expected to accelerate. Managed care, once the main hope for controlling both private and public health expenditures, has become unpopular with both the public and health care providers. As a result, many of its cost containment features have been weakened, while nearly all "novel" approaches to cost containment emphasize increased cost sharing, an approach that managed care was intended to supplant.

Although the cost control measures of managed care are weakening just as cost pressures are about to intensify, the question is not *whether* there will be limits on utilization of, or access to, health care, but *how* limits will be imposed. Will Congress curtail eligibility for government programs?

Will availability and generosity of private insurance narrow? Will patients' choice of providers and treatments diminish? Will out-of-pocket expenditures rise steeply as many new services and medications are excluded from full coverage? How will novel diagnostic tests and treatments find a place in a market that is dominated by large private and public purchasers and by consumers who pay a larger share of the costs out of pocket? The answers to these questions will determine the future shape of the health care system, the distribution of the financial burdens of health care, the breadth of access to care, and, ultimately, the level and distribution of health of the population.

The U.S. health system is often described as a patchwork of private and public funding, with uneven health insurance coverage. Private spending flows largely through employer-sponsored health insurance for workers and their families. Government programs focus on the elderly, the disabled, and the poor. Some of the challenges these two parallel systems will face in the years ahead are distinct, but others are common to both. Americans, like citizens of every other developed nation, have sought protection from the financial consequences of illness and disability. They have found this protection through a unique mix of public and private insurance.

Demographic Change

Increased longevity has raised projections of the elderly population, but large increases have been foreseen for years. Agreement about the challenge has not led to consensus about how to deal with it. All developed nations face sharp increases in the proportion of the population that is elderly. Between 2000 and 2040, the population ages sixty-five and over in the United States is projected to rise from its current share of about 12 percent of the total population to nearly 21 percent.[11] The support ratio—the ratio of working-age adults to children and the elderly—will correspondingly decline. With population aging, health care spending will tend to increase because the elderly are more likely than the young to have chronic conditions and to use health care heavily. In the United States, as in nearly all the rest of the developed world, public funds finance much of the cost of health care for the elderly. The elderly also impose a financial burden on both public and private pension systems. Although increased longevity and improved health mean that people have the physical capacity to work to older ages than in the past, people have chosen to retire at ever earlier ages in much of Western Europe and several other wealthy nations.[12] Some evidence suggests that retirement ages in the United States stopped falling in the mid-1980s and have risen slightly since then. Unless the future elderly build up reserves to support pension and health costs—through voluntary private saving or mandatory public saving—future taxpayers will be required to shoulder higher taxes or benefits will have to be cut.

Thus population aging has two overriding implications for the health care system. The first is that demand for care will grow. In the United States this demand will take several forms, among them rising Medicare and Medicaid outlays, increased burdens on those employers who continue to provide supplemental health care coverage for their retirees, and growing out-of-pocket payments. Demographic trends also shape and, in important respects, constrain the debate on how policy should change in response to the evolving needs of the American population. Delivering on currently promised Social Security and Medicare benefits for a growing elderly population will require higher taxes. Whether future workers will be willing to pay them is not certain. What is certain is that any expansion of benefits will require economies in the provision of promised services, new sources of revenue, or a decision by workers to extend their working lives.

Private Sector Financing

Effective health insurance reduces risk, but it also weakens incentives to control the level and growth of health care spending. Insurance subsidizes care at the time it is used. Consumers use more of any good or service, including health care, that is subsidized.[13] Conventional insurance also encourages health care research and biases it toward quality-improving, rather than cost-reducing, innovation. The history of health insurance in America may be read as a lengthy series of experiments to find cost control mechanisms to offset the weakening of the price discipline of the market that is inherent in insurance.

Protection from financial risk may be most important, but it is only one of many factors that explain the spread of health insurance. The freedom to ignore most of the costs of care when making medical decisions can mitigate one source of distress at times of serious illness or injury.[14] Insurance also benefits providers by increasing the demand for their services; for this reason, physicians and hospitals actively promoted establishment of the Blue Shield and Blue Cross plans. Organized labor elevated guaranteed health benefits to the status of a prize to be won through collective bargaining. Finally, the exclusion from personal income and payroll taxes of health insurance premiums paid by employers lowered the cost of workplace-based group plans relative to both individually purchased insurance and directly purchased health care.

Although these motivations are decades old, contemporary private health insurance differs enormously from mid-twentieth-century plans. Private insurance plans of the 1950s and 1960s—so-called indemnity plans—typically provided specified benefits to patients who were hospitalized or who used outpatient services. Nearly all doctors and hospitals were paid on a fee-for-service basis. Indemnity insurance and unmanaged fee-for-service health insurance declined in popularity as their premiums increased. Many people enrolled in HMOs and other managed care plans in the 1980s and early 1990s, but not always out of choice. Managed care plans typically limited the selection of hospitals and physicians eligible for reimbursement, while reducing financial incentives for the provision of more and more expensive health services. Many enrolled out of necessity when their employers stopped offering traditional plans. Over time, many people became disillusioned with HMOs and other forms of aggressively managed care, and soon employers became concerned about growing employee resentment of the restrictions of managed care. The rise in HMO enrollment ended in the mid-1990s. As a result of these trends and fears of actual and threatened lawsuits, managed care organizations have relaxed some of the restrictions they used to control the volume and cost of care.

HYBRID ARRANGEMENTS. Disillusionment with managed care has not led to a renaissance of traditional health insurance, however. Instead, hybrid arrangements, such as point of service (POS) plans, preferred provider organizations (PPOs), and self-directed health plans, have become more prominent. POS plans offer HMO care along with partial coverage for out-of-network care.[15] Patients enrolled in PPO plans can reduce their out-of-pocket payments by obtaining care from an approved provider, who typically agrees to offer services at a discount or to submit to various cost-reducing administrative procedures. They may have to pay substantially more if they obtain care from an out-of-network provider. Self-directed or consumer-directed health plans, which limit the employer's liability for health expenditures, have emerged recently as alternatives to managed care and traditional insurance. These plans include a catastrophic insurance component that pays claims after a high deductible is met. Unlike traditional catastrophic insurance, the new plans include an allowance to help cover small medical outlays. This allowance resides in an individually controlled account whose balances can be carried forward to future years. Both the insurance and savings account components can be customized by the employer and allow considerable choice for the employee; a variety of investment or savings vehicles, for example, can be part of the savings account. The boundaries between different types of insurance have blurred. Traditional HMOs, such as Kaiser Permanente, claimed that relatively low-cost preventive and early outpatient care would save money by reducing the need for costly hospital care. Subsequently, both managed care plans and traditional health insurers adopted diverse techniques to control health care use, such as requiring prior authorization for some hospitalizations and major procedures and placing restrictions on access to specialists.

COST SHARING. Because patients dislike explicit restrictions and employers fear rising costs, private insurance is steadily increasing deductibles and copayments—the share of payments borne directly by patients. The RAND Health Insurance Experiment demonstrated that the use of services declines when the patient's share of costs increases.[16] The deductible—and other specific features of the plans—determine how tightly the plan controls expenditures. People who expect their health expenditures for the year to remain below the deductible level are likely to be particularly price sensitive. Once expenses near or exceed the deductible, the insured person loses much of the financial incentive to control use. At that point, patient cost sharing is limited to the copayments. Many insurance plans also place caps on the copayments, removing cost as a consideration for enrollees who have very high expenditures. All plans that provide complete or near complete protection once costs exceed a given level need additional ways to control use. This need is particularly acute for severely ill patients treated in intensive care settings, whose expenditures routinely exceed limits on out-of-pocket costs. The most important disadvantage of increased cost sharing as a control mechanism is that it erodes protection from financial risk.

Self-directed plans are one manifestation of the trend toward using cost sharing to limit outlays. Employers who offer such plans often do so as part of a *defined-contribution* approach to health benefits. Under defined-contribution plans, an employer contributes a fixed amount toward each employee's health insurance premium. Employees who choose more expensive plans pay the full incremental cost themselves. The goal is to make the employee's choice among health plans "cost conscious." Under traditional plans, in contrast, employers pay part or all of the cost of more expensive plans.

PPOs and other health plans are also increasing cost sharing, particularly for prescription drugs. This method of cost control can impose severe hardships on the chronically ill, victims of costly acute conditions, and those who place a very high value on costly health services. These groups prefer less restrictive forms of health insurance, such as traditional insurance and PPO plans, and are likely to find higher premiums, copayments, and deductibles quite unattractive.

Because the interests, health conditions, and financial circumstances of subscribers vary so much, no single type of plan will appeal to everyone. Some people will be unsatisfied with any plan that denies them nearly complete payment for care from any specialist they choose. Others will readily accept restrictions on choice of providers and limitations on covered medications in exchange for low premiums and out-of-pocket expenses. In fact, the plan that an individual prefers may change as his or her health or financial circumstances change. In the competition among health plans, one or a few may eventually emerge as the choice of a large majority of Americans, but this has not happened yet. The lack of consensus helps to explain why political support for single-payer plans is so limited.

The competition from which a consensus may eventually emerge will be heavily influenced by *adverse selection*—the tendency for plans with broad coverage to attract sicker and more costly patients than are drawn to more restrictive plans. Adverse selection creates the risk that generous plans will gradually become unaffordable, even if large numbers of people prefer them. The market cannot eliminate adverse selection without outside regulation, even if risk adjustment mechanisms (the variation of premiums based on ex ante estimates of each insured person's expected health outlays) are refined. Nor will markets by themselves produce subsidies for high-risk men, women, and children, or for the poor.

The challenge of private health insurance is to produce health insurance plans that offer risk protection to a broad segment of Americans and that can compete fairly. Rising costs and refinements in the ability of insurers to discriminate risk will make that challenge more daunting in the coming years. Today most Americans favor health plans that give them an extensive choice of providers and unrestricted coverage—with correspondingly high premiums and extensive patient cost sharing. In the coming years, more and more Americans will seek lower-cost plans that sacrifice choice or other aspects of coverage, and others will conclude that the cost of any plan available to them is excessive. Although the demand for generous health plans is likely to remain strong among upper-income Americans, increasingly health plans will be scrutinized for the value they provide and their ability to meet the specific needs of potential enrollees.

THE UNINSURED. At any point in time, a diverse and changing group of approximately 40 million Americans lacks health insurance. Some are without insurance briefly. Many are workers between jobs who are unable to pay or choose not to pay for an extension of the insurance for which their previous employers paid. Others are young and relatively healthy and have decided that health insurance is not worth its cost. Still others are self-employed or work for small employers who do not offer health insurance. Some recoil at the high price of individually purchased insurance, lack knowledge about the available alternatives, believe they can obtain care from a hospital if they need it, have chronic diseases severe enough to make private insurance unaffordable but not so disabling that they qualify for Medicare, or are just too poor to afford insurance.

A large body of literature shows that the uninsured receive considerable medical care, but less than do insured people in similar health. The uninsured are less likely than the insured to be under the continuous care of a primary care physician or to have health problems detected and treated early. They are also less likely to undergo screening for cancer, to receive preventive care for cardiovascular disease, or to undergo cardiac catheterization or invasive treatment for coronary artery disease. They are more likely to be treated in emergency rooms and less likely to receive appropriate follow-up care.[17]

Despite the expectation that extension of coverage to the uninsured would improve health outcomes, effects of insurance on health outcomes have been hard to detect. Studies that purport to show that the uninsured have worse health outcomes than the insured are all "observational"—that is, they lack well-constructed control groups that would allow the effects of health insurance to be distinguished from the consequences of other characteristics of insured individuals. This shortcoming is serious, because the lack of insurance is not random. Uninsured patients have worse hospital outcomes, are less likely to receive certain forms of care when they are sick, and have higher mortality rates in general. Although poorer health outcomes among the uninsured could result from the lack of insurance, they could also stem from other characteristics: the age, income, health risks, and chronic diseases of people who become uninsured differ from those who remain insured.[18] Furthermore, the effects of expanding insurance coverage would surely depend on how it is done. For example, Medicaid beneficiaries receive care that is qualitatively different from that received by commercially insured patients or by Medicare beneficiaries.

An emerging reason for concern about incomplete coverage is the possibility that the uninsured will find it increasingly difficult to secure even basic care, as providers face tightening cost controls and intensified competition. Furthermore, uncompensated care places an undue burden on some health care institutions, many of which are already under financial stress. The lack of insurance can also be seen as a sign that health care is unaffordable for many Americans.

Government Programs

Although government health programs do not cover most Americans, per capita public spending for health care in the United States rivals that of countries whose public programs serve everyone. In 1999 U.S. public programs spent about $1,968 per capita, about 45 percent of total health care spending. That sum exceeded total median per capita health expenditures, public and private, of $1,764 in thirty industrial countries.[19] The federal government accounted for about 70 percent of all public expenditures for health care in 2000, mostly through the Medicare ($224 billion) and Medicaid ($118 billion) programs. The states spent an additional $84 billion on Medicaid. Spending through other federal and state programs constituted an additional $160 billion.

MEDICARE. Although per capita private and public health care spending have grown at similar rates in the past and may be expected to do so in the future, government health programs face quite different challenges from those confronting private health insurance. Medicare, which insures nearly all Americans sixty-five years of age and older, along with the disabled and people with end-stage renal disease, faces the daunting burden of growing numbers of beneficiaries. The number of enrollees is projected to double between 2002 and 2035;[20] if expenditures per enrollee grow at historical rates, the growth of Medicare expenditures will far outstrip the tax base that supports the program. By 2012, Medicare hospital insurance (Part A) outlays are expected to exceed revenues. Projections indicate that the Hospital Insurance Trust Fund will be depleted by 2026.[21] Outlays for Medicare's supplemental medical insurance (Part B), which covers physician and selected other services, are projected to rise even faster than those for Part A.

More than two-thirds of the elderly also have either public or private insurance that supplements Medicare. Such supplementation usually pays some or all of Medicare's deductibles and coinsurance. Many supplemental plans provide additional services, such as limited coverage for outpatient prescription drugs. Medicare has never paid for most outpatient prescription drugs. This omission pains many seniors, as the costs of drugs have climbed and pharmaceuticals have become increasingly central to medical care. Republicans and Democrats agree on the desirability of a prescription drug benefit for the elderly and disabled, but they disagree on how large a public subsidy to provide for such benefits and how to administer the benefit.

The absence of coverage for outpatient prescription drugs is not the only gap in Medicare coverage, although it may be the most glaring. Deductibles and coinsurance under Medicare are higher than under most private insurance plans. A seriously ill beneficiary without supplemental coverage faces potentially ruinous out-of-pocket financial expenses. Furthermore, Medicare provides only limited long-term care services. Medicare covers some home care services but pays only for a limited number of visits. It covers nursing home care, but only in a skilled nursing facility after a hospital stay of three days or more and for no more than 100 days.

The challenge before Congress is to modernize benefit coverage and administration of a program enacted to the standards of private insurance plans prevailing nearly forty years ago, while at the same time closing a large projected long-term deficit in the current system. Because the cost of updating the benefit package, reducing cost sharing, and closing the deficit are certain to exceed any savings that may be achievable through administrative reforms, the problem is how to cover the costs. The only options are higher premiums on beneficiaries, higher taxes on workers, or increased general revenue support of Medicare at a time when the rest of the government's budget confronts seemingly intractable deficits.

MEDICAID. The federal government and the states divide the costs of Medicaid, which serves the indigent elderly, blind and disabled, and poor parents and children. The federal government covers half of Medicaid costs in most states and more than half in some.

Medicaid covers long-term care for those who meet income and asset tests, including those who become medically indigent by depleting their assets to pay for health care. Thus the 26 percent of Medicaid beneficiaries who were aged or disabled accounted for 71 percent of expenditures in

1998. In 1999 Medicaid accounted for 47 percent of all nursing home expenditures, and Medicare accounted for an additional 11 percent.[22] Medicaid coverage remains uneven across the United States. It also constitutes a major fiscal burden on states, supportable when economic times are good, but a staggering responsibility when recession depletes revenues and swells the ranks of recipients. Because it is targeted toward the poor, Medicaid has never been a model for national health insurance in the United States. But despite its limitations, it remains an important safety net program, and many plans for incremental expansion of health insurance coverage would do so by making more low-income Americans eligible for Medicaid. Predictions that comprehensive health care reform would lead to Medicaid's demise seem less plausible now than they did in the 1980s and early 1990s.

MANAGED CARE IN MEDICARE AND MEDICAID. In the early 1990s, when rising health expenditures were at the top of the political agenda, Medicare and Medicaid both began to move away from traditional fee-for-service medicine, much as did private insurance plans. But the two government programs then followed quite different paths. Under legislation dating back to the 1980s, Medicare agreed to pay HMOs—and other so-called risk contractors that provide all Medicare services for a flat fee—95 percent of the average cost of serving Medicare patients in the counties where the HMOs operate. Congress reasoned that if such plans could operate more cheaply than traditional fee-for-service Medicare, the taxpayer should share in the savings. In practice, the resulting payments have varied widely from county to county. In some, payments have been so generous that HMOs could provide not only the services Medicare required but also prescription drug coverage, dental care, and other services. The HMOs also often waived the large copayments that Medicare imposed on hospital patients.

As a result, the proportion of Medicare beneficiaries in managed care plans grew steadily until 1998, when it peaked at 16 percent. In light of the extra services that HMOs provided, this modest enrollment rate requires explanation. To begin with, some states had few or no HMOs. Payments in some counties were too low to induce HMOs to offer coverage to Medicare patients. But low enrollment rates, even in counties where HMOs actively sought Medicare beneficiaries, also indicate that most Medicare beneficiaries were loathe to surrender the flexibility and choice under traditional Medicare, even in exchange for an extended menu of benefits.

Medicare's HMO enrollments declined after 1998. The Balanced Budget Act of 1997 included incentives to encourage Medicare beneficiaries to enroll in HMOs, but it had unintended consequences. To control rising Medicare costs, the legislation restricted payments to HMOs in counties where payments were much above average. It also imposed new regulations on HMOs. These rule changes coincided with a general backlash against the restrictions that many HMOs imposed on access to care. In response, some HMOs and other risk contractors curtailed extra services, and many withdrew entirely from Medicare. Enrollments dropped to 12 percent of Medicare beneficiaries by 2002.

With so few beneficiaries enrolled in HMOs and other risk contractors, Medicare cost control depends on the success of cost containment efforts in the traditional program, where the federal government controls prices but has few tools to control use. Cost control efforts have therefore focused on restricting the fees of doctors, hospitals, and other providers. As reimbursements fall, however, providers increasingly warn that they may refuse to serve Medicare patients for what they regard as inadequate fees.

RISK SELECTION. Many plans to reform Medicare would give enrollees freedom to choose among alternative insurance arrangements, including HMOs.[23] Any proposal to encourage beneficiaries to enroll in lower-cost alternatives to traditional Medicare, like competing private health insurance plans, must face the vexing problem of *risk selection*. Risk selection is the name for actions health plans take to attract clients who will generate relatively low costs. Health insurance polices often include features to encourage favorable risk selection—for example, offering reimbursement for services that are highly valued by relatively healthy enrollees, such as fitness programs and extensive pediatric benefits, while limiting reimbursement for "out-of-network" specialists and highly advanced forms of care for chronic or serious illnesses. To the extent that any one plan succeeds, others must absorb the remaining enrollees with above-average costs. If competition is to work effectively, however, price differences among plans should reflect each plan's real costs of providing services, not its ability to enroll low-cost patients. At least in theory, perfectly risk-adjusted premiums would eliminate the incentive of plans to try to attract low-cost patients. Under risk adjustment, the plan receives a different premium for each enrollee based on his or her expected medical costs. Although this ideal is easy to state, developing adequate risk adjustment procedures has proven extremely difficult.

With imperfect risk adjustment, the choice of health plan can lead to a "death spiral." Whenever lower-cost beneficiaries can save money by choosing health plans that attract relatively few high-cost beneficiaries, the plans that enroll the most high-cost enrollees are forced to raise premiums. Premium increases, in turn, drive ever-rising numbers of low-cost enrollees to choose other options. These movements force the plan with the higher-risk population to become even more costly, which again leads to higher premiums and further exit by low-risk clients. Eventually, the premium in the high-cost plan becomes exorbitant, and the plan dies.

To overcome the problem of adverse selection, nearly all proposals to reform Medicare financing call either for community rating—the practice of charging every household of the same size and composition the same premium in a given geographic area—or paying each provider risk-adjusted premiums. Whether methods of risk adjustment, which are being continuously refined and improved, will become adequate to prevent competition based on risk selection remains unclear. But the success of Medicare plans based on competition will hinge on adequate methodologies and better data, such as detailed clinical information systems.[24]

In contrast to Medicare, Medicaid enrollment in plans that provide all services for a fixed monthly payment per enrollee has risen continuously, from 10 percent in 1991 to 57 percent in 2001. The most likely explanation for the difference between Medicaid's and Medicare's HMO enrollment is that Medicare beneficiaries may choose between HMOs and other risk contracts, on the one hand, and the traditional fee-for-service plan, on the other. In contrast, Medicaid enrollees in many states must accept whatever arrangements the state imposes or go uninsured. The lack of choice in Medicaid reflects the gulf between the political influence of Medicaid and Medicare beneficiaries. Because it covers nearly every American who reaches age sixty-five, along with many others who are disabled or have end-stage renal disease, Medicare has a large and politically powerful constituency. Medicaid enrolls the poor and enjoys less political support, and neither the federal government nor the individual state bears full responsibility for the program. Although policymakers continue to be concerned about coverage and expenditures under Medicaid, their efforts to address shortcomings and fill gaps in the Medicare program, such as the lack of prescription drug coverage, are far more visible. The seemingly impossible task of extending benefits while controlling costs is made even more challenging by political opposition to measures that would directly lower

Medicare expenses, such as an increase in the age of eligibility or added cost sharing for individuals with relatively high incomes.

Medical Innovation

Most of the health gains during the second half of the twentieth century were attributable to improved medical care. Most of the improvement in medical care resulted from innovations—better biomedical science and improved clinical practice. These advances included spectacular innovations in health care that greatly improved the detection and treatment of both rare and common diseases, such as magnetic resonance imaging, genetically engineered growth factors, and highly effective drugs for the treatment of depression, gastroesophageal reflux, high blood cholesterol, and HIV disease.[25] Although true breakthroughs, such as the polio vaccine and antibiotics, are infrequent, incremental improvements in diagnostic procedures and treatments are not, and their combined effects can be dramatic. The accumulation of incremental advances has greatly improved the outcomes of complex procedures such as organ transplantation, coronary artery bypass surgery, and high-dose chemotherapy (bone marrow transplantation) for acute myeloid leukemia and multiple myeloma. Technological progress in medicine is continuing and may be accelerating. It is a source of hope for the prevention, effective treatment, and cure of disease.

IMPORTANCE FOR HEALTH EXPENDITURES NOW AND IN THE FUTURE. Some innovations reduce spending on medical care, but most do not. One government agency attributes nearly all of the age- and price-adjusted growth in per capita medical spending in recent decades to technological innovation.[26] Such innovations often have their greatest impact long after they are introduced, when patients who would have received an older, inexpensive treatment or none at all receive more, or more expensive, care. Such shifts typically occur when the use of a new drug, device, or operation spreads beyond the narrowly defined populations in which it was introduced. For example, middle-aged men with chronic stable angina pectoris were the first routine beneficiaries of coronary artery bypass graft surgery. With experience and incremental clinical innovations, however, the same procedure now benefits patients with other conditions, such as heart attacks, and in other demographic groups, such as the elderly, who were initially deemed unsuitable for it. Although these and other innovations in treating coronary disease may have raised expenditures per patient, they have reduced the price of achieving important health outcomes, such as surviving hospitalization.[27] Similarly, the automated implantable cardioverter-defibrillator is poised to achieve broad dissemination. Initial clinical trials demonstrated its efficacy in patients with intractable cardiac arrhythmia who were at extremely high risk of sudden cardiac death, and subsequent trials demonstrated their efficacy in broader patient populations.[28]

INTERACTION OF RESEARCH AND HEALTH CARE FINANCE. Federal support of biomedical research (more than $20 billion in fiscal 2001 for the National Institutes of Health alone) and research investments by manufacturers and other private companies (billions more) stimulate the development of new technologies and approaches to health care, each of which has consequences for health expenditures and outcomes. For-profit corporations invest in research because they expect it to lead to the development of biomedical goods and services that will bring future revenues and profits.

U.S. insurers directly invest little in biomedical research. But they have a powerful indirect effect on research investment because they influence demand for and revenues from medical innovations. Because insured consumers pay only a fraction of the price of care, price is less important to them than it is in other markets. Other characteristics of new services, such as convenience, safety, and efficacy—that is, quality—assume greater importance. The tendency of insurance to increase demand at a point in time is well known,[29] but the most important effect of insurance on health care spending may be through its long-term influence on the development of new forms of care. By subsidizing demand, health insurance not only raises investment in medical research, but also changes the character of that investment, encouraging research on quality-improving innovations rather than cost-reducing ways to accomplish the same health outcomes as older interventions.[30]

Imagine how the market for automobiles would have developed if a third party had provided automobile insurance that paid 80 percent of the cost of new cars. The third party would recover the cost of this insurance by taking a portion of each insured person's pre-tax earnings.[31] Apart from those without auto insurance, anyone who wanted an automobile could buy one at one-fifth of the market price. Such insurance would influence both the number and types of cars people bought. People would replace cars more often, and they would buy higher-quality cars than they do in today's automobile market. A Lincoln or a Mercedes would cost buyers little more than a Chevrolet or a Honda, and sales of luxury automobiles would rise. Auto manufacturers would focus their product development on quality enhancements, such as big engines and luxurious interiors, rather than on cost-reducing manufacturing changes. Quite possibly, Chevrolets and Hondas would either disappear or become far more luxurious. The quality-adjusted price of automobiles might fall,[32] but since only high-quality cars would be sold, the average price of a car would rise. The costs of car insurance would rise inexorably. The well insured might welcome the steady improvements in the quality of luxury cars, but many would be better off with simpler automobiles and higher take-home pay.

There can be little doubt that the high expenditures on health care have encouraged technological innovation that has dramatically improved the well-being of Americans. Most people with health insurance in the United States are surely better off with today's health care at today's prices than they would be if they had 1980 health care at 1980 prices. This observation, however accurate, offers little guidance for policy. The appropriate question is whether Americans would be better off today if the demand for medical care had been more strongly influenced by price and biomedical research had been shaped by such a payment system. In that scenario, both the health care system and the specific technologies it provided would be different. The character of technological advance would have been different and probably somewhat slower, the price and total cost of health care would have been considerably lower, a larger fraction of Americans would have been able to afford health insurance, and consumption of other goods and services would have been higher. Overall, welfare might well have been higher.

AVERAGES VERSUS MARGINS. Debates about technological progress in health care often confuse two distinct issues. One concerns the *average* improvement in health: are we better off today than in the past? The other concerns *marginal* improvement: if we spend more on health care, how much better off will we be? The key difference is that average improvements include care providing the greatest benefits along with care producing minimal or no benefits. We believe that average improvements over time have been large, but that marginal improvements from the last dollars we now spend are small. The progress that medical science has made in preventing and treating coronary heart disease is striking, but it is not evidence that implanting a stent (a mesh tube used to keep partially occluded arteries open) in patients with single-vessel, minimally symptomatic coronary disease is worth the cost.

The distinction is important because most thoughtful proposals for the reform of health care financing and delivery are intended to alter spending and incentives at the margin, cutting "flat-of-the-curve" practices. To the extent that they succeed, their effects are measured by marginal changes, not averages. Nearly all health reforms include demand-side incentives—increases in the share of costs that patients bear directly—or supply-side incentives such as those embedded in capitation and other forms of managed care, or a combination of the two. Demand-side incentives are based on the belief that patients or their families can make informed, rational decisions about which care is best for them. Supply-side incentives are based on the rationale that health care providers can find efficient ways to deliver care if they are rewarded for doing so. The RAND Health Insurance Experiment found that both increases in cost sharing and enrollment in a health maintenance organization reduced utilization, without any clear evidence that health outcomes suffered. Although this study was conducted years ago, it remains the sole randomized trial of alternative forms of health insurance in the United States and lends some assurance that, despite the imperfections of these approaches to health care financing, they do not limit care indiscriminately. The "average" change in health due to technological advances is thus a poor measure of the effects of policies that selectively reduce utilization, such as those tested in the RAND experiment.

MEDICAL INNOVATION—A DILEMMA. In the U.S. health care market, government regulation is pervasive, insurance subsidizes consumption, and producers enjoy monopoly power through patents or proprietary information. The goals of health care policy—to provide coverage for the currently uninsured, to hold down health care costs, and to promote innovation—are frequently in conflict.

The desirability of government intervention is widely accepted. Government-granted patents, for example, protect manufacturers from direct competition for several years, allowing them to recover development costs. Market exclusivity, maintained under government-granted patents or proprietary information, enables companies to charge more than production costs, making it possible for them to pay for research out of profits. Even classic monopoly pricing, under which all buyers are charged the same high price, might not be sufficient to ensure profits.[33] Sometimes the recovery of research and development costs requires companies to engage in price discrimination—the practice of setting prices for different buyers according to their willingness to pay.[34] Prices for drugs and medical devices, supported by subsidized demand, may bear little relation to the (often low) marginal production costs. The market price—the sum of the patient's copayment and insurance payment—for highly effective innovations with no close substitutes can be very high without seriously eroding demand. Since well-insured patients can pay a great deal, the interaction between insurance and patents on drugs and devices enables companies to make large profits on successful products. Prolonging patent lives and broadening patent protection extend barriers to competition and can greatly increase those profits. But both policies raise prices and thereby curb consumption. Narrowing or shortening patent protection lowers profits and boosts consumption.

This trade-off creates a dilemma. If promoting innovation were not a consideration, consumers would be better off if patents did not exist and any company was free to produce any product. Such a policy, however, would diminish the flow of new drugs and devices by removing much of the incentive to invest in research and the development of new products.

The trade-off between maximizing current consumer welfare and promoting the future flow of new drugs is at the heart of most policy debates about pharmaceuticals. Policies that would lower drug prices—mandating drug discounts and controlling prices, for example—are worth pursuing only if the immediate benefit from lowering prices and increasing the availability of drugs today compensates for the harm from reducing the future flow of new products. Those who would maintain or extend current guarantees of market exclusivity and who favor policies to preserve high prices for branded drugs typically emphasize the importance of profits to fund the research that will lead to future products.

Recent and projected increases in drug prices heighten the salience of this trade-off. No simple guidelines can determine how to resolve it. Recent increases in prescription drug expenditures and the rise of copayments for drugs are both certain to make demand more sensitive to price.[35] People with health insurance will pay a greater share of the costs of medication out of pocket, and the uninsured will pay all of the costs out of pocket. The increase in personal payments will tend to reduce consumption of prescription drugs, while the introduction of new products will have the opposite effect.[36] Health plans and pharmaceutical benefits managers are also likely to try to hold down prices by negotiating price discounts from drug companies in return for policies that favor the products of those companies. Pharmaceutical companies will find it increasingly difficult to compete on quality alone, especially for drugs and devices that face competition from similar products, as consumers themselves demand evidence of value before spending their own money on health care.

Growth in the number and costs of beneficial drugs and devices is likely to cause political pressure to prevent or attenuate a widening disparity between people who are well insured or wealthy enough to afford innovations and those who are not. Medicine has a long and generally honorable history of price discrimination. Doctors traditionally have provided free or heavily discounted care to the needy, and drug companies have charged lower prices to those less able or willing to pay full price. Many recent developments, however, have made traditional price discrimination less feasible. The thinner margins on commercial health insurance contracts have made hospitals less willing and able to provide free or heavily subsidized care. With the rise of bulk purchasing by health plans and pharmacy benefits managers, fewer purchasers have truly price-inelastic demand for pharmaceutical products. Paradoxically, it is the solitary uninsured buyer who must pay undiscounted prices for drugs or for health care.

Current research in genomics is expected to lead to highly targeted but expensive therapies. Without a dramatic change in health care financing, only the wealthy and well insured will be able to afford such innovations when they are first introduced. As the number of health care have-nots grows, the pressure for comprehensive health care reform may increase.

Conclusion

There was a time when serious analysts could argue that "all medical care that is effective should be free to all."[37] No country can follow that precept today. Eliminating ineffective care, according to some policy advocates, is key to reducing health expenditures. Yet even if ineffective care is eliminated, the continued introduction of effective new forms of medical care will guarantee continued growth in spending. The chief problems facing the U.S. health care system today are setting priorities for choosing among effective forms of care and finding the means to pay for such care.

How can the most promising medical advances be developed and made widely available? The first step will be to identify those that are most promising. The Food and Drug Administration evaluates the safety and efficacy of new interventions, but not their effectiveness in alternative clinical settings or their cost implications. Today such information, when available at all, is often fragmentary. Several organizations—the Evidence-Based Practice Centers of the Agency for Healthcare Research and Quality, the

Cochrane Collaborative, the Blue Cross–Blue Shield Association, Kaiser Permanente and other health plans, and some large provider groups— assess medical technologies. The heavy preponderance of private sector efforts is less a sign of thriving private initiative than of inadequate government funding. Although these efforts produce a great deal of reliable information about the effectiveness and value of new medical technologies, the information is neither comprehensive nor readily accessible to the public. There is a compelling need for a well-funded, semi-autonomous agency to carry out technology assessment in health care. A center for the assessment of new and existing technologies could help physicians, hospital administrators, private insurance companies, government agencies, and the public to distinguish innovations that are truly valuable from those that provide small or no benefit at great cost.

We recommend the creation of a National Center for the Assessment of Medical Technologies, with an annual budget of $1 billion, financed by a small levy (less than one-tenth of 1 percent) on all health care spending. The center would sponsor and conduct research and serve as a repository for diverse data and health information. It would help to develop and disseminate systematic knowledge about the effectiveness and value of medical technologies, providing the information that health care providers and patients need to make decisions about when to use both new and established technologies.

The source of funding is critical. There is little chance that private, voluntary contributions would be sufficient to finance such a center. The temptation for individual firms and organizations to "free ride" on the contributions of others would be too great. On the other hand, a conventional government agency, subject to the vagaries of annual appropriations and vulnerable to political pressures whenever research results ran contrary to the interests of powerful constituencies, would lack the independence essential for its dual mission, that is, to develop and disseminate systematic knowledge about the value of medical technologies, and, through credible evaluations, to confer legitimacy on the efficient delivery of care. A federal program with a secure and adequate funding base, accountable to the public yet, like the Federal Reserve Board, insulated from excessive pressure from interest groups, will be needed to fulfill this mission.

Sometimes the most important contributions of scientific advances are not embodied in treatments and diagnostic procedures. Scientific advances can lead to new insights into the best ways to use existing technologies— or to modify behaviors—to improve health. A particular genetic variant associated with a disease like rheumatoid arthritis, for example, might trigger disease only in individuals exposed to high levels of certain amino acids. The best preventive for the disease might consist of dietary restrictions rather than gene therapy or a targeted drug. Because most diseases result from an interaction of genes and the environment, there will usually be multiple potential targets for intervention. The best approach should be determined by considering both the effectiveness and the cost of all promising alternatives, whether the approach is the modification of a gene or its products or something as simple as a change in diet or exercise regimen.

Because the gene-environmental interactions that seem to underlie much chronic disease are difficult to study, particularly when multiple genes contribute to the risk of disease, discovering the best approach to treatment will often be expensive. A pharmaceutical or device manufacturer might readily support research on the effectiveness of its product, whether the motivation is a regulatory requirement or simply an opportunity to demonstrate that its treatment is best. But there is no similar payoff from research on nonmedical approaches to disease prevention or even to research on the effects of generic drugs. We recommend increased public support from government and private foundations for the investigation of the interactions between genes and the nonmedical determinants of health.

Identifying the best approaches to care is a necessary first step, but this information must be used to be effective. The next step is to find ways to pay for effective care. Even with improved information about new technologies, the combination of medical innovation and the aging of baby boomers will almost certainly lead to further increases in health spending. There is every prospect that, if care is financed and organized the way it is today, the availability of care will depend on the willingness and ability of the economy to fund the increases out of taxation. In the coming decade people will pay a larger share of health care bills in the form of higher insurance premiums and especially more out-of-pocket payments. The higher out-of-pocket payments will encourage people to use the forms of care that they believe represent the best value, but this trend will contribute to widening inequality in the utilization of health care. Without a dramatic change in the ways that Americans finance health care, this trend will continue for the foreseeable future.

A thoughtful response to rising inequality in the use of medical care will not simply strive to equalize access. The societal interest in equal access to interventions that substantially reduce mortality or prevent disability is much greater than it is for marginally effective interventions. Furthermore, access to medical care must be balanced against other societal needs, including support for the poor, education, housing, and public safety. We face a world of medical opportunity and of challenge. In the coming decade, dilemmas posed by the health care system will test our values, our institutions, and our ability to apply rationality and compassion to intractable problems—not to solve them, but to do better than we now do.

Notes

1. Benjamin Disraeli, *House of Commons* (1873).

2. Kenneth G. Manton and XiLiang Gu, "Changes in the Prevalence of Chronic Disability in the United States Black and Nonblack Population above Age Sixty-five from 1982 to 1999," *Proceedings of the National Academy of Sciences,* vol. 98, no. 11 (2001), pp. 6354–59.

3. Daniel Callahan, *False Hopes: Why America's Quest for Perfect Health Is a Recipe for Failure* (Simon and Schuster, 1998), pp. 21, 37.

4. Francis Fukuyama, *Our Posthuman Future* (Farrar Straus and Giroux, 2002).

5. David Mechanic, "Disadvantage, Inequality, and Social Policy," *Health Affairs* (Millwood), vol. 21, no. 2 (2002), p. 51.

6. Angus Deaton, "Policy Implications of the Gradient of Health and Wealth," *Health Affairs* (Millwood), vol. 21, no. 2 (2002), p. 15.

7. Ichiro Kawachi and Bruce P. Kennedy, *The Health of Nations: Why Inequality Is Harmful to Your Health* (New Press, 2002); Ichiro Kawachi and others, eds., *The Society and Population Health Reader* (New Press, 1999); Angus Deaton, *Health, Inequality, and Economic Development* (Cambridge, Mass.: National Bureau of Economic Research, 2001); Angus Deaton, *Relative Deprivation, Inequality, and Mortality* (Cambridge, Mass.: National Bureau of Economic Research, 2001); Angus Deaton and Christina Paxson, *Mortality, Income, and Income Inequality over Time in Britain and the United States* (Cambridge, Mass.: National Bureau of Economic Research, 2001); Deaton, "Policy Implications of the Gradient"; Merete Osler and others, "Income Inequality, Individual Income, and Mortality in Danish Adults: Analysis of Pooled Data from Two Cohort Studies," *British Medical Journal,* vol. 324, no. 7328 (2002), pp. 13–16; Roland Sturm and Carol R. Gresenz, "Relations of Income Inequality and Family Income to Chronic Medical Conditions and Mental Health Disorders: National Survey," *British Medical Journal,* vol. 324, no. 7328 (2002), pp. 20–23.

8. The second and third measures are approximations. We assume that age- and sex-specific life expectancies are the same for people who died at a given age as for those who did not die. This assumption is doubtless incorrect, but the numbers in table 5-3 do provide informative contrasts among the three measures and the interactions between sex and the measures.

9. Organization for Economic Cooperation and Development (OECD), *OECD Health Data 2001: A Comparative Analysis of Thirty Countries* (Paris, 2001).

10. Uwe E. Reinhardt and others, "Cross-National Comparisons of Health Systems Using OECD Data, 1999," *Health Affairs,* vol. 21, no. 3 (2002), pp. 169–81.

11. Council of Economic Advisers, *Economic Report of the President, 2002* (U.S. Government Printing Office, 2002).

12. Jonathan Gruber and David Wise, eds., *Social Security Programs and Retirement around the World* (University of Chicago Press, 1999).

13. Kenneth. J. Arrow, "Uncertainty and the Welfare Economics of Medical Care," *American Economic Review,* vol. 53, no. 5 (1963), pp. 941–73; Mark. V. Pauly, "The Economics of Moral Hazard," *American Economic Review,* vol. 58, no. 3 (1968), pp. 533–39.

14. Victor Fuchs, "From Bismarck to Woodcock: The 'Irrational' Pursuit of National Health Insurance," *Journal of Law and Economics,* vol. 19 (August 1976), pp. 347–59.

15. Henry J. Kaiser Family Foundation and Health Research and Educational Trust, *Employer Health Benefits: 2001 Annual Survey* (Menlo Park, Calif.: Henry J. Kaiser Family Foundation, 2001).

16. Joseph P. Newhouse and others, "Some Interim Results from a Controlled Trial of Cost Sharing in Health Insurance," *New England Journal of Medicine,* vol. 305, no. 17 (1981), pp. 1501–07.

17. Committee on the Consequences of Uninsurance, *Care without Coverage: Too Little, Too Late* (Washington: Institute of Medicine, 2002); Jack Hadley, *Sicker and Poorer: The Consequences of Being Uninsured* (Menlo Park, Calif.: Henry J. Kaiser Family Foundation, 2002).

18. Likewise, the age, income, health risks, and chronic diseases of people who become insured differ from those who remain uninsured.

19. Stephen Heffler and others, "Health Spending Projections for 2001–2011: The Latest Outlook," *Health Affairs* (Millwood), vol. 21, no. 2 (2002), pp. 207–18; Reinhardt and others, "Cross-National Comparisons of Health Systems"; OECD, *OECD Health Data 2001.*

20. Boards of Trustees, Federal Hospital Insurance and Federal Supplementary Medical Insurance Trust Funds, *2002 Annual Report of the Boards of Trustees of the Federal Hospital Insurance and Federal Supplementary Medical Insurance Trust Funds* (Baltimore, Md.: Center for Medicare and Medicaid Services, 2002).

21. Boards of Trustees, *2002 Annual Report.*

22. Mark Eberhardt and others, *Health, United States, 2001* (U.S. Government Printing Office, 2001).

23. Jack. A. Meyer and E. K. Wicks, eds., *Covering America: Real Remedies for the Uninsured* (Washington: Economic and Social Research Institute, 2001).

24. Wynand P. M. M. Van de Ven and Randall P. Ellis, "Risk Adjustment in Competitive Health Plan Markets," in Anthony J. Culyer and J. P. Newhouse, ed., *Handbook of Health Economics,* vol. 1A (Amsterdam: Elsevier, 2000), pp. 755–845.

25. Victor R. Fuchs and Harold C. Sox, "Physicians' Views of the Relative Importance of Thirty Medical Innovations," *Health Affairs* (Millwood), vol. 20, no. 5 (2002), pp. 30–42.

26. Sally T. Burner and Daniel R. Waldo, "National Health Expenditure Projections, 1994–2005," *Health Care Financing Review,* vol. 16, no. 4 (1995), pp. 221–42. These estimates attribute to technology cost increases that are not attributable to demographic change or to general or health sector–specific price inflation.

27. David M. Cutler and others, "Are Medical Prices Declining? Evidence for Heart Attack Treatments," *Quarterly Journal of Economics,* vol. 113, no. 4 (1991), pp. 991–1024.

28. Antiarrhythmics versus Implantable Defibrillators (AVID) Investigators, "A Comparison of Antiarrhythmic-Drug Therapy with Implantable Defibrillators in Patients Resuscitated from Near-Fatal Ventricular Arrhythmias. The Antiarrhythmics versus Implantable

Defibrillators (AVID) Investigators," *New England Journal of Medicine,* vol. 337, no. 22 (1997), pp. 1576–83; Alvin Mushlin and others, "The Cost-Effectiveness of Automatic Implantable Cardiac Defibrillators: Results from MADIT (Multicenter Automatic Defibrillator Implantation Trial)," *Circulation,* vol. 97, no. 21 (1998), pp. 2129–35; Gillian D. Sanders and others, "Potential Cost-Effectiveness of Prophylactic Use of the Implantable Cardioverter Defibrillator or Amiodarone after Myocardial Infarction," *Annals of Internal Medicine,* vol. 135, no. 10 (2001), pp. 870–83; Arthur J. Moss and others, "Prophylactic Implantation of a Defibrillator in Patients with Myocardial Infarction and Reduced Ejection Fraction," *New England Journal of Medicine,* vol. 346, no. 12 (2002), pp. 877–83.

29. Arrow, "Uncertainty and the Welfare Economics"; Pauly, "The Economics of Moral Hazard."

30. Burton A. Weisbrod, "The Health Care Quadrilemma: An Essay on Technological Change, Insurance, Quality of Care, and Cost Containment," *Journal of Economic Literature,* vol. 29, no. 2 (1991), pp. 523–52.

31. Economists are agreed that workers pay for employer-purchased health insurance through reduced wages. The cost of this insurance is reduced because it is not subject to individual income taxes or payroll taxes. The key point, however, is that the cost of the insurance is not increased by the use of medical services or—in the example given in the text—by the purchase of automobiles. It therefore is equivalent to a subsidy at the time the service is purchased.

32. One of the few rigorous attempts to measure quality-adjusted price change for a medical technology demonstrated that the real cost of treating a heart attack fell over time. Cutler and others, "Are Medical Prices Declining?"

33. Normal monopoly pricing requires that price be set so that the marginal revenue (computed as the difference between the product of quantity sold times price at one price level and that at a slightly higher or lower price) just equals the marginal cost of production.

34. Monopoly pricing without price discrimination normally reduces the quantity demanded. If price discrimination is perfect, so that all buyers are charged prices just equal to what a good is worth to them, sellers will maximize profits if they sell to everyone who values the product at a price at least equal to the marginal production cost. That means that sales will be the same as they would be in competitive markets, where a uniform price equals marginal production cost.

35. National Institute for Healthcare Management, *Prescription Drug Expenditures in 2000: The Upward Trend Continues* (Washington, 2001), pp. 1–24.

36. Brenda Motheral and Kathleen A. Fairman, "Effect of a Three-Tier Prescription Copay on Pharmaceutical and Other Medical Utilization," *Medical Care,* vol. 39, no. 12 (2001), pp. 1293–304.

37. Archibald L. Cochrane, *Effectiveness and Efficiency: Random Reflections on Health Services* (London: Nuffield Provincial Hospitals Trust, 1972).

WILLIAM G. GALE
PETER R. ORSZAG

6

Private Pensions:
Issues and Options

Oに OF THE MOST striking economic transitions over the past century has been the creation of a lengthy retirement period at the end of most working lives. In 1900, nearly two out of every three men aged sixty-five or older were in the work force.[1] By 2000, fewer than one in five among this age group was in the labor force.[2] An extended retirement is a historic advance in economic well-being, but it creates new challenges for public policy.

Over the past century, the United States has developed government programs and encouraged private institutions to ensure that elderly households have adequate income and health care during retirement. Social Security, established in 1935, covers more than 95 percent of workers. It provides basic, assured income support to retirees (and to the disabled and survivors), but was never intended to provide for all retirement needs.[3]

Other than Social Security, the primary saving vehicles for most households are pensions and saving plans favored by tax incentives, which form a second tier of retirement income.[4] Tax incentives for employer-based pensions originated in 1921. The use of pensions expanded during World War II because pension contributions were exempt from wage controls and

We thank Manijeh Azmoodah, David Gunter, and Matthew Hall for excellent research assistance, and Henry Aaron, Robert Cumby, Peter Diamond, Mark Iwry, Maya MacGuineas, Michael Orszag, and two referees for valuable comments and discussions.

were deductible under the rapidly growing income tax. The spread of pensions continued after the war, and rules governing them have been modified repeatedly. The creation of Keogh accounts in 1962 and Individual Retirement Arrangements (sometimes called Individual Retirement Accounts or IRAs) in 1974 expanded eligibility for tax-sheltered saving plans beyond the employer-based system.

In 1998, pensions and tax-preferred saving plans covered more than 70 million workers. These plans received more than $200 billion in new contributions, had total assets of more than $4 trillion, and provided one-fifth of the income of the elderly.[5] Relative to Social Security, pension coverage is less universal—only about half of workers are covered at any one time, and about two-thirds are covered at some point in their career. Coverage is particularly low among lower earners. Because pensions are intended to replace earnings rather than meet basic needs, pension income is distributed less equally than Social Security.

Other financial assets, proceeds from businesses, and home equity constitute a third source of retirement income. Apart from housing equity, however, these assets are concentrated among a few, relatively affluent retirees.

This multitier approach to retirement saving has enabled millions of retirees to enjoy a financially secure retirement. Poverty among the elderly, which was higher than among the nonelderly until 1994, has now fallen to roughly the same level as among nonelderly adults.

However, retirement programs now face significant challenges. Social Security is projected to run a long-term deficit that will require benefit adjustments or new revenues. Even now, Social Security replaces only a modest fraction of earnings for most workers, and that fraction is destined to decline for retirement at any given age under current law (see table 6-1). Medicare faces equally serious financial challenges. These problems underscore the importance of private pensions and other tax-sheltered saving plans in meeting the needs of tomorrow's retirees.

In light of these circumstances, the central goal of the private pension system should be to encourage or provide *adequate* and *secure* retirement income in a *cost-efficient* and *equitable* manner. To meet this goal, pensions must achieve several intermediate objectives.

First, they should increase households' saving for retirement. The central motivation for using the tax system to encourage pensions is the belief that without incentives, people would save too little to provide themselves with adequate retirement income.[6] How many people save inadequately for

Table 6-1. *Scheduled Replacement Rates from Social Security for Workers Retiring at 65*[a]

Percentage of earnings replaced

Year attaining age 65	Low earner	Medium earner	High earner	Maximum earner
2003	55.6	41.3	34.8	29.6
2010	52.4	38.8	32.2	26.5
2020	52.1	38.7	32.0	25.6
2040	48.9	36.2	30.0	24.0

Source: 2003 OASDI Trustees Report, table VI.F11.

a. In 2003, the low earner is assumed to earn $15,629; the average earner is assumed to earn $34,731; the high earner is assumed to earn $55,569; and the maximum earner is assumed to earn $87,000.

retirement is controversial, but at least a significant minority of the population falls into this category. Some are myopic and do not plan ahead. Some with modest incomes may save little because they have little hope of saving more than the benefits they would receive under means-tested government income security programs for the poor elderly. Saving incentives succeed in any meaningful sense only if they increase the saving of those who would have saved too little in their absence.

Second, pensions should boost national saving—the sum of public and private saving. National saving contributes to economic growth, and increased growth would make Social Security and Medicare easier to finance. Pensions increase national saving, however, only to the extent that the contributions represent saving that would not have occurred anyway and only to the extent that the increase in private saving exceeds the reduction in tax revenues resulting from the tax incentives. Private saving is not increased when people shift assets into the tax-preferred pensions or reduce other saving that they would have undertaken.[7]

Third, pensions should induce efficient handling of risk. Long-term financial commitments, such as those represented by pensions, are inescapably risky. The recent stock market collapse and corporate scandals underscore those risks. While people are working and accumulating pensions, the risks include the possibility of unemployment, slowed growth of wages, a decline in asset values, unanticipated inflation, and disappointing yields. The final three risks persist during the pay-out stage, after the worker has retired. In addition, workers face the risk that they may outlive their assets in some pension plans.

Fourth, the increasing burdens on workers to support a growing retired population suggest that pensions should not promote early retirement and, in fact, should encourage continued work. Extended working lives are now feasible because of increasing longevity and improved health.

Finally, the pension system must be sufficiently simple and otherwise attractive enough to induce employers to offer pension plans and workers to participate in them. This is a considerable task because of inherent conflicts in the design of pension policy.

Considerable controversy surrounds the extent to which the current pension system attains these goals and, to the extent that it does not, how the system should change. In this chapter, we describe the current system of pensions and tax-deferred saving, evaluate its ability to meet the goals described above, and discuss options for reform.

A Brief Overview of Pensions and Tax-Preferred Saving

Pensions and tax-favored saving plans come in several different forms. In *defined contribution* (DC) plans, employers and/or employees contribute a specified portion of a worker's current salary into an account belonging to the individual worker. Employer contributions are excluded from the employee's current taxable income. In the most common DC plans— 401(k) plans, named for the section of the Internal Revenue Code that authorizes them—employees' contributions are also excluded from current personal income tax. Employer contributions may be independent of the workers' contributions, but many companies match a percentage of the worker's contribution. A typical formula would have the employer contribute an amount equal to 50 percent of the first 6 percent of salary that the worker contributes. Employers provide a menu of approved investments, and workers are free to choose among them. At retirement, the worker simply receives the account balance, which is the sum of deposits and all investment income. Workers may withdraw the funds as a lump sum or convert them to an annuity (that is, a periodic payment that lasts as long as the annuitant is alive). In either case, withdrawals are taxed as ordinary income. Employees generally may borrow against these accounts or make hardship withdrawals before retirement. Workers who leave their jobs before retirement typically may roll the funds into an IRA (or their new employer's plan) or cash out the balances. If the funds are withdrawn before legislated ages, workers are subject to penalties in addition to income taxes. Minimum distribution rules also require workers to begin withdrawing funds once they are retired and have reached a certain age. Under *defined benefit* (DB) plans, employers commit to paying workers with sufficient job tenure an annual retirement benefit that usually depends on years of service and a measure of a worker's average salary. A typical formula might provide an annual benefit equal to 1 percent times the number of years the worker stayed at the firm times the average salary over the worker's five highest-paid years at the firm. The employer funds these benefits by making pretax contributions to a pension fund for all employees. Employees typically do not make contributions. Employees pay income tax when the benefits are paid. The Pension Benefit Guaranty Corporation insures defined benefit payments up to $42,954 a year for sixty-five-year-olds in 2002.[8] Employees typically do not have access to the funds before retirement.

Even this short description indicates that DC and DB plans differ in numerous ways (see table 6-2). In a DB plan, workers have few choices: they are enrolled in the plan, the employer makes contributions, and a benefit is paid when the worker retires. In a DC plan, workers have numerous choices: workers decide whether to participate and how much to contribute; they have some (though typically limited) discretion on how to allocate the funds across investment options, when to withdraw the funds, and in what form to take the withdrawal.

The distribution of financial risks also differs. Workers bear the risk associated with fluctuations in asset prices under DC plans. Such plans impose few risks on employers, whose responsibilities end with their contributions. Under DB plans, by contrast, employers bear the direct investment risk. Here, employers must make whatever deposits are necessary to keep reserves equal to the accrued value of pension liabilities. When asset prices fall and interest rates drop—which increases the present discounted value of accrued liabilities—the required deposits may be large enough to significantly affect the financial solvency of the sponsoring company. This problem arose for many large companies in 2002 and 2003. This does not mean that workers bear no risks in DB plans, though. Firms can pass some of the risks on to workers by changing the future benefit formula if the pension fund goes sour.

Retirees under most DB plans have traditionally received annuities, though increasingly they are paid as lump sums. Most DC participants have taken their benefits as lump sums.[9] Participants who choose not to

Table 6-2. *Characteristics of Employer Pension Plans*

Feature	Traditional defined benefit	Defined contribution/401(k)	Cash balance plan
Funding	Employer	Employee and employer	Employer
Financial market risk borne by	Employer	Employee	Employer
Benefits determined by	Years of service and final or highest average pay	Contributions (based on current wages) and investment returns on those contributions	Pay credits (based on current wages) and interest credits
How benefits are typically paid at retirement	Annuity	Lump sum	Annuity or lump sum
Access to funds for current workers prior to retirement	No	Yes (through loans and hardship withdrawals)	No
Guaranteed by PBGC	Yes	No	Yes

annuitize their balances run the risk of outliving their pension benefits. Annuities usually are not indexed for inflation. As a result, their value erodes over time, but generally payments are not terminated before the pensioner (or the pensioner and spouse, under joint-and-survivor annuities) dies.

DC plans treat frequent job changers better than DB plans do. Typically, DC benefits accrue and vest faster than do DB benefits. Whether job changers leave their balances at their old employer or transfer the funds to an IRA (or their new employer's plan), the balances continue to grow as investment returns accumulate. In contrast, DB benefits are typically frozen in nominal terms when workers switch employers. The real value of benefits actually falls over time because of inflation.

DB plans offer employers the flexibility to structure pension-accrual patterns to encourage job retention at some points in the career and retirement at other points. DC plans offer firms less opportunity to structure pensions to encourage or discourage retirement. *Cash balance* plans and other so-called hybrid plans have been designed at least in part to capture key benefits of both DB and DC plans (see table 6-2). Cash balance plans are legally classified as DB plans because the employer owns the assets, makes the investment choices, bears the direct investment risk, and is required to maintain adequate reserves. But the worker's accrual of pension rights resembles that of DC plans. The employer credits the workers' accounts with contributions, typically set as a percentage of current earnings. The employer also provides a credit based on the account balance and a specified interest rate. Workers accrue (notional) account balances. Workers who switch jobs before retirement may withdraw or transfer the account balances to other tax-sheltered accounts. The interest credit rate under a cash balance plan is specified in advance, rather than depending on financial market performance as under DC plans, but employers may change the interest credit rate over time.

In addition to the employer-sponsored plans noted above, many people contribute to tax-sheltered accounts under several different arrangements. The most widely used are Individual Retirement Arrangements, or IRAs. Self-employed individuals may contribute to Keogh plans, which operate as do defined contribution plans, except that there is no employer. Funds placed in such accounts are not taxed when deposited, investment income accrues tax free, and withdrawals are taxed as ordinary income. The main exception is the so-called Roth IRA, under which the income used to finance contributions is subject to income tax, but investment returns and withdrawals are not taxed.[10] In each case, account holders decide how much to invest, what investments to make, and when to withdraw the balances. They also bear all financial market risk.

Aggregate Trends

Defined contribution plans have been increasingly dominant since 1975 (see table 6-3). Between 1975 and 1998, the number of defined contribution plans more than tripled and the number of active participants more than quadrupled. During the same period, the number of defined benefit plans fell by almost half and the number of active participants fell by one-quarter. Defined contribution plans accounted for more than 80 percent of contributions to pensions in 1998, compared with just over one-third in 1975.

From the mid-1970s to the mid-1980s, DC plans largely supplemented older DB plans. Since the mid-1980s, DC plans appear to be displacing

Table 6-3. *Shift of Pension System toward Defined Contribution Plans,*
1975, 1998

	1975			1998		
	DB	DC	DB share of total (percent)	DB	DC	DB share of total (percent)
Number of plans	103,346	207,748	33.2	56,405	673,626	7.7
Active participants	27,214	11,217	70.8	22,994	50,335	31.4
Plan assets, 1998 ($ million)	563,429	224,259	71.5	1,936,600	2,085,250	48.2
Contributions, 1998 ($ million)	73,453	38,842	65.4	34,985	166,900	17.3

Sources: Department of Labor, Pension and Welfare Benefits Administration, *Private Pension Plan Bulletin: Abstract of 1995 Form 5500 Annual Reports,* no. 8 (Spring 1999); Department of Labor, Pension and Welfare Benefits Administration, "Coverage Status of Workers under Employer Provided Plans," 2000 (available at www.dol.gov/pwba/programs/opr/CWS-Survey/hilites.html); and authors' calculations. Nominal figures for 1975 were converted into 1998 dollars using the CPI-U.

DB plans. Almost all new DC pension plans have been 401(k) plans. Notably, overall pension coverage rates have been flat over the entire period since 1975.[11]

Several factors help explain the shift to DC plans. Employment has shifted from unionized industries, where defined benefit plans were common, to nonunionized industries, where they are relatively rare. The burden of government regulations on DB plans has increased, relative to DC plans. Tax policy provided that worker contributions to 401(k) plans, but not to DB plans, were tax deductible. Perceptions of increased worker mobility may also have increased the perceived attractiveness of DC plans, which are more beneficial for frequent job changers, as noted above.[12]

Increasingly, DB plans are cash balance plans. BankAmerica originated cash balance plans in 1985. Although the idea attracted little interest at first, by 1999 cash balance plans accounted for about 15 percent of all DB assets.[13] Several considerations may explain the shift to cash balance plans. Many design features of cash balance plans are attractive to both employers and employees. Some critics allege that companies have adopted cash balance plans to reduce their pension obligations, and some companies have indeed reduced pension costs by converting to a cash balance plan, but others have actually increased pension funding following the conversion.[14]

Who Benefits from Pensions?

The tax advantages associated with pension contributions in 2002 reduced the present value of tax revenues by more than $190 billion.[15] That is, they provided taxpayers with a tax cut of $190 billion in present value. The size of this tax advantage underscores the fact that the United States makes a substantial investment in pension subsidies.

Determining who benefits from pensions and by how much is complicated. Some workers elect not to participate in pension plans.[16] Among participants, contribution rates vary. In addition, pension benefits are not free. Both economic theory and empirical studies show that workers pay for pensions through lower wages than they would otherwise earn. But it is not clear whether the match between pension accruals and wage adjustments occurs at the level of the worker, the firm, or the industry.[17] A further issue is that the value of the tax breaks on pensions depends on the level and pattern of tax rates over workers' lifetimes.

Despite these difficulties, however, the broad pattern of distributional consequences is clear. High-income households are more likely to be covered by a pension. They are more likely to participate if they are eligible. The share of salary contributed, given participation, increases with earnings. Tax deferral is worth more to high-bracket than to low-bracket filers, a feature that is reinforced by the fact that high earners are likely to face a larger drop in marginal tax rates in retirement than are low earners.

COVERAGE. Roughly 50 percent of full-time private-sector wage and salary workers have been covered by a pension. This fraction has changed little since the early 1970s, when the Employee Retirement Income Security Act (ERISA) was enacted.[18] Pensions covered fewer than one-fifth of workers with less than a high school degree in 1999, compared with almost two-thirds of workers with a college degree. Pensions covered only 6 percent of workers earning less than $10,000 a year, compared with 76 percent of workers earning more than $50,000 a year.[19] Pension coverage is generally high among full-time workers at large and medium-sized firms. About 85 percent of those in the labor force who worked and lacked pension coverage had low income, did not work full time, worked for a small company, or were relatively young.[20] Roughly three-quarters of the uncovered population worked for an employer that did not sponsor a pension plan in 1999.[21]

PARTICIPATION RATES. While participation is automatic for workers covered under DB plans, it is usually optional under 401(k) plans. In 1993, two-thirds of workers who were offered the opportunity to participate in a 401(k) plan did so. Participation was significantly higher for higher-earning workers.[22] Only 6 percent of taxpayers eligible to make deductible contributions to an IRA did so in 1996.[23]

Why is participation so low? For low earners, the answer may be income that is too low to permit saving after payment for necessities. Yet 60 percent of households at or below the poverty line indicate that they save at least something.[24] Experience with a program that provides tax breaks and matching funds to encourage saving among participating low-income families suggests that poor families will save if presented with financial incentives to do so.[25] A more plausible explanation for low participation rates is that tax incentives for retirement are meager for low-income households. Tax deferral means little to people whose tax rate is low or even zero.[26]

Another important factor is a lack of financial education. Only 32 percent of the work force has even tried to figure out how much saving is needed for retirement, according to a 2002 survey.[27] Financial education appears to be particularly effective at increasing saving levels. Students who are exposed to financial decisionmaking courses in high school, for example, tend to have greater wealth when adults. Employer-provided financial education also tends to generate higher saving. Households that have planned for retirement tend to save more than other households, even controlling for income and other characteristics.[28]

Inertia also matters. Participation rates are lower if workers must make an affirmative decision to join a 401(k) plan or an IRA than they are if workers are presumed to participate unless they elect not to do so. Inertia and the "power of suggestion," it appears, play an important role in determining saving patterns.[29]

CONTRIBUTION RATES. Contribution rates also vary across workers participating in a 401(k) plan: participating low-income workers typically contribute a smaller percentage of their pay to 401(k)-type pension plans than higher-income workers. Among workers aged eighteen to sixty-four with a 401(k) plan in 1992, for example, the average employee contribution rate (excluding employer matches) was 3.7 percent of pay for those with household income less than $25,000 and 7.9 percent of pay for those with household income exceeding $75,000.[30]

Evaluating the Pension System

The key objectives of the pension system include increasing retirement saving and national saving, handling risk efficiently, and encouraging later retirement. The key constraint on reaching these goals is to keep the pension system simple—to encourage participation in a voluntary system—and affordable. How does the current system stack up?

Adequacy of Wealth Accumulation

Although there is some controversy, most studies have found that at least some U.S. households are saving too little and therefore arrive at retirement with insufficient wealth to maintain their current living standards. Not surprisingly, the studies typically find that the problem is more serious among families with modest incomes.[31]

Pensions and tax-deferred saving plans represent substantial assets, but whether and how much they increase wealth accumulation is less clear. Pension contributions increase private wealth, but only if they are financed by a reduction in current consumption. Contributions do not increase private wealth if they are financed by reductions in other saving the household would have done anyway, by transfers from taxable to tax-preferred accounts or by increased borrowing.

The empirical evidence on this issue is mixed. Most studies of DB plans find a strong impact of pensions on a household's overall wealth. However, these studies contain a variety of statistical biases that exaggerate the effect, and efforts to control for those biases have produced estimates that are substantially smaller.[32] Even the studies that find that only a small share of overall contributions represents net additional saving, however, indicate that DB pension plans can help increase wealth accumulation by low- and middle-income households, which often have little in the way of other assets.

The effects of 401(k) plans are equally controversial. Early studies found that 401(k) plans significantly increased wealth accumulation, but a number of more recent studies using better statistical techniques have found the effects to be substantially smaller or nonexistent. Several recent studies have found that contributions to 401(k) plans by lower- and middle-income households represent net additions to saving, while contributions by high-income households tend to represent asset reshuffling rather than new saving.[33]

These studies examined the effects of pensions and tax-deferred accounts on private saving and did not account for the loss of public saving from reduced tax collections, which would offset some or all of any positive effect on private saving.[34]

The results regarding the effects of pensions on saving correspond in an interesting way to findings on the adequacy of individual retirement saving. Higher-income households are generally saving adequately for retirement and are most likely to have pensions, but their pension contributions represent less new saving and more asset shifting (and, hence, tax avoidance) than do the pension accumulations of lower earners. Conversely, lower-income households are less likely to be saving adequately for retirement and are less likely to have pensions than are higher earners, but their pension contributions are more likely to represent net additions to saving.

These findings indicate problems with the current pension system as well as opportunities for reform. The problem is that pension benefits accrue disproportionately to high-income households while creating little improvement in the adequacy of saving for retirement and little increase in national saving. By contrast, lower- and middle-income households gain less from the pension system, but these benefits—where they exist—appear both to increase saving and to help households who would otherwise save inadequately for retirement. The objective of reform should be to encourage expanded pension coverage and participation among low- and middle-income households, a step that would boost national saving and build wealth for households, many of which are currently saving too little.

Risk

Distributing fairly and efficiently the risks associated with retirement saving is as important as increasing saving. Workers in DC plans face two main sources of risk: investment returns on their asset balances over their career and the possibility of outliving their resources. In DB plans, companies bear the direct investment risk, but workers face some risk because benefits depend on future wage growth and job tenure, and because companies can alter plan features.

Investment risks are central to both DC and DB plans. In DC plans, workers typically decide how to invest the assets and therefore bear the burden of uncertain asset returns. Most individual workers do not appear well equipped to deal with these risks. Only half of Americans know the difference between a stock and a bond. Only 12 percent know the difference between a load and a no-load mutual fund. Only 16 percent understand the details of an IRA.[35] At an even more basic level, only 20 percent of adults can correctly determine change using prices from a menu.[36] Such financial naiveté fosters investment blunders, such as the failure to diversify investment portfolios or to annuitize an accumulated balance on retirement.

Given most workers' lack of financial sophistication, the historic shift toward DC plans creates serious risks. Not the least is the shift of financial risk bearing from employers to workers. The booming stock market of the 1980s and 1990s obscured these risks, but recent stock price declines and financial collapses have dramatically revealed them. The Enron controversy also highlighted the practice at many large firms of encouraging employees to hold much of their pension assets in stock of the same company that employs them. Workers invested almost 20 percent of 401(k) assets in their own employers' stock in 2000.[37] This failure to diversify is unwise because if the company fails, the workers lose not only their jobs, but also much of their savings. Even if the firm does not fail, the worker will have taken on excessive risk by concentrating so much wealth in one asset. Precisely because many of these concentrated holdings are due to the decisions of workers rather than the plan sponsors, the misallocation of assets raises concerns about the soundness of worker-determined investment allocations.

In DB plans, companies rather than workers bear the direct financial risks. The drop in stock prices and in interest rates during 2001 and 2002 caused DB pension funds among S&P 500 companies to become underfunded at the end of 2002 for the first time since 1993. The shortfall exceeded $200 billion.[38] The share of U.S. plans with assets below a common measure of their liabilities rose from 18 percent in 1999 to 31 percent in 2001 and to 62 percent in early 2002.[39] These changes have dramatically increased companies' minimum funding requirements for their defined benefit plans.[40] Some analysts suggest that the increase in funding requirements—whether from a drop in equity prices or as a result of falling interest rates—together with increased annual contribution rates required as work forces age could prove to be the death knell for DB plans.[41]

Although employers bear the direct risk of fluctuating investment returns in DB plans, they can shift some risk to workers by freezing the current plan and replacing it with another plan, possibly a cash balance plan. To be clear, firms may not renege on accrued benefits. But the rate of accrual under DB plans increases with age and job tenure, while the contribution rate under DC or cash balance plans benefits is determined by the employer. This difference means that shifting from a traditional DB plan to a cash balance plan normally reduces future benefit accrual for many workers. Without special transitional provisions, therefore, workers in their fifties and to some extent those in their forties may be penalized by a switch to a cash balance plan.[42]

The financial difficulties companies with DB plans faced starting in 2002 and the drop in asset prices for workers with DC plans underscore the investment risk inherent in a pension plan, which, by its very nature, entails commitments that span many decades. Someone has to bear those risks. Because corporations have unlimited lives and can pool risks over time more easily and cheaply than most individuals, having individual workers bear these risks may be more costly than having firms bear them.[43] The question for public policy is how much of these risks should be borne by companies through defined benefit plans, by individual workers through defined contribution plans, or by society.

The uncertainty of future wage growth and job tenure is another source of pension risk for workers under defined benefit plans. Under the typical DB formula, benefits accrue slowly when workers are young and more rapidly at the end of their careers. The benefit from working at one job for forty years is typically much greater than the combined benefits from working at four jobs for ten years each. For this reason, losing or changing jobs lowers pension benefits under traditional DB plans more than under DC or cash balance plans.

Retirees face other pension risks. DC plans typically provide a lump sum at retirement. This practice is increasing among DB plans, but it is still less common than in DC plans. Retirees who do not use the lump sum to buy an annuity risk outliving their retirement savings. Few retirees buy annuities, however, for at least five reasons. First, annuities are expensive. Because those who buy annuities tend to live longer than average, insurance companies can avoid losses only by pricing annuities 10–15 percent higher than would be necessary if every customer had average life expectancy. Second, private insurers typically do not offer inflation-adjusted annuities. Instead, the purchasing power of annuities, which are normally fixed in nominal terms, falls as prices rise. Third, some workers appear not to understand the insurance aspect of an annuity, and others may place an unduly high value on lump sums relative to a flow of income over time. Fourth, some workers may want to use their accumulated retirement funds to leave bequests for their children. Finally, workers already are partially annuitized through Social Security and Medicare and may prefer to keep some of their existing assets in liquid form. The reluctance to purchase annuities in the private market, combined with the ongoing relative shift away from DB plans and toward DC plans, raises important issues about how well retirees will insure themselves against poverty in very old age.[44]

Retirement

Employers have frequently structured DB plans to encourage early retirement by making the lifetime, present value of pension payments decline if workers delay retirement after a specified age. In 1993–94, almost 75 percent of private-sector workers in medium- and large-scale enterprises with defined benefit plans could claim benefits as early as age fifty-five. The monthly benefit is typically smaller if benefits are claimed before a standard retirement age, often age sixty-five, but the present value of *lifetime* benefits is often higher the sooner benefits are claimed, because the reduction in each payment is more than offset by the longer period of payment. Several studies have suggested that such provisions cause earlier retirement than would otherwise be the case.[45]

DC plans contain no such incentive for early retirement. Some evidence suggests that the shift from DB to DC plans has delayed retirement by one to two years.[46] The shift to cash balance plans should also reduce the incentive for early retirement, as cash balance plans are also neutral regarding the timing of retirement. Companies that convert traditional DB plans to cash balance plans have often removed early retirement subsidies at the same time.[47]

Complexity

Pension rules are notoriously complex. Needless complexity increases the costs that employers face in sponsoring pensions and hampers workers' understanding of plan provisions, reducing coverage and participation rates. The source of much of this complexity is the multiplicity of conflicting pension objectives. There is an inherent tension between encouraging people to save adequately, which suggests that their choices would otherwise be less than ideal, and giving workers choices regarding their pensions, which is a more successful strategy if workers do make optimal choices. Policy makers seek to ensure that the tax breaks that encourage pensions are used equitably across income and demographic groups and do not create tax shelters that erode the tax system. A government agency, the Pension Benefit Guaranty Corporation, insures DB pensions, so the government also has an interest in keeping plans actuarially sound and prudently invested. Since the programs are voluntary, policymakers need to keep the rules as simple as possible.

Because the goal of pensions is adequate retirement saving, rather than unlimited all-purpose saving, DC plans have maximum contribution limits and DB plans have maximum benefit levels to hold down the revenue costs. To focus the subsidy on retirement saving, rather than bequests, participants face minimum distribution rules in retirement. Companies that offer DB plans are subject to both minimum funding requirements—to ensure that the plans are adequately financed—and maximum contribution limits—to ensure that companies do not pile up deductible contributions in years when tax rates are high.[48] Employers face complicated nondiscrimination rules intended to ensure that low-income workers receive a fair share of the tax benefits.[49]

These well-intentioned provisions collectively conflict with the need to keep pensions simple. Congress has sought to ameliorate excessive complexity in recent years by providing "safe harbors" and other exceptions from the complicated rules that apply to pensions in general.[50] The provisions relieve the administrative burden for some and substitute "rough justice" for finely tuned equity. Unfortunately, they also stir more letters into the alphabet soup of the pension system.

Reform Options

It is easy to say that pension reform should increase individual and national saving, improve the allocation of risk, rationalize retirement incentives, and promote simplicity. Achieving those goals is difficult, however. Because pensions serve conflicting objectives, changes often involve trade-offs among alternative, desirable goals. Measures to increase saving by lower- and middle-income households, for example, are likely to increase complexity. Because the pension system is voluntary, onerous administrative burdens may cause employers to drop pension plans altogether. Finally, regardless of whether the employer or the employee makes the contributions to a pension, workers ultimately bear the burden of pension contributions. Increased pension saving thus corresponds to a reduction in current take-home pay, and that inevitable cost can undermine efforts to improve the pension system.

The Economic Growth and Tax Relief Reconciliation Act of 2001 (EGTRRA) included a series of important changes to the pension and IRA laws. Among other things, the act raised the limits on contributions to IRAs and 401(k) plans, increased the maximum benefit payable under defined benefit plans, and increased the maximum amount of compensation that could be considered in determining pension benefits. The act also created a new Roth 401(k), modeled after the Roth IRA. Under a Roth 401(k), contributions would be made on an after-tax basis, would accumulate tax free, and could be withdrawn without tax. With few exceptions, the changes do not score highly when ranked against the goals described above. The provisions are disproportionately aimed at higher earners and are therefore unlikely to boost the adequacy of retirement income or to increase national saving. The legislation also allows defined benefit plans to provide even larger subsidies for early retirement than under previous law. The impact on simplicity is mixed. One bright spot is that EGTRRA also created a "saver's credit" that provides saving incentives for households with moderate income, as is discussed further below.

Over the past several years, pension experts have proposed various basic structural reforms of the pension system. We describe two.

The Groom/Shoven Plan

Theodore Groom of the Groom Law Group and John Shoven of Stanford University propose to eliminate the detailed requirements and limits on contributions applying to qualified pension plans.[51] They would raise the limits on tax-deductible contributions by employers to both DB and DC pensions.[52] Under current law, contributions and benefits under a qualified plan can be based on compensation only up to $200,000. Groom and Shoven would eliminate this cap, allowing much higher current contributions and benefits for those earning more than $200,000.[53] They would also replace current rules that prevent employers from giving disproportionate benefits to highly compensated employees with a simple requirement that each feature of a plan be effectively available to all workers, though not all workers would have to use them. They would also remove the minimum distribution requirements that retirees withdraw specified proportions of accumulated pension balances starting at a specific age.

The Groom-Shoven plan scores well on simplification. By increasing potential contributions and removing the minimum distribution rules, it would move the tax system substantially toward a consumption tax and would likely increase pension contributions among high-income households. However, the plan would have little effect on private saving because higher-income households could simply shift assets from currently taxable accounts into the expanded tax-preferred accounts, which does not increase private saving. The asset shifts, moreover, would reduce government revenue, which would increase government borrowing, a drain on national saving. Furthermore, by loosening the nondiscrimination rules, the proposal could reduce participation among lower- and middle-income households.

In short, the Groom-Shoven proposal would exacerbate the fundamental problems with the current pension system: that it provides expensive and substantial benefits to households that do not need them and do not use them to increase their own saving, and it affords small incentives and small benefits to households that can and do use pensions to increase their own retirement income to adequate levels and to increase national saving.

The Halperin/Munnell Plan

Daniel Halperin of Harvard Law School and Alicia Munnell of Boston College would also expand tax incentives for higher earners, but only as part of a comprehensive plan meant to increase the participation and benefits for rank-and-file employees at companies that offer pension plans.[54] Halperin and Munnell note that pension income is now taxed less heavily than are other forms of saving and that higher earners already receive the bulk of these tax advantages. They also note that increased pension coverage and participation is needed most for lower- and middle-income households, but that traditional pension incentives are least effective in that income range.

To remedy this situation, Halperin and Munnell propose a progressive, government-sponsored, matched savings program aimed at lower-income workers who face low or zero marginal income tax rates and therefore receive little if any benefit from the current tax-preferred status of pensions.

Because Social Security and the new accounts would provide sufficient retirement income for most lower-income workers, Halperin and Munnell would exclude workers earning less than $20,000 a year from employer-sponsored pension plans and the nondiscrimination rules. For other workers, this proposal would substantially tighten nondiscrimination rules by requiring each company to provide uniform coverage and benefits to all full-time employees; current rules allow employers to exclude a significant share of full-time rank-and-file workers.[55] The plan would require sponsors of 401(k) plans to make substantial contributions for all participants.

Halperin and Munnell would also eliminate so-called "integration" provisions, under which companies link private pensions to Social Security benefits so that company plans replace a smaller fraction of low earnings than of high earnings (Social Security benefits do the opposite). They would also encourage certain types of defined benefit plans, including cash balance plans, and provide incentives for annuitization. Finally, they would finance these changes with a 5 percent tax on the investment earnings of pension plans.[56]

Many features of the Halperin-Munnell proposal would increase national saving. By raising coverage of and participation by lower- and middle-income households, it would concentrate incentives to save on those least likely to shift assets from taxable to tax-sheltered accounts and to those most in need of increased retirement wealth accumulation. The plan would also promote a shift from traditional DB to cash balance plans, which would improve retirement incentives. But it would complicate, rather than simplify, the pension system, as new rules would be required for the government-sponsored savings accounts, and it would allow companies to exclude workers earning less than $20,000 a year. Furthermore, its proposed tax on the investment earnings of pension plans is not politically viable at the current time. In the absence of that tax, the plan would reduce government revenue, and its effects on national saving would therefore be less clear.

Incremental Reforms

In the absence of sweeping reforms, certain incremental changes could move the pension system in the right direction. The reforms listed here deal primarily with improving defined contribution plans and cash balance plans.

CREATE PROGRESSIVE SAVING CREDITS. Current tax incentives for saving are weak or absent for low- and moderate-income workers whose income is taxed either at a low rate or not at all. A direct government subsidy that supplements saving at a rate higher for low-income than for high-income savers could encourage saving by people who now save little for retirement. EGTRRA created a "saver's credit" of up to 50 percent of up to $2,000 in contributions to IRAs and 401(k) plans made by married couples earning less than $30,000 and single filers earning less than $15,000. The credit phases out for filers with higher incomes. Unfortunately, the saver's credit is likely to be of limited value because it is not refundable and therefore provides no saving incentive to families with no income-tax liability after other deductions and credits.[57] Furthermore, the credit phases out at modest incomes. For example, a married couple with combined earnings of $45,000 a year receives only a $200 tax credit for depositing $2,000 into a retirement account. Finally, the credit is scheduled to terminate in 2006. To have much effect on saving, the incentives should be refundable, permanent, and available to filers with modestly higher incomes.[58]

CHANGE THE DEFAULT CHOICES IN 401(K) PLANS. A seemingly minor change in rules governing 401(k) plans could massively increase savings. Richard Thaler of the University of Chicago and Shlomo Benartzi of UCLA have suggested that people will save more if they are asked to commit a portion of future pay raises to saving than if asked to cut current spendable income to save more immediately. To implement this insight, they persuaded a mid-sized manufacturing company in 1998 to adopt a plan, "Save More Tomorrow" (SMT), under which employees commit to allocate a part of future pay raises to saving. The contribution rate is automatically increased with each pay raise until it reaches a preset maximum (such as the legally allowable maximum). Employees may withdraw from the plan at any time. The first implementation of the SMT plan caused contribution rates to more than triple, from 3.5 percent to 11.6 percent, over the course of twenty-eight months.[59]

EXPAND FINANCIAL EDUCATION. Measures to improve financial education and investment advice provided to workers are overdue. The Employee Retirement Income Security Act (ERISA) requires employers to ensure that workers have "sufficient information to make informed decisions" about pensions, but prohibits plan sponsors from providing specific investment advice to participants. Unfortunately, the general financial education allowed under ERISA is too abstract to be of much use for many workers. We believe that a measure, considered by the Senate after the Enron debacle, to allow third-party financial advisors to provide such advice, merits early adoption.[60]

DIVERSIFY. Employee decisions were largely responsible for the excessive concentration of pension investments in shares of their own employers, although the problem arose in part because of restrictions imposed by employers on sales of shares. ERISA limits employer stock to no more than 10 percent of assets of DB plans, but exempts DC plans from these rules. In fact, many companies use company stock as their employer match in the

401(k) plan, and some then restrict sales of such stock by the employee.[61] Congress in 2002 considered a bill that would have forced employers to let workers sell employer stock after three years (by which point the law generally requires that the employee be vested with the matched funds).[62] In addition to this provision, workers should at least have the option to diversify their portfolios after they have vested. A stronger measure—to prohibit employer shares as the default option for matching funds—merits serious consideration, although it would be strongly opposed by employers. Under this option, employers would not be allowed to use their own shares to provide matching funds, although, of course, workers would be free to buy company stock with their own contributions.[63]

SIMPLIFY PENSION RULES. Two of the most complicated areas of the pension tax code are the minimum distribution rules and the nondiscrimination rules. The minimum distribution rules require that workers begin to draw down their accumulated pensions by age seventy and a half, or when they retire, whichever is later.[64] These rules are intended to ensure that the tax incentives provided for pensions and IRA contributions are actually used to finance retirement rather than to accumulate estates.

Progress has recently been made in simplifying the minimum distribution rules.[65] Some have argued that policymakers should either eliminate (as in Groom-Shoven) or drastically loosen (as in a bill reported out of the House Committee on Ways and Means in 2002) the minimum distribution rules. A better alternative—to exempt a modest amount per individual, say $25,000 or $50,000, from the rules—would allow most retirees to avoid the rules altogether without creating an overwhelming incentive to use retirement tax incentives primarily as an estate-building mechanism, since the exemption would be relatively modest compared with the estate desired by many high-income individuals.

The nondiscrimination rules are intended to ensure that the generous tax incentives granted to qualified pension plans benefit low- and moderate-income workers as well as highly compensated workers. In practice, however, the rules allow significant disparities. They are also complex and costly to administer, and it is not obvious that they achieve their intended effect. As an alternative, a minimum contribution regime could reduce administrative costs while still ensuring that lower earners shared in the benefits provided to qualified plans. Under one proposal, for 401(k) plans, employers would be required to contribute a flat percentage of earnings for all employees, and workers would be permitted, but not required, to contribute up to some multiple of the employer's contribution. This rule would both simplify regulation and ensure some contribution for all earners, including those who make no voluntary contributions.[66]

EXPAND CASH BALANCE PLANS. In principle, cash balance plans offer several advantages over traditional DB plans and 401(k) plans. Unlike traditional DB plans, they do not penalize workers who switch jobs, and they do not encourage early retirement.[67] As with DC plans, changing jobs does not reduce pension accumulation, and the timing of retirement does not affect the value of lifetime benefits. Unlike 401(k) plans, however, the rate of return is guaranteed in the short term, and direct financial market risk falls on the company—and on the Pension Benefits Guaranty Corporation, if the pension plan becomes insolvent. Because workers have less access before retirement to accumulations in cash balance plans than to those in 401(k) plans, funds are more likely to be available to support retirement consumption. Furthermore, participation rates are usually higher in cash balance plans than in 401(k) plans because enrollment is automatic in the former and voluntary in the latter. For all of these reasons, cash balance plans seem particularly attractive based on several of our principles.

A number of practical problems have arisen with regard to cash balance plans, however.[68] Not only have some companies used cash balance plans to reduce their pension obligations, but other companies have reduced or even suspended accruals, sometimes for extended periods.[69] Some employers have provided workers with inadequate explanations of what shifts to cash balance plans mean.[70] Finally, cash balance plans are not typically indexed to inflation, potentially exposing participants to significant inflation risk.

Legislated disclosure rules and restrictions on transitional changes could reduce current worker suspicion about employers' motives in shifting to cash balance plans. These rules should limit the period after the switchover when workers do not accrue additional pensions. These no-accrual periods frequently arise because cash balance plans do not have subsidies for early retirement. Elimination of such subsidies is actually a socially attractive feature of cash balance plans, as pensions should not subsidize early retirement, but their withdrawal is unpopular with directly affected workers.[71]

MINIMIZE UNNECESSARY LEAKAGE FROM LUMP-SUM DISTRIBUTIONS. Reducing the withdrawal of assets from pension funds before retirement could boost both national saving and retirement security. Currently, unless a departing worker affirmatively asks for a cash distribution, pension rules require that companies roll over accounts of more than $1,000 but less than $5,000 into an IRA established by the company on behalf of the worker. In addition, the employee may direct that the account balance be rolled over to another employer plan or to a specified IRA.[72] This provision encourages rollovers and could help broaden pension coverage if businesses establish IRAs for the millions of workers who change jobs. An increase in the withholding and penalty taxes applied to distributions from pension plans would encourage rollovers. These desirable effects should be balanced against the legitimate reasons some workers have to withdraw funds before retirement.

Conclusion

As the baby boomers near retirement, the nation's pension system is wobbling. It covers only half the work force at any point in time. It is complex. Its impact on national saving and the adequacy of retirement saving are suspect, despite the substantial costs it imposes on the federal treasury. Even those who end up with a pension frequently receive meager benefits. The rules provide significant tax incentives to households who would save sufficiently for retirement even in the absence of such incentives. The shift of the pension system from DB plans to DC plans has provided workers with more choice and flexibility. But it has also exposed individual workers, who often lack the financial education necessary to make informed decisions, to more pension risks.

Recent policy shifts have exacerbated these shortcomings. A change of course is necessary to enlarge the number of workers who reach retirement with sufficient assets to sustain the living standards to which they have become accustomed. Major reforms may be desirable, but they require a measure of political consensus that is as scarce in pension policy as it is elsewhere in American political life. Incremental reforms—from improving the default options under 401(k) plans to encouraging the responsible growth of cash balance plans, encouraging diversification and financial education, and expanding the low-income saver's credit—would be important steps in the right direction.

Notes

1. Dan McGill, Kyle Brown, John Haley, and Sylvester J. Schieber, *Fundamentals of Private Pensions,* 7th ed. (University of Pennsylvania Press, 1996), p. 5.

2. Bureau of Labor Statistics, Labor Force Statistics from the Current Population Survey, Series ID: LFU606501 (1). Available at http://data.bls.gov/cgi-bin/srgate, accessed January 28, 2003.

3. Other programs also directly support the elderly. Medicare provides hospital insurance and the opportunity to purchase supplementary medical insurance. Supplemental Security Income and disability insurance provide benefits to poor elderly households and those with disabled individuals, respectively.

4. The tax advantage takes one of two forms. Under one approach, deposits are made from after-tax income, but investment earnings and withdrawals are not taxed. Under the alternative approach, deposits are made from before-tax income; investment earnings are untaxed when earned, but withdrawals are taxed as ordinary income. These two approaches are equivalent if the taxpayer is in the same tax bracket at all times, and if the *before*-tax amount contributed to the former approach is equal to the before-tax amount contributed to the latter approach (which means that the amount initially deposited in the account under the former approach, in which after-tax dollars are initially deposited, is smaller than the amount deposited in the account under the latter approach).

5. Department of Labor, Pension and Welfare Benefits Administration, *Private Pension Bulletin: Abstract of 1998 Form 5500 Annual Reports*, no. 11 (Winter 2001–2002), table A1; and Employee Benefit Research Institute, "Income of the Elderly, 1998," January 2000.

6. Under a personal income tax, the tax rules applicable to pensions and to other "tax-sheltered" saving involve subsidies. Under the income tax, all income, whether it is currently consumed or saved, should be taxed as earned. Against this standard, pensions are "tax favored," in the sense that tax is not imposed at the time the worker's net pension wealth increases. Many analysts, however, favor a tax on consumption rather than income. For those who favor taxation of consumption, not income, the tax treatment of pensions and other sheltered income is not a concession, but rather a step toward a superior principle of taxation. It is not our purpose here to evaluate the various positions in this debate, but merely to point out that perspectives on the current tax system intersect with the partly independent debate about how best to design pensions.

7. Note that it is possible that national saving would increase without improving retirement income adequacy if private saving increased by more than the reduction in public saving, but the private saving was undertaken only by those already well prepared for retirement.

8. Pension Benefit Guaranty Company, "Benefits." Available at www.pbgc.gov/about/BENEFITS.htm, accessed January 29, 2003.

9. Jeffrey R. Brown and Mark J. Warshawsky, "Longevity-Insured Retirement Distributions from Pension Plans: Market and Regulatory Issues," paper presented at the conference "Public Policies and Private Pensions," sponsored by the Brookings Institution, Stanford Institute for Economic Policy Research, and TIAA-CREF Institute, September 2000.

10. Eligibility for traditional IRAs among those covered by employer-provided plans is limited to married filers with adjusted gross income below $64,000 in 2002 and single filers with adjusted gross income below $44,000. There is no income limit, however, for those who are not covered by an employer-provided pension (unless the worker's spouse is covered, in which case the income limit is equal to the limit on Roth IRAs). Individuals not eligible for the traditional IRA may contribute to a nondeductible IRA, where the contributions are made from after-tax income, but assets accrue untaxed, and only the excess of

withdrawals over contributions is taxed. Eligibility for the Roth IRA, regardless of whether the worker or spouse is an active participant in an employer-based pension, is limited to married filers with incomes below $160,000 and single filers with income below $110,000. Leonard E. Burman, William G. Gale, and David Weiner, "The Taxation of Retirement Saving: Choosing between Front-Loaded and Back-Loaded Options," *National Tax Journal,* vol. 54, no. 3 (September 2001).

11. William G. Gale, Leslie E. Papke, and Jack VanDerhei, "Understanding the Shift from Defined Benefit to Defined Contribution Plans," paper presented at the conference "ERISA after 25 Years: A Framework for Evaluating Pension Reform," sponsored by the Brookings Institution, the Stanford Institute for Economic Policy Research, and the TIAA-CREF Institute, September 1999.

12. See Robert Clark and Ann McDermed, *The Choice of Pension Plans in a Changing Regulatory Environment* (American Enterprise Institute, 1990); Alan Gustman and Thomas Steinmeier, "The Stampede toward Defined-Contribution Pension Plans: Fact or Fiction," *Industrial Relations,* vol. 31, no. 2 (Spring 1992), pp. 361–69; Richard Ippolito, "Explaining the Growth of Defined-Contribution Plans," *Industrial Relations,* vol. 34 (January 1995), pp. 1–20; Richard Ippolito, "Disparate Savings Propensities and National Retirement Policy," in *Living With Defined-Contribution Plans* (University of Pennsylvania for the Pension Research Council, 1998), pp. 247–72; and Gale, Papke, and VanDerhei, "Understanding the Shift from Defined Benefit to Defined Contribution Plans."

13. Christine Williamson, "Up, Up and Away: Cash-Balance Catches Fires," *Pensions and Investments,* May 31, 1999. A survey of about 1,000 major U.S. employers found that the proportion of very large DB plans that were cash balance plans rose from 6 percent in 1995 to 16 percent in 1999. Hewitt Associates *SpecBook,* cited in Paul Yakoboski, "Overview of the Defined-Benefit System," presented at the EBRI-ERF Policy Forum, "The Next 25 Years of ERISA: The Future of Private Retirement Plans," December 1, 1999.

14. One of the potential motivations for adopting a cash balance plan instead of a 401(k) plan involves the reversion tax that applies to terminations of defined benefit plans. If a plan sponsor terminates a defined benefit plan, it must decide what to do with the excess assets—the plan's current assets less its measured future liabilities. If the firm tries to bring these assets back into the corporation, the assets are subject to a 50 percent reversion tax. If the firm transfers the assets to a defined contribution plan, the assets are still taxed (albeit at a lower rate). A firm may therefore find it prohibitively expensive from a tax perspective to terminate a defined benefit plan and replace it with a defined contribution plan. Instead, the firm can avoid the tax altogether if it converts the defined benefit plan to a cash balance plan. Since the cash balance plan is technically classified as a defined benefit plan under law, the switch can be designed to avoid "terminating" the previous defined benefit plan and thereby triggering the reversion tax. Richard Ippolito and John Thompson, "The Survival Rate of Defined Benefit Plans: 1987–1995," *Industrial Relations* 39 (April 2000), pp. 228–45.

15. Budget of the U.S. Government, Fiscal Year 2004, Analytical Perspectives, table 6-4, p. 112.

16. Note also that the worker who is covered by a private pension but chooses not to participate still obtains a benefit from the pension plan; specifically, he or she obtains the option to participate. The extent to which this option is considered a benefit implies that coverage, even without participation, provides some value.

17. If the adjustment occurs at the level of the firm or a broad group of workers within the firm, pensions with less than 100 percent participation redistribute compensation from nonparticipants to participants. Under this assumption, a firm offers a pension to a group of workers and reduces the group's aggregate wages accordingly. Group members who do not participate are then actually made worse off by the pension (at least without putting a value on the option to participate): their wages are lower than they would otherwise be, but they do not receive the benefits of pensions. Workers who do participate (or who participate more extensively, by contributing a higher share of their salary) are made better off because they experience a wage reduction that is smaller than the pension benefits they receive.

18. The coverage figures apply to individual workers at a given point in time. Coverage rates are somewhat higher over a lifetime and on a household rather than individual worker basis. For example, roughly two-thirds of households are covered by a pension at some point during their careers. According to data from the Health and Retirement Survey, which provides information on the income and wealth holdings of people born between 1931 and 1941 and therefore currently in their peak retirement years, 65.6 percent of households had positive pension wealth. See Alan Gustman and others, "Pension and Social Security Wealth in the Health and Retirement Study," in James P. Smith and Robert J. Willis, eds., *Wealth, Work, and Health: Innovations in Measurement in the Social Sciences* (University of Michigan Press, 2000).

19. These figures include both part-time and full-time workers. See Department of Labor, Pension and Welfare Benefits Administration, "Coverage Status of Workers under Employer Provided Plans," 2000. Available at www.dol.gov/pwba/programs/opr/CWS-Survey/hilites.html.

20. General Accounting Office, "Private Pensions: Implications of Conversions to Cash Balance Plans," GAO/HEHS-00-185 (September 2000).

21. Peter Orszag and Robert Greenstein, "Toward Progressive Pensions: A Summary of the U.S. Pension System and Proposals for Reform," presented at the conference "Inclusion in Asset Building: Research and Policy Symposium," Washington University, St. Louis, September 21–23, 2000. Several factors explain the absence of pension plans in many firms, especially small businesses. For example, surveys of small businesses suggest that administrative costs and the complexity of the pension tax code are important factors—but perhaps not the most important factors—in discouraging them from offering pension plans. The surveys suggest that somewhat more important explanations include the preference of workers for other forms of compensation or the uncertainty of the firm's future prospects.

22. Department of Labor, Social Security Administration, Small Business Administration, and Pension Benefit Guaranty Corporation, *Pension and Health Benefits of American Workers* (1994), table C7. The participation figures apply only to whether a worker makes a contribution to a 401(k), not to the relative *size* of that contribution. General Accounting Office, "401(k) Pension Plans: Many Take Advantage of Opportunities to Ensure Adequate Retirement Income," GAO/HEHS-96-176, 1996, table II.4.

23. Paul Smith, "Complexity in Retirement Savings Policy," *National Tax Journal,* vol. 55, no. 3 (September 2002), pp. 530–54.

24. Jeanne M. Hogarth and Chris E. Anguelov, "Can the Poor Save?" *Proceedings of Association for Financial Counseling and Planning Education* (2001).

25. Michael Sherraden, "Asset Building Policy and Programs for the Poor," in Thomas

Shapiro and Edward Wolff, eds., *Assets for the Poor: The Benefits of Spreading Asset Ownership* (New York: Russell Sage Foundation, 2001).

26. For moderate-income workers, the rules for taxation of future Social Security benefits may reduce the tax advantage associated with 401(k) contributions. A portion of Social Security benefits is subject to income tax, but only if income exceeds certain thresholds. Jagadeesh Gokhale, Lawrence Kotlikoff, and Todd Neuman, "Does Participating in a 401(k) Raise Your Lifetime Taxes?" NBER Working Paper 8341 (June 2001). The authors argue that the net tax effect from contributing to the 401(k) may actually be positive (that is, contributions raise lifetime taxes) because the tax benefit from the 401(k) is outweighed by the cost from the increased taxation of Social Security benefits. Their examples, however, assume that workers make the maximum allowable contribution to a 401(k) and that Social Security benefits are claimed at age sixty-five. The vast majority of workers, however, do not contribute the maximum amount to a 401(k) and also claim benefits before age sixty-five; relaxing those assumptions makes it much less likely that the net effect of contributing to a 401(k) is to raise lifetime taxes.

27. Employee Benefit Research Institute, 2002 Retirement Confidence Survey, Summary of Findings; available at www.ebri.org/rcs/2002/index.htm.

28. B. Douglas Bernheim, Daniel M. Garrett, and Dean M. Maki, "Education and Saving: The Long-term Effects of High School Financial Curriculum Mandates," NBER Working Paper 6085 (July 1997); B. Douglas Bernheim and Daniel Garrett, "The Determinants and Consequences of Financial Education in the Workplace: Evidence from a Survey of Households," NBER Working Paper 5667 (1996); Patrick J. Bayer, B. Douglas Bernheim, and John Karl Scholz, "The Effects of Financial Education in the Workplace: Evidence from a Survey of Employers," NBER Working Paper 5655 (July 1996); Annamaria Lusardi, "Explaining Why So Many People Do Not Save," Center for Retirement Research Working Paper 2001-05, Boston College (September 2001).

29. Brigitte C. Madrian and Dennis F. Shea, "The Power of Suggestion: Inertia in 401(k) Participation and Savings Behavior," NBER Working Paper 7682 (May 2000). Madrian and Shea studied 401(k) participation rates among employees in a large corporation before and after a change in the default option. Before the change, workers had to elect to participate in the 401(k); after the change, they were automatically enrolled unless they explicitly requested to opt out. The authors found that 401(k) participation increased dramatically after the change. Since none of the other features of the plan changed, the purely rational model of economic behavior has difficulty explaining the results.

30. General Accounting Office, "401(k) Pension Plans: Many Take Advantage of Opportunities to Ensure Adequate Retirement Income," GAO/HEHS-96-176, 1996, table II.4.

31. Eric M. Engen, William G. Gale, and Cori E. Uccello, "The Adequacy of Household Saving," *Brookings Papers on Economic Activity, 2:1999*, pp. 65–165. The authors emphasize that levels of savings adequacy are actually higher than most studies suggest because the studies ignore uncertainty and suffer from other biases. An important issue involves home equity, which represents the most significant asset for the vast majority of families. According to the Census Bureau, the home ownership rate among those sixty-five years and older was 80 percent in 2000, relative to 41 percent among those under thirty-five and an overall rate of 67 percent. Some elderly families may be willing to move out of

their home, or reduce their equity in their home, in order to finance consumption during retirement, and that could significantly affect savings adequacy levels. But Venti and Wise argue that housing wealth is typically not used to support nonhousing consumption during retirement. See Steven F. Venti and David A. Wise, "Aging and Housing Equity," in Olivia S. Mitchell and others, eds., *Innovations in Managing the Financial Risks of Retirement* (University of Pennsylvania Press, 2002).

32. William G. Gale, "The Effects of Pensions on Household Wealth: A Reevaluation of Theory and Evidence," *Journal of Political Economy,* vol. 106, no. 4 (August), pp. 70–23; Orazio Attanasio and Susann Rohwedder, "Pension Wealth and Household Saving: Evidence from Pension Reforms in the UK," The Institute for Fiscal Studies Working Paper W01/21, September 2001.

33. A recent study that controls for biases in previous work shows that contributions from households with income below $40,000 tend to represent net additions to saving, whereas contributions from households with higher income tend to represent substitution of other saving, existing assets, or debt for increased tax-preferred 401(k) balances. In recent years, however, households with income below $40,000 held between 10 and 20 percent of 401(k) assets, suggesting that only a small share of 401(k) contributions to date has represented new saving. Eric M Engen and William G. Gale, "The Effects of 401(k) Plans on Household Wealth: Differences across Earnings Groups," Brookings, August 2000. Other studies that find small effects of 401(k)s on wealth accumulation include Eric M. Engen, John Karl Scholz, and William G. Gale, "Do Saving Incentives Work?" *Brookings Papers on Economic Activity, 1:1994,* pp. 85–151; Eric M. Engen, William G. Gale, and John Karl Scholz, "The Illusory Effect of Saving Incentives on Saving," *Journal of Economic Perspectives,* vol. 10, no. 4 (1996), pp. 113–38; Daniel Benjamin, "Does 401(k) Eligibility Increase Saving? Evidence from Propensity Score Subclassification," mimeo, London School of Economics, 2001; Gary V. Engelhardt, "Have 401(k)s Raised Household Saving? Evidence from the Health and Retirement Survey," Aging Studies Program Paper 24, Center for Policy Research, Maxwell School of Citizenship and Public Affairs, Syracuse University, June 2001; and Karen M. Pence, "401(k)s and Household Saving: New Evidence from the Survey of Consumer Finances," Federal Reserve Board of Governors, December 2001. Studies that find significant effects of 401(k)s on wealth accumulation include James Poterba, Steven Venti, and David Wise, "Do 401(k) Contributions Crowd Out Other Personal Saving?" *Journal of Public Economics,* vol. 58, no. 1 (September 1995), pp. 1–32; and James Poterba, Steven Venti, and David Wise, "How Retirement Saving Programs Increase Saving," *Journal of Economic Perspectives,* vol. 10, no. 4 (1996), pp. 91–112.

34. Tax subsidies for pensions result in lower revenues at the time the contribution is made and higher revenues when the funds are cashed in and income taxes are paid. Because of the value of deferral and the shift of funds to lower tax rates, congressional committees and the Department of the Treasury consider the effect on revenue to be negative. Some have argued that under certain circumstances the net revenue effect is positive. See Brianna Dusseault and Jonathan Skinner, "Did Individual Retirement Accounts Actually *Raise* Revenue?" *Tax Notes,* February 7, 2000, pp. 851–56; and Martin Feldstein, "The Effects of Tax-Based Saving Incentives on Government Revenue and National Saving," *Quarterly Journal of Economics,* vol. 110, no. 2 (May 1995), pp. 475–94.

35. Arthur Levitt, "The SEC Perspective on Investing Social Security in the Stock Market," John F. Kennedy School of Government, October 19, 1998.

36. B. Douglas Bernheim, "Financial Illiteracy, Education, and Retirement Saving," in Olivia Mitchell and Sylvester Schieber, eds., *Living with Defined-Contribution Pensions* (University of Pennsylvania Press, 1998), p. 42.

37. Sarah Holden and Jack VanDerhei, "401(k) Plan Asset Allocation, Account Balances, and Loan Activity in 2000," Investment Company Institute *Perspective*, vol. 71, no. 5 (November 2001). The 20 percent share results primarily from heavy concentrations of employer stock at large firms. Alicia H. Munnell and Annika Sundén, "401(K)s and Company Stock: How Can We Encourage Diversification?" Center for Retirement Research at Boston College, Issue in Brief 9, July 2002.

38. David Zion and Bill Carcache, "The Magic of Pension Accounting," Credit Suisse First Boston, September 27, 2002, p. 13.

39. The measure of liabilities is the so-called current liability, which represents an estimate of the benefits that would be paid from the plan if it were immediately terminated. The figures in the text are based on a survey conducted by Watson Wyatt Worldwide, and they do not reflect the effects of the Job Creation and Worker Assistance Act. See Watson Wyatt, "Pension Plans and Interest Rates: Short-term Relief, Long-Term Uncertainty," available at www.watsonwyatt.com/us/news/featured/usmarkets.asp. The Job Creation and Worker Assistance Act of 2002 temporarily raised the interest rate that firms could use to compute their pension liabilities; the increase in the allowable interest rate reduces the plan's liabilities for this purpose, but does not change the underlying reality. For a discussion of why this change was unwarranted, see Peter Orszag and David Gunter, "Note On Proposed Change in Assumed Interest Rate for Defined-benefit Pension Plans," Brookings, February 2002.

40. For further discussion of potential future problems in funding defined benefit plans, see Sylvester Schieber and John Shoven, "The Consequences of Population Aging," in Sylvester Schieber and John Shoven, eds., *Public Policy toward Pensions* (New York: Twentieth Century Fund, 1997).

41. Sylvester Schieber, "The Employee Retirement Income Security Act: Motivations, Provisions, and Implications for Retirement Security," paper prepared for the conference "ERISA after 25 Years: A Framework for Evaluating Pension Reform," September 1999.

42. A related controversy has arisen because some firms have converted their traditional defined benefit pension plan to a cash balance plan in a manner that creates "wear-aways," which have been the subject of much criticism by unions and other employee groups. Under a wear-away, the pension benefit provided by the new plan is initially lower than the accrued benefit provided under the old plan, so that a worker's total accrued pension benefit does not increase as he or she continues working. The accrued benefit under the old plan, which is higher than the cash balance value during the wear-away period, is legally protected. Therefore, if the worker left the firm during the wear-away period, he or she would be entitled to a higher pension than the cash balance account would suggest.

43. Because we are focusing on private pensions, we do not explore the more difficult question of whether the government is better able to handle these risks through social insurance than are individual workers or their employers.

44. Lump-sum payouts from 401(k) plans may become even more common in the future because the IRS has recently changed the relevant regulations to allow lump sums as the sole withdrawal option in a 401(k) plan. On the high cost of annuities, see Olivia Mitchell, James Poterba, and Mark Warshawsky, "New Evidence on the Money's Worth of Individual Annuities," *American Economic Review,* vol. 89, no. 5 (December 1999); and Mamta Murthi, J. Michael Orszag, and Peter Orszag, "The Value for Money of Annuities in the UK: Theory, Experience, and Policy," in Robert Holzmann and Joseph E Stiglitz, eds., *New Ideas about Old Age Security* (World Bank, 2001). Many insurers now offer so-called variable annuities, which are backed by common stocks, real estate, or other assets that can increase in value as the economy grows. Such annuities also carry a significant risk of falling in value, possibly sharply, if the value of underlying assets declines. For this reason, they are unsuitable investments for people who must depend on the annuity income to support their basic living standard. For a discussion of preferences for lump-sum payments, see Richard H. Thaler, "Some Empirical Evidence on Dynamic Inconsistency," as reprinted in Richard H. Thaler, *Quasi-Rational Economics* (New York: Russell Sage Foundation, 1994); and David Fetherstonhaugh and Lee Ross, "Framing Effects and Income Flow Preferences," in Henry J. Aaron, ed., *Behavioral Dimensions of Retirement Economics* (Brookings, 1999), p. 203. The relative shift toward defined contribution plans also raises questions about gender equity: under defined benefit plans, which are governed by the antidiscrimination standards in federal labor law, the annuities provided to a male and a female with the same earnings history are equal despite the longer life expectancies (on average) for females. The annuities that can be purchased with the proceeds from a 401(k), however, are governed by state insurance laws, which generally allow different annuity prices for males and females. Sheila Campbell and Alicia H. Munnell, "Sex and 401(k) Plans," Center for Retirement Research at Boston College, Just the Facts on Retirement Issues, no. 4, May 2002. In effect, the annuities provided under defined benefit plans subsidize females, on average; the movement from defined benefit plans to 401(k) plans removes this subsidy and thus, all else being equal, involves redistribution from females to males.

45. Ann C. Foster, "Early Retirement Provisions in Defined-benefit Pension Plans," *Compensation and Working Conditions,* Department of Labor, December 1996, pp. 12–17. For example, in 1993–94, the average uniform percentage reduction per year of early retirement among those plans with a uniform percentage reduction formula was 4.8 percent, which is lower than the reduction factor applied to Social Security benefits, which is roughly actuarially fair. Ibid., table 2, p. 14. Other plans include provisions such as a "30 and out" rule, under which a worker with thirty years of service can receive the full retirement annuity from the plan regardless of age. See Kyle Brown and others, "The Unfolding of a Predictable Surprise" (Watson Wyatt Worldwide, 2000), p. 2; Lawrence Kotlikoff and David Wise, "The Incentive Effects of Private Pension Plans," in Zvi Bodie, J. Shoven, and D. Wise, eds., *Issues in Pension Economics* (University of Chicago Press, 1987); Lawrence Kotlikoff and David Wise, "Employee Retirement and a Firm's Pension Plans," in David Wise, ed., *The Economics of Aging* (University of Chicago Press, 1989); and Robin Lumsdaine, James Stock, and David Wise, "Retirement Incentives: The Interaction Between Employer Provided Pensions, Social Security, and Retiree Health Benefits," NBER Working Paper 4613 (1994).

46. Leora Friedberg and Anthony Webb, "The Impact of 401(k) Plans on Retirement," University of California at San Diego Economics Discussion Paper 2000-30, November 2000.

47. Robert L. Clark and Sylvester J. Schieber, "Taking the Subsidy out of Early Retirement: The Story behind the Conversion to Hybrid Pensions," in Olivia S. Mitchell and others, eds., *Innovations in Managing the Financial Risks of Retirement* (University of Pennsylvania Press, 2002).

48. The rules regarding how DB plans may calculate pension liabilities are also split between trying to ensure adequate funding—which generally militates toward more contributions sooner—and limiting tax avoidance—which generally suggests contributions be limited and come later in the worker's career.

49. For example, the "permitted disparity" rules allow integration of the employer's pension plan with Social Security. By integrating the plan with Social Security, the firm is allowed to provide higher contributions to high-income workers without triggering the nondiscrimination rules that normally apply. (In effect, the pension component of the integrated plan discriminates in favor of high earners, but that regressivity is considered to be compensated by the progressivity of the Social Security system.) As another example, the "cross-testing" rules allow a defined contribution plan to be evaluated for nondiscrimination purposes as if it were a defined benefit plan. The effect is often to allow older, higher-paid executives to enjoy a larger share of overall pension contributions in the plan. See Peter Orszag and Norman Stein, "Cross-Tested Defined-Contribution Plans: A Response to Professor Zelinsky," *Buffalo Law Review*, vol. 49 (2001), pp. 628–74, for further discussion of the cross-testing rules.

50. Examples include the Simplified Employee Pension (SEP) and the Savings Incentive Match Plan for Employees (SIMPLE), as well as the safe-harbor nondiscrimination rules for 401(k)s.

51. Theodore Groom and John Shoven, "How the Pension System Should Be Reformed," paper prepared for the conference "ERISA after 25 Years: A Framework for Evaluating Pension Reform," September 1999.

52. At the time Groom and Shoven drafted their plan, EGTRRA had not yet been passed. Many of the Groom-Shoven provisions, however, would raise benefit and contribution limits even relative to the new, higher levels embodied in EGTRRA.

53. The elimination of the compensation limit would also affect the amount of funding that companies are allowed under the tax code. Currently, for the purposes of computing their funding requirements for tax purposes, companies are not allowed to take into account future indexation of the compensation limit. As a result, workers with wages well below the compensation limit may be projected to earn wages in the future that exceed the nonindexed level of the limit. Addressing this problem does not require increasing the real value of the compensation limit, however. It would be better addressed by allowing firms to project the expected indexation of the compensation limit for the purposes of computing their funding requirements.

54. Daniel I. Halperin and Alicia H. Munnell, "How the Pension System Should Be Reformed," paper prepared for the conference "ERISA after 25 Years: A Framework for Evaluating Pension Reform," September 1999.

55. For example, under current law, the allowable degree of disparity between contributions for higher-income executives and rank-and-file workers is defined by two mathematical tests: the "ratio percentage" test and the "average benefit" test. A pension plan must generally conform to one of these tests to meet the nondiscrimination rules and thereby qualify for pension tax preferences. Under the ratio percentage test, the firm calculates the

percentage of highly compensated employees (defined essentially as those earning more than $90,000) covered by the pension plan. To pass the ratio percentage test, the plan's coverage rate for *non*-highly compensated employees must be at least 70 percent as high as the percentage for the highly compensated workers. In other words, if 80 percent of the highly compensated workers are covered, at least 56 percent (70 percent of 80 percent) of rank-and-file workers also must be covered. If a plan fails the ratio percentage test, it still qualifies if it passes the average benefit test. The average benefit test requires that the plan include and exclude employees under a reasonable business classification system, that the classification be nondiscriminatory (which is determined by a much weaker version of the ratio percentage test), and that the average benefit of the rank-and-file workers (measured as a percentage of pay) be at least 70 percent of the average benefit (as a percentage of pay) of the highly compensated employees.

56. This part of the Halperin/Munnell plan resembles the universal savings account plan proposed by the Clinton administration.

57. For example, a married couple with two children who claimed the standard deduction in 2002 started owing income tax (after the child credit) at an adjusted gross income of $31,850, which is *above* the $30,000 threshold for the 50 percent credit rate. Furthermore, the income threshold is not indexed to inflation, meaning that fewer and fewer families could even potentially benefit from the nonrefundable credit.

58. The Clinton administration proposed universal savings accounts (USAs) in 1999. The USA program would have provided an automatic tax credit to taxpayers between eighteen and seventy years old who had at least $5,000 in earnings and adjusted gross income below $80,000 for married filers ($40,000 for single filers). The program would also have provided a matching, refundable tax credit for voluntary contributions to the account. The retirement savings account (RSA) proposal, put forward in 2000, would have provided a matching credit for contributions made to retirement savings accounts by workers between the ages of twenty-five and sixty with earnings of at least $5,000 and adjusted gross incomes of less than $80,000 a year for married filers ($40,000 for single filers).

59. Richard H. Thaler and Shlomo Benartzi, "Save More Tomorrow: Using Behavioral Economics to Increase Employee Saving," working paper, August 2001. Almost all workers (98 percent) continued with the plan through two pay raises; the vast majority (80 percent) remained through three pay raises. Even those who withdrew from the plan did not cut their contribution rates back to the original levels; instead, they froze their contribution rates rather than allowing future increases. One problem with expanding the SMT plan is that it is unclear whether such automatic escalations are allowed under extant regulation. Some Treasury Department officials have informally indicated that such plans are indeed allowed, but there has been no official confirmation, and there is at least some concern in the private sector about the lack of clarity.

60. The House considered an alternative that would permit the plan sponsor to provide investment advice. We believe that this alternative is inferior, as it creates a conflict of interest that is subject to abuse.

61. Munnell and Sundén, "401(K)s and Company Stock: How Can We Encourage Diversification?"

62. After the passage of EGTRRA, employer matches must vest with workers in full after three years or vest on a sliding scale between years two and six.

63. This more aggressive approach would pose difficult problems with regard to Employee Stock Ownership Plans (ESOPs), a form of retirement plan designed to concentrate holdings in company stock. For further discussion of the role of employee stock ownership plans and the views of corporations, see Olivia S. Mitchell and Stephen P. Utkas, "Company Stock and Retirement Plan Diversification," Pension Research Council Working Paper 2002-4, Wharton School, University of Pennsylvania, March 2002.

64. The rules for distributions from traditional IRAs are slightly different. Distributions from IRAs are required to begin by age seventy and a half regardless of whether the owner is retired. No minimum distribution rules apply to Roth IRAs until the death of the owner. For further discussion of the minimum distribution rules and various proposals to loosen them, see Jay A. Soled and Bruce A. Wolk, "The Minimum Distribution Rules and Their Critical Role in Controlling the Floodgates of Qualified Plan Wealth," *Brigham Young University Law Review*, no. 2 (2000), pp. 587–625; and Jeffrey R. Brown and others, "Taxing Retirement Income: Nonqualified Annuities and Distributions from Qualified Accounts," *National Tax Journal*, vol. 52, no. 3 (September 1999), pp. 563–92.

65. See United States Department of Treasury, *Internal Revenue Bulletin,* 2001-11 (March 12, 2001), p. 865.

66. For example, elective deferrals by workers could be limited to three times the employer's uniform percentage contribution for all workers. If the employer contributed 5 percent of earnings, each employee could deposit up to 15 percent of compensation, which would be subtracted from taxable income in the year of the deposit. See Orszag and Stein, "Cross-Tested Defined Contribution Plans."

67. In addition, cash balance plans redistribute pension benefits from workers with relatively steep earnings profiles to those with relatively flat earnings profiles (for any given present value of lifetime wages), compared with a traditional defined benefit plan. In particular, for any given level of lifetime wages and overall pension costs, workers with wages rising more steeply over their careers would receive a relatively larger benefit from a traditional defined benefit plan, and workers with flatter earnings profiles over their careers would receive a relatively larger benefit from a cash balance plan. The intuition is that the interest credits in a cash balance plan raise the importance of wages early in a career; the final pay aspect of a traditional defined benefit plan raises the importance of wages later in a career. The available evidence suggests that more educated workers tend to have steeper earnings profiles than less educated workers; see Barry Bosworth, Gary Burtless, and C. Eugene Steuerle, "Lifetime Earnings Patterns, the Distribution of Future Social Security Benefits, and the Impact of Pension Reform," Center for Retirement Research Working Paper 1999-06, Boston College, December 1999.

68. One controversial issue not examined in the text is whether cash balance plans violate the age discrimination rules in ERISA, the Internal Revenue Code, or the Age Discrimination in Employment Act. See Patrick J. Purcell, "Pension Issues: Cash-Balance Plans," Congressional Research Service, November 1, 2002, p. 12.

69. This problem occurs through the creation of "wear-aways," which have been the subject of much criticism by unions and other employee groups. See note 42.

70. EGTRRA included a limited disclosure provision requiring that firms disclose amendments (including conversions to cash balance plans) that reduce the rate of future accruals of benefits. The provision is less aggressive than others that had been considered at

the time; the version of the tax legislation that passed the Senate, for example, would have required firms to provide examples illustrating the effects on classes of employees and to provide a benefit estimation tool kit to workers to allow them to compute more personalized estimates of the effects. These provisions were contained in S. 896, the Restoring Earnings to Lift Individuals and Empower Families (RELIEF) Act of 2001.

71. A separate question involves the transition to the new rules, however. It may be necessary to perpetuate early retirement subsidies during a transition to the cash balance plan in order to be fair to the current workers and to improve the political viability of the cash balance approach. Clark and Schieber, "Taking the Subsidy out of Early Retirement."

72. The Treasury Department had earlier issued administrative guidance that authorized (but did not require) plans to roll over distributions of accounts up to $5,000 to an IRA established by the plan sponsor on behalf of an employee who does not express a preference regarding the disposition of the funds. See Revenue Ruling 2000-36.

JAMES M. LINDSAY
AUDREY SINGER

7

Changing Faces:
Immigrants and Diversity
in the Twenty-First Century

HERMAN MELVILLE EXAGGERATED 160 years ago when he wrote, "You cannot spill a drop of American blood without spilling the blood of the world."[1] However, the results of the 2000 Census show that his words accurately describe the United States today. Two decades of intensive immigration are rapidly remaking our racial and ethnic mix. The American mosaic—which has always been complex—is becoming even more intricate. If diversity is a blessing, America has it in abundance.

But is diversity a blessing? In many parts of the world the answer has been no. Ethnic, racial, and religious differences often produce violence—witness the disintegration of Yugoslavia, the genocide in Rwanda, the civil war in Sudan, and the "Troubles" in Northern Ireland. Against this background the United States has been a remarkable exception. This is not to say it is innocent of racism, bigotry, or unequal treatment—the slaughter of American Indians, slavery, Jim Crow segregation, and the continuing gap between whites and blacks on many socioeconomic indicators make clear otherwise. However, to a degree unparalleled anywhere else, America has knitted disparate peoples into one nation. The success of that effort is visible not just in America's tremendous prosperity, but also in the patriotism that Americans, regardless of their skin color, ancestral homeland, or place of worship, feel for their country.

America has managed to build one nation out of many people for several reasons. Incorporating newcomers from diverse origins has been part of its experience from the earliest colonial days—and is ingrained in the American culture. The fact that divisions between Congregationalists and Methodists or between people of English and Irish ancestry do not animate our politics today attests not to homogeneity but to success—often hard earned—in bridging and tolerating differences. America's embrace of "liberty and justice for all" has been the backdrop that has promoted unity. The commitment to the ideals enshrined in the Declaration of Independence gave those denied their rights a moral claim on the conscience of the majority—a claim redeemed most memorably by the civil rights movement. America's two-party system has fostered unity by encouraging ethnic and religious groups to join forces rather than build sectarian parties that would perpetuate demographic divides. Furthermore, economic mobility has created bridges across ethnic, religious, and racial lines, thereby blurring their overlap with class divisions and diminishing their power to fuel conflict.

The tremendous changes the United States is experiencing in its racial and ethnic mix—changes that promise to continue for several decades—will test these forces that knit Americans together. At a minimum, the rapid growth in the size of America's Latino and Asian communities as a result of immigration means that our national narrative on diversity will no longer be only, or perhaps even primarily, about whites and blacks. It will also increasingly be about what this chapter focuses on—immigrants and their progeny, many of whom do not fit neatly into either racial category. Diversity in the twenty-first century will still be about race, but it will involve a palette with more hues. How well America succeeds in weaving its newcomers into its social fabric will do much to determine whether the American experiment with diversity continues to be a success.

In this regard, some observers warn that our new, more complex American mosaic spells great trouble. In this telling of the newest episode in the long story of American diversity, the United States is becoming too diverse, too quickly. We are exceeding our capacity to absorb newcomers, creating new societal divisions, and destroying the ineffable ties that bind us together as Americans. If we fail to slow demographic change by curtailing or even halting immigration, say the pessimists, we risk destroying America.

Fears of fragmentation have a long lineage in American history. Substitute "Italian" and "Pole" for "Asian" and "Latino," and today's warnings would sound familiar to Americans living one hundred years ago. Of course, claims need not be novel to be right, and America's past success at incorporating newcomers does not guarantee future success. Yet fears that increasing diversity due to immigration will be America's undoing are overblown. Americans may have become more tolerant of cultural differences, but that hardly means that the forces of assimilation have evaporated. The remarkable geographic mobility of immigrants and the willingness of Americans to marry and have children across racial and ethnic lines bring people together. True, increased diversity will change who we are; immigration always has. Nevertheless, rather than witnessing the death of America, we are more likely to relearn one of the abiding lessons of American history: it is possible to build one nation out of many people.

By the same token, however, diversity should not be romanticized. Yes, it enriches and energizes society; but it also creates stresses, many of which reflect the consequences of immigration. If ignored, these stresses could be disruptive. The remedy here, however, is not to keep immigrants out. Instead, it is to worry about what happens to them once they arrive. Whether by encouraging immigrants to become citizens, facilitating their economic and social mobility by providing them with more opportunities for English-language and vocational training, or introducing them to the ways of the bureaucracy, both government and civil society can do more to help them and their offspring become full members of American society. The fiscal costs of such policies are small; their long-term benefits for national unity are substantial.

America's increasing diversity also poses challenges for affirmative action. Although affirmative action was designed to redress the legacy of discrimination against African Americans and certain other minorities, its beneficiaries increasingly are people who arrived in the United States after the civil rights revolution began. Meanwhile, the growing number of multiracial Americans increasingly complicates affirmative action's static racial and ethnic categories. Defenders of race-based affirmative action often claim that the gains in racial equality would quickly evaporate without it. Such claims, however, underestimate the degree to which the principle of nondiscrimination has become rooted in American society—to the extent that many minorities oppose racial and ethnic preferences. Conversely, substantial support exists across racial and ethnic lines for class-based affirmative action policies. That convergence points to an opening to experiment with policies that might diminish the centrality of race and ethnicity in American life while promoting the interests of all disadvantaged Americans, regardless of their skin color or ancestral homeland.

America's Changing Faces

Americans could once be neatly categorized as either white or black. Today our national portrait is increasingly enriched with Asian, Latino, and multiracial faces. Three developments are responsible: large-scale immigration from Asia and Latin America; higher birth rates among some racial and national groups; and a growing number of interracial unions. One result of these three trends is that ethnicity, national origin, and race will remain a key feature of American identity, as it has been throughout U.S. history. At the same time, however, the changing racial and ethnic mix is not being felt uniformly across the United States or across generations. Nonetheless, the change is extensive, extending even to whom and how we worship.

John and Caroline Smith Meet Juan Carlos Guzman and Zheng Tian

A precise picture of America's growing diversity is hard to draw. One problem is that almost every census for the past two hundred years has changed the way it collected racial and ethnic data. For instance, the Census Bureau did not ask a question about Hispanic background until 1980. The 2000 Census gave people for the first time the option to identify themselves as being of more than one race. Because of these methodological changes, racial and ethnic data are not strictly comparable over time. Further complicating matters, the Census Bureau asks separate questions about race and Hispanic background. So while Americans routinely talk about "whites," "blacks," and "Hispanics" (or "Latinos") as distinct groups, they are not mutually exclusive categories in census data. In particular, a person who self-identifies as "Hispanic" could be of any race. This creates classification problems. Should someone who identifies as "Black" and "Hispanic" be counted as black (which means undercounting the number of Hispanics); or as Hispanic (which means undercounting the number of blacks); or as both (which means overcounting blacks and Hispanics relative to everyone else); or be placed in a new category of "Black Hispanics" (which means undercounting both groups)?

With these methodological difficulties in mind, table 7-1 shows how America's racial and ethnic composition changed over the last three decades of the twentieth century.[2] In 1970, nearly 99 percent of U.S. residents could be characterized as either solely white or solely black. By contrast, in 2000 the percentage of the population identifying itself as either white or black had fallen to slightly less than 88 percent, even though the black share of the population actually rose a percentage point. The more than

Table 7-1. *U.S. Population by Race, Age, and Hispanic Background, 1970–2000*
Percentage[a]

Category	1970	1980	1990	2000	Difference, 1970–2000
Race					
Total					
White	87.4	83.2	80.3	75.1	−12.3
Black	11.1	11.7	12.0	12.3	1.2
Other[b]	1.4	5.2	7.6	12.5	11.1
Children[c]					
White	84.8	78.6	75.1	68.6	−16.2
Black	13.7	14.7	15.0	15.1	1.4
Other[b]	1.5	6.7	9.9	16.3	14.8
Adults[d]					
White	88.9	84.9	82.2	77.4	−11.5
Black	9.8	10.5	11.0	11.4	1.6
Other[b]	1.4	4.5	6.8	11.2	9.9
Ethnicity					
Hispanic background[e]	. . .	6.4	9.0	12.5	6.1[f]

Sources: Census of Population 1980, Characteristics of Population, vol. 1, ch. B, part 1; Census of Population and Housing, 1990: Summary Tape File 3 on CD-ROM; Census 2000 Summary File 1.

a. Rounding may affect totals.

b. For 1970, 1980, and 1990, "Other" refers to individuals who marked any race other than black or white, which included American Indian, Eskimo or Aleut, Asian and Pacific Islander, and some other race. In 2000, "Other" refers to American Indian and Alaska Native, Asian, Native Hawaiian, and some other race. In addition, the 2000 Census allowed individuals to mark more than one race; those individuals are included in the "Other" category.

c. Children defined as 0–17 years.

d. Adults defined as 18 and older.

e. Hispanic or Latino ethnicity is collected separately from race in the Census. Hispanics may be of any race; therefore race and Hispanic background are not additive.

f. Difference between 1980 and 2000.

twelve percentage point decline in the white share of the population was accompanied by a substantial rise in the share of the population that identified a race other than white or black only, such as Asian, American Indian, or multiracial. The share of this "Other" category rose from 1.4 percent in 1970 to 12.5 percent in 2000.

The growing share of the Other category reflects three growth trends. One is tremendous growth in the size of the Hispanic community. As table 7-1 shows, the percentage of U.S. residents identifying themselves as Hispanic stood at 12.5 percent in 2000, nearly double that of 1980. Although

48 percent of Hispanics identified themselves as white, 42 percent identi-fied their race as Other. The second trend is the growing number of Asians in the United States. Between 1980 and 2000, Asians more than doubled as a percentage of the total population, rising from 1.7 percent to 3.6 per-cent (counting those who identify their race as Asian alone) or 4.2 percent (counting people who say they are Asian alone or Asian and some other race). The third trend is the growing number of multiracial individuals. Some 6.8 million people, or 2.4 percent of the population, identified themselves in the 2000 Census as being of two or more races. Nearly three out of four of these multiracial individuals marked one of their races as white. The most common combination was of white and "some other race" (32.3 percent); white and American Indian and Alaska Native (15.9 per-cent); white and Asian (12.7 percent); and white and black or African American (11.5 percent).

Although the data on race and Hispanic background show that Amer-ica is becoming more diverse, in a way they also understate that diversity. As the number of Asians and Hispanics has increased, the composition of their communities has broadened as well. People of Chinese and Japanese descent historically dominated America's Asian community. Chinese remain America's largest Asian community, but the Filipino, Asian Indian, Vietnamese, and Korean communities have all exceeded the Japanese com-munity in size. As for Hispanics, established Mexican, Puerto Rican, and Cuban populations have been joined in the past three decades by substan-tial numbers of Dominicans, Guatemalans, Salvadorans, and Colombians. Although these communities are nowhere near as linguistically or culturally diverse as America's Asian population, they nonetheless represent a variety of nationalities with distinct histories and experiences. In that respect, these populations are not as unified as the labels "Asian," "Hispanic," or "Latino" suggest.[3]

What Happened?

What accounts for America's increasing racial and ethnic diversity? One driver is immigration. Between 1970 and 2000, the United States experi-enced the largest influx of immigrants since the classic era of immigration brought some 30 million newcomers to U.S. shores between 1880 and 1930. In the 1970s, 4.5 million immigrants arrived legally in the United States, more than one and a half times the total of the 1960s. The number topped 7.3 million in the 1980s and 9.1 million in the 1990s.[4] These legal immigrants were joined by millions who entered the United States illegally.

Figure 7-1. *Regional Origin of Legal Immigrants, Beginning and End of the Twentieth Century*

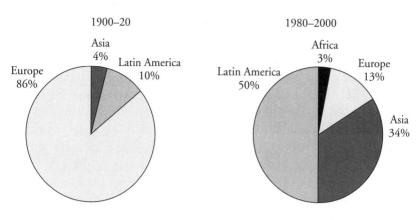

Source: U.S. Immigration and Naturalization Service, *Fiscal Year 2000 Statistical Yearbook.*

For obvious reasons, no one knows how many undocumented aliens have entered the country over the past two decades or how their numbers varied from year to year. The best estimates put the number of people living illegally in the United States in 2000 between 7 and 8.5 million.[5]

Immigration today differs from the classic era of immigration in a key way: the source countries for immigrants have changed. A century ago, most immigrants came from Europe. Most of the rest came from other parts of the Americas.[6] Very few came from Asia. This regional (and racial) distribution reflected deliberate government policy. Beginning with the Chinese Exclusion Act of 1882 and lasting until the Immigration Act of 1965, U.S. immigration policy deliberately sought to keep out Asians. Today, however, the regional mix of immigrants looks vastly different. Figure 7-1 shows that 85 percent of legal immigrants to the United States during the first two decades of the twentieth century originated in Europe, largely southern and eastern Europe. In the last two decades of the century, in contrast, 87 percent of legal immigrants came from outside of Europe, with half from Latin America alone.

Family formation among immigrants after they arrive in the United States is the second part of the story of increasing diversity. Immigrants tend to be young adults. So they arrive in America during the years in which they begin to start families, and their children become a piece of the

American patchwork of race and ethnicity. Moreover, some immigrant groups, particularly those from Latin America, have higher fertility rates than native-born Americans, including native-born Latinos. While non-Hispanic white women on average give birth to 1.9 children over the course of their lifetime, and black women, 2.1 children, Hispanic women bear on average 3.2 children. (The total fertility rate of Asian-American women falls between that for non-Hispanic white women and black women: 2.0 children.)[7] These two realities explain why one in five babies born in 2000 had a foreign-born mother even as the foreign born accounted for only one in nine U.S. residents in 2000. These trends are also the major reason why minority children accounted for 98 percent of the increase in the size of the child population in the United States between 1990 and 2000.[8]

The third factor responsible for increasing diversity is interracial unions. The fading of social taboos on interracial sex has meant a corresponding rise in the number of interracial children. The 2000 Census found that children were twice as likely as adults to be multiracial; about 4 percent as compared with 2 percent of adults.[9] Nearly 6 percent of all marriages in 2000 crossed ethnic or racial lines (or both), up from 3 percent in 1980. One out of every four marriages involving a Hispanic or an Asian is mixed. In California, nearly one out of every twelve non-Hispanic whites who marries does so to an Asian or a Hispanic.[10] By one estimate, one-fifth of all adult Americans already have a close family member who is of another race than their own. The rate is even higher for nonwhites.[11] The existence of multiracial children today will help perpetuate America's increasing ethnic and racial diversity tomorrow. As today's multiracial children reach adulthood, the United States is likely to see an even larger upsurge in multiracial identity as it becomes more socially acceptable and as they have multiracial children of their own.

Geographical Differences

Although the United States has become more racially and ethnically diverse, that diversity is not being felt uniformly throughout the country. More than three-quarters of people who identified themselves as "Hispanic" in the 2000 census lived in seven states: California, Texas, New York, Florida, Illinois, Arizona, and New Jersey. Half lived in just two: California and Texas.[12]

One unsurprising result of the geographical concentration of Hispanics is that they constitute substantial portions of the population in metropolitan areas with established Latino populations such as Los Angeles, New York, Chicago, and Miami. What is surprising is the extraordinarily high growth rate of Hispanics in cities and regions where few Latinos historically have lived. For example, several metropolitan areas in the Southeast— Atlanta, Raleigh-Durham, Greensboro, and Charlotte to name the top four—saw their Hispanic populations increase by more than 900 percent over the past twenty years. Many more metropolitan areas, especially in newer settlement areas, are absorbing Latinos in their suburban areas. In 1990, Hispanics living in the one hundred largest metropolitan areas were split equally between central city and suburban residence. Over the next decade the Latino suburban population grew 71 percent, raising the share of Hispanics who live in the suburbs to 54 percent in 2000.[13]

Asians are even more geographically concentrated than Hispanics. According to the 2000 Census, six in ten people who identified themselves as Asian alone live in just five states: California, New York, Texas, Hawaii, and New Jersey. Slightly more than one in three live in California alone. Conversely, in forty-one states, the Asian share of the population falls below the national average of 3.6 percent. Thus, while one in ten residents of New York City is Asian, only one in a hundred Detroit residents is.[14]

Generational Differences

Increasing racial and ethnic diversity is also not being felt uniformly across generational lines. As table 7-1 shows, the share of the population that is other than solely white or black is 5 percentage points higher among children than among adults. The fact that younger Americans are more likely to be Asian or Hispanic than older Americans can be seen in the census data on median age. In 2000, the median age of the total U.S. population was 35.3 years. This was up from 28.0 years in 1970, and the change reflects the aging of the Baby Boom generation and the fact that it was followed by the Baby Bust generation. In contrast to the country as a whole, the median age of the Hispanic population in 2000 was 25.9 years, or slightly more than nine years younger.[15] Meanwhile, the median age of people who identified themselves as Asian alone was 32.7 years, and the median age of those who identified themselves as Asian in combination with one or more other races was 31.1 years.[16] Again, one consequence of the greater racial and ethnic diversity among younger Americans will be to perpetuate increased diversity.

Church, Temple, and Mosque

America's increasing racial and ethnic diversity has also meant increasing religious diversity, a fact that September 11 helped spotlight.[17] Exactly how much America's religious make-up has changed is difficult to pinpoint. Federal law prohibits the Census Bureau from asking questions about religious faith, and methodological questions plague most other estimates. Still, three things are clear. First, the number of Americans who describe themselves as Buddhists, Hindus, and Muslims grew sharply in the 1990s. The American Religious Identification Survey found that the number of adults in the United States who described themselves as Hindus tripled between 1990 and 2001. The number who described themselves as Buddhists and Muslims more than doubled.[18]

Second, Buddhists, Hindus, and Muslims constitute a tiny percentage of the U.S. population. For instance, Islamic organizations place the number of Muslims in the United States at 6 million to 7 million—roughly equivalent to America's Jewish population—though other, more systematic studies say the number is at best half that.[19] Even at the higher number, however, Muslims constitute less than 2.5 percent of the total U.S. population. On a related point, Muslims in the United States are most likely to be African American or of South Asian, not Arab, descent; most Arab Americans are Christian. Buddhists and Hindus constitute less than 1 percent of the population.

Third, in religious affiliation, Americans remain overwhelming Christian. In 2001, roughly eight in ten Americans described themselves as Christian, down only slightly from nine in ten a half century earlier.[20] Virtually all Latino immigrants are Christian, with the vast majority being Catholic. If Americans do become decidedly less Christian in their religious affiliations in coming years, it will be because they convert to other religions or cease being religious, not because of immigration.

What Not to Worry About

Is America's growing diversity a cause for celebration, indifference, or alarm? To judge by the current state of American politics, the answer would seem to be celebration. The U.S. economy is remarkably productive, in part because of the contributions of immigrants. America has not erased the legacy of Jim Crow, but it has moved far beyond the days of Bull Connor. What was once white solid support for racially discriminatory laws has given way to strong opposition.[21] Although black mobility remains a concern, African Americans have made substantial economic and social progress. Despite frequent claims that whites, blacks, Asians, and Latinos all see the world differently, polls show that on most issues their views are more similar than different. This is especially true with regard to questions about the quality of life in the United States, the appeal of American political values, and the duties of individual Americans.[22]

Yet for many observers, America's successes today mask an underlying deterioration in its polity.[23] The exact nature of the perceived peril varies by author, although it almost inevitably involves anticipated social fractures triggered by immigration. Some pessimists worry that the United States is taking in too many immigrants. Others worry less about sheer numbers and more that the social forces that once encouraged immigrants to assimilate have dissipated, making it impossible to sustain a cohesive society. Still others worry that America's increased diversity will exacerbate regional and generational schisms.

It is impossible to refute these arguments, especially since most of them are vague about when their predictions will come true. There certainly is no reason to believe that greater diversity must make America stronger. Through bad luck, ill will, or incompetent public policy, growing diversity could produce the social and political calamities that pessimists fear. But disaster is neither preordained nor likely. While the diversity story comes with bad news, there is also considerable good news. Indeed, what may be most surprising about the pessimists' arguments is their lack of confidence in the resiliency of the American society they trumpet.

America Is Full Up

One fear, voiced more openly after September 11, is that the United States is exceeding its capacity to absorb new immigrants. If history is any guide, such fears are misplaced. As figure 7-2 shows, the portion of the U.S. population that is foreign born increased substantially over the last three decades of the twentieth century. In 2000, roughly one out of nine U.S. residents was born abroad, up from one in twenty in 1970. This was still below the one-in-seven figure reached in the first few decades of the twentieth century. Put differently, during the classic era of immigration, immigrants arrived at a rate of 6.3 per thousand people in the U.S. population. Today the rate of immigration, including illegal migrants, is less than 4 per

Figure 7-2. *Foreign-Born Population and Percent of Total Population of the United States, 1900–2000*

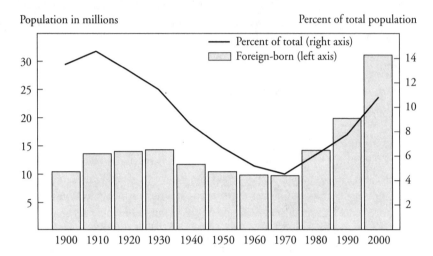

Population in millions   Percent of total population

Source: "Profile of the Foreign-Born Population in the United States: 1997," Current Population Reports, Special Studies P23-195, figure 1-1; U.S. Bureau of the Census, Census 2000.

1,000 members of the U.S. population.[24] Raw numbers alone, then, would suggest that the United States has yet to reach the point at which it can no longer absorb more newcomers.

Of course, the trend of the past three decades could continue or even accelerate. Pessimists fear what the writer Sergio Troncoso has trumpeted, namely, that "unlike the episodic waves of Irish, Italian and Jewish immigrants, Latin-American immigrants to the United States will be a constant and significant stream into this country. Forever."[25] On one level, this claim is true. Unless immigration law is entirely rewritten, continued immigration from Latin America is a certainty because immigration policy favors family unification.[26] No one can deny that if the percentage of the population that was foreign born surged well beyond levels experienced a century ago it could overwhelm America's absorptive capacities. That upper limit may be quite high, however. In 1999 the foreign-born as a share of the total population stood at 24.6 percent in Australia and 19.2 percent in Canada. Both countries enjoy economic prosperity and social peace.[27]

Moreover, it is not inevitable that immigration into the United States will remain at levels witnessed in the 1990s, let alone increase. Trends can and do change. Tougher enforcement of immigration laws and a prolonged economic recession in the United States could depress immigration levels. So too could deliberate U.S. efforts to use trade policy and economic assistance to promote economic growth in Latin America, especially in Mexico (the largest source country), thereby reducing the supply of immigrants heading north looking for jobs. (Only two Latin American countries number in the top ten recipients of U.S. foreign assistance, and none receives more than $200 million annually.)[28] European immigration to the United States dwindled after World War II not because Europeans were barred from entering the country, but because their economic prospects at home improved. Finally, immigration flows might drop if Washington adopted new policies that made it harder for people to immigrate to the United States. Although September 11 pushed immigration to the forefront of the political agenda, neither the White House nor Congress has attempted to change the rules regulating who can immigrate to the United States. The focus instead has been on tightening the rules governing the admission of business, tourist, and student visitors.[29]

Immigration flows—both legal and illegal—may in fact already be slowing, at least temporarily, because of the end of the 1990s economic boom. One possible indicator of this decline is the number of applicants for the annual diversity immigrant visa "lottery." This program makes available 50,000 green cards to persons from countries with low rates of immigration to the United States. Applications fell to 9 million for the one-month application period immediately following the September 11 terrorist attacks compared with the previous period a year earlier, when 13 million applied.[30] Another possible indication of slowing immigration may be found in the apprehensions of illegal immigrants along the U.S.-Mexican border. Apprehensions hit 1.8 million in FY2000, before dropping to 1.2 million in FY2001, marking the first major decline after a decade of increases.[31] These apprehension data should be viewed cautiously, because they reflect the government's commitment to enforcement as much as immigration flows. It is significant, then, that during the first half of 2002, when border security tightened in response to September 11, apprehensions ran at only half the rate of a year earlier.[32]

Immigrants Will Not Assimilate

Most pessimists admit that the current level of immigration is not by itself a problem. They argue instead that the problem is that the character of immigration and the context in which it is occurring differ radically from

America's historical experience. What is said to make today different from yesterday varies by observer. Some worry that Asian and Latino immigrants come from "alien" cultures.[33] Others argue that an information economy frustrates assimilation. Education was not critical to the blue-collar manufacturing economy of the early 1900s, enabling immigrants to get ahead by dint of their hard work. Now the U.S. economy resembles an hourglass—many high-paying, knowledge-intensive jobs at the top, many low-paying, low-skilled jobs at the bottom, and little in between.[34] Still other observers argue that inexpensive air travel, cheap telephone service, and the Internet encourage immigrants and their offspring to remain tied to their ancestral homeland. Finally, many observers worry that the rise of multiculturalism means that immigrants have arrived at a time when the forces that once encouraged assimilation have ebbed.[35]

None of these claims is new.[36] Fears that immigrants will not assimilate predate the Constitution. Benjamin Franklin complained in the early 1750s that Germans arriving in Philadelphia "will shortly be so numerous as to Germanize us instead of our Anglifying them . . . . [They] will never adopt our Language or Customs, any more than they can acquire our Complexion."[37] Thomas Jefferson worried several decades later that most immigrants would come from European countries ruled by monarchs. "They will bring with them the principles of the governments they leave, imbibed in their early youth; or, if able to throw them off, it will be in exchange for an unbounded licentiousness, passing, as is usual, from one extreme to another. It would be a miracle were they to stop precisely at the point of temperate liberty."[38] A century later, Senator Henry Cabot Lodge warned that immigration threatened "a great and perilous change in the very fabric of our race," and Representative Martin Dies urged the quarantining of "this Nation against people of any government in Europe incapable of self-government for any reason, as I would against the bubonic plague."[39]

Claims that the structure of the American economy would trap immigrants and their offspring in low-paying jobs were common a century ago.[40] While today's technology is better, yesterday's immigrants did not sever their ties to their homelands on reaching America. Anyone reading one of the more than two hundred Norwegian-language newspapers in the United States in the late 1800s might have concluded that Norwegian immigrants would never become Americans.[41] The desire to carve out ethnic enclaves separate from the English-speaking majority appeared long before the rise of multiculturalism. "In the first half of the nineteenth century, several German societies were formed with the express intention of so concentrating immigration in particular areas that they could, in effect, take over. One German spoke for many when he dreamed of Pennsylvania becoming 'an entirely German state where . . . the beautiful German language would be used in the legislative halls and the courts of justice.'"[42]

The long lineage to fears of immigration highlights an often-overlooked fact: America has been a diverse and multiethnic society for much of its history. Today the children of Irish, Italian, Greek, and Polish immigrants are often depicted as members of a common white European (or Anglo) culture. But when those immigrants arrived on U.S. shores, the native-born saw them as physically distinct, culturally alien foreigners who hailed from lower races.[43] The federally sponsored Dillingham Commission, which released a forty-two-volume report on immigration in 1910–11, argued that Slavic immigrants were prone to "periods of besotted drunkenness [and] unexpected cruelty" and that southern Italian immigrants had "little adaptability to highly organized society."[44] The children and grandchildren of these immigrants nonetheless became Americans, suggesting that some skepticism is in order regarding claims that today's immigrants and their offspring will not.

Still, pessimists insist today is different. Evaluating all the potential differences between then and now would consume an entire book. Nevertheless, two claims are worth exploring in depth: that today's immigrants are less interested in joining mainstream American society and that society increasingly encourages them to stand apart.

Have today's immigrants lost interest in assimilating? Polling data suggest not. An extensive *Washington Post* poll of Latino immigrants found that nearly nine in ten "believe it is important to change so they can fit into larger society."[45] Foreign-born parents are more likely than native-born parents to believe that a person who settles in the United States but refuses to learn English or who never stands during the national anthem at public events is "a bad citizen."[46] Studies of immigrant high-school students find that "two-thirds of those interviewed believe that hard work and accomplishment can triumph over any prejudice they've experienced, and about that many (the figure varies slightly with age) say there is no better country than the United States."[47] Of course, these results may simply reflect immigrants' telling pollsters what they think they are supposed to say. But if so, that suggests immigrants have already internalized key elements of American civil life.

The tangible sign of the desire to fit into American society can be seen in efforts to learn English. Despite frequent claims that today's newcomers refuse to learn English, and despite the prevalence of the Internet and cable television (or perhaps because of them), today's immigrants and their off-spring are learning English as fast as or faster than their predecessors one hundred years ago. The language shift has been so rapid in some communities that children have difficulty communicating with their own parents.[48]

The shift to English is occurring most rapidly among Asian immigrants. They are fewer in number and speak such a wide range of languages that it is difficult for them to sustain self-contained language enclaves. Latinos may retain their native tongue longer than Asians do, but they too are mastering English. While 73 percent of first-generation Latinos say they speak primarily Spanish at home, only 17 percent of the second generation and just 1 percent of the third generation say they do. Just as important, whereas only 37 percent of first-generation Latinos say they can read a newspaper or book in English very well or pretty well, the number jumps to 90 percent for the second generation.[49]

However, do Latinos and Asians see themselves as Americans? Pessimists point to polling data that suggest that for Latinos—evidence on Asian attitudes is scarce—the answer is no. For example, a 1999 *Newsweek* poll found that Latinos over thirty-five years old were most likely to identify themselves as American; those under thirty-five were more likely to identify as Hispanic or Latino.[50] Another poll found that 54 percent of Latino teens identify themselves as "Hispanic Only" or "More Hispanic than American."[51] A third poll found that only 33 percent of U.S. residents of Asian descent say they are culturally American.[52]

Pessimists assume these responses say something about political allegiance. But do they? It is more likely that they reflect the reality that these groups have different cultural heritages. For instance, the same poll that found that only 33 percent of Asians said their culture and traditions were uniquely American also found that just 54 percent of African Americans—who, after all, are not immigrants—thought that their traditions were quintessentially American. Oddly enough, residents of Latin American descent (61 percent) and Middle Eastern descent (64 percent) were more likely than African Americans to see themselves as culturally American.[53]

The fact that ethnic identification might not have the political significance often assigned to it helps explain why the public reaction to September 11 ran directly contrary to what the pessimists' arguments predicted. The country did not descend into ethnic squabbling, with Asian and Latino Americans repudiating "Anglo" foreign policy. Americans, regardless of their race and ethnicity, were instead remarkably unified.

September 11 did not produce ethnic divisions because the social forces encouraging assimilation are far stronger than pessimists recognize. True, the old assimilationist model that sought, sometimes aggressively, to mold immigrants and their offspring into model Americans has fallen by the wayside. But it is not clear that becoming an American ever depended on schools' providing a daily dose of biographies of Teddy Roosevelt, recitations from Longfellow, or demonstrations on how to fold the flag.[54] As David Hackett Smith and others have shown, existing cultures always exert tremendous influence on newcomers, even when they arrive in substantial numbers.[55] This is probably especially true for a culture like America's, whose traits of liberty, individuality, and prosperity are so appealing. Indeed, to an extent usually not appreciated, in pursuing their own self-interest, American social, economic, and political institutions unconsciously encourage assimilation.

This process may be most evident in the actions of the Democratic and Republican parties. For both parties, the drive to win Latino and Asian votes has been and will continue to be a matter of political survival. The Republicans learned that firsthand in the 1990s, when their decision to run on an anti-immigrant platform helped turn them into the minority party in California, the country's most populous and electorally valuable state. With the country split down the middle in recent national elections, both parties know that whoever makes the biggest inroads among Latino and Asian voters will hold the upper hand in future elections. (The national Latino vote is projected to increase from 5.9 million in 2000 to about 7.9 million in 2004, or by about a third.)[56] In turn, Democratic and Republican efforts to recruit Latinos and Asians into the political process will accelerate their integration into American society.

These efforts are having results. The number of Latinos registered to vote more than doubled between 1980 and 2000, as did the number who actually voted.[57] The number of Latinos elected to public office has also increased. In 2003, there were 22 Latino members of Congress (excluding nonvoting delegates) and 217 state legislators.[58] The first figure had tripled and the second more than doubled from two decades earlier. Latinos have made even greater strides at the local level.[59] Asian Americans also show greater political activity. Among those registered to vote, Asian-American turnout rates are comparable to those of non-Hispanic whites in midterm elections and only slightly lower in presidential elections.[60] The number of Asian Americans holding elected office at the local, state, or federal levels rose from 106 in 1978 to 503 in 1998.[61] These successes will undoubtedly be emulated and thereby further the assimilation of immigrants and their offspring.

Efforts by Democrats and Republicans to reach out to immigrants and their offspring are (and will be) mimicked by other institutions in American society. Organizations as diverse as the U.S. military, the AFL-CIO and its affiliated unions, the Episcopal and Presbyterian churches, and local PTAs have made it a priority to reach out to immigrant communities. The reason is simple—membership organizations must find new members or see themselves decline, and immigrant communities are a rich target for recruits. While self-interest rather than altruism drives these organizations, the net effect is to incorporate immigrants and their offspring into American society.

Demographic Balkanization

A third set of fears is that increased diversity is pushing the United States toward "demographic balkanization."[62] The argument here proceeds from the indisputable fact that increasing diversity is not being felt uniformly across the United States. Some worry that ethnic settlement patterns are creating a demographic divide that will soon pit cosmopolitan melting-pot states on the American littoral against a largely non-Hispanic white heartland. As one writer puts it: "We are seeing the emergence of two different Americas: One that is young, urban hip, and multiracial, and another that is aging, village traditional, and mostly white."[63] Over time, the argument goes, this demographic divide will become more politically salient. The two Americas will have an increasingly difficult time understanding each other because their interests and values will diverge.

Others see a different demographic divide. They note that today's immigrants and their offspring are disproportionately Hispanic, or, more exactly, disproportionately Mexican. They have settled primarily in California and the Southwest, displacing the native born and swamping other immigrant groups. So the coming demographic divide will not pit the coasts against the heartland, but Mexican America against everyone else. The journalist Peter Brimelow warns that the United States faces the resurgence of "a threat thought extinct in American politics for more than a hundred years: secession."[64] Harvard political scientist Samuel Huntington concurs: "Mexican immigration looms as a unique and disturbing challenge to our cultural integrity, our national identity, and potentially to our future as a country."[65] Grist for these claims can be found in the talk of La Reconquista by some Latino activists. The editor of *Latina* magazine proclaims: "The United States of the 21st century will be undeniably ours. Again."[66]

Talk of secession is far-fetched. While it is true that Iowa will not look like California or Florida any time soon, politics in the United States has never rested on demographic homogeneity for its political success. Nor are future regional demographic differences likely to be as sharp as pessimists claim. Historically, immigrants and their offspring disperse from traditional gateway cities over time in search of better jobs and quality of life. Today's immigrants are repeating that pattern. Moreover, the fact that many recent immigrants are bypassing traditional gateway communities and settling in areas that historically have seen few immigrants is effectively blurring the dividing line between a "browning" littoral and a "white" heartland. This dispersion is robbing the demographic differences that will persist of their political relevance.

Probably the only way that the fears of demographic balkanization could be realized is if American society made ethnicity politically relevant. As the political scientist Rodolfo de la Garza has said, "The cohesion of the group will be a function of how society deals with the group. If society decides that being a Hispanic is no more significant than being an Italian, then the group will be as cohesive as Italians, which means not very much."[67] Americans have mostly taken this approach. The irony is that pessimists would do the opposite. By emphasizing the "otherness" of immigrants, and especially of Mexicans, they could well help produce the future they fear.

Generational Conflict

A final set of fears targets the consequences of generational differences in diversity. Again, as table 7-1 shows, Asians and Latinos constitute a greater share of younger Americans than of older Americans. This creates the possibility that the intergenerational bargains that underlie much of government policy will collapse. Will elderly whites support the spending needed to educate children to whom they have no ethnic ties? Will Asian and Latino workers support generous cost-of-living increases for retirees with European surnames? In both cases, otherwise "ordinary" intergenerational conflict could take on a sharper ethnic and racial edge—poisoning politics and intensifying social divisions.

Although such clashes could emerge in some localities, are they in the offing nationwide? One reason for doubt is that the tendency of ethnic groups to concentrate mitigates intergenerational conflict. In cities and towns where Latinos or Asians emerge as new majorities, the racial or ethnic edge to intergenerational conflict disappears. A more fundamental reason is that the intergenerational argument exaggerates the depth of division in society. Age does not neatly separate whites from nonwhites, or Latinos from non-Latinos, or newcomers from natives. All groups have children. Everyone ages. Moreover, on many specific programs, more unites Americans of diverse racial and ethnic backgrounds than divides them. Retirees may be disproportionately non-Hispanic whites, but elderly Latinos are far more likely to rely on Social Security for all their income.[68]

Of course, politicians could fail to recognize that such common interests exist, or they could decide for cynical reasons to sow the seeds of racial and ethnic division rather than promote unity. No doubt some of each will happen. But to focus on how things could go wrong is to miss the fact that the dominant political winds are blowing in precisely the opposite direction. Again, both Democrats and Republicans are seeking Latino and Asian votes today—just as their predecessors sought to woo Irish, German, and Italian immigrants. These efforts to build winning coalitions are far more likely to blur divisions among groups than to intensify them, thus minimizing the chances that generational cleavages will mirror ethnic and racial ones.

What to Worry About

Pessimists exaggerate the problems created by America's growing diversity, but they are right that it poses challenges. One such challenge is encouraging immigrants to become citizens and full participants in American society. Another is ensuring that no racial or ethnic group finds itself bypassed by economic growth. A third is dampening the social conflict that diversity can produce. These challenges have no simple solutions. Meeting them requires a mix of strategies and by necessity will involve the efforts of federal, state, and local government as well as those of business and community-based groups. Because each of these three challenges is intimately tied up with the question of immigration, meeting them also requires rethinking the traditional American approach to immigrants, which worries greatly about how many should come, but cares little about what happens to them when they get here.

Citizenship and Legal Status

American political culture has always expected immigrants to become citizens. U.S. naturalization laws are generally more liberal than those of other industrialized democracies. The nationality of an immigrant's parents is immaterial, and immigrant offspring born in the United States are American citizens at birth. Any immigrant who has legal permanent residency or refugee status is eligible to naturalize after residing in the United States for five years (or less for special categories of immigrants), passing an English and civics exam, filing the appropriate paperwork, and paying a fee of $260 (in 2003).

However, nothing compels immigrants to become citizens. Whether today's immigrants are less inclined to seek citizenship than their predecessors—and if so, by how much—is unclear. The most commonly cited statistic is the Census Bureau's calculation of the proportion of foreign-born residents living in the United States who have gained citizenship. It dropped from 63.6 percent in 1970 to 37.4 percent in 2000. This simple figure does not, however, establish that immigrants have become less interested in citizenship. Historically, immigrants become more likely to seek citizenship the longer they live in the United States. The average foreign-born resident in 2000 had lived in the United States six years fewer than the typical immigrant in the 1970s. The Census Bureau calculates that this difference in length of residency accounts for roughly a third of the drop since 1970 in the percentage of the foreign-born population that is naturalized.[69]

Further reducing the usefulness of statistics on the percentage of the foreign born who are naturalized is the implicit assumption that all foreign-born residents are eligible for citizenship or, to be more precise, that the percentage who are has not changed. The first assumption is clearly wrong, and the second almost certainly is. The more than 30 million foreign-born residents of the United States fall into five broad groups: naturalized citizens (estimated at roughly 30 percent of the foreign-born); legal permanent residents (also roughly 30 percent); refugees and asylees (7 percent); nonimmigrant residents (3 percent) such as foreign students and temporary workers; and undocumented residents (28 percent), a category that includes people who entered the United States clandestinely as well as those who enter legally for a temporary stay but fail to leave when their time is up.[70] The size of the nonimmigrant and undocumented categories and the fact that both have grown substantially over the past three decades are significant because neither group is eligible for citizenship. When the nonimmigrant and undocumented populations are excluded, naturalization exceeds 50 percent even before controlling for length of residency in the United States.

While simple statistics like the percentage of the foreign-born who are naturalized create the mistaken impression that interest in citizenship has plummeted, there are still reasons to worry that the desire to naturalize might be declining or might decline in the future. One reason is that advances in communication, transportation, and information technology are making it much easier for immigrants to maintain close ties with people and institutions in their home countries.[71] As has always been the case, many immigrants arrive in the United States with the intention of one day returning home. (The rates of return among sojourners actually appear to be lower today than they were before World War II.)[72] The greater ease with which immigrants can maintain ties to their communities of origin and the ease and speed with which they can return there encourage the belief that residence in the United States will be temporary. For those immigrants who do return, these close ties are a blessing. But for those whose temporary residence becomes permanent, often without their consciously thinking about it, those same technological advances could slow their complete integration into American society.

Equally important is the pull side of the equation. Although Americans rhapsodize about the importance of citizenship, they have fallen out of the practice of encouraging immigrants to become citizens. Washington has not made it a policy priority. Presidents and members of Congress seldom mention the issue, and public outreach to immigrant communities is minimal. The Immigration and Naturalization Service (INS), the agency long responsible for naturalization, sometimes seemed designed to discourage it. By all accounts, it was one of the worst run in the federal government. The agency struggled throughout the 1990s with a backlog of unprocessed citizenship applications, and the wait for approval in the recent past exceeded two years in some parts of the country.[73] Given the frustration the native-born express about their dealings with government, it would hardly be surprising if immigrants took the INS's failings as a sign that the government did not value their citizenship aspirations.

The failure to encourage naturalization matters. Citizenship is by no means a cure-all, nor is it appropriate for guest workers or immigrants who are true sojourners. But for immigrants who have put down roots in the United States, citizenship is essential to becoming a full member of society, even if in every other way they have integrated and their native-born children are citizens. The obvious problem is that without citizenship they are shut out of the political process. The fact that almost 40 percent of adult Latinos are not U.S. citizens is the main reason that one out of every eight

U.S. residents in 2000 was a Latino, but only one in every fourteen potential voters was.[74] If immigrants remain outside the political process, the loss is twofold. They lose the opportunity to influence public policy to reflect their interests and values; and society loses the opportunity to incorporate them fully into the community.[75]

Government and civil society thus should make it a higher priority to encourage immigrants to naturalize. All signs indicate that immigrants would be receptive to such encouragement. The INS stumbled in the 1990s partly because so many immigrants wanted to naturalize. Many immigrants rushed to naturalize in the second half of the 1990s because legislative changes denied welfare benefits to noncitizens. Regardless of whether they used public assistance, immigrants realized that without citizenship they could not claim full rights in American society. As a result, the percentage of the foreign-born population who had naturalized in 2000 was actually 2 percentage points higher than it was only three years earlier.[76] Similarly, citizenship applications jumped 65 percent in the first eight months after September 11.[77] For some immigrants, naturalization was an act of patriotism; for others it was a way to protect themselves against a political backlash.

Efforts to encourage naturalization may have some bumps ahead in the new plan that abolished the INS and transferred its responsibilities to the new Department of Homeland Security. Immigrants now will file citizenship and other immigration documents with the Bureau of Citizenship and Immigration Services (formerly INS Services) in the Department of Homeland Security. Whether the department responsible for keeping terrorists out will manage to be welcoming to immigrants remains an open question. Even if the Department of Homeland Security succeeds in striking the proper balance between these different objectives, many immigrants are likely to regard the changes with trepidation, at least in the short term, because they worry it signals a fundamental change in America's embrace of newcomers.

Democrats and Republicans at all levels of government need to compensate for this mixed message. The president should create an office of citizenship within the White House to coordinate federal, state, local, and private efforts to promote citizenship. The new Bureau of Citizenship and Immigration Services, in keeping with the INS's charge under the 1990 Immigration and Nationality Act "to promote the opportunities and responsibilities of United States citizenship," should greatly expand its outreach efforts to immigrant communities and undertake periodic naturalization campaigns.[78] Public service announcements and other forms of public outreach should send the message that immigrants are wanted as citizens, that America is inclusive both in theory and in practice. Emphasis should be placed on making sure that naturalization rules and procedures are reasonable, transparent, and nondiscretionary.[79] Funding for citizenship classes and naturalization programs should also be increased, and volunteers recruited to usher immigrants through the process.

Civil society also has a major role to play. Ethnic associations can do much to encourage their fellow ethnics to become citizens. Churches, sports clubs, and neighborhood organizations can also be vehicles to promote naturalization, not to mention the kinds of political participation that turn formal citizenship into substantive citizenship.[80] Private companies and labor unions can play a role as well, even if only by facilitating their employees' efforts to naturalize. The Chicago office of AT&T, for example, responded to employee requests and worked with the regional INS office to distribute naturalization applications and study guides and to provide space for naturalization ceremonies.[81]

However, policies aimed at those who are here legally are not enough. Washington must also face up to the issue of those who are here illegally. Proposals to simply expel undocumented residents are unworkable. The American public almost certainly would not tolerate a policy of mass expulsions, especially since so many undocumented residents have American spouses or children and have put down roots in the community. By the same token, leaving millions to continue living in the shadows of society does not serve America's long-term interests. The fact that undocumented workers are unable to work in the open means they must work for less (which in turn depresses the wages of the low-skilled native-born as well). Their inability in many states to obtain a driver's license or open a bank account impedes their ability to upgrade their skills or to build capital. The net effect is to increase the chances that they and their offspring will be locked into underclass status.

The wise approach would take the undocumented foreign-born out of the shadows and put them on the path to citizenship. Policy should be redesigned to allow undocumented immigrants to earn legal status based on their years of residence, work history, and lack of a criminal record. In a nod to the argument that a blanket amnesty would reward law breaking, undocumented workers who regularize should be required to pay a fine in addition to the application fees that all new entrants must pay. Such a policy of "earned adjustment" should be coupled with a new temporary work visa program for Mexican nationals.[82] Mexico is the largest source country of undocumented workers, and the cross-border flow is likely to continue as long as the sizable wage differential between the two countries persists. One perverse result of not having a temporary work visa program that reflects actual market forces is that migrants who make it across the border have a greater incentive to stay in the United States.[83] It also means that Washington has less knowledge about who is crossing its borders, thereby increasing the security threat to the United States. The Bush administration had been moving toward an overhaul of the guest-worker program with Mexico before September 11. It should reconsider doing so now.

Economic Progress

A second challenge in America's increasing diversity is economic—ensuring that no ethnic group is locked into an underclass. There are signs of trouble on this front, especially for Latino immigrants and their offspring. Between 1980 and 1999, the average annual earnings of all Hispanics declined by 10 percent relative to all workers. To put that in perspective, over the same period the average annual earnings of African Americans held steady relative to the entire population, while those of Asians were actually higher than those of the work force as a whole.[84]

A substantial education gap underlies the economic gap between immigrants and the native born. Although some immigrants are well educated—an immigrant is more likely than a native-born American to hold a Ph.D.—many are poorly educated and low skilled—which is why immigrants are also more likely than the native-born not to have a high-school diploma.[85] Those with lower education attainment most likely arrived in the United States having already completed their schooling in their home country, where the education standards tend to be lower.

The nativity gap—that is, the difference between those youth born in the United States and those who arrived as children—helps explain why Latino youth lag behind on key education indicators. Thirty-one percent of Hispanic boys fail to obtain their high school diploma, nearly triple the rate for African American boys (12.1 percent) and four times the rate for non-Hispanic white boys (7.7 percent). Hispanic girls fare only slightly better, with 23 percent dropping out, compared with 13 percent of African American girls and 6.9 percent of non-Hispanic white girls.[86] Latinos who come to the United States as teens come primarily to work and not to attend school; in fact, because of their high work hours, they are the highest paid segment of the youth labor force.[87]

These economic and education data are disturbing, but not surprising. Most immigrant groups initially fare poorly relative to the native born. The economic and education attainments of Irish immigrants in the 1840s or Italian immigrants in the 1890s hardly augured well. Nor have the prospects of native-born Americans always looked encouraging. In the 1950s, two-thirds of whites in California were high-school dropouts, and a quarter lived in poverty.[88] Fifty years later their children worry that new immigrants will form a hostile underclass. But their own history shows that socioeconomic profiles are not set in stone.

There is also positive news on the economic front. Even proponents of reducing immigration agree that immigrants make significant progress over time.[89] While Hispanics' earnings have fallen relative to those of the population as a whole in recent years, their average annual earnings held steady between 1980 and 1999.[90] This is noteworthy because it coincided with a rapid influx of low-skilled Latino immigrants, which depressed Hispanic earnings potential. By the time second-generation Hispanic workers reach prime working age (beyond twenty-five years old), they fare at least as well as African Americans, though worse than whites and Asians.[91] Moreover, Hispanics have the highest labor force participation rate of any ethnic or racial group. This commitment to work, rather than an inherent hostility to education, helps explain the high drop-out rates among Hispanic youth.[92] Indeed, higher levels of education appear to be why native-born second-generation Latinos (that is, those with at least one immigrant parent) fare better economically than their foreign-born counterparts.[93]

The public policy challenge is to institute measures to encourage positive economic trends while discouraging bad ones. This is not to argue that it is possible to have an immigrant-specific economic policy. How immigrants and their offspring fare will depend largely on how the overall economy fares. Robust economic growth will make it easier for immigrants and their offspring to get ahead; sluggish economic growth will make it harder. By the same token, poor immigrants and their offspring will benefit from the same policies that will help poor white and blacks—better public schools, more job training opportunities, and less onerous tax policies.

Nevertheless, modest steps can and should be taken to promote economic mobility among immigrants and thereby provide a substantial long-term payoff for the country as a whole. Some of these steps do not directly target the problems of the second generation, which largely mirror those of the offspring of native-born, low-skilled parents. But helping immigrants move up the economic ladder may be the single biggest thing society can do to help their children succeed. Moreover, while Washington has a key role to play in funding many of these initiatives, state and local government, and civil society as well, have the lead role to play in their design and implementation.

One such step would be to make a sizable investment in English-language training. Despite the importance of English in facilitating economic progress among immigrants—not to mention their overall integration—federal and state support for adult English as a second language (ESL) programs is low. Washington distributed $460 million to state governments in fiscal year 2001 to fund adult education programs. Much of this money funds GED preparation classes and literacy programs for English speakers, not ESL programs.[94] The unsurprising result is that the demand for English-language classes far outstrips the supply. New York City, for instance, offered substantially fewer English-language classes for immigrants in 2000 than it did in 1990, even though the city welcomed nearly 1 million immigrants in the intervening decade.[95] California and Texas officials estimate that the demand for English-language classes exceeds supply by nine to ten times.[96] Failing to meet this demand represents a missed opportunity to foster economic independence, integrate immigrants into society, and strengthen the pathways to citizenship—all of which would strengthen social cohesion.

Efforts to expand English-language training should seek to make it reasonably convenient for immigrants to attend; classes offered only during working hours or that require long commutes to a central campus are self-defeating. Finding new ways to increase English instruction are also important. Combining English-language training with other activities, such as Head Start programs, can improve the chances that immigrants will enroll.[97] In industries such as construction, where immigrants have clustered, some private firms have offered English-language training to their employees. Major corporations and trade unions have also gotten into the act. Boeing and the International Association of Machinists have joined forces to provide ESL classes to workers.[98] These efforts should be encouraged and emulated.

Government and civil society should also invest substantially in services designed to educate immigrants about the intricacies of America's financial system. Mastering the use of credit, building up home equity, and investing for the future have always been keys to building financial security in the United States over the long term and providing for the next generation.[99] Yet most new immigrants arrive in the United States with no experience with savings and checking accounts, let alone credit cards, mortgages, or investments in the stock and bond markets. Programs that teach newcomers basic financial practices can play a critical role in helping them gain a foothold in the American economy and develop financial security. Such programs can also improve the physical security of immigrants. Some local police departments have reduced incidents of burglary and robbery in immigrant neighborhoods by teaming with area banks to persuade immigrants to use the banking system rather than keeping cash in their homes. All these efforts have a substantial multiplier effect. As immigrants learn to navigate the U.S. financial system, they can become guides for other immigrants.

Investment in community college education and vocational training also needs to be expanded. For poorly educated immigrants and their offspring, community college courses designed to teach marketable skills can assist their efforts to climb the rungs on the economic ladder. Making vocational programs work requires more than just offering classes. It also requires holding classes near where immigrants live and at times they can attend, reaching out to immigrants to inform them of opportunities, and finding instructors who speak their native language. Like English-language training and financial education, vocational training is by no means a cure-all. But such deliberate nuts-and-bolts attempts to encourage the clear desire immigrants have to get ahead can significantly improve the chances that they will succeed.

A final and more long-term strategy for minimizing the chances that immigrants and their offspring get locked into an economic underclass is to invest more in early childhood education. A key element here is federal programs such as Early Head Start (which targets children between the ages of one and three) and Head Start (which targets children between ages three and six). Both have been shown to strengthen the cognitive and language skills of preschoolers, giving them a firmer foundation on which to begin their formal education.[100] Of course, these successes can be undone in later years by badly run, unsafe, and underfinanced schools—a problem whose solution requires broader education reform efforts. Still, early childhood education could be an important key to helping many children climb beyond their modest beginnings.

Social Conflict

Diversity enriches American society, but it also sows the seeds of social conflict.[101] Immigration presents particular problems. Newcomers change existing communities, sometimes overnight; threaten established interests; and place new demands on government. The native-born often resist, seeking to stave off what they see as threats to their way of life. Thus Long Island homeowners protest the "atrocities" that illegal immigrants are inflicting on their town, and a North Carolina town responds to an influx of Latinos by inviting David Duke to speak against U.S. immigration policy.[102] African Americans may feel particularly threatened. Their hard-fought efforts to gain political power may be eclipsed by a growing Latino vote, and poor blacks in many local labor markets face increased competition for lower-skilled jobs. The potential friction between natives and newcomers is nothing new. Americans often imagine that their ancestors made a smooth transition from immigrant to citizen. In practice, the transition has always been marked by contention and conflict.

Rather than ignoring this potential for conflict, Americans should confront it. In social policy as in medicine, an ounce of prevention is worth a pound of cure. Waiting until former Klansmen are asked to address town meetings before responding makes the task of building ties between newcomers and natives that much harder. Nontraditional immigrant settlement areas should be particular targets because they have little infrastructure to absorb new immigrants.

The federal government can help cities and towns defray the costs associated with a rapid influx of immigrants. Education costs are probably the highest priority, given the cultural and fiscal impact immigrants can have on local schools. A federal program to handle this challenge already exists, the Emergency Immigrant Education Program (EIEP). Enacted in 1984, it provides impact aid to school districts that experience a surge in the number of foreign-born students who have been attending U.S. schools for three years or less. The money can be used for a variety of purposes, ranging from increasing parental involvement to tutoring or buying books. The program has never been fully funded, however. In FY 2001 its funding amounted to only $150 million, or about $186 per eligible student—well below the $500 per student that Congress initially authorized.[103] Funding EIEP at its authorized level—or better yet, increasing both the authorized and the appropriated amounts—would help cities and towns better adjust to the emergence of new immigrant communities.

Although the federal government has a role to play, much of the work of preventing conflict needs to be done at the state and local level. That is where the impact of immigration is most deeply felt and where appropriate responses can be most effectively fashioned. States should follow the lead of Maryland, Massachusetts, and Illinois in creating offices designed to reach out to immigrant communities. These offices should help identify emerging problems, serve as a source of policy ideas for local governments, and coordinate state, local, and community-based programs. Their goal should be to help newcomers meld into the community by acting as bridges to local institutions such as schools, government offices, and hospitals as well as by helping the community overcome fears of newcomers. The kinds of outreach that should be encouraged are diverse. Some cities and towns have set up task forces to advise newcomers about local laws (especially on zoning, a source of much friction) and how to navigate the government bureaucracy. Many local police forces now engage in community policing, making deliberate efforts to reach out to immigrant communities and to solicit their feedback and involvement in law enforcement. In other localities, community groups have sponsored formal employment centers to ease the tensions created by immigrant day laborers who seek employment by congregating in front of stores and major intersections. Of course, these and similar efforts to smooth interactions between new and established communities will not eliminate social conflict. But they can diminish it substantially, thus increasing the chances that America's growing diversity will be far less wrenching than it otherwise could be.

Affirmative Action

Even as government and civil society act to address the stresses and strains associated with immigration, America's growing diversity is complicating one of its most controversial policies—race-based affirmative action. Affirmative action policies are in place in several arenas: job hiring and promotion, government contracts, and college and university admissions. Intended to remedy the injustices of slavery and Jim Crow, affirmative action assumed that racial group affiliation made individuals presumptively eligible or ineligible for benefits. It also rested on the presumption that people can be sorted into mutually exclusive racial categories. That may have been possible in 1970, when virtually all of Americans were identified as either black or white. It is much harder to do three decades later, when racial and ethnic identities have multiplied and a growing segment of the population is multiracial.

From its earliest days, affirmative action applied not just to African Americans, but to Asians, Hispanics, and American Indians as well.[104]

Because these minority populations were so small in the 1960s, the consequences of making them eligible for preferences attracted little discussion or dispute. The post-1960s surge in immigration, however, confronted government officials with the task of deciding—usually without any public debate—which specific nationalities qualified under the vague labels of "Asian" and "Hispanic."[105] This has produced numerous oddities. For instance, people of Spanish, Pakistani, and Portuguese heritage qualified (at least for some programs), but those of Bosnian, Iranian, and Moroccan descent did not. Yet even as the beneficiaries of affirmative action expanded, the American political debate on the merits of racial preferences remained framed in black-white terms. Neither the Clinton administration's 1995 review of affirmative-action policies nor the final report of the U.S. Commission on Immigration Reform mentioned the issue of immigrant participation.[106]

The decision to allow respondents to select more than one race on the 2000 census adds another layer of complexity. With six major racial categories to choose among—white, black or African American, American Indian and Alaska Native, Asian, Native Hawaiian and other Pacific Islander, and some other race—there are now more than sixty-three possible racial combinations. (Adding Hispanic background to the mix in turn doubles the number of possible combinations.) This raises the question of how people who are white and something else should be treated for affirmative action purposes. The Clinton administration's answer, which the Bush administration accepted, is that "Mixed-race people who mark both White and a non-white race will be counted as the latter for purposes of civil rights monitoring and enforcement."[107]

While affirmative action has adapted to America's changing demography, those adaptations complicate an already imperfect system. Furthermore, these adaptations add three new complaints to the traditional ones that racial preferences are always wrong, that they primarily help affluent minorities rather than poor ones, and that they were intended to be temporary.[108] First, if affirmative action is intended to remedy past discrimination, why should immigrants and their offspring be eligible for affirmative action at all? This policy is especially questionable when some national groups that have qualified, such as Asian Indians, are more prosperous than the average American. Second, the decision to count mixed-race individuals as nonwhite enshrines into policy the one-drop rule of race that segregationists had championed. This accentuates, rather than diminishes, the importance of race even as it creates the odd outcome whereby some people who consider themselves non-Hispanic whites become eligible for affirmative action. (Roughly 25 percent of those who identify themselves as black and white consider themselves white, as do roughly half those who say they are of mixed Asian-white descent.)[109] Third, expanding affirmative action may actually defeat its original purpose of helping African Americans. By hiring Asians, Latinos, or black immigrants, employers can meet affirmative action goals while continuing to discriminate against native-born blacks.[110]

The debate over the future of affirmative action takes place against a backdrop of mixed public attitudes toward it. Diversity is widely accepted as a social good. However, preferences for ethnic and racial minorities in hiring and school admissions have long been unpopular with whites. Nonwhites are not of a single mind on affirmative action's merits, either. Blacks have always been the policy's strongest supporters, though their support is neither axiomatic nor monolithic.[111] Asians and Hispanics—though not Asian or Hispanic elites—have expressed ambivalence.[112] This partially explains why efforts to end affirmative action, such as successful referenda in California in 1996 and in Washington in 1998, produced no sizable political backlash. The California case is the more remarkable of the two, given the state's tremendous diversity and the size of its nonwhite population. Substantial portions of the nonwhite community have been more attached to the notion of nondiscrimination than to the idea of racial preferences.

How the debate over affirmative action evolves depends greatly on the actions of the U.S. Supreme Court. In recent years the Court has narrowed the conditions under which affirmative action plans are permissible in hiring practices, though it has stopped short of declaring them unconstitutional. The issue will soon be joined, at least in the area of higher education. In December 2002 the Court agreed to hear challenges to the University of Michigan's undergraduate and law school admissions policies.

Many proponents of affirmative action fear that if the Supreme Court rules that ethnic and racial preferences are unconstitutional, the floodgates of discrimination will open, wreaking havoc on an increasingly diverse American society. This pessimism, while understandable, exaggerates things. It overlooks the robustness of civil rights law, which is far more important to guaranteeing minority rights than affirmative action. Equally important, it fails to recognize how profoundly racial attitudes and behavior have changed since the days of the civil rights movement. This was acutely evident in the intense public pressure on Senator Trent Lott to step down as Senate majority leader in late 2002 after he made remarks seemingly endorsing segregation. The country's reaction to September 11, which emphasized inclusion rather than exclusion, is further evidence. Contrary to fears of a sharp backlash against Arab and Muslim Americans, the number of bias incidents remained remarkably small.[113]

Moreover, the public pressure on government to have universities and bureaucracies that look like the American people would continue. For that reason, class-based affirmative action policies—that is, initiatives designed to help lower-income groups, regardless of their race or ethnic origin—may replace race-based ones.[114] In the wake of decisions to end the use of ethnic and racial preferences in higher education, both California and Texas adopted plans to guarantee places at one of its university campuses to a set percentage of the top students in every high-school graduating class in the state. (Florida also has instituted a percentage plan.) These policies effectively benefited the graduates of poorer school systems and reversed the decline in nonwhite undergraduate enrollment that had occurred immediately after racial preferences were jettisoned.[115] These government policies will invariably be supplemented by private-sector initiatives. For instance, in 2002 a consortium of companies such as Boeing, GlaxoSmithKline, and McGraw-Hill joined to help universities retain and increase their diversity in the event affirmative action is ruled unconstitutional. The companies' motive was not altruism, but self-interest: they calculate that a work force that reflects the same racial and ethnic diversity as their customer base will benefit their corporate bottom lines.[116]

What if the Supreme Court finds that the University of Michigan's admissions policies are, or could with modification be, constitutional? In this instance, should the government look for practical ways to diminish its reliance on racial and ethnic preferences? Good arguments for considering class-based (or class- plus race-based) rather than race-based affirmative action are provided by the current policy's drift away from its original purposes, its ambivalent support among nonblack minorities, its elevation (rather than reduction) of the importance of race, the strength of the nondiscrimination principle in American society, the economic and social gains blacks have made over the past three decades, and the difficulties of administering ethnic and racial preferences in a society in which people do not fit into mutually exclusive categories.

A shift toward class-based policies could help bridge the racial and ethnic divides that current policies aggravate. Polls show that need-based policies enjoy support across all racial and ethnic groups.[117] (Prominent African

American intellectuals such as Orlando Patterson and Cornel West have endorsed the idea as well.)[118] Class may be a near-taboo word in American politics, and many Americans may persist in believing they live in a class-free society. However, they also understand intuitively what social scientists have amply documented—regardless of color or surname, which side of the tracks you grow up on greatly affects your life prospects. Most people support the idea of taking steps to make the playing field more level, provided that all disadvantaged groups stand to benefit.

In America, however, race still matters. Therefore, class-based affirmative action alone will not be a magic bullet. The percentage plans that California and Texas university systems adopted did not reverse the decline in minority enrollments in their state's graduate and professional schools. In the University of California system, African American and Latino enrollment at the flagship Berkeley and Los Angeles campuses still lags behind what it was before race-based affirmative action was halted.[119] Critics argue that percentage plans depend on continued racial segregation at American high schools to succeed in producing diversity at the college level. To the degree that percentage plans create incentives to desegregate they might be seen as a social good, not only because integration has a value in itself, but also because the non-Hispanic white majority would presumably have a greater stake in seeing minority schools succeed. However, if percentage plans are deemed objectionable, they can be replaced by alternative schemes that would target preferences at the graduates of schools in poor communities or at the residents themselves.

At the same time, race-conscious policies have obvious flaws. What distinguishes a class-based strategy is that it is neutral toward race and ethnicity, but not indifferent to them. To the extent that race and ethnicity are tied to income—and they are in the United States—need-based policies help advance racial and ethnic groups without being exclusively about race. That is an important virtue in an increasingly diverse American society in which policies that make racial and ethnic differences more politically salient do more harm than good.

However, because class-based affirmative action is not a cure-all—and because race for good reason remains a politically volatile subject in American society—decisions to move away from race-based affirmative action should be embedded in a broader set of policies aimed at helping minorities. This is something the Bush administration notably failed to do when it decided to oppose the University of Michigan's admissions policies. At a minimum, colleges, businesses, and government should develop better outreach and mentoring programs and provide more scholarships for lower-income students. Ultimately, however, government at all levels must confront the problem of failing public schools. Failing to take such steps would both ask class-based policies to do too much and send a signal that many minorities will read as evidence that white America is indifferent to their plight. That would feed ethnic and racial tensions rather than help ease them.

The Future of Diversity

The American mosaic is changing. Our national portrait is no longer painted solely in shades of black and white, but in Technicolor. We are becoming more Asian, Latino, and multiracial. That trend would continue even if we closed our borders tomorrow. The diversity created by three decades of relatively high immigration is self-sustaining. The children of today's immigrants and the willingness of Americans to look beyond racial and ethnic lines in choosing mates will see to that.

Will these diverse faces still cohere as a nation? One reason for optimism is that America has succeeded many times in the past in melding different groups into one nation. The American creed of liberty, justice, and equality for all under law adds a powerful force for assimilation. True, many immigrants discovered on arriving that the native born dismissed them as inferiors, too culturally alien ever to become Americans. Yet if we as a society have often fallen short of our ideals, we have not abandoned them. Instead, we have struggled to translate them into reality.

Our governmental and societal institutions should continue that tradition and reach out to immigrants, urge them to become citizens, and welcome them into the American family. Government and civil society should also move proactively to institute policies and programs designed to lessen the friction that arises when newcomers meet natives, thereby helping to diminish the political conflicts that can arise from diversity.

Our ideals alone, however, are not responsible for the success of American diversity. Equally important has been the reality of economic mobility. Immigrants historically have found that they could climb the ladder of economic success no matter how humble their origins. This mobility prevents racial, ethnic, and religious divisions from coinciding with class divisions and diminishes the potential for conflict. Conversely, when economic mobility has been denied to people based on their race or ethnicity—most notably African Americans—diversity has become a source of social unrest.

There may be no surer way to guarantee that any ethnic, racial, or religious group will reject integration into American society than to deny its members the tools and opportunities they need to achieve the American dream. A test for American society in the coming decades, then, will be whether it can continue to facilitate the economic mobility of immigrants and their offspring. This process could, of course, be left to the magic of the market. But given what is at stake, and given the understandable concerns that the avenues for economic mobility may be narrower in an information economy than they were in a manufacturing economy, it makes far more sense for government to abandon its traditional laissez-faire approach to immigrants. Washington needs to take the lead by sizably increasing its investment in English-language training, expanding vocational and early childhood education opportunities, and moving affirmative action away from race-based preferences to class-based ones. However, the responsibility is not Washington's alone. State and local governments, as well as nonprofit organizations and private firms, have key roles to play in promoting economic mobility.

Proposals to encourage citizenship, minimize frictions between natives and newcomers, and promote economic mobility are easy to dismiss because they involve mundane everyday tasks and require only modest amounts of spending. They admittedly lack the grandeur of a war on poverty or a trillion-dollar tax cut. Yet much like an aspirin a day, they could produce substantial benefits over the long term. This is not just because some of these proposals would increase the quality of the nation's human capital, which, as Lawrence Katz, Claudia Goldin, and Bradford DeLong show in chapter 2 of this volume, is crucial to the country's long-run economic health. On a deeper level, they would demonstrate once again that America's great strength as a society lies in its diversity.

Notes

1. Herman Melville, *Redburn: His First Voyage* (Penguin, 1977), p. 238.

2. Audrey Singer, "America's Diversity at the Beginning of the Twenty-First Century: Reflections from Census 2000," Brookings, April 2, 2002 (www.brook.edu/views/papers/singer/20020402.htm [accessed February 2003]).

3. See, for example, Amitai Etzioni, "Inventing Hispanics," *Brookings Review*, vol. 20 (Winter 2002), pp. 10–13; Amitai Etzioni, *The Monochrome Society* (Princeton University Press, 2001); and Peter Skerry, "E Pluribus Hispanic?" *Wilson Quarterly*, vol. 16 (Summer 1992), pp. 62–73.

4. U.S. Immigration and Naturalization Service, *Fiscal Year 2000 Statistical Yearbook*, "Immigrants, Fiscal Year 2000," table 2, pp. 7–9 (www.ins.usdoj.gov/graphics/aboutins/statistics/IMM00yrbk/IMM2000.pdf [accessed February 2003]).

5. The 7 million figure is from U.S. Immigration and Naturalization Service, "Estimates of the Unauthorized Immigrant Population Residing in the United States: 1990–2000," January 2003 (www.ins.usdoj.gov/graphics/aboutins/statistics/Illegals.htm [accessed February 2003]). The 8.5 million figure is from Michael E. Fix and Jeffrey S. Passel, "Testimony before the Subcommittee on Immigration and Claims Hearing on 'The U.S. Population and Immigration,'" Committee on the Judiciary, U.S. House of Representatives," Urban Institute, August 2001 (www.urban.org/urlprint.cfm?ID=7321 [accessed February 2003]).

6. U.S. Immigration and Naturalization Service, *Fiscal Year 2000 Statistical Yearbook*, "Immigrants, Fiscal Year 2000," table 2, pp. 7–9 (www.ins.usdoj.gov/graphics/aboutins/statistics/IMM00yrbk/IMM2000.pdf [accessed February 2003]).

7. Mary M. Kent and Mark Mather, "What Drives U.S. Population Growth?" *Population Bulletin*, vol. 57 (December 2002), p. 10 (www.prb.org/Content/NavigationMenu/PRB/AboutPRB/Population_Bulletin2/57.4_USPopulationFINAL.pdf [accessed February 2003]).

8. William P. O'Hare, "The Child Population: First Data from the 2000 Census," Annie E. Casey Foundation and the Population Reference Bureau, June 2001, p. 13 (www.aecf.org/kidscount/trends_children.pdf [accessed February 2003]).

9. Mary M. Kent and others, "First Glimpses from the 2000 U.S. Census," *Population Bulletin*, vol. 56 (June 2001), p. 14 (www.prb.org/Template.cfm?Section=PRBLibrary&template=/ContentManagement/ContentDisplay.cfm&ContentID=7502 [accessed February 2003]).

10. U.S. Census Bureau, "Table FG3. Married Couple Family Groups" (www.census.gov/population/socdemo/hh-fam/p20-537/2000/tabFG3.txt [accessed February 2003]); and Roberto Suro, "Mixed Doubles," *American Demographer*, vol. 21 (November 1999), pp. 58–59.

11. Joshua R. Goldstein, "Kinship Networks That Cross Racial Lines: The Exception or the Rule?" *Demography*, vol. 36 (August 1999), pp. 399–407.

12. Betsy Guzmán, "The Hispanic Population," U.S. Census Bureau, *Census 2000 Brief*, May 2001, pp. 2–3 (www.census.gov/prod/2001pubs/c2kbr01-3.pdf [accessed February 2003]).

13. Roberto Suro and Audrey Singer, "Latino Growth in Metropolitan America: Changing Patterns, New Locations," Census 2000 Survey Series, Brookings Institution Center on Urban & Metropolitan Policy and the Pew Hispanic Center, July 2002 (www.brook.edu/dybdocroot/es/urban/publications/surosinger.pdf [accessed February 2003]).

14. Figures derived from Jessica S. Barnes and Claudette E. Bennett, "The Asian Population: 2000," *Census 2000 Brief*, February 2002, tables 2 and 3.

15. Guzmán, "Hispanic Population," p. 7.

16. Barnes and Bennett, "Asian Population," p. 8.

17. See Diana Eck, *A New Religious America: How the Most "Christian Country" Has Now Become the World's Most Religiously Diverse Nation* (Harper Collins, 2001).

18. Barry A. Kosmin, Egon Mayer, and Ariela Keysar, *American Religious Identification Survey 2001*, Graduate Center of the City University of New York, p. 13.

19. On the dispute over measuring the number of Muslims living in the United States, see Bill Broadway, "Number of U.S. Muslims Depends on Who's Counting," *Washington Post*, November 24, 2001, p. A1; David Cho, "Evangelicals Help Pace U.S. Growth in Church Attendance," *Washington Post*, September 17, 2002, p. A3; Gustav Niebuhr, "Studies Suggest Lower Count for Number of U.S. Muslims," *New York Times*, October 25, 2001, p. A16; John Schwartz, "Numbers Games: Go Figure," *New York Times*, November 11, 2001, p. E4; and Tom W. Smith, "The Muslim Population of the United States: The Methodology of Estimates," *Public Opinion Quarterly*, vol. 66 (Fall 2002), pp. 404–17.

20. Gallup Polling Organization, "Easter Season Finds a Religious Nation," April 13, 2001; Gregg Easterbrook, "Religion in America: The New Ecumenicalism," *Brookings Review*, vol. 20 (Winter 2002), p. 46; and Kosmin, Mayer, and Keysar, *American Religious Identification Survey 2001*, p. 12.

21. Among others see Howard Schuman, Charlotte Steeh, and Lawrence Bobo, *Racial Attitudes in America: Trends and Interpretations* (Harvard University Press, 1985), pp. 74–89.

22. For extensive documentation on this point, see Etzioni, *The Monochrome Society*, chap. 1.

23. Peter Brimelow, *Alien Nation: Common Sense about America's Immigration Disaster* (Random House, 1995); Georgie Ann Geyer, *Americans No More: The Death of Citizenship* (Atlantic Monthly Press, 1996); and Patrick Buchanan, *The Death of the West: How Dying Populations and Immigrant Invasions Imperil Our Country and Civilization* (Thomas Dunne Books/St. Martin's Press, 2002).

24. Douglas S. Massey, "The New Immigration and Ethnicity in the United States," *Population and Development Review*, vol. 21 (September 1995), pp. 646–47.

25. Sergio Troncoso, "Latinos Find America on the Border of Acceptance," *Newsday*, July 8, 2001, p. B8.

26. On the future of Mexican immigration into the United States, see Douglas S. Massey, Jorge Durand, and Nolan J. Malone, *Beyond Smoke and Mirrors: Mexican Immigration in an Era of Economic Integration* (Russell Sage Foundation, 2002).

27. "The Longest Journey: A Survey of Migration," *Economist*, November 2, 2002, p. 4.

28. Organization for Economic Cooperation and Development, *Aid and Debt Statistics, Donor Aid Charts, United States,* January 3, 2002 (www.oecd.org/gif/M000000000/M00000299.gif [accessed February 2003]).

29. Muzaffar Chishti, "Immigration and Security Post-September 11," *Migration Information Source, 2002* (www.migrationinformation.org/Feature/display.cfm?ID=46 [accessed February 2003]).

30. U.S. Department of State, "Results of the Diversity Immigrant Visa Lottery (DV-2001), Office of the Spokesman, May 10, 2001, and June 18, 2002.

31. U.S. Immigration and Naturalization Service, *Fiscal Year 2001 Statistical Yearbook*, table 57 (2002), (www.ins.gov/graphics/aboutins/statistics/ENF2001.pdf [accessed February 2003]).

32. Mary Jordan, "Mexicans Caught at Border in Falling Numbers," *Washington Post*, May 24, 2002, p. A27.

33. See, for example, Brimelow, *Alien Nation*, p. 268; and Samuel Huntington, "The Special Case of Mexican Immigration: Why Mexico Is a Problem," *American Enterprise*, vol. 11 (December 2000), p. 22.

34. For arguments that new immigrants face a more challenging economic environment, though not necessarily by scholars hostile to immigration, see Herbert J. Gans, "Second-Generation Decline: Scenarios for the Economic and Ethnic Futures of the Post-1965 American Immigrants," *Ethnic and Racial Studies*, vol. 15 (1992), pp. 173–92; Christopher Jencks, "Who Should Get In?" *New York Review of Books*, November 29, 2001, pp. 57–63; Jencks, "Who Should Get In? Part II," *New York Review of Books*, December 20, 2001, pp. 94–102; Massey, "The New Immigration," pp. 643–44; and Alejandro Portes and Min Zhou, "The New Second Generation: Segmented Assimilation and Its Variants," *Annals of the American Academy of Political and Social Science*, no. 530 (November 1993), pp. 74–96.

35. See, for instance, Michael Barone, *The New Americans: How the Melting Pot Can Work Again* (Regnery, 2001), pp. 11–13; Brimelow, *Alien Nation*, p. 19; and Geyer, *Americans No More*, pp. 203–11.

36. Among others, see John Higham, *Strangers in the Land: Patterns of American Nativism, 1860–1925*, 2d ed. (Rutgers University Press, 1988); Maldwyn Jones, *American Immigration* (University of Chicago Press, 1960); and David M. Reimers, *Unwelcome Strangers: American Identity and the Turn against Immigration* (Columbia University Press, 1998), chap. 1.

37. Benjamin Franklin, "Observations Concerning the Increase of Mankind, Peopling of Countries, &c," in Leonard W. Labaree and others, eds., *The Papers of Benjamin Franklin*, vol. 4 (Yale University Press, 1959), p. 234.

38. Thomas Jefferson, *Notes on the State of Virginia* (University of North Carolina Press, 1955), pp. 84–85.

39. Quoted in Higham, *Strangers in the Land*, pp. 144, 171.

40. See Joel Perlmann and Roger Waldinger, "Immigrants, Past and Present: A Reconsideration," in Charles Hirschman, Philip Kasinitz, and Josh DeWind, eds., *The Handbook of International Migration* (Russell Sage Foundation, 1999), pp. 233–34.

41. There are only three Norwegian-language newspapers in the United States today. Greg Johnson, "Ethnic Papers Far from Foreign in California," *Los Angeles Times*, July 9, 2001, p. 1.

42. Bill Bryson, *Made in America: An Informal History of the English Language in the United States* (William Morrow, 1996), p. 135. See also Leonard Dinnerstein and David Reimers, *Ethnic Americans: A History of Immigration* (Columbia University Press, 1999), pp. 41–44.

43. Barone, *New Americans*, especially pp. 47–48, 143, 228–30. See also Noel Ignatiev, *How the Irish Became White* (Routledge, 1995).

44. *Immigration Commission Dictionary of Race and Peoples* (U.S. GPO, 1911), pp. 74, 129. See also John M. Lund, "Boundaries of Restriction: The Dillingham Commission," *UVM History Review*, vol. 6 (December 1994), pp. 40–57.

45. Amy Goldstein and Roberto Suro, "A Journey in Stages," *Washington Post*, January 16, 2000, p. A24.

46. "Distinct Views on the Proverbial Melting Pot," *American Demographics*, vol. 22 (December 2000), p. 24.

47. Tamar Jacoby, "Second-Generation Question Mark," *American Enterprise*, vol. 11 (December 2000), p. 34.

48. See Alejandro Portes and Rubén G. Rumbaut, *Legacies: The Story of the Immigrant Second Generation* (University of California Press, 2001).

49. Goldstein and Suro, "A Journey in Stages," p. A24.

50. John Leland and Veronica Chambers, "Generation Ñ," *Newsweek*, July 12, 1999, p. 54.

51. Rebecca Gardyn, "Habla English?" *American Demographics*, vol. 23 (April 2001), p. 55.

52. John Fetto, "An All-American Melting Pot," *American Demographics*, vol. 23 (July 2001), pp. 8–9.

53. Ibid.

54. For an impassioned defense of the old assimilationist model, see Victor Davis Hanson, "Do We Want Mexifornia?" *City Journal*, vol. 12 (Spring 2002), pp. 12–23.

55. David Hackett Fischer, *Albion's Seed: Four British Folkways in America* (Oxford University Press, 1989).

56. "Mobilizing the Vote: Latinos and Immigrants in the 2002 Midterm Election," National Council of La Raza, November 2002, p. 4 (nclr.policy.net/proactive/newsroom/release.vtml?id=21984 [accessed February 2003]).

57. Figures derived from data in U.S. Census Bureau, *Voting and Registration in the Election of November 1980* (1982), pp. 12–13; and U.S. Census Bureau, *Voting and Registration in the Election of November 1998* (2000), p. 5. See also "Mobilizing the Vote" and "Mobilizing the Latino Vote: Tapping the Power of the Hispanic Electorate," National Council of La Raza, July 2002 (nclr.policy.net/proactive/newsroom/release.vtml?id=21380 [accessed February 2003]).

58. Personal Communication, National Association of Latino Elected Officials, January 31, 2003.

59. *2001 National Directory of Latino Elected Officials* (Los Angeles: NALEO Educational Fund, 2001), p. vii.

60. Pei-te Lien, "Asian Pacific-American Public Opinion and Political Participation," *PS: Political Science and Politics*, vol. 34 (September 2001), p. 625.

61. Carol Ness, "Blacks Fear Losing Their Political Clout in State," *San Francisco Chronicle*, June 17, 2001, p. A17. See also James S. Lai and others, "Asian Pacific-American Campaigns, Elections, and Elected Officials," *PS: Political Science and Politics*, vol. 34 (September 2001), pp. 611–17.

62. See, for example, William H. Frey, "Immigration and Internal Migration 'Flight' from US Metropolitan Areas: Toward a New Demographic Balkanization," *Urban Studies*, vol. 32 (May 1995), pp. 733–57; William H. Frey, "Immigration, Domestic Migration, and Demographic Balkanization in America: New Evidence for the 1990s," *Population and Development Review*, vol. 22 (December 1996), pp. 741–63; and William H. Frey, "The Diversity Myth," *American Demographics*, vol. 20 (June 1998), pp. 39–43.

63. Brad Edmondson, "Immigration Nation," *American Demographics*, vol. 22 (January/February 2000), p. 32.

64. Brimelow, *Alien Nation*, p. 268.

65. Huntington, "Special Case of Mexican Immigration," p. 22.

66. Christy Haubegger, "The Legacy of Generation Ñ," *Newsweek*, July 12, 1999, p. 61.

67. Quoted in Maria Puente and Martin Kasindorf, "The Hispanic Experience: Unique, Evolving," *USA Today*, September 7, 1999, p. 14A.

68. Julie Kosterlitz, "Boomers, Say Hola," *National Journal*, August 14, 1999, p. 2363.

69. U.S. Census Bureau, *Profile of the Foreign-Born Population in the U.S.: 2000* (2001), pp. 20–21 (www.census.gov/prod/2002pubs/p23-206.pdf [accessed February 2003]).

70. The precise size of the undocumented population is unknown, and while the federal

government tracks how many people enter the United States on nonimmigrant visas, it does not track who leaves, changes legal status, or illegally overstays the terms of a visa. The estimate for refugees and asylees includes both those who have become citizens and those who have not. See Fix and Passel, "Testimony before the Subcommittee on Immigration and Claims Hearing."

71. See, among others, Nancy Foner, *From Ellis Island to JFK: New York's Two Great Waves of Immigrants* (Yale University Press and Russell Sage Foundation, 2000); Nancy Foner, "What's New about Transnationalism? New York Immigrants Today and at the Turn of the Century," *Diaspora*, vol. 6 (February 1997), pp. 355–75; Luis Guarnizo, *Los Dominicanyork: The Making of a Binational Society* (Sage Publications, 1994); Nina Glick Schiller, Linda Basch, and Cristina Szanton Blanc, *Towards a Transnational Perspective on Migration: Race, Class, Ethnicity and Nationalism Reconsidered* (New York Academy of Sciences, 1992).

72. Michael Jones-Correa, *Between Two Nations: The Political Predicament of Latinos in New York City* (Cornell University Press, 1998).

73. Audrey Singer, "U.S. Citizenship Applications at All-Time High," *Population Today*, vol. 27 (October 1999), p. 5.

74. Amie Jamieson, Hyon B. Shin, and Jennifer Day, "Voting and Registration in the Election of November 2000," U.S. Census Bureau, *Current Population Reports*, February 2002, table A, p. 5 (www.census.gov/prod/2002pubs/p20-542.pdf [accessed February 2003]).

75. Survey research shows that Latino citizens are on average three times more likely than non-Latino citizens to engage in nonelectoral forms of political participation. See David L. Leal, "Political Participation by Latino Non-Citizens in the United States," *British Journal of Political Science*, vol. 32 (April 2002), pp. 353–70.

76. The difference is statistically significant. Census Bureau, *Profile of the Foreign-Born Population in the U.S.: 2000*, p. 21.

77. U.S. Immigration and Naturalization Service, *Fiscal Year 2002 Monthly Statistical Report*, June 28, 2002 (www.ins.usdoj.gov/graphics/aboutins/statistics/msrmay02/index.htm [accessed February 2003]).

78. The INS initially set out to do this with the Citizenship USA program, which it launched in 1995. That initiative quickly gave way to an effort to reduce the accumulating backlog of naturalization applications. That in turn led to charges that the Clinton administration rushed the naturalization process to swell the voting rolls with people who would be likely to vote for Democrats. See Inspector General, Department of Justice, "An Investigation of the Immigration and Naturalization Services' Citizenship USA Initiative," July 31, 2000.

79. See T. Alexander Aleinikoff and Douglas Klusmeyer, *Citizenship Policies for an Age of Migration* (Carnegie Endowment for International Peace, 2002).

80. Ibid., pp. 57–58.

81. See U.S. Commission on Immigration Reform, *Becoming an American: Immigration and Immigrant Policy*, September 1997, p. 47.

82. For proposals along these lines, see Daniel T. Griswold, "Willing Workers: Fixing the Problem of Illegal Mexican Immigration to the United States," Trade Policy Analysis 19, Cato Institute, Center for Trade Policy Studies, October 15, 2002 (www.freetrade.org/pubs/pas/tpa-019es.html [accessed February 2003]); and Demetrios G. Papademetriou, "A Grand Bargain: Balancing the National Security, Economic, and Immigration Interests

of the U.S. and Mexico," Migration Policy Institute, Washington, April 2002 (www. migrationpolicy.org/files/bargain.pdf [accessed February 2003]).

83. Massey, Durand, and Malone, *Beyond Smoke and Mirrors*, p. 45.

84. John Maggs, "The Economics of Being Hispanic," *National Journal*, August 14, 1999, pp. 2359–61.

85. See George Borjas, *Heaven's Door: Immigration Policy and the American Economy* (Princeton University Press, 1999).

86. Dana Canedy, "Troubling Label for Hispanics: Girls Most Likely to Drop Out," *New York Times*, March 25, 2001, p. 1.

87. Richard Fry and B. Lindsay Lowell, "Work or Study: Different Fortunes of U.S. Latino Generations," Pew Hispanic Center, Washington, May 2002, p. 21 (www.pewhispanic.org/ site/docs/pdf/phc_report_final_gens_&_labor_market_-_final_copy.pdf [accessed February 2003]).

88. Maria Puente and Martin Kasindorf, "Hispanic Experience: Unique, Evolving," *USA Today*, September 7, 1999, p. A1.

89. See, for example, Steven A. Camarota, "The Slowing Progress of Immigrants: An Examination of Income, Home Ownership, and Citizenship, 1970–2000," Center for Immigration Studies *Backgrounder*, Washington, March 2001, p. 7 (www.cis.org/articles/2001/back401.pdf [accessed February 2003]).

90. Derived from data in U.S. Census Bureau, "Historic Income Tables—People (Table P-43D) Work Experience—Workers of Hispanic Origin," May 8, 2001; U.S. Census Bureau, "Historic Income Tables—People (Table P-43) Workers (Both Sexes Combined All Races)," September 21, 2001; and U.S. Census Bureau, "Historic Income Tables—People (Table P-43) Work Experience—Workers of Asian Origin," September 20, 2001 (www.census.gov/hhes/income/histinc [accessed February 2003]).

91. Fry and Lowell, "Work or Study," p. 21.

92. One poll found that 67 percent of Hispanic parents say that education is the single most important factor determining economic success, higher than African American parents (45 percent) or parents overall (35 percent). Jodi Wilgoren, "College Education Seen as Essential," *New York Times*, May 4, 2000, p. A23.

93. Fry and Lowell, "Work or Study," p. 12.

94. Michael Fix, Wendy Zimmerman, and Jeffrey S. Passel, "The Integration of Immigrant Families in the United States," Urban Institute, Washington, July 2001, pp. 50–51 (www.urban.org/UploadedPDF/immig_integration.pdf [accessed February 2003]).

95. *Eager for English: How and Why New York's Shortage of English Classes for Immigrants Should Be Addressed*, New York Immigration Coalition, New York, undated, p. 1. See also, Jim O'Grady, "A Shortage of Seats to Learn Miss Liberty's Tongue," *New York Times*, May 6, 2001, p. 4.

96. Interviews with officials in the California Department of Education and the Texas Education Agency, August 2001.

97. See "Celebrating Cultural and Linguistic Diversity in Head Start," Commissioner's Office of Research and Evaluation and the Head Start Bureau, U.S. Department of Health and Human Services, April 2000, p. xi (www.acf.dhhs.gov/programs/core/pubs_reports/diversity/celebrating.pdf [accessed February 2003]).

98. See U.S. Commission on Immigration Reform, *Becoming an American*, p. 45.

99. See Michelle Miller-Adams, *Owning Up: Poverty, Assets, and the American Dream* (Brookings, 2002).

100. See Jay Mathews, "Early Head Start Offers an Edge," *Washington Post*, June 4, 2002, p. A9.

101. See Peter Skerry, "Beyond Sushiology: Does Diversity Work?" *Brookings Review*, vol. 20 (Winter 2001), pp. 20–23; and Peter Skerry, "Do We Really Want Immigrants to Assimilate?" *Society*, vol. 37 (March/April 2000), pp. 61–62.

102. Eric Schmitt, "Pockets of Protest Are Rising against Immigration," *New York Times*, August 9, 2001, p. A12; and Susan Sachs and Al Baker, "Few Local Issues at Anti-Immigrant Gathering," *New York Times*, August 5, 2001, p. 30.

103. Fix, Zimmerman, and Passel, "Integration of Immigrant Families," pp. 45–46.

104. Among other studies of the origins and evolution of affirmative action, see Hugh Davis Graham, *Collision Course: The Strange Convergence of Affirmative Action and Immigration Policy in America* (Oxford University Press, 2002); and John Skrentny, *Ironies of Affirmative Action: Politics, Justice, and Culture in America* (University of Chicago Press, 1995).

105. See, for example, Greg Sangillo, "Who's Hispanic?" *National Journal*, June 8, 2002, pp. 1699–1702.

106. Graham, *Collision Course*, chap. 6.

107. Office of Management and Budget, "Guidance on Aggregation and Allocation of Data on Race for Use in Civil Rights Monitoring and Enforcement," OMB Bulletin No. 00-02, March 9, 2000.

108. See Graham, *Collision Course*, chap. 7.

109. Peter H. Schuck, "Affirmative Action: Don't Mend It or End It—Bend It," *Brookings Review*, vol. 20 (Winter 2002), p. 27.

110. See Jennifer Lee, "The Racial and Ethnic Meaning behind *Black*: Retailers' Hiring Practices in Inner-City Neighborhoods," in John David Skrentny, ed., *Color Lines: Affirmative Action, Immigration, and Civil Rights Options for America* (University of Chicago Press, 2001); and Michael Lichter and Roger Waldinger, "Producing Conflict: Immigration and Management of Diversity in the Multiethnic Metropolis," in Skrentny, ed., *Color Lines*.

111. See Charlotte Steeh and Maria Krysan, "Affirmative Action and the Public, 1970–1995," *Public Opinion Quarterly*, vol. 60 (Spring 1996), pp. 128–58.

112. See Davis, *Collision Course*, p. 16; Seymour Martin Lipset, "Affirmative Action and the American Creed," *Wilson Quarterly*, vol. 16 (Winter 1992), pp. 52–62; Paul M. Sniderman and Edward C. Carmines, *Reaching beyond Race* (Harvard University Press, 1997).

113. The FBI recorded 481 hate crimes against Muslims in 2001, up from 28 in 2000. See Federal Bureau of Investigtation, *Crime in the United States—2000* (U.S. GPO, 2001), p. 60 (www.fbi.gov/ucr/cius_00/00crime2.pdf [acessed February 2003]); and Federal Bureau of Investigation, *Crime in the United States—2001* (U.S. GPO, 2002), p. 60 (www.fbi.gov/ucr/01cius.htm [accessed February 2003]).

114. For an extended discussion of how class-based affirmative action policies would work, see Richard D. Kahlenberg, *The Remedy: Class, Race, and Affirmative Action* (Basic Books, 1997), esp. chaps. 5 and 6.

115. Sean Cavanaugh, "Slowly, UC System Begins to Accept More Minority Students," *Education Week*, April 24, 2002, p. 16; Piper Fogg, "U. of California Admits More Minority

Students," *Chronicle of Higher Education*, April 19, 2002, p. A26; "Sweat, Not Blood," *Economist*, April 20, 2002, p. 30; and Jim Yardley, "The 10 Percent Solution," *New York Times*, April 14, 2002, p. A28.

116. Jennifer Merritt, "Wanted: A Campus That Looks Like America," *BusinessWeek*, March 11, 2002, pp. 56–58. See also Erin Kelly and Frank Dobbin, "How Affirmative-Action Became Diversity Management: Employer Response to Antidiscrimination Law, 1961–1996," in Skrentny, ed., *Color Lines*.

117. Among others, see Carol Swain, Kyra R. Greene, and Christine Min Wotipka, "Understanding Racial Polarization on Affirmative Action: The View from Focus Groups," in Skrentny, ed., *Color Lines*; Sniderman and Carmines, *Reaching beyond Race*; and Paul M. Sniderman and Edward G. Carmines, "The Moral Basis of a Color-Blind Politics," in Christopher H. Foreman, ed., *The African-American Predicament* (Brookings, 1999), pp. 175–201.

118. Orlando Patterson, "Affirmative Action" in Foreman, ed., *The African American Predicament*, pp. 45–60; and Cornel West, *Race Matters* (Beacon Press, 1993), pp. 95–96.

119. Admissions of black and Latino students at the University of Texas at Austin were not substantially lower in 2002 than when affirmative action policies were still in place. However, given that the percentage of college-aged blacks and Hispanics in Texas grew from 44 percent in 1990 to 52 percent in 2000, minority representation has not kept pace with the growth of minority youth in Texas. See Adam Liptak, "Racial Math: Affirmative Action by Any Other Name," *New York Times*, January 19, 2003, p. 4.1.

HOWARD GRUENSPECHT
PAUL R. PORTNEY

8

Energy and
Environmental Policy

G OVERNMENT ORGANIZATION CAN hinder or facilitate the formation
of sound public policy. Few policy areas better illustrate the interaction of structure and substance than do energy and the environment. Energy and environmental policies are almost inextricably intertwined, and the connections are tightening as concern grows over global warming caused by energy-related greenhouse gas emissions. Yet the organization of the federal government agencies that make policy in these areas does not reflect this interdependence. It is time to deal with this problem.

The cost of poor coordination has been high. Agencies with narrow statutory missions focus on one part of the energy and environmental policy puzzle. They routinely fail to identify and resolve potential conflicts among policies. They often miss significant opportunities to develop and implement strategies that can simultaneously advance both energy and environmental objectives.

Diffusion of authority across multiple agencies has especially hampered the development of energy policy. Even well-informed citizens might assume that the Department of Energy (DOE) has the primary role in shaping policies that determine the nation's demand for oil, the fuels and technologies used to generate its electricity, the reliability of its energy supply systems, and the domestic production of energy. Yet many of the key decisions in these areas rest with agencies concerned primarily with objectives outside the realm of energy policy. The Department of Transportation, for example, is responsible for fuel-economy standards. The Environmental Protection Agency (EPA) establishes vehicle emissions standards and regulates the content and performance of motor fuels. The Treasury Department designs energy tax policies. Each of these agencies influences the nation's demand for oil far more than does the DOE. Similarly, EPA policies governing emissions from power plants have a dominant impact on fuel choices and turnover of capital stock in the nation's electricity supply infrastructure. Although the DOE does have a lead role in research and development (R&D) of advanced energy supply and efficiency technologies, it has virtually *no* authority to influence the most fundamental energy questions facing the nation.

It is not hard to illustrate the interactions between energy and environmental policies. Electricity generation—particularly from coal—accounts for a substantial share of many important air pollutants. Motor vehicles used for personal transportation and trucking are also major emitters. While non-energy activities are major sources of water pollution and solid and hazardous wastes, power plants, petroleum refineries, and petrochemical plants are also significant sources of these pollutants.

Not only does the use of energy create (and occasionally contribute to the solution of) environmental problems, but our environmental laws and regulations largely determine the types of energy we use and where and how we use them. These policies are deficient in important respects that we outline in this chapter, and these deficiencies, in turn, flow in significant measure from the way policymaking agencies are organized. Specifically, the goals of U.S. environmental policy are rather clearly focused. Each of the major statutes under which the EPA regulates spells out reasonably clear goals and criteria for rule-making. In contrast, the goals of U.S. energy policy are diffuse. The Department of Energy has little statutory authority to direct energy policy, and its budget is unsuited to the task of shaping America's energy future.

We set ourselves three tasks in this brief chapter. We outline the respects in which energy and environmental policy are all but inseparable and describe the way in which the EPA and the DOE are organized. We then examine organizational barriers to coherent energy and environmental policymaking and what might be done to address them. We were tempted to consider options for a wholesale reorganization of the government structures for federal energy and environmental policymaking. However, such reorganizations generate large transition costs as responsibilities are shifted.

The difficulty of reconciling different bureaucratic cultures is still apparent twenty-five years after separate agencies were merged to form the DOE, and the debate regarding creation of a Department of Homeland Security underscored the difficulty. For these reasons, we focus on organizational changes intended to improve the effectiveness of the DOE and foster inter-agency coordination.

Within the DOE, we suggest consolidating bureaucracies that focus on a single fuel or exclusively on demand-side or supply-side concerns, because such consolidation would facilitate development of policies to promote a secure, affordable, and environmentally responsible supply of energy to the country. Instead, we recommend that energy program offices be restructured along sectoral lines. On the interagency level, we consider ways to provide agency staff with incentives to identify and resolve conflicts between energy and environmental programs at the earliest possible date rather than to "dig foxholes" to defend uncoordinated energy and environmental policies. Finally, we identify several policies that could advance energy and environmental goals more effectively than do current policies.

We recognize that advocates of a clean environment and advocates of energy independence are likely to regard a call for government reform not as an answer to their prayers but as a diversion. We believe that both groups need to recognize that their objectives are closely intertwined and that a well-designed government structure is a prerequisite to improved policy.

Energy and the Environment: Where Do We Stand?

U.S. energy consumption has grown steadily for half a century, interrupted only during a four-year period between 1979 and 1983, when energy-price shocks and economic weakness caused total energy use to fall. Economic output and energy use grew at comparable rates between 1950 and 1970. Since then, growth of the economy has outpaced the increase in energy use. In 2000 energy use in all forms totaled 99 quads (quadrillion British thermal units), but energy consumption per dollar of real output was 44 percent lower than it was in 1970 (see table 8-1).[1]

The share of fossil fuels in total energy consumption is likely to rise over the next several decades despite growing use of renewable energy sources such as wind because today's major nonfossil sources of energy—nuclear energy and hydropower—are likely to account for a falling share of energy use and will provide a declining amount of energy once significant retirements of

Table 8-1. *U.S. Energy Consumption, 2000*

Source	Quads
Oil	38
Natural gas	24
Coal	23
Nuclear	8
Hydroelectric	3
Biomass (wood, waste, alcohol)	3
Geothermal, wind, solar	< 1

existing nuclear plants begin. We examine here the environmental implications of increased reliance on fossil fuels.

The environment has improved markedly since the early 1970s, whether measured by emissions or ambient concentrations of pollutants. Between 1970 and 1998, emissions of sulfur dioxide, volatile organic compounds, carbon monoxide, and lead fell 37, 42, 31, and 98 percent, respectively. Emissions of nitrogen oxides increased 17 percent over this period, with nearly all of the increase occurring between 1970 and 1975. Recently implemented and pending policies are reducing emissions of nitrogen oxides and sulfur dioxide even further.[2]

Reductions in air pollutant emissions over the past three decades have brought many metropolitan areas into full compliance with ambient air quality standards. They have also sharply reduced the severity and number of violations in areas still classified as being out of attainment. Trends in water quality have also been favorable. Since 1970 the proportion of lakes and rivers deemed to be safe for fishing and swimming, classified using criteria established by the Clean Water Act, has doubled from one-third to nearly two-thirds of all water bodies.

Despite these generally favorable trends, significant additional reductions in emissions will be needed to meet current and newly established environmental goals. More than 90 million Americans still live in areas where the ambient air quality standard for smog is violated on more than one day a year, the criterion used to classify attainment status. Under new, more stringent air quality standards for smog and particulates issued in 1997, and recently upheld by the U.S. Supreme Court, both the number of areas classified as being out of attainment and the proportion of total U.S. population living in such areas will likely increase.

Current Structure for Energy Policymaking

Many citizens undoubtedly believe that the Department of Energy and its secretary have primary authority over energy policy and regulation, just as the Environmental Protection Agency and its administrator have over environmental issues. The reality is quite different: authority over energy issues is widely dispersed across federal agencies, and the vast majority of the DOE's resources and personnel are focused on activities almost wholly unrelated to energy. For example, the Federal Energy Regulatory Commission, rather than the DOE, regulates wholesale natural gas and oil pipelines. The Department of the Interior controls leasing of coal, oil, and gas resources on federal lands, as well as offshore oil and gas development in federal waters outside the three-mile limit. The Department of Transportation, through the National Highway Safety Traffic Administration, sets vehicle fuel-economy standards, one of the few policy levers that could significantly affect the demand for oil. The EPA regulates environmental quality under statutes that in many cases require a single-minded pursuit of environmental quality without regard to the resulting consequences for energy.

Thus the DOE's mission—notwithstanding its name—is largely unrelated to energy supply and demand. Only $2.8 billion, less than 15 percent of the DOE's $21.3 billion budget in fiscal 2002, serves an energy resources mission. The vast majority of DOE staff in the energy resources area manage technology R&D programs and have little or no expertise on energy policy issues.[3] The DOE is also responsible for operation of the strategic petroleum reserve, but decisions regarding its use require a presidential determination under highly restrictive statutory criteria. National security activities related to nuclear weapons and naval reactors, and the environmental remediation of facilities used in these programs, account for most of the DOE's budget; they have combined annual appropriations in excess of $14 billion. Basic science activities at national laboratories and universities, another major DOE mission, are funded at $3.3 billion.[4]

Structure for Environmental Decisionmaking

A reorganization of the executive branch by President Richard Nixon in 1970 led to the creation of the Environmental Protection Agency. Before then, the Department of Health, Education, and Welfare handled air pollution, the Department of the Interior dealt with water pollution, the Department of Agriculture regulated pesticides, and the Atomic Energy Commission set radiation standards. The EPA is organized largely according to the environmental media through which problems manifest themselves: air, water, drinking water, land contamination, pesticide residues on foodstuffs, and so on.

Seven major statutes spell out, in quite general terms, the goals of policy, the tools available to the EPA to pursue these goals, the kinds of penalties the EPA can impose on violators, and the role that lower levels of government play in implementing policy.[5] This statutory situation contrasts markedly with that of the DOE and its role in energy policy.

The laws governing EPA activities clearly spell out what the EPA is supposed to accomplish. Under the Clean Air Act, for example, the EPA administrator sets "national ambient air quality standards" for six common air pollutants—standards that are to provide an "adequate margin of safety" against "adverse health effects," paying particular attention to "sensitive populations." In addition, the EPA sets what are called "new source performance standards" that mandate the types of pollution control equipment, acceptable fuels, or other technical specifications for any new facility, including power plants, factories, and—increasingly—even small businesses like dry cleaners or auto paint shops.

The Clean Water Act specifies that the ultimate goal of policy is to ensure that water is "fishable and swimmable." It would reach this goal through the equivalent of new source performance standards, as well as controls on current water polluters such as municipal waste treatment plants, factories, and even farmers and land developers. Each of the five other statutes enunciates reasonably clear—if often unobtainable—goals and spells out the types of regulations that the EPA must promulgate, dates by which the standards must be issued, dates by which compliance is supposed to be ensured, and penalties available to the EPA and the Justice Department in the event of failure to comply.

The resulting regulations have become an important part of the political landscape. They run to thousands of pages in the Code of Federal Regulations and have generated significant costs and benefits to affected parties. In its 2002 report to Congress, the Office of Information and Regulatory Affairs of the Office of Management and Budget estimates that federal environmental regulations in 2001 forced expenditures of $120 billion to $203 billion annually for compliance but created annual benefits worth $120 billion to $1.8 trillion.[6]

All of this regulatory activity generates controversy, including disagreements about the appropriate role of the federal government vis-à-vis the states, the proper weight for economic considerations in environmental standard-setting, and the extent to which environmental regulations can be considered illegal barriers to international trade. But three points are not in dispute. First, the EPA has clear authority to regulate as a result of the powers delegated to it by Congress, and this authority has been regularly reaffirmed by higher courts. Second, the authorizing legislation spells out the goals of federal environmental policy. Third, at least some of the most important goals lend themselves to quantification. For instance, progress in attaining the air quality standards is quite measurable. In fact, each and every year the EPA issues a report detailing this progress.[7] Similarly, the EPA reports at least periodically on the fraction of the nation's waters that have met the appropriate water quality goals, the percentage of municipal drinking water systems that meet drinking water standards, the status of sites on the National Priorities List (the collection of hazardous waste sites targeted for cleanup under the superfund law), and the share of active ingredients in pesticides that have been tested and registered under the Federal Insecticide, Fungicide, and Rodenticide Act.

How Energy Use Can Create Environmental Problems

Fossil energy accounts for most air pollutant emissions—93 percent of sulfur dioxide emissions, 95 percent of nitrogen oxide emissions, 85 percent of carbon monoxide emissions, and 48 percent of volatile organic compound emissions. These pollutants are associated with significant air quality concerns. Sulfur dioxide and nitrogen oxide emissions contribute to acid rain and to fine particulate pollution, which has been associated with elevated mortality. Nitrogen oxide and volatile organic compounds are both precursors of ground-level ozone, commonly referred to as smog. Energy production and use contribute to toxic air pollution and create radioactive wastes that require careful management.

Energy activities also significantly affect water quality. The production of oil and gas and the use of the nation's surface waters to cool energy facilities can affect water quality and water resources both above and below the earth's surface. Moreover, the transport, storage, and handling of oil products can involve accidental releases to water bodies. Major spills, such as the 1989 oil spill near Valdez, Alaska, are infrequent, but minor spills and chronic discharges can also present significant water quality problems.

The impact of energy activities on land use is another concern. Many of the nation's fossil energy resources are located on public lands or off-shore; and environmental and aesthetic considerations may preclude their development. Renewable energy sources, such as hydropower, wind, solar, and biomass energy, do not emit greenhouse gases, as does fossil energy, but they affect a much larger quantity of land per unit of energy provided. Finally, routes for electricity transmission lines and natural gas pipelines and gathering systems may intersect federal lands or wetlands where access may be restricted for environmental reasons. An estimated 90 percent of the oil and gas pipeline rights-of-way in the western United States are dependent to some extent on right-of-way authorizations on public lands.[8]

Of the many environmental concerns raised by the use of fossil energy, the emission of greenhouse gases is the most difficult to address. The Intergovernmental Panel on Climate Change found in 2001 that the earth's climate has been changing over the past century and that human activities are contributing to this change.[9] The atmospheric concentration of carbon dioxide, the most important greenhouse gas, has increased from a preindustrial level of roughly 280 parts per million to a current level of 370 parts per million. U.S. energy-related emissions of carbon dioxide increased 36 percent between 1970 and 2000, with three-quarters of the increase occurring after 1985. These increases have tracked trends in the use of fossil fuels. Furthermore, while other emissions from fossil fuel combustion can be controlled through technological means at modest cost, no practicable technology now exists to control carbon dioxide emissions. Currently, reduction in energy-related carbon dioxide emissions within the United States can be achieved only through policies that reduce the use of energy or shift the energy mix in favor of low- and no-carbon fuels, including natural gas, nuclear power, and renewable energy.[10]

The United States accounts for approximately 25 percent of global energy use and world GDP, but only 5 percent of the world's population. Accordingly, the United States uses about the global average of energy per dollar of GDP, but U.S. per capita energy use far exceeds the global average. Energy-related carbon dioxide emissions constitute more than 80 percent of total U.S. greenhouse gas emissions. Until technological options for the removal and permanent storage of the carbon content of fossil fuels are available, any policy decisions to limit energy-related carbon dioxide emissions based on environmental considerations will directly affect the composition and level of energy use. Conversely, energy policies designed to influence the mix of fuels and overall level of energy use will determine energy-related carbon dioxide emissions.

How Environmental Policies Affect Energy Options

Environmental policies can influence the choices regarding what technologies to adopt and what fuels to use. They can affect decisions regarding when to replace or close energy plants. By requiring downtime for emission control retrofits and constraining maintenance activities, they can affect price volatility in energy markets. In this section we describe how environmental policies have affected the electric power sector, motor fuels markets, and vehicle fuel-economy technology.

Electric Power

Power plants are required to reduce pollution if they are located in areas that do not meet air quality standards or if their emissions contribute to violations of the standards in downwind areas. Plants sometimes meet standards by installing pollution control equipment. In other cases, they may burn natural gas instead of coal or shift production away from coal-fired plants with high emissions rates. Use of such strategies changes the mix of fuels used to generate power.

The New Source Review (NSR) is an important environmental program that significantly affects power plants and other major energy facilities. The program applies to any new source whose potential emissions at full use are high enough to qualify it as a major source of pollution.[11] The program also applies to any change at an existing major source that increases emissions. Sources subject to the NSR must secure a permit before beginning construction or modification and must achieve emissions rates that reflect the performance of the best-available emissions control technology. NSR sources in areas that do not meet national ambient air quality standards must also show that other sources of pollution have been reduced by the same amount of pollution added by the new source.

Experience over the past twenty-five years has shown that this approach is excessively costly and may be environmentally counterproductive. The reason for this is that it motivates companies to keep old (and dirty) plants operating and to hold back on investments in new (and cleaner) power generation technologies. The reduction in flexibility and disincentive to turnover also conflicts with energy policy goals by "crowding out" otherwise attractive investment in new energy technologies.

The current application of the NSR to existing plants also raises several serious problems.[12] First, although old plants typically emit most of the pollution in any sector, the NSR does not provide a continuous and effective incentive for reducing emissions at these plants. As a result, many of the most cost-effective opportunities to reduce emissions are simply not exploited. Second, because "modifications" trigger a lengthy and costly process, the NSR actually discourages improvements and efficiency upgrades at old plants. Since adjusting the existing equipment to perform better can reduce pollution as well as save money, the chilling effect of the NSR program can be both economically and environmentally harmful. It can also discourage legitimate maintenance projects, which can adversely affect the reliability of the electricity supply system.

Motor Fuels Markets

Environmental regulations also play an important role in the markets for motor fuels. How gasoline is formulated affects the level of pre- or post-combustion emissions covered by national air quality standards, the performance of emissions control equipment, the level of toxic emissions not covered by air quality standards, and the economic value of particular additives and blendstocks. Between 1970 and 1990, public policy regarding gasoline formulation focused on the elimination of lead. The national shift to unleaded fuels facilitated the use of catalytic converters, which reduced tailpipe emissions of hydrocarbons, carbon monoxide, and nitrogen oxides but were rendered ineffective by leaded gasoline. It also dramatically reduced concentrations of lead in the environment, perhaps the greatest boon to public health from any environmental law or regulation.

The Clean Air Act Amendments of 1990 established additional fuel-formulation requirements to reduce smog and carbon monoxide even further and to promote the use of ethanol and other fuel oxygenates. In contrast to the phaseout of lead, which was national, the 1990 requirements were targeted at areas that failed to meet air quality standards for carbon monoxide or ground-level ozone, effectively splitting the national gasoline market into distinct segments for conventional, oxygenated, and reformulated gasoline.

Subsequent state and local action further segmented markets. California adopted its own, more stringent, reformulation requirement for gasoline sold throughout the state, which took effect in June 1996. Several Midwestern states used a combination of tax incentives and regulations to create a market for reformulated gas made with ethanol produced from locally grown agricultural crops, instead of with methyl tertiary butyl ether (MTBE), an additive used in most reformulated gas as a source of oxygen and octane. In order to stay within prescribed volatility limits, reformulated gas made with ethanol must be manufactured using a special low-volatility gasoline blendstock.[13] In March 1999 California announced a ban on gasoline formulated with MTBE to be effective in 2003.[14] Following its lead, sixteen additional states have enacted plans to ban or limit the use of MTBE. Several reviews of recent gasoline-price spikes have suggested that fuel formulation requirements, particularly those that increased the balkanization of regional markets, contributed significantly to price volatility.[15]

Vehicle Emissions Standards

Since the 1970s federal standards limiting the emissions rates for volatile organic compounds, nitrogen oxides, and carbon monoxide have reduced emissions of these pollutants from cars and light trucks, although vehicle miles traveled increased nearly 140 percent over the same period.[16] The sharp reduction in emissions rates, now roughly 1 percent of pre-1974 levels, occurred as vehicle fuel economy and performance were also improving.

Recently, however, tightened standards for emission of conventional pollutants have obstructed the use of advanced diesel engines, a technology that is widely used in Europe to improve fuel economy and reduce greenhouse gas emissions. As of 2002, more than 35 percent of new cars sold in Europe were diesel powered, compared to less than 1 percent in the United States.

Diesel technology figured prominently in the plans of the Partnership for a New Generation of Vehicles, a cooperative research and development program of the "Big Three" U.S. automakers and U.S. government agencies and laboratories, launched in 1993. The partnership sought to achieve technological breakthroughs and, by 2004, to produce prototypes of a car capable of getting up to 80 miles per gallon—three times greater than the average fuel efficiency of the 1993 midsize family sedan—but with no adverse impact on performance, size, utility, safety, emissions, and total cost of ownership.

The goals for fuel economy, cost, and performance, combined with the time frame of the program, led participants in the partnership to focus their efforts on vehicles that combined electric motors with advanced diesel engines—a type of hybrid powertrain. The program set aggressive targets for emissions rates but, in response to growing concern regarding the potential health effects of fine particulate pollution, adjusted them downward in

1997. However, in May 1999, the EPA proposed new "Tier 2" emissions standards for motor vehicles, including a nitrogen oxide standard of 0.07 gram per mile, significantly below the 0.20 gram per mile target used in the partnership program and in present and planned European standards. The National Research Council panel overseeing the partnership's efforts concluded that these standards effectively precluded the use of advanced diesel engines.[17] The EPA may well have made the right decision, as recent literature suggests that diesel particulate emissions may have health effects that merit extremely stringent controls. But the need for coordinating emissions control and fuel efficiency strategies is clear.

Organizing Energy and Environmental Policies: Experience of Other Countries

Like the United States, nearly all other major industrial countries have a national ministry focused on environmental protection. However, the United States is virtually alone in having an energy policy function located outside of a ministry with broad jurisdiction over industrial or economic activity. The most direct explanation is that the U.S. government does not have any broad industrial policy, as other countries do. Nonetheless, lessons from abroad may prove instructive.

Case Studies

The lead role for energy policy rests with the Ministry of Economics and Technology in Germany, with the Department of Trade and Industry in the United Kingdom, with the Ministry of Economic Affairs, Finance, and Industry in France, and with the Ministry of Economy, Trade, and Industry (METI, formerly MITI) in Japan. These ministries typically exercise much greater influence over energy-intensive industries and power generators than does the U.S. Department of Energy. They also have more input into the development of national tax and subsidy policies, levers that give them power to influence energy use.

In Japan, the Agency of Natural Resources and Energy within the METI is responsible for the rational development of mineral resources, for the assurance of a stable supply of energy, for the promotion of efficient energy use, and for the regulation of the electric power and other energy industries. It is also responsible for energy R&D, including nuclear energy R&D, which until recently was handled through an independent science and technology agency.

Energy is only one aspect of the METI's broad mission, which encompasses industrial, trade, and technology policies and consumer affairs. Japan's lackluster economic performance over the past decade has somewhat dimmed the reputation of the METI (and the MITI) as a masterful designer of industrial, trade, and investment policies responsible for Japan's postwar economic miracle. Nevertheless, the METI retains its role as one of the most powerful ministries in Japan's government structure. To say that the DOE does not have a comparable position is an understatement.

The experience of Denmark illustrates the evolution of government organization to address the interaction of energy and environmental policy issues. Until 1994 the Danish Energy Agency functioned as a stand-alone ministry primarily responsible for energy policy. Its functions included planning the supply of power, heat, and natural gas; regulating oil and gas exploration and production activities; promoting the technological development and use of wind and other renewable energy technologies; managing energy conservation campaigns, appliance efficiency labeling, and subsidy programs to promote efficiency; and negotiating agreements for industrial investment in energy-efficiency capital in return for carbon tax rebates. In 1994 the Energy and Environmental Protection Agencies were placed within a single entity, the Ministry of Environment and Energy. The new agency was responsible for administration and research in the areas of national environmental protection and energy planning. The government's strong environmental orientation was reflected in aggressive policies to limit the use of fossil fuels, including the imposition of a carbon tax, as well as aggressive policies to promote the use of wind energy. By 2001 wind power accounted for 13 percent of total electricity generation in Denmark, and there were plans to develop significantly more generation from offshore wind farms. The situation changed quickly, however, following elections held in November 2001 that replaced the Social Democratic government with one led by conservative parties. The new government quickly moved responsibility concerning energy matters to the Ministry of Economic and Business Affairs, emulating the organizational approach used in most other industrial countries. The new government has maintained Denmark's commitment to popular environmental goals, such as ratification and implementation of the Kyoto Protocol, which limits emissions of greenhouse gases. However, energy policy is less subservient to environmental policy goals under the new regime. Plans have already been announced to scale back support for offshore wind power and for clean energy activities in developing countries.

Lessons for the United States

In considering lessons that might be drawn for the United States, it is important to recognize that fundamental differences in government structure make getting the organization right even more important here than abroad. Almost without exception, the other industrial democracies are parliamentary systems, constitutionally biased toward quick decisionmaking and action. The majority party or coalition of parties, which controls both the legislative and executive powers, holds a clear, unambiguous, and unimpeded mandate to govern. It need not negotiate, bargain, and compromise. Such governments can make and carry out authoritative, binding decisions. In this setting, organizational differences and impediments to a preferred policy direction can be readily overcome.

The American system, in contrast, is constitutionally biased toward the operation of numerous checks and balances. Departments and agencies carry out their distinct activities within highly prescriptive statutory mandates that can only be changed through an arduous legislative process that generally requires substantial consensus. Agencies that alter policies under their direct control in the interests of broader policy coherence may find their actions challenged in the courts. Each agency is subject to oversight by particular committees of Congress, each with distinct policy preferences that govern their legislative and oversight actions. In areas where jurisdiction is unclear, each interest group goes to great lengths to move authority toward agencies and committees perceived to be sympathetic to its position. Of equal importance, no government agency has the power over industrial decisions that is routinely accorded to bureaucrats in Europe and Japan.

These differences are particularly apparent for the emerging issue of global warming. Energy interests want legislation to originate in the Senate Energy and Natural Resources Committee and be administered by the DOE. Environmentalists generally prefer that legislation originate in the Senate Environment and Public Works Committee and be administered by the "greener" EPA.[18] Congress needs to rise above this battle of interests to develop a framework that pays more than lip service to the coordination of energy and environmental policy.

Current Execution of Energy and Environmental Policies

Energy and environmental policies have taken radically different paths for thirty years. Environmental policies and programs generally focus on the attainment of quantified objectives for concentrations or emissions of ambient pollutants. The Clean Air Act, for example, requires each region in which a national ambient air quality standard is violated to develop a plan to meet the standard. Jurisdictions with particularly poor air quality are provided a longer period in which to comply, but they are subject to more stringent limits on the introduction of additional major sources of pollution. Areas that do not develop suitable plans risk imposition of a federal plan. Moreover, each jurisdiction is required to show continuous progress in reducing emissions that contribute to violations of the standards. Areas that do not make the required progress face sanctions that include the loss of federal highway funding.

The oil-price shocks of the 1970s initially sparked highly interventionist energy policies. Complex oil-price controls were implemented. The use of natural gas for power generation was restricted—one of the main reasons America today relies so heavily on coal for electricity generation. Massive R&D programs were launched for alternative energy technologies such as nuclear breeder reactors, coal-based synfuels, and oil production from shale. Vehicle fuel-economy standards were established. These policies reflected the conventional wisdom of the day that oil and natural gas supplies were "running out" and that real oil prices would double or rise even more over the following two decades relative to their 1980 level.[19]

During the 1980s and 1990s, a consensus emerged favoring increased reliance on market-oriented policies. This change in approach both contributed to, and was supported by, the moderation in prices and the increase in energy supplies. The Federal Energy Regulatory Commission took the lead in opening markets to competition, as competitive gas markets produced abundant supplies of gas at prices far below the "take or pay" price for marginal supplies of regulated gas only a few years earlier. Global oil markets were also responsive to market forces. Real world prices in the range of $50 a barrel (1996 dollars) in the early 1980s spurred both a large increase in production in areas other than the Middle East and a significant slowdown in the growth of demand. Prices fell and have averaged about $20 a barrel in real terms since 1986.

Energy policies built around the attainment of quantified goals have become unfashionable for several reasons. Many of the most prescriptive energy policies of the 1970s failed and resulted in large economic costs. The market-oriented policies that supplanted them were generally successful. And doubts have intensified regarding the significance, or even the existence, of nonenvironmental externalities that would justify interference in private markets. The goals of energy policy now are typically stated in general terms, such as the need for energy that is affordable, reliable, clean, secure, and efficient. In contrast to environmental policies, there are no universally accepted measures of progress toward these goals.

The difficulty of specifying the meaning of energy security is illustrative. One commonly cited indicator is the proportion of total petroleum consumption that must be imported or the share of imports from unstable areas. These measures are quite imperfect, however. The vulnerability of the U.S. economy to oil-price shocks, which seems to be the primary policy concern regarding oil markets, depends on the intensity of petroleum use throughout the industrial world, not just on U.S. imports in total or from the Middle East. Even if U.S. petroleum production rose enough to eliminate imports, a shock in world oil markets would still raise domestic prices and harm the economy because U.S. petroleum suppliers would charge the same price as other suppliers. The same would be true if imports from the Middle East ended and the United States came to rely primarily on "safer" sources of imports—in fact, most U.S. petroleum imports are already from "safe" regions. The point is simply that a shock anywhere in the world will be felt throughout an integrated world oil market.[20]

Energy-price volatility is not, of course, restricted to oil markets. The economic impacts of a disruption in the electricity system are potentially enormous. The value of unscheduled outages is typically estimated in the range of $3,000 to $20,000 per megawatt-hour. Even the low end of this range is nearly 100 times the typical wholesale price of power and nearly ten times the prices experienced in California during the worst of last year's market meltdown. The events of September 11 highlight a new risk to energy security: the possibility of terrorist attacks on energy infrastructure. One perhaps unintended consequence of the lack of agreed measures of energy security or other energy policy objectives is that they are likely to be sacrificed when they conflict with concrete and measurable goals not related to energy.

Large-Scale Organizational Changes

Although it is possible, in principle, to make good policy regardless of the organizational framework, well-designed administrative structures can facilitate the sorts of communication and policy coordination that energy and environmental policy so sorely need. Here we describe a variety of organizational changes that could advance this objective.

Reorganization of the Department of Energy

The DOE's energy programs are organized according to the primary sources of fuel. The offices of fossil energy, nuclear energy, and energy efficiency and renewable energy each independently promote electricity generation technologies within their respective domain, with little or no reference to a common vision of the nation's future electricity supply. These technology-oriented programs largely ignore the design of wholesale power markets and institutions governing the transmission system. We believe that these fuel-based organizations should be placed within an Office of Electricity that would encompass nuclear, fossil, and renewable energy technologies as well as programs related to uranium and coal fuels that are used almost exclusively to generate electricity. Such an office could provide a comprehensive perspective on supply options and policies affecting electricity markets. It could improve on the current ad hoc approaches used to address such issues at higher departmental levels.

A similar approach should be followed in other areas. In light of the fact that more than two-thirds of petroleum is used for transportation, DOE programs in vehicle technology, alternative fuels, and oil should be consolidated into an Office of Transportation Energy. Such a broadened authority would be in a position to consider actions on both the demand and supply sides of the petroleum fuels market. Other offices could focus on industrial energy (which currently accounts for nearly one-third of total U.S. energy use) and residential and commercial energy.

Reorganization along these lines could improve coherence in the design of energy policies and R&D programs, while avoiding the significant transition costs and political controversies associated with the broader reorganization initiatives we describe next.

Limited Interagency Reorganization of Energy Functions

Beyond internal reorganization, the DOE could be expanded to include additional responsibilities that go to the heart of energy policymaking. The power to set fuel-economy standards for passenger cars (now set by Congress) and light-duty trucks (now set by the National Highway Traffic Safety Administration) could be moved to the DOE. Congress should also consider moving some or all of the responsibility for the leasing of energy resources from the Department of the Interior to the DOE. While economic regulation of the electricity and natural gas markets should undoubtedly remain with the Federal Energy Regulatory Commission, the

DOE could also play a larger role in determining the location of critical energy infrastructure, such as major electric transmission lines, because new federal authority is needed in cases where the states fail to agree on the location of energy facilities that cross state boundaries and are needed to ensure reliable and efficient energy systems.

Integration of Energy and Environmental Functions

The limited interagency reorganizations outlined above would provoke considerable controversy. An even more ambitious proposal—combining the EPA and the DOE into a single Department of Energy and the Environment—would provoke even more. In theory, at least, such a change would force the trade-offs inherent in energy and environmental policy-making to be confronted earlier in the policy process. It would be more difficult to propose policies that further environmental goals, for instance, while taking inadequate account of their effects on the availability of energy. Conversely, proposals that enhance domestic energy supplies at the expense of environmental quality would be unlikely to get as far as they do under the current "stovepipe" system.

Even this merger of energy and environmental policy formulation would not obviate the need for interagency review, however. The departments of transportation, agriculture, interior, and commerce, among others, could quite conceivably object to a proposal emanating from a Department of Energy and the Environment. In such a case, the dispute would be resolved by the Cabinet Council or other decisionmaking body that a political administration uses to balance conflicting objectives. Thus, one might argue, why not maintain separate departments and let the issues be debated at this higher level since such a debate is likely to take place with other agencies anyway. Moreover, one cannot even be sure that a single cabinet department would result in fully vetted and balanced policies. To illustrate, the EPA was created in large part out of the recognition of important interconnections among the control of air pollution, water pollution, and solid and hazardous wastes. For example, air pollution can be reduced by "scrubbing" chemicals from the flue gases of electricity-generating stations and other industrial facilities, but this generates vast amounts of solid waste. Yet the most persistent criticism is that the EPA is unable to regulate in an integrated way that ensures that it does not create a bigger problem by solving a smaller one. In other words, a Department of Energy and the Environment would not automatically get the balancing right.

Perhaps the biggest obstacle to the creation of a Department of Energy and the Environment would be the political cost to be paid. The agencies proposed for inclusion in such a department would fear a loss of power and likely resist consolidation. More important, the congressional committee and subcommittees with jurisdiction over the would-be merged agencies would surely react negatively. Such a combination would dilute or eliminate the power that the chairs of authorizing, appropriations, and oversight committees or subcommittees have over agencies or parts of agencies. Since these positions are often key to the ability of legislators to raise campaign support, any consolidation would be extraordinarily difficult politically.

Enhanced Coordination Mechanisms

Options focused on improving collaboration and coordination across agency boundaries could provide some of the benefits of comprehensive reorganization while avoiding the large transition costs and wrenching political battles associated with that path. One way to improve coordination would be to establish formal requirements for policy and regulatory developers in each agency to assess the impact of proposed actions on energy and environmental objectives that fall within the primary purview of other agencies. EPA's "cost of clean" analysis, which periodically estimates the out-of-pocket compliance costs associated with the Clean Air Act, is an example. Other environmental statutes could be extended to consider energy-related opportunity costs. Executive Order 13211 of May 2001, which directs agencies in the executive branch to prepare and submit a statement of energy effects for their "significant energy actions," also moves in this direction.

State experience further illustrates how to promote collaboration and improve coordination across agencies. California has centralized the administration and oversight of the siting process for major energy facilities at the California Energy Commission, while continuing to allow agencies with substantive expertise in each functional area—air and water quality, for example—to play the primary role in its part of the approval process. Beginning in 2000, this process approved significant amounts of new generating capacity when the need for generation became apparent.

Finally, fruitful collaboration among state-level energy and environmental agencies has occurred on an informal basis. The recent development of initiatives to curb greenhouse gas emissions in several states is particularly notable. These collaborations have occasionally extended to the regional level. Regular consultations between the New England states and the Canadian maritime provinces on energy and environmental issues have resulted in common initiatives to curb greenhouse gas emissions. Although it may be more difficult to overcome the capture of agencies by narrow constituencies at the federal level, these initiatives could nonetheless provide some useful lessons.

Policy Opportunities

Modest changes in government organization coupled with improved coordination should allow policymakers to exploit some of the policy opportunities that have heretofore been missed.

Get to the Frontier First

While some environmental and energy policy objectives are in conflict, many are not. Environmentalists have strongly opposed proposals to increase energy security in oil markets by expanding access to public lands for energy development. Instead, they have favored large legislated increases in automobile fuel-economy standards, an approach that itself has been blocked by those concerned about possible adverse effects on automakers and their employees, vehicle choice, and safety. The polarized debate surrounding this issue ignores the reality that neither of these two approaches will do much to prevent oil-price spikes and resulting economic slowdowns. To address this linkage, the government must abandon the outmoded view that the roughly 550-million-barrel strategic petroleum reserve should be used only for some undefined "emergency," not as a way of altering market prices. After all, if the energy security problem is fundamentally related to jumps in energy prices, shouldn't moderating those prices be a central policy goal? In the past some analysts called for treating the reserve as a publicly provided source of supplemental supply that the private sector can bid for through options contracts like those that already exist in commodity exchanges. That approach needs to be dusted off and seriously considered, together with a small excise tax on all petroleum consumption to pay for operating the reserve.

Quantification of Energy Objectives

A strong consensus has emerged that markets should drive energy choices and that past programs to direct or limit fuel choices were flawed. For example, the Fuel Use Act prohibited the use of natural gas to generate new electric power for more than a decade under the false premise that North

America was "running out" of gas. This law led directly to large additions of coal-fired capacity between 1975 and 1990 that otherwise would not have been built. These plants are significant sources of greenhouse gases and conventional pollutants. Such examples have led to the realization that it is neither realistic nor appropriate to establish strictly binding targets for our energy system. Market-like institutions can actually help to achieve energy objectives, as experience with tradable allowances in the environmental field illustrates. For example, tradable allowances could be used to promote renewable energy, which can advance the objectives of both fuel diversity and emissions reduction (clean energy). Several states have recently adopted what is called a renewable portfolio standard, under which retail electricity sellers are required to cover a specified fraction of their sales with energy generated from renewable energy sources. The Senate version of energy legislation in the last (107th) Congress included a renewable portfolio standard at the federal level that incorporates an "escape valve" through which the quantitative target for renewable energy is automatically relaxed if the cost premium relative to conventional energy exceeds 1.5 cents per kilowatt-hour. The escape valve eliminates the risk that establishment of the standard will create an open-ended exposure to higher costs comparable to that which might be incurred under a completely inflexible mandate. This approach could be extended to other areas of energy policy, but only if a consensus can be reached regarding the quantification of goals.

Early Identification of Potential Trade-Offs

Experience with the Partnership for a New Generation of Vehicles highlights the need for early identification of potential conflicts between energy and environmental objectives. That program pursued an approach to producing highly fuel-efficient vehicles that ultimately was precluded by the EPA's Tier 2 emissions standards.

Early action to determine the compatibility of new energy technologies with environmental standards is especially important for technologies to reduce greenhouse gas emissions from the energy sector. For example, hydrogen can be extracted from natural gas or coal and then used to generate electricity or as an alternative to petroleum as a vehicle fuel. Provided that the carbon content of the primary fuel is captured and sequestered, this fuel cycle virtually eliminates emissions of both conventional pollutants and greenhouse gases. However, large technological challenges must be overcome to make the widespread use of hydrogen possible, and cost estimates are highly uncertain.

R&D can narrow the uncertainties about technology and cost, but it cannot eliminate uncertainties that emerge from environmental policy itself. Hydrogen extracted from fossil fuels with removal and sequestration of the carbon content will always be more expensive than combustion of the source fossil fuel that vents carbon dioxide to the atmosphere, even under the most favorable conditions. For that reason, hydrogen cannot be competitive unless a significant economic value is attached to carbon dioxide reduction. Moreover, the environmental implications of leading carbon dioxide storage options, such as sequestration in deep saline aquifers, and the compatibility of these options with existing EPA rules for regulating injection wells, are also highly uncertain. While uncertainties, such as those related to the stringency of future limits on greenhouse gas emissions, cannot be eliminated, it should be possible to learn more about the environmental performance of sequestration and its compatibility with existing environmental rules by permitting and carrying out pilot sequestration projects.

Promoting Turnover of Capital Stock

We explained earlier how the New Source Review program slowed the replacement of inefficient energy facilities. One way to reduce reliance on NSR would be to cap total pollution emissions and establish an allowance trading system under which increases in emissions at one plant could be offset by reductions at another. The sulfur dioxide program in the 1990 Clean Air Act, which has successfully achieved targeted emissions reductions with a minimum of litigation, can serve as a model. No matter how emissions are initially allocated across plants, the owners of existing plants and those wishing to build new ones will face the correct incentives for deciding when to retire old plants and invest in new ones. It would also create correct incentives regarding the use of alternative fuels and technologies to reduce pollution. Requirements for localities to meet ambient air quality standards would remain in effect. Such standards would prevent a concentration of emissions allowed under the cap in any geographic region that would conflict with the need to protect public health with an adequate margin of safety.

Other regulatory modifications could promote the turnover of capital stock in a manner that serves both environmental and energy objectives. The owner of a major energy plant affected by a new environmental standard could be granted a somewhat extended period in which to bring the facility into compliance in exchange for a firm and enforceable commitment to retire the facility following the extension. The short-run environmental cost of such a policy arises from the possibility of a modest delay in reductions of the targeted pollutant. However, retirement of an old facility, once it occurs, will often reduce emissions of many other pollutants as well as achieve larger reductions in the targeted pollutant. For example, a new gas-fired power plant that would most likely replace an existing coal plant under today's market conditions would emit substantially less sulfur dioxide, nitrogen oxides, mercury, particulates, and carbon dioxide than the coal plant, even if it were retrofitted with advanced emissions controls. Thus it is quite possible that the retirement option, if taken, can produce positive results—from both an environmental and an energy perspective—by helping to accelerate the replacement of dirty old plants with clean new ones.

Conclusion

Energy and environmental objectives have always been highly interdependent. The interdependencies are becoming even more important as concern grows over the role of energy-related greenhouse gas emissions in causing changes in global climate. Although close coordination of energy and environmental policies is important, current policies are often in needless conflict. The U.S. system of checks and balances hampers the development of coherent policies. Government reorganization is all the more important as a factor influencing policy development.

Reallocating and reorganizing energy-related responsibilities within the existing Department of Energy could help to promote more balanced policy development. A reorganization that integrates the responsibilities for energy and environmental policy in a single agency would force the trade-offs inherent in energy and environmental policymaking to be confronted earlier in the policy process. However, the controversy likely to surround such a reorganization and the fact that it would not obviate the need to coordinate energy and environmental policies with other government agencies lead us to shy away from this path.

Whether or not energy functions are reorganized, energy and environmental policies can be made more consistent while making energy policies more effective. Before contemplating trade-offs between energy and environmental objectives in the name of energy security, we should get the most out of other available energy security mechanisms, such as our strategic petroleum reserve. Quantification of energy goals would improve decisionmaking. So would market-oriented tools, such as tradable allowances, that have proven to be highly effective instruments of environmental policy. Perhaps most important, existing interagency processes can be redesigned to reward early identification and resolution of conflicts between energy and environmental objectives. This step would help to avoid situations in which regulatory uncertainties compound technological uncertainties and impede the development of energy technologies that can advance both energy and environmental objectives.

Notes

1. Energy data are from Energy Information Administration, *Annual Energy Review 2001*, DOE/EIA-0384 (Washington, November 2002) and Energy Information Administration, *Renewable Energy Annual 2001*, DOE/EIA-0603 (Washington, November 2002).

2. Environmental data are from Environmental Protection Agency, *National Air Quality and Emissions Trends Report, 1999*, EPA 454/R-01-004 (Washington, March 2001).

3. Within its energy mission, the DOE's activities fall into six major areas: research and development of advanced energy supply and energy-efficiency technologies; development of energy-efficiency standards for residential appliances and commercial equipment and for model (not mandatory) residential building codes; federal energy management; dissemination of energy information; and development of a permanent repository for civilian nuclear waste. Research and development of advanced energy supply and energy-efficiency technologies are the major use of financial resources in the energy mission, accounting for approximately $2 billion in budgeted expenditures. Renewable energy and energy-efficiency technologies currently receive the bulk of this R&D funding.

4. Budget information from the DOE and the Office of Management and Budget websites: www.energy.gov and www.whitehouse.gov/omb. See Department of Energy, *FY 2003 Budget Documents* (www.mbe.doe.gov/budget/03budget/index.htm [posted February 2002; accessed June 2002]) and Office of Management and Budget, "Draft Report to Congress on the Costs and Benefits of Federal Regulation" (www.whitehouse.gov/omb/inforeg/cbreport.pdf [posted March 28, 2002; accessed January 7, 2003]).

5. The statutes are the Clean Air Act, the Clean Water Act, the Federal Insecticide, Fungicide, and Rodenticide Act, the Safe Drinking Water Act, the Resource Conservation and Recovery Act, the Toxic Substances Control Act, and the Comprehensive Environmental Response, Compensation, and Liability Act (also known as the superfund law). For a thorough overview of federal environmental policy, see Paul Portney, "EPA and the Evolution of Federal Regulation," in Paul R. Portney and Robert Stavins, eds., *Public Policies for Environmental Protection*, 2d ed. (Washington: Resources for the Future, 2000). Terry Davies and Jan Mazurek also identify several less significant environmental laws under which the EPA is delegated certain authority. See Terry Davies and Jan Mazurek, *Pollution Control in the United States: Evaluating the System* (Washington: Resources for the Future, 1998).

6. See Office of Management and Budget, "Draft Report to Congress."

7. See Environmental Protection Agency, *National Air Quality and Emissions Trends Report*.

8. Testimony of Rebecca Watson, assistant secretary, land and minerals management, Department of the Interior, before the Resources Subcommittee on Energy and Mineral Resources of the House of Representatives, July 16, 2002.

9. R. T. Watson and the Core Writing Team, eds., *Climate Change 2001: Synthesis Report* (Geneva, Switzerland: Intergovernmental Panel on Climate Change, 2001).

10. Coal has nearly twice the carbon content per unit of energy as natural gas, with oil falling roughly in the middle. Technologies to capture and sequester the carbon content of fossil fuels are being actively studied. Even under optimistic scenarios, except for limited applications where carbon sequestration can be used to boost oil and gas production, the significant capital costs and energy penalties associated with these technologies could only be justified if a high social value were attached to reducing carbon emissions.

11. The cutoff value used to determine whether a source is major generally varies between 10 and 100 tons of emissions per year, depending on the source and the severity of any air quality problem where the source is located.

12. In 1999 several high-profile enforcement actions were initiated alleging that major electric utilities had evaded NSR requiremens by imporperly classifying upgrade and life-extension projects as activities that do not count as major modifications under the EPA's rules.

13. Reformulated gasoline requires a minimum of 2.1 percent oxygen by weight, which can be met using 5.8 percent ethanol by volume or an 11.7 percent MTBE by volume. However, reformulated gas must also have a reid vapor pressure (RVP) less than 7 to limit evaporative emissions. Since RVP is much higher for ethanol than for MTBE (18 versus 8), reformulated gas requires a lower RVP blendstock if it is made with ethanol than if it is made with MTBE.

14. In March 2002 California governor Gray Davis issued an executive order delaying the effective date of the ban on MTBE by at least one year. The governor cited concerns about the adequacy of gasoline supply and the potential for gasoline-price spikes, which in his view were exacerbated by the refusal of the Bush administration to waive the oxygenate requirement in the federal Clean Air Act. Howard Gruenspecht and Robert Stavins, "New Source Review under the Clean Air Act: Ripe for Reform," *Resources*, no. 147 (Spring 2002), pp. 19–23.

15. Tancred Lidderdale and Aileen Bohn, *Demand and Price Outlook for Phase 2 Reformulated Gasoline, 2000* (Washington: Energy Information Administration, 1999); Tancred Lidderdale, *MTBE, Oxygenates, and Motor Gasoline* (Washington: Energy Information Administration, 2000); Joanne Shore, *Supply of Chicago/Milkwaukee Gasoline, Spring 2000* (Washington: Energy Information Administration, 2000).

16. *Ward's Motor Vehicle Facts and Figures* (Southfield, Mich.: Ward's Communications, 2001), p. 70.

17. National Research Council, *Review of the Research Program of the Partnership for a New Generation of Vehicles: Sixth Report* (Washington: National Research Council, 2000).

18. In the 108th Congress, environmentalists want the Commerce, Science, and Transportation Committee, chaired by John McCain (R-Ariz.), to take the lead on legislation to cap greenhouse gas emissions.

19. See, for example, International Energy Workshop and Society of Petroleum Engineers surveys of experts cited in Morris A. Adelman, *The Genie out of the Bottle: World Oil*

since 1970 (MIT Press, 1993). This conventional wisdom proved to be quite wrong: real oil prices over the 1996–2000 period were more than 60 percent below their 1980 level.

20. Neither increased domestic production nor reduced demand is likely to change the U.S. oil security situation anytime soon. Even highly controversial additional sources of supply, such as opening of the Arctic National Wildlife Refuge, would provide added peak production of (at most) one million barrels daily after passage of more than a decade. Such an increment would be a tiny part of the world oil market and current U.S. imports. On the demand side, the recent report of the National Research Council (see NRC, *Effectiveness and Impact of Corporate Average Fuel Economy [CAFE] Standards* [Washington: National Academy Press]) finds significant potential to increase fuel economy without adverse impacts on safety, but only if higher efficiency requirements for new vehicles are phased in over many years. It would take additional time to turn over the existing fleet of vehicles. Even in the most aggressive scenarios, higher efficiency would only slow, not reverse, the projected growth in consumption of motor fuels.

IVO H. DAALDER
JAMES M. LINDSAY

9

Power and Cooperation: An American Foreign Policy for the Age of Global Politics

THE AGE OF GEOPOLITICS in American foreign policy is over; the age of global politics has begun. Throughout the twentieth century, traditional geopolitics drove U.S. thinking on foreign affairs: American security depended on preventing any one country from achieving dominion over the Eurasian landmass. That objective was achieved with the collapse of the Soviet Union. Now the United States finds itself confronting a new international environment, one without a peer competitor but that nonetheless presents serious threats to American security. The terrorists who struck the World Trade Center and the Pentagon neither represented a traditional state-based threat nor were tied to a specific geographical location. Nevertheless, nineteen people with just a few hundred thousand dollars succeeded in harming the most powerful nation on earth.

For more than three centuries, the dynamic of world politics was determined by the interplay among states, especially the great powers. Today, world politics is shaped by two unprecedented phenomena that are in some tension with each other. One is the sheer predominance of the United

The authors would like to thank James Steinberg, Strobe Talbott, the participants in the American Foreign Policy Round Table at the Brookings Institution, and the participants in a seminar organized by the Rockefeller Brothers Foundation for their comments and suggestions on earlier versions of this chapter. The authors are also indebted to the Carnegie Foundation and the Hewlett Foundation for their support.

States. Today, as never before, what matters most in international politics is how—and whether—Washington acts on any given issue. The other is globalization, which has unleashed economic, political, and social forces that are beyond the capacity of any one country, including the United States, to control.

American primacy and globalization bring the United States great rewards as well as great dangers. Primacy gives Washington an unsurpassed ability to get its way in international affairs, while globalization enriches the American economy and spreads American values. But America's great power and the penetration of its culture, products, and influence deep into other societies breed intense resentment and grievances. Great power and great wealth do not necessarily produce greater respect or greater security.

American leaders and the American people are now grappling with the double-edged sword that is the age of global politics: how to maximize its rewards while minimizing its dangers. In this debate, there is little disagreement over whether the United States should be engaged in world affairs. Both America's extensive global ties and its vulnerability to outside forces make disengagement and isolationism impossible. Nor is there much disagreement on the purpose of American engagement. America's interests are best served by a continually expanding liberal international order, one in which increasing numbers of people share the benefits of open markets and democratic governments.

Much of the current American foreign policy debate is about how Washington should achieve the goals of safeguarding and expanding the liberal international order. This debate, in turn, revolves around the relative importance of the two defining features of the age of global politics. One view (which we call *Hegemonist*) maintains that American primacy is the key to securing America's interests—and that it is both possible and desirable to extend the unipolar moment into a unipolar era. Hegemonists emphasize the threats posed by tyrants and terrorists—and the technologies of mass destruction both seek to acquire. They believe the United States should unabashedly exercise its power to defeat these threats, and they see formal international arrangements as impeding rather than enabling this effort. By contrast, a second view (which we call *Globalist*) argues that globalization has greatly expanded the range of foreign policy problems while limiting the effectiveness of the unilateral exercise of American power. Globalists believe that global challenges can be addressed only together with other nations and emphasize the need for international cooperation—especially through formal institutions and organizations.

The debate between Hegemonists and Globalists came to a head in the months leading up to the war in Iraq. The two views coincided on the desirability of disarming Iraq of its weapons of mass destruction (WMD) and of ousting Saddam Hussein. But they disagreed over how to accomplish these goals. The Bush administration, espousing a strong Hegemonist view, argued that Saddam's weapons of mass destruction and ties to terrorist organizations posed an unacceptable threat to American security, to regional stability, and to international order, and that a change of regime in Baghdad was the only sure way to defeat this threat. America would undertake that effort—if necessary alone—in the confident belief that it could both quickly end Saddam's rule and create a new strategic situation in the Middle East that would be demonstrably better and more stable than what existed before. A brutal dictatorship would be removed from power, weapons of mass destruction would be found and destroyed, and a powerful example would be set for others who might threaten U.S. interests with weapons of mass destruction or support for terrorist organizations. In the end, the Bush administration believed, even those who opposed war would come to believe that it had been worthwhile.

In contrast, Globalists argued that the Bush administration was setting a dangerous precedent by ignoring the concerns of many other nations, including of some of America's closest allies, that a preemptive war against Iraq would prove highly destabilizing. A war and the subsequent American occupation of Iraq could fuel Arab and Muslim resentment of the United States, enhance recruitment of young men to the terrorist cause, and further unsettle already fragile regimes facing strong Islamist opposition to their rule. Globalists also worried that the administration's failure to convince a majority of the UN Security Council, as well as many of its most important allies, that a preemptive war was not merely the right but the only course of action would fatally undermine the international security institutions that had underpinned U.S. foreign policy for more than half a century.

The Hegemonist view triumphed in Iraq. The Bush administration went to war with token international support (only Britain made a militarily significant contribution), yet succeeded in ousting Saddam Hussein swiftly and with relative ease. The full consequences of the war have yet to play out, but one thing is already certain: George W. Bush has embarked on a revolution in foreign policy, abandoning decades-old traditions of how America should engage abroad (we discuss this revolution in our forthcoming Brookings book, *America Unbound: The Bush Revolution in Foreign Policy*). His revolution is in many ways compelling. However, it comes with very high risks and potentially very high costs. At the same time, Globalists offer an alternative that is equally unsatisfactory. Not every problem has an international or multilateral solution—and even those that do require the prudent, but consistent, exercise of power to ensure cooperative endeavors remain effective.

The problem with the current debate about American foreign policy is that it often presumes an either/or choice between the Hegemonist emphasis on power and the Globalist emphasis on cooperation. In fact, however, an effective foreign policy in the age of global politics must *combine* power and cooperation. Power is fundamental to America's ability to achieve its foreign policy objectives. American leaders must be willing to wield it in defense of core interests, even at the price of alienating friends and allies. Yet a policy that rests solely on compelling others to bend to Washington's will is doomed. Many of the most pressing problems cannot be solved by unilateral U.S. action. Moreover, the sustainability of American primacy ultimately depends on the extent to which others believe it is used to further not only U.S. interests, but theirs as well. That requires using America's power in concert with friends and allies to make existing international rules and institutions more effective, to forge new structures of cooperation to deal with emerging challenges and opportunities, and to make sure that agreed rules and norms are effectively enforced. It is only through such cooperative efforts, backed by the judicious use of power, that the United States can create a world order that is conducive to its interests.

The Demise of Geopolitics

For much of the twentieth century, American foreign policy sought as its first priority to ensure that no single country dominated the key centers of strategic power in Europe and Asia—primarily western Europe, Russia, and northeast Asia. (The Persian Gulf was added in the 1970s when the strategic importance of oil became apparent.) That was the purpose of America's entry into two world wars, and that was why it engaged in a four-decade-long cold war with the Soviet Union. But this "Long War," as Philip Bobbitt has called it, was not just about Eurasia's geostrategic centrality in American foreign policy.[1] It also reflected an ideological conflict that pitted liberalism against fascism and communism.[2] The strategic need to prevent any rival from dominating the Eurasian power centers was therefore coupled to the political need to defeat totalitarian threats to the American—indeed, the Western—way of life.

The collapse of communism and the disintegration of the Soviet Union thus represented a dual victory for American foreign policy in the Long War. Liberalism won the battle of ideas—even leading to the notion of "the end of history."[3] With the collapse of the Soviet empire came the end of the last serious challenge for territorial dominion over Eurasia. American foreign policy had thus achieved its primary objective.

During the 1990s, a period now remembered as the post–cold war era, American foreign policy focused on consolidating the victory of the Long War. Together with its European allies, the United States set out to create, for the first time, a peaceful, undivided, and democratic Europe.[4] That effort is now all but complete. The European Union—which, with the formal accession of ten new members in 2004, will encompass most of Europe—has become the focal point for European policy on issues ranging from trade and monetary policy, through agricultural and immigration policy, to judicial and foreign affairs. NATO has evolved from a collective defense organization into Europe's main security institution—helping to stabilize the Balkans, transforming military practices with no fewer than twenty-seven partnership countries, and forging new relationships (including by expanding its membership) with erstwhile adversaries. A new relationship with Russia is being forged after ten years of intensive effort.

Progress has been slower, though still significant, in Asia, the other core area of strategic concern. U.S. relations with its two key regional partners, Japan and South Korea, continue to form the foundation of regional stability. Democracy is well rooted in many parts of the region, notably in South Korea, the Philippines, and Taiwan. Economic engagement is slowly creating ties that bind a surging China into the global economy.

The success of American policy in consolidating the victory in the Long War means that no power—not Russia, not Germany, not a united Europe, and not China or Japan—today threatens to dominate Eurasia. Geopolitical calculations have not disappeared entirely from American foreign policy, or from the foreign policies of other countries. Washington will continue to assess traditional state threats, and for many countries such considerations will remain dominant. However, the central geopolitical imperative that drove American foreign policy for almost one hundred years is no more. Some analysts, fixated on the old geopolitical context, predict that the United States will retreat from engagement by withdrawing its military forces from Europe and possibly even Asia.[5] That prediction ignores the profound change that has occurred in world politics: geopolitical considerations have given way to global ones. In the new age of global politics, American foreign policy will no longer pivot on geography. The threat Afghanistan posed to the United States was not tied to its geographical location, and al Qaeda can be just as deadly whether it is located in Pakistan, the Philippines, or Portland, Oregon.

The Age of Global Politics

The age of global politics has two defining characteristics: American primacy and globalization. American dominance means the United States has far greater influence over world politics than any other country. Globalization has been both beneficial (stimulating increased prosperity, greater democratization, and better protection of human rights) and destructive (causing global environmental damage, the proliferation of weapons of mass destruction, the spread of infectious diseases, and the expansion of international crime and terrorist organizations). The United States, perhaps more than any other country, has reaped the benefits of globalization. But despite its unrivaled power, it is not immune from globalization's pernicious effects.

America as the Global Power

The United States is the world's only truly global power.[6] One key pillar of America's power is its overwhelming military strength, which the war in Iraq vividly demonstrated. Only the United States can send bombers from its heartland on a round-trip mission to attack targets anywhere around the globe and do so with great stealth, precision, and destructive force. Only the United States can quickly dispatch its ground forces in large numbers to any battlefield in the world and defeat any traditional foe. Only the United States can deploy a truly blue-water navy across every ocean—complete with twelve mammoth aircraft carriers, each housing a modern air armada larger than the entire air force of most countries. Such is the cumulative effect of the trillions of dollars the United States has invested in its military over the past six decades.

A huge gap separates the capabilities of the U.S. military from those of other nations. After declining somewhat in the previous decade, U.S. defense spending is once again rising rapidly. Annual spending stood at $355 billion in 2003 and may reach as high as half a trillion dollars a year by the end of the decade.[7] As a result, the spending gap between the United States and the rest of the world is great and growing. The United States now accounts for nearly four in every ten dollars the world spends on defense, and its major European and Asian allies account for nearly half the remaining six dollars. In 2003, the United States spent as much on defense as the next eleven countries combined. The 2003 defense spending *increase* of $37.5 billion was almost as large as Britain's *entire* defense budget and three-quarters the size of China's. U.S. defense spending is forty times greater than the amount the three "axis of evil" countries—Iraq, Iran, and North Korea—spend on their militaries in 2001.[8]

Most remarkably, the United States has attained its military dominance at relatively little effort. Defense spending takes a smaller share of the U.S. gross domestic product than it did a decade ago. Even after the White House and Congress added 12 percent to the defense budget for 2003, U.S. defense spending stood at only 3.5 percent of GDP, or about half the cold war highs. "Being Number One at great cost is one thing," Yale University historian Paul Kennedy marvels. "Being the world's single superpower on the cheap is astonishing."[9]

Another pillar of America's power is its economy. It is the world's largest. After nearly two decades of economic expansion, it accounts for 31 percent of the world's total output, a larger share than in 1950.[10] To be sure, the economic gap is smaller than the military gap, especially if the United States is compared with the European Union (which on economics often behaves as a single actor). Nevertheless, America's dominance is still remarkable. The U.S. economy in 2000 was equal in size to that of the next four national economies (Japan, Germany, France, and Britain) combined, and it accounted for almost half the GDP of the G-7 countries.[11] While China is modernizing rapidly and Russia may have turned the corner, the size of their economies is comparable, respectively, to those of Italy and Belgium—not the United States.

America's primacy comes at a cost. Its great power means it affects the interests of others, and it often does so without intending to or even noticing that it has. This gives other countries and groups a great stake in what the United States does. Decisions made solely for narrow domestic political purposes often have profound implications for millions abroad. Subsidies for Midwestern wheat farmers mean lower market prices for growers in Argentina, and protection for textile mills in the Carolinas means less employment for shirt makers in Lahore and Capetown. America's great influence also enables countries to blame it, fairly or unfairly, for many of their ills. But those countries, being far less powerful, are necessarily driven to accept the inevitable or resort to unconventional responses. The same dynamic animates terrorists like those who struck on September 11.[12]

Still, America's military and economic predominance enables it to exert tremendous influence in world affairs. This does not mean it always gets what it wants. Some objectives may simply exceed American capabilities, while others may entail a price not worth paying. Nevertheless, when Washington really wants something and is willing to work with others, it often gets its way—witness the UN Security Council's unanimous vote in November 2002 demanding that Iraq accept tough new weapons inspections. In many cases, moreover, the United States does not need to wield its power overtly to bend others to its will. Countries often calculate that Washington will ultimately get its way, making resistance pointless and potentially costly. Better then to give before Washington takes. Even when countries refuse to concede, because of either principle or domestic politics, their opposition is often more rhetorical than substantive. Despite repeatedly warning that the demise of the ABM Treaty would produce dire consequences, Russia, China, and all of America's allies did little more than grumble when the Bush administration announced in December 2001 that the United States was withdrawing from the treaty.

There is more to America's influence than compelling others, by virtue of its hard—military and economic—power to conform their policies to Washington's liking. The United States also possesses what Joseph Nye has called "soft power."[13] This power derives from American values and culture, as well as from its success in using hard power. Soft power enables Washington to set the international agenda, to define the terms of debate, and to structure agreed outcomes by getting others to want what the United States wants. Hard power provides the foundation for soft power, but there can be a trade-off between the two. Relying excessively on hard power can actually diminish America's soft power. If other countries feel bullied or bossed around by Washington, they are less likely to follow its lead. This is what occurred in the run up to the war in Iraq, when the louder Washington shouted, the more other countries opposed its ways.

Can the United States sustain its international predominance over the next quarter century? By its nature, power is relative—whether America remains dominant depends on what happens to its capabilities and to those of others. Economically, the United States is not likely to maintain its current share of global output indefinitely, but its share is unlikely to shrink substantially any time soon. The U.S. economy has proven itself at least as adept as those of its major competitors in realizing the productivity gains from the revolution in information technology. Europe and Japan face substantially tougher demographic challenges than does the United States. With lower birth and mortality rates, they face labor shortages and severe budgetary pressures.[14] China and Russia both have yet to prove they can develop the political institutions needed to sustain economic growth.

Militarily, there is little prospect that any country or group of countries will spend enough to compete with the United States, let alone surpass it in the next two or three decades. The reason is not just, or even mainly, that the military gap is so large; instead, it is because few countries have sufficient incentive to try to match the United States militarily, and those that have an incentive lack the resources to succeed. The motivations for challengers are weak because America has no territorial ambitions. Furthermore, it has tended to use its power in ways that serve others' interests in addition to its own. Since many of its potential competitors do not see the United States as a significant threat, they are far more likely to bandwagon than to balance American power.[15] Those who do regard the United States as a threat lack the capacity to match it; their alternatives are to submit or to respond asymmetrically. As long as this continues, America's relative power will remain larger than that of any other country or group of countries—and a return to the age of geopolitics will be unlikely.

Just as important as how much power other countries can wield is how they intend to use the power they do have. Even if Europe unites fully, which will take decades, the extensive transatlantic ties forged by more than a half century of close cooperation ensure that few Americans will see this Europe as a threat to their security, just as few Europeans will have an interest in threatening the United States.[16] It matters that a Soviet Union that defined itself in opposition to the West has given way to a Russia striving to emulate Western ways and developing closer ties to the United States. For the same reason, China's political evolution holds immense consequences for American primacy. A world populated with powerful friends is more hospitable than one populated with powerful adversaries or nations that resent American highhandedness and are reluctant to follow American leadership.

Globalization

The twin, and in significant ways the rival, to the reality of American primacy is globalization. Countries around the globe are now increasingly interconnected, and these ties permeate all of their societies.[17] The consequence for Americans, as September 11 dramatically illustrated, is that distant developments can profoundly affect their security, prosperity, and way of life.

Globalization is not a new phenomenon—nor is it necessarily irreversible.[18] Economic interconnectedness increased rapidly in the decades before World War I, mainly as a result of technological innovations that reduced the cost of transportation (such as the steam engine) and information (the telegraph). The Great War, Great Depression, and Great

(Russian) Revolution disrupted many of these ties, and it was many decades before they were rebuilt.[19] At the same time, globalization is not simply an economic phenomenon.[20] Greater interconnectedness among countries can involve sociocultural, military, and environmental links as well as economic ones. These too are not new. The spread of Buddhism, Christianity, and Islam across the globe over the millennia created ties that continue to influence world politics today. The Dutch Navy sailed the Seven Seas four centuries ago, and the even mightier British Royal Navy subsequently extended the Union Jack to the far reaches of the globe. Fatal diseases like smallpox spread across borders and continents long ago—from Egypt in 1350 B.C. to China in A.D. 49 and on to Europe (700s), the Americas (1500s), and finally to Australia in 1789.

Although globalization is not unprecedented, two characteristics distinguish what we are witnessing today from anything that preceded it. One is the sheer speed and volume of cross-border contacts.[21] To take just one example, the United States one hundred years ago received a few million foreign visitors annually. Most traveled by boat for weeks to reach American shores. Today the United States welcomes more than 330 million foreign visitors each year, the vast majority of whom reach America within hours of leaving home.[22]

The second, and in many ways more important, characteristic of today's globalization is that it is taking place across multiple dimensions simultaneously. The most well known is growing economic interdependence. The numbers are stunning. Since the early 1970s, economic globalization has exploded. The average daily turnover in foreign exchange markets totaled roughly $15 billion in 1973. In April 2001, daily foreign exchange flows averaged more than $1.2 trillion. Total world exports increased nearly eighteen-fold between 1970 and 1999.[23] As a result, trade in 2002 accounted for 25 percent of total global economic output, double its share in 1970.[24] Total worldwide inflows of foreign direct investment stood at $59 billion in 1982. Two decades later, the figure was $735 billion.[25] Mergers and acquisitions (M&As) involving companies located in different countries surged as well. In 1987 there were 14 cross-border M&As worth more than $1 billion apiece. These transactions totaled $30 billion and accounted for 40 percent of the value of all cross-border M&As. Fourteen years later, there were 113 cross-border M&As that exceeded $1 billion apiece. These deals totaled $378.1 billion, or 64 percent of all cross-border M&As.[26]

Economic globalization has been accompanied in recent decades by military globalization. For centuries distance nullified military advantages and provided buffers in geopolitical competition. Modern technology changed that. With the development of ocean-spanning missiles in the 1960s, the United States and the Soviet Union gained the ability to destroy each other in as few as thirty minutes. Their monopoly on such destructive force proved temporary. With the widespread diffusion of military technology, many states now have the capability to manufacture chemical, biological, nuclear, and other weapons of mass destruction, as well as to build the ballistic and cruise missiles needed to deliver them.[27] Equally important, globalization has eroded the monopoly states once had on organized violence. Some international organized crime syndicates and terrorist organizations now wield sophisticated arsenals, and they have demonstrated an ability to harm even the most powerful states.

The communications revolution ushered in by the development of satellite television, wireless communications, and the Internet has fostered not just military and economic globalization but social globalization as well. The cost of transmitting information instantaneously across the globe has become negligible—thus enabling almost infinite amounts of information to be sent instantly to almost anywhere around the world.[28] Political ideas and practices can now spread with a speed once unimaginable as groups and movements emulate what they see elsewhere. States in turn find it harder, though not impossible, to control the information that reaches their citizens.[29]

In addition to economic, military, and social globalization, we are also experiencing rapid environmental globalization. Global temperatures are rising as modern economies increasingly emit greenhouses gases.[30] By 2002, more than 20 million people around the world had died of HIV/AIDS and another 60 million were infected.[31] The CIA estimates that by 2010 between 50 and 75 million people in just five countries (China, Ethiopia, India, Nigeria, and Russia) will be HIV-infected—far outstripping the number of cases in sub-Saharan Africa, where the ravaging effects of the disease have until now been most notable.[32] Nor are these isolated developments. As William Clark observes, "More and more kinds of human activities, undertaken by more and more people in more and more parts of the world, are imposing more and more impacts on other people at transcontinental scales. Moreover, those impacts are increasingly interactive."[33] As if to prove the import of this warning, the virus that causes severe acute respiratory syndrome (SARS) sprang up in Asia in 2003 and spread rapidly, creating worldwide fears of a global pandemic.

The prophets of globalization have trumpeted its positive features. The increased flow of goods, services, and capital across borders stimulates economic activity and enhances prosperity. Annual growth rates among the more globalized economies averaged 5 percent a year during the 1990s; the less globalized saw their economies contract by an average of 1 percent a year over the same period.[34] The spread of ideas across the Internet and other global media has empowered people around the globe to challenge autocratic rulers and seek to advance human rights and democracy. People's cultural horizons are broadened as Texans discover the delights of sushi, and Muscovites, the humor of *Seinfeld*. Growing interconnections can even lessen the chance of war. Fearing that a war with Pakistan would disrupt ties to large, U.S.-based multinationals, India's increasingly powerful electronic sector successfully pressed New Delhi in mid-2002 to deescalate its conflict with Pakistan.[35]

Globalization also brings new perils and challenges to the United States. September 11 is only the most notable example. A computer hacker in the Philippines can temporarily disrupt the Internet and inflict billions of dollars of losses on e-commerce operations around the world. Speculators can produce a run on the Thai baht, the ripple effects of which can plunge economies as far away as Russia and Brazil into recession, robbing American exporters of markets and costing American jobs. The accumulation of carbon dioxide and other greenhouse gases in the atmosphere from newly booming economies can warm the globe, possibly flooding coastal plains and turning mountain meadows into deserts.

Foreign Policy Consequences

Whether benign or malign, the effects of globalization demonstrate the wrongheadedness of the neoisolationist argument that American security and prosperity lie in minimizing America's political involvement abroad.[36] Much of America's prosperity today rests on a world order made possible by active U.S. engagement. In a globalizing world the United States cannot insulate itself from problems elsewhere. Interconnectedness is most obvious with challenges such as global warming, infectious diseases, and collapsing biodiversity. It also characterizes security problems, where American disengagement can lead to escalating conflict that affects U.S. interests (think Bosnia in the early 1990s or the Israeli-Palestinian conflict since

2001) without necessarily easing resentment of the United States. The fact that globalization wears an American face, and will continue to do so even if all U.S. troops come home, means that some abroad will continue to harbor grievances against the United States. In striking the World Trade Center, al Qaeda was signaling its hatred not just of what Americans do but of who they are and the values they represent.[37]

So America must be engaged abroad. There is actually considerable agreement in the United States not just on the need for engagement, but also on its purpose. America should seek to deepen and expand the existing liberal international order, thereby widening the circle of "winners" that have a stake in a system that has served Americans so well. This, after all, is the sentiment behind both the Clinton administration's "strategy of engagement and enlargement" and the Bush administration's pursuit of "a balance of power in favor of freedom."[38] The appeal of these calls is understandable—most Americans are instinctively Wilsonian.[39] They believe, for good reason, that an international order based on rule of law, constitutional democracy and human rights, and free enterprise would serve both American values and interests. Such an order would not eliminate conflict; market democracies are perfectly capable of squabbling among themselves. But it would diminish the frequency and severity of violent conflict within and between states, encourage prosperity, and increase the prospects of cooperative action to meet common challenges.

Yet this outward consensus hides vigorous disagreements over how to deepen and expand the liberal international order. Two main schools of thought exist. Each has different policy priorities and offers different assessments of what primacy and globalization mean for American foreign policy. Hegemonists—the word is from the Greek *hegemonia*, which means "leadership"—on the one hand emphasize American primacy. They see a world in which American power is threatened by the combination of terrorism, rogue states, and weapons of mass destruction—rather than, as traditionally, by the ambitions of other great powers. They look to America's preponderance of power to defeat this threat and, thus, to safeguard America's security as well as the security of its allies and friends. They see the confident exercise of that power—with few constraints on America's freedom of action—as the essence of American foreign policy. Globalists, on the other hand, emphasize globalization. They see a world in which threats to the security of individuals from problems such as HIV/AIDS, global warming, and international crime now supplement, if not supplant, threats to the security of nations. None of these problems respects national boundaries.

That is why Globalists emphasize international cooperation—preferably in the form of formal institutions, treaties, and international law—as the preferred means of American foreign policy.

Hegemonists

September 11 confirmed what Hegemonists—the dominant voice in George W. Bush's administration—have long maintained: the world is a dangerous place. Hegemonists believe, however, that unlike the past, when other great powers posed the gravest threat, the danger today derives from rogue states bent on harming America, its friends, and its allies. President Bush explained the threat in his "axis-of-evil" speech: "By seeking weapons of mass destruction, these regimes pose a grave and growing danger. They could provide these arms to terrorists, giving them the means to match their hatred. They could attack our allies or attempt to blackmail the United States."[40] The fundamental priority of American foreign policy therefore must be to defeat this new enemy—by bringing terrorists to justice, removing tyrants from power, and ensuring that technologies of mass destruction do not fall into the wrong hands. Hegemonists often acknowledge that the United States has other foreign policy goals—like promoting democracy and human rights and dealing with environmental and other global challenges. But they generally regard them as secondary to the need to defeat America's enemies.

Hegemonists see America's primacy as the key to achieving its foreign policy goals. Preponderant power enables the United States to achieve its goals without relying on others. As Charles Krauthammer, a forceful Hegemonist voice, argues, "An unprecedentedly dominant United States . . . is in the unique position of being able to fashion its own foreign policy. After a decade of Prometheus playing pygmy, the first task of the new [Bush] administration is precisely to reassert American freedom of action."[41] In short, the flexibility that arises out of the reality of U.S. dominance is the best guarantor of American security. September 11 only underscored the vital importance of maintaining the freedom to act as Washington sees fit. As President Bush argued in rejecting advice that he take account of allied views in conducting the war on terrorism, "At some point we may be the only ones left. That's okay with me. We are America."[42]

The premium Hegemonists place on freedom of action leads them to view international institutions, regimes, and treaties with considerable skepticism. Such formal arrangements inevitably constrain the ability of the United States to make the most of its primacy. This is not to say

Hegemonists rule out working with others. Rather, their preferred form of multilateralism—to be indulged in when unilateral action is impossible or unwise—involves building ad hoc coalitions of the willing, what Richard Haass calls "multilateralism à la carte."[43] Three key judgments underlie this instrumental view of multilateralism.[44] One is that existing formal institutions do not work when it comes to dealing with tough cases, which are the only ones that truly matter.[45] Another is that formal institutions do not create significant spillover effects that help American foreign policy more broadly by creating a shared sense of interests among member countries. The third is that different issues can be dealt with separately. Potential coalition partners will not refuse to join a U.S.-led ad hoc coalition simply because Washington has refused to cooperate on issues that matter to them. America should act on the basis of its own interests, and Hegemonists expect others to do likewise.

These views lead Hegemonists to take an unsentimental view of U.S. friends and allies. The purpose of allied consultations is not so much to forge a common policy, let alone build goodwill, as to persuade others of the rightness of the U.S. cause. As Secretary of State Colin Powell told European journalists, President Bush "makes sure people know what he believes in. And then he tries to persuade others that is the correct position. When it does not work, then we will take the position we believe is correct, and I hope the Europeans are left with a better understanding of the way in which we want to do business."[46] A better definition of what William Safire has called "consultative unilateralism" would be hard to find.[47]

Because primacy enables the United States to pursue and defend its interests as it pleases, Hegemonists like Krauthammer argue "explicitly and unashamedly for maintaining unipolarity, for sustaining America's unrivaled dominance for the foreseeable future."[48] This perspective is not new. Its intellectual predicate was laid out in a 1992 Pentagon study prepared by several people who occupy key positions in George W. Bush's administration—including Vice President Dick Cheney, Paul Wolfowitz (now deputy secretary of defense), Lewis Libby (the vice president's chief of staff), and Zalmay Khalilzad (a top National Security Council official). That study, according to a draft leaked to the *New York Times* in March 1992, maintained that U.S. national security policy after the cold war should seek to preclude "the emergence of any potential future global competitor."[49] Ten years ago, the public outcry that greeted the leaked report led the first Bush administration to order a new study softening much of the power rhetoric. Today, an equally ambitious statement of American power and priorities stands at the heart of George W. Bush's *National Security Strategy:* "Our [military] forces will be strong enough to dissuade potential adversaries from pursuing a military build-up in hopes of surpassing, or equaling, the power of the United States."[50] In other words, the United States can best achieve its objectives if it prevents others from acquiring the power to oppose it when interests clash. A better definition of American hegemony would be hard to find.

Beyond this core objective of preserving and enhancing American power, Hegemonists disagree among themselves, however, over how to use American primacy to extend the reach of the liberal international order.[51] So-called democratic imperialists argue that the United States should actively deploy its overwhelming military, economic, and political might to remake the world in its image. In doing so, they believe, the United States will serve other nations' interests as well as its own.[52] They call for unseating authoritarian regimes, by force if necessary, and they unabashedly embrace the idea of "nation-building on a grand scale."[53] Assertive nationalists, by contrast, scorn nation-building. They doubt that America can create what others are unable to build for themselves. Assertive nationalists see the purpose of American power as more limited—to deter and defeat potential threats to the nation's security.[54] Because these threats also threaten others, America's willingness to stare them down enhances not only U.S. security but international security as well—thereby making possible a liberal international order.

Despite these differences, Hegemonists agree on one thing: power remains the coin of the realm in world politics. The terrorist threat notwithstanding, their world remains one dominated by self-interested, sovereign nation-states, a world that in important ways has not changed since the signing of the Treaty of Westphalia. They dismiss complaints about unilateralism. They argue that if the United States leads, others will follow. And they justify all of this on the basis of their belief that America is a unique power and others see it so.

The war in Iraq represented the logical culmination of this perspective. The Bush administration's argument for the war was couched in terms of needing to prevent an even more deadly terrorist attack on the United States than Osama bin Laden had launched on September 11—as would be any attack using weapons of mass destruction. Terrorists were most likely to acquire such weapons from rogue states—which was why going after the states that supported terrorists and possessed weapons of mass destruction became the linchpin of the administration's war on terrorism.

As Bush argued days before he ordered U.S. forces into action, "Saddam Hussein has a long history of reckless aggression and terrible crimes. He possesses weapons of terror. He provides funding and training and safe haven to terrorists—terrorists who would willingly use weapons of mass destruction against America and other peace-loving countries. . . . Attacks of September the 11th, 2001 showed what the enemies of America did with four airplanes. We will not wait to see what terrorists or terrorist states could do with weapons of mass destruction."[55]

Although Bush was willing to address the Iraqi threat by enlisting international support through the United Nations, he was determined to act regardless of whether other countries supported him. So he challenged the United Nations to demonstrate its relevance by enforcing the resolutions the Security Council had passed demanding that Iraq be disarmed completely of all its weapons of mass destruction and all but the shortest-range ballistic missiles. An intensive diplomatic effort produced a unanimous resolution giving Iraq "one final opportunity" to disarm. Within months the administration affirmed what it had believed all along—namely, that Iraq would not voluntarily disarm. And while a majority of the Security Council, close allies, and much of the rest of the world believed that intrusive inspections ought to be given more time, the Bush administration decided that war offered the only viable solution. It refused to be constrained by the views of other countries or the collective view of international institutions of which America was a part. It was utterly convinced that ousting Saddam from power was essential for America's security. And it had the power to do so virtually on its own.

By going to war in Iraq, ousting Saddam with relative ease, and taking full responsibility for Iraq's reconstruction, the Bush administration put into practice the Hegemonists' contention that American power is the driving force of world politics. It is on this point that their critics, the Globalists, dissent.

Globalists

September 11 confirmed for Globalists that globalization has fundamentally changed the nature of the threats the United States faces as well as the means needed to address them. Globalization—including advances in information technology, integrated financial markets, the diffusion of technology, and the permeability of borders—made the attacks possible. Globalists therefore argue that American foreign policy priorities should be reordered to address the nonstate threats arising from globalization.

America should focus on disrupting global terror networks (which have proven capable of spectacular attacks that kill thousands), halting the spread of infectious diseases like HIV/AIDS (which each year kills more people than do all the world's many violent conflicts), slowing global climate change (which threatens to flood coastal zones where the vast majority of people live and transform agricultural regions into deserts), preventing the proliferation of the technology of mass destruction (which can make even the weakest a deadly danger to the strongest), and stopping international crime syndicates and narcotraffickers (which are destablizing many countries around the world and robbing many millions of people of a future). In addition to addressing the dark side of globalization, Globalists argue the necessity of exploiting the opportunities it presents—by securing access to open markets to enhance the prosperity of all and improving the human condition through vigorous efforts to protect human rights and promote democracy.

Whereas Hegemonists focus on how American primacy frees the United States to pursue its interests as it sees fit, Globalists stress how globalization curtails America's ability to use its power to influence events. They argue that globalization creates opportunities and challenges that cannot be harnessed or blocked by American action alone. The cooperation of others is needed to defeat terrorists, preserve biodiveristy, stop the spread of infectious diseases, and deal with other new foreign policy problems. But it is not just the issues themselves that limit the usefulness of American power. It is also that globalization is diffusing power away from nation-states. As Jessica Mathews argues, "National governments are not simply losing autonomy in a globalizing economy. They are sharing powers—including political, social, and security roles at the core of sovereignty—with businesses, with international organizations, and with a multitude of citizens groups, known as nongovernmental organizations (NGOs). The steady concentration of power in the hands of states that began in 1648 with the Peace of Westphalia is over."[56] NGOs, which also encompass crime cartels and terrorist groups, are more nimble than states and frequently succeed in frustrating their policies.[57] What Hegemonists miss by ignoring the changing policy agenda and rise of NGOs, or so the Globalists contend, is that even the most powerful state is losing its ability to control what goes on in the world. As a major Globalist text argues, "Few of today's foreign policy challenges are really amenable to unilateral action—to truly 'going it alone.' In most instances, cooperating with other countries and with international institutions is less an option than a necessity."[58]

While Globalists agree that globalization has made multilateralism essential to a successful foreign policy, they disagree on the nature of multilateral action. Global institutionalists look to supranational institutions as the key to solving problems that cannot be handled at the national level. They favor strengthening existing international organizations and treaties and creating or negotiating new ones where none now exist. They also would make securing international cooperation through such formal channels a precondition for most U.S. action abroad. For most institutionalists the driving idea is that formal international arrangements are needed because the United States cannot achieve its goals without them. For others, though, there is the additional consideration of Lord Acton's famous dictum: "Power corrupts and absolute power corrupts absolutely." They worry that American primacy, if left unchecked and unconstrained, would create far more harm than good.

Global populists, who dominate the antiglobalization movement, share this suspicion of unchecked American power. But they are equally suspicious of the existing international order. They believe that foreign policy fundamentally reflects corporate rather than national interests. They argue that globalization moves jobs from countries with high labor costs to countries with low labor costs, spurs volatility and speculation in international financial markets, and encourages the erosion of national health, safety, and environmental standards—all trends that enrich economic elites and harm ordinary people. Rather than providing a solution, global populists argue that existing international institutions amplify the harm because corporate interests helped write their rules. Thus for global populists, strengthening international institutions as institutionalists propose is not only insufficient but also dangerous. Instead, international institutions must be strengthened *and* democratized so that they respond to the needs and interests of those whom globalization is leaving behind. The main vehicles for forcing these changes are transnational networks of protest, which ironically are made possible by the very globalization they are seeking to tame.[59]

Where global institutionalists and populists look to the role that international organizations can play in addressing global challenges, transnationalists emphasize cross-border networks of NGOs.[60] Although these networks are typically decentralized—having no top, no center, and no hierarchy—they are nonetheless capable of coordinated and effective action. Among other things, they now provide "more official development assistance than the entire UN system (excluding the World Bank and the

International Monetary Fund)."[61] In pointing to the importance of NGOs, transnationalists do not deny the relevance of international organizations. Contrary to global institutionalists, however, they reject the view that NGOs merely follow in the wake of supranational institutions. Talk of states enlisting the help of "nonstate actors suggests a hierarchical disposition and a measure of state control that may not always match reality or advance effective policy. Often states will and should be the coordinators or main actors in [public-private] partnerships. But in many cases, that pecking order will be neither possible nor desirable."[62]

The differences that separate global institutionalists, global populists, and transnationalists pale, however, beside the differences each has with Hegemonists. Globalist criticisms of hegemonist thinking were on display in the months leading up to the war in Iraq. Many Globalists argued that the principal threat to American security was not Iraq and its weapons of mass destruction, but the transnational network of terrorists that operated independent of Baghdad and other state-sponsors of terrorism. The Bush administration sought to counter this criticism by linking al Qaeda and Saddam Hussein. Most Globalists found the White House's evidence to be unpersuasive; hence they remained skeptical that the best way to confront the terrorist threat was to oust Saddam from power.[63] Rather, most Globalists argued that invading Iraq would inflame anti-American sentiments in the Middle East and bolster al Qaeda's recruiting effort. Far from making terrorism less likely, these critics argued, a war against Iraq would increase the chances of future attacks.

Aside from questioning the wisdom of an invasion of Iraq, Globalists strongly opposed the way in which the Bush administration played its diplomatic hand. When the president and his senior advisers challenged the United Nations to demonstrate its relevance, they made clear that meant accepting America's position that Saddam Hussein had to be removed from power. All along, the administration said it would act alone if necessary. The only choice it offered other nations was to join or get out of the way. Issuing such an ultimatum, Globalists argued, alienated many friendly countries and undercut the effort to build a large international coalition against Baghdad. They recognized that America's military power would likely enable it to oust Saddam with little assistance from others. However, they believed that broad international support would be necessary to legitimize the invasion, as well as to lessen the burden and enhance the prospects for success of the large-scale nation-building effort that would have to follow the war. In the end, the Bush administration failed to secure the support of many of its traditional allies. Although the war was easily won, Globalists argued that the Bush administration's diplomatic approach left the United States with few friends eager to help in the rebuilding effort.

In sum, Globalists believe that Hegemonists want to play by rules appropriate for the days of Metternich and not those of the microchip. The array of threats now facing the United States is far broader than and different in kind from those of three decades ago, let alone a century ago, when power considerations dominated all. Unilateral American action will ultimately prove ineffective, if not counterproductive and dangerous, because other countries and nonstate actors have many levers with which to frustrate U.S. policy. Washington can achieve its interests only if it recognizes the limits to what its primacy brings and, rather than dictating to others, agrees to work with them to address the manifold challenges of globalization.

Melding Power and Cooperation

Hegemonists and Globalists are both right in important ways. Hegemonists are right that the threat from terrorism, rogue states, and weapons of mass destruction is real and must be confronted. Power remains essential to success in this international endeavor, as in many others. Though five decades of concerted U.S. and allied efforts may have transformed Europe into a Kantian zone of perpetual peace where the rule of law has triumphed, military might continues to hold sway in much of the rest of the world. True, no country, not even China, poses the same sort of geostrategic threat to the United States that first Germany and then the Soviet Union did. Still, threats of lesser order abound, from Pyongyang to Teheran to Damascus, and U.S. military and economic power will be needed to contain, if not extinguish, them.

For their part, Globalists are right that globalization has greatly broadened America's foreign policy agenda and created new opportunities for Washington to lead in efforts to revamp existing international institutions and build new ones. Issues such as infectious diseases, poverty, and poor governance are important not just because they offend our moral sensibilities, but because they threaten our security. Globalists are also right to remind us of the limits of American power. Many crucial problems defy unilateral solutions. Preventing or slowing global climate change requires many countries—not just the United States—to cut their greenhouse gas emissions.

Stemming WMD proliferation entails agreement by those who possess the requisite technologies not to transfer them. Success in fighting terrorism with a global reach hinges on international cooperation in law enforcement, intelligence, and the controlling of financial flows. American power cannot sustain the positive consequences of globalization on its own. Economic globalization rests on an intricate web of international trade and financial institutions. Without the cooperation of others to extend, develop, and improve these institutions, the benefits of globalization, which help to underwrite American power, would erode.

Yet on the whole the Hegemonist and Globalist approaches are both incomplete. Each offers a pinched list of the challenges facing the United States. Few Americans would call American foreign policy successful if it defeated al Qaeda but allowed the international economy to collapse, or vice versa. Both Hegemonists and Globalists think about the foreign policy agenda in selective rather than comprehensive terms. Hegemonists focus on threats to American power, while Globalists worry about the challenges arising from globalization. Neither keeps at the forefront the overarching objective of maintaining and expanding the liberal international order.

America's priorities should flow from that overarching goal. In particular, American foreign policy should give highest priority to those issues that have potentially systemic consequences for the liberal international order, either by drawing the United States back into an age of geopolitics or by determining whether the age of global politics comes to be defined by its opportunities or its dangers. A return to the age of geopolitics would confront America with a peer competitor and greatly complicate efforts to meet the challenges that arise from globalization. At the same time, it matters greatly to the United States whether globalization produces the expanding prosperity and freedom that its prophets trumpet or the apocalyptic nightmare that September 11 foreshadows. As the concluding section discusses at length, this criterion suggests a list of priorities that blends elements of both the Hegemonist and Globalist agendas.

On the matter of means, Hegemonists and Globalists err in assuming that foreign policy must emphasize either power or cooperation. Globalists often forget that the formalized international cooperation they seek demands more than good will. It also requires the willingness and ability to mobilize countries to cooperate and to enforce the agreed upon rules of behavior. However, that requirement, as Mancur Olsen demonstrated years ago, runs into a fundamental collective action problem—if the potential costs of action are great and the benefits are widely shared, few will be willing to incur the costs. That is where overwhelming power, and a willingness to provide for public goods, makes a crucial difference.[64] Here the United States is exactly what Madeleine Albright said it was—the "indispensable nation."[65] To take just one example, it was only the Bush administration's willingness to act, unilaterally if necessary, that pushed the members of the Security Council in November 2002 to face up to their responsibility to compel Baghdad to abide by its international obligations to rid itself of weapons of mass destruction. Without American primacy—or something like it—it is doubtful that the rule of law can be sustained.

By the same token, Hegemonists are mistaken to think that the United States can dictate its policy preferences to the rest of the world, confident that others will inevitably follow. The cumulative effects of behaving like the "SUV of nations," as Mary McGrory puts it—"hog[ging] the road and guzz[ling] the gas and periodically run[ning] over something"—are substantial.[66] It spurs resentment among even America's closest allies, resentment that, as the German and South Korean elections in 2002 demonstrated, prompts efforts to frustrate U.S. policy objectives or to ignore them. By early 2000, Washington's bullying, rather than Baghdad's noncompliance, had become the major issue for most members of the Security Council, including close allies like France, Germany, and Mexico. As a result, the Bush administration failed to gain majority support—let alone approval—for going to war against Iraq. All this comes with costs. Increasingly, Europe sees its role not as an American partner but as a brake on the improvident exercise of U.S. power. It has sought to create new international regimes, which in part reflect its own weakness, but are also often designed to limit America's recourse to its hard power (and disliked by Washington precisely for that reason).[67]

This is not to say that the United States will automatically lose its ability to lead others if it decides to act unilaterally. After all, America's allies rallied around it after September 11 and despite their irritation over the Bush administration's dismissal of the Kyoto Protocol and its intention to withdraw from the ABM Treaty. Instead, it underscores the degree to which America's ability to sustain its primacy depends on its own actions. The more others question America's power, purpose, and priorities, the less influence America has. If others try to counter the United States and delegitimize its power, Washington will need to exert more effort to reach the same desired end, assuming it can reach its objective at all. If others step aside and leave Washington to tackle common problems as it sees fit, the cost of foreign policy will increase. The American public, always wary of being played for a sucker, might balk at paying the price.

Rather than undoing American primacy, then, cooperation is critical to sustaining it. The most obvious benefit is that by working with others Washington can spread the costs of action over more actors, enabling it to do more with less and reassuring Americans that they are doing no more than their fair share. On a deeper level, however, cooperation diminishes the need to compel others to act in America's interests and convinces them instead that doing so is in their own interest. As Samuel Berger, National Security Adviser to President Bill Clinton, observes:

> There is a difference between power and authority. Power is the ability to compel by force and sanctions, and there are times we must use it, for there will always be interests and values worth fighting for. Authority is the ability to lead, and we depend on it for almost everything we try to achieve. Our authority is built on qualities very different from our power: on the attractiveness of our values, on the force of our example, on the credibility of our commitments, and on our willingness to listen to and stand by others. There may be no real threat to our power today. But if we use power in a way that antagonizes our friends and dishonors our commitments, we will lose our authority—and our power will mean very little.[68]

Washington understood this lesson well in the years immediately following World War II, when, as John Ikenberry has shown, "The United States spun a web of institutions that connected other states to an emerging American-dominated economic and security order."[69] For nearly half a century, these institutions have been "America's secret empire."[70]

The fundamental task for American foreign policy in the age of global politics is to replicate this success in melding power and cooperation. America needs to use its primacy to increase the capacity of the international community to meet its common challenges by building lasting structures of cooperation. Doing so maximizes the likelihood that Americans will find themselves in a world in which countries will see they can achieve their goals by working with the United States rather than against it. It also maximizes the chances that the world community will share not just America's interests but also its responsibilities.

A successful blend of power and cooperation entails two tasks. The first is to extend and adapt existing international arrangements that have proven effective in meeting common challenges, revitalize those that do not work well, and create new ones where necessary. Although Hegemonists routinely denigrate international institutions as ineffective, the fact is they can and do promote American interests, as the work of the United Nations, the World Trade Organization, and the International Monetary Fund (to mention only three) attests. At the same time, developing cooperative arrangements does not axiomatically mean creating formal international organizations or writing new treaties. More flexible structures, such as the Missile Control Technology Regime, the Australia Group, and the Nuclear Suppliers Groups, are also possible. The formality of cooperation matters less than its being regularized, lasting, and thus predictable. Cooperative structures that provide for repeated interactions over time create the opportunity to turn separate national interests into shared ones. NATO, to take another example, helped knit Western Europe together during the cold war and is now extending the boundaries of the European zone of peace. By relying heavily on ad hoc coalitions that disperse once the stated mission is achieved, Hegemonists forfeit opportunities to build on the common interests that exist among the United States and its allies and potential partners—thus risking not having partners when you need them.

The second task facing Washington is to strengthen, where possible, the ability of existing or new institutions and arrangements to monitor and compel compliance. If Hegemonists have been too quick to dismiss regularized structures for cooperation as obstacles to American foreign policy, Globalists have been too quick to declare victory once new rules and institutions are established. Cooperation is not an end in and of itself; it is a means to an end. Rules and institutions that can be ignored at will contribute nothing to shaping or constraining how states behave. Conversely, when robust means exist to monitor behavior, voluntary compliance is more likely to occur and coalitions to compel compliance are easier to build.

The point of using American primacy to build cooperative structures is not to give foreign capitals a veto over American foreign policy, as Hegemonists fear. It is instead to make the most of American power by maximizing the number of potential partners for the United States and deflating the grievances that others have against it. Washington has a strong long-term interest in acting—and being seen by others as acting—cooperatively to create arrangements, institutions, and norms in which everyone has a stake. Nor is it to suggest that multilateral action should always trump unilateral action, as Globalists hope. To argue that American foreign policy should be either unilateral or multilateral is to posit a false choice as well as to confuse means with ends. Unilateralism can be put to good or bad uses. The Globalists who denounced President Bush for ending American support for the Kyoto Protocol did not criticize the Nunn-Lugar program because it was a unilateral effort. Likewise, multilateralism can produce a modern-day Kellogg-Briand Treaty just as easily as it produces a Gulf War coalition or a World Trade Organization.

In sum, Hegemonists and Globalists have much to learn from each other. The United States does not have the luxury of worrying only about physical threats to its security or the freedom to focus only on human tragedies abroad. Power without willing cooperation veers toward diktat and breeds resentment and resistance. Cooperation without power produces posturing, not progress. A wise foreign policy for the age of global politics would keep these lessons in mind.

A Foreign Policy for the Age of Global Politics

In the age of global politics, American foreign policy should focus as a matter of priority on those issues that will determine Washington's success in sustaining and expanding the liberal international order. Five issues stand out—defeating global terrorist organizations that are able and willing to launch catastrophic attacks; extending the economic and political benefits of globalization to as many people as possible; encouraging the other great powers to work together to support a liberal international order; stemming and ultimately reversing WMD proliferation; and confronting threats to the global environment, starting with climate change. In each instance, the United States should seek to achieve these priorities by melding American primacy and international cooperation.

These priorities do not exhaust the list of issues on the American foreign policy agenda. Problems such as regional conflict and the spread of HIV/AIDS may not have systemic consequences, but Washington will inevitably address (and should address) these and other issues. The impulse to do so will be not merely humanitarian, but also strategic and political. Regional conflicts drive WMD proliferation in most instances, while HIV/AIDS can decimate societies and leave governments incapable of preventing terrorists from operating on their soil. Likewise, when Washington asks for help on issues that matter to it, other countries will naturally ask what Washington is doing on issues that matter to them. The American foreign policy agenda will thus always overflow with tasks to complete. Yet a successful foreign policy ultimately recognizes what its main priorities should be, and time and energy ought to be invested accordingly, even if that means having at times to make tough choices.

Combatting Catastrophic Terrorism

The first priority of American foreign policy is to disrupt and defeat terrorist organizations bent on catastrophic terrorism. In the 1980s and 1990s, the United States experienced numerous terrorist attacks but never made counterterrorism a top priority. The reason was simple. Most attacks took place overseas and resulted in few American deaths. Al Qaeda changed all that. No one now doubts its desire to inflict catastrophic harm on the United States. Unfortunately, while Operation Enduring Freedom denied al Qaeda a base of operations in Afghanistan, it did not eliminate its ability to operate. Moreover, even if al Qaeda were to disappear, the threat of catastrophic terrorism would remain. Left unchecked, globalization and the diffusion of technology will increasingly enable the angry few to inflict grievous harm on the many. The most feared dangers come with WMD proliferation. However, as we now know, terrorists do not need nuclear warheads or smallpox viruses to kill thousands of Americans. And if such attacks targeted key transportation nodes or brought down other critical infrastructure, the American economy could be sent into a tailspin, taking the world economy down with it.[71]

Efforts to disrupt and defeat catastrophic terrorism must emphasize both the shield and the sword. The shield consists of preventive, protective, and responsive efforts at home—starting with better defenses at the borders, expedited information flows among intelligence and law enforcement agencies, improved domestic intelligence capabilities, vigorous protection of the most critical infrastructure, robust consequence management programs, and a more responsive organization to manage all these efforts.[72] Better defenses at home are not enough, however; they must be complemented by the sword of vigorous U.S. action abroad. That includes destroying terrorist training camps, detaining (or, if necessary, killing) terrorist operatives, stepping up intelligence collection, enhancing bilateral and multilateral intelligence and law enforcement cooperation, and encouraging states to get out of the business of sponsoring terrorism. The latter requires a mix of strategies that will vary depending on the country in question. At times—Afghanistan being the clear case—it may require military action, either alone or in concert with others. More often, it will involve political and economic pressure, which will be all the more effective if Washington succeeds in obtaining the support of other countries.

As Afghanistan has underscored, an effective counterterrorism effort also requires policies aimed at helping failed states. As the Bush administration's *National Security Strategy* wisely points out, "America is now threatened less by conquering states than by failing ones."[73] Failed and failing states give terrorists grievances to exploit and places to operate. Efforts to prevent states from failing—or rebuilding those that have—include diplomatic engagement aimed at helping to resolve civil conflict, aid for postconflict reconstruction, trade and debt relief, and counterterrorism assistance.[74] Such efforts are most likely to work if they are coordinated, if not conducted jointly, with America's major allies.

Extending the Benefits of Globalization

The United States has a profound interest in seeing the economic, political, and social benefits of globalization extended to as many people as possible. America's prosperity, and hence its power, is intimately bound up with the health of the international economy. Lowering trade barriers, reducing the international financial system's volatility, and helping developing countries become successful market economies benefit the U.S. economy in the long term, as Americans learned to their profit when they helped rebuild Europe and Japan after World War II. At the same time, a world in which the largest possible number of countries are successful market democracies is likely to pose the fewest threats to American security. It is not just that democracies are less likely to wage war against fellow democracies, though the evidence on that score is impressive.[75] It is also that collapsing economies and the denial of liberty help fuel threats to Americans. Economic failure and dashed aspirations in poor countries breed resentment of the United States, which is often portrayed as causing and benefiting from their misery, and authoritarian regimes frequently encourage anti-Americanism to deflect public criticism of their own misrule. Terrorist groups like al Qaeda gladly exploit the resulting anger to justify their attacks and to secure aid and comfort for their operatives.

Promoting democracy is, of course, easier said than done. It takes decades, if not generations, to achieve the stability and predictability associated with mature democracies like those in North America and Western Europe. Indeed, the transition from authoritarian to democratic rule is generally difficult and often offers antidemocratic forces an opportunity to exploit the openness to their own ends. As a result, appeals to nationalism, anti-Americanism, and religious fundamentalism tend to flourish during times of transition.[76] Moreover, elections alone do not a democracy make.

Absent a concomitant commitment to liberal constitutionalism, elections can produce what Fareed Zakaria has called illiberal democracies.[77] Early elections often bring to power the very antidemocratic forces that democratic governance is supposed to undermine. However, none of these difficulties should deter the United States from making the promotion of democracy and human rights a top priority. Even if, in the short run, authoritarian governments like Saudi Arabia and Pakistan provide crucial support for other U.S. foreign policy objectives, backing governments like these has significant long-run costs—including, most important, turning alienated local populations from potential friends into actual foes.

Efforts to build democracy must start by recognizing these obstacles. Democracy is not a matter of holding one or even two elections, but instead requires the emergence of a civil society that not only supports but demands to be governed in ways that reflect the desires of all the people. The populace also requires a certain level of education in order to make informed choices. That, in turn, requires the establishment of an independent media and the creation of civic associations of many kinds. Finally, a certain minimal level of economic development will have to be achieved— people concerned solely with getting food on the table for their families have little time for helping build the underlying structures of democracy. All of this will take time and effort, and while outside assistance is important, the crucial effort must be made by the people themselves. The United States can help by encouraging governments—especially otherwise friendly ones—to open up their societies to the democratic aspirations of its people. It should also provide the resources necessary for individuals and groups within these countries to take the educational and organizational steps on which ultimate success depends.

Crucial to the success of any democracy-building effort is a concomitant commitment to economic development and liberalization. As Richard Haass has rightly observed, "Market-based economic modernization helps usher in elements of democracy: the rule of law, transparent decision-making, the free exchange of ideas. Yet it is just as true that these elements of democracy sustain and accelerate economic growth. This need not be a sequential path, such as economic development followed by political liberalization. When political and economic freedom go hand in hand, they strengthen each other."[78] How can economic modernization be encouraged?[79] Part of the answer, for sure, is a much greater U.S. commitment to foreign assistance. The United States still spends only half a penny of every federal dollar on foreign aid, and it ranks dead last among all western countries in foreign assistance spending as a percentage of GDP. President Bush's proposal to increase U.S. aid spending by 50 percent will help—but that is still a paltry sum given the requirements that exist around the world. Yet, even a much greater commitment to foreign aid will not guarantee economic development. Equally, if not more, important are changes on the trade front, as Lael Brainard and Robert Litan explain in chapter 10 of this volume. For domestic political reasons, the United States tends to be most protectionist in areas such as agriculture and textiles where developing countries actually have products to sell. In 2000, President Bill Clinton sought to reverse that trend when he signed the African Growth and Opportunity Act, which opened the U.S. market to African-produced clothing made from non-American textiles. Yet, rather than extending this limited step to other parts of the world and additional products, Washington more recently reversed course by imposing new barriers on textiles and steel and granting huge agricultural subsidies to American farmers. While these protectionist measures help domestic producers, they hurt U.S. consumers and foreign producers—many of them in the poorest countries. Domestic political realities mean that Washington must help American workers and industries most affected by opening markets, but neither subsidization nor protectionism offers a long-term answer. The only way other countries and people are going to embrace the benefits of globalization is if the cost of doing so is not disproportionately borne by the least fortunate in the world.

Encouraging Great Power Support for a Liberal International Order

A third priority for Washington is to encourage Europe, Russia, China, and Japan to work in concert with the United States to support and extend the liberal international order. A return to the era of geopolitics, in which rival powers vied for domination, would doom the chances of expanding the community of market democracies. Not only would geopolitical calculations reclaim their traditional prominence in American foreign policy; the problems that arise out of globalization would be greatly magnified. The war on terrorism would look much different if, say, China were giving sanctuary to al Qaeda. If trade wars among economic giants were to replace the common commitment of the world's largest economies to breaking down the last remaining barriers to the free flow of goods and services across the globe, continued prosperity for all would suffer a mighty blow.

The challenge for American foreign policy is twofold. First, Washington must maintain mutually supportive relations with its allies in Europe and

Asia. The basis for such relations will necessarily differ from what it was in the past, when a common adversary provided the necessary glue for maintaining a united front. Then there was no practical alternative to alliance for America, Europe, or Japan. Now there is. American power gives Washington the ability to achieve many of its goals with little regard for other nations. Europe can, as it has for the past decade, continue to focus on extending the zone of peace and prosperity further eastward largely on its own. Japan will likely continue for some time to focus inward as it figures out how an aging society and stagnant economy can recover its past dynamism.

Nevertheless, the drifting apart of erstwhile allies has both short- and long-term costs. Many of the most important global challenges—terrorism, global warming, poverty—can be dealt with only if the major powers cooperate. Moreover, rancor, especially between the United States and Europe, ultimately could lead to competition for power and global leadership.[80] Even if America could win such a competition, the inevitable costs suggest that wise policy would work now to avoid it. The value of seeking cooperation from America's most important partners, even when their contribution is not strictly required, lies precisely in maintaining mutually supportive relations and avoiding the drift that over time can turn into destructive rivalry. That is why accepting Europe's offers of military assistance in helping to defeat the Taliban in Afghanistan was important and why seeking Europe's support in helping to stabilize postwar Iraq has benefits that extend beyond the limited military contribution Europe can make. Conversely, that is why the Bush administration's early decisions to walk away from cooperative endeavors to strengthen nonproliferation regimes, curtail greenhouse gas emissions, and promote international justice harmed America's long-term interests.

The second, more difficult challenge is to foster the integration of Russia and China into the liberal international order. Fortunately, recent trends have been encouraging. Both Russia and China are embracing free-market economics, Russia has partially democratized, and China's communist rulers have allowed greater political openness at the local level (while continuing to hold power tightly at the national level). Moreover, Moscow and Beijing used September 11 as an opportunity to recast their foreign policies. Both decided early that they had more to gain by cooperating with America's war on terrorism than by resisting it. This cooperation prompted President Bush to argue that "the international community has the best chance since the rise of the nation-state in the seventeenth century to build a world where great powers compete in peace instead of perpetually prepare for war."[81]

The task is to exploit this opportunity and ultimately make it too costly for Moscow and Beijing to reverse course. That will require that both countries succeed in converting the closed command economies and totalitarian systems of yesteryear into vibrant, open market democracies. The transition will not be easy. Both economies are slowly becoming integrated into the liberal international economic order, and both are experiencing wrenching social change as a result. Russia's democratization process has been fitful and incomplete. Its appalling human rights abuses in Chechnya underscore just how far Moscow still has to go. China's communist rulers have allowed greater political openness at the local level, but they have refused to abandon any notion of one-party rule or to open power at the national level. Although Washington has only a limited ability to influence these trends, it should do as much as it can to encourage economic openness and political democracy. As it has with China, the United States should extend the benefits of free trade to Russia through its entry into the World Trade Organization. Washington must also be forthright and uncompromising about the importance of political liberalization and the protection of human rights. Ultimately, however, it will be up to the Chinese and Russian people to press their leaders to provide them with the full benefits of economic and political liberalization.

Stemming WMD Proliferation

American foreign policy must work to stem and, ultimately, reverse the proliferation of weapons of mass destruction. This objective is obviously related to the goal of stopping catastrophic terrorism. The spread of chemical, biological, and nuclear weapons to more nations also poses grave dangers to American interests. Although it often goes unnoticed, one of Washington's great foreign policy triumphs in recent decades was its success in persuading most countries either not to start nuclear and other weapons programs (think Germany and Japan) or to abandon ones they had (think South Africa and Brazil). Now Washington confronts a small number of holdouts, countries such as Iran and North Korea, that refuse to abide by their international obligations not to develop these weapons. Should these countries develop robust WMD capabilities—especially nuclear capabilities and the means to deliver them—they may become emboldened to threaten the United States or, more likely, its friends and allies. That development could easily undo the success Washington has had in slowing and in some instances even reversing the spread of WMD as some countries decide that they need them to deter potential attackers. The result could be a rapid acceleration in proliferation, thereby creating more opportunities for WMD to be used or sold to, or stolen by, terrorist organizations.

Washington should take several unilateral steps to diminish the WMD threat. Maintaining a robust military provides a powerful deterrent to rogue state attacks. U.S. political and economic pressure can be wielded against potential proliferators, and preemption can defeat attacks before they occur. Missile defense can backstop a preemptive strategy, both by denying adversaries the potential for blackmail and by defeating any missile launches that actually take place.[82] Consequence management strategies can mitigate, and in the case of biological weapons perhaps even defeat, an attack. However, such unilateral strategies are inherently limited. Deterrence through retaliation means little to stateless terrorists willing to die for their cause. The political and military feasibility of preemption is often in doubt.[83] Missile defenses are hardly perfect, and in any case provide no protection against bombs on trucks or container ships. Consequence management efforts could prove ineffective against nuclear or biological attacks.

As a result, unilateral efforts must be combined with concerted multilateral efforts to stem WMD. Past efforts on this score are a major reason that more countries have shut down their nuclear, chemical, and biological weapons programs during the past two decades than have acquired them. The list of initiatives Washington should pursue is long. It should go beyond the Moscow Treaty and negotiate a new arms reduction accord with Russia that encompasses tactical as well as strategic weapons and that requires and verifies the actual destruction of warheads.[84] It should ratify the Comprehensive Test Ban Treaty, which among other things would create a worldwide monitoring system for detecting nuclear explosions, including sensors in countries such as Russia, China, and Iran that are closed to U.S. intelligence. It should work with U.S. allies to expand the successful Nunn-Lugar Cooperative Threat Reduction program beyond Russia to secure stockpiles of fissile and radioactive material elsewhere around the world.[85] It should seek to strengthen the Biological and Chemical Weapons Conventions and increase the authority of the International Atomic Energy Agency to make it harder for countries to cheat.

Treaties alone are not enough, however. They must be backed by the willingness of the international community to insist on compliance. It is here where power, including the threat or use of force, becomes critical. Violations that go unpunished breed further violations and the collapse of the regime. Here American primacy will be pivotal. It may be the natural order of things that most countries will turn a blind eye to noncompliance, calculating either that someone else will take care of the problem or that the problem will never touch them. U.S. leadership is essential to preventing countries from shirking their obligations. America's willingness to participate in and work through multilateral regimes will provide important legitimacy for its efforts to enforce compliance.

Sustaining the Global Environment

Washington's final priority must be to confront threats to the global environment. The largest problem is climate change. It is now agreed that the earth is warming and humans are at least partly responsible.[86] No one knows how rapidly the climate might change and with what consequences. It could change slowly and mildly, giving humans ample time to adapt. It could also change rapidly and catastrophically. Even if the United States can adapt to a new climate, much of the rest of the world—and many of its plants and wildlife—may not. That would be a humanitarian disaster of unimaginable proportions. It also would almost surely threaten American security and prosperity. Stable countries could collapse, either because their people migrate in massive numbers in search of jobs and food or because they are overwhelmed with migrants. Markets for American goods could disappear as entire economies crumble. These threats make it critical, if only as a matter of insurance, for the United States to act to limit the extent and consequences of climate change.

There are unilateral actions the United States could take to begin to address the problem of global warming. It should raise fuel economy standards for cars and trucks—which produce roughly one-third of U.S. carbon dioxide emissions. It should require firms to reduce emissions of methane and rare industrial gases that are far more potent than carbon dioxide in absorbing heat. And it should invest heavily in technology that promises to reduce emissions—such as bioreactors and fuel cells—and trap them—such as carbon capture, storage, and sequestration technologies. Such steps would have the added benefit of reducing the vulnerability of the U.S. economy to price shocks in the international oil markets—thus helping to sustain American primacy.

However, unilateral action will never be enough to combat climate change. The emissions of heat-trapping gasses from developing countries will soon exceed those from industrialized countries, negating the benefits of any reduction in U.S. emissions. Moreover, success in promoting the expansion of free-market democracies might actually exacerbate the climate change problem. All other things being equal, economic growth produces higher emissions.

To say multilateral action is necessary is not to endorse the Kyoto Protocol. The Bush administration is right that Kyoto's backers are championing an institutional and multilateral solution that is probably unworkable.[87] The protocol fails to include the developing world, consider the cost of emissions reductions, provide a reliable enforcement mechanism, or even produce substantial emissions reductions. The Bush administration has failed to deliver on its promises to advance its own proposals for countering global warming, thereby confirming fears that it does not take the problem seriously. But the principles that should guide such a policy can be identified: they should seek eventual global participation and create arrangements that are cost-effective, verifiable, and enforceable.[88] The policy should encourage the transfer of clean energy technology to developing countries to minimize the emissions produced by their economic growth. And U.S. policy will inevitably need to help developing countries adapt to climate change. The concentration of heat-trapping gases in the atmosphere is so high today that climate change would likely continue for decades even if emissions were reduced drastically.

Conclusion

We live in an age of global politics—an age in which America's foreign policy choices are influenced by America's unprecedented primacy and a globalization that at once sustains and threatens that primacy. Many of the most beneficial consequences of globalization—from opening markets that spread prosperity to opening minds that spread American ideals—help the United States extend its power and influence to the farthest reaches of the globe. However, the same forces that make possible American primacy also unleash potentially catastrophic threats. Rogue regimes now have access to the technologies of mass destruction—not least because the technology trade among them is brisk and uncontrolled. Angry young men, filled with hatred for a country many depict as the Great Satan, can exploit the permeability of borders and ease of modern communications to deliver punishing blows.

The challenge for Washington in this new age is to use America's power to extend the benefits and reduce the dangers of globalization. To succeed in this effort, it will not be enough to rely solely on American primacy, as Hegemonists contend. Too many of the most important challenges facing America now and in the years ahead require the cooperation of others to be tackled successfully. But a stated commitment to multilateral cooperation, as Globalists demand, will not ensure success either. Effective cooperation often is a function of American power—including the power not to work within agreed institutional structures to achieve important foreign policy goals. Instead, the challenges of the global age require a foreign policy that puts America's primacy at the service of cooperative efforts. Used wisely, power begets effective cooperation; in turn, effective cooperation sustains the very power that makes such cooperation possible.

Iraq is a case in point. American power proved crucial in persuading the fourteen other members of the UN Security Council to pass a resolution demanding that Baghdad disarm. Perhaps more skillful diplomacy might have persuaded more countries (including a majority on the Security Council) in early 2003 that war was the only way left to secure Baghdad's disarmament. But there is little doubt that American power was absolutely essential to producing Saddam Hussein's ouster. And now American power is essential to ensuring that Iraq emerges from the war, years of sanctions, and decades of brutal dictatorship as a stable, secure, united, free, and prosperous country.

This is not, however, a task America can accomplish on its own—and to the extent it tries to do so it is bound to fail. The legitimacy of the effort, its acceptability within Iraq and the wider region, requires that others be centrally involved. The United States has neither the capacity nor possibly even the will to ensure success in what will likely be the most difficult and ambitious nation-building exercise since Germany and Japan. Other countries have vast resources and experience, and many international institutions—from the United Nations and NATO to the European Union and the World Bank—can play crucial roles in the effort. American power will be vital to bring these elements together in a cooperative effort to rebuild Iraq, but in no way can it substitute for them.

Ensuring success in Iraq should be a priority for American foreign policy for many years to come. It would vindicate the Bush administration's belief that ousting Saddam Hussein was the right thing to do—even though many at home and most abroad believed it had been done in a profoundly wrong way. Leading a cooperative international effort to rebuild

Iraq would also vindicate those who believe that many of America's foreign policy goals cannot be achieved without effective international cooperation. Most of all, succeeding in Iraq would advance the central goal of American foreign policy: to sustain and expand the liberal international order. That, indeed, must remain the overarching objective of American foreign policy. By that standard, defeating catastrophic terrorism, extending the benefits of globalization, encouraging great power support of a liberal international order, stemming the spread of weapons of mass destruction, and sustaining the global environment are the right priorities for an America astride the global age.

Of course, these priorities will at times conflict with one another. Defeating terrorist organizations may sometimes require that Washington work with governments that do not respect individual liberty or trade in technologies of mass destruction, just as encouraging economic growth could accelerate the emission of carbon dioxide and other gases responsible for climate change. But though trade-offs will have to be made, these five priorities will more often reinforce each other. Stemming WMD proliferation would reduce the chances of catastrophic terrorism. Promoting economic prosperity and democracy could help diminish the popular grievances that terrorists seek to exploit. Stopping catastrophic terrorism and mitigating the potential effects of global warming would diminish the potential for major disruptions of the international economy. And all of these goals will be aided significantly if Europe, Japan, China, and Russia cooperate with rather than obstruct efforts to achieve them.

Notes

1. Philip C. Bobbitt, *The Shield of Achilles: War, Peace, and the Course of History* (Knopf, 2002), pp. 21–61.

2. This point is developed in Michael Mandelbaum, *The Ideas That Conquered the World: Peace, Democracy, and Free Markets in the Twenty-First Century* (Public Affairs, 2002).

3. Francis Fukuyama, "The End of History?" *National Interest*, no. 16 (Summer 1989), pp. 3–35.

4. For details, see Ivo H. Daalder, "The United States and Europe: From Primacy to Partnership?" in Robert J. Lieber, ed., *Eagle Rules? Foreign Policy and American Primacy in the Twenty-First Century* (Prentice Hall, 2001), pp. 70–96; Ivo H. Daalder and James M. Goldgeier, "Putting Europe First," *Survival*, vol. 43 (Spring 2001), pp. 71–91; and Philip H. Gordon, "Bridging the Atlantic Divide," *Foreign Affairs*, vol. 82 (January/February 2003), pp. 70–83.

5. See, for example, John J. Mearsheimer, *The Tragedy of Great Power Politics* (Norton, 2001), pp. 392–400.

6. For useful overviews, see Stephen G. Brooks and William C. Wohlforth, "American Primacy in Perspective," *Foreign Affairs*, vol. 81 (July/August 2002), pp. 20–33; Paul Kennedy, "The Eagle Has Landed," *Financial Times*, February 2, 2002, p. 1; Robert J. Lieber, "Foreign Policy and American Primacy," in *Eagle Rules?* pp. 1–15; Joseph Nye, *The Paradox of American Power* (Oxford University Press, 2002), pp. 1–40; and William Wohlforth, "The Stability of a Unipolar World," *International Security*, vol. 24 (Summer 1999), pp. 9–22. See also Michael O'Hanlon's chapter 11 in this volume.

7. Michael O'Hanlon, "Too Big a Buck for the Bang," *Washington Post*, January 6, 2003, p. A15.

8. International Institute for Strategic Studies, *The Military Balance 2002/2003* (Oxford University Press, 2002), pp. 332–37.

9. Kennedy, "The Eagle Has Landed."

10. *World Development Indicators 2002* on CD-ROM, produced by the World Bank.

11. Ibid.

12. Richard K. Betts, "The Soft Underbelly of American Primacy: Tactical Advantages of Terror," *Political Science Quarterly*, vol. 117 (Spring 2002), pp. 19–36.

13. Joseph Nye, "Soft Power," *Foreign Policy*, no. 80 (Fall 1990), pp. 153–72.

14. See "Half a Billion Americans?—Demography and the West," *Economist*, August 24, 2002, pp. 19–22.

15. On the importance of threat perceptions in determining balancing behavior, see Stephen Walt, *The Origins of Alliances* (Cornell University Press, 1987).

16. For a contrary view, see Charles Kupchan, *The End of the American Era: U.S. Foreign Policy and the Geopolitics of the Twenty-First Century* (Knopf, 2002).

17. For an excellent discussion of the globalization phenomenon, see Robert Keohane and Joseph Nye, "Introduction," in Joseph Nye and John Donahue, eds., *Governance in a Globalizing World* (Brookings, 2000).

18. On globalization as a long-term trend in human affairs, see Nayan Chanda, "Coming Together: Globalization Means Reconnecting the Human Community," *YaleGlobal*, November 19, 2002 (http://yaleglobal.yale.edu/about/essay.jsp [accessed January 2003]).

19. For a comprehensive review of the literature on whether globalization today is different from a century ago, see Michael D. Bordo, Barry Eichengreen, and Douglas A. Irwin, "Is Globalization Today Really Different than Globalization a Hundred Years Ago?" Working Paper 7195 (Cambridge, Mass.: National Bureau of Economic Research, June 1999) (www.nber.org/papers/w7195 [accessed January 2003]).

20. For a good economic analysis of globalization, see Gary Burtless and others, *Globaphobia: Confronting Fears about Open Trade* (Brookings, 1998).

21. Thomas Friedman, *The Lexus and the Olive Tree* (Farrar Strauss Giroux, 1999), p. xiv.

22. *The National Strategy for Homeland Security* (Office of Homeland Security, The White House, July 2002), p. 21 (www.whitehouse.gov/homeland/book/index.html [accessed January 2003]).

23. Nye, *Paradox of American Power*, p. 86; and Bank of International Settlements, Press Release, October 9, 2001.

24. *Statistical Abstract of the United States, 1990*, 110th ed. (U.S. Census Bureau, 1990), p. 829; *Statistical Abstract of the United States, 2001*, 121st ed. (U.S. Census Bureau, 2001), p. 829; and "United We Fall," *Economist*, September 28, 2002, p. 24.

25. *UNCTAD World Investment Report 2002: Transnational Corporations and Export Competitiveness*, pp. 3–4.

26. Ibid., p. 12.

27. For an overview, see Joseph Cirincione (with Jon Wolfstahl and Miriam Rajkumar), *Deadly Arsenals: Tracking Weapons of Mass Destruction* (Carnegie Endowment for International Peace, 2002).

28. Viktor Mayer-Schönberger and Deborah Hurley, "Globalization of Communication," in Nye and Donahue, eds., *Governance in a Globalizing World*, pp. 135–51. For a brilliant dissection of the impact of social globalization, see Friedman, *The Lexus and the Olive Tree*.

29. See Stephen M. Walt, "Fads, Fevers, and Firestorms," *Foreign Policy*, no. 121 (November–December 2000), pp. 34–42.

30. Robert T. Watson and others, *Climate Change 2001: Synthesis Report* (Geneva: Intergovernmental Panel on Climate Change, 2001) (www.ipcc.ch/pub/SYRspm.pdf [accessed January 2003]).

31. UNAIDS, *Report on the Global HIV/AIDS Epidemic* (Geneva, July 2002), pp. 22, 44 (www.unaids.org/epidemic_update/report_july02/english/contents.html [accessed January 2003]).

32. National Intelligence Council, *The Next Wave of HIV/AIDS: Nigeria, Ethiopia, Russia, India, China* (Central Intelligence Agency, ICA 2002-04D, September 2002), p. 7.

33. William C. Clark, "Environmental Globalization," in Nye and Donahue, eds., *Governance in a Globalizing World*, p. 94.

34. Bill Emmott, "A Survey of America's World Role," *Economist*, June 29, 2002, p. 20.

35. Tom Friedman, "India, Pakistan, and GE," *New York Times*, August 11, 2002, sec. IV, p. 13.

36. See, among others, Patrick J. Buchanan, *A Republic, Not an Empire: Reclaiming America's Destiny* (Regnery, 1999); Eugene Gholz, Darly G. Press, and Harvey M. Sapolsky, "Come Home, America: The Strategy of Restraint in the Face of Temptation," *International Security*, vol. 21 (Spring 1997), pp. 5–48; Eric Nordlinger, *Isolationism Reconfigured: American Foreign Policy for a New Century* (Princeton University Press, 1995); and Benjamin Schwarz and Christopher Layne, "A New Grand Strategy," *Atlantic Monthly*, vol. 289 (January 2002), pp. 5–23.

37. See Daniel Benjamin and Steven Simon, *The Age of Sacred Terror* (Random House, 2002), esp. chaps. 1–5.

38. *A National Security Strategy of Engagement and Enlargement* (The White House, July 1994); and *The National Security Strategy of the United States of America* (The White House, September 2002) (www.whitehouse.gov/nsc/nss.html [accessed April 2003]).

39. See Mandelbaum, *Ideas That Conquered the World*, esp. chap. 1.

40. President George W. Bush, "State of the Union Address," January 29, 2002 (www.whitehouse.gov/news/releases/2002/01/20020129-11.html [accessed January 2003]).

41. Charles Krauthammer, "The New Unilateralism," *Washington Post*, June 8, 2001, p. A29.

42. Quoted in Bob Woodward, *Bush at War* (Simon & Schuster, 2002), p. 81.

43. Quoted in Thom Shanker, "White House Says the U.S. Is Not a Loner, Just Choosy," *New York Times*, July 31, 2001, p. A1.

44. On the distinction between instrumental and formal multilateralists, see Robert Kagan, "Multilateralism, American Style," *Washington Post*, September 13, 2002, p. 39.

45. As Krauthammer argues, "The history of paper treaties—from the prewar Kellogg-Briand Pact and Munich to the post–Cold War Oslo accords and the 1994 Agreed Framework with North Korea—is a history of navieté and cynicism, a combination both toxic and volatile that invariably ends badly." Charles Krauthammer, "The Unipolar Moment Revisited," *National Interest*, no. 70 (Winter 2002/03), p. 13. See also John Bolton, "Should We Take Global Governance Seriously?" *Chicago Journal of International Law*, vol. 1 (Fall 2000), pp. 205–22; and Charles Krauthammer, "Arms Control: The End of an Illusion," *Weekly Standard*, November 1, 1999, pp. 21–27.

46. Quoted in "Old Friends and New," *Economist*, June 1, 2002, p. 28. See also Woodward, *Bush at War*, p. 281.

47. William Safire, "Friendly Dissuasion," *New York Times*, May 3, 2001, p. A25.

48. Krauthammer, "The Unipolar Moment Revisited," p. 17.

49. "Excerpts from Pentagon's Plan: 'Prevent the Re-Emergence of a New Rival'," *New York Times*, March 8, 1992, p. A14. On the influence of this study on current administration thinking, see Nicolas Lemann, "The Next World Order," *New Yorker*, April 1, 2002, pp. 41–44.

50. *The National Security Strategy of the United States*, p. 30.

51. For a similar assessment of the strains in Hegemonist thinking, see Stanley Hoffmann, "The High and the Mighty," *American Prospect*, January 13, 2003, pp. 28–32.

52. Robert Kagan, "The Benevolent Empire," *Foreign Policy*, no. 111 (Summer 1998), p. 28. Paul Wolfowitz expressed this sentiment thus: "The way we define our interest there's a sort of natural compatibility between the United States and most countries in the world." See "Deputy Secretary Wolfowitz Interview with the Los Angeles Times," April 29, 2002 (www.defenselink.mil/news/May2002/t05092002_t0429la.html [accessed January 2003]).

53. Robert Kagan, "Iraq: The Day After," *Washington Post*, July 21, 2002, p. B7.

54. For a discussion of the divisions between democratic imperialists and assertive nationalists on the specific question of Iraq, see Ivo H. Daalder and James M. Lindsay, "It's Hawk vs. Hawk in the Bush Administration," *Washington Post*, October 27, 2002, p. B3.

55. "President Bush Discusses Iraq in National Press Conference," March 6, 2003 (www.whitehouse.gov/news/releases/2003/03/20030306-8.html [accessed May 2003]).

56. Jessica T. Mathews, "Power Shift," *Foreign Affairs*, vol. 76 (January/February 1997), p. 50.

57. For an excellent analysis of al-Qaida as an NGO, see Tod Lindberg, "How to Fight a Superpower," *Weekly Standard*, December 31, 2001/January 7, 2002, pp. 31–35. See also Moisés Naim, "The Five Wars of Globalization," *Foreign Policy*, no. 134 (January–February 2003), pp. 29–37.

58. Stewart Patrick, "Multilateralism and Its Discontents: The Causes and Consequences of U.S. Ambivalence," in Stewart Patrick and Shepard Forman, eds., *Multilateralism and U.S. Foreign Policy* (Boulder, Colo.: Lynne Rienner, 2002), p. 25.

59. See Moisés Naim, "Lori's War: An Interview with Lori Wallach," *Foreign Policy*, no. 118 (Spring 2000), pp. 28–55; and Jay Mazur, "Labor's New Internationalism," *Foreign Affairs*, vol. 79 (January/February 2000), pp. 79–93.

60. A variant of this idea is "transgovernmentalism," which holds that the key transnational networks involve government agencies linked to their counterparts abroad. See

Anne-Marie Slaughter, "The Real New World Order," *Foreign Affairs*, vol. 76 (September/October 1997), pp. 183–97.

61. Mathews, "Power Shift," p. 53.

62. P. J. Simmons and Chantal de Jonge Oudraat, "From Accord to Action," in P. J. Simmons and Chantal de Jonge Oudraat, eds., *Managing Global Issues: Lessons Learned* (Carnegie Endowment for International Peace, 2001), p. 720.

63. The most extensive attempt to link Iraq and al Qaeda came during Secretary Powell's UN Security Council presentation on Iraq's violations of its international commitments. Colin Powell, "Remarks before the United Nations Security Council," New York, February 5, 2003 (www.state.gov/secretary/rm/2003/17300.htm [accessed May 2003]).

64. Mancur Olsen, *The Logic of Collective Action* (Harvard University Press, 1965).

65. "Remarks by the President in Announcement of New Cabinet Officers" (Office of the Press Secretary, The White House, December 5, 1996).

66. Mary McGrory, "Pit-Stop Presidency," *Washington Post*, October 27, 2002, p. B7.

67. See Robert Kagan, "Power and Weakness," *Policy Review*, no. 113 (June/July 2002), pp. 3–28; and Josef Joffe, "Who's Afraid of Mister Big?" *National Interest*, no. 64 (Summer 2001), pp. 43–52.

68. Samuel R. Berger, "A Foreign Policy for the Global Age," *Foreign Affairs*, vol. 79 (November/December 2000), p. 39.

69. John Ikenberry, "Getting Hegemony Right," *National Interest*, no. 63 (Spring 2001), p. 21.

70. Emmott, "A Survey of America's World Role," p. 20.

71. See "America—Still Unprepared, Still in Danger" (New York: Council on Foreign Relations, 2002) (www.cfr.org/pdf/Homeland_TF.pdf [accessed January 2003]); and Stephen E. Flynn, "America the Vulnerable," *Foreign Affairs*, vol. 81 (January/February 2002), pp. 60–75.

72. For details, see Michael O'Hanlon and others, *Protecting the American Homeland: A Preliminary Analysis* (Brookings, 2002).

73. *National Security Strategy of the United States*, p. 1.

74. See Susan Rice, "The Bush National Security Strategy: Focus on Failed States," Brookings Policy Brief 11 (January 2003).

75. The literature supporting this proposition is vast. See especially David A. Lake, "Powerful Pacifists: Democratic States and War," *American Political Science Review*, vol. 86 (March 1992), pp. 24–37; John M. Owen, "How Liberalism Produces Democratic Peace," *International Security*, vol. 19 (Fall 1994), pp. 87–125; and Bruce M. Russett, *Grasping the Democratic Peace: Principles for a Post–Cold War World* (Princeton University Press, 1993).

76. Edward D. Mansfield and Jack Snyder, "Democratization and War," *Foreign Affairs*, vol. 74 (May/June 1995), pp. 79–97.

77. Fareed Zakaria, "The Rise of Illiberal Democracy," *Foreign Affairs*, vol. 76 (November/December 1997), pp. 22–43. See also Mandelbaum, *Ideas That Conquered the World*, pp. 241–76.

78. Richard N Haass, "Towards Greater Democracy in the Muslim World," Address at the Council on Foreign Relations, December 4, 2002 (www.state.gov/s/p/rem/15686.htm [accessed January 2003]).

79. For details, see Lael Brainard and Robert Litan's chaper 10 in this volume.

80. See Ivo H. Daalder, "Are the United States and Europe Heading for Divorce?" *International Affairs*, vol. 77 (July 2001), pp. 553–69; and Kupchan, *End of the American Era*, esp. chap. 4.

79. George W. Bush, "Introduction," *The National Security Strategy of the United States*, p. ii.

80. See James M. Lindsay and Michael E. O'Hanlon, *Defending America: The Case for Limited National Missile Defense* (Brookings, 2001).

81. On the difficulties of preemption, see International Institute for Strategic Studies, "The Bush National Strategy: What Does 'Pre-emption' Mean?" *Strategic Comment*, vol. 8 (October 2002), pp. 1–2.

82. On the shortcomings of the Moscow Treaty, see Ivo H. Daalder and James M. Lindsay, "One-Day Wonder: The Dangerous Absurdity of the Bush-Putin Arms Treaty," *American Prospect*, August 26, 2002, pp. 13–15; and Ivo H. Daalder and James M. Lindsay, "A New Agenda for Nuclear Weapons," Brookings Policy Brief 94 (February 2002).

83. See Dick Lugar, "Eye on a Worldwide Weapons Cache," *Washington Post*, December 6, 2001, p. A39.

84. See *Climate Change Science: An Analysis of Some Key Questions* (National Academy Press, 2001) (http://books.nap.edu/html/climatechange/climatechange.pdf [accessed January 2003]); and Watson, *Climate Change 2001: Synthesis Report*.

85. For criticisms of Kyoto, see James M. Lindsay, "Global Warming Heats Up," *Brookings Review*, no. 19 (Fall 2001), pp. 26–29; and David G. Victor, *The Collapse of the Kyoto Protocol and the Struggle to Slow Global Warming* (Princeton University Press, 2001).

86. Warwick J. McKibbin and Peter Wilcoxen, *Climate Change Policy after Kyoto: Blueprint for a Realistic Approach* (Brookings, 2002).

LAEL BRAINARD
ROBERT LITAN

10

A Global Economic Agenda for the United States

S EPTEMBER 11 WAS a defining event for America's strategic posture. In subtler ways it called attention to the nation's international economic posture, demonstrating that our international engagement is not a matter for debate but a fact of our time. After the attack, manufacturing lines ground to a halt as just-in-time inputs were held at border crossings, tarmacs, and loading docks. Corporate executives sharply circumscribed air travel and revisited security procedures at overseas plants. And some foreign reactions showed a disturbing readiness to interpret the attack as a comeuppance for an arrogant superpower pushing its brand of globalization on a resentful world.[1]

The well-being of the United States depends far less on geographical isolation in this age of globalization than on the ability to shape the international system. Securing the homeland will require extensive cooperation from nations around the world and a sustained effort to strengthen the perceived legitimacy of America's preeminence in the international economic order. The question now is not whether the United States should remain engaged, politically and economically, with the rest of the world, but how it should do so. Can this country pursue a coherent policy agenda that not only advances the national interest but also fosters the interests of citizens of other countries, especially in the poorest nations? We believe it can, through judicious management of foreign aid, expansion of the globe's vibrant trading system, and institutional reforms to improve the stability and efficiency of capital across national borders.

Relieving Poverty

One of the few silver linings in the new environment is the emergence of broad bipartisan support among U.S. officials for expanding development aid. The case for doing so is powerful, but only if aid is directed to governments with a demonstrated commitment to development through a transparent and accountable process. Aid should support investments with high social return—such as basic health, primary education, sanitation, environment, and rural infrastructure. Yet despite growing support among U.S. policymakers and a convergence of goals at the international level, U.S. budget pressures or political considerations could derail increased development spending or shunt it into activities that do not serve economic development.

A Second Chance for Aid?

U.S. development aid fell steadily for decades—from more than 3 percent of total budget outlays in 1962, at the time of the Cuban missile crisis, to roughly one half of 1 percent by 2001.[2] U.S. per capita foreign aid spending of $34 a year is far below the industrial country average of $67.[3] Several reasons account for the decline.

For one thing, there is deep disillusionment over aid's many failures. For decades, much of the debate on addressing global poverty centered on how much foreign aid to provide and through what means. But in the 1990s, critics contrasted the stunning economic successes of East Asian countries—where aid has amounted to less than 2 percent of GDP—with the dismal economic performance of countries in sub-Saharan Africa, where foreign economic aid exceeded 10 percent of national income for decades. To be sure, South Korea and Taiwan, for example, benefited from massive U.S. assistance, but growth was also robust in other Asian nations that received little official aid. Interest in aid also diminished because the end of the cold war meant that foreign assistance was no longer justified to reward allies in the fight against communism. Finally, large and persistent U.S. budget deficits led to significant cuts in discretionary spending, at home and abroad.

The pendulum now seems to be swinging the other way. Aid activists have developed a powerful four-part recipe for mobilizing public support:

the adoption of a simple, compelling goal, champions with strong name recognition, coalitions that transcend national borders and span the political spectrum, and a focus on high-profile international gatherings. The first big shift came in 1998, when the global rock star Bono of U2 made common cause with Pope John Paul II to persuade leaders of the richest nations to forgive the debt of the poorest nations. A similarly eclectic coalition, including Bill Gates and leading economists, helped direct world attention to the HIV/AIDS pandemic. In 2000, even as Congress cut U.S. budget authority for development aid overall, President Bill Clinton won congressional authorization for nearly $1 billion for debt forgiveness and the global fight against HIV/AIDS, and Congress has granted further increases during the Bush administration.[4]

The campaign against terrorism has provided a potentially powerful political rationale for foreign assistance that had been missing since the end of the cold war: namely, that by strengthening foreign economies, foreign aid may weaken incentives for residents of poor nations to turn to terrorism. Indeed, it is no coincidence that just before the Monterrey Summit in May 2002, several months after 9/11, President George W. Bush proposed an increase in total U.S. development aid of $5 billion by 2006.[5] Leading Democrats sounded a similar call.

The shift in the politics of aid presents a rare opportunity to make real progress in fighting the debilitating poverty that holds too many in its grip. Although many American taxpayers find the humanitarian case for aid alone compelling—with as many as 3 billion people living on less than $2 a day—polls have indicated less support for foreign aid than for all other major government activities, including welfare for the U.S. poor.[6] But it is critical to invest aid funds wisely—avoiding the repeat of past mistakes—or risk another backlash.

Making Aid More Effective

Although superficially appealing, the new security rationale for development aid—that it will help in the fight against terrorism—is far from airtight. The links between poverty, inequality, and terrorism, at best, are weak and indirect. The masterminds and perpetrators in the attacks on the United States were largely educated and from middle-class backgrounds in relatively affluent, but politically repressive, Middle Eastern societies. Their dissatisfaction is rooted more in frustration with the political and economic paralysis in their countries than in poverty itself. However, poverty surely is a critical ingredient in the failed states such as Afghanistan and Somalia that host terrorist training camps. Poor education coupled with despair help to explain the resonance of terrorist ideology for some in the Islamic world.

Even where the linkage between terrorism and poverty may be strong, it is important to be realistic about the case for aid. The record of foreign assistance in promoting growth has been poor when political considerations have dictated its allocation. Aid to corrupt foreign leaders who were "with us" in the cold war has led to the many horror stories of corrupt leaders using aid to line their own pockets or fund pet projects. In too many cases, U.S. aid dollars have been used to curry favor with foreign leaders without in any way advancing democracy, improving health and education, or promoting economic growth. Using foreign assistance in this way may have been justified for foreign policy or national security reasons, but it should not be confused with promoting economic development.

In the current environment, the primary goal of development as distinct from politically directed aid should be to help recipient nations reduce poverty and generate growth. This outcome is most likely when governments are committed to reform, policymaking is transparent, leaders are accountable, and macroeconomic policies are sound. Humanitarian aid and postconflict assistance may be justified even when these conditions are not satisfied, but then it may be necessary to bypass official channels and work through nongovernmental organizations.

The record also suggests that aid fails when it does not respect the power of the market. Previous approaches that supplanted market mechanisms, such as forced industrialization, filling investment financing gaps, investing in industrial infrastructure, and creating monopoly quasi-governmental organizations in agricultural marketing and distribution proved disappointing. Even experiments with sensible goals, such as population control and mandatory education, largely failed because they took a top-down approach (establishing school buildings) rather than providing good incentives at the individual level (eliminating school fees).[7] The economics of development aid largely follows the logic of government intervention more broadly: effective policies correct market failures and align market returns with social returns.

In fact, there is strong evidence that aid has improved welfare in the poorest nations, even though income gaps between rich and poor countries remain wide. Figures 10-1 through 10-4 show narrowing gaps between rich and poor nations on life expectancy, child survival, and literacy. The charts show the world divided into five groups with approximately equal population arrayed on the basis of per capita income in 1960 from poorest

Figure 10-1. *Per Capita Income Relative to Richest Quintile, 1960, 1997*

Percent

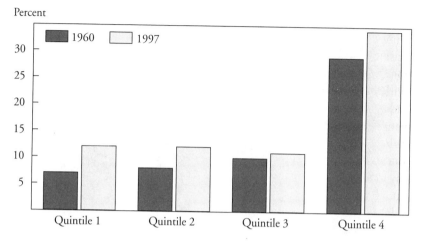

Source: Authors' calculations based on Alan Heston, Robert Summers, and Bettina Aten, Penn World Table Version 6.1 database (University of Pennsylvania, Center for International Comparisons, October, 2002) [hereafter Penn World Table database]; and World Bank, World Development Indicators database (Washington, various years).

Note: Richest quintile per capita income increases from $9,711 in 1960 to $23,114 in 1997 in 1995 dollars.

Figure 10-2. *Life Expectancy Relative to Richest Quintile, 1960, 1997*

Percent

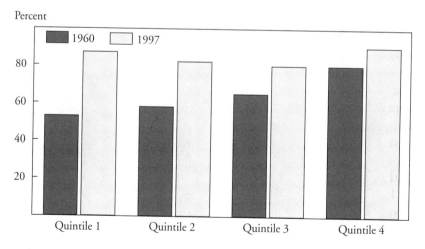

Source: Authors' calculations based on Penn World Table database and World Development Indicators database.

Note: Richest quintile life expectancy increases from 69 years in 1960 to 76 years in 1997.

Figure 10-3. *Child Survival Rate Relative to Richest Quintile, 1960, 1997*

Percent

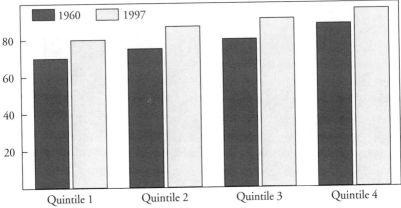

Source: Authors' calculations based on Penn World Table database and World Development Indicators database.

Note: Richest quintile child survival rate increases from 962 per thousand in 1960 to 987 per thousand in 1997.

Figure 10-4. *Adult Literacy Rates, 1970, 1998*

Percent

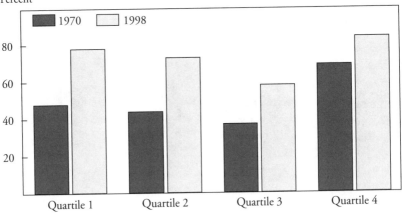

Source: Authors' calculations based on Penn World Table database and World Development Indicators database.

Note: Quartiles made up of lower- and middle-income countries. "Possibility frontier" presumed to be 100 percent.

to richest. They compare outcomes in the poorer four quintiles against the "possibility frontier" represented by the richest quintile.[8] Between 1960 and 1997, income for the poorest three quintiles remained less than one-eighth that of the richest quintile, and even the fourth quintile achieved income averaging barely one-third of that of the richest quintile.[9]

In contrast to slow progress in reducing economic inequality, gaps in health and education have narrowed faster than have income gaps. Life expectancy in the poorest quintile increased from 53 percent in 1960 to 87 percent in 1997 of life expectancy in the richest quintile, even as life expectancy in the richest quintile increased from 69 to 76 years (figures 10-2 and 10-3). Adult literacy rates also rose faster between 1970 and 1998 in the poorest countries (figure 10-4).[10] These differences suggest there has been better dissemination and adoption of health and education technologies and know-how across borders—in part through the provision of foreign aid—than of broader production technologies, and this is true for all initial income groups. On a more sober note, however, it also suggests that health and literacy improvements, while necessary, are unlikely to be sufficient for producing sustained economic growth.

Many of these gains from development assistance efforts are in danger of being reversed by the global scourge of HIV/AIDS, which claimed over 3 million lives in 2002 alone.[11] AIDS has disproportionately afflicted the regions of the world least able to shoulder the enormous financial and institutional burden associated with preventing and treating the disease, with sub-Saharan Africa, the world's poorest region, showing the highest prevalence rates.[12] UNAIDS, the United Nations agency devoted to the epidemic, estimates that average life expectancy in sub-Saharan Africa is now fifteen years lower than it would have been without AIDS.[13] The disease has already left in its wake 11 million orphans across the continent, with estimates reaching 25 million by the end of the decade.[14] And AIDS has undermined advances in economic productivity, straining already insufficient public health budgets and leaving private and public sector employers struggling to hire and train replacements for dying and debilitated workers. The problem is compounded because afflicted individuals are far more vulnerable to the numerous other diseases ravaging the continent, such as TB, malaria, and cholera. And the epidemic is spreading quickly throughout the world, with Asia and the Caribbean experiencing dramatic increases in infection rates.

The AIDS epidemic makes the case for development assistance that much more urgent, and failure to combat the disease costs not only the lives of those infected but also undermines the effectiveness of all development efforts. President Bush, at the urging of Congress and a broad coalition of AIDS activists, has recognized this urgent need, pledging $15 billion over the next five years to the global fight against AIDS.[15] The fiscal 2004 budget request includes approximately $2 billion in funding for global AIDS programs.[16] Development experts welcome these increases in funding but warn that they represent a fraction of the funding that is needed.[17] And the president's proposal commits just one-tenth of the new funds to the Global Fund for AIDS, Tuberculosis, and Malaria, an international organization widely recognized as a model of international cooperation. The new funding for global AIDS programs represents a step in the right direction, but it is extremely important that these funds do not supplant existing programs dedicated to improving public health. Although AIDS is certainly the largest public health challenge of our time, tuberculosis still claims 2 million lives a year and malaria another 1 million. An estimated 1.5 million children in Africa die each year from pneumonia, two-thirds of whom could be saved by simple and inexpensive antibiotics, and another 2 million children worldwide die each year from dehydration associated with diarrhea.[18]

The proportion of total world aid devoted to health, education, and sanitation has risen to nearly one-third—nearly one-half for U.S. bilateral aid (figures 10-5 and 10-6). This emphasis is consistent with good economics and development experience. Official intervention works best where markets produce inferior outcomes. For example, markets on their own provide too little of goods that generate large benefits for people other than the direct consumers. Market underprovision is prevalent in basic health and education, as evidenced by considerable (although varying) government involvement in these areas in rich nations. Basic health services provide such "external" benefits because they reduce the possibility of contagious illness. Basic education facilitates productivity growth and democratic processes. Thus, there is a strong humanitarian case for using development assistance to subsidize the provision of health services, education, and other goods that generate large external benefits in the poorest nations.[19]

There is also a compelling *economic* case for international action when public goods are regional or global in nature so that even well-governed, wealthy nations would underprovide them because some of the benefit falls outside national borders. This is particularly true for global public goods whose benefits are enjoyed globally and cannot be captured by any single country. But the strong economic rationale for subsidizing international

Figure 10-5. *Social Sector Aid as Percentage of World Total Aid,*
1973–2000

Percent

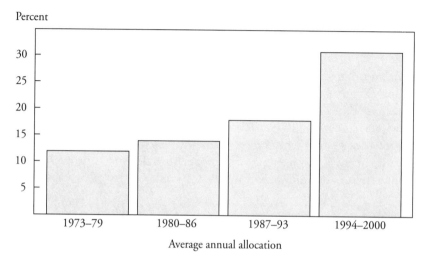

Average annual allocation

Source: Authors' calculations based on Organization for Economic Cooperation and Development, Creditor Reporting System database (2002).

Figure 10-6. *Social Sector Aid as Percentage of U.S. Bilateral Total Aid,*
1973–2000

Percent

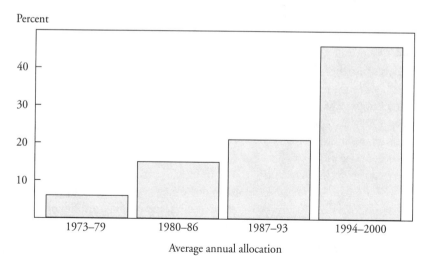

Average annual allocation

Source: Authors' calculations based on OECD, Creditor Reporting System database.

public goods, strictly speaking, applies to a rather narrow set of goods, such as the complete eradication of a disease such as smallpox, which not only eliminates the disease but also obviates the need for future spending on vaccinations.[20] For development assistance, a more practical threshold is whether a good is undersupplied because important regional or global spillovers are not taken into account.

A much broader class of challenges meets this bar, such as cross-border spillovers in the spread of infectious disease. Research on diseases that are present worldwide, but endemic in poor countries, is typically profitable only if the diseases are also prevalent in countries rich enough to pay for the cost of treatment. Rich countries can aid poor nations by subsidizing research or by guaranteeing a market for drugs developed privately that deal with diseases found mostly in poor nations.[21]

A Special Role for Knowledge

Most of the benefits of new knowledge accrue to people other than the person who develops the knowledge. The gap between private and social value of an innovation can be huge. The economic and social returns to the research and development now called the Green Revolution were enormous. This collection of innovations, which increased nutrients to crops and improved their resistance to diseases, insects, and birds, massively increased agricultural productivity in India, China, and other nations and banished the specter of hunger and famine for billions of people. Ironically, the backlash against genetically modified foods that began in Europe and shows signs of spreading to developing nations could curtail future research, sacrificing further increases in agricultural productivity. The dispute between the European Union and the United States over agricultural biotechnology has already caused leaders of some African nations to turn away food assistance in the midst of deepening famine.

The potential for research to increase the productivity of tropical agriculture and to find diagnoses and treatments for diseases that disproportionately or exclusively affect the poorest nations is vast. Currently, the social and economic costs of malaria and other tropical diseases are staggering.[22] Governments of wealthy nations combine public funding for basic research and development with patent and copyright protection for intellectual property to encourage the development of scientific knowledge. But poor nations have neither adequate public resources to subsidize research nor the promise of private returns to make intellectual property invest-ments attractive. Thus a key challenge for international development is to foster research on the particular challenges faced by poor nations.[23] The United States should offer some mixture of public funding and tax incen-tives for basic and applied research that would benefit developing nations. Developed nations should commit to buy vaccines when they are devel-oped and possibly offer sales tax credits to guarantee innovators a future stream of revenues.

What to do about research in pharmaceutical products is particularly troublesome. Intellectual property laws are designed to strike a balance between encouraging innovation (by enabling investors to charge prices well above production cost on new drugs to recover their research invest-ments) and ensuring that valuable innovations and treatments are widely available. In recent years, especially in the last round of global trade talks, the United States tried to extend to the international level rules that pro-tect intellectual property, reflecting the rapid transmission of science and technology across borders. But these efforts subsequently were attacked for denying lifesaving medicines to the poorest nations.

There is a real tension between addressing the research shortfall on dis-eases disproportionately afflicting the poor and improving the accessibility of medicines to poor nations. Additional research effort can be encouraged partly by extending intellectual property protection, or the length of time a given producer enjoys a monopoly on a particular drug, as is currently done for "orphan" drugs in the wealthy nations. But ensuring broad access requires pricing at cost, which undercuts the value of the intellectual prop-erty monopoly. For a limited class of internationally agreed-on health emergencies, when medicines are already in production in response to demand in rich nations, it is not hard to reconcile these goals by segment-ing markets in rich and poor nations. This option requires that drugs sold to or produced in poor nations cannot be re-exported to rich nations. If this safeguard could be ensured, producers in rich nations could maintain profit margins through relatively high-priced sales in middle- and upper-income nations' markets, while allowing the same drugs to be made avail-able in poor nations at much lower prices. For diseases where rich-country demand is low, it may be necessary to combine incentives on the "push" side, such as directly subsidizing research and development, and incentives on the "pull side," such as commitments to purchase drugs for distribution in poor nations.

Emerging International Consensus

Broad agreement has emerged at the international level that aid programs driven by the diverse agendas of donors are likely to fail. A central determinant of the success of development programs is the commitment of recipient governments to national development strategies that are designed in a transparent process that involves key stakeholders. These home-grown strategies can serve as funding vehicles for bilateral and multilateral support, facilitating coordination and reducing administrative complexity for beneficiary governments.

The World Bank's Poverty Reduction and Growth Strategy process illustrates this approach. This program, supported by the International Monetary Fund (IMF) and regional development banks, directs resources freed up by debt forgiveness toward nationally determined social investments. Beneficiary nations present spending plans and assistance needs in the context of an overall strategy to reduce poverty and support growth. The Poverty Reduction Strategy process is intended to ensure that domestic budget resources support the same objectives as aid does. The World Bank's program encourages the inclusion of nongovernmental organizations in the formulation of these plans.

The emphasis on international public goods and on coordinating donor efforts is reflected in the emergence of global trust funds directed at particular programmatic goals. These include the Global Environmental Facility at the World Bank, the Highly Indebted Poor Countries Debt Relief trust fund, and the Global Fund to Fight AIDS, Tuberculosis, and Malaria. They provide a mechanism for pooling funds from public and private donors who agree on eligibility criteria and objectives. In the health field, this arrangement draws on a rich history of successful "campaign-style" initiatives targeting a particular disease or set of interventions. The campaign approach has important advantages: the goal is clear, results are measurable, technical expertise is well defined, and single-issue focus provides a good marketing vehicle. A pool of committed funds assures poor countries that money will be forthcoming for programs consistent with program objectives. The multilateral nature of these funds also has shortcomings, however: delay in implementation and some rigidity, because of the need for time-consuming negotiations to achieve agreement among all donors. Trust funds are likely to be most effective for a limited set of programs for which broad donor participation is critical—as in debt relief, when creditors' pledges are completely interdependent—and the goal is broadly shared by all the donors.

The growing international consensus on aid is embodied in a set of eight Millennium Development Goals (MDG) adopted at the United Nations Millennium Summit in September 2000 for achievement by 2015 (box 10-1).[24] The international adoption of specific, numeric development targets is historically unprecedented and untested. A group chaired by former Mexican president Ernesto Zedillo and including former U.S. Treasury secretary Robert Rubin has estimated the price tag for achieving the MDG at an additional $50 billion a year. This is nearly double the current annual international aid level of $54 billion, $35 billion of which goes to the world's poorest nations.[25] The annual U.S. share of any additional aid amounts would be between $8.5 billion (based on the U.S. share of IMF and World Bank capital) and $20.7 billion a year (based on the U. S. share in OECD donor GDP of 41.3 percent).[26]

The State of Play

The Bush administration has pledged to increase bilateral development assistance through a Millennium Challenge Account (MCA) starting in 2004 and reaching $5 billion annually above current assistance levels by 2006. Recipient nations would be required to meet eligibility criteria in good governance, economic freedom, and investment in health and education.[27] Continued eligibility would be contingent on achievement of measurable results.[28] This initiative presents an enticing opportunity to transform U.S. development assistance, but success will hinge on several design elements.

PROGRAM EMPHASIS. That the MCA should support areas such as basic health, primary education, clean water, and sanitation, which are included in the MDG and in the Bush administration's proposed eligibility criteria, is generally accepted. Whether the MCA should support all of the areas encompassed by the eligibility criteria is more controversial. Such a charge could extend to private sector development and democratic institution building, or to areas covered by the MDG but not by the MCA eligibility criteria, such as protecting the environment. We believe that prospects for success are highest if the program starts with a narrow focus on those areas where foreign assistance has a strong track record and progress is easy to measure, such as basic health, primary education, water, sanitation, and the

---

Box 10-1. *UN Millennium Development Goals*

Goal 1. Eradicate extreme poverty and hunger.
1. Halve, between 1990 and 2015, the proportion of people whose income is less than one dollar (PPP) a day.
2. Halve, between 1990 and 2015, the proportion of people who suffer from hunger.

Goal 2. Achieve universal primary education.
3. Ensure that, by 2015, children everywhere, boys and girls alike, will be able to complete a full course of primary schooling.

Goal 3. Promote gender equality and empower women.
4. Eliminate gender disparity in primary and secondary education, preferably by 2005, and in all levels of education no later than 2015.

Goal 4. Reduce child mortality.
5. Reduce by two-thirds, between 1990 and 2015, the under-five mortality rate.

Goal 5. Improve maternal health.
6. Reduce by three-quarters, between 1990 and 2015, the maternal mortality ratio.

Goal 6. Combat HIV/AIDS, malaria, and other diseases.
7. Have halted by 2015 and begun to reverse the spread of HIV/AIDS.
8. Have halted by 2015 and begun to reverse the incidence of malaria, (tuberculosis), and other major diseases.

Goal 7. Ensure environmental sustainability.
9. Integrate the principles of sustainable development into country policies and programs and reverse the loss of environmental resources.

---

environment. Capacity and institution building should also be emphasized through the grantmaking process.

COUNTRY ELIGIBILITY. The focus on measurable results and objective criteria should help avoid the politically directed spending decisions of years past. Setting ambitious eligibility criteria will create powerful and benign incentives and ensure that aid money flows to the highest yielding

10. Halve by 2015 the proportion of people without sustainable access to safe drinking water.

11. By 2020 have achieved a significant improvement in the lives of at least 100 million slum dwellers (as measured by sanitation and access to secure tenure).

Goal 8. Develop a global partnership for development

12. Develop further an open, rule-based, predictable, nondiscriminatory trading and financial system. Includes a commitment to good governance, development, and poverty reduction—nationally and internationally.

13. Address the special needs of the least developed countries. Includes tariff and quota-free access for least-developed countries' exports; enhanced program of debt relief for HIPCs and cancellation of official bilateral debt; and more generous [official development assistance] for countries committed to poverty reduction.

14. Address the special needs of landlocked countries and small-island developing states.

15. Deal comprehensively with the debt problems of developing countries through national and international measures in order to make debt sustainable in the long term.

16. In cooperation with developing countries, develop and implement strategies for decent and productive work for youth.

17. In cooperation with pharmaceutical companies, provide access to affordable essential drugs in developing countries.

18. In cooperation with the private sector, make available the benefits of new technologies, especially information and communications.

Source: www.developmentgoals.org.

environments. But it is important to develop complementary strategies for helping "near miss" countries address weak areas and for providing assistance to weaker performing nations with compelling needs.[29] Instead, the administration proposal would progressively broaden the pool of eligible countries by expanding the per capita income scale so that lower-middle-income countries would be competing for the funds by the third year of operation. Since this group contains countries that currently receive large amounts of politically directed economic assistance, such as Egypt, Jordan, and Columbia, this move increases the risks that the allocation of the new aid could be influenced by political considerations, rather than narrowly targeting it on impoverished good performers.

LOCAL OWNERSHIP AND ACCOUNTABILITY. The demonstrated connection between the commitment of recipient governments to a development program and the effectiveness of aid suggests that local governments and nongovernmental organizations, not donor country bureaucrats, should be responsible for program design.[30] This approach would place the MCA in the position of evaluating competing proposals from potential recipients and measuring results, rather than designing programs. To be sure, many potential beneficiaries will need funding and technical assistance to develop high-quality proposals, but that is quite different from designing the aid program for them.

INSTITUTIONAL HOME. The administration has proposed establishing an independent agency overseen by an interagency board on the model of such small independent agencies as the Overseas Private Investment Corporation (OPIC) and the Export-Import Bank (Ex-Im). OPIC provides guarantees against "political risk" (such as governmental expropriations) to U.S. investors when they make direct investments abroad. The Ex-Im Bank helps to provide financing of U.S. exports. While the objectives or the need for both agencies, at times, have been questioned in the past, both are generally seen as efficient, hence the most likely reason the administration looks at them as models for a new agency to oversee the new development initiative. While a new agency does not come with the encrusted bureaucratic habits of an established organization, using one to channel the MCA funds threatens to add to the confusing plethora of U.S. government entities, eligibility criteria, and reporting conditions that already confront developing nations. Moreover, it begs the question of redefining USAID's mission and does not address overlap between the two organizations on the ground.

FUNDING. Although aid advocates and officials from poor nations applauded the announcement of the MCA, an undercurrent of skepticism persists. It can be summed up in the phrase from the movie *Jerry McGuire*: "Show me the money." In Monterrey, Mexico, the president committed to a 50 percent increase in assistance to developing countries, resulting in a $5 billion annual increase by fiscal year 2006. Thus, according to the plan, the MCA would not be fully funded until after the end of President Bush's current term. Administration officials issued an important further clarification that the new assistance would total $10 billion cumulatively in the three years 2004 to 2006. Subsequently, in June 2002, the White House issued an update showing "illustrative funding levels" for the Millennium Challenge Account of $1.7 billion in fiscal year 2003, $3.3 billion in 2004, and $5 billion in 2006.[31] The administration's fiscal 2004 budget contains $1.3 billion for the MCA. Although by recent standards this is an extremely large single-year increase in bilateral development assistance, it nonetheless falls short relative to the administration's previous statements. The fiscal 2004 request of $1.3 billion is more than 20 percent below the illustrative funding level, which puts a greater burden on the following two years to achieve the remaining $8.7 billion cumulative increase.[32]

Strengthening the Trading System

Trade policy is one of America's most powerful tools for boosting living standards at home and abroad, but it is also one of the most difficult to deploy because of inevitable distributive trade-offs. For more than 200 years, the source of mutual gain among trading partners has been well understood by economists. As each nation concentrates on production of those goods and services in which it is comparatively most efficient, specialization increases total world production. In addition, the opportunity for each nation to sell to all increases the scope for economies of scale. At the same time, economists have long understood that some workers and sectors within countries suffer losses in adjusting to trade liberalization, even as others benefit.

Trade among nations has expanded enormously since the end of World War II. The volume of world trade has increased by roughly a factor of fourteen.[33] International investment has increased twelvefold in the past two decades alone.[34] This expansion did not occur by accident. The nations of the world have engaged in eight separate rounds of negotiations to lower barriers to trade and investment. The first such round, involving twenty-three nations, began in 1947 and led to the creation of the General Agreement on Tariffs and Trade later that year. The eighth round, which began in 1986 in Punta Del Este, Uruguay, involved 125 nations and was completed successfully in 1994. The Uruguay Round established the World Trade Organization (WTO) in 1995 as the successor to GATT and endowed the WTO with increased powers to enforce free trade and to see that remaining limitations are not abused

Strengthening the multilateral trading system and major regionwide initiatives should be top priorities for the U.S. trade agenda. A new round of global trade talks was launched at a conference in Doha, Qatar, in November 2001. It holds great promise of stimulating economic growth for both poor and rich nations, including the United States, but only if it results in the liberalization of markets in sectors that have historically proved difficult: agriculture, services, and labor-intensive manufactures. But building political support for such a demanding trade initiative will be difficult. In the meantime, we will probably see still greater emphasis on bilateral accords driven by opportunity rather than strategy.

Because reducing trade barriers among all nations simultaneously is complex and extraordinarily difficult, pairs or small groups of nations often achieve faster and broader-reaching results by negotiating reductions in trade barriers among themselves. Such bilateral and plurilateral negotiations sometimes increase trade—especially when they reinforce "natural" trade patterns—those that would occur in the absence of any policy barriers. But they may also divert trade from outsiders to members of the narrow group. To the extent that reductions in trade barriers among groups of nations increase trade, they too can contribute to increased economic growth. But to the extent that they divert trade, they can reduce the efficiency of worldwide production by diverting trade from relatively low-cost suppliers that are outside the group and therefore subject to relatively high trade barriers. Unfortunately, bilateral agreements often do not serve—and may sometimes hinder—achievement of a well-designed trade strategy. Not only may they divert, rather than create, trade, they also divert the time of negotiators and the energy of political leaders from potentially more important multilateral efforts and regional initiatives—for example, in the Western Hemisphere.

Trade Tremors

Support for globalization was already precarious by 2001. After the attacks on the World Trade Center and the Pentagon, many predicted a further pendulum swing against trade. [35] And indeed, for the year overall, growth of trade virtually ceased and foreign investment declined sharply. Yet most experts agree these declines were already in the works, reflecting economic slowdowns in the United States, the European Union, and Japan, and the worldwide collapse of the information technology sector.

Nonetheless, the terrorist attacks served as a wake-up call for many trade supporters around the world by reinforcing the direct interest of the wealthier nations in rectifying inequities, real and perceived, that seemed to hinder millions of the world's poor from reaping the potential benefits of globalization. Sensing an opportunity to advance the agenda of trade liberalization, U.S. Trade Representative Robert Zoellick declared that trade would be a central element in America's campaign against terror. A month later, President Bush declared, "The terrorists attacked the World Trade Center, and we will defeat them by expanding and encouraging world trade."[36]

The emphasis on international coalition building in the wake of the terrorist attacks created enormous momentum for the successful launch of global trade talks at the WTO ministerial meeting in Doha, Qatar, in November 2001. The decision to locate the ministerial meeting in Qatar had been long since made, but the determination to follow through and hold this high-level international gathering in the Middle East was courageous and symbolically important, especially since Qatar is one of a handful of states in the region to have joined the WTO. Moreover, the designation of the outcome as "the Doha Development Agenda" helped to reinforce the commitment of those participating to focusing on problems of the developing world. Both the European Union and the United States made important procedural concessions to the developing countries to ensure a successful launch.

Whether WTO members will be able to convert procedural into substantive achievements is a large open question, however. The areas subject to the new round of negotiations touch on difficult areas, such as farm subsidies, protection of textile jobs, the sovereign right to deploy trade remedies, and the relationship between trade agreements and labor and environmental standards. The negotiations also raise contentious distributive issues associated with intellectual property.

The developments in the United States since Doha have been mixed. The U.S. Congress enacted legislation in 2002 granting the president trade promotion authority, following eight years of stalemate, while significantly expanding assistance to U.S. workers displaced by trade.[37] Trade promotion authority or fast track is essentially a procedural deal whereby Congress agrees to streamline its approval process for future trade agreements in return for enhanced congressional oversight of negotiations. On the downside, the vote in the House of Representatives on the legislation was characterized by greater partisanship than has yet been seen on a trade vote and won by razor-thin margins of three votes, purchased at the expense of reductions in trade benefits for Caribbean Basin countries. The process left deep divisions at home and sent a confusing signal to foreign trading partners, whose satisfaction with the U.S. promise to negotiate future trade liberalization was tempered by the rollback of trade benefits for the Caribbean Basin.

Meanwhile, both the Doha agreement and the grant of trade promotion authority (TPA) express a commitment to proceed with negotiations, but the negotiations will be much harder because they must address concrete trade measures and will require concessions in sectors where identifiable jobs and livelihoods are directly on the line. And so far, whenever concrete sectional trade-offs have arisen—whether on farm subsidies, steel, Canadian lumber imports, or textiles market access—the Bush administration has adopted policies that restrict trade. The United States is by no means unique in this divergence between its broader national interests and a reluctance to accept painful sectoral dislocation when the economy is under stress. The European Union was strongly tempted to oppose agricultural liberalization supported by other WTO members in Doha, and Japanese farmers have a long record of strenuously resisting opening this sector to international competition.

Sustaining a genuine focus on smoothing the rough edges of the global trading system while continuing to open markets, helping to give the hundreds of millions who live in desperate poverty a stake in the international system, and maintaining environmental and labor standards constitutes a formidable and surpassingly important set of challenges. Even the compelling national security rationale of vanquishing terrorism may not be enough to overcome the competing domestic pressures. While the harsh realities faced by the developing countries are real, so too are the American jobs at stake in the short term as the United States seeks to liberalize the world economy. It is a distinct understatement to characterize the problem or reaching an agreement as challenging. Trade policy has always presented hard trade-offs between the losses faced by those in sectors vulnerable to international competition and the greater but more diffuse national interest in a more competitive and productive economy—and in a more peaceful, prosperous, and equitable world.

America's Agenda for the WTO

Strengthening the multilateral trade system should be America's top trade priority for economic and geostrategic reasons. As a global power, America has a vital interest in a liberal international economic order. The WTO, the only global trade forum that represents nations from all regions and levels of development, is dedicated to achieving this objective. America's ability to influence rules of commerce and trade opportunities of poor nations is vastly greater through the WTO than through a series of piecemeal arrangements. Producers should be looking globally for the best market opportunities, not for the best special deal negotiated between governments. This principle holds especially for agricultural subsidies and protection, which received special dispensation under GATT, even as tariffs, quotas, and other barriers to trade in other commodities fell.

America should pursue reduction in trade barriers in sectors that historically have been shielded by special treatment, including agriculture, services, and labor-intensive manufactures, as well as locking in open markets in high-growth, technology-intensive sectors. In these areas, a "development" agenda and U.S. national interests coincide. The United States and other industrial nations can offer market access to developing nations on the condition that developing nations adopt reforms conducive to expanded trade and economic growth. Although industrial nations tend to be in the spotlight in the debates over agriculture and such labor-intensive manufactures as apparel, in fact, barriers and subsidies in these sectors are very high in many middle-income countries. Reducing these trade barriers will not only improve market access but will also reduce wasteful distortions.[38]

THE STAKES. Estimates of the potential gains from trade liberalization are huge. According to the World Bank, full liberalization of merchandise trade would be worth $355 billion annually, with more than half accruing to developing nations.[39] By contrast, annual assistance flows currently total $50 billion. No other single policy instrument can deliver a 1 percent permanent boost to world income and a nearly 3 percent boost to income in developing countries.[40] This gain is more than twenty-five times current inflows of foreign direct investment. And gains from trade do not require a return flow of interest or dividend payments. And the estimated gains are significantly higher when services liberalization is also considered.

The evidence that trade access makes a difference is overwhelming. In 2000, President Clinton signed into law the African Growth and Opportunity Act (AGOA). In the first year alone, the island nation of Madagascar doubled its clothing exports to the United States, and Lesotho doubled its manufacturing employment on the strength of improved export opportunities.[41] Overall, over the first two years, the AGOA region increased total trade in nonfuel goods with the United States by 25 percent, and an additional $1 billion of investment flowed to the region.[42]

AGRICULTURE. Agricultural reform alone accounts for two-thirds of the estimated $355 billion gain in world income.[43] But it faces daunting political obstacles. The OECD countries pay their farmers more than $300 billion a year in subsidies, more than five times total spending on overseas development assistance and greater than the national income of all sub-Saharan African nations combined.[44] The average cow in European Union nations receives $2.20 a day in government support.[45] At the same time, 3 billion people live on less than $2 a day.[46] The EU's sugar subsidies have depressed world prices by 17 percent. Because of these subsidies, sugar exports from the European Union to Algeria and Nigeria have displaced exports from lower-cost Mozambique, where the sugar industry is the top employer.[47]

Cuts in agricultural subsidies in developed nations could materially improve living standards for the three-quarters of the world's poor who live in rural areas. But the obstacles to achieving further meaningful market opening are also huge. The interests of the main negotiating countries are not well aligned. For the EU, Japan, and Korea, the critical objective is to postpone the day of reckoning for agricultural barriers and subsidies. Agricultural subsidies are the most costly item in the EU budget but they are fiercely protected, especially by France. Reducing these subsidies is risky and difficult. Given the admission of Poland, whose farmers would qualify for budget-busting subsidies under the current formula, debate within the European Union on this tendentious issue may be unavoidable. But pressure to lower subsidies enough to open markets to imports from poor nations would complicate an already difficult puzzle. If agricultural concessions are to prove acceptable, EU negotiators will need to win compensating concessions in such areas as environmental protection, competition policy, and foreign investment rules, which key developing countries oppose.

One of the more controversial subjects of the negotiations is food safety. Powerful EU constituencies want to materially limit WTO jurisdiction to protect the power of national governments to ban the import of genetically modified agriculture products. They argue that such prerogatives are essential when science cannot absolutely exclude the possibility of harm. Toward that end, they seek guarantees that WTO rulings will be subordinate to multilateral environmental agreements. But developing countries fear that European countries will use these provisions as protectionist loopholes to deny access to their agricultural products.

Meanwhile, U.S. interests in agriculture are somewhat mixed. The United States shares with key agricultural exporters such as Canada, Australia, New Zealand, Argentina, and Uruguay a strong interest in liberalizing world markets for major commodities such as grains, poultry, and meat. However, increases in domestic agricultural subsidies approved by Congress and President Bush in 2002 are projected to bring the totals to $190 billion during the next decade.[48]

"DEEP" INTEGRATION. As traditional trade barriers have been lowered or eliminated, policies once regarded as entirely domestic in character have emerged as important influences on trade and investment flows, such as antitrust policy, taxation of "domestic" corporations, and intellectual property laws. Negotiating agreements on these policies—so-called deep integration—is challenging because international rules frequently impinge on domestic sovereignty. Dismantling the obvious trade barriers is hard enough, but deep integration requires even greater circumspection. Tariffs and quotas are internationally similar, but national institutions, practices, and laws differ enormously.

Experts cannot agree across countries on just which subjects to include under "competition policy." Nor can they specify, other than the most rudimentary steps to increase transparency and possibly prohibit cross-border cartels, how the WTO can usefully coordinate the laws, regulations, and prohibitions that nations have put in place to maintain open and fair domestic competition. If the WTO intrudes too far into areas traditionally considered domestic, its actions could undermine support for the multilateral trading system even among key supporters (as the ruling that U.S. tax exemption of profits on foreign export sales of certain U.S. corporations violates WTO rules threatens to do).[49]

The deep-integration agenda also faces opposition from most developing nations, who do not consider these domestic regulatory issues central to their development prospects. Many actively oppose them on principle or because they found it costly and difficult to implement the ambitious rules changes mandated by the Uruguay Round.

THE ROCKY ROAD AHEAD. Using the next round of trade agreements to advance a market access agenda would serve the economic and security interests of the United States. But for the reasons just mentioned success is not ensured. To complicate matters, although the developing countries are effective as a group in opposing agreements, their positive agendas are in reality diverse. For example, while Uruguay and Argentina view agricultural market access as the biggest prize, other developing countries wish to shelter their agricultural sectors from international competition. Manufacturing interests are similarly mixed. Egypt effectively bans garment imports, despite WTO obligations not to do so.[50] India maintains one of the most tightly closed markets in the world, according to the American Textiles Manufacturers Institute.[51] While countries such as China seek expanded access for textiles and apparel, where trade barriers remain high, other developing nations would lose if the United States, the European Union, and Canada dismantled quotas that currently guarantee them shares of these markets. To complicate matters further, all of the advanced industrial nations seem committed to expand the preferential trade access they extend to the poorest nations, but this special access is opposed by many middle-income countries, which see themselves as the losers.

In sum, the upcoming multilateral trade round is likely to be arduous, with uncertain results. Global trade negotiations have become vastly more complicated since the first round in 1947, which included 25 countries and was completed in two years. With WTO membership now at 145, the current four-year target for completing all but two of the agreements looks distinctly optimistic. Nonetheless, the fragility of the current trading system and the interrelationships among the WTO round and the multiplicity of regional and bilateral initiatives now under way make failure too costly to contemplate. If the WTO path toward liberalization is discounted as too cumbersome and contentious, the inevitable result will be an increase in protectionism and trade disputes. Further liberalization could be confined to regional and bilateral trade deals that are likely to exclude the biggest (China, India) and poorest (sub-Saharan Africa, Central Asia) nations and threaten to divert rather than to expand trade.

More Agreements May Not Necessarily Be Better

Bilateral trade deals are gaining increasing prominence in U.S. trade policy. Although the growing emphasis on bilateral agreements is touted as a spur to further multilateral opening and an insurance policy if multilateral talks falter, there is a risk that country-by-country free-trade agreements (FTAs) will become the central element of U.S. trade policy. Indeed, USTR Robert Zoellick declared that pursuit of multiple free trade agreements is a strategy of "competition in liberalization."[52] He bemoaned that "the United States has been falling behind the rest of the world in pursuing trade agreements. Worldwide, there are 150 regional free-trade and customs agreements; the United States is a party to only three." Zoellick declared that the United States must catch up with its competitors in securing preferential trade agreements or compromise the country's leadership in the international arena.[53] By the end of 2002, the Bush administration had indicated its intent to pursue seven bilateral and regional FTAs involving thirty-nine countries (not including Mexico and Canada, which have already signed the North American Free Trade Agreement—NAFTA).

There is a long-standing debate on whether the proliferation of free trade agreements on balance is good or bad for the global trading system and for individual nations. Some seem willing to engage in trade relations with any willing partner. Others condemn all bilateral trade arrangements as detrimental to free trade. Experience suggests the truth lies in between. We suggest a simple principle—that "running up the score" on bilateral trade agreements is ill advised, but that the United States should selectively pursue free trade agreements that advance U.S. national interests broadly defined. These interests include not only U.S. commercial interests but also the establishment of a prosperous and open international community.

Bilateral and plurilateral free trade agreements—that is, agreements with one nation or with a small group of nations—can advance free trade in various ways. They can achieve deeper and broader liberalization relative to multilateral agreements and spur a virtuous cycle of competitive market opening. They also can be justified where they reinforce "natural" trade patterns.

Trade between two nations is natural if it would occur in a world from which all trade barriers have been removed. For instance, trade occurs naturally between markets where freight costs are low. A trading pattern is not natural if it arises only because of remaining trade barriers. When only some barriers are removed, trade may be shifted from nations that are natural trading partners to ones who trade only because trade barriers to outsiders remain. Regional FTAs can reinforce natural or efficient trade ties and help anchor peace among neighbors, as with the European Union. But such agreements also carry risks. They demand enormous political effort, as some domestic interests typically suffer losses from such agreements. Resulting domestic backlash can undermine broader liberalization. In addition, agreements with one or a few nations can obstruct progress on multilateral treaties. Such local free trade agreements should be pursued only if the economic and security gains warrant the political cost, if they contribute to a dynamic that strengthens the multilateral trade framework, and if more trade liberalization results than could be achieved in a multilateral context.

It is not clear that the FTA agenda of the Bush administration meets either of these tests. If successful, agreements under negotiation at the end of 2002 would require congressional votes on at least seven separate trade agreements. The direct economic stakes are not in all cases compelling: the thirty-nine additional countries covered by those FTAs account for only 6.4 percent of world production and 12 percent of U.S. exports. Neither are the foreign policy stakes in some cases. Only four of the thirty-nine countries merit a mention in the Bush administration's National Security Strategy;[54] only one of the potential FTA partners is a moderate Islamic nation; and none is a former communist state making the transition to democracy and free market capitalism.

The three potential agreements in the Western Hemisphere can clearly be justified from a strategic perspective. Nurturing the seeds of democracy and market reform are manifestly in U.S. interests in this hemisphere. Anchoring Latin American economies in a framework of internationally agreed trade rules and an expanded market will help to attract productive investment, reduce the scope for government meddling, and promote broadly shared prosperity. Although the foreign policy rationale for the FTAA is strong, the economic gains to the United States are likely to be modest. The Western Hemisphere overall accounts for 38 percent of U.S. trade, but all but 7 percent of that trade is with Canada and Mexico, the United State's partners in NAFTA.[55] Securing congressional agreement on the FTAA will carry a high political price tag, as experience with NAFTA ratification shows. Furthermore, progress in the FTAA may have to wait for progress in the Doha round, as Brazil insists that FTAA negotiations include reductions in agricultural subisidies and consideration of remedies for trade disputes that the United States will want to hold for the global negotiations.

The Bush administration concluded negotiations with Singapore and signaled its intent to negotiate agreements with Australia, Morocco, Central

America, and southern Africa. In the Pacific, the Bush administration has not advanced a compelling rationale for pursuing separate U.S.-Australia and U.S.-Singapore trade agreements while not demonstrating a willingness to contemplate similar agreements with other interested trading partners, such as New Zealand and Taiwan.

The deficiency of the Bush administration's "trade agreement by the numbers" approach is also striking in the case of the Middle East. The United States has one free trade agreement with an Islamic nation in the Middle East—Jordan. Although the United States has very low direct economic stakes, the Bush administration has justified the possible agreement with Morocco as "our second with an Arab, Muslim country."[56] But this justification seems like a slim reed on which to base a trade policy toward this region of the world. A serious Middle East trade strategy would address the reasons why key Middle Eastern economies are not well integrated into the international economy and remain outside of the WTO. Such a strategy would use the lure of potential access to U.S. markets to encourage domestic economic reform and integration among the region's underdeveloped economies. Spurring economic reform in the Middle East is in the U.S. national interest. Promoting economic integration would encourage growth and could foster political modernization in that region. But reaching a trade agreement with just one country—Morocco—that is already among the most open in the region is not the way to achieve these objectives.

It is likely that the current approach will stimulate a competition in liberalization, but it may not be the desired type. So far, there has been no propitious shift in negotiating positions at the WTO as a result—direct or indirect—of the new U.S. emphasis on bilateralism. But there is increased competition to consummate bilateral deals with the United States. Already, Egypt has begun exploring the prospects for a bilateral trade deal after assessing the implications of the agreement with Jordan and negotiations with Morocco.[57] Taiwan is intensifying its interest in an FTA with the United States, partly as a defensive move in anticipation of trade diversion from the U.S.-Singapore agreement.[58] New Zealand is anxious that it would lose out if the United States and Australia finalize a deal. And indeed there is no compelling rationale to reject such overtures, since the administration's stated standards are not very discriminating: "the U.S. wants to have agreements in regions throughout the world . . . with countries that have demonstrated a willingness to open markets . . . to encourage reform."[59]

Domestic Adjustment

Trade produces domestic losers and winners. The winners include businesses and workers in export-oriented industries and consumers as a class, and especially lower-income consumers. The losers include businesses and workers in import-competing industries, whose losses are arguably more concentrated (in some cases extending to lifetime earnings, pension benefits, health coverage) than the gains. In principle, everyone would be better off, or at least no worse off, from trade if the winners compensated the losers. In practice, in the United States, the losses associated with trade are compensated only in small part. U.S. policymakers began recognizing the importance of providing at least some compensation when, forty-one years ago, Congress enacted and President John F. Kennedy signed a program of trade adjustment assistance (TAA) designed to help workers laid off because of trade by giving them extended unemployment insurance benefits. Such assistance is more important in the United States than in other developed nations because the U.S. social safety net is thinner and more porous than are the social and economic protections elsewhere. Unfortunately, TAA has never worked well, for several reasons. Perhaps most fundamentally, it is very difficult in a market economy that is constantly producing winners and losers to determine whether a company failed or a particular worker became unemployed because of international trade or domestic market competition. To make this determination, TAA instituted a certification process that has been criticized for delaying adjustment and introducing unwarranted uncertainty. Nor have compulsory training requirements for displaced workers, added in the 1980s, helped workers as they were designed to do, since workers entering training programs do not know whether they will secure jobs upon completion.

In 2002, Congress passed legislation making important improvements to the TAA program (as part of the overall TPA legislative package). It includes a 65 percent advanceable and refundable tax credit to cover the cost of health care premiums for displaced workers and their families. It expands TAA eligibility to "secondary" workers—defined as those employed at plants supplying 20 percent or more of their sales or production to a factory that is closed because of increased trade. The assistance will now be available to workers who lose their jobs when their company moves production to another country with which the United States has a free trade agreement or to another country if approved by the secretary of labor.

In addition, the 2002 legislation also took a significant first step to address a troubling problem—the fact that less-skilled workers displaced by trade typically suffer major wage reductions when, and if, they are re-employed. Congress approved a narrow version of "wage insurance," limited to older displaced workers, who face particular difficulties changing careers. At an annual cost of $50 million, the 2002 legislation promised to pay displaced workers over age fifty up to $10,000 over two years to compensate them for the wage differential between a job lost to trade and a new, lower-paying job.[60] Because assistance is paid only after qualified workers actually take a new job, this form of assistance should strongly encourage job search and placement. If this program succeeds in promoting, rather than impeding, worker adjustment, it should be expanded to cover all displaced workers at an estimated annual cost of $3–4 billion.[61]

The International Finance Agenda

The first half of the 1990s witnessed remarkable progress in integrating many nations into the international financial system. Private capital flows to emerging markets quintupled, from $46 billion in 1990 to more than $235 billion in 1996.[62] But a series of damaging financial crises—affecting Mexico in 1995, Southeast Asia, Russia, and Brazil in 1997–99, and Argentina, Turkey, and Brazil (among others) in 2001–02—underscored two challenges. First, integrating emerging markets into the world financial system remains an elusive goal, with important challenges unresolved. Second, because world financial markets are tightly linked, problems in one nation can spill over to others with potentially catastrophic consequences for world trade and investment.

Why Instability Abroad Matters

U.S. national interests can be damaged in several ways by instability far from its shores. The Russian default and devaluation in August-September 1998 triggered volatility in stock exchanges around the world, underscoring the tight linkage among world financial markets. The financial crises that roiled South Korea in 1998 and Turkey in 2001 threatened the political stability of important U.S. regional allies. Furthermore, as the largest investor in the International Monetary Fund (IMF) and the World Bank, the United States has a large interest in how the resources of those organizations are used. Reducing the frequency and severity of such crises is thus an urgent goal for U.S. policymakers.

Instability in the Western Hemisphere

By mid-2002, Brazil and Argentina, the largest and most populous economies in South America, were mired in financial turmoil. Several other Latin American countries were similarly afflicted. The situation in Argentina was dire. Production had fallen precipitously. The banking system had ceased to function. Unemployment exceeded 20 percent. By some estimates, poverty afflicted 50 percent of the population. In December of 2001, Argentina defaulted on $141 billion in private sector debt—the largest sovereign default in history. And in November 2002, Argentina went into arrears on a World Bank loan, joining a small group of nations including Somalia, Iraq, and Zimbabwe—strange bedfellows for this former financial market darling.

Meanwhile, Argentina's neighbor, Brazil, found itself in financial distress. As we discuss, although that country's central government had recently run budget surpluses, the provincial governments were continuing to run up debts. With investors running for the exits in neighboring Argentina, Brazil had to pay increasingly onerous premiums, in the form of high interest rates, on its debt.

WHAT WENT WRONG. Argentina and Brazil got into trouble for different although related reasons. After a long history of high inflation, Argentina in 1991 tied the value of its currency to the U.S. dollar as a way of conveying to the international financial community its determination not to permit future inflation. Subsequently, the U.S. dollar appreciated relative to the currencies of Argentina's other major trading partners. As a result, Argentina's exports were increasingly noncompetitive on world markets. Nonetheless, Argentina stubbornly retained the peg to the U.S. dollar. In addition, Argentina's central and provincial governments, as well as private businesses, borrowed heavily from abroad, leading to debt obligations that Argentina was unable in the end to honor.

Brazil had discontinued its policy of trying to hold the exchange rate of its currency at a fixed level during an earlier period of financial distress. It had also undertaken a difficult program of fiscal discipline that produced a surplus of between 3 percent and 4 percent of GDP in the primary budget—the government balance excluding debt service. Because of these steps, Brazil might have suffered no international financial problems but for contagion from Argentina's debacle and uncertainty about the outcome of pending presidential elections.

Although their policies diverged in the late 1990s, Argentina and Brazil shared an unfortunate history of having rapidly accumulated public debt earlier in the 1990s. Much of it was held by foreigners and denominated in dollars, and much of it carried short maturities that exposed both nations to adverse shifts in market sentiment. Argentina doubled its external-debt-to-GDP ratio—from 23 percent to 47 percent of GDP—during relatively good economic times from 1993 to 1998.[63] The resulting debt service and the need to roll over outstanding debt left Argentina little flexibility when its economic fortunes deteriorated. Meanwhile, Brazil's public sector debt nearly doubled during the 1990s, to about 60 percent of GDP. While less of Brazil's public debt is denominated in dollars and held by foreigners relative to Argentina, Brazil's externally held share of about 40 percent left it also vulnerable to changes in international market sentiment.

The Argentine and Brazilian crises set off alarm bells among supporters of the liberal international economic order. There was growing risk of sustained popular backlash against market-oriented reform policies. An even more ominous possibility was that economic turmoil could reverse progress toward democratization in these and other nations with long histories of authoritarian regimes.

Crisis Management

The financial turmoil in two star Latin American performers also contributed to growing criticism of the approach toward financial stabilization used by the IMF and its key shareholders, prime among them the United States. This approach—dubbed "the Washington consensus"—entails deregulation, privatization, international economic integration, and fiscal and monetary restraint. Critics of these policies pointed to the difficulties in South America's two largest nations as evidence that this approach should be modified or abandoned.

The plight of Argentina and Brazil raises difficult questions. In retrospect, it is clear that international financial authorities tolerated, and even blessed, fiscal policies that led to unsustainable debt burdens in Argentina and Brazil. This experience highlights a fundamental problem. When economic times are good, markets willingly accommodate heavy national borrowing. The IMF can do very little other than preach sound finance to wayward nations. Furthermore, Brazil's recent history suggests that currently sound policies may not keep nations out of trouble if previous policies have been imprudent. At a time when Brazil's fiscal stance was austere by any measure, spillover from Argentina and political uncertainty raised

Brazil's cost of public borrowing by 1100 basis points in the space of a few short months, pushing what had previously seemed a manageable debt burden into unsustainable territory.

Second, the two crises illustrate starkly a major piece of unfinished business from the financial crises of the 1990s: determining the appropriate roles in crisis resolution of financing from the official sector relative to the private sector.[64] The traditional policy reaction to financial crises consisted of hard currency loans from the IMF and other sources, conditioned on commitments by the recipient government to adopt specific policies, usually including a restrictive domestic monetary and fiscal policy. This prescription became increasingly controversial because the required assistance grew dramatically and private capital outflows often offset official capital inflows.

Concern also arose that the availability of assistance could contribute to instability by lulling lenders and borrowers into a belief that international assistance from official sources would always bail them out. Why should a bank worry about the riskiness of a particular loan or a nation how much it borrows if the IMF or some consortium of nations will always come to the rescue? This problem, which crops up with many kinds of insurance, is called "moral hazard." But balanced against this concern is that allowing nations to default on their obligations can create enormous disruption because no international mechanism exists for resolving debt claims quickly and in an orderly and predictable manner.

As the international financial crisis of 1998–99 ran its course, there was increasing recognition that, somehow and someway, private investors had to bear some part of the loss when a country could not service its debt. By the same token, it became clear that no single approach would work for every circumstance. Bailouts—the provision of official financial assistance by international financial institutions and possibly creditor governments— were sometimes necessary. In other cases, bail-ins—the restructuring of debt by private lenders—were critical as an alternative to or in conjunction with official support. The past half decade has provided several instructive experiences with bail-ins. "Voluntary" exchanges, in which the sovereign debtor offers alternative debt instruments to lenders on a purely voluntary basis, typically failed, while unilateral exchanges dictated by debtor governments without an international seal of approval have a more mixed record. Concerted debt rollovers blessed and orchestrated by the international financial authorities have been successful in some cases.

As it emerged from the Asian financial crisis of 1998–99, the United States pursued a policy of intentionally leaving the determination of the appropriate balance between official support and private sector involvement to a "case-by-case" consideration. In contrast, the Bush administration entered office proclaiming the end of large IMF bailouts. Yet, as it has turned out in practice, the actual course of policy during the Bush administration has been confusing. Faced with possible default in important countries, the U.S. Treasury blessed large IMF assistance for Argentina and Turkey in 2001. In fact, the assistance given these nations was greater relative to the size of the economies involved than what had been given before. When it became clear the Argentina program would not suffice, the administration conditioned further financial support on the willingness of private lenders to restructure private sector claims, but the U.S. Treasury did nothing significant to assist in organizing the necessary conversations with creditors. The process foundered, whereupon the administration effectively withdrew from the field and Argentina defaulted on its private sector debt in December 2001.

The administration's approach toward Brazil revealed similar inconsistency. The U.S. Treasury secretary categorically ruled out support for Brazil on July 28, 2002.[65] Eight days later the same Treasury Department blessed a $30 billion IMF financing program for Brazil—the largest in history.[66] Disbursement of the funds was made conditional on policies of the incoming government. In contrast, the IMF did not insist that the private sector make any commitments to extend lending exposures, a curious omission given the economic climate. The only private contribution to the plan consisted of loose assurances by executives of sixteen major banks to maintain credit lines to Brazil.[67]

INTERNATIONAL BANKRUPTCIES. These zig-zags in official policy took place against the backdrop of an equally confused debate over IMF policy governing private sector involvement in crisis resolution. The international financial authorities are faced with a difficult challenge of establishing a set of rules to ensure private investors will take into account the true risk of default in making their initial decision without exacerbating panic when crisis hits and the rules are carried out. In a domestic context, this balance is struck by bankruptcy law. The problem is that private lenders are generally unwilling to lend funds to troubled nations unless they are assured of extremely high interest rates. They might be willing to make such loans if they knew their loans would receive favored treatment in the event of a general default, but provisions in loan agreements with previous lenders generally preclude such assurances. Loans with such assurances could improve the prospects that previous lenders will eventually be paid because timely assistance can help prevent default. But without agreed-on rules on what to do if a country effectively goes bankrupt, it is unclear how to encourage potential private lenders to step forward without degrading commitments to previous lenders, which could exacerbate creditors' panic when a nation's financial condition becomes precarious.

Several proposals are currently under discussion among financial experts. More modest proposals focus on modifications to bond contracts to make it easier for a majority of bondholders to agree to changes to the terms or to ensure that bonds would automatically roll over in the event of financial crisis. Since only new issues would have such provisions, however, they would be inferior to outstanding claims, so that investors likely would demand an interest premium to hold them. So far, no nation—including the most advanced economies that have advocated this approach—has been willing to be the first to incorporate these features.

Bolder proposals attempt to replicate some of the features of U.S. Chapter 11 bankruptcy procedures. IMF Deputy Managing Director Anne Krueger in late 2001 proposed that the IMF fill a role in international defaults analogous to the courts in civil bankruptcies. This sovereign debt restructuring mechanism (SDRM) proposal was fiercely criticized by the international financial community, which claimed it would undermine the rights of existing bondholders.[68] The Bush administration initially rejected the IMF proposals for a SDRM in favor of the kinds of voluntary terms in bond contracts just described. A few months later, at a time of great volatility in Latin American financial markets, the administration reversed itself and endorsed a somewhat softer version of the IMF plan.

Meanwhile, investors have come to expect a greater likelihood that their claims will be restructured if sovereign borrowers get into financial trouble. By the end of 2002, the dominant concern was that private capital flows for emerging nations are drying up owing to a pervasive decline in investors' appetite for risk. This situation poses serious threats to development in many poor nations.

It is hoped that the current debate over bankruptcy versus official bailouts will be succeeded by a finer-grain consideration of a "combination approach" in which IMF official support for countries unable to service their sovereign debt is made contingent on private sector involvement.

Underpinning official support with private sector involvement is critical not only because it can help make programs sustainable but also because it will improve investors' assessment of risk in the first place. The restructuring of private sector claims will take different forms, varying from commitments to extend maturities, to more systematic rescheduling and, in extreme cases, to write-downs.

Such an agreed framework is more likely to emerge if the United States, as the dominant member of the IMF and the largest world economic power, pursues a policy that is consistent, proactive, and engaged.

Risks from the Advanced Economies

One feature of the global economic outlook in 2002 contrasts sharply with the earlier periods of financial instability during the 1990s—the threat of instability originating in the developed world. Such instability threatens not only poor nations but the international financial system as a whole. With Japan continuing in a decade-long recession and German economic weakness slowing growth throughout the Euro area, the risks associated with the U.S. outlook are particularly troubling. These include continued fallout from the boom and bust in technology, telecommunications, and media markets; the worldwide drop in stock prices because of persistent economic weakness, and the corporate governance scandals in the United States; the enormous and growing current account imbalance in the United States; a sharp fiscal deterioration; and geopolitical uncertainty. The IMF, in trying to confront these problems, is largely ineffectual, and the seven large nations that compose the G7 can do little more than exhort one another to practice policy virtue.

CORPORATE GOVERNANCE. It is ironic that the United States, which in the late 1990s pilloried Asian nations for "crony capitalism," found itself in late 2001 and throughout 2002 awash in more corporate fraud and mismanagement than it had seen since the Great Depression. The exemplars of these scandals—the failure of Enron, followed shortly by disclosures of accounting misrepresentations at Worldcom, Xerox, Global Crossing, Bristol-Myers-Squibb, and other major companies—contributed to sliding stock prices during much of 2002. As each new disclosure emerged, confidence evaporated in a system of financial markets regulation that Americans only a few years before had urged other nations to emulate. After serving as a safe haven for foreign investors throughout the 1980s and 1990s, U.S. markets lost some of their luster. Portfolio and direct investment from abroad plummeted by more than half, from $763 billion in 2000 to $315 billion in 2002.

U.S. policymakers have a long history of reacting to crises with reforms. The crisis in corporate disclosure and governance has proved no exception. In less than a year, Congress enacted and the president signed sweeping reform legislation that created a new quasi-government agency to oversee the auditing profession; restricted auditors from engaging in nonaudit businesses; significantly toughened criminal and other penalties for corporate fraud and misrepresentations; speeded disclosure of insider security trading; and prohibited corporate loans to executives. The legislation came shortly after the Securities and Exchange Commission had implemented new disclosure requirements and the New York Stock Exchange had proposed sweeping corporate governance reforms for companies listed on the exchange (requiring a majority of board directors to be independent, shareholders to approve executive compensation packages, and audit committees of boards of directors to hire and fire outside auditors).

Nonetheless, as this book went to press, several questions remain unanswered about the depth of the U.S. commitment to real reform. It remains widely recognized that despite a $100 million increase in its budget, the SEC remains woefully underfunded and understaffed to deal with the magnitude of the job before it. The chairman of the new accounting oversight board still had not been chosen, and concerns were still prevalent about how effective that new board would be in any event.

ACCOUNTING. Over the longer term, one other key disclosure issue remains unresolved. Will the United States continue to require all publicly held companies whose shares are traded on U.S. exchanges to report their financial condition according to Generally Accepted Accounting Principles (GAAP), or will foreign and domestic companies be permitted to use the International Accounting Standards (IAS) that are accepted elsewhere around the world? In some respects, the IAS may provide greater safeguards than does GAAP. For example, critics claim that Enron could not have engaged in the abusive practices under IAS that GAAP permitted.[69] Enron would not have been able to expand so rapidly and take on such much debt under IAS rules, which most likely would have required consolidation of the many "special purpose entities" that Enron created to keep much debt off its balance sheet. In addition, the growing globalization of capital markets strengthens the case for a single set of reporting standards worldwide, which is what IAS is well on the way to becoming. By 2005, public companies in the European Union must report their condition using IAS. Other countries around the world have adopted or plan to adopt international standards. The Enron affair and the trends abroad give impetus to those who have been arguing that IAS should replace GAAP or, at the least, be recognized as a legitimate mode of reporting in the United States, without a requirement that financial results reported under IAS be "reconciled" with U.S. GAAP.

Most observers believe that two standards should continue to coexist but that differences should be narrowed. Such important differences as the accounting for stock options and reporting of corporate profits would be harmonized. Nonetheless, others believe that competition between the two standards is healthy. Companies could use either standard without restriction. Investors, it is argued, would keep both standard-setting bodies on their toes. Such competition might reduce the role of political influence, which has been apparent in the setting of U.S. GAAP for some time—most notably with respect to the congressional rejection in the 1990s of the effort by the Financial Accounting Standards Board (which oversees GAAP) to require companies to list employee stock options as an expense at the time they are granted.[70]

On theoretical grounds, competition has the stronger case than a harmonized approach. On practical grounds, however, harmonization is likely to carry the day. Both the FASB and the International Accounting Standards Board (which oversees IAS) announced in the fall of 2002 an initiative to pursue harmonization of the two standards. For the immediate and near future, that will be the course—although it is questionable how stable any set of harmonized standards will be over the long run.

U.S. Imbalances

After serving as the anchor and locomotive of the world economy throughout the 1990s, the U.S. economy may become a source of instability, owing to the enormous increase in U.S foreign indebtedness and the potential for disorderly adjustment in America's growing external imbalance. During the late 1990s, the United States was a major magnet for the world's capital. With strong productivity growth and a booming stock market, America seemed like a great investment—certainly better than stagnating Japan, sluggishly growing Europe, and risky emerging markets. The dollar more or less steadily appreciated 30 percent relative to the yen between late 1999 and early 2002 and by 33 percent vis-à-vis the euro between its introduction in early 1999 and early 2002.[71] Matching the capital account surplus was a growing current account deficit, which has remained at or above 3.6 percent of GDP since 2000, reaching 5 percent in the second quarter of 2002.[72]

Current account deficits of the current and projected future magnitudes raise some concern. A current account deficit of just 3.4 percent of GDP in 1987, after all, precipitated a sharp drop in the value of the dollar and a lagged turnaround in the current account, which returned below 2 percent in 1989.[73] If continued domestic recession and loss of confidence in U.S. corporate governance cause investors to flee, the value of the U.S. dollar could fall sharply, forcing a major reduction in U.S. net imports. Because the U.S. economy is so large relative to the rest of the world, a drop in net imports of a few percent of U.S. GDP can have major effects on other nations.

The signs in early 2003 are not encouraging. The borrowing requirements of the U.S. federal government have sharply increased, as the budget has moved from a surplus of $236 billion in fiscal year 2000 to an estimated $304 billion deficit in fiscal year 2003, with deficits now projected to total $1.08 trillion cumulatively over the next five years.[74] As American manufacturers have confronted weakening markets at home and have looked abroad to fill their order books, they have raised concerns about the loss of export competitiveness because of the "strong dollar."[75] As capital markets have reacted to these events, the dollar has weakened, and so far the decline has been gradual and orderly.[76] However, the composition of U.S. borrowing bears watching. The proportion of foreign capital coming into the U.S. market in the form of direct investment or committed capital fell from 39 percent in 1998 to 17 percent in 2001. A growing share of external borrowing is taking the form of short-term capital that can reverse direction rapidly.[77] Ironically, continued bad economic news in Japan and Europe has been good news for the United States as an investment haven. The gradual pace with which the value of the dollar has fallen through early 2003 along with continued strong productivity growth, and the continued willingness of foreign investors to hold U.S. securities suggest a soft landing—a gradual reduction in the current account deficit. But important risks remain.

Conclusion

In a global age marked by insecurity and uncertainty, one thing is clear: the United States must remain a committed player on the global stage, taking an active role in shaping the international financial architecture and leading the international effort to help developing countries overcome desperate poverty and become integrated and productive members of the global economy. Concerns over the global future abound: from the developing countries of sub-Saharan Africa to the emerging economies of Latin America, to our staunchest allies in Europe. The United States must use foreign assistance as an effective mechanism for generating real improvements in the lives of the world's poor. Trade policy must be viewed as an instrument that, when employed judiciously, can balance the needs of the developed world's workers and the developing world's citizens eager for an opportunity to take part in the global marketplace. The United States must sustain the political will to move forward in the multilateral negotiations of the WTO. Success is crucial for the future of the global trading system and for U.S. economic dynamism, and the United States must avoid being sidetracked by more easily fashioned bilateral and regional agreements. The United States must take an active role in reforming the international financial architecture to achieve the appropriate balance between investor risk and reward, and to improve the stability of capital flows to the emerging markets. And where developed economies overseas stagnate and falter, it is especially important that the United States remain committed to its own reforms, buoying investor confidence by improving the accountability of business and pursuing fiscal responsibility.

Notes

1. Chicago Council on Foreign Relations/German Marshall Fund, "Worldviews 2002 Survey," October 2002 (www.worldviews.org [February 2003]).

2. Isaac Shapiro and Nancy Birdsall, "How Does the Proposed Level of Foreign Economic Aid under the Bush Budget Compare with Historical Levels? And What Would Be the Effects of Bush's New 'Millennium Challenge Account'?" Center for Global Development and Center on Budget and Policy Priorities, March 19, 2002 (www.cbpp.org/3-14-02foreignaid.htm [February 2003]).

3. Average for 1999–2000, in 1999 dollars. Jean-Claude Faure, "Development Co-Operation, 2001 Report," *DAC* [*Organization for Economic Cooperation and Development*] *Journal*, vol. 3, no. 1 (2002).

4. Lael Brainard, "With Help From the Famous, Foreign Aid Resurges," *Los Angeles Times*, June 26, 2002, p. 13.

5. President George W. Bush, remarks at the Inter-American Development Bank, Washington, March 18, 2002.

6. Chicago Council on Foreign Relations/German Marshall Fund, "Worldviews 2002 Survey."

7. William Easterly, *The Cartel of Good Intentions: Bureaucracy versus Markets in Foreign Aid*, Working Paper 4 (Washington: Center for Global Development, March 2002).

8. Thus, for instance, some countries' populations are split between two quintiles. Gary Burtless compares income quintiles in "Is the Global Gap between Rich and Poor Getting Wider? (Brookings, June 17, 2002).

9. Progress in reducing income inequality is greater if income gaps are measured among people, rather than among nations. The reason is that incomes have grown more rapidly in the world's two most populous nations—China and India, which together account for about 40 percent of the planet's population—than in other poor nations. There is an extensive literature on income inequality trends; the conclusions are extremely sensitive to the data set and the unit of analysis. For both sides of the income inequality and poverty debate, see Surjit S. Bhalla, *Imagine There's No Country: Poverty, Inequality and Growth in the Era of Globalization* (Washington: Institute for International Economics, 2002); Martin Ravallion, *Inequality Convergence*, Working Paper 2645 (Washington, World Bank, July 21, 2001); Branko Milanovic, "World Income Inequality in the Second Half of the Twentieth Century," World Bank Paper (Washington, June 2001); and Xavier Sala-I-Martin, *The Disturbing 'Rise' in Global Income Inequality*, Working Paper 8904 (Cambridge, Mass.: National Bureau of Economic Research, April 2002).

10. Owing to lack of consistent literacy data for highest-income countries, figure 10-4 divides only the low- and middle-income countries into quartiles. Here, the "possibility frontier" is presumed to be 100 percent adult literacy.

11. "AIDS Epidemic Update," UNAIDS (www.unaids.org/worldaidsday/2002/press/Epiupdate.html [December 2002]).

12. "Sub-Saharan Africa Fact Sheet 2002," UNAIDS (www.unaids.org/worldaidsday/2002/press/factsheets/FSAfrica_en.doc [February 2003]).

13. *Report on the Global HIV/AIDS Epidemic 2002* (Geneva: UNAIDS, 2002).

14. "The AIDS Crisis," DATA (www.datadata.org/abouthiv.htm?1044892188078 [February 2003]).

15. President Bush, "State of the Union Address," January 28, 2003.

16. Lael Brainard, "The Administration's FY04 Budget Request for Global Poverty and AIDS: How Do the Numbers Stack Up?" February 4, 2003 (www.brookings.edu/views/papers/brainard/20030204.pdf [February 2003]).

17. Sheryl Gay Stolberg and Richard W. Stevenson, "Bush AIDS Plan Surprises Many, but Advisers Call It Long Planned," *New York Times*, January 30, 2003, p. A1; and Paul Blustein, "Activists Hail President's Call for More Funding to Fight AIDS," *Washington Post*, January 29, 2003, p. A12.

18. "Childhood Diseases in Africa," Fact Sheet 109 (Geneva: World Health Organization, March 1996) (www.who.int/inf-fs/en/fact109.html [February 2003]); Rehydration Project (www.rehydrate.org/diarrhoea/index.html [February 2003]).

19. By analogy, markets produce excessive quantities of goods that produce external costs. Prices of goods produced by processes that generate pollution seldom incorporate the costs that pollution imposes on people other than the consumer.

20. *Macroeconomics and Health: Investing in Health for Economic Development: Report of the Commission on Macroeconomics and Health* (Geneva: World Health Organization, December 2001).

21. Michael Kremer, "A Purchase Commitment for Vaccines," in Inge Kaul, Katell Le Goulven, and Mirjam Schnupf, eds., *Global Public Goods Financing: New Tools for New Challenges, A Policy Dialogue* (United Nations Development Programme, 2002).

22. Even when the marginal cost of the knowledge needed for disease prevention or treatment is negligible (the composition of a vaccine), the actual cost of putting that knowledge into practice may be considerable (including production, specialized shipment, storage, and handling, on-the-ground distribution, trained personnel, and education and mobilization of local communities).

23. Lael Brainard, "What Is the Role for Health in the Fight against International Poverty?" in Kurt Campbell and Philip Zellikow, eds., *Biological Security and Global Public Health* (W.W. Norton and Company, forthcoming).

24. See www.developmentgoals.org (February 2003).

25. Organization for Economic Cooperation and Development, *The DAC Journal Cooperation 2001 Report,* vol. 3, no. 1 (Paris, 2002).

26. The lower figure is based on U.S. IMF and World Bank subscriptions, which make up approximately 17 percent of both IMF total member quotas and the World Bank's International Bank for Reconstruction and Development (IBRD) total subscriptions. "IMF Members' Quotas and Voting Power, and IMF Governors," January 24, 2002 (www.imf.org/external/np/sec/memdir/members.htm [April 2002]); and "International Bank for Reconstruction and Development Subscriptions and Voting Power of Member Countries," September 19, 2001 (www.worldbank.org/about/organizations/voting/kibrd.html [April 2002]). The upper figure is based on the U.S. share of OECD income based on Development Assistance Committee members' 2000 gross national income. Faure, "Development Co-Operation, 2001 Report." Of the $50 billion the panel estimates a gap of $10 billion a year to achieve the health targets. The World Health Organization Commission on Macroeconomics and Health puts the price tag on health at more than double that amount, estimating it will cost the international community roughly $22 billion by 2007 or an additional 1 percent of GDP to reach two-thirds of the population affected by HIV/AIDS and target the major communicable diseases and perinatal conditions in low-income countries. WHO, *Macroeconomics and Health.*

27. All of these issues are covered in much greater detail in Lael Brainard "Transforming Foreign Assistance: Compassionate Conservatism Confronts Global Poverty," *Washington Quarterly*, vol. 26, no. 2 (Spring 2003), pp. 149–69.

28. "A New Compact for Development," White House Fact Sheet, March 2002 (www.whitehouse.gov/news/releases/2002/03/20020314-4.html [February 2003]).

29. Steve Radelet, "Beyond the Indicators: Delivering Effective Foreign Assistance through the Millennium Challenge Account," Center for Global Development, September 10, 2002 (http://www.cgdev.org/nv/MCA_indicators.pdf [February 2003]).

30. And indeed, many experts are advocating a so-called foundation model for the MCA. Lael Brainard, Carol Graham, Nigel Purvis, Steven Radelet, and Gayle E. Smith, *The Other War: Global Poverty and the Millennium Challenge Account* (Brookings, forthcoming).

31. "Millennium Challenge Account Update," White House Fact Sheet, June 3, 2002 (www.fas.usda.gov/icd/summit/WH%20MCA%20Fact%20Sheet%206-3-02.pdf [February 2003]).

32. Brainard, "The Administration's FY04 Budget Request for Global Poverty and AIDS."

33. "The Guardian of Free Trade," *BBC News Economy Reports*, May 18, 1998 (http://news.bbc.co.uk/1/hi/business/business_basics/96032.stm [February 2003]).

34. *World Investment Report 2002: Transnational Corporations and International Competitiveness* (New York: United Nations, 2002).

35. Stephen Roach, "Back to Borders," *Financial Times*, September 28, 2001, p. 20.

36. President George W. Bush, *Address on the War Effort*, California Business Association Breakfast, Sacramento, California, October 17, 2001.

37. Lael Brainard and Hal Shapiro, "Trade Promotion Authority Formerly Known as Fast Track: Building Common Ground on Trade Demands More than a Name Change," *George Washington International Law Review*, forthcoming.

38. Jagdish Bhagwati and Arvind Panagariya, "The Truth about Protectionism," *Financial Times*, March 30, 2001, p. 21.

39. *Global Economic Prospects and the Developing Countries: Making Trade Work for the World's Poor* (Washington: World Bank, 2002).

40. The estimated gain to developing countries is $184 million. Percentages based on 2000 GDP figures from "World Development Indicators 2002," CD-ROM database (Washington: World Bank, 2002).

41. Ed Gresser, "A World of Opportunity," *Blueprint Magazine*, September 10, 2001.

42. Office of the U.S. Trade Representative, "President Bush and USTR Zoellick Open First U.S.-Sub-Saharan Africa Trade Forum: Strong Growth in Trade between the United States and Africa is Creating 'Hope and Opportunity'" October 29, 2001 (www.ustr.gov/releases/2001/10/01-90.htm [February 2003]).

43. *Global Economic Prospects and the Developing Countries.*

44. "Towards More Liberal Agricultural Trade," *OECD Policy Brief*, November 2001 (www.oecd.org/pdf/M00022000/M00022532.pdf [February 2003]).

45. "Facts about the Common Agriculture Policy," Catholic Fund for Overseas Development (http://www.cafod.org.uk/tradejustice/capfaq.shtml#3 [April 2003].

46. *World Development Report, 2000/2001: Attacking Poverty* (Oxford University Press, 2001).

47. Oxfam, "Stop the Dumping! How EU Agricultural Subsidies Are Damaging Livelihoods in the Developing World," Oxfam Briefing Paper 31 (October 2002).

48. Dan Morgan, "Farm Bill Gains Senate Approval; 10-Year Price Tag Is $190 Billion," *Washington Post*, May 9, 2002, p. A9.

49. WT/DS 108/12, "U.S. Tax Treatment for Foreign Sales Corporations," October 5, 2000.

50. Howard Schneider, "Egypt Starts to Slip on Its Way toward Financial Reform," *Washington Post*, January 26, 2002, p. A20.

51. "The Importance of Trade Negotiations in Fighting Foreign Protectionism," statement of the American Textile Manufacturers Institute to the Subcommittee on Trade, hearings before the House Committee on Ways and Means, 106 Cong. 1 sess., February 11, 1999.

52. Robert B. Zoellick, remarks at the National Foreign Trade Council, July 26, 2001.

53. Robert B. Zoellick, "Falling Behind on Free Trade," *New York Times*, April 14, 2002, sec. 4, p. 13.

54. *The National Security Strategy of the United States of America* (White House, September 2002).

55. Lael Brainard, "Trading Places," *International Economy* (July–August 2001), pp. 34–37.

56. Remarks by Robert Zoellick at "Press Roundtable Questions and Answers with Ambassador Robert B. Zoellick," Port of Spain, Trinidad and Tobago, September 11, 2002.

57. Karen DeYoung, "Egypt Asks U.S. for Trade Pact, Aid Boost; Possible War in Iraq Fuels Other Requests," *Washington Post*, February 8, 2003, p. A15.

58. "Taiwan's Economics Minister Calls for Early FTA Signing with U.S.," *Asia Pulse*, January 20, 2003.

59. "Zoellick Sees Bilateral Negotiations with Morocco This Year," *Inside U.S. Trade*, May 24, 2002.

60. The bill also includes a program for assisting unemployed workers to purchase medical insurance, which addresses another source of workers' anxiety.

61. Lori Kletzer and Robert Litan, "A Prescription to Relieve Worker Anxiety," Policy Brief 73 (Brookings, March 2001).

62. David Folkerts-Landau, Donald J. Mathieson, and Garry J. Schinasi, "International Capital Markets: Developments Prospects and Key Policy Issues" (Washington: International Monetary Fund, 1997), p.13.

63. "IMF Concludes Article IV Consultation with Argentina," International Monetary Fund Public Information Notice 00/84, October 3, 2000 (www.imf.org/external/np/sec/pn/2000/pn0084.html [February 2003]); and "IMF Concludes Article IV Consultation with Argentina," International Monetary Fund Public Notice No. 98/9, February 23, 1998 (www.imf.org/external/np/sec/pn/1998/pn9809.html [February 2003]).

64. For more detailed discussion see Lael Brainard, "Capitalism Unhinged," *Foreign Affairs*, vol. 81, no. 1 (January-February 2002), pp. 192–98; and Peter B. Kenen, *The International Financial Architecture: What's New, What's Missing* (Washington: Institute for International Economics, 2001).

65. Paul Blustein, "Tough Talk Aside, the Aid Flows; Global Crises Melt the Bush Administration's Resistance to Bailouts," *Washington Post*, August 6, 2002, p. E1.

66. Tony Smith, "O'Neill Encourages Brazil in I.M.F. Talks," *New York Times*, August 6, 2002, p. C4.

67. Paul Blustein, "Banks Vow to Maintain Brazil Credit; Pledge Gives a Boost to IMF Bailout Effort," *Washington Post*, August 27, 2002, p. E1.

68. "Battling Over the Bankrupt," *Economist*, October 5, 2002; and "Major Financial Groups Blast IMF Proposal for Debt Crisis," *Agence France Press*, December 18, 2002; "Debt Restructuring Plan Sparks Trouble—Emerging Market Creditors Are at Loggerheads with the IMF Over the Latter's Proposal to Overhaul Debt Restructuring," *Banker*, October 1, 2002.

69. George Benston and others, *Following The Money: The Enron Failure and the State of Corporate Disclosure* (AEI-Brookings Joint Center for Regulatory Studies, March 2003).

70. Ibid.

71. Federal Reserve Bank of St. Louis, FRED Database, "Exchange Rates, Balance of Payments and Trade Data Tables" (http://research.stlouisfed.org/fred/data/exchange.html [February 2003]).

72. Bureau of Economic Analysis, U.S. International Transactions Accounts Data, table 1 (www.bea.gov/bea/international/bp_web/simple.cfm?anon=408&table_id=1&area_id=3 [February 2003]).

73. Ibid.

74. *Historical Tables, Budget of the United States Government, Fiscal Year 2004* (Executive Office of the President, Office of Management and Budget, 2003).

75. Edmund L. Andrews, "Strong Dollar Runs Into Renewed Resistance," *New York Times*, October 18, 2002, p. C1.

76. The result has been increased volatility and some weakening of the dollar, which fell roughly 12 percent against the yen and the euro between February and July of 2002. Federal Reserve Bank of St. Louis, "Exchange Rates, Balance of Payments and Trade Data Tables."

77. Bureau of Economic Analysis, U.S. International Transactions Accounts Data, table 1.

MICHAEL O'HANLON

11

Military Policy:
Getting the Best Bang
for the Bucks

Frequent disagreement about how the United States should employ its military forces abroad obscures a remarkable measure of agreement between Republicans and Democrats on the size and composition of U.S. military forces. Although as a presidential candidate George W. Bush charged that his White House predecessor had cut military spending too much, the strategic plan of September 2001 drafted by Donald Rumsfeld, President Bush's secretary of defense, retained the force structure and personnel totals of the Clinton administration with only small changes. Consensus does not necessarily equate with correctness, however. It is important, therefore, to consider whether the U.S. military should be significantly larger or smaller than current policy calls for. Just as critical are questions about how the U.S. military should modernize and adapt to a world of new threats and challenges.

I shall argue in this chapter that given the range of its obligations, the United States cannot significantly cut the size of its main combat forces. With few exceptions, any reductions in personnel should result from efficiencies in how the combat forces are maintained and supported, not from reductions in their number. The current forces of the American military are still needed, even if they resemble those of the cold war. For a variety of reasons, maintaining the current force structure will necessitate some increase in military spending. Through judicious choices, however, we should be able to avoid the huge increases in defense spending contemplated by the Bush administration for 2004 and beyond. Having inherited a national security budget of about $320 billion in 2001, President Bush would increase it to $503 billion in 2009, based on his plan released in February of 2003. Part of the increase is due to inflation, part to the war on terror, part to increasing costs for activities such as military health care, and part to the need to replace aging weapons bought largely during the Reagan years. These factors are all legitimate. Nevertheless, they do not explain about $50 billion of the projected $180 billion increase in annual funding.

The era of budget cuts in defense is decidedly over. Yet, in real-dollar terms it should be possible to hold the line at roughly $400 billion a year for the rest of the decade, only slightly above the initial appropriation for 2003 of roughly $385 billion (that figure excludes at least $65 billion for the costs of the war against Iraq, subsequent stabilization operations, and continuing missions in Afghanistan). In current or nominal dollars, the national security budget—including Department of Energy nuclear weapons activities, as well as Department of Defense resources, but not including homeland security activities outside of DoD—would reach about $450 billion in 2009, but no higher.

Why the United States Needs a Large Military

Over the long haul, military spending should be determined by America's role in protecting its global interests and in leading alliances that encompass some sixty countries on six continents. It has major security interests in western and central Europe, the Middle East, the Persian Gulf, the Indonesian Straits, and the industrial centers of Northeast Asia, and lesser but still important security concerns in Latin America and Africa. The span of U.S. interests requires global reach for American military capabilities. The U.S. armed forces provide the glue for an alliance system involving most of the world's major economies. They preserve stability for investment and commerce worldwide. They discourage the proliferation of weapons of mass destruction. America's forward positioning enhances this nation's capacity to project power and to prevail in wars it might be forced to fight. Better still, the dominant power of the U.S. military probably lowers the odds that many such wars will even occur.

Sweeping changes in U.S. defense capabilities and budgets would do more harm than good. A "fortress America" approach, designed to defend only the homeland and key waterways, might cost no more than $100 billion a year. But by ignoring the indisputable fact that the well-being of the United States is directly affected by what happens abroad, such a posture would repeat the isolationist blunders of the late 1930s. Even less drastic reductions would generally be imprudent. Trying to sustain global strategic obligations with, say, 1 million active-duty personnel instead of 1.4 million would be unwise. Such a reduction would enable the U.S. military to handle just one major war at a time rather than two. It would run American troops ragged, drive many excellent men and women out of the armed forces, and ultimately demoralize those who remained. It would also probably weaken deterrence and increase the risk that major conflicts could break out. Such a scaled-down military also would probably compel reductions in U.S. peacekeeping operations. Although critics of the United States accuse it of unilateralism, the fact remains that most of our allies can offer only limited help in conducting global military missions, constraining the Pentagon's options for reducing its forces.

At the opposite extreme, a return to force levels maintained during the cold war would require something like a 50 percent increase in personnel and a real-dollar defense budget of $600 billion. Some might argue that even though cold-war force levels are unnecessary, it would be desirable to restore forces to the levels the first Bush administration planned: roughly 1.6 million instead of 1.4 million active-duty troops. However, such an increase would add at least $50 billion to a defense budget that will have to rise significantly in the years ahead simply to maintain current force levels. There can be little doubt that added forces would increase U.S. capabilities, but the risks against which such forces would provide protection are so remote that the added costs would probably be a waste. The current armed forces should be able to adapt to the foreseeable problems of the post–cold war environment; indeed, they have already adapted more than most recognize.

To complete its reorientation to twenty-first century threats and challenges, however, the Pentagon needs to adopt a more selective approach to weapons modernization. It should also continue to economize through base closures and other operational reforms, make modest reductions in some personnel as new capabilities permit, and, given the past half-decade's already-generous increases in pay and benefits, limit further increases in military compensation.

Fundamentals

The current U.S. defense establishment is smaller than it has been in the past, but it is large and extremely expensive by international standards. It is also extensively engaged around the world.

The United States has one-third fewer military personnel now than it did during the cold war (see table 11-1). This force is still big, but hardly disproportionate compared with those of other countries. China has twice as many people under arms. Several other nations, including India, Russia, and North Korea, have armed forces with more than one million people. Furthermore, as a proportion of the national population, the scale of the American military is not notably different from the average of its major allies.

Although U.S. armed forces are not unusually large by these measures, the U.S. defense budget is by far the largest in the world, roughly equal to those of the world's next fifteen or so countries combined, many of which are U.S. allies (see figure 11-1 and table 11-2). If the Bush administration has its way, the defense budget measured in inflation-adjusted dollars will soon approximate levels reached during the Vietnam War and the Reagan years. At the same time, U.S. defense spending as a percent of gross domestic product, at just over 3 percent, is modest by historical standards. None of these comparisons goes to the fundamental question: is U.S. defense spending sufficient to meet U.S. commitments and obligations around the world without being excessive?

The United States has a larger military presence outside its borders than does any other country—more than a quarter million U.S. troops even in

Table 11-1. *Defense Personnel, 1990–2000*
Millions

Component	1990	2000	1990–2000 (percentage change)
Active	2.1	1.4	−32
Reserve	1.1	0.9	−23
Civilian	1.1	0.7	−35

Source: For active component, as of June 30, 2000, Office of the Secretary of Defense, http://web1.whs.osd.mil/mmid/military/ms0.pdf (September 14, 2000). For reserve and civilian component, as of September 30, 1999, William Cohen, *Annual Report to the President and Congress* (Department of Defense, February 2000), appendix C-1.

Figure 11-1. *U.S. Defense Budget, 1950–2006*

Billions of 2003 dollars

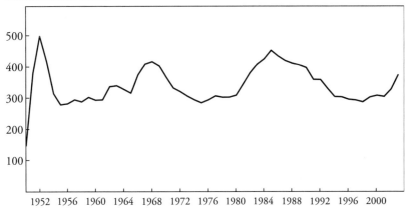

Source: *National Defense Budget Estimate for FY 2003,* March 2002.

Table 11-2. *Global Distribution of Military Spending, 2001*
Billions of U.S. dollars

United States and its major security partners	Defense spending
United States	322.4
NATO's remaining 18	173.2
Major Asian allies[a]	57.4
Other allies[b]	34.8
Other key friends[c]	68.0
Others	
Russia	63.7
China	46.0
"Rogue states"[d]	9.3
All remaining countries	60.4
Total	835.2

Source: International Institute for Strategic Studies, *The Military Balance 2002/2003* (Oxford University Press, 2002), pp. 332–37.

a. Japan, South Korea, and Australia.

b. New Zealand, Thailand, Philippines, and the Rio Pact countries minus Cuba.

c. Austria, Egypt, Israel, Ireland, Jordan, Kuwait, Oman, Qatar, Saudi Arabia, Sweden, Switzerland, and Taiwan.

d. Cuba, North Korea, Iran, Iraq, and Libya.

Table 11-3. *U.S. Military Personnel in Foreign Areas, 1986–2001*
Thousands of troops

Country or region	1986	1996	2001
Germany	250	49	71
Other European countries	75	66	42
Europe, afloat	33	4	5
South Korea	43	37	38
Japan	48	43	40
Other Asia-Pacific countries	17	1	1
Afloat in East, South, and Southeast Asia, plus all forces in Persian Gulf/North Africa	36	30	40
Western hemisphere	22	12	14
Miscellaneous	1	1	4
Global total	525	240	255
Percentage of total active-duty strength	24	16	19

Source: Department of Defense, *Worldwide Manpower Distribution by Geographical Area*, September 30, 2001, September 30, 1996, and September 30, 1986. All available at http://web1.whs. osd.mil/mid/military/miltop/htm. Numbers may not add up to totals due to rounding.

peacetime—but this number is down by half from cold war levels (see table 11-3). Most of the reductions were in Germany. In East Asia, force levels are similar to their cold war levels. About 25,000 troops are present now in the vicinity of Afghanistan and the Arabian Sea. A large force is in the Persian Gulf as of this writing, but even before the recent buildup, another 25,000 forces were typically in that region as well.

As noted above, Republicans and Democrats generally agree about the broad contours of American force levels and weaponry. Secretary Rumsfeld's 2001 Quadrennial Defense Review reaffirmed the active-duty troop levels of about 1.4 million that were maintained during the Clinton administration. Rumsfeld canceled the Army's Crusader artillery system and proposed additional initiatives—ranging from missile defense to increased research and development funding—and new military command structures, but he retained most of the Clinton agenda for weapons modernization. After September 11, he sought and received a great deal more budget authority than President Clinton's defense plan called for, but there can be little doubt that a Democratic president would also have boosted defense spending under the circumstances. In most respects, Secretary

Rumsfeld has left the overall size of the military, its combat force structure, and its main weapons programs largely as his predecessor proposed.[1]

The Importance of Remaining Dominant

The United States plays a unique role in promoting global security. Although critics sometimes disparage that role as hegemonic or unilateralist, the existence of a responsible superpower confers enormous benefits on the international community. To begin with, a superpower can deter aggression. War between major countries is rare in today's international system, largely because of U.S. influence. Having a single superpower also discourages costly military buildups by other nations, which realize that they have little prospect of becoming militarily dominant in their own regions. Friends and allies, moreover, gain protection from U.S. military might and hence are less likely to engage in arms racing or acquire nuclear weapons (though they sometimes go too far and "free ride").

Of course, the United States benefits as well. It is this fact, not altruism, that explains U.S. willingness to incur the costs necessary to sustain military dominance and to deploy its military strength globally. Isolationism once led the United States to disregard its interests in European and East Asian stability. This detachment encouraged aggressors in 1939. The cold war had its share of open conflicts, but major power conflict did not occur, and the United States eventually prevailed in the larger contest. It did so in large part because it remained resolute and militarily strong during the four decades of East-West confrontation. A steadfast stance can enable the United States to defend its interests and help preserve global stability today. Rather than pay huge costs in dollars and lives after a major war breaks out, we have decided to pay an insurance premium—remaining involved in the international security system, even at considerable expense, to avoid what could be much worse.

Global Reach

The justification for deploying U.S. power abroad has not waned in a world in which hostile regimes and terrorist organizations seek access to weapons of mass destruction. The United States cannot be the Earth's sole policeman, but without its leadership and military muscle, the rest of the international community is generally incapable of restraining despots and rogues. Of course, the United States sometimes acts in self-interested ways, but by any objective assessment, it has defined that self-interest in a manner that, for the most part, is benign by the standards of other great powers throughout history.

The reach of America's involvement with other nations is striking. Treaties and alliances bind the United States to scores of allies or security partners. No other country comes close to having a comparable network. The United States has security partnerships on every continent but Antarctica. No other country has made comparable pledges. Most important, these commitments are serious. With the notable exception of Britain, no other nation has the capacity or the will to enforce even the limited security guarantees or resolutions it has signed in treaties or incurred under international auspices such as the Security Council of the United Nations.

Those who question the wisdom of so broad a set of commitments should note that it seems to be working. Despite occasional acrimony among allies, the western alliance system for decades has been remarkably powerful and unified. The United States and its alliance partners are responsible for some 75 percent of global GDP and about the same fraction of global military spending—unprecedented among the major alliances of history. No less important, with the partial exception of President Chirac's France, other nations in that system show no interest in leaving it or in competing with the United States for control. Indeed, powers such as Russia and India seem more intent on joining the club—or at least working with it in most instances—than on breaking it up. In sum, the payoff to the considerable investment by the United States is large and global. It lowers the probability of major military competition between countries and promotes political and economic cooperation among them. This remarkable state of affairs owes a great deal not only to American statecraft, but to American military prowess.[2]

Thus the United States has reason to dedicate to its military more resources than does any other country. Hawks and doves alike mostly agree on this point. Even those who would like to spend less typically favor sums in excess of $200 billion—still several times as much as Russia or China spend and equal to the aggregate military spending of the world's next half dozen powers. Furthermore, the closer one looks at the military and political situations in particular regions, the stronger the argument for America's far-flung military presence becomes.

Sensitive Areas

Consider Europe, the Far East, and the Persian Gulf. At first glance, it may seem hard to understand why European countries, which include five of the world's seven largest economies, still require the physical presence of heavily armed U.S. forces. The once fearsome hordes of the Warsaw Pact, after all, no longer threaten anyone. Europe's major powers no longer engage in military competition. They probably would not do so even if U.S. troops sailed home. Russia wants to join Europe, not threaten it. German governments severely limit military involvements outside their borders. Britain, France, Italy, Spain, Portugal, and the Netherlands have long since given up their old colonial aspirations. Nuclear weapons in the hands of responsible European governments represent no cause for alarm, even if their spread to more European powers would set an undesirable precedent.[3]

The case for maintaining long-standing U.S. deployments in the Korean peninsula is also clear: a stubborn dictatorship across the thirty-eighth parallel continues to pose a menace. Even in that context, however, the South Korean economy is twenty times larger than that of its northern neighbor. Why, then, do the South Koreans not simply protect themselves, instead of relying to a significant extent on American security guarantees? The same might be asked about the world's second largest economy, Japan, which has the wealth and technical sophistication to defend itself. As for the Persian Gulf, its countries presumably have to sell their oil to the rest of the world regardless of whether they are aligned with the West, indifferent toward it, or even antagonistic toward it. Why do America's armed forces have to be entrenched there, too?

Answers to these questions are not difficult. As far as Europe is concerned, two millennia of history suggest that there is at least a small chance of a revival of great-power competition in Europe at some future time. Even if the risk that Europe might revert to form is remote, it is not worth running, particularly when a U.S. decision to withdraw from, say, the North Atlantic Treaty Organization would save little, probably no more than $5 billion a year. The savings are so small because U.S. military units based in Europe do more than contribute to European security. For example, U.S. heavy armor based in Europe was deployed to the Persian Gulf for Operation Desert Storm, and U.S. bases in Germany helped form an "air bridge" from the United States during Operation Iraqi Freedom. Hence, the price of the U.S. military commitment to Europe is not the cost of an additional 100,000 personnel under arms—most of those troops would remain in the U.S. armed forces anyway—but only the extra logistical expense of maintaining a foothold overseas, and some of that cost is borne by our allies.[4]

Even more important, maintaining a strong alliance system helps the United States globally. European allies have been of help in the Balkans and Afghanistan; they will be willing to help in a postwar stabilization effort in Iraq as well. If the United States surrendered its military presence in Europe, it would weaken NATO and lessen the tendency for European countries to assist it in overseas missions.[5] Some realignment of U.S. forces in Europe makes sense, perhaps moving some from Germany to eastern Europe. But large overall cuts are not advisable.

The savings from U.S. disengagement from Northeast Asia would be larger, but so too the adverse consequences. If the United States pulled out of Japan and South Korea and abandoned the defense of Taiwan, a host of dangerous dynamics could easily ensue. North Korea could be tempted to invade South Korea. Even if war did not result, the two Koreas would likely rush to develop nuclear weapons in substantial numbers. Japan would not stand idly by. Tensions over maritime resources and disputed islands throughout Northeast Asia would intensify. Taiwan would also have an incentive to acquire nuclear weapons as insurance against an attack from the Chinese mainland. Such an effort by Taiwan might provoke China to launch a preemptive strike. In short, up to four more powers in the region might join the nuclear club. The risk of war between the two Koreas and of armed strife between Taiwan and China would increase sharply.[6] Unlike the risk of great-power confrontation in Europe, these dangers would be palpable, and if war resulted, U.S. economic interests would suffer greatly, as would America's global interests in limiting the proliferation and use of weapons of mass destruction.

A U.S. decision to pull back from the Persian Gulf would give despots a green light to pursue acquisitions of weapons of mass destruction and also, quite possibly, to maraud in the neighborhood. Whether the flow of oil from the Gulf would be disturbed is unclear, but an emboldened government in a place like Iran could try to blackmail its neighbors and, perhaps, the industrial world with threats to use a biological or nuclear arsenal and to seize the region's oil fields.[7] In short, vacating the Middle East is not an option U.S. policymakers dare consider, even if the defeat of Saddam Hussein's regime affords opportunities for cutting back U.S. forces in certain places, such as Saudi Arabia.

Getting By with Less?

With these broad considerations in mind, could the U.S. military perform its essential tasks for much less than $400 billion annually? The answer is: no.

If a volunteer army, navy, and air force are to function, each branch must attract enough volunteers to sustain its ranks. That means, in turn, that salaries, fringe benefits, and working conditions must be adequate to attract enough new recruits and re-enlistments. Pay must increase periodically to keep pace with rising wage levels throughout the economy. Other perquisites have to meet prevailing standards—even if, as in the case of health care, costs persistently rise faster than inflation or earnings. Salaries could be lower if the nation reinstituted the draft, but that course would threaten the quality of what is by far the best military in history and would go against a trend among U.S. allies to end conscription and develop more professional militaries. The cost of modern weapons and equipment is not only high, but also likely to keep going up, even if some cost savings can be achieved through the application of modern electronics. The military also needs to buy a lot of equipment during the next several years to replace large stocks purchased during the Reagan years. That equipment is now wearing out or becoming unreliable. In addition, the U.S. military edge hinges on maintaining technological superiority.

For these reasons, the costs of maintaining a military force of approximately the current size will rise faster than inflation, unless countervailing economies can be realized. To be sure, some strategic choices could permit cuts in the size and cost of the military. Unless the United States retreats from its principal obligations overseas, however, significant savings are impossible.

Fighting Two Wars at a Time

U.S. armed forces are now supposed to be able to fight two full-scale wars at once. Although a two-war scenario is improbable, this capacity is important, as again became apparent during recent simultaneous crises over Iraq and North Korea. It permits us to fight one war without letting down our guard everywhere else, which would undercut deterrence and perhaps increase the likelihood of a second conflict. Retaining this capability, or something close to it, is prudent (even though Secretary Rumsfeld rightly modified the requirement somewhat in his 2001 quadrennial review to a somewhat less rigorous standard that no longer envisions two all-out and simultaneous victories). It will be prudent even in a world without Saddam

Hussein, since threats will still remain—in other parts of the Persian Gulf, Korea, the Taiwan Strait, and Central Asia.

Burden Sharing

Shifting defense responsibilities to our allies is an idea that is attractive in the United States, but prospects for doing so to any significant degree are not good. In theory, our western European friends could develop more capacity to project power in the event of another war in the Persian Gulf. Other rich countries such as Japan and less prosperous ones such as Russia and many African states could increase their capacity to perform peacekeeping and humanitarian functions. (Russia's considerable airlift fleet would come in handy for such purposes.) In practice, however, the near-term prospects for extensive burden sharing are dim. Improvements would be helpful, but, realistically speaking, they will not significantly relieve current demands on American forces. The enhanced participation of allies might aid a shift to a somewhat less strenuous two-war capability, but it is not credible to think it conducive to substantial force reductions. To be sure, the United States should press for a more balanced distribution of burdens within its various alliances. It should, however, keep aspirations in check.

It may seem surprising that possibilities for burden sharing are currently so limited. After all, America's allies together spend almost as much on defense as does the United States. Several of our allies are endowed with strong military traditions. Many have competent military personnel and a high-tech industrial base. The problem is largely political. Other nations often believe, perhaps unrealistically at times, that the use of force is less important today than it once was. They also have strong incentives to free-ride on U.S. commitments. Furthermore, several European countries are encumbered by fiscal deficits that preclude big defense buildups. Moreover, European nations respond to our calls for greater commitments by citing their substantial contributions to peacekeeping missions as evidence that they are already bearing a considerable share of the defense burden.

Germany and Japan are disinclined to remilitarize, and their former adversaries, including Americans, who remember World War II, hesitate to press them to abandon this reticence. Some African militaries have the will to take on more work in their regions, so as to avoid a recurrence of catastrophes like the genocidal violence in Rwanda in 1994, but they lack the means. Recent U.S. and European programs to train African forces have emphasized peacekeeping, not more complex assignments. Only about

15,000 troops have been trained to date.[8] These programs should be expanded, but doing so will take time.

Some progress has been made in other ways. European militaries are developing the combined capacity to deploy up to 60,000 troops at a considerable geographic distance and to sustain them there for a year. The Europeans are moving toward maintaining volunteer, professional armies that will be less constrained by legal or constitutional restrictions on out-of-country deployment than were conscripted forces. Japan is slowly enlarging its interpretation of which military missions are consistent with its post–World War II constitution. And, as already noted, U.S., British, and French programs are helping African militaries improve their skills—though the programs currently are poorly funded and should be expanded.

The bottom line, however, is that right now the United States holds at least two-thirds of the world's deployable military power and almost all of its top-of-the-line projectable force. Even as allied capabilities increase gradually, U.S. armed forces will retain the lion's share of global capability—and responsibilities—for years to come.[9]

National Missile Defense

How national missile defense (NMD) affects the U.S. defense budget depends on the type of system contemplated. An effective missile defense is hard to build and could also strain relations with other major powers—though fallout over U.S. withdrawal last year from the ABM Treaty was much less serious than many feared. Furthermore, NMD cannot protect the United States against what may be its most immediate risk—that of global terrorism. Missile defense would not have prevented the events of September 11. It will do nothing to stop similar attacks in the future. A suicidal missile strike by a hostile nation against the United States is much less likely than a suicidal terrorist act requiring far less technological finesse.

These arguments undercut the case for attempting to build a massive, supposedly impregnable defense for the United States. Doing so would be extremely costly and provide at best only one form of protection. But a limited defense looks like a smart buy.[10] It could forestall nuclear blackmail from a North Korean or Iranian ICBM. Defenses against shorter-range missiles like SCUDs certainly make sense, too.

A large-scale, multitiered missile defense against ICBMs would cost a bundle. The Congressional Budget Office (CBO) estimates that a national defense aimed at stopping an attack from an established nuclear power could cost as much as $200 billion or even more.[11] When added to current programs for theater defense against shorter-range missiles, the *annual* costs for missile defense could reach or even exceed $20 billion, compared with current outlays of $8 billion. However, if the NMD program were aimed only at the problem posed by rogue states, costs would be substantially lower—perhaps on the order of $10 billion a year for all types of missile defense. That would fund a robust theater missile defense capability and a limited national defense system. This would put it within the price tag of procuring, say, a new fleet of submarines, fighter jets, or helicopters.

Peacekeeping and Peace Enforcing

Some analysts hold that the United States should leave peacekeeping operations entirely to other countries. However, America should remain a player in peacekeeping as well as more muscular but related activities such as humanitarian military intervention. "Peacekeeping" forces are not mere observers. They stabilize volatile zones. They provide a *preventive* military presence, often reducing the need for larger-scale intervention. Because peacekeepers are often in part a trip wire, they cannot be composed exclusively of troops from countries that could never credibly follow up with a large-scale intervention if needed. In various locations, a credible preventive force requires at least some U.S. participation, since the world knows that America—perhaps only America—has the means quickly to back up its peacekeeping contingents with far more force if circumstances warrant.[12] U.S. participation in this case encourages other nations to participate in peacekeeping missions; some nations that would otherwise be unwilling to put their soldiers in harm's way will do so if U.S. troops are present.

At any rate, other countries already carry out most of the world's peacekeeping activity. The United States has deployed its forces in the Balkans, but even there, U.S. troops have totaled only about 15 percent of NATO forces. In Afghanistan, American troops have not contributed anything to the international security assistance force to date, though of course they have assumed primary responsibility for defeating the Taliban and al Qaeda.

Curtailing peacekeeping missions could produce some budget savings—roughly $2 billion to $4 billion a year (not counting costs of any stabilization mission in Iraq), according to Pentagon and CBO estimates, if all were eliminated. But these costs are less than many like to claim. The Clinton administration was said to have initiated more than fifty peacekeeping actions over eight years. However, most of the Clinton administration's missions were simply renewals of existing ones, not brand-new deployments. Its only major peacekeeping missions were in the Balkans, Haiti, and Somalia. A number of missions have been mischaracterized as peacekeeping when they were not. The list of so-called peacekeeping missions includes deterrent actions directed at Iraq, for instance. Still other missions were tiny operations involving only dozens or at most hundreds of troops lasting days or weeks. Peacekeeping has been a chore for the U.S. armed forces, but it has also been within its capabilities in general (though stabilizing Iraq could be a different story).[13]

Finally, an end to U.S. peacekeeping expeditions would permit only small reductions in the armed forces. No major unit in the U.S. military is devoted exclusively to peacekeeping, nor is the U.S. military explicitly sized and structured with peacekeeping in mind. On average, perhaps one brigade of ground forces was involved in peacekeeping at any time during the 1990s (out of about forty brigades in the active-duty force, including Marine Corps equivalents). It might have been possible to avoid the cost of paying for the people, equipment, training, and other costs of preparing that one brigade for peacekeeping—or even two or three. However, such a policy would not have reduced the overall number of U.S. servicemen and -women by more than a couple of percent.

China

Some critics of defense spending ask why the United States needs to pour $400 billion into defense now that it faces no rival like the former Soviet Union. Dealing with the Taliban, Slobodan Milosevic, or Saddam Hussein—foes that lack modern military capabilities—should not, the critics say, require so vast an expenditure.

These skeptics underestimate the ability of seemingly weak adversaries to resist effectively on or near their own territory. Vietnam was a big and costly lesson, Somalia a smaller but still significant one. Operation Iraqi Freedom was not a cakewalk. Furthermore, not all future foes of the United States will necessarily be weak. Surely, China, with its rapidly growing economy, enormous population, aspiration for greater geopolitical influence, and desire to retake Taiwan, by force if necessary and possible, is a case in point. True, hawks sometimes overstate the current threat from China, but there is little question that China will grow stronger and eventually could pose a serious challenge. Moreover, any foreseeable clash between China and the United States would probably occur close to Chinese shores, with the tactical advantages of proximity on China's side.

Table 11-4. *Basic Military Data on China, Taiwan,
and the United States, 2000*

Type of military capability	China	Taiwan	United States
Population (millions)	1,240	22	273
Active-duty military personnel (millions)	2.5	0.38	1.37
Reserve personnel (millions)	1.2	1.66	1.3
Active Army/Marines (millions)	1.8	0.246	0.640
Active Air Force (millions)	0.42	0.068	0.361
Active Navy (millions)	0.230	0.068	0.370
Annual defense spending (billions of 1998 U.S. dollars)	38 (46 in 2001)	14	300
Heavy armor—tanks, armored personnel carriers, large artillery	30,000	4,000	35,000
Combat jets (number of advanced jets)	4,000 (50)	600 (340)	4,000 (4,000)
Major ships (number of aircraft carriers)	53 (0)	37 (0)	130 (12)
Attack submarines (number of advanced subs)	69 (9)	4 (0)	55 (55)
Nuclear weapons (all types)	300	0	10,000

Sources: Bates Gill, "Chinese Defense Procurement Spending: Determining Intentions and Capabilities," in James R. Lilley and David Shambaugh, eds., *China's Military Faces the Future* (New York: M. E. Sharpe, 1999), pp. 197–211; International Institute for Strategic Studies, *The Military Balance 1999/2000* (Oxford University Press, 1999); Lane Pierrot, *Planning for Defense: Affordability and Capability of the Administration's Program* (Washington: Congressional Budget Office, 1994), p. 22; Office of Naval Intelligence, *Worldwide Challenges to Naval Strike Warfare* (U.S. Navy, 1996), p. 29.

Chinese power does not require an additional U.S. buildup, but we should not let our guard down, either.

To better understand this mixed message about Chinese capabilities, consider some select facts on the regional military balance. China has more people under arms by far than does any other nation. Its defense spending may now rank second in the world.[14] Taiwan has a much smaller and considerably less costly military, though it is tenth in the world in total defense spending, and its reserve forces are actually larger than those of China (see table 11-4). Fortunately, Taiwan's troops are generally better trained than China's. Although Taiwan's defense technology is of uneven quality, it certainly surpasses China's. Taiwanese foreign arms purchases in the 1990s were seven times larger than those of China.[15]

The Chinese military has traditionally focused on internal and border security more than on operations beyond its frontiers. The Pentagon estimates that no more than 20 percent of China's nearly two million ground troops are mobile even within the mainland itself. Considerably fewer could deploy abroad, given their dearth of logistical capacity, including trucks, construction and engineering equipment, mobile depots, hospitals, and fuel storage.[16] Although the Taiwan Strait is just 100 miles wide, this moat is currently sufficient to preclude an invasion of Taiwan by China because China has little airlift, sealift, and amphibious capacity. Its amphibious vessels can now move about 10,000 to 15,000 troops with their equipment, including perhaps 400 armored vehicles. Airlift could move another 6,000 troops, or perhaps somewhat more counting the possibility of helicopter transport.[17] These numbers are small compared with Taiwan's military strength. Thus China almost surely lacks the capacity to mount a successful invasion of Taiwan.[18]

The military position of the People's Republic of China will no doubt improve, but probably not soon. China's defense industry remains mediocre.[19] Much of that nation's defense budget is devoted to paying, training, and supplying its huge forces.[20] The Defense Intelligence Agency estimates that only 10 percent of China's armed forces will have "late–cold war" equivalent hardware even by 2010.[21] China's ability to establish air superiority in a hypothetical war against Taiwan seems remote—a constraint that would further complicate the work of any expeditionary force facing Taiwanese ground troops, artillery, and armor.

China does not need to invade Taiwan to threaten it, however. China could attack with missiles or impose a naval blockade. Beyond the Taiwan issue, moreover, China could lay claim not only to islands in the South China Sea, but also to the surrounding waterways—an action the United States would find unacceptable. In time, China will undoubtedly play a larger part on the world stage, reversing centuries of subjugation and intimidation by outside powers. China potentially has the resources to modernize its military in ways that Iraq, Iran, or North Korea cannot.[22]

For the present, the United States can readily deal with the threats that China could plausibly pose. However, that presupposes maintaining a military of roughly the current size and structure.

Getting By with $400 Billion?

The United States may not be able to reduce its armed forces without giving up a great deal of clout in international relations, but it can continue to play its prominent global role and still basically hold the line on military spending. The trick lies in allocating resources more efficiently. Here are some suggestions on where to begin.

Technology

The promising performance of American high-technology weapons in the 1991 Persian Gulf War and the marked improvement during the Afghan campaign and Operation Iraqi Freedom have convinced many defense analysts that a revolution in military affairs is under way. The "revolution" thesis holds that further advances in precision munitions, real-time data dissemination, and other modern technologies, if combined with appropriate war-fighting doctrines and organization, can transform warfare. The unprecedented pace of technological change, many observers hold, will sharply alter the size and composition of our military forces, perhaps saving a lot of money in the long run.[23]

The optimism needs tempering. Change in military technology is fast, but may not outpace that of the past half-century. Enthusiasts think it will, once strategy catches up with technology. But the military in recent decades has been appropriately cautious in replacing war-fighting concepts that have served the nation well, even when satellites, stealth, precision-guided munitions, advanced jet engines, night-vision equipment, and other remarkable new capabilities came on stream.[24] A measured and balanced approach to modernization has fostered the very technologies that currently promise so much for the future.[25]

True believers in the "revolution" thesis invoke "Moore's law"—the trend of the number of transistors on a semiconductor chip to double every eighteen months. They arbitrarily extrapolate from this trend in computer chips and predict equally rapid progress in entirely different realms of technology.[26] Advances in electronics and computers, however, do not imply comparably rapid changes in the basic functioning of tanks, ships, aircraft, rockets, explosives, and energy sources—that is, in the traditional hardware that makes the military machine run and that will still be needed in the future to provide mobility, battlefield protection, and certain types of firepower.

So remaking the military radically would be neither cheap nor particularly prudent. But the right use of technology can, indeed, allow some economies. Operation Enduring Freedom in Afghanistan, Operation Iraqi Freedom, and several missions before them have demonstrated the potential for modernizing basic systems at modest costs. In Afghanistan, relatively inexpensive investments—for example, Global Positioning Systems (GPS) guidance kits attached to "dumb bombs," unmanned aerial vehicles (which cost a fraction of what manned fighters do), and real-time data links between various sensors and weapons platforms—produced formidable results. Similar technologies were instrumental in the downfall of Saddam Hussein.

The Clinton administration spent an average of $50 billion a year on equipment. The procurement budget climbed to $70 billion in 2003 and is slated to increase slightly in 2004 before rising to $100 billion in 2009 (in constant 2003 dollars). If it reaches and remains at that level, it might be adequate to buy and sustain a force like the one now planned by the Pentagon, according to the Congressional Budget Office.[27] Much of this increased cost will be unavoidable. While $100 billion seems like a fortune, it actually only restores the defense procurement budget to its historical norm in real terms.

Nonetheless, does the Pentagon's weapons-modernization plan make sense? Is such a cost necessary? Despite Bush's presidential election campaign promise to "skip a generation" of weaponry, his Pentagon has canceled only one major weapon system (the Army's Crusader howitzer), and that was not even a particularly expensive system. Although procurement budgets will need to continue rising, the rapid increases implied by current plans are not essential. Economies can almost certainly be found through expanded applications of modestly priced technologies, such as the weapons and communications systems used in Afghanistan.

The Bush plan fails to set clear priorities. The administration proposes to replace major combat systems throughout the force structure with systems typically costing twice as much. A more discriminating and economy-minded modernization strategy is in order.[28] Such a strategy would equip only part—not all—of the armed forces with the most sophisticated and expensive weaponry. That high-end or "silver bullet" component, as the CBO has dubbed it, would hedge against new contingencies, such as a rapid modernizing of the Chinese military. The rest of the U.S. military establishment would be equipped primarily with relatively inexpensive upgrades of existing weaponry, including better sensors, munitions, computers, and communications systems. Instead of purchasing, say, 3,000 joint strike fighters, the military would buy about 1,000 and would buy upgraded versions of current planes, such as new F-16 Block 60 aircraft, and perhaps even some unmanned combat aerial vehicles in a few years, to meet its needs.

Last, the development of new weapons could be done more economically. This facet of the Pentagon's budget has historically accounted for somewhere between 10 and 15 percent of overall defense spending. President Bush has rightly emphasized research and development, and recent budgets added large sums for R&D. Current real spending on research, development, testing, and evaluation already exceeds the levels of Bush senior's administration and roughly equals those of the peak Reagan years. That reflects an unwillingness to set priorities and a continuation of too many big-ticket weapons development programs, ranging from fighter jets to missile defense and other systems, not all of which are essential.

Pay and Operations

Other savings in such budget accounts as personnel and operations accounts are possible. No one seriously advocates cutting military pay. Good compensation is essential for attracting and keeping people of high quality in the military. But the growth rate of compensation, over and above ordinary cost-of-living increases, is in need of restraint. The Pentagon has a huge payroll: 1.4 million active-duty troops, about 650,000 civilians, nearly 1 million reservists, at a total cost that will soon approach $150 billion a year in salaries and fringe benefits. Military compensation has never been higher in inflation-adjusted dollars. For most military personnel, pay, including perquisites such as housing and tax breaks, at least matches that of civilians of comparable age, education, and experience. These comparisons do not even include the especially generous retirement and health care benefits of the military. Partly as a result of increased compensation, recruiting and retention have improved markedly in recent years.[29] Any additional increases (above cost-of-living adjustments) should be targeted at those few technical specialties where the Pentagon still has trouble attracting and retaining the right people.

The operations and maintenance account poses more complex problems. This category includes upkeep of equipment, a wide range of support activities (including various aspects of operating military bases), and health care costs. These costs have been rising fast in recent years.[30] Some savings in these areas are already in the works. Congress has agreed to authorize an additional round of base closures in 2005.[31] Since the cold war ended, U.S. military forces have shrunk by more than one-third, yet domestic base capacity has been reduced only 20 percent. Once retrenchment of base capacity is completed, annual savings of at least $3.5 billion annually will result. To these savings could be added possible gains from overhauling military health care services. The system could become more efficient if the independent health programs of each military service were merged and if a small copayment for military personnel and their families were introduced.

Savings might be $2 billion or more per year.[32] Other reductions in spending on operations and maintenance are possible. For example, creating incentives for local base commanders to find efficiencies in their operations—by letting them keep some of the savings for their base activities—could reduce annual spending by several billion dollars within a decade.[33]

Operation Iraqi Freedom

In March and April 2003, American and British forces (aided by smaller contributions from Australia and a few other countries) decisively defeated Saddam Hussein's regime in Iraq. What do the early results from that conflict tell us about future U.S. defense planning and priorities?

What Happened

On the evening of March 19 Washington time, coalition forces began the war. The most visible event on that date was the apparently unsuccessful attempt to kill Saddam Hussein with an air strike on a bunker in Baghdad that he was believed to be occupying. But even before that strike, special forces had moved into Iraq in large numbers and begun offensive operations. Within a day, earlier than expected, coalition main ground forces began to move into Iraq from Kuwait. The decision to hasten their movement northward was based in part on Iraq's decision to start firing missiles at U.S. forces in Kuwait, in part on fear that Iraqi forces would begin to set oil wells on fire in southeastern Iraq.

Early days of the war went generally well. Coalition special forces secured many key facilities; Saddam's military failed to accomplish any significant missile or other strikes against coalition forces and friendly countries such as Kuwait and Israel; U.S. and U.K. ground forces achieved impressive advances into Iraq. However, by the beginning of the second week of the war (Sunday March 23/Monday March 24), some problems developed. Iraqi irregulars, also known as Saddam fedayeen, began to harass coalition supply lines in the southeast, exploiting the fact that they could hide in cities that coalition armored forces had chosen not to control even though their supply lines sometimes passed near or through them. The absence of the 4th Mechanized Infantry Division, which was to have entered Iraq via Turkey until Ankara denied the United States permission to use its territory for ground operations at the last minute, seemed to hurt the coalition cause. Other units, such as armored cavalry regiments designed to protect coalition flanks, were not present either.

These difficulties were not as serious as critics alleged. Iraqi irregulars could harass, but not seriously threaten, coalition logistics operations. Even if the United States and the United Kingdom had needed to await the arrival of the 4th Infantry Division and other forces via Kuwait, there would have been little strategic cost to the delay. Devoting more coalition forces to those choke points and vulnerable roadways where fedayeen could easily approach essentially solved the problem.

By the third week of the war (starting March 30–31), coalition forces regained the momentum. Not only had they largely solved their logistics problems, but they had begun to devise tactics for engaging the Republican Guard divisions outside of Baghdad. In the ensuing few days, they decimated those formations.

By the end of that week and the beginning of the fourth week of battle (starting April 6–7), coalition forces reached Baghdad and began to establish a real presence in Basra. Initial probing raids uncovered a surprisingly weak Iraqi resistance. Coalition commanders then exploited that weakness and pressed their attack. Baghdad fell, and promptly so did Mosul, Kirkuk, and Tikrit, Saddam's hometown. The problem in most of Iraq became one of restoring order and providing humanitarian relief, not defeating Saddam's forces. Roughly 160 U.S. and U.K. forces died in the war, fewer than the number of coalition losses (240) in Operation Desert Storm in 1991.

The Chief Elements of the Strategy

What can we say about the historical importance of Operation Iraqi Freedom? Clearly, answering the question of what worked and what did not will provide important lessons for the future of warfare as well as for the future of American defense policy.

This victory was traceable to the well-trained personnel as much as to the advanced technology of today's U.S. and U.K. armed forces. Traditional combat skills mattered as much as new ways of warfare. This conclusion argues against pursuing a hasty defensive revolution. And despite much commentary to the contrary, the invasion force was reasonably large—reminding us that quantity still has a quality all its own.

—"Shock and Awe." Air strikes during the war's first forty-eight hours were less decisive than hoped. Their basic logic did make sense, though. Selectively hitting military targets while sparing civilian infrastructure was a prudent tactic perfected after the U.S. experience in Afghanistan, Kosovo, and Desert Storm. Avoiding attacks against regular Iraqi military units was smart, because these forces were much less loyal to Saddam than the Special Republican Guard, Republican Guard, and fedayeen units. In the end, the shock and awe concept was scaled back. Given the degree to which Iraqi forces had become accustomed to coalition bombing in the preceding decade, it is not clear that shock and awe would have worked as advertised in any event.

—Special Operations raids. These were actually more impressive than the early air campaign. Even before the formal expiration of President Bush's forty-eight-hour deadline to Saddam, dozens of small special operations teams were deploying throughout much of Iraq and beginning to attack key sites. They disrupted Iraqi command and control, seized oil infrastructure, took hold of airfields in western Iraq in regions where SCUD missiles might have been launched at Israel, and prepared the way for regular coalition forces. These operations were brave, creative, and successful.

—Bypassing southeastern cities while rushing to Baghdad. This approach was not new; it dates back to Germany's blitzkriegs of World War II. But it became controversial when critics wondered if we had enough boots and tanks on the ground to carry out so rapid a move. The criticism was right, yet exaggerated. In a worst case, waiting a couple of weeks for the 4th Mechanized Infantry Division and other units to arrive would have done little harm to the broader strategy.

—Decimating air-ground attacks against the Republican Guard. By the last days of March and early days of April, U.S. forces were severely damaging Iraqi Republican Guard divisions deployed outside of Baghdad. Saddam made a major mistake in keeping them there, and his forces paid an enormous price. There were some tactical innovations on the part of the coalition. Basically, though, that fight was won by sheer military excellence and a devastating display of combined-arms warfare on the part of U.S. Army, Air Force, Navy, and Marine Corps personnel.

—The fights for Baghdad and Basra. These were very well done. Neither protracted patience nor immediate all-out attack would have been wise. Attempting to seize the cities quickly would probably have produced high casualties. Waiting patiently for reinforcements would have given Saddam's forces confidence as well as time to regroup and devise new tactics. So the middle ground—using increasingly assertive "reconnaissance-in-force" operations to gain information, disrupt Saddam's forces, embolden the Iraqi population to resist Saddam's regime, and engage selectively in firefights against elite Iraqi forces—was the right way to go.

Lessons for Future Defense Planning

The war to overthrow Saddam had two principal outcomes that are relevant to future defense planning.

First, the war demonstrated that high-technology systems are important, but excellence in traditional soldiering, ranging from combined-arms warfare to urban combat, still matters a great deal. This means that no radical or extreme ideas about changes in warfare should be adopted as lessons of the conflict.

After satellite-guided bombs and special forces stole the show in Afghanistan, tanks and infantry troops starred as much as anything in Operation Iraqi Freedom. Coalition forces were just as large, relative to the size of their Iraqi foe as they were in Desert Storm in 1991. The Powell Doctrine, which called for engaging in combat only with overwhelming force, was hardly repudiated by the Iraq war.

Second, although Saddam's regime is no longer a threat, a two-war capability remains prudent. The Iraq war provides no grounds for a radical change in the size or the composition of the U.S. military. While the list of likely contingencies may now include fewer possible wars in which large ground forces would likely be needed, several scenarios could require substantial Army and Marine contributions. A war in Korea is not out of the question. At the same time, more speculatively but hardly implausibly, stabilization missions may be required in a place like South Asia (after an Indo-Pakistani war over Kashmir, for example, or a partial collapse of Pakistan) or in parts of Indonesia or the Philippines (should instability or terrorism become a problem on some parts of their archipelagos, for example). For the coming one to five years, stabilizing Iraq is itself likely to require substantial U.S. ground forces—at least one to two divisions at a time, necessitating a rotation base of at least three to six divisions to sustain that effort over a period of years.

Conclusion

Whether Americans like it or not, global security and stability hinge on their willingness to support a robust American military establishment. Without the U.S. military, much of today's troubled world would be less peaceful and prosperous than it is. That the United States spends more on defense than any other country is not surprising. We can afford to do so,

Table 11-5. *Estimated Pentagon Costs in the War on Terrorism, 2002–04 and After*[a]
Billions of dollars

Category of expense	2002[b]	2003 (estimated)	2004 (and thereafter)
Combat air patrols within U.S.	1.5	0.75	0.75
Airport, other domestic security	0.5	0.1	0.1
Base protection, U.S. and abroad	4.0	4.0	4.0
Intelligence, other costs	4.0	4.0	4.0
War in Afghanistan, related operations elsewhere	21	10	0
War in Iraq	0	50–75	0
Postwar mission in Iraq	0	10–20	15–25
Northern Command Headquarters	0	0.2	0.2
Total	31	80–115	25–35

Sources: Dave Moniz, "Fewer Jet Patrols over U.S. Sought," *USA Today*, January 15, 2002, p. 1; Correspondence from Media Relations, National Guard Bureau Public Affairs Office, November 14, 2001, and April 22, 2002; Congressional Budget Office, *Costs of Operation Desert Shield* (1991); Department of Defense, "FY 2002 Supplemental Request to Continue the Global War on Terrorism" (March 2002); Tony Capaccio, "Afghan War, Defense Cost $6.4 Billion since September 11, Pentagon Says," Bloomberg.com, January 22, 2002.

a. This table excludes the costs of national ballistic missile defense and possible future national cruise-missile defense.

b. In the last three weeks of fiscal year 2001 and 2002, the Pentagon received about $31 billion in additional funds for the struggle against terrorism: $13.8 billion in a 2001 emergency supplemental, $3.4 in the first 2002 emergency supplemental, and $14 billion in a later supplemental in July 2002.

and we are generally getting our money's worth. Radical reductions in defense expenditures are an option only if Americans are willing to take their chances with a world more dangerous than it already is.

Secretary of Defense Donald Rumsfeld's proposed strategic and budget plan, however, would push the military budget higher than is warranted. Recent increases in defense spending have been justified, particularly in the aftermath of September 11. But the war on terrorism does not explain most of the additional increases the Bush administration still seeks (see table 11-5). Congress should recognize the elements of extravagance and correct them. Further real spending increases need not be large. American power, after all, rests on economic strength, not just on the might of our armed forces.

Notes

1. Rumsfeld stated an intention to retain, at least for the foreseeable future, 10 active-duty Army divisions, roughly 20 Air Force fighter wings (specifically, 46 active squadrons and 38 reserve squadrons, with 4 squadrons being in the typical wing), 3 Marine Corps divisions and associated air wings, 12 Navy aircraft carriers and 11 associated air wings, 116 additional surface combatants, 55 attack submarines, and more than 100 bombers. That agenda includes three major fighter jet programs, two major attack helicopters, submarine and destroyer and aircraft carrier programs, an Army plan to develop medium-weight forces in contrast to its current heavy and light forces, the V-22 Osprey tilt-rotor aircraft for the Marine Corps, and many other weapons systems with a total price tag approaching $1 trillion. See Secretary of Defense Donald H. Rumsfeld, "Quadrennial Defense Review Report," Department of Defense, September 30, 2001 [available at www.defenselink.mil], pp. 22–23; and U.S. Department of Defense, "News Release: Fiscal 2004 Department of Defense Budget," February 3, 2003 [available at www.defenselink.mil].

2. See, for example, John G. Ikenberry, "Institutions, Strategic Restraint, and the Persistence of American Postwar Order," *International Security*, vol. 23, no. 3 (Winter 1998/99), pp. 43–78; Michael W. Doyle, *Ways of War and Peace: Realism, Liberalism, and Socialism* (W.W. Norton, 1997).

3. See Richard H. Ullman, *Securing Europe* (Princeton University Press, 1991).

4. William C. Wohlforth, "The Stability of a Unipolar World," *International Security*, vol. 24, no. 1 (Summer 1999), pp. 5–41.

5. The allies contributed more than many Americans acknowledge, but it is hard to imagine the Europeans' providing enough combat punch to produce the desirable outcomes that occurred in Bosnia in 1995 and Kosovo in 1999. For more on these conflicts, see Ivo H. Daalder, *Getting to Dayton* (Brookings, 2000); Benjamin S. Lambeth, *NATO's Air War for Kosovo* (Santa Monica, Calif.: RAND, 2001); Tim Judah, *Kosovo: War and Revenge* (Yale University Press, 2000); General Wesley K. Clark, *Waging Modern War* (New York: Public Affairs, 2001).

6. See Aaron L. Friedberg, "Ripe for Rivalry: Prospects for Peace in a Multipolar Asia," and Richard K. Betts, "Wealth, Power, and Instability: East Asia and the United States after the Cold War," *International Security*, vol. 18, no. 3 (Winter 1993/1994).

7. See Thomas L. McNaugher, *Arms and Oil* (Brookings, 1985); Congressional Budget Office, *Limiting Conventional Arms Exports to the Middle East* (U.S. Congress, 1992).

8. Testimony by William M. Bellamy, Principal Deputy Assistant Secretary, Bureau of African Affairs, Department of State, before the House Committee on International Relations, Subcommittee on Africa, July 12, 2001; Eric G. Berman and Katie E. Sams, *Peacekeeping in Africa: Capabilities and Culpabilities* (Geneva, Switzerland: United Nations Institute for Disarmament Research, 2000), pp. 267–376.

9. For backup on those estimates, see John E. Peters and Howard Deshong, *Out of Area or Out of Reach? European Military Support for Operations in Southwest Asia* (Santa Monica, Calif.: RAND, 1995); Michael O'Hanlon, "Transforming NATO: The Role of European Forces," *Survival*, vol. 39, no. 3 (Autumn 1997), pp. 5–15; Congressional Budget Office, *NATO Burdensharing after Enlargement* (Washington, 2001).

10. For more on this, see James M. Lindsay and Michael E. O'Hanlon, *Defending America: The Case for Limited National Missile Defense* (Brookings, 2002), pp. 17–20; James M.

Lindsay and Michael E. O'Hanlon, "Limited National and Allied Missile Defense," *International Security*, vol. 26, no. 4 (Spring 2002), pp. 190–96.

11. Congressional Budget Office, *Estimated Costs and Technical Characteristics of Selected National Missile Defense Systems* (Washington, 2002).

12. See Ashton B. Carter and William J. Perry, *Preventive Defense* (Brookings, 1999), pp. 8–64.

13. Laurinda Zeman, *Making Peace while Staying Ready for War* (Washington: Congressional Budget Office, 1999), p. 10.

14. The text statement is based on the most widely accepted estimates of actual expenditures, as opposed to misleadingly low official figures. U.S. government estimates of China's military spending are about twice those produced by the International Institute for Strategic Studies. See Arms Control and Disarmament Agency, *World Military Expenditures and Arms Transfers 1996* (1997), p. 65. For an explanation of the methodologies involved, see pp. 186–92; and International Institute for Strategic Studies, *The Military Balance 1995/96* (London: Oxford University Press, 1995), pp. 270–75.

15. Bates Gill and Michael O'Hanlon, "China's Military, Take 3," *National Interest*, no. 58 (Winter 1999/2000), p. 118.

16. William S. Cohen, "The Security Situation in the Taiwan Strait," Report to Congress pursuant to the FY99 Appropriations Bill (Department of Defense, 1999), p. 11.

17. International Institute for Strategic Studies, *The Military Balance 1999/2000* (London: Oxford University Press, 1999), pp. 187–88; Cohen, "The Security Situation in the Taiwan Strait," p. 9; William S. Cohen, "Future Military Capabilities and Strategy of the People's Republic of China," Report to Congress pursuant to the FY98 National Defense Authorization Act (Department of Defense, 1998), pp. 15–16; and Edward B. Atkeson, "The People's Republic of China in Transition: An Assessment of the People's Liberation Army," Land Warfare Paper 29, Institute of Land Warfare, Association of the U.S. Army, Alexandria, Va., 1998, p. 11.

18. In the words of one Pentagon assessment, "China probably has never conducted a large-scale amphibious exercise which has been fully coordinated with air support and airborne operations." Cohen, "Future Military Capabilities and Strategy of the People's Republic of China," p. 15.

19. Richard A. Bitzinger, "Going Places or Running in Place? China's Efforts to Leverage Advanced Technologies for Military Use," in Colonel Susan M. Puska, ed., *People's Liberation Army After Next* (Carlisle, Pa.: U.S. Army War College, 2000), pp. 9–54.

20. See Tim Huxley and Susan Willett, *Arming East Asia*, Adelphi Paper 329 (Oxford: Oxford University Press, 1999), pp. 75–77.

21. Lieutenant General Patrick M. Hughes, "Global Threats and Challenges: The Decades Ahead," Statement for the Congressional Record, Defense Intelligence Agency, Washington, February 1999, p. 10; Avery Goldstein, "Great Expectations: Interpreting China's Arrival," *International Security*, vol. 22, no. 3 (Winter 1997/98), p. 46; and John Wilson Lewis and Xue Litai, "China's Search for a Modern Air Force," *International Security*, vol. 24, no.1 (Summer 1999), p. 87. The country's attack submarine fleet is large but includes only nine vessels that could be viewed as relatively modern—and five of those, in the nuclear-powered Han class, are said to be noisy and unreliable. Eric McVadon, "PRC Exercises, Doctrine and Tactics Toward Taiwan: The Naval Dimension," in James R. Lilley and Chuck Downs, eds., *Crisis in the Taiwan Strait* (Washington: National Defense

University, 1997), p. 261. The People's Liberation Army is likely to add only twenty to thirty top-notch fighter aircraft to its air force annually in the years ahead. It is having trouble completing the development of its indigenous F-10 fighter program and may not be able to produce such aircraft until after 2010, if the program succeeds at all. There are doubts about China's ability to maintain and effectively operate even the modest number of advanced fighter jets it will be able to acquire. Kenneth W. Allen, "PLAAF Moderniza-tion: An Assessment," in Lilley and Downs, eds., *Crisis in the Taiwan Strait*, pp. 232–40; Jonathan Brodie, "China Moves to Buy More Russian Aircraft, Warships, and Sub-marines," *Jane's Defence Weekly,* December 22, 1999, p. 15; and Office of Naval Intelli-gence, *Worldwide Challenges to Naval Strike Warfare* (U.S. Navy, 1996), p. 29.

22. Thomas J. Christensen, "Posing Problems without Catching Up: China's Rise and Challenges for U.S. Security Policy," *International Security*, vol. 25, no. 4 (Spring 2001), pp. 5–40.

23. See, most notably, Admiral William A. Owens with Ed Offley, *Lifting the Fog of War* (New York: Farrar, Straus, and Giroux, 2000).

24. Martin Van Creveld, *Technology and War: From 2000 B.C. to the Present* (Free Press, 1989). Trevor Dupuy uses yet another categorization scheme, different from those of Kre-pinevich, Van Creveld, and others, to understand the history of military innovation. He groups all progress since 1800 together under the title of "the age of technological change." See Trevor N. Dupuy, *The Evolution of Weapons and Warfare* (Fairfax, Va.: HERO Books, 1984).

25. For sound warnings about both dismissing the "revolution in military affairs" hypothesis and jumping on the bandwagon too enthusiastically, see Colin S. Gray, *The American Revolution in Military Affairs: An Interim Assessment* (Camberley, England: Strate-gic and Combat Studies Institute, 1997), pp. 5–7, 33–34; for a reminder that militaries must always be innovating and changing, see Jonathan Shimshoni, "Technology, Military Advantage, and World War I: A Case for Military Entrepreneurship," *International Security*, vol. 15, no. 3 (Winter 1990/91), pp. 213–15.

26. National Defense Panel, *Transforming Defense* (Washington, 1997), pp. 7–8.

27. See Lane Pierrot, *The Long-Term Implications of Current Defense Plans* (Washing-ton: Congressional Budget Office, 2003). The CBO actually considers a range of possi-ble long-term procurement requirements, depending on various assumptions about cost and the service lives of equipment, with annual averages ranging from $85 billion to $130 billion.

28. See Lane Pierrot, *Budgeting for Defense: Maintaining Today's Forces* (Washington: Congressional Budget Office, 2000).

29. See Richard Fernandez, *What Does the Military "Pay Gap" Mean?* (Washington: Con-gressional Budget Office, 1999), esp. p. 32.

30. Gregory T. Kiley, *The Effects of Aging on the Costs of Operating and Maintaining Mil-itary Equipment* (Washington: Congressional Budget Office, 2001). Congressional Budget Office, *Paying for Military Readiness and Upkeep: Trends in Operation and Maintenance Spending* (U.S. Congress, 1997).

31. Some optimists tend to exaggerate the savings from possible base closings, however. Wayne Glass, *Closing Military Bases: An Interim Assessment* (Washington: Congressional Budget Office, 1996).

32. See Ellen Breslin-Davidson, *Restructuring Military Medical Care* (Washington, Congressional Budget Office, 1995); Russell Beland, *Accrual Budgeting for Military Retirees' Health Care* (Washington: Congressional Budget Office, 2002).

33. Robert F. Hale, *Promoting Efficiency in the Department of Defense: Keep Trying, but Be Realistic* (Washington: Center for Strategic and Budgetary Assessments, 2002).

STEVEN SIMON # 12

The New Terrorism

Presidents Bill Clinton and George W. Bush responded to the 1998 bombings of two U.S. embassies in East Africa and the 2001 attacks on the World Trade Center and the Pentagon by arguing that the perpetrators had used the cloak of religion to justify fundamentally cynical acts of violence. Blaming evil rather than religion for these catastrophes served useful domestic and foreign policy purposes for both presidents. They wanted to limit any anti-Muslim backlash at home and make it easier for Arab leaders and politically vulnerable European governments to cooperate with Washington.

The men responsible for the embassy bombings and the September 11 attacks, however, would not have recognized this portrait of themselves as secular evildoers using religion as a cover to legitimate indiscriminate attacks against political adversaries. They saw their attacks as acts of religious devotion. Mohammed Atta, the probable ringleader of the September 11 hijackers, instructed his fellow conspirators to see the attacks as a form of worship, conducted in God's name and in accordance with God's wishes. The enemy was the infidel, and the opposing ideology was "western culture."[1] It is the specifically religious nature of al Qaeda's motivation that distinguishes this group and makes it more threatening to the United States than other types of terrorist groups.

The "new" terrorism that al Qaeda represents may coexist with the eth-nonationalist and ideological political violence typical of the post–World War II period.[2] Indeed, it shares with traditional terrorism objectives that could be described as political, insofar as religiously motivated terrorists are vying for power in order to implement their goals. However, unlike the "old" terrorism of the Provisional Irish Republican Army (IRA), the Red Brigades, or even the Palestine Liberation Organization, al Qaeda and Islamic militant organizations that have adopted its worldview are moti-vated by religious concerns. Some within this broad movement find in an apocalyptic narrative the explanation for their oppression and the promise of redemption. For them, a charismatic leader like Osama bin Laden can acquire a messianic cast. The combination of apocalypticism and messia-nism can be particularly incendiary.

While the new terrorists do have secular political objectives in mind, they express these interests as religious issues. The new terrorists see them-selves as sacred warriors engaged in a cosmic struggle. In contrast, while a traditional terrorist group like the IRA may be fueled by historical Catholic-Protestant enmity, its overriding objective—a united Ireland—is unabashedly secular. Al Qaeda certainly wants to purge the Middle East of American political, military, and economic influence, but this goal is sub-sidiary to a far more sweeping religious agenda: a "defensive jihad" to exter-minate a rival system that is seen as an existential threat to Islam. Because the conditions that gave rise to the new terrorism that al Qaeda represents are likely to endure for many years, understanding them and their implica-tions for policy is imperative. This chapter probes both the historical and the policy domains to highlight some of the key issues facing the United States.

The Fabric of the New Terrorism

The rise of religiously motivated terrorism has been extensively docu-mented. Its most important element is the organic connection between religious precepts and the pursuit of mass casualties, first noted in the 1990s by RAND Corporation terrorism expert Bruce Hoffman.[3] Mono-theistic faiths such as Judaism, Christianity, and Islam make exclusive claims to valid identity and access to salvation. The violent imagery em-bedded in their sacred texts and the centrality of sacrifice in their liturgical traditions establish the legitimacy of killing as an act of worship with redemptive qualities. These narratives often ordain the annihilation of rivals and forbid the taking of prisoners or booty. The enemy must be erad-icated, not merely suppressed.

In periods of deep cultural despair, eschatology—speculation in the form of apocalyptic stories about the end of history and the dawn of the kingdom of God—can capture the thinking of a religious group. In some instances, apocalyptic communities adopt a relatively passive stance, keeping themselves pure for the new era and watching for "signs of the hour." In other cases, the community might initiate the great epochal battle to show itself worthy of God's intervention. History abounds with instances of religious communities' immolating themselves and causing terrible suffering in an attempt to spur the onset of a messianic era.[4] The sacred narratives of these apocalyptic communities explain their oppressed condition as the result of their infidelity to God. These narratives also furnish a ready formula for future triumph. In the Jewish tradition, the archetypal event is the Hasmonean victory over Syrian-Greek invaders;[5] for Christians, it is the story of the Book of Revelation, which transforms Christ into a ruthless warrior; and in Islam, it is the magnificent conquests of the seventh and eighth centuries and the victory of Saladin over the Crusaders in the twelfth century. In each case, a religious community believed it had reached the nadir of degradation and was on the brink of a resurgence that would culminate in a final triumph over its enemies. This prospect warranted and required violence on a massive scale. It is this impulse that makes weapons of mass destruction (WMD) so appealing to members of apocalyptic groups.

Recent history has also witnessed extraordinary episodes of messianic zeal. In the mid-1980s, a group of Israeli settlers, convinced that salvation must be at hand after the profound disappointment of the Camp David Accords, plotted to destroy the Dome of the Rock, the eighth-century mosque that sits atop the Haram al Sharif in Jerusalem. They prepared for three years, assembled powerful explosives, and devised a plan to gain access to the site. The conspirators apparently saw the presence of the mosque on the Temple Mount as a sign of Jewish sinfulness and believed that its destruction would spark an Arab invasion. This in turn would necessitate an Israeli nuclear response, which would result in the Armageddon the Bible says will precede the end of history. They believed that the normal rules of politics would be suspended in the wake of this audacious act. The kingdom of God would be established, and Jewish supremacy would be restored in the lands conquered by the ancient Israelite kings. The fact that the plot was never carried out because the conspirators could not get rabbinical permission underscores the religious motivation of the proposed attack.[6]

Although Timothy McVeigh seems not to have regarded himself as a religious person, he thought that white Christian civilization in the United

States was on the verge of catastrophe, and he was attracted to like-minded groups with an explicitly religious orientation. Inspired by the Turner Diaries, a popular modern apocalypse penned by the late William L. Pierce under the pseudonym of Andrew Macdonald, McVeigh believed that destruction of the Murrah Federal Building in Oklahoma City would ignite a popular revolution in the United States that would stave off catastrophe, decimate Jews and other miscreants, and establish perfect justice and tranquility in a racially and religiously pure America. Like other apocalypticists, he was convinced that history had reached a tipping point and that great contending forces could be realigned by a decisive act. Since the Oklahoma City attack, U.S. authorities have disrupted numerous conspiracies intent on creating catastrophic damage or revolution, including an attempt in 1999 to detonate two twelve-million-gallon propane tanks just outside Sacramento.

The Tokyo sarin gas attacks in 1995 provided intriguing evidence of the effect Christian apocalyptic thinking can have on a nonmonotheistic faith—in this case Buddhism. The leader of Aum Shinrikyo, the group that carried out the attacks, was obsessed with the prospect of an imminent end to the existing world order. He had directed his followers to use chemical and biological weapons defensively at least twice before the subway attack to stymie law enforcement investigations into the group's activities. Although his precise motive for precipitating the 1995 attack has not been determined, he seems to have intended either to initiate the final confrontation between good and evil or to win converts by vindicating his own claims that such weapons would be used in Armageddon. Whichever the case, the crucial factor was his conviction that the world was in crisis, that the apocalypse was imminent, and that he or his group would survive in a messianic role.[7]

The Doctrinal Potency of al Qaeda

The brand of thinking that animated the Israeli settlers, Timothy McVeigh, and Aum Shinrikyo surfaces in al Qaeda's ideology and actions. However, al Qaeda's thinking includes other important components that make it significantly more dangerous. To fully grasp the worldview of al Qaeda and its leader, Osama bin Laden, it is essential to start with the writings of a thirteenth-century Muslim jurisconsult, Taqi al-Din ibn Taymiyya.

Ibn Taymiyya was a professor of Hanbali law, one of the four major schools of Sunni Islamic jurisprudence, and a prolific writer on religious and public policy matters. Two of his concepts have exercised an enormous influence over Islamic revolutionary or reform movements. The first was his elevation of jihad—not the spiritual struggle that many modern Muslims take it to be, but physical combat—to the rank of the canonical five pillars of Islam (declaration of faith, prayer, almsgiving, Ramadan fast, and pilgrimage to Mecca). The second was his argument that jihad was justified not just against external, non-Muslim opponents, but also against Muslim rulers who do not enforce *sharia* law in their domains. By elevating jihad's importance and reforging it as a weapon to use against Muslims as well as infidels, ibn Taymiyya planted a seed of revolutionary violence in the heart of Islamic thought.

As the Ottoman Empire consolidated, ibn Taymiyya's arguments fell into disfavor. They were revived first in Arabia in the eighteenth century by Muhammad ibn Abd al-Wahhab, who found in ibn Taymiyya's writings arguments that resonated with his own desire to return Islam to its basics. Ibn Abd al-Wahhab's efforts to promote his beliefs made him powerful enemies. He eventually sought the help and protection of a local sheikh, Muhammad ibn Saud. An alliance of power and faith was born. Over the next two hundred years it produced the modern Saudi state as well as Saudi Wahhabism, Islam's most rigid and puritanical branch.

Saudi Arabia's own history shows that Ibn Abd al-Wahhab's jihadist impulse and high standard of piety could make government rule difficult. In 1929, the new Saudi state had to forcibly suppress a revolt by Wahhabi militants known as the Ikhwan. Fanatical Wahhabi puritanism, however, did not die. Instead, it fused with an outbreak of apocalyptic speculation, prompted by the 1,500th anniversary of the *hijra* in 1979, to produce the seizure of the Grand Mosque in Mecca. During the takeover, an Ikhwan warrior was declared the messiah before thousands of hajjis. Many believed his claim. Days passed before the apocalyptic rebels could be rooted out of the mosque cellars, a bloody task accomplished with the technical assistance of French special forces.[8]

Ibn Taymiyya's ideas were revived again in Egypt in the mid-twentieth century by Sayyid Qutb, a writer and former government official. Qutb married ibn Taymiyya's arguments about jihad and illegitimate Muslim rulers to the idea of *jahiliyya*. Muhammad had used the term *jahiliyya* to denote the barbarity that existed in Arabian society before Allah's revelation. Some twentieth-century Islamic thinkers used it to describe Muslim lands of their own era that, they argued, submitted to human law and ignored God's law. In merging these ideas, Qutb argued that human rule—

government that legislates its own behavior—is illegitimate. Muslims must answer to God alone. The supremacy of human law, especially by those who paid lip service to Islam, was apostasy; the very presumption that there could be human rule over Muslims implied a denial of God's authority over humankind and was therefore heretical. Such a government was the legitimate target of jihad. A truly Islamic society could arise only by destroying *jahili*—non-Islamic and therefore barbarous—rule. The responsibility of jihad would fall to a vanguard of true believers, who would kill the *jahili* rulers and lead fellow Muslims into a new golden age.

Egyptian president Gamal Abdel Nasser had Qutb hanged in 1965. However, Qutb's incendiary ideas underpinned two decades of violence in Egypt, including the assassination of Anwar Sadat in 1981, a low-key war against Coptic Christians, and the slaughter of western tourists at Luxor in 1997. The Egyptian government eventually and bloodily suppressed the groups that carried out this campaign—Egyptian Islamic Jihad (EIJ) and al Gamaat al Islamiyya, or the "Islamic Group" (IG). The surviving militants fled abroad, well aware of Cairo's notoriety for torture and summary execution and taking advantage of Europe's lax laws regarding asylum.

Al Qaeda merges the Egyptian and Saudi sides of the jihad movement. The Egyptian side is represented by second-in-command Ayman al-Zawahiri, who served three years in prison following Sadat's assassination; the Saudi side is represented by bin Laden himself. As the theological descendants of ibn Taymiyya, Ibn Abd al-Wahhab, and Qutb, they see themselves as engaged in a legitimate jihad against both infidels and apostate Muslim rulers. They also see themselves as having the religious sanction necessary to carry out their jihad.

Al Qaeda's emphasis on jihad strikes an increasingly popular chord in parts of the Muslim world. Islamic bookshops and websites, as well as sermons in mosques, all offer stories redolent of apocalyptic thinking. Some of these stories tell of cataclysmic battles between Islam and the United States, NATO, Israel, and sometimes the European Union. As in the scriptural precedents for these stories, global battles seesaw between infidel and Muslim victory until some devastating act, usually the destruction of New York by nuclear weapons, brings the Armageddon to an end and leads the survivors to convert to Islam.[9] Echoes of this motif, as well as other characteristics of apocalyptic narrative—such as dream interpretation, the participation of angels in battle, and the mass conversion of infidels to the faith of the triumphant believer—can be seen in al Qaeda's videos and in texts such as Mohammed Atta's last instruction.[10]

Of course, not every Muslim in the Middle East reads such stories, and not everyone who does takes them literally. But some people do see apocalyptic imagery as an accurate vision of the future and will attempt to enact it. Indeed, the destruction of the twin towers may have been one such attempt.[11] Furthermore, the historical record shows that apocalyptic movements, especially when animated by a messianic leader, try to realize their eschatological visions even in the face of contradictory evidence and hopeless circumstances. In the process, they can wreak considerable havoc.

Fields of Jihad: Al Qaeda's Geopolitical Reach

There are many reasons why the Islamic world is such fertile ground for al Qaeda's radical message.[12] These include low or nonexistent economic growth in many Islamic countries, falling wages and increasing unemployment, low literacy rates and low yield from investment in education, relentless but unsustainable urban growth, and diminishing environmental resources, especially water.[13] These problems coexist with resentment against the intrusion of offensive western ideas, habits, and commercial products. Television coverage of violence perpetrated on Muslims in Palestine and elsewhere reinforces a widespread sense of injustice and victimization and in turn underlines Islam's inability to defend itself. The absence of alternatives to the mosque as a forum for expressing political discontent explains why these primarily secular grievances gain a religious voice. However, the mobilization of religious imagery and terminology transforms secular issues into substantively religious ones. This process puts otherwise negotiable political issues beyond the realm of bargaining and biases political processes toward violent outcomes.

The political power of religion in the Islamic world has led some pivotal states, in particular Egypt and Saudi Arabia, to use religious symbols to buttress their own legitimacy. By validating the religious transmogrification of a secular agenda, however, these governments have perversely conferred authority on the very clerical opposition that threatens their power and impedes the modernization programs that might, over the long term, improve the quality of life for their citizens. This validation also implicitly certifies the jihadists' justifications for violence. The Islamists, of course, failed in their bids to seize power in Egypt, Saudi Arabia, and elsewhere in the Arab world. These governments controlled the political process, used torture and blackmail, and doled out concessions to siphon off antiregime sentiment. Their apparent victory might prove illusory, however, as

Islamists dominate public discourse and shape the debate on foreign and domestic policy.[14]

The need to cater to Islamist sentiment to preserve their own security dictates that many Arab governments tolerate and even endorse extreme anti-American views. At the same time, strategic circumstances compel these states to provide diplomatic or other practical support for U.S. policies that offend public sensibilities. It is no small wonder that Egyptians and Saudis constitute the backbone of al Qaeda and that Saudi Arabia spawned most of the September 11 attackers.

Egypt and Saudi Arabia are not the only countries that are home to religiously motivated militants. Islamists have now dispersed to multiple "fields of jihad" with striking geographical scope. Al Qaeda developed ties to Sunni radicals in Lebanon and has attempted to forge an alliance with Hamas in Gaza and the West Bank.[15] An underground Islamist group in Jordan worked with al Qaeda on the unsuccessful Millennium Plot in 2000 to destroy a major hotel in Amman and to massacre Christian tourists at various sites. More recently, militants connected to al Qaeda have engaged Jordanian forces in running gunfights in Ma'an. In Southeast Asia, Afghan-trained Indonesians and Malaysians implicated in the September 11 attacks conspired with Singaporean Muslims to carry out large-scale terrorist attacks against U.S., British, and Israeli installations in Singapore. They have also staged attacks against churches in the Philippines. By cultivating close ties to a weak regime in Jakarta, jihadists have gained protection against arrest or extradition. They were therefore unhindered in the planning and execution of the October 2002 Bali bombing that killed 187 and wounded hundreds of others.

In Central Asia, al Qaeda has penetrated, funded, and indoctrinated the Islamic Movement of Uzbekistan, which has become a full-fledged jihadist organization. In Pakistan, jihadists with apocalyptic instincts nearly achieved their goal of provoking a nuclear exchange between India and Pakistan.[16] There is evidence that former senior officials and officers of Pakistan's nuclear program met with bin Laden and discussed the feasibility of a so-called dirty bomb.[17] In North Africa, the jihadists of the Algerian Armed Islamic Group (GIA), who venerate ibn Taymiyya and killed 40,000 Algerians in the 1990s, share al Qaeda's ideology and believe that all Algerian society is *jahili*. Although the group has been decimated, its religious ideology does not permit surrender. Residual slaughters still occur, and videotapes of GIA atrocities circulate widely in Europe as recruitment propaganda for the global jihad. East Africa emerged as a key field of jihad in the mid-1990s and was the site of two audacious attacks, one in August 1998 against U.S. embassies in Kenya and Tanzania and another in November 2002 against a hotel and an airplane used by Israeli tourists. Each attack consisted of separate, simultaneous strikes, an al-Qaida signature.

Europe, with its growing Muslim population, may turn out to be the most crucial field of jihad. Virtually total lack of parliamentary representation, unequal access to education, employment, housing and social services, and the failure of societal integration have turned many young European Muslims against the states in which they live. The problem is especially severe in the United Kingdom. Approximately 3,000 British youths went to Afghanistan and Kashmir during the 1990s. Two polls in 2001 revealed that close to a majority of young Muslims felt no obligation to bear arms for Britain but would fight for bin Laden.[18] In radical mosques in the United Kingdom, preachers tell their congregations that they are living in the Abode of War. The Muslim prison population in the United Kingdom doubled in the 1990s. Angry young Muslims become radicalized in jail, and some alienated Christian youths, like the Shoe Bomber, Richard Reid, convert. If there were any doubts about the ability of al Qaeda or any of its successors to be both far-flung and in close contact, these sobering facts put them to rest.

The United States remains the prime target of al Qaeda's religious zeal and apocalyptic mentality. Suleiman Abu Ghaith, the al Qaeda spokesman, has said that there can be no truce until the group has killed 4 million Americans, whereupon there will be an opportunity for others to convert to Islam.[19] Al Qaeda videotapes recovered in Afghanistan in August 2002 show that the group has been seeking WMD and has experimented with chemical and perhaps biological weapons.

Blunting the Jihadists' Appeal

Fundamental causes of the new terrorism, to the extent that one can speak of them, defy direct and immediate remedial action. Although Egypt's birth rate has declined slightly, the population in the Middle East as a whole will increase by about one-third over the next fifteen years. In places like Gaza, it will grow by nearly 70 percent. At the same time, the median age is dropping. Given the correlation between youth and political instability, the youth bulge embedded in the overall population increase raises the potential for unrest and radicalization.

Potable water is projected to decrease by two-thirds by 2015. Cities will likely grow much faster than governments' capacity to enhance social welfare programs, let alone extend vital infrastructures for sanitation, transportation, housing, power, and water. Even in oil-producing countries, where unemployment is already high, the combination of a natural cap on energy prices, inflated wage structures, poor education, and heavy government subsidies will ensure that socioeconomic conditions deteriorate in the medium term.[20] In many areas of the Muslim world, there will be only one refuge from filth, noise, and heat: the mosque.[21]

Economists agree that the way out of the morass is to develop institutions that facilitate the distribution of capital and create opportunity. They do not know, however, how to create such institutions. Western countries can help diminish poverty somewhat with foreign aid and technical assistance, but these measures will not correct structural problems. The transition from agricultural to industrial economies has invariably been plagued by violence, as the experiences of Russia and China make clear. Postwar experience suggests that the corresponding transition in the Middle East is not likely to differ, despite the region's unique history and fossil fuel endowment.

Political scientists also do not know how to persuade people in the Middle East to view the United States more favorably, thereby substantially shrinking the pool of disaffected youth from which terrorists recruit. The obstacles go beyond language. Decades of official lies and a controlled press have made Arab publics understandably skeptical of the claims of any government, especially one already presumed to be hostile to Muslim interests. Western news media similarly lack credibility. Only al-Jazeera and even more popular networks like Middle East Broadcasting, which do not offer evenhanded coverage, are heeded. Moreover, people assess the truth of information they receive on the basis of its chain of transmission. If the individual links are held to be trustworthy, then the transmitted claim is taken to be true, even if it might seem absurd to an outsider. This explains the tenacity of the widespread belief that the Israeli intelligence agency, Mossad, destroyed the World Trade Center on September 11.

Further compounding the problem is the fact that many respected critics of the United States in places like Saudi Arabia have considerable credibility of their own. They demonstrate an ostensibly profound understanding of U.S. policies and society while offering a powerful and internally consistent explanation for their country's descent from the all-powerful, rich supplier of oil to the West to a debt-ridden, faltering economy, protected by Christian troops and kowtowing to Israel. These are difficult narratives to counter, especially in a society where education about the West has diminished in quality, travel abroad is increasingly constrained by budgetary and cultural factors, and one out of five university students majors in religious studies.

The prominent role that clerics play in shaping public opinion presents additional obstacles to improving perceptions of America. The people who represent the greatest terrorist threat to the United States follow the preaching and guidance of Salafi clerics—the Muslim equivalent of fundamentalists in the Christian context. Neither secular Americans nor even non-Salafi American Muslims are considered legitimate interlocutors in Salafi discourse. Although some Salafi preachers have forbidden the waging of jihad because it harms Muslim interests, their underlying assumptions are that jihad *qua* holy war against non-Muslims is fundamentally valid and that governments in the Islamic world that do not enforce *sharia* must be opposed. The absence of an authoritative moderate clerical establishment amplifies this basic problem. Finally, the general shift of religious discourse to the right has forced the remaining institutional sources of orthodoxy in the same direction. Thus there are no moderate institutions that could help ensure the propagation in the mosque of a more sympathetic attitude toward the United States.

The prognosis for effecting broad societal change that diminishes the jihadists' appeal, therefore, is poor. The world is getting more religious; Islam is the fastest growing faith; religious expression is generally becoming more assertive and apocalyptic thinking more prominent.[22] Apocalyptic ends require spectacular means, which WMD attacks promise. These weapons are certain to become more widely available to groups that believe they are engaged in a cosmic war. In the meantime, democratization is at a standstill, and radicalizing poverty is likely to increase as resources diminish and populations grow larger and younger. Key governments in Egypt, Saudi Arabia, Pakistan, and Indonesia will be unwilling or unable to oppose antiwestern, religiously based popular feeling. Immigration, conversion, and inept social policies will intensify parallel trends in Europe. The West, in particular the United States, does not know how to inject, from the outside, institutional reform to improve economies that have disengaged from the globalization process, nor can it enforce democratization. Even if it could, the short-run risks to American interests would be large.

At least for now, dialogue does not appear to be an option because of dynamics within the Muslim world that are impervious to outside influence. Western cultural penetration that generates resentment—and which bears the face of America—will continue because of global market forces and the inability of western governments to control them.[23] Jihadists could conceivably argue that they have a concrete political agenda: cessation of U.S. support for Israel, the withdrawal of U.S. troops from Saudi Arabia, and a broader American disengagement from the Islamic world. But U.S. and allied conceptions of their strategic interests will make such demands difficult, if not impossible, to accommodate.

Reducing Vulnerability to the New Terrorism

In the face of a global adversary with maximal goals and in the absence of a bargaining option or means to redress severe economic and societal conditions that may or may not motivate attackers, the United States is confined primarily to a strategy of defense, deterrence by denial, and, where possible, preemption. Deterrence through the promise of retaliation is not possible with a group—or group of groups—that is widely dispersed, controls little or no territory, and invites attack both to prove its merit and to demonstrate to coreligionists that the West is indeed intent on subjugating Muslims.

By the mid-1990s, the possibility that terrorists might launch WMD attacks on U.S. soil was clear to the Clinton administration. Its Presidential Decision directives 39, 62, and 63 emphasized that in the absence of a localized, identifiable threat it would be essential to focus on remedying vulnerabilities, particularly in critical infrastructure and aviation.[24] A host of factors prevented the Clinton administration from fully implementing this broad guidance before it left office.[25] September 11 and the more recent confirmation of al Qaeda's pursuit of chemical weapons may alter perceptions of the strategic context sufficiently to prompt sustained efforts to provide greater security for the American homeland.

The possibility of a WMD attack on U.S. soil requires Americans to think differently about threats and how to respond. Surprise attack will be the natural order of things. After generations of effort to reduce the risk of surprise attack through national technical means and negotiated transparency measures, surprise is no longer something simply to be managed. The warning problem will be further intensified by the genuine creativity al Qaeda has shown, its experimental recruitment of Europeans and Americans, and its demonstrated ability to stage attacks from within the United

States. American planners will have to jettison wishful preconceptions that contributed to the shock of September 11. After that attack, senior U.S. officials said they had not judged al Qaeda capable of attacking U.S. territory and that they had examined the aviation threat, but only with respect to small commuter aircraft.

Comparable cognitive shackles explain America's failure to foresee the Japanese attack on Pearl Harbor. In that case, analysts understood that an attack was likely—as they did before September 11—but assumed it would take place in Southeast Asia rather than in Hawaii. Thomas C. Schelling's introduction to Roberta Wohstetter's classic work on Pearl Harbor sums up the problem this way: There "is a tendency in our planning to confuse the unfamiliar with the improbable. The contingency we have not considered seriously looks strange; what looks strange is therefore improbable; what is improbable need not be taken seriously."[26] Thinking carefully about the unlikely—"institutionalizing imaginativeness"—is by definition a paradox, but nonetheless essential.[27]

In a world where warning is scarce and invariably ambiguous, it will be necessary to probe the enemy both to put it off balance and to acquire evidence of its intentions. The United States has done this clandestinely against hostile intelligence agencies, occasionally with remarkable results. Al Qaeda is a harder target, so this approach will take time to cohere. Such probes, however, need not be confined to covert operations. They could, for example, take the form of military action against al Qaeda-affiliated cantonments, such as those in Yemen. Raids by special forces could yield documentary evidence, prisoners, materiel, and equipment that could illuminate al Qaeda planning, disrupt preoperational activity, and possibly derail terrorist attacks.[28] This is one feasible form of preemption. Preemptive strikes against WMD development, production, storage, or deployment sites, such as the one carried out in August 1998 on the al Shifa pharmaceutical plant in Khartoum, would constitute the other.

These are not the only conceptual departures the new terrorism will dictate. A decade of al Qaeda activity within the United States has erased the customary distinction between the domestic and the foreign in the domain of intelligence and law enforcement. Whatever the results of the establishment of a Department of Homeland Security, the relationship between the Central Intelligence Agency (CIA) and the Federal Bureau of Investigation (FBI)—or whatever may replace it—will have to change. Only a more integrated organization can adapt to the seamlessness of the transnational arenas in which terrorists operate.

The new threat will also require a rebalancing of civil liberties and security. How sweeping this process turns out to be will depend largely on whether there are successful attacks, or at least convincing attempts, in the future.[29] Although the death of privacy is already near, thanks to the properties of the Internet and the tenacity of marketers, expediting its demise and curtailing civil liberties will require the public's broad acceptance. If that is to happen, Americans will have to be convinced that these changes are unavoidable and limited to the need to deal with proximate threats. They will need to see bipartisan consensus in Congress and between Congress and the White House. They will also need to see clear evidence that politicians are committed to minimizing the rebalancing of civil liberties and security in the direction of security.

The new terrorism has also vitiated the distinction between the public and private sectors. Al Qaeda has targeted the American population and infrastructure and, as was widely noted after September 11, used our infrastructure against us. Reducing vulnerabilities will be essential, if only because the inevitability of ambiguity in warning would otherwise require a perpetual state of heightened readiness. Such readiness would impose unacceptable opportunity costs on the civilian world. It is one thing to upgrade and maintain readiness at a military installation in response to a warning; it is quite another to expect the American people to stay on the alert at a practically infinite number of potential targets.

An additional complication is civilian ownership of the infrastructure targeted by al Qaeda.[30] What the U.S. government does not own, it cannot completely defend. As the Clinton administration discovered with respect to aviation and computer networks, the owners do not necessarily share the government's perception that the terrorist threat is acute and are often in a political position to resist regulation. This epiphany generated the gospel of public-private partnership, which is only now finding acceptance in the realm of cybersecurity. This approach will have to be extended to all potentially vulnerable critical infrastructures in the United States. The delicate governmental process of obtaining the cooperation of corporate owners, monopolies, and even local authorities, however, will be impeded by an imperfect understanding of which infrastructures are truly critical and which apparently dispensable infrastructures interact to become critical.

Defense of these infrastructures will also present hair-raising challenges. The U.S. government is not on the lookout for Warsaw Pact armored regiments moving out of garrison or specially configured Soviet railway cars. It is looking for a lone individual in a visa line. This is a daunting task.

Unlike the armored regiment, which has one, known purpose—warfare—and an unmistakable configuration (tanks, armored personnel vehicles, and cargo vehicles) and whose location and equipment disclose the use for which it is intended (garrison duty, maintenance, exercise, or attack), officials do not know where to look or, more important, what that lone individual looks like.

Technology will simplify this needle-in-the-haystack problem to some extent by making it possible to collect and store detailed characteristics of large numbers of people and match these characteristics to the people in that visa line. Biometrics, data mining, superfast data processing, and video surveillance will be indispensable to identifying the terrorist before he (or she) reaches the target.[31] The lamentable cost of locating terrorists by archiving personal and distinctive information will be borne by a great mass of harmless individuals.[32]

In addition to locating people, the United States will need to devise ways to block or intercept WMD delivery vehicles. The United States cannot do this alone. The cruise-missile threat, for instance, requires the cooperation of suppliers, which means an active American role in expanding the remit of the Missile Technology Control Regime, which sets guidelines regarding the transfer of missiles and related technologies. The use of shipping containers to smuggle WMD will require new or improved technologies for bulk-cargo screening and tamper-proof seals as well as new procedures, such as loading shipping containers under observation and in "sterile" zones.[33] Terrorist use of crop dusters to disseminate toxins will require that security rules now affecting passenger carriers be extended to general aviation. Conversion kits now for sale (for about $75,000) that can effectively turn an airplane into a cruise missile or anthrax sprayer must be stringently controlled. Corresponding efforts are needed to reduce the large number of man-portable surface-to-air missiles now floating around the globe and to install in commercial aircraft countermeasures to disable them, even if such countermeasures are expensive.

Nuclear weapons components themselves must be kept out of terrorists' hands. The largest source of fissile material is in Russia. Cooperative Threat Reduction (CTR), a program under which the United States has been buying surplus fissile material or helping the Russians render it useless for weapons, is vital. Following through on the Bush administration's new commitment to this program with generous multiyear funding will be essential to American security. CTR is not a panacea, however. Other necessary measures include stanching the brain drain from Russia, paying for the elimination of plutonium, and stepping up security at storage sites in Russia and elsewhere. At the same time, U.S. policy must work to prevent North Korea and Pakistan from emerging as potential sources of nuclear material or weapons for terrorists.

Remote detection of WMD—especially nuclear materials—that have successfully reached the United States is crucial. Emergency response teams will need to be able to pinpoint the location of a device, identify its type, and know in advance how to render it inoperable once it is seized.[34] Local authorities will have to detect and identify biological and chemical agents that have been introduced into the environment. New techniques will be needed for rapid development and production of genetically engineered vaccines to stop local attacks from becoming national—and ultimately global—epidemics. Special medical units, which will be on standby to relieve local health-care personnel who become exhausted or are killed, will require nurturing.

Some offensive opportunities will exist for dealing with an elusive enemy. They will require impeccable intelligence, however, and this is difficult to generate. Afghanistan's remote jihadist training camps and the cohesion and tradecraft of the groups that constituted al Qaeda made penetration forbiddingly complicated. Nevertheless, the changing nature of al Qaeda creates opportunities. As the group disperses geographically and picks up Muslims and converts to Islam who have been long-term western residents, penetration may become easier. The more they look like us, the more we look like them. As the jihadists expand their pool of operatives, human intelligence—"humint"—may become more easily available to intrepid moles from American intelligence agencies or from liaison services in Europe and the Middle East. The presence of American convert John Walker Lindh among the jihadists in Afghanistan, the deployment of British convert Richard Reid as a field operative, and the apparent recruitment by al Qaeda of American convert Jose Padilla suggest intriguing possibilities for creative intelligence agencies.

Probes along the lines discussed earlier would also provide useful intelligence that could be integrated with newly acquired humint and the highly reliable signal intelligence—"sigint"—already being collected by the National Security Agency. Yet another source of potentially vital intelligence is the jihadists picked up by local authorities in foreign countries on the basis of intelligence provided by the United States and then shipped to their countries of origin (or, if under U.S. indictment, directly to the United States) for interrogation and presumably trial. This three-way choreography often works well and has led to the disclosure of jihadist attack plans. There are cases, however, in which the authorities of the country where the suspect is residing do not wish to permit an arrest, for fear of terrorist retaliation, domestic political problems, or diplomatic frictions with other countries. Fear of diplomatic repercussions or of a fracas on the ground in the process of what is frankly a kidnapping has also deterred the United States from exercising its asserted right to "render" such suspects into American custody. In the wake of September 11, the United States may want to reassess the risks and benefits of these extraordinary renditions.[35]

Without revoking the longstanding executive order prohibiting assassination, the United States should also consider targeted killing, to use the Israeli phrase, of jihadists known to be central to an evolving conspiracy to attack the United States or obtain WMD or who are attempting to carry out an attack. As a practical matter, the intelligence value of such a person alive generally outweighs the disruptive benefits of his death, assuming that U.S. or friendly intelligence services can be relied on to keep him under surveillance. But this will not always be the case. When it is not, targeted killing falls reasonably under the right to self-defense. A policy departure of this kind is unsavory. However, in a new strategic context, in which jihadists are intent on mass casualties, unsavory may not be a sensible threshold. The November 2002 assassination of al Qaeda operatives in Yemen with Hellfire missiles launched from a remote-controlled Predator suggests that the Bush administration has already crossed this line, as it has with some forms of torture.[36]

The organizational and technological demands of defensive and offensive measures to counter the new terrorism will cost a great deal of money in an era of federal budget deficits, looming crises in social security and health care, and ballooning defense spending. Adding to the budgetary crunch is the Bush administration's commitment to building an expansive missile defense system, which could cost upward of $200 billion over twenty-five years. This program will compete directly with as yet unknown funding requirements for homeland security and the war on terrorism. Other things being equal, the United States should have an effective defense against ballistic missile attack. The question is whether this is a more likely threat than jihadist use of WMD—delivered by plane, train, automobile, or the U.S. postal service—against the United States. In January 2002, George Tenet, the director of Central Intelligence, released a new National Intelligence Estimate that concluded the United States was more likely to be attacked by "ships, trucks, airplanes, or other means" than by ballistic missiles. The estimate also put the risk of attack by cruise missiles or unmanned aerial vehicles, which the planned missile defense system is not designed to counter, as higher than that from ballistic missiles.[37] More broadly, a sustainable homeland defense and the war on terrorism will depend on a reliable funding stream that does not crowd out nondefense programs essential to America's quality of life.

Broader Strategies for Dealing with the New Terrorism

The link between socioeconomic trauma in the Middle East and terrorism lies in the way that the imagery of poverty fuels the anger of middle-class terrorists. Revolutionaries from the mid-nineteenth century through the end of the twentieth were similarly motivated. The precise connection is far from transparent. Nevertheless, the United States will have to explore ways to improve the standard of living and the environment in poorer countries where government incapacity, illiteracy, and lack of infrastructure render indigenously generated economic restructuring and reform impossible. Institution building and development of basic skills and infrastructure should still be pursued, but not at the expense of assistance that more efficiently reduces the despair of downtrodden populations.

Allied Cooperation

International cooperation is indispensable to countering the jihadist threat. The United States cannot do it alone. This cliché becomes truer every day, as American counterterrorism officials secure authorization from more and more foreign governments to survey ports and terminals that ship cargo and passengers to the United States, and as al Qaeda, or its successors, disperses to more than sixty countries around the world.

Many of these countries will cooperate with the United States because it is in their self-interest to do so; they do not want jihadists on their soil any more than Americans do on theirs. A durable and effective counterterrorism campaign, however, requires not just bare-bones cooperation, but also cooperation at the political level and coordination of broad military, diplomatic, economic, and security policies. Bureaucracies must understand that cooperation with their American counterparts is expected. This kind of robust, wholesale working relationship is what produces vital large-scale initiatives: a common diplomatic approach toward problem states; a sustainable program of economic development for the Middle East; changes in domestic policies that lessen the appeal of jihadism to Muslim diaspora communities;

improvement of border controls; and tightened bonds among the justice ministries, among the law enforcement, customs, and intelligence agencies, and among special operations forces on the front lines. Whether this level of burden sharing can be generated and sustained depends on the prospective give and take among the players. Since September 11, the United States has not seemed too concerned about the sensitivities of its allies and, thus far, has not paid a serious penalty in terms of allied cooperation in the war against terrorism even as France, Germany, and others opposed the march to war in Iraq. The scale of the September 11 disaster and the Bush administration's blend of resolve and restraint in the war on terrorism have combined to offset the disappointment of America's allies in Washington's go-it-alone posture. However, as the war on terrorism grinds on, especially against the background of a war with Iraq that was deeply unpopular in much of the world and a postwar reconstruction effort that could go awry, goodwill may evaporate. To rebuild goodwill, the United States would be wise to forgo some its own preferences in matters related to trade and treaties in order to ensure allied support in the inevitable crises in the war on terrorism.

Although such bilateral horse trading usually involves a common currency—concessions by one party in the security realm are rewarded with security cooperation by the other—the challenge posed by the war on terrorism demands that the overall tenor of U.S. relations with other countries take a careful tone. America is in rather bad odor nowadays in much of the world, especially in the Middle East. Resentment abroad may perhaps be the unavoidable fate of being the lone superpower. Nevertheless, the more Washington can do to counter its villainous image, the more cooperation it will get from other governments sensitive to their own domestic public opinion.[38]

Israel and the Palestinians

Since the heyday of the Middle East peace process under Ehud Barak's Labor government in the late 1990s, the jihadists have exploited the Israeli-Palestinian conflict to boost their own popularity. The stratagem has worked. The jihadists are seen as sticking up for Palestinian rights while Arab governments do nothing. Direct, energetic U.S. diplomatic intervention would do much to take the wind out of jihadist sails. Such a tangible demonstration of the U.S. government's concern for the plight of Palestinians would also make it easier for Middle Eastern governments to cooperate with Washington in the war on terrorism.

Bush administration officials have been reluctant to get deeply involved in the Middle East peace process, in part because they believe President Clinton's concerted efforts to get an agreement at the 2000 Camp David summit were premature and contributed to the outbreak of the *intifada*. The Bush team is also pessimistic about prospects for agreement and fears becoming entangled in a drawn-out, venomous negotiation between irreconcilable parties. This entanglement, they worry, will distract them from higher priorities and embroil them in the domestic political disputes that inevitably arise when Israel comes under pressure from Washington. Taken together, these are powerful incentives to stay disengaged. Still, the administration has been drawn in by degrees and announced its support for the creation of a Palestinian state. If the war on terrorism is now America's highest priority, then more vigorous—and admittedly risky— involvement in the peace process is required. At this juncture, concern over the political hazards and distractions of intervention must be subordinated to the more urgent need to defang the jihadist argument that the United States is complicit in the murder of Palestinian Muslims.[39]

Democratization

The problems created by America's ties to authoritarian regimes are vexing because the structure of the international system of states requires governments to deal with other governments. The painful reality is that Washington must continue to engage with the regimes now in power in Cairo and in Riyadh. It can, however, try gingerly to renegotiate the implicit bargain that underpins its relations with both Egypt and Saudi Arabia.

The old bargain is structured something like this: Egypt supports the U.S. approach to the Middle East peace process, and Saudi Arabia provides oil at a reasonable price and takes Washington's side in its confrontation with Iraq. In return, Washington lets Egyptian and Saudi leaders run their countries the way they want, even if this entails the growth and export of Islamic militancy and the regimes' deflection of public discontent onto the United States and Israel. With jihadists in pursuit of nuclear weapons, this arrangement no longer looks appealing.

The new bargain should be negotiated along these lines: Cairo and Riyadh should begin to take measured risks to lead their publics gradually toward greater political responsibility and away from Islamist thinking (and action) through greater political participation and encouragement of secular opposition parties, freedom of expression, and judicial independence. Saudi Arabia should be asked to cease its Wahhabi-ization of the

Islamic world. Both countries should be pressed to reform their school cur-
ricula—and enforce standards—to ensure a better understanding of western history and to encourage respect for other cultures. At the same time,
they should focus more consistently on the welfare of their people, with
increased financial and technical assistance from the West. In this admittedly utopian scenario, the leaders of both countries should use their newly
won credibility as democratizers to challenge Islamist myths about the
United States and the supposed hostility of the West toward Islam. In sum,
the culture of demonization should be challenged across the board, with an
eye toward laying the groundwork for liberal democracy.

In this new bargain, the United States would establish contacts with
moderate opposition figures in Egypt, Saudi Arabia, and perhaps one or
two other Arab countries. These governments would object, and Washington would have to be ready for a backlash. Nor would such contacts guarantee the automatic respect of the opposition. When the Bush administration threatened Cairo in 2002 with a minor sanction in response to the
continued imprisonment of Saad Eddin Ibrahim, a noted academic
regarded as a regime opponent, Egyptians on the left and the right criticized the United States for interfering in Egypt's domestic affairs.

Nevertheless, encouraging civil society in this way promises two benefits. First, Washington would get a better sense of what is occurring on the
ground. Second, it would over time gain a measure of credibility with, and
perhaps even understanding from, its critics. For this effort to bear fruit,
however, the United States has to communicate its efforts throughout the
Middle East by using regional media efficiently, something for which there
is no tested strategy.[40] The key audience must be the young, technocratic
elite whose alienation from the United States leads them to tolerate if not
support terrorist attacks against America. As the Jordanian journalist Rami
Khouri has said, the issue is not the Arab street, but the Arab basement.[41]

Change will not come rapidly. Regimes in Cairo and Saudi Arabia face
problems, largely self-inflicted, that cannot be surmounted readily without
serious risks to their stability. An infatuation in the Arab world with great
quests impedes productive domestic policy initiatives.[42] Moreover, democratic transitions generally depend on reformers' within the regime establishing common cause with the moderate opposition. This depends, in turn,
on a high degree of trust and mutual confidence. The moderate opponents
of the regime must believe that the reformers can control the hardliners in
the military and security services. The reformers within the government
must believe that the moderate opposition can control its radical wing. They

must also be confident that the opposition's commitment to democracy is genuine. In the Middle East, where virtually all the opposition forces are Islamists of one stripe or another, such confidence is scarce. In the absence of this high degree of trust, neither party will run the risk of a "pacted transition," and the public will certainly be reluctant to support it.[43]

The United States, in any case, is not entirely free to insist on the new bargain. The ouster of Saddam Hussein makes it possible that Washington can play Baghdad off against Riyadh, thereby limiting the Saudi regime's leverage. Still, Saudi Arabia remains a major player in the Persian Gulf and in the broader Arab world.[44] Furthermore, reliance on Saudi Arabia's oil and its variable production capacity is not going away.[45] Egyptian cooperation vis-à-vis Israel will likewise remain essential, endowing Cairo with the strategic "rent" that helps the regime rule without the participation of its population.[46] Nevertheless, incremental change must start sometime and somewhere.[47] It will not happen without steady American pressure and persistent attempts to persuade rulers in Cairo and Riyadh that the long-term interests of their countries would be served best by a new bargain. Given the looming demographic, economic, and environmental trends facing the region, the sooner these new deals are struck, the better.

Conclusion

Al Qaeda presents the United States, and western democracies more generally, with a serious, possibly transgenerational threat, with causes that are multidimensional and difficult to address. The situation is hazardous, but not hopeless. The United States possesses enormous wealth, has capable allies, and stands on the leading edge of technological development that will be key to survival. A strategy that blends military, intelligence, law-enforcement, diplomatic, and economic tools will see America through.

For the next few years, the objective of such an integrated strategy should be to contain the threat, in much the same way that the United States contained Soviet power throughout the cold war. Al Qaeda and its emulators must be prevented from doing their worst, while the United States and its allies wear down their capabilities and undermine the support they derive from their religious followers. The United States, in particular, must counter the rhetoric of its own citizens who are prone to mirror the adversary's combative religious impulse with their own. Success will require broad domestic support for this containment strategy and the dedication of a strong coalition abroad. These two key ingredients—bipartisanship and prudent diplomacy—must ultimately be secured by whatever administration occupies the White House.

The challenge the United States faces is stiff, but it is no greater than the challenges the United States confronted in the twentieth century. The U.S. first reaction to September 11 is and indeed must remain its own self-defense: bolstering homeland security, denying al Qaeda access to failing or hostile states, dismantling networks, and developing a horizontal law-enforcement and intelligence network to better cope with al Qaeda's flat, decentralized structure. Not all vulnerabilities can be identified and even fewer remedied, and al Qaeda need not be good all the time, but lucky only once with a weapon of mass destruction to trigger an existential crisis for the United States and its allies. The United States and its partners also need to persuade Muslim populations that they can prosper without either destroying the West or abandoning their traditions to the depredations of western culture. That is a long-term project. American and allied determination in war against apocalyptic—and therefore genocidal—religious fanatics must be coupled with a generosity of vision about postwar possibilities. Islam's warm embrace of the West is too stark a reversal to expect in the foreseeable future. However, it is feasible to lay the foundation for a lasting accommodation by deploying the considerable economic and political advantages of the United States and its allies.

Notes

1. For the English text, see "Written instructions link hijackers on 3 flights," at www.cnn.com/2001/US/09/28/inv.document.terrorism [accessed January 2003]. For the Arabic original, see www.abc.net.au/4corners/atta/resources/ documents/instructions1.htm [accessed January 2003]. For a detailed exegesis of the essentially cultic terms of the text, see Kanan Makiya and Hassan Mneimneh, "Manual for a Raid," in Robert B. Silvers and Barbara Epstein, eds., *Striking Terror in America's New War* (New York: New York Review of Books, 2002), p. 324.

2. There is an ongoing debate about the relative primacy of religion and politics in the motivation and purpose of the new terrorists. The spectrum of views is evident in "America and the New Terrorism: An Exchange," *Survival*, vol. 42 (Summer 2000), pp. 156–72. In general, observers tend to look at this phenomenon through the lenses of their respective disciplines. Political scientists place greater weight on political concerns and agendas, while sociologists of religion see belief, doctrine, and scriptural imagery as more central to behavior. For the latter approach, see Mark Juergensmeyer, *Terror in the Mind of God: The Global Rise of Religious Violence* (University of California Press, 2001).

3. Bruce Hoffman, "Holy Terror: The Implications of Terrorism Motivated by a Religious Imperative," RAND Paper P-7834, 1993 (www.nwcitizen.com/publicgood/reports/ holywar3.htm [accessed January 2003]); Bruce Hoffman, *Inside Terrorism* (Columbia

University Press, 1998); Bruce Hoffman, "Old Madness, New Methods: Revival of Religious Terrorism Begs for Broader U.S. Policy," *Rand Review* 22 (Winter 1998-99), pp. 12–7 (www.rand.org/publications/randreview/review.index/terrorism.html [accessed January 2003]); and Bruce Hoffman, "Terrorism and Weapons of Mass Destruction: An Analysis of Trends and Motivations," RAND Paper P-8039-1, 1999. For earlier efforts to develop this argument, see David C. Rapoport, "Messianic Sanctions for Terror," *Comparative Politics*, vol. 20 (January 1988), pp. 195–223; and David C. Rapoport, "Fear and Trembling: Terrorism in Three Religious Traditions," *American Political Science Review*, vol. 78 (September 1984), pp. 658–77.

4. The succession of messianic Jewish revolts within the Roman Empire from 66 A.D. to 117 A.D. led to the destruction of most Jewish communities in North Africa, the Aegean, Egypt, and Mesopotamia after inflicting significant casualties among neighboring gentile populations. See E. Mary Smallwood, *The Jews under Roman Rule from Pompey to Diocletian*, 2d ed. (Leiden: E. J. Brill, 2001), pp. 389–427. Interestingly, the revolt under Hadrian (115 A.D.) was sparked by the emperor's ban on circumcision, which he issued as a modernizing initiative in a globalized context. On the messianic component of these revolts, it is still worth consulting Edward Gibbon's vivid account based on contemporary Greek and Latin records in *The History of the Decline and Fall of the Roman Empire*, vol. 1, ed. David Wormersley (London: Allen Lane, 1776, 1994), pp. 514–20.

5. These battles are commemorated by the holiday of Hanukkah and underlie the bloody apocalyptic of the biblical book of Daniel. For the background on these remote events, see Lester L. Grabbe, *Judaism from Cyrus to Hadrian*, vol. 1 (Minneapolis: Fortress Press, 1992), pp. 221–307. The nature and origins of the apocalyptic genre, as well as its salient characteristics, are sketched in John J. Collins, *The Apocalyptic Imagination*, 2d ed. (Grand Rapids: William B. Eerdmans, 1998), pp. 1–42.

6. Yigal Amir, Yitzhak Rabin's killer, believed that he had rabbinical authority to kill the prime minister in the form of two edicts (din rodef and din moser) that circulated widely in the orthodox settler community. He told interrogators that he would not have acted without such authorization. See Ehud Sprinzak, *Brother against Brother: Violence and Extremism in Israeli Politics from Altalena to the Rabin Assassination* (Free Press, 1999). In similar fashion, the conspirators in the first World Trade Center and landmarks plots insisted on a fatwa from the blind Sheikh, Umar abd al Rahman, before carrying out attacks. See Steven Simon and Daniel Benjamin, "America and the New Terrorism," *Survival*, vol. 42 (Spring 2000), pp. 59–75.

7. A solid scholarly interpretation from a religious studies' perception of these events, and especially of Shoko Asahara's evolving views in the years leading up to the 1995 attack, is offered in Ian Reader, *Religious Violence in Contemporary Japan: The Case of Aum Shinrikyo*, Monograph Series 82 (Copenhagen: Nordic Institute of Asian Studies, 2000).

8. For an informed account of this dramatic event, see Joseph A. Kechichian, "Islamic Revivalism and Change in Saudi Arabia: Juhayman al Utaybi's 'Letters' to the Saudi People," *Muslim World*, vol. 86 (January 1990), pp. 1–6; and Joseph A. Kechichian, "The Role of the Ulema in the Politics of an Islamic State: The Case of Saudi Arabia," *International Journal of Middle Eastern Studies*, vol. 18 (February 1986), pp. 53–71.

9. This is a new field of study that lags well behind cognate research on American revivalism and fundamentalism. Dr. David Cook, a historian of Islam at the University of Chicago, was kind enough to share his pioneering study of these texts, which he is preparing

for publication under the provisional title Between Hope and Hatred: Contemporary Muslim Apocalyptic Literature. See also David Cook, "America, the Second 'Ad: Prophecies about the Downfall of the United States," which can be found on Boston University's Center for Millennial Studies website (www.mille.org/scholarship/papers/ADAM.html [accessed January 2003]).

10. On dreams, see bin Laden's remarks at www.cnn.com/2001/US/12/13/tape.transcript/ [accessed January 2003] and those of another ranking al Qaeda figure in Peter Finn, "Arrests Reveal Al-Qaida's Plans," *Washington Post*, June 16, 2002, p. A1. Angels fighting alongside believers in eschatological scenarios or disposing of infidels on Judgment Day feature in Quranic narratives bin Laden uses. See his 1996 Declaration of War against America in any one of its countless appearances on the Internet, for example, www.terrorismfiles.org/individuals/declaration_of_jihad3.html [accessed January 2003]. Mass conversion to Islam on Judgment Day is a common theme. See bin Laden's "Letter from Usamah bin Muhammad bin Laden to the American People," which was apparently first circulated in fall 2002 (www.waaqiah.com/letterbinladen.htm [accessed January 2003]). See also note 11 below.

11. See www.al-qiyamah.org/al-qiyamah/surah_20-21.htm [accessed January 2003], where a moderate cleric interprets S.57 in an apocalyptic mode as a prophecy of the destruction of the World Trade Center. Safar al Hawali, the Saudi cleric, also indulges in apocalyptic discourse, drawing on multiple scriptural sources—Christian and Jewish—to create a complex narrative. On the complex symbolism of the attack, see Daniel Benjamin and Steven Simon, *The Age of Sacred Terror* (Random House, 2002), pp. 156–61.

12. On the relationship between socioeconomic distress and mobilization of radical feeling, see Mark Tessler, "The Origins of Popular Support for Islamist Movements: A Political Economy Analysis," paper presented at the Seminar on Political and Economic Islam, Washington, May 19, 1992, cited in Alan Richards, "Economic Imperatives and Political Systems," *Middle East Journal*, vol. 47 (Spring 1993), pp. 217–27.

13. For a recent assessment of these conditions, see the 2002 United Nations Development Program, "Arab Human Development Report," available in English and Arabic at www.undp.org/rbas/ahdr/ [accessed January 2003].

14. For a detailed analysis of how diverse Islamist groups have come to dominate public discourse in key Arab states, see Emmanuel Sivan, "The Clash within Islam," *Survival*, vol. 45 (Spring 2003), pp. 25–44.

15. Arieh O'Sullivan, "Bin Laden Ring Planned Mass Terror Campaign," *Jerusalem Post*, August 22, 2000, p. 1.

16. The two sides came closer to catastrophe in 1999 than is generally recognized. See Bruce Riedel, "American Diplomacy and the 1999 Kargil Summit at Blair House," Policy Paper Series, Center for the Advanced Study of India, University of Pennsylvania, 2002, at www.sas.upenn.edu/casi/reports/RiedelPaper051302.htm [accessed January 2003]. Conversations with government officials, who would not consent to be quoted for this article regarding the 2002 crisis, indicated that Islamabad believed it could effectively decapitate and disarm India in a first strike. This confidence complicated U.S. diplomatic efforts to defuse the crisis. This fragmentary anecdotal evidence regarding Pakistan's nuclear posture, alongside what is known about the views of Islamic militants in Pakistan, informs the judgment that the jihadists nearly got the Armageddon they sought. During an address to military veterans, Pakistani president Pervez Musharraf intimated that he was prepared to use

nuclear weapons had Indian forces crossed the country's border. See "Pakistan Was Prepared to Use Nuclear Weapons," Associated Press, December 30, 2002.

17. See Peter Baker, "Pakistani Scientist Who Met bin Laden Failed Polygraphs, Renewing Suspicions," *Washington Post*, March 3, 2002, p. A1; Toby Harnden, "'Pakistani Scientists Gave bin Laden Nuclear Advice," *Daily Telegraph*, December 13, 2001, p. 12; David E. Sanger, "Nuclear Experts in Pakistan May Have Links to Al Qaeda," *New York Times*, December 9, 2001, p. A1; and Farrah Stockman, "A Disenchanted Researcher's bin Laden Tie," *Boston Globe*, December 16, 2001, p. A35.

18. In a Sunday *London Times* survey of British Muslims, 40 percent of respondents approved of al Qaeda's attacks on September 11, 2001. In another poll conducted by a London radio station with a predominantly Pakistani audience, 98 percent of respondents under the age of forty-five said they would not fight for Great Britain, while 48 percent said they would do so for bin Laden. See Melanie Phillips, "Britain Ignores Angry Muslims within at Its Peril," *Sunday Times* (London), November 26, 2001, p. 4.

19. Suleiman Abu Ghaith, "Why We Fight America," June 12, 2002 (www.memri.org/bin/articles.cgi?Page=archives&Area=sd&ID=SP38802 [accessed January 2003]).

20. See National Intelligence Council, "Global Trends 2015: A Dialogue about the Future with Nongovernment Experts," December 2000 (www.cia.gov/nic/pubs/index.htm [accessed January 2003]). For updated population figures see www.census.gov/main/www/popclock.html.

21. See Alan Richards, "Socio-Economic Roots of Radicalism," *Naval War College Review*, vol. 55 (Autumn 2002), pp. 22–38.

22. See the most recent religion survey conducted under the auspices of the Pew Forum on Religion and Public Life at pewforum.org/publications/[accessed January 2003]. The Pew survey returns tend to confirm earlier findings in the most authoritative source in a field where data are difficult to collect and interpret; see David B. Barrett, George T. Kurian and Todd M. Johnson, eds., *A Comparative Survey of Churches and Religions in The Modern World*, vol. 1, 2d ed. (Oxford University Press, 2001).

23. It is worth noting in this context that World Trade Organization accession will obligate Saudi Arabia to open the kingdom to U.S.-owned cinemas and Hollywood movies. This is a prime example of America's heedless pursuit of economic gain in the face of clear security risks and, at the same time, an example of the incompatibility of economic reform and the Wahhabi interpretation of Islamic law.

24. Excerpts from, and fact sheets describing, the Clinton administration's Presidential Decision directives 39, 62, and 63 are available at www.fas.org/irp/offdocs/pdd/index.html [accessed January 2003].

25. The best sources of information on how the U.S. government responded to the rise of al-Qaida are the "Findings of the Final Report of the Senate Select Committee on Intelligence and the House Permanent Select Committee on Intelligence Joint Inquiry into the terrorist attacks of September 11, 2001," December 11, 2002 (intelligence.senate.gov/findings.pdf) [accessed January 2003]; and Benjamin and Simon, *Age of Sacred Terror*, chaps. 6–8.

26. Roberta Wohlstetter, *Pearl Harbor: Warning and Decision* (Stanford University Press, 1962), pp. vii–ix.

27. See Dennis Gormley, "Enriching Expectations: 11 September's Lessons for Missile Defense," *Survival*, vol. 44 (Summer 2002), p. 23.

28. The November 2002 missile attack against al Qaeda personnel in Yemen might be regarded as such a probe.

29. As a practical matter, the Bush administration has begun to eliminate constraints on domestic surveillance that had impeded counter-terrorism efforts before September 11, 2001. See David Johnston, James Risen, and Neil A. Lewis, "Threats and Responses: The Law," *New York Times*, November 30, 2002, p. A1.

30. See Michael E. O'Hanlon and others, *Protecting the American Homeland* (Brookings, 2002), esp. chap. 4.

31. An initial application of this technology took place in Tampa, Florida, in January 2001 at the so-called "Snooper Bowl," where the faces of all 72,000 spectators at the Super Bowl were scanned when they entered the stadium and compared with a database of criminals. See "Uncle Sam and the Watching Eye," *Economist*, September 22–28, 2001, p. 32.

32. The Bush administration's "Total Information Awareness" initiative, for example, is intended to monitor all private communications and business transactions. On the public anxiety this is producing, see Jeffrey Rosen, "The Year in Ideas: Total Information Awareness," *New York Times Magazine*, December 15, 2002, p. 128.

33. See Stephen E. Flynn, "America the Vulnerable," *Foreign Affairs*, vol. 81 (January/February 2002), pp. 60–75; and Stephen E. Flynn, "Beyond Border Control," *Foreign Affairs*, vol. 79 (November/December 2000), pp. 57–68.

34. This remains a vexing issue. See Barton Gellman, "In U.S., Terrorism's Peril Undiminished," *Washington Post*, December 24, 2002, p. A1.

35. The pace of renditions has picked up in recent months, suggesting that the Bush administration has fully embraced this counterterrorism tool. See ibid.

36. Dana Priest and Barton Gellman, "U.S. Decries Abuse but Defends Interrogations," *Washington Post*, December 26, 2002, p. A1.

37. The unclassified National Intelligence Estimate is at www.cia.gov/nic/pubs/other_products/Unclassifiedballisticmissilefinal.htm [accessed January 2003]. Director of Central Intelligence George Tenet's testimony on these issues is at www.cia.gov/cia/public_affairs/speeches/speeches.htm [accessed January 2003].

38. On how people elsewhere around the globe view the United States, see "What the World Thinks in 2002" (Washington: Pew Research Center for the People & the Press, 2002) (people-press.org/reports/display.php3?ReportID=165 [accessed January 2003]). For a summary of the Pew report, see Adam Clymer, "World Survey Says Negative Views of U.S. Are Rising," *New York Times*, December 4, 2002, p. A22.

39. A demonstration of American regard for an issue that mobilizes Muslim and Arab opinion is obviously not a magic bullet. It will not convince those who have crossed the line to violence or win over Salafis who object to any non-Muslim authority within the historical lands of Islam. It might not even dent the perception widespread in the Islamic world that the Jews control the United States, a view probably strengthened by the November/December 2002 broadcasts on al-Jazeera and al Manar of "Knight without a Horse," a dramatization based on the Protocols of the Elders of Zion. It will, however, limit the pool of recruits to violence and give regional governments the breathing room to help the United States in the war on terrorism. Also, President Bush's February 26, 2003, speech on the future of Iraq, in which he pledged to bring about a Palestinian state, suggests that the White House understands the link between radicalism and American policy toward the Israeli-Palestinian conflict. See www.whitehouse.gov/news/releases/2003/02/20030226-11.html.

40. The Bush administration started and subsequently abandoned a high-profile television campaign aimed at winning the hearts and minds of the Islamic world. See Vanessa O'Connell, "U.S. Suspends TV Ad Campaign Aimed at Winning over Muslims," *Wall Street Journal,* January 16, 2003, p. A1.

41. Quoted in Thomas L. Friedman, "Under the Arab Street," *New York Times,* October 23, 2002, p. A23.

42. The "great quest" barrier to democratization is discussed in John Waterbury, "Democracy without Democrats? The Potential for Political Liberalization in the Middle East," in Ghassan Salame, ed., *Democracy without Democrats? The Renewal of Politics in the Muslim World* (London: I. B. Tauris, 1994).

43. This term was coined by Adam Przeworski. There is a vast literature on democratization. Much of it focuses on Latin America and eastern Europe, where, unlike most of the Middle East, the process has actually taken root. Broadly speaking, analysts agree that it is a multistage transformation that takes place over relatively long periods of time. Przeworski argues that there are two main phases: extrication from authoritarian rule and the constitution of democracy. Where the military and security establishments are in control, the first phase can take considerable time; where there is strong civilian or party control over the security apparatus—as in eastern Europe—or the military establishment is swept away in the wake of military catastrophe—as in Greece or Argentina—transition can move quickly into the second phase. To the degree his schema is applicable to the Middle East, there is little hope of a swift or bloodless transition to democracy. See Adam Przeworski, *Democracy and the Market: Political and Economic Reforms in Eastern Europe and Latin America* (Cambridge University Press, 1991).

44. As in other states with rentier economic structures, oil also underpinned the state-society contract that has enabled the Saudi royal family to exclude most of its subjects from participation in the country's politics. As Saudi Arabia's economic situation crumbles and the state can no longer pay for its obligations under this contract, it will have to be renegotiated. Indeed, this renegotiation is already under way, albeit in a tentative and nearly invisible manner. See International Institute for Strategic Studies, "Saudi Arabia's Political Dilemmas," *Strategic Comments,* vol. 7, no. 10 (December 2001); and Mamoun Fandy, *Saudi Arabia and the Politics of Dissent* (MacMillan, 1999), pp. 22–60. On the political economy of regional rentier states, see Kirin Aziz Chaudhry, *The Price of Wealth: Economics and Institutions in the Arab World* (University of California Press, 1999).

45. See Jeff Gerth, "Growing U.S. Need for Oil from the Mideast Is Forecast," *New York Times,* December 26, 2002, p. A24.

46. For a brisk and up-to-date reformulation of this concept, see Mick Moore, "Political Underdevelopment," paper presented at the 10th anniversary conference of the Development Studies Institute, London School of Economics, London, September 7–8, 2000 [on file with author].

47. This is well understood in Washington, where the State Department has announced a "U.S.-Middle East Partnership Initiative" intended, among other things, to spur education, economic reform, and private sector development and to strengthen civil society. The success of this well-intentioned effort will likely be impeded by the regional perception that American rhetoric is triumphalist and solipsistic and by the extremely small amount of money ($29 million) the Bush administration has allocated to the project. The main elements of the partnership initiative can be viewed at www.state.gov/r/pa/prs/ps/2002/15923pf.htm [accessed January 2003].

STUART TAYLOR 13

Rights, Liberties, and Security

WHEN DANGERS INCREASE, liberties shrink. This has been our history, especially in wartime, when our government most clearly needs muscular investigative and detention powers to protect the security on which our most fundamental liberties depend. And now the United States faces dangers without precedent: a mass movement of militant Islamic terrorists—including some 20,000 men trained at Osama bin Laden's camps in Afghanistan[1]—who crave martyrdom, hide in shadows, are fanatically bent on slaughtering as many Americans as possible and using nuclear truck bombs to obliterate New York, or Washington, or both, if they can. Such a bomb could kill the president, vice president, and most of the Cabinet, Congress, and Supreme Court, among tens or hundreds of thousands of others, possibly without leaving a clue about the source of the attack.

How can the United States avert such a catastrophe? And how can we hold down the number of lesser mass murders of dozens, hundreds, or thousands of Americans? A more pro-Arab or pro-Muslim foreign policy would not end the threat and might increase it.[2] Our best hope of avoiding apocalyptic loss of life is to prevent al Qaeda or other terrorist groups or states from getting and smuggling nuclear, biological, or chemical weapons into this country. But we need be unlucky only once to fail in that. Time is not on our side. And terrorists can kill a great many of us with conventional bombs and weapons. So no matter how much we invest in hardening our targets, ultimately we can hold down casualties only if we find and lock up (or kill) as many as possible of the hundreds or thousands of al Qaeda terrorists whose modus operandi is to infiltrate U.S. society and avoid attention until they strike.

And the only way to do that is aggressive use of surveillance, informants, searches, seizures, subpoenas, wiretaps, arrests, interrogations, detentions, modern information technology, and, sometimes, group-based profiling. Those are the same investigative and detention powers and techniques that are so tightly restricted by the web of laws, judicial precedents, administrative rules and media-driven cultural norms that were developed in sunnier times to protect civil rights and civil liberties.[3] Despite significant modifications since 9/11, which civil libertarians hyperbolically decried, many of these rules remain unchanged. To deal with the deadliest terrorists in history, the United States is armed with investigative powers and legal rules calibrated largely for dealing with drug dealers, bank robbers, burglars, and ordinary murderers. Americans are also stuck in habits of mind that have not yet fully processed how dangerous our world has become or how ill-prepared our traditional legal regime is to meet the new dangers.[4]

This is not to advocate truly radical revisions of civil liberties. Nor is it to applaud all of the revisions that have already been made. Some of them seem unwarranted and even dangerous, as critics (including this writer) have pointed out.[5] But this chapter departs from most commentaries on the balance between liberty and security since 9/11—which argue (plausibly, on some issues) that the United States has gone too far in expanding government power—by contending that in important respects the nation has not gone far enough.[6] Among the central theses:

Civil libertarians have underestimated the need for broader investigative powers, exaggerated the dangers that such powers pose to our fundamental liberties, and ignored Alexander Hamilton's injunction in the first of the *Federalist Papers* that "the vigor of government is essential to the security of liberty." Judicious expansion of the government's powers to find suspected terrorists would be less dangerous to freedom than risking possibly preventable attacks or a reactive upsurge in the use of incarceration without due process of law. We should worry a bit less about being wiretapped or searched or spied on or interrogated or data-mined and more about being blown to bits or seeing innocent people put behind bars.

Well-designed legislation to protect security is also good for liberty, especially in the long run. Stubborn adherence to the civil liberties status quo would probably damage our most fundamental freedoms far more in the long run than would judicious modifications of rules that are less (or not at all) fundamental. The current restrictions on the government's wiretapping powers, for example, are worth nothing to people murdered by terrorist bombers who might have been stopped by wiretaps. Our freedom to travel is protected no less by the government powers that make travel safe than by the Constitution's limits on the government's power to restrain our movements. Careful congressional action based on robust national debate is more likely to be sensitive to our fundamental liberties and to the Constitution's checks and balances than unilateral expansion of executive power.[7] Courts are more likely to check executive excesses if Congress sets limits for them to enforce.[8] Government agents are more likely to respect our fundamental liberties if freed from rules that create unwarranted obstacles to doing their jobs. And successful prevention of terrorist mass murders is the best hope for avoiding a panicky stampede into police-state measures that are now unthinkable but could suddenly become unstoppable.[9]

Finally, Congress and the nation need to undertake a far more candid, searching, and systematic reassessment of civil liberties rules and cultural norms. The objective should be to prevent as many terrorist murders as possible without undue damage to America's most fundamental freedoms. The methods should include a willingness to consider modifying rules that have until recently seemed immutable; a determination to expand governmental powers only insofar as the likely counterterrorism benefits outweigh the costs to liberty—including the risk that seemingly small steps could send us down slippery slopes; effective safeguards against the risks of abuse inherent in all new government powers; and the substitution of robust national debate and congressional action for what has so far been largely ad hoc presidential improvisation. (Rather than attempting to cover all of the important civil liberties issues that now loom large, which would take several chapters, this chapter focuses on the core powers to investigate and detain suspected terrorists.)[10]

Even if all of the measures suggested are adopted, the revised rules would be more libertarian than the laws of all or almost all other nations and far more libertarian than our own rules were from 1789 until, say, 1970. And for all its flaws, "the U.S. was not a fascist dictatorship before Ted Kennedy and Jimmy Carter rode to the rescue."[11]

In this chapter I examine how some of the current restraints on the government's investigative and detention powers impede the fight against today's terrorists and how an attitude of reflexive resistance to any increase in government power to pursue terrorists can blind people to the magnitude of the terrorist threat.[12] I respond to the main objections to expanding investigative and detention powers and explore how to enlarge the most important investigative and detention powers while setting boundaries to minimize overuse and abuse, in part through a proposed Terrorism Prevention Act. I argue that the government should use group-based profiling to screen large numbers of people in pursuit of a few terrorists when—and only when—the public safety benefits seem clearly to outweigh the costs of inconveniencing or humiliating those individuals who fit the profile.

Several important rules and practices have already been changed. The USA Patriot Act of October 2001 included numerous provisions enhancing the government's electronic surveillance, search and seizure, and other investigative powers and lowering barriers to information sharing among law enforcement and intelligence agencies, in terrorism investigations and (to some extent) ordinary criminal matters.[13] The act also increased the government's powers to detain and deport aliens, combat money laundering, and prosecute alleged terrorists.[14]

In May 2002, Attorney General John Ashcroft relaxed the administrative rules that since 1976 have restricted the FBI's powers to monitor public meetings and other activities of political and religious groups that might be involved in terrorism, to plant informers, and to cruise the Internet fishing for clues of possible terrorist or criminal activities.[15]

The Bush administration has also adopted more questionable and far-reaching measures by executive fiat, without significant congressional or public input. The most radical example is the administration's stunning assertion of unilateral power to seize any and all people it labels "enemy combatants" and keep them in solitary confinement for months, years, perhaps decades—even if they are U.S. citizens, and even if they were arrested in this country—without giving them any opportunity, ever, to tell their side of the story to a court, lawyer, or the public.[16] Thus would the administration bypass Congress and negate the bedrock right of every U.S. citizen to be at liberty unless the government can show an independent court hard evidence justifying detention. A federal appeals court upheld this unprecedented policy in January 2003.[17] But another federal judge flatly rejected in another case the government's claim that alleged enemy combatants have no right to tell their side of the story or to the assistance of counsel, ever.[18] The Supreme Court should do the same. It should remember Justice Robert H. Jackson's words of forty-one years ago—"No penance would ever expiate the sin against free government of holding that a President can escape control of executive powers by law through assuming his military role"—and call a halt to this flirtation with tyranny.[19]

Recalibrating the Balance between Liberty and Security

The courts, Congress, the president, and the public have from the beginning of the nation demarcated the scope of protected rights, in practice if not always in theory, "by a weighing of competing interests. . . . the public-safety interest and the liberty interest," in the words of Judge Richard A. Posner of the U.S. Court of Appeals for the Seventh Circuit. "The safer the nation feels, the more weight judges will be willing to give to the liberty interest." The more threatened the nation feels, the more weight will and should be given to the security interest.[20]

The nation feels—and is—gravely threatened today. "A year after 9/11, America remains dangerously unprepared to prevent and respond to a catastrophic terrorist attack on U.S. soil," a task force headed by former senators Gary Hart and Warren Rudman warned in October 2002. "In all likelihood, the next attack will result in even greater casualties and widespread disruption to our lives and economy."[21] Our nuclear arsenal and conventional military hegemony, which have succeeded in deterring attacks by other nations, will not deter terrorists who crave martyrdom or who may hope to escape retaliation by committing mass murder anonymously, especially if they can launch a nuclear or biological attack.

Some suggest that because our terrorist enemies lack the military power of nation-states, and because our own military is unchallengeable, and because Congress has not declared war, it is a misnomer to call the fight against terrorism a "war" and a mistake to resort to emergency powers.[22] Such reasoning is wrong, except in the sense that the absence of any risk of territorial occupation or immediate threat of anarchy makes unnecessary any resort to the most sweeping of emergency powers, such as suspending the writ of habeas corpus or imposing martial law.[23] Indeed, the broad resolution passed by Congress three days after September 11, 2001, authorizing the president to use "all necessary and appropriate force" in response to the attacks was the constitutional equivalent of a declaration of war.[24]

But whatever we call the terrorist threat, it is indistinguishable from war in the need for extraordinary governmental powers to protect us from enemies who have already caused more carnage on the home front than any other foreign enemy has inflicted since at least the war of 1812. That is the reality underlying Justice Sandra Day O'Connor's (perhaps premature) assertion in a September 28, 2001, speech that "we're likely to experience more restrictions on our personal freedom than has ever been the case in our country."[25] This is not the first time we have been threatened with infiltration by agents of hostile foreign organizations or with weapons of mass destruction. But never before have we faced an enemy committed to invading our nation by stealth, lurking among us and murdering as many of us as possible, and that counts millions of militant Islamists around the globe as potential recruits. And never before has the risk of attack with weapons of mass destruction been so high.[26]

Legal Obstacles to Catching and Detaining Terrorists

Some of our rules on civil liberties make it too hard to catch and detain terrorists. Indeed, overly broad restrictions on investigative powers and the cultural taboo against racial (and national-origin) profiling share responsibility—along with human error and organizational dysfunctions—for the government's failure to prevent the September 11 attacks. Consider some hypothetical scenarios for the future:

—The FBI receives an anonymous tip identifying an apartment in Trenton, N.J., where the same terrorists who prepared the anthrax-laced letters that convulsed the nation in the fall of 2001 are said to be preparing more such letters and planning an anthrax attack on the New York City subway. Could the FBI get a warrant to search or wiretap the apartment? Quite possibly not: under the Supreme Court's interpretation of the Fourth Amendment, an anonymous tip generally falls well short of the "probable cause" necessary to justify searching a home, apartment, or car.[27] Even if the tipster claims there is a hidden bomb, it would arguably be illegal for an FBI agent to search the apartment or even to set up a Geiger counter on the sidewalk outside.[28]

—An FBI agent stakes out the apartment, sees two men emerge and head off in opposite directions. The agent follows one to a mailbox, watches him mail an envelope, approaches him, grabs him when he tries to flee, and arrests him when he resists. What should the agent do next? Can he press the man aggressively for information about where his companion was going? Current Supreme Court case law, while ambiguous, is widely interpreted as saying: read him his *Miranda* rights; ask no questions if he requests a lawyer; and—unless there is "probable cause" linking him to criminal activity—release him to go about his business.[29]

—The FBI learns from a wiretap that an al Qaeda terrorist driving an orange truck has a bomb that he plans to detonate somewhere in Manhattan in two hours. The FBI and local police want to search all orange trucks in the area. But the chance that any one of the dozens or hundreds of orange trucks would be the one with the bomb would be far too small to amount to the probable cause required to search a vehicle without consent by the Supreme Court's Fourth Amendment case law. (Indeed, the police who stopped hundreds of white vans to look for the sniper who terrorized the Washington, D.C., region in October 2002 may well have violated rulings suggesting that in the absence of a traffic violation, police may stop a car only if they have a reasonable suspicion that evidence of crime will be found *in that car*.)[30]

—Another nineteen al Qaeda terrorists try to smuggle nineteen bombs in checked bags into nineteen airliners on a given morning. How many might succeed? It is unclear at present, because it is difficult to assess the credibility of the government's claim that it now tests virtually all checked bags effectively for evidence of explosives. But if nineteen terrorists had attempted such an operation during the six to twelve months after September 11, most of them might well have succeeded, thanks in large part to the Bush administration's ban (or purported ban) on racial *or* national-origin profiling in airline security screening. The bases for this estimate are the apparent ease with which competent terrorists can dodge the behavioral profiles that are now in use and reports that as late as July 2002, only a small percentage of checked bags were screened for bombs in any way.[31]

It would be crazy to adhere to such rules in the face of the enormous dangers to the public safety presented by modern terrorism. "The old adage that it is better to free 100 guilty men than to imprison one innocent describes a calculus that our Constitution—which is no suicide pact—does not impose on government when the 100 who are freed belong to terrorist cells that slaughter innocent civilians, and may well have access to chemical, biological, or nuclear weapons," in the words of Harvard Law School's Laurence H. Tribe.[32] The question is not whether we should increase governmental powers to meet such dangers. The question is which powers to increase and how much.

There is, of course, much room for disagreement about whether any particular rule change will bolster security enough to be worth the cost to liberty. But the cliché that (as rendered by the columnist Molly Ivins) "we can't make ourselves safer by making ourselves less free" cannot withstand analysis.[33] It is beyond dispute that the government needs *some* investigative power to fight terrorism—for example, the power to search a truck if five credible eyewitnesses swear that it contains a ticking time bomb. It follows as the night the day that giving the government *more* investigative power—for example, the power to search the truck even if only one credible eyewitness, or a single, anonymous tipster claims that it contains a ticking time bomb—is likely to make us at least somewhat safer. It would also make us a tiny bit less free from government surveillance, by increasing the risk of subjecting innocent people's trucks and cars to searches based on unreliable evidence. The question is whether the security benefit of any specific increase in governmental power is likely to outweigh its cost to liberty. Such questions cannot be answered with mathematical precision. But the burden of justifying measures that might make us safer (and a little bit less free) should be less onerous now—with the terrorist threat to domestic security at an all-time high—than in recent decades.

The nation felt a lot safer from terrorist attacks during the 1960s and 1970s, when we placed previously unheard-of restrictions on law enforcement and intelligence agencies. The weight on the public safety side of the scales seemed relatively modest then. The isolated acts of violence by groups like the Weather Underground and Black Panthers—which had largely run their course by the mid-1970s—were a minor threat compared with those of our enemies today. Suicide bombers were virtually unheard of. The possibility that foreign terrorist groups could get their hands on nuclear or other doomsday weapons seemed remote. The main foreign threat on the home front came from Soviet spies who could at most effectuate incremental changes in a strategic balance well within the stalemate zone.

Meanwhile, the threat to civil liberties posed by broad law enforcement powers and an imperial presidency had been dramatized by Watergate and by the disclosures of some of the ugliest abuses of power in our history: FBI director J. Edgar Hoover's spying on politicians; his wiretapping (with then-attorney general Robert F. Kennedy's approval) and harassment of Rev. Martin Luther King Jr.; the FBI's Cointelpro program, which sent infiltrators to disrupt and harass antiwar and radical groups by spreading lies about them and their leaders; the U.S. Army's domestic spying program, and more. Overseas there had been the secret bombing of Cambodia, CIA-orchestrated coups d'etat, and amateurish CIA assassination plots against Fidel Castro, Patrice Lumumba, and others.

The Supreme Court, Congress, and the Ford and Carter administrations set out to curb the powers that had been abused. The justices consolidated and in some ways extended the Warren Court's revolutionary restrictions on government powers to search, seize, wiretap, interrogate, and detain suspected criminals (and terrorists). They also reined in the president's internal security powers by barring warrantless searches and wiretaps of domestic radicals as unconstitutional in 1972.[34] Congress barred warrantless wiretaps of suspected foreign spies and terrorists—a previously untrammeled presidential power—by adopting the Foreign Intelligence Surveillance Act of 1978 (FISA), which in the years predating the September 11 attacks proved a more potent restraint than had previously been supposed.[35]

During the same period, in 1976, Edward Levi, President Gerald Ford's attorney general, clamped down on domestic surveillance by the FBI with detailed administrative rules to curb infiltration of radical groups and surveillance and monitoring even of their public activities. Under the so-called Levi guidelines, agents now needed special justifications even to clip newspaper articles, fish through Internet chat rooms, attend public meetings or religious observances, or assemble files about people.[36] (These were the rules that Ashroft relaxed in May 2002.) And all the while, budding lawyers and journalists were educated to think that the nation had more to fear from the FBI, CIA, and racist cops than from criminals or foreign enemies.[37]

Rights: Immutable or Not?

It is comforting to think that the rules protecting our civil liberties are etched in constitutional stone. And it is easy to think so in ordinary times because these rules usually evolve so gradually, with courts rationalizing incremental (and not-so-incremental) adjustments as logical extensions of established precedents and with politicians vowing to make us safer with no sacrifice of freedom. All this helps account for the remarkable staying power of the tiresome cliché that if we dilute our civil liberties in any way, "then the terrorists will have won."

But in fact the Constitution's most important clauses deliberately define our fundamental rights in majestically vague and malleable terms that leave ample room to develop and modify detailed rules in light of experience and evolving needs. The Supreme Court, the primary expositor of constitutional rights, has fine-tuned and revised its detailed interpretations of these rights throughout its history. So has Congress.

Civil liberties expanded more often than they contracted during the second half of the twentieth century, when we faced no domestic security threat nearly as lethal as al Qaeda. One such expansion was the Supreme Court's sudden announcement on June 13, 1966, of the *"Miranda* rules," which had existed nowhere in the country the day before and had only a tenuous connection to the language, history, or intent of the Fifth Amendment. Those rules sharply curbed governmental power to interrogate arrested suspects, by suppressing any evidence obtained without benefit of the now-familiar warnings: "You have a right to remain silent," and so forth.[38] Most law enforcement agencies have grown comfortable with *Miranda,* and many do not consider it an insuperable obstacle to obtaining confessions from common criminals. But *Miranda* and related decisions, especially the one barring any questioning after a suspect asks for a lawyer, may pose a very serious obstacle to interrogating a trained terrorist.[39] It is probably no coincidence that *Miranda*—written by the same Earl Warren who twenty-four years previously had helped herd Japanese Americans into detention camps—and the other major Warren Court decisions curbing the government's investigative powers came when the notion that aggressive interrogation might sometimes be essential to prevent mass murders by international terrorists was almost unimaginable. Now the potential for successful interrogation to save a great many lives is all too clear.[40]

Interpretation of the Fourth Amendment's ban on "unreasonable searches and seizures" has also fluctuated greatly during the past one hundred and fifty years, as the Supreme Court's understanding of what is "unreasonable" has evolved to accommodate social and technological change. In 1928, for example, the Court held that the Constitution posed no obstacle to warrantless governmental wiretapping of anyone, anywhere, for any reason.[41] Then, in 1967, the justices overruled the 1928 decision and held for the first time that a wiretap was a "search" barred by the Fourth Amendment unless the government could obtain a warrant based on probable cause to believe that the proposed wiretap would produce evidence of crime.[42]

That same year, however, the same justices extinguished one of the oldest Fourth Amendment rights by completing the gradual evisceration of an 1886 decision that had barred all searches and subpoenas for documents, articles of clothing, or other "privacies of life"—also known as "mere evidence"—as distinguished from contraband.[43] This "mere evidence" rule was widely seen by 1967 as an intolerable obstacle to prosecution of white-collar criminals and street thugs alike. Indeed, had the Court retained this rule while holding wiretaps to be searches, wiretaps (which always seek "mere evidence") would be unconstitutional. So would all subpoenas for documents, such as those designed to find the truth about the Enron and Worldcom frauds. Those who see constitutional rules as fixed and immutable should consider that the logic of their position would revive the mere evidence rule and thus cripple efforts to investigate suspected terrorists and white-collar criminals alike.

Opponents of even modest trimming of civil liberties rules in the wake of September 11 often quote a Benjamin Franklin maxim: "Those who would give up *essential* liberty to purchase *a little temporary* safety deserve neither liberty nor safety."[44] But Franklin's qualifying words (italicized here) carry the clear implication that some liberties are less fundamental to a free society than others, and that those may properly be diluted for real gains in security.

In the hierarchy of rights mentioned in the Declaration of Independence—"life, liberty and the pursuit of happiness"—life comes first. And liberty's core—the right not to be wrongfully imprisoned—is more fundamental than the right not to be forced to talk and the rights now collected under the rubric of "privacy," which include freedom from unwarranted searches and wiretaps. These are more important than our interests in lesser forms of privacy such as freedom from being monitored in public activities and banking and business transactions, which are not constitutional rights. Near the bottom comes our interest in freedom from such minimal impositions as being singled out for a toilet-kit inspection while boarding an airliner.

Government Inefficiency and the Need for New Powers

Opponents of expanding the government's powers are quick to point out how inefficiently the FBI and other agencies have used the powers they have already. Some take this to the extreme of suggesting that if these agencies were not such bunglers, they would have no problem getting the job done with no dilution of civil liberties. One respected civil libertarian lobbyist who has spent his career opposing proposed expansions of the FBI's investigative powers has reported saying to himself, as he watched the World Trade Center burn, "They have screwed up so bad. With all the powers and resources that they have, they should have caught these guys."[45] (The possibility that the FBI might have caught these guys if it had had the additional powers that civil libertarian lobbyists have fought so hard to deny it apparently did not cross his mind.) Because the government "screwed up," such civil libertarians suggest, it should be given little or no new power. Such reasoning has a strong grip on the civil libertarian mindset. But it rests on four glaring logical fallacies that should be apparent no matter how inept the intelligence agencies may have been.

To suggest that there is no point in making it easier for error-prone human beings to prevent future attacks because they have failed in the past amounts to punishing the nation's people for the perceived flaws of their government. This is about as logical as it would be to argue that the role of human error in spoiling so many ballots in Florida in election 2000 means that there is no point in making it easier for voters to mark ballots correctly.

Although we can immediately change legal rules to make it easier for fallible federal agencies to protect us, it will take years to make the agencies dramatically less fallible. *Of course* they are notorious for their weaknesses in analyzing—and their habitual aversion to sharing—the massive data they have collected about al Qaeda and other terrorist groups. *Of course* government bureaucracies made grievous mistakes, and they will never be infallible.[46]

The agencies' inefficiencies are attributable in part to the legal restrictions so stoutly championed by civil libertarians and by the culture that these restrictions have fostered. Their aversion to sharing information, for example, was forged in the crucible of civil liberties rules that erected formidable legal obstacles to such intelligence sharing.[47] These rules have now been relaxed, by the USA Patriot Act and an important appeals court decision.[48] But a culture cannot be so quickly changed. Similarly, the "paralytic fear of risk-taking" at FBI headquarters was partly attributable to the career-blighting consequences of any accusations of violating civil liberties rules or doing anything that might be labeled (or mislabeled) racial profiling.[49] It is perverse to erect a procedural obstacle course in the path of the agents assigned to protect us from terrorists and then to complain that they are not smart enough to clear all the obstacles.[50] No matter how smart or dumb they may be, we need rules that are forgiving enough to help them help us stay alive.

Finally, even assuming that it is more important to make the government smarter and more efficient than to give it new surveillance powers, we should do both. More data are better than less. And the FBI, the CIA, and the White House would still be hobbled by some of the current restrictions even if they miraculously did everything right from now on. In short, judicious expansion of the government's powers is essential to limiting our future casualties. The notion that we should do nothing because the government is not perfect and nothing can make us entirely safe is a counsel of despair.

Abuse of Power and Overreaction

Past abuse and distrust of the George W. Bush administration must not paralyze the nation's response to new dangers. A frequent civil libertarian theme is that our history shows that wartime emergency powers are prone to overuse and abuse. Abraham Lincoln suspended *habeas corpus* and imposed martial law. Peaceful antiwar activists were prosecuted for sedition during and after World War I. President Franklin D. Roosevelt and Congress mandated the shameful herding of 110,000 Japanese Americans, the majority of them U.S. citizens, into detention camps during World War II. Communists and their associates were prosecuted, hauled before congressional committees, hounded out of jobs, and otherwise harassed during the McCarthy era. Not to mention the Alien and Sedition acts of 1798, which made criticism of the government a federal crime.

But that past wartime emergency measures were excessive does not mean that no wartime expansion of governmental power can ever be justified. The measures noted—perhaps except for Lincoln's initial order suspending habeas corpus—were unjustified because they were disproportionate to the relatively tiny threat of violent subversion at home. Now, however, the nation faces a threat of mass murder by enemies lurking in our midst that is without precedent, even during the Civil War. Never has the admonition that the Constitution is not a suicide pact been more apt.[51]

This is not to deny the views of many critics (including this writer) that some Bush administration officials seem especially prone to overuse and abuse any new powers.[52] In his November 2001 order authorizing the creation of special military commissions to detain and prosecute any noncitizen alleged to be an international terrorist—a reasonable step if accompanied by meaningful judicial review and other guarantees of procedural fairness—the president sought to foreclose judicial review and specified few credible procedural protections.[53] He dismissed as "legalisms" arguments that detainees at Guantanamo Bay who claimed to be charitable workers rather than enemy combatants should be given even the most minimal due process.[54] When it turned out that a number of suspected members of al Qaeda were U.S. citizens, including one arrested in Chicago, the military took custody of two of them as well—declaring them "enemy combatants," incarcerating them in military brigs, denying them access to lawyers, claiming the power to hold them indefinitely, and telling courts they "may not second-guess" the military's legal or evidentiary basis for doing the same to anyone it chooses.[55] Meanwhile, Ashcroft cloaked his post–9/11 preventive detention regime in unprecedented secrecy and accused critics of giving aid and comfort to the enemy.[56]

Why risk repeating the abuses of the past by unleashing an administration that is so fond of unchecked executive power and seems so insensitive to civil liberties? Because the alternative to trimming civil liberties is risking the preventable loss of countless lives to terrorism—an evil of far greater magnitude than any conceivable abuse of power by this administration. And because carefully drawn legislation would *not* unleash the administration: while authorizing and legitimizing the powers the government needs, it would also set boundaries, provide safeguards against abuse, and rein in unilateral expansions of presidential power.

The nation has a collection of internal and external watchdogs far more formidable than ever before: inspectors general in all major departments and agencies, the Justice Department's Office of Professional Responsibility, congressional investigators, a gaggle of liberal and conservative civil liberties groups, and the news media, which have never been more powerful. These institutions are staffed largely by lawyers, journalists, and others who have been inculcated with distrust of governmental power.[57] Any official tempted to emulate J. Edgar Hoover by playing politics with wiretap transcripts or by harassing nonviolent dissidents would risk media evisceration, removal, disgrace, lawsuits, even prosecution. These protections may help explain why nothing close to the Hoover or Nixon abuses has occurred during the nearly thirty years since they left the scene, and why this tough-talking administration has not emulated the programs of repression launched during the world wars and the McCarthy era.[58] In addition, more safeguards could be created.[59]

An Emergency with No End in Sight

The risk of terror attacks is unlike past wars in that it could continue for decades, and any new powers might well become permanent. Therefore, it is often said, Congress should be especially hesitant to take steps that we could come to regret.[60] This is true as far as it goes. But the executive unilateralism already under way can have just as lasting an impact as an act of Congress, with less sober deliberation, less careful vetting, less democratic legitimacy, and less transparency.[61]

If Congress leaves our civil liberties to the unchecked discretion of the Bush administration and its successors, they will continue to invoke sweeping visions of executive power and bend the law to do whatever they consider useful in the fight against terrorism. They will also be tempted to give the military an ever-increasing role on the home front—a potentially dangerous trend in a conflict that sprawls across the line between war and domestic law enforcement. Although the courts may provide some restraint, they will show great deference to presidential and military judgments, especially if Congress does not assert itself.

So the alternative to legislation striking a new balance between liberty and security is not preservation of the current rules. The alternative is unilateral executive circumvention or overriding of these rules—even, perhaps, creeping martial law.

The Balances Congress Should Strike

Only a handful of the standard law-enforcement investigative techniques have much chance of penetrating and defanging secretive, disciplined terrorist groups like al Qaeda cells: infiltrating them through informants and undercover agents; finding them and learning their plans through surveillance, searches, and wiretapping; detaining them before they can launch terrorist attacks; and interrogating those detainees.

As of September 11, and to a large extent today, all but the first (infiltration) were tightly restricted not only by Supreme Court precedents (sometimes by mistaken or debatable readings of them), statutes, and administrative rules, but also by the taboo against any screening or investigative technique that could be called racial profiling (often inaccurately). Several problems were caused by these rules and by this taboo. Possible solutions follow.

For one thing, the nation could further ease restrictions on searches and electronic surveillance. As the preceding examples suggest, the Supreme Court's Fourth Amendment case law does not distinguish clearly between a routine search for stolen goods or marijuana, on the one hand, and a preventive search for a bomb or a vial of anthrax, on the other. To search a dwelling, obtain a wiretap, or do a thorough search of a car or truck without consent, the government must generally have "probable cause" to believe that the proposed search will uncover evidence of crime, which is often, if incorrectly, interpreted in the sense of more-probable-than-not. These rules make little sense when the purpose of the search is to prevent mass murder.

Federal agents and local police need more specific guidance than the Supreme Court can quickly provide. Congress should provide it, in the form of legislation relaxing for international terrorism investigations the usual restrictions on searching, seizing, and wiretapping. The USA Patriot Act, as interpreted by a special federal appellate court, has already made it easier for the government to obtain a FISA warrant in cases in which its primary purpose is not merely to gather intelligence on suspected foreign spies and terrorists but also to prosecute them.[62] But while the act went too far in some ways, it did not go far enough in others.[63] It left in place an unduly stringent burden of proof to obtain a warrant to search or wiretap suspected terrorists, both under FISA and under the rules that govern ordinary criminal searches and wiretaps.[64]

This problem was a critical—although widely ignored—cause of the FBI's famous failure to seek a warrant during the weeks before September 11 to search the computer and other possessions of Zacarias Moussaoui, the alleged "twentieth hijacker." He had been locked up since August 16, technically for overstaying his visa, based on a tip about his strange behavior at a Minnesota flight school. The FBI had no basis for obtaining an ordinary criminal search warrant, which would have required "probable cause" to believe that he had committed a crime. It did have ample reasons to *suspect* that Moussaoui—who has since admitted being a member of al Qaeda—was a dangerous Islamic militant plotting airline terrorism.[65] Indeed, one official in the FBI's Minneapolis office told an official at FBI headquarters on August 27, 2002, that he was trying to make sure that Moussaoui "did not take control of a plane and fly it into the World Trade Center." The response from headquarters: "You don't have enough to show he's a terrorist."[66] No warrant was sought.

Congressional and journalistic investigations of the Moussaoui episode have focused on the intelligence agencies' failure to put together the Moussaoui evidence with other intelligence reports that should have alerted them that a broad plot to hijack airliners might be afoot. These critics have virtually ignored the undue stringency of the legal restraints on the government's powers to investigate suspected terrorists. Until these shortcomings are fixed, they will seriously hobble our intelligence agencies no matter how efficient they are.

It must be emphasized that "our current surveillance rules are neither constitutionally required, nor traditionally American."[67] From the time of FDR until 1978, the government could have searched Moussaoui's possessions without judicial permission, by invoking the president's inherent power to collect intelligence about foreign enemies. The FISA changed that, barring searches or wiretaps of suspected foreign agents or terrorists unless the attorney general could obtain a warrant from the special FISA court. The provision most relevant to Moussaoui requires the warrant application to show "probable cause" to believe not only that the target is a foreign terrorist, but also that he is a member of an international terrorist "group."[68]

Coleen Rowley, a lawyer in the FBI's Minneapolis office, argued passionately in a widely publicized May 21, 2002, letter to FBI Director Robert S. Mueller III that the information about Moussaoui satisfied this FISA requirement. Congressional investigators have said the same thing.[69] FBI headquarters officials have disagreed, because before September 11 there was no evidence linking Moussaoui to al Qaeda or any other identifiable terrorist group.[70] Although some experts argue that the FISA does not require that the terrorist group be identifiable, they—unlike FBI headquarters—are not privy to the FISA court's precedents, which are cloaked in secrecy. . . . FBI officials were also understandably gun-shy about going forward with a legally shaky warrant application in the wake of the FISA court's excoriation of an FBI supervisor in the fall of 2000 for perceived improprieties in his warrant applications.[71] The bottom line is that even if the FBI had done everything right, it was and is at least debatable whether its information about Moussaoui was enough to support a FISA warrant. And even if the FBI had sought a FISA warrant in late August 2001, the protracted approval process may well have been incomplete as of September 11.

More important for future cases, it is clear that FISA—even as amended by the USA Patriot Act—would not authorize a warrant in any case in which a suspected foreign terrorist is a lone wolf, or the FBI cannot find evidence of any confederates. So if we want to be sure that the next Zacarias Moussaoui's possessions are searched, fixing the FBI will not necessarily do the trick. We will also need to fix the law.[72]

One way of doing so would be to amend FISA to include the commonsense presumption that any foreign terrorist who comes to the United States is probably acting for (or at least inspired by) some international terrorist group.[73] A second option would be to lower the burden of proof from "probable cause" to "reasonable suspicion." A third—which could be extended to domestic as well as international terrorism investigations—would be to authorize a "preventive" search or wiretap of anyone the government has reasonable grounds to suspect of preparing or helping others prepare for a terrorist attack. To minimize any temptation for government agents to use this new power in pursuit of ordinary criminal suspects, Congress could prohibit the use in any prosecution unrelated to terrorism of any evidence obtained by such a preventive search or wiretap.[74]

The Supreme Court seems likely to uphold any such statute as consistent with the ban on "unreasonable searches and seizures." While the

Fourth Amendment says that "no warrants shall issue, but upon probable cause," warrants are not required for many types of searches, are issued for administrative searches of commercial property without "probable cause" in the traditional sense, and arguably should never be required.[75] Even in the absence of a warrant or probable cause, the justices have upheld searches based on "reasonable suspicion" of criminal activities, including brief "stop-and-frisk" encounters on the streets and car stops. The Court has upheld mandatory drug testing of certain government employees and transportation workers whose work affects the public safety and of certain high school students even when there is no particularized suspicion at all. It has reasoned in these cases that such searches serve the government's "special needs, beyond the normal need for law enforcement." The quintessential special need is preventing harm to the public safety.[76]

Exaggerated Fear of Big Brother

"The telescreen received and transmitted simultaneously," wrote George Orwell in *1984*. "Any sound that Winston made, above the level of a very low whisper, would be picked up by it; moreover, . . . he could be seen as well as heard. . . . How often, or on what system, the Thought Police plugged in on any individual wire was guesswork. It was even conceivable that they watched everybody all the time."[77] Such chilling images have filled many Americans with a reflexive horror of being bugged, wiretapped, or (now) screened by the FBI's fearsomely named Carnivore program, which sifts through computer networks for evidence of crime or terrorist plots. That horror was also fed by Hoover's abuses of the wiretapping power and by the use of warrantless wiretaps by presidents Franklin D. Roosevelt, Harry S. Truman, Lyndon B. Johnson, and Richard M. Nixon for political ends.

So any proposal to increase the government's wiretapping powers provokes fears of unleashing some kind of Big-Brother-Hoover-Nixon monster to spy on, harass, blackmail, and smear political dissenters and others. Libertarians point out that the tappers and buggers will overhear intimacies and embarrassing disclosures that are none of the government's business. That is characteristic of wiretaps, which indiscriminately capture all conversations on the tapped phones (or computers), including those of innocent people who are not the targets.[78]

Such concerns argue for taking care to broaden wiretapping and surveillance powers only as much as seems a reasonable bet to prevent terrorist acts. But broader wiretapping authority is not all bad for civil liberties.

It is a more accurate and in some ways more benign method of penetrating terrorist cells than the main alternative: planting and recruiting informers, which is a dangerous, ugly, and unreliable business, and one in which the government is already free to engage without limitation. The narrower the government's surveillance powers, the more it will rely on informers.

Moreover, limiting the government's power to collect information through wiretapping is not the only way to protect against misuse of the information. Other safeguards (such as penalties for misuse and the watchdogs just mentioned) are less damaging to the counterterrorism effort. And the FBI has little incentive to waste time and resources on unwarranted snooping. Only so many agents can be assigned to spend their days listening to wiretaps, and they must justify any and all taps and bugs to their superiors as well as the courts.

Nor is the FBI likely to invest many resources in targeting the innocent activities of political and religious groups for those less intrusive forms of government surveillance that have never been restricted by the Fourth Amendment. These methods include monitoring radical groups' public activities, infiltrating them, fishing through bank and business records for information about them, following their postings on public Internet sites, and using informants. Ashcroft's May 2002 orders loosening the restrictions on such activities that had been imposed by the 1976 Levi guidelines provoked an outcry from civil libertarians and Arab and Muslim groups.[79] The outcry seems understandable but excessive.

Critics warned that undercover FBI agents would be snooping around mosques run by militant mullahs, fishing for information. But if (for example) the mullahs are militant enough to speak sympathetically of Osama bin Laden—which would suggest a possible predisposition to harbor terrorists—the FBI *should* keep an eye on them. The first World Trade Center bombing, in 1993, was plotted at the Al-Farooq mosque in Brooklyn. *Newsweek* has reported that "hundreds of mosques in U.S. Muslim communities" are controlled by Saudi-funded fundamentalists who believe in "a pure, self-contained Islamic state" and "embrace the idea . . . that Christians and Jews are enemies."[80] So it should not be surprising that FBI headquarters has ordered the fifty-six field offices to tally the number of mosques in their areas as part of their assessment of "vulnerability" to terrorist attack. While the potential for abuse is clear, and no individual mosque should be targeted for investigation simply because it is a mosque, the cries of "witch hunt" from the American Civil Liberties Union are unwarranted.[81]

Indeed, to keep the specter of Big Brother in perspective, it is worth recalling that until 1978, when FISA was adopted, the president had *unlimited* power to wiretap suspected foreign spies and terrorists. This did not make America a police state. And despite the government's already vast power to comb through computerized records of banking and commercial transactions and much else done in the computer age, the vast majority of the people who have seen their privacy or reputations shredded have not been wronged by rogue officials. They have been wronged by media organizations, which do far greater damage to far more people with far less accountability.

Two decades ago, in *The Rise of the Computer State,* David Burnham wrote, "The question looms before us: can the United States continue to flourish and grow in an age when the physical movements, individual purchases, conversations and meetings of every citizen are constantly under surveillance by private companies and government agencies?"[82] It can. It has. And now that the computer state has risen indeed, the threat of being watched by Big Brother or smeared by the FBI or disinformed by a new Cointelpro seems a lot smaller than the threat of being blown to bits or poisoned by terrorists.

The Case for Coercive Interrogation—and against Torture

The same Zacarias Moussaoui whose possessions would have been searched but for FISA's undue stringency epitomizes another problem: the perverse impact of the rules—or what are widely assumed to be the rules—restricting interrogations of suspected terrorists.

"We were prevented from even attempting to question Moussaoui on the day of the attacks when, in theory, he could have possessed further information about other co-conspirators," Coleen Rowley complained in a little-noticed portion of her May 21 letter to Mueller.[83] The reason was that Moussaoui had requested a lawyer. To the FBI that meant further interrogation would violate the Fifth Amendment rules laid down by the Supreme Court in *Miranda* and subsequent cases. Former FBI director Louis Freeh has testified that "before we interviewed detained foreign national al Qaeda members in East Africa in connection with the embassy bombings, FBI agents gave them their *Miranda* rights."[84]

It is not hard to imagine such rules (or such an interpretation) leading to the loss of countless lives. Suppose that Moussaoui had been part of a team planning a second wave of hijackings later in September, and that his resistance could have been cracked.[85] Or suppose that the FBI learns tomorrow, from a wiretap, that another al Qaeda team is planning a big terrorist attack sometime next month and arrests an occupant of the wire-tapped apartment.

We all know the drill. Before asking any questions, FBI agents (and police) must give the suspect *Miranda* warnings: "You have a right to remain silent," and so forth. And if the suspect asks for a lawyer, all inter-rogation must cease until the lawyer arrives (and tells the suspect to keep quiet). This seems impossible to justify when one is dealing with people suspected of planning mass murder. But it is the law, isn't it?

Actually, it is not the law, even though many judges think it is, along with most lawyers, federal agents, police, and cop-show mavens. Actually, one does not have a right to remain silent. The most persuasive interpre-tation of the Constitution and the Supreme Court's precedents is that agents and police are free to interrogate any suspect without *Miranda* warnings; to spurn requests for a lawyer; to press hard for answers; and—at least in a terrorism investigation—perhaps even to use hours of inter-rogation, verbal abuse, isolation, blindfolds, polygraph tests, death penalty threats, and other forms of psychological coercion short of torture or physical brutality. Maybe even truth serum could be used. While this behavior seems at odds with the language of some precedents—not to mention hundreds of TV cop shows—it was the view of three of the most liberal justices in modern history, and the Court may confirm it in a pend-ing case, *Chavez v. Martinez*.[86]

The Fifth Amendment self-incrimination clause says only that no per-son "shall be compelled in any criminal case to be a witness against him-self." This clause prohibits forcing a defendant to testify in a criminal case and also indirectly making him a witness against himself through the pros-ecution's use of compelled pretrial statements. The Fifth Amendment does not prohibit compelling a suspect to talk. Nor does *Miranda*, which held only that in determining whether a defendant's statements (and informa-tion derived from them) may be used against him in a criminal prosecu-tion, courts must treat all interrogations of arrested suspects as inherently coercive unless the warnings are given.[87]

Courts typically ignore this distinction because in almost every litigated case the question is whether a criminal defendant's incriminating state-ments should be suppressed at his trial. There is no need to focus on whether the constitutional problem is the conduct of the interrogation, or the use in a prosecution of evidence obtained, or both. And as a matter of verbal shorthand, it is a lot easier to say "the police violated *Miranda*" than to say "the judge would be violating *Miranda* if he or she were to admit the defendant's statements into evidence."

But the war against terrorism has suddenly increased the significance of this previously academic question. In terrorism investigations, it will often be more important to get potentially life-saving information from a suspect than to obtain incriminating statements for use in court.[88] Fortunately, the Supreme Court said in 1990 that "a constitutional violation [of the Fifth Amendment's self-incrimination clause] occurs only at trial."[89] It cited an earlier ruling that the government can obtain court orders compelling reluctant witnesses to talk and can imprison them for contempt of court for refusing if it first guarantees them immunity from prosecution on the basis of their statements or any derivative evidence.[90] These decisions support the conclusion that the self-incrimination clause "does not forbid the forcible extraction of information but only the use of information so extracted as evidence in a criminal case," as another federal appeals court ruled in 1992.[91]

Of course, even when the primary reason for questioning a suspected terrorist is prevention, the government could pay a heavy cost for ignoring *Miranda* and using coercive interrogation techniques: this would sometimes make it difficult or impossible to prosecute extremely dangerous terrorists.[92] But terrorism investigators may be able to get their evidence and use it too, if the Court—or Congress, which unlike the Court would not have to wait for a proper case to come along—extends a 1984 precedent creating what the justices called a "public safety" exception to *Miranda*. That decision allowed use at trial of a defendant's incriminating answer to a policeman's demand (before any *Miranda* warnings) to know where his gun was hidden.[93]

Those facts are not a perfect parallel for most terrorism investigations because of the immediate nature of the danger (an accomplice might pick up the gun) and the spontaneity of the officer's question. And as Rowley testified, "In order to give timely advice" about what an agent can legally do, "you've got to run to a computer and pull it up, and I think that many people have kind of forgotten that case, and many courts have actually limited it to its facts."[94]

But when the main purpose of the interrogation is to prevent terrorist attacks, the magnitude of the danger argues for a broader public safety exception, as Rowley implied.[95] Congress should neither wait until the justices have a proper case in which to clarify the law nor assume that they will reach the right conclusions without prodding. It should make the rules as clear as possible as soon as possible. Officials like Rowley need to know that they are free to interrogate suspected terrorists more aggressively than they might imagine. While a law expanding the public safety exception would be challenged, it would contradict no existing Supreme Court precedent and—if carefully calibrated to apply only when the immediate purpose is to save lives—would probably be upheld.[96]

Would investigators routinely ignore *Miranda* and engage in coercive interrogation—perhaps extorting false confessions—if told that the legal restraints are far looser than has been supposed? The risk would not be significantly greater than it is now.[97] Police would still need to comply with *Miranda* in almost all cases for fear of jeopardizing any prosecution. While that would not be true in terrorism investigations if the public safety exception were broadened, extreme abuses such as beatings and torture would violate another clause of the Fifth Amendment (and of the Fourteenth Amendment). That is the due process clause. The Supreme Court has ruled that suspects have a substantive due process right to be free from police practices "so brutal and so offensive to human dignity" that they "shock the conscience."[98]

Should even torture be allowed if the information sought might save many lives? "Let's assume you think someone is going to blow up the World Trade Center," Justice Antonin Scalia asked during a December 4, 2002, oral argument. "Could the police beat him with a rubber hose?"[99] Harvard Law School's Alan Dershowitz makes a strong case for judicially supervised use of torture in rare cases.[100] Surely, he and like-minded thinkers say, torturing a captured terrorist would be morally and legally justified if that were the only hope for finding a ticking nuclear time bomb that could kill 100,000 people.

Although it is tempting to duck the difficulty of such questions by taking refuge in the rationale that torture is ineffective at extracting reliable information, this conclusion seems incorrect. Torture has clearly worked in some cases and has almost certainly saved lives.[101] And as Dershowitz points out, there is an element of hypocrisy in a we-don't-torture rule. U.S. authorities have gladly accepted information from friendly foreign intelligence agencies that use torture and have been known to deliver suspects into the hands of such agencies to be tortured and then returned. And two former Afghan prisoners at the U.S. air base at Bagram, Afghanistan, named Abdul Jabar and Hakim Shah, told the *New York Times* that between interrogations they were kept standing in cold cells for two weeks, day and night, naked (in Shah's case), hooded, arms chained to the ceiling, feet shackled, and sleepless, with guards kicking them or shouting at them to keep them awake. The deaths of two other Bagram detainees are under investigation as homicides, caused in one case by what a U.S. military pathologist called "blunt-force injuries to lower extremities complicating coronary artery disease." The man was twenty-two.[102]

It would nonetheless be a mistake to codify in any act of Congress an explicit exception to the absolute (or near-absolute) rules against torture.[103] Unlike *Miranda* and other rules just discussed, the rule against torture is much more than a prophylaxis against abuses of authority; torture *is* an abuse of authority, viscerally horrifying to civilized people and condemned by the moral codes of all civilized societies. The ticking-nuclear-time-bomb hypothetical is extremely unlikely ever to occur in the real world, because it is almost always impossible to be confident in advance that a suspect has potentially life-saving information that can be extracted by torture and only by torture. Nor could a "torture exception" be defined narrowly enough to prevent overuse.

Would we want our government torturing suspects like Moussaoui because they might possibly know something about planned attacks? What about John Walker Lindh? What about a suspect who may be a terrorist— or may not be? If the hope of saving 100,000 lives justifies torture, what about 1,000? Or 100? Or 10? Or one? This slope is too slippery. It is better to have an element of hypocrisy in our national policy by accepting information that we suspect may have been extorted through torture overseas than to risk drifting toward systematic brutality on American soil.[104]

In the unlikely event that the ticking-nuclear-time-bomb hypothetical ever does become reality, one can only hope that conscientious investigators would do what it takes to avert catastrophe. They might—or might not—be in technical violation of the law.[105] But in any event, prosecutorial discretion would argue against any effort to punish them. If prosecuted, they could invoke the seldom-raised common-law defense of necessity and could expect sympathetic jurors and, if necessary, executive clemency.[106]

Bringing Preventive Detention Inside the Law

Of all the enhanced governmental powers that must be considered after September 11, preventive detention—incarcerating people because of their perceived dangerousness even when they are neither convicted nor charged with any crime—would represent the sharpest departure from centuries of Anglo-American jurisprudence and come closest to the methods of a police state.[107]

But the case for some kind of preventive detention has never been as strong. Al Qaeda's capacity to inflict catastrophic carnage dwarfs any previous domestic security threat. Its "sleeper" agents are trained to avoid criminal activities that might arouse suspicion. So the careful ones cannot be arrested on criminal charges until it is too late. And their lust for martyrdom renders criminal punishment ineffective as a deterrent.

Without preventive detention, the Bush administration would apparently have no solid legal basis for holding the two U.S. citizens now in military brigs in this country as suspected "enemy combatants" or for holding the more than 600 noncitizens at Guantanamo Bay and others in Afghanistan and perhaps elsewhere. Nor would it have had a solid legal basis for detaining any of the nineteen September 11 hijackers if it had suspected them of links to al Qaeda before they struck. Nor could it legally have detained Moussaoui—who *was* suspected of terrorist intent but was implicated in no provable crime or conspiracy—had he had not overstayed his visa.

Without preventive detention, the Clinton administration would have had no legal basis to detain Osama bin Laden in 1996 if, as some have claimed, Sudan had offered to hand him over. (Former officials deny that such an offer was made.) Despite intelligence reports that bin Laden was training terrorists and planning attacks on the United States, the government lacked sufficient admissible evidence to mount a convincing prosecution.[108]

What should the government do when it is convinced of the suspect's terrorist intent but lacks admissible evidence of any crime? Or when a criminal trial would blow vital intelligence secrets? Or when ambiguous evidence makes it a tossup whether a suspect is harmless or a member of al Qaeda? What should it do with suspects like Jose Padilla, who was arrested at Chicago's O'Hare airport in May 2002 and has been in military detention since June because he is suspected of (but not charged with) plotting a radioactive "dirty-bomb" attack on Washington, D.C.? Or with an otherwise unremarkable (hypothetical) Pakistani graduate student in chemistry who has downloaded articles about how terrorists might use small planes to start an anthrax epidemic and shown an intense but unexplained interest in crop dusters?

Only four options exist: let such suspects go about their business unmonitored until (perhaps) they commit mass murders; assign agents to tail them until (perhaps) they give the agents the slip; bring prosecutions without solid evidence, risking acquittals; and preventive detention. The latter could theoretically include not only incarceration but milder restraints such as house arrest or restriction to certain areas combined with agreement to carry, or to be implanted with, a device enabling the government to track the suspect's movements at all times.

As an alternative to preventive detention, Congress could seek to facilitate prosecutions of suspected "sleepers" by stretching the already broad concept of criminal conspiracy so far as to make it almost a thought crime and by allowing use of secret or now-inadmissible evidence.[109] But that would have a harsher impact on possibly innocent terrorism suspects than would preventive detention and could weaken protections for all criminal defendants.

"No civilized nation confronting serious danger has ever relied exclusively on criminal convictions for past offenses. Every country has introduced, by one means or another, a system of preventive or administrative detention for persons who are thought to be dangerous but who might not be convictable under the conventional criminal law."[110] While the herding of 110,000 Japanese Americans into detention camps during World War II is almost universally condemned today as the greatest abuse of civil liberties since slavery, the simultaneous confinement of German and Italian aliens found to be enemy sympathizers—based on individualized investigations and hearings—was far more defensible in theory, if still excessive in practice.[111]

The best argument against preventive detention of suspected international terrorists is history's warning that any such system will be abused, could expand inexorably—especially in the panic that might follow future attacks—and has such terrifying potential for infecting the entire criminal justice system and undermining the Bill of Rights that the nation should never start down that road. What is terrorist intent, and how may it be proved? Can it be discerned through a suspect's advocacy of a terrorist group's cause or by association with its members or sympathizers? If preventive detention is okay for people suspected of, but not charged with, terrorist intent, what about people suspected of homicidal intent, violent proclivities, or dealing drugs?

These are serious concerns. But the dangers of punishing dissident speech, guilt by association, and overuse of preventive detention could be controlled by careful legislation. This would not be the first exception to the general rule against preventive detention. The others have worked fairly well. They include pretrial detention without bail of criminal defendants shown to be dangerous,[112] civil commitment of people found dangerous by reason of mental illness,[113] and medical quarantines, an ancient practice that may once again be necessary in the event of bioterrorism. All in all, the danger that a preventive detention regime for suspected terrorists would take us too far down the slippery slope toward a police state is simply not as bad as the danger of letting would-be mass murderers roam the country.

In any event, we already have a preventive detention regime for suspected international terrorists—three regimes, in fact: two at home and one at Guantanamo Bay. All were created and controlled by the Bush administration without congressional input and with little regard for the law, the rights of the many (mostly former) detainees who are probably innocent, or international opinion:

—The administration has incarcerated for months, in military brigs, two U.S. citizens whom it calls "enemy combatants" but has charged with no crime and given no semblance of due process. The government refuses to let them see lawyers or judges on the ground that such meetings would frustrate interrogation efforts. One is Jose Padilla, the Detroit-born Mexican American street gang alumnus arrested in Chicago. The other is Yaser Esam Hamdi, a Louisiana-born Saudi Arabian who was captured in Afghanistan and taken first to Guantanamo and then the United States.

Preventive detention of enemy combatants, including U.S. citizens, seems to be constitutionally valid under wartime precedents, including the 1942 Supreme Court ruling in the now-famous case of the German saboteurs that enemy combatants, regardless of citizenship, "are subject to capture and detention as prisoners of war."[114] Two courts have so held in recent decisions involving Padilla.[115] But that does not justify the administration's complete denial of due process to *suspected* enemy combatants captured in the United States, like Padilla and Hamdi, or the "sweeping proposition . . . that, with no meaningful judicial review, any American citizen alleged to be an enemy combatant could be detained indefinitely without charges or counsel on the government's say-so," in the words of a federal appeals court.[116]

The administration says that it does not have to prove anything to anyone, ever. It claims that even U.S. citizens arrested in this country—who may have far stronger grounds than battlefield detainees for denying that they are enemy combatants—are entitled to no due process whatever, once the government puts that label on them. This argument is virtually unprecedented, probably wrong as a matter of law (as one judge has already held), and indefensible as a matter of policy.[117] It brings to mind James Madison's assertion in *Federalist* 47 that "the accumulation of all powers legislative, executive and judiciary in the same hands . . . may justly be pronounced the very definition of tyranny."

—Ashcroft's roundup in the fall of 2001 of more than 1,200 mostly Muslim noncitizens clearly involved preventive detention in many cases. Although 765 of them were charged with mostly minor immigration violations and another 134 with federal crimes, most of them would apparently not have been detained had they been (say) Norwegians.[118] At least 44 were held under the material-witness statute, which apparently was used in many cases as a pretext for preventive detention rather than to obtain testimony.[119] (More than 300 others were detained by state and local officials.) This when-in-doubt-detain approach effectively reversed the presumption of innocence in the hope of disrupting any planned follow-up attacks. We may never know whether it succeeded in this vital objective. But we do know this: not one of these 1,200-plus detainees has been charged with any role in the September 11 attacks, and only a handful have been charged with having any connection to terrorist groups.[120]

However necessary this dragnet may have been in the immediate aftermath of September 11, the legal and moral bases for holding hundreds of apparently harmless detainees, sometimes without access to legal counsel,[121] in conditions of unprecedented secrecy, seemed less and less plausible as weeks and months went by. (By mid-2002, most of them had been deported or released.)[122] Many "material witnesses," never identified by the government, were held for far longer than necessary to secure their testimony.[123] That was preventive detention in disguise. Worse, the administration reportedly treated many if not most of the detainees shabbily and some abusively.[124] The accounts of some former detainees have spawned plausible suggestions that before releasing innocent men, officials deliberately sought to break their spirits, through what could be called psychological torture, to make sure they were holding nothing back.[125]

— The Pentagon has incarcerated more than 600 Arab and other prisoners captured in Afghanistan for many months at Guantanamo—which was apparently chosen to avoid the jurisdiction of all courts—as "unlawful combatants." International law authorizes detention of enemy combatants (lawful and unlawful alike) until hostilities have ended, and the same rule logically applies when the enemy is a foreign terrorist organization. But the administration has violated at least the spirit of the 1949 Geneva Conventions by refusing to create a fair, credible process for determining which of these men are in fact enemy combatants, which are unlawful combatants, and which are neither.[126]

There is a better way to handle such cases. It is past time for Congress to step in and authorize a regime of temporary preventive detention for suspected international terrorists, while circumscribing that regime and specifying strong safeguards against abuse.

A Proposed Terrorism Prevention Act

The tentative outlines of a proposed Terrorism Prevention Act are as follows:

—To augment the government's investigative powers, the attorney general should be authorized to obtain a judicial warrant for a physical search, wiretap, or other electronic surveillance whenever he or she can produce evidence establishing reasonable grounds to believe that the proposed action might save lives by preventing an international terrorist attack.

—To guard against overuse and abuse of these new powers, any evidence obtained *solely* by the authority of this law should be inadmissible in any criminal proceeding other than prosecutions for crimes involving or related to terrorism.

—To facilitate interrogation of suspected international terrorists, federal agents should be instructed that they may dispense with *Miranda* warnings, refuse to honor requests for counsel, and vigorously interrogate persons they have reasonable grounds to suspect of having information that might prevent a terrorist attack. Compelled statements would be inadmissible in any prosecution of the speaker, by operation of the Fifth Amendment. But not all statements taken without *Miranda* warnings or access to counsel are compelled.[127]

—To replace the Bush administration's various ad hoc preventive detention regimes, Congress should authorize the government to detain suspected foreign terrorists arrested inside the United States if, and only if, they are charged with crimes, or with immigration violations, or held under material witness warrants, or assigned to military detention as enemy combatants based on a presidential order subject to appropriate judicial review, or the following requirements are satisfied:[128] One, the attorney general certifies that he has reasonable grounds to believe that the suspect is an active participant in an international terrorist group that seeks to murder Americans; his release would lead to or facilitate life-threatening acts of terrorism; and prosecution is not currently an option, because the government cannot prove him guilty of a crime or because the evidence is inadmissible or too sensitive for a public trial.[129] Two, the government may detain and interrogate such suspects without access to legal counsel for no more than twenty days. Three, individuals not criminally charged within twenty days should be promptly compensated for lost wages and other economic costs, plus a reasonable additional sum for each day in detention. Four, after twenty days, the government must release each uncharged detainee unless it can win a six-month extension by convincingly establishing the preceding criteria for detention at a hearing before a special federal court. The detainee should have the rights to counsel, to any known exculpatory evidence, to contest the government's claims, and to call witnesses. All evidence probative to a reasonable person should be considered, even if it is not admissible in a criminal trial. Proceedings should be public except for properly classified evidence. Five, after the six months, and each succeeding six months, the government must release each uncharged detainee unless it can justify continued detention at a similar hearing based on the same three criteria (noted under "one" above) and any new evidence or relevant facts. All detainees must be released within three years unless they are criminally charged. And finally, all detainees must be held in comfortable, nonpunitive quarters and compensated as specified above unless criminally charged or unless the court rules that the circumstances do not warrant compensation.

—A different, more deferential legislative scheme would be appropriate for the foreign detainees captured on foreign battlefields who are at Guantanamo. The Bill of Rights does not apply on foreign battlefields. And the risk of error in identifying enemy combatants is not as great as in the domestic context. But they should at least be given an opportunity to challenge their enemy-combatant designations in some kind of military tribunal.

—To provide for accumulation of judicial expertise and clear, consistent case law, Congress should expand the FISA court's jurisdiction to encompass all issues arising under these provisions. It should also require that all of that court's proceedings be public except to the extent that the government can show that public access to a certain proceeding might endanger lives or the national security.

—A new agency should be created to monitor the government's compliance with civil liberties and civil rights in the war against terrorism, with the power to investigate complaints, initiate its own investigations, subpoena witnesses and documents, and report findings to the president, the attorney general, Congress, and the public.[130] (In contrast to the prosecutors named under the late, unlamented Independent Counsel Statute, this agency should be headed by a Senate-confirmed presidential appointee and should have no prosecutorial powers of its own.)

These proposals are offered as a starting point for the debate the nation should be having. Reasonable people will disagree about how best to recalibrate the liberty-security balance. The most important point is that a free people should resolve these questions not by executive fiat but by law.

An Irrational Taboo: Group-Based Profiling and Cost-Benefit Analysis

In a July 10, 2001, memo e-mailed to FBI headquarters, an agent in Phoenix, Kenneth J. Williams, expressed alarm about Muslim militants at an aeronautical school who were showing unusual interest in airport security. The agent suggested that perhaps they had been sent by Osama bin Laden to prepare for terrorist activities. Williams urged a nationwide review of Middle Eastern men enrolled in such schools. This suggestion echoed a May 1998 memo by an FBI pilot reporting that he had seen "large numbers of Middle Eastern males receiving flight training at [Oklahoma] area airports" and that this occurrence "could be related to planned terrorist activity," such as using light planes to spread chemical or biological agents.[131]

Yet FBI headquarters did nothing. Among the reasons suggested by some FBI officials: "the worry that such an effort might be criticized in Congress as racial profiling."[132] This excuse has been plausibly dismissed by some congressional investigators and others as a rationalization for inattention and incompetence. But it does seem that the FBI had been especially gun-shy about complaints about racial profiling, and that "we've made people so frightened of doing their jobs because they have to be politically correct that they avoid the obvious."[133] The FBI had been excoriated in the media and Congress since 1999 based on the (apparently untrue) claim that racial profiling had been the basis for targeting Taiwan-born nuclear scientist Wen Ho Lee for investigation on a never-substantiated suspicion of spying for China.[134] Some of the same critics turned on a dime last spring and criticized the FBI for failing to be more suspicious of Middle Eastern men in flight schools—failing, that is, to engage in profiling based on national origin.

(Group-based profiling may be defined as choosing a person for investigation or scrutiny based on the belief that members of a group to which he or she belongs—be it gender, nationality, race, or religion—are more likely than the population at large to commit certain crimes or terrorist acts.)

On September 11, nineteen young Middle Eastern men boarded four coast-to-coast domestic flights, without incident. All or some were carrying razor-sharp box cutters or knives and had bought high-priced seats near the cockpit; four had attended flight schools in the United States; and two were named on the government's "watch list" of suspected terrorists.[135] Why did the airlines and security screeners see nothing amiss?

First, at the behest of Arab American and civil-libertarian lobbyists, security screeners were—and apparently still are—under orders to treat such Middle Eastern men with no more suspicion than Vermont boy scouts with Swiss Army knives or Iowa grandmothers with knitting needles. The government's security screening rules, initially adopted by the Clinton administration after a debate that "focused on civil liberties, not effectiveness," strictly prohibited inclusion of national origin (or race, ethnicity, religion, or even gender) among the traits and behaviors used as components of its multifactored airline security profile, the Computer-Assisted Passenger Pre-Screening System (CAPPS).[136] Second, security screeners might not even have seen the box cutters because—in a further concession to hypersensitive passengers who might cry "discrimination"— the same rules barred manual searches of those passengers who *were* flagged by CAPPS; only checked bags were to be screened.[137] Third, the "watch list" was unavailable to the airlines and security screeners in part because— in yet another concession to civil libertarians—the same rules barred inclusion of law-enforcement or intelligence data in CAPPS.[138]

Politically correct fundamentalism had triumphed over rationality. (And not only in airline security.)[139] This approach achieved its goal of minimizing passenger complaints about profiling.[140] It did not work so well at preventing mass murder.

Yet so powerful is the taboo that has arisen in recent years against anything that could correctly or not be called racial profiling that the Bush administration publicly embraced the Clinton administration's approach to airline security profiling *even after* September 11.[141] "I'm against using race as a profiling component," declared Ashcroft—who is not known for devotion to civil liberties—five days after the September 11 hijackings.[142] He added that he considered such profiling unconstitutional, a position sharply at odds with the most relevant Supreme Court precedent.[143] He has avoided addressing the distinctions among racial, religious, and national-origin profiling, which are often, although incorrectly, equated. And FBI Director Robert Mueller testified at a June 6, 2002, congressional hearing that the FBI "is against, has been and will be against any form of profiling."[144]

These official preachments are contradicted by Justice Department and FBI practices, including the above-noted FBI headquarters order that field offices tally the number of mosques in their areas. This contradiction between announced policy and official practice creates dangerous confusion among both government agents—who may fear being hung out to dry for following orders—and citizens.[145]

Ashcroft's Justice Department has given dispositive weight to national origin—and indirectly to religion—in other counterterrorism activities. Almost all of the more than 1,200 immigrants and foreign visitors detained in the fall of 2001 in connection with the investigation into the September 11 attacks were from Islamic nations. Another Ashcroft program sent FBI agents to interview more than 5,000 (later increased to 8,000) male noncitizens between the ages of eighteen and thirty-three who had arrived from Islamic nations in the past two years. A third program targeted some 5,000 noncitizens from the Middle East who have ignored deportation orders to be hunted down, ahead of some 300,000 people from other nations who have done the same. A fourth program requires several thousand students and other temporary residents from twenty-five Islamic nations to be fingerprinted and photographed to determine whether they are suspects in terrorism or other criminal investigations.[146]

Such forms of national-origin profiling impose greater burdens on those targeted than being required to open one's toilet kit to security screeners—far, far greater burdens, in the cases of those incarcerated. Whether any or all of these programs produce enough benefits to justify the burdens—and the resentments that flow from them—depends on fact-intensive analyses likely to vary from one program to the next. The efforts to interview the 8,000 men seem to have worked fairly well and brought relatively few complaints.[147] The fingerprinting and photographing may be too selective to do much good or to warrant the offense to visitors from the twenty-five Islamic nations. Some Arab Americans and Muslims from abroad have told searing tales of beatings and other abuses by police investigators, and some express fear of being interned en masse as Japanese Americans once were.[148] But whatever the merits, Ashcroft is knee-deep in national-origin profiling, or something close to it.[149] As he should be, subject to the need for more robust safeguards against abuse.

There are worse things than Ashcroft's inconsistencies on group-based profiling. One is Transportation Secretary Norman Mineta's foolish consistency. He has stubbornly stuck with the Clinton administration's color-blind, religion-blind, national-origin-blind approach to airline security profiling. This in the face of facts showing that the *only* effective protection during the months after September 11 against bombs concealed in luggage would have been to maximize the odds that the tiny fraction of bags that were searched include those of men from the Muslim nations known to supply most of al Qaeda's recruits.

Mineta (who as a child was sent to World War II detention camps for Japanese Americans) declared on national television in December 2001 that his policy was to give the same scrutiny to seventy-year-old white women as to young Muslim men.[150] His public information office said in July 2002 that "we do not use racial, ethnic, national origin or gender factors to profile people."[151]

Opposition to racial profiling is an understandable and in many cases a correct reaction to our history of racial discrimination, to the offensiveness to many people of even the most unintrusive forms of profiling, and to the manifest lack of justification for the most notorious form of profiling: the police practice of stopping African American motorists for "driving while black" and pressuring them to submit to "voluntary" searches for drugs. Arab Americans and Muslims do not want to be treated similarly. Nor should they be: stopping drivers perceived to be Arabs or Muslims for drug searches would be just as indefensible.

But while national-origin profiling is in the same neighborhood as racial profiling, it is not the same thing. An airline security profile including national origin as a component could be designed to exclude Arab Americans: a brown-skinned Muslim born in the United States to Lebanese immigrants, for example, would not fit the profile if his or her voice exuded no trace of foreign origins.[152] More important, that group-based profiling is usually unjustified does not mean that it is always unjustified.[153] Stopping black (or brown) drivers for drug searches based on a racial profile is wrong; stopping airline passengers who are known or suspected to be from the Islamic world for weapon and bomb searches after September 11 is right. So is giving special scrutiny to Islamic-world students at flight schools.

The basis for these distinctions is cost-benefit analysis. On the benefit side, reducing the risk that terrorists will murder planeloads of people is infinitely more important than finding some minuscule percentage of the tons of illegal drugs flowing through the country. On the cost side, politely asking a fraction of all passengers to take off their shoes and submit to "wanding" and manual searching of their bags is at worst a minor annoyance—and one that is already imposed on people of all ethnicities, based on random selection and behavioral profiling, whether or not national origin is also used as a profiling component. The burden is trivial compared with the inconvenience to and humiliation of black drivers pulled over by grim-faced police, often at night, sometimes in the rain, and pressured to get out "voluntarily" and submit to the ransacking of their cars.

Stopping innocent black drivers on highways also smacks of—and sometimes involves—old-fashioned racial harassment.[154] By instilling distrust among many African Americans whose cooperation law enforcement needs, this practice imposes heavy costs not only on liberty but also on public safety. These costs so clearly outweigh any benefits of race-based car stops—which have very little effect, if any, on the flow of illegal drugs—as to create a growing consensus that the practice should end.[155] Although Arab American leaders warn that airline profiling also foments distrust of the authorities, many Arab Americans disagree. They understand their own interests in not being blown to bits or flown into skyscrapers.[156]

The best airline security would be foolproof searching of all passengers and their baggage by high-tech machines, which would make it possible to dispense with all forms of profiling. But we are not there yet. Effective security still depends on choosing the small percentage of passengers and bags to be closely searched through the most educated possible guesses about which passengers are most likely to be terrorists.

The most serious argument against national-origin profiling in airline security is that it would be ineffective.[157] This seems superficially plausible but is ultimately unconvincing. It is true that any profile designed to fit Muslims from abroad based on physical appearance and voice would be overinclusive and underinclusive, given the diverse races, skin tones, languages, and nationalities of the world's 1.2 billion Muslims and the outward resemblance of many Muslims to non-Muslims. Nor would a national-origin profile fit American-born jihadists such as Jose Padilla (a Hispanic American) and John Walker Lindh (white), or Europeans such as Richard Reid (London-born suspect of an English mother and Jamaican father, who is charged with trying to blow up an airplane with explosives hidden in his shoes), or, perhaps, Muslims of African ancestry born in France, such as Moussaoui.

But still, the mathematical probability that a man who looks and sounds like Mohammed Atta will turn out to be a terrorist—while tiny—is far greater than the chance that a person who looks and sounds like Colin Powell, or Dick Gephardt, or Henry Kissinger, or Strom Thurmond, or Michael Jordan, or Hillary Rodham Clinton will turn out to be one. Young men are more likely to be terrorists than old women. Recent immigrants or visitors are more likely to be terrorists than twenty-year frequent flyers who use corporate travel agencies. Militant Muslims are far more likely to be terrorists than any other religious or ethnic group. And most militant Muslims were born or raised in the nations of the Islamic world.

The leading airline security experts in the world—those at El Al Israel, who have shut out Islamic terrorists since 1968—use such profiling systematically. And although El Al's interview-based screening system may be too time consuming for exact replication in the United States, most European airlines also use group-based profiling. Some American experts also endorse such profiling—though in muted terms, because most or all serve political masters like Mineta.[158]

The government's profiling system (CAPPS), as characterized by Mineta, recklessly averts its eyes from these realities, focusing instead on behaviors that well-trained terrorists can easily avoid and on identification documents that they can easily forge or steal. The government is still "dependent on antiquated software that assumes terrorists book flights by paying with cash, buy one-way tickets or catch flights at the last minute."[159] Al Qaeda is not that stupid. Not so easily avoided or disguised are the outwardly observable badges of probable Islamic-world origin: skin color, facial features, use of language, and accent, although these characteristics are far from foolproof evidence. A profile taking account of these traits, as well as suspicious behaviors, would be a powerful deterrent to future airline terrorism by almost all Islamic terrorists.

It is sometimes suggested that focusing on airline terrorism falls into the trap of fighting the last war instead of preparing for the next one. And it is true that more bomb-detection equipment, fortified cockpit doors, sky marshals, and the prospect of resistance from passengers and crew may deter future hijackings and bombing attacks on airliners. This has made the need for national-origin profiling less urgent than it was before and during the first few months after September 11. But the system is still far from perfect.[160] And until it is, the ban, or purported ban, on national-origin profiling will put thousands of lives at unnecessary risk.

September 11: What Might Have Happened

It is conceivable, although far from clear, that some or all of the September 11 hijackings could have been prevented had the rules proposed here been in force then. As we have seen, some of the government's most widely publicized failures turn out to be rooted at least partly in its efforts to avoid violating the taboo against racial profiling and to comply with unduly restrictive civil liberties rules.

If federal law had encouraged the FBI, CIA, and other agencies to share information and work together to pursue suspected terrorists, they might have seen the significance of the scattered clues that in hindsight point to the September 11 attacks. And if they had done that, the attacks might have been prevented. Or so some FBI officials have claimed.[161]

If the FBI had done the proposed nationwide investigation of Middle Eastern men in flight schools, it might have developed suspicions about some of the nineteen hijackers, as the Minneapolis office did about Moussaoui. And if a preventive detention statute had been on the books, the government could have locked them up.

If the FBI had been free to search Moussaoui's computer and other belongings after arresting him on August 16, 2001, it would have found the names and phone numbers of two of the September 11 hijackers and the al Qaeda cell in Hamburg that planned the attacks, detailed information on crop dusting and Boeing 747 jetliners, and more.[162] "It's at least possible we could have gotten lucky and uncovered one or two more of the terrorists in flight training prior to September 11," FBI lawyer Coleen Rowley wrote last May.[163]

If the government's watch list of suspected terrorists had been checked against the names of people making airline reservations, the two hijackers whose names were on the watch list would have been identified when they made their reservations in August 2001. This would have prevented those two from boarding the flight that crashed into the Pentagon, probably aborting that hijacking. And if the government had plugged the same two names into a modest "data-mining" system of the kind deplored by some civil libertarians, most or even all of the other seventeen hijackers might have been identified before September 11.[164]

If security screeners had used a profile designed to include passengers who appear to have been raised in Islamic nations, all nineteen hijackers would probably have been flagged for special scrutiny. If the CAPPS rules had called for wanding their persons and searching their carry-on bags by hand, all or most of their box cutters would probably have been found. Although FAA rules did not then bar such small knives, some security officials suggested that they would have confiscated box cutters anyway.[165] And had security screeners been trained to pay special attention to Middle Eastern men, they might have been suspicious to find several of them carrying box cutters onto the same airliner.

If all of these safeguards had been in place, we might have seen a less catastrophic ending. Or we might not have. Definitive conclusions cannot be reached with confidence.

What is clear is that our overriding goal now should not be to restrict governmental powers so severely as to make abuses like Hoover's or Nixon's impossible—though we must guard against such abuses. Nor should it be to stamp out any semblance of politically incorrect profiling—though we should use such profiling sparingly. Our overriding goal now should be to increase our chances of finding the next Mohammed Atta, searching the possessions of the next Zacarias Moussaoui, and locking them up before it is too late.

Notes

1. James Risen and Dexter Filkins, "Threats and Responses," *New York Times,* September 10, 2002, p. A1.

2. Barry Rubin, "The Real Roots of Arab Anti-Americanism," *Foreign Affairs,* vol. 81 (November-December 2002), pp. 73–85. ("Arab and Muslim hatred of the United States is not just, or even mainly, a response to actual U.S. policies—policies that, if anything, have been remarkably pro-Arab and pro-Muslim over the years. Rather, such animus is largely the product of self-interested manipulation by various groups within Arab society, groups that use anti-Americanism as a foil to distract public attention from other, far more serious problems within those societies.")

3. "Civil rights" and "civil liberties" have somewhat different connotations, but the phrases are used interchangeably in this chapter.

4. "I think that the most important single step that we could have taken, had not taken, that we still need to take, is a change in mindset. . . . You have to change the way you think. . . . We're not organized [for this war] because we don't want to be. In the last 100 years, we have had a great record of success protecting our national security when it was threatened by some of the most ferocious powers on earth, without really sacrificing our open society. We don't want the FBI to talk to the CIA. We don't want the National Security Agency listening in on the conversations of American citizens. We don't want prosecutorial information shared with nonprosecutors. And as a result, we have designed a system that is not functional for this fight." Philip Bobbitt, quoted in Todd S. Purdom, "Getting More than One Step Ahead of an Attack," *New York Times,* May 26, 2002, sec. 4, p. 5. Bobbitt, a professor at the University of Texas with expertise in constitutional law and military strategy, has served in the Carter White House, the George H.W. Bush State Department, and the Clinton National Security Council.

5. For example, see note 52.

6. For example, Stephen J. Schulhofer, *The Enemy Within: Intelligence Gathering, Law Enforcement, and Civil Liberties in the Wake of September 11,* A Century Foundation Report (Century Foundation Press, August 2002); Lawyers Committee for Human Rights, "A Year of Loss: Reexamining Civil Liberties Since September 11" (New York, September 2002); and David Cole, "Enemy Aliens and American Freedoms," *Nation,* September 23, 2002, pp. 20–23.

7. Indeed, even the hastily passed USA Patriot Act, no model of careful deliberation,

expanded the administration's power to detain suspected terrorists much less than it had requested and much less than it has since sought to do by executive fiat. See Dan Eggen, "Justice Made Limited Use of New Powers, Panel Told," *Washington Post*, October 18, 2002, p. A11; USA Patriot Act, sec. 412, 8 USC 1226A(a)(5) (authorizing detention of suspected alien terrorists for up to seven days without charges).

8. See *Youngstown Sheet & Tube Co. v. Sawyer*, 343 U.S. 579, 635–38 (1952) (Jackson, J., concurring) ("When the President acts pursuant to an express or implied authorization of Congress, his authority is at its maximum, for it includes all that he possesses in his own right plus all that Congress can delegate. . . . When the President acts in absence of either a congressional grant or denial of authority, he can only rely upon his own independent powers, but there is a zone of twilight in which he and Congress may have concurrent authority, or in which its distribution is uncertain. Therefore, congressional inertia, indifference or quiescence may sometimes, at least as a practical matter, enable, if not invite, measures on independent presidential responsibility. In this area, any actual test of power is likely to depend on the imperatives of events and contemporary imponderables rather than on abstract theories of law. . . . When the President takes measures incompatible with the expressed or implied will of Congress, his power is at its lowest ebb, for then he can rely only upon his own constitutional powers minus any constitutional powers of Congress over the matter. Courts can sustain exclusive presidential control in such a case only by disabling the Congress from acting upon the subject. Presidential claim to a power at once so conclusive and preclusive must be scrutinized with caution, for what is at stake is the equilibrium established by our constitutional system" (footnotes omitted).

9. Matthew Brzezinski, "Fortress America," *New York Times Sunday Magazine*, February 23, 2003, pp. 28, 40. (We may come to think nothing of American citizens who act suspiciously being held without bail or denied legal representation for indeterminate periods or tried in courts whose proceedings were under seal.")

10. Among the issues omitted here are immigration and deportation; the use of biometric identifiers, including national identity cards with DNA fingerprints; the Justice Department's policy of monitoring consultations between some detainees and their lawyers; its congressionally aborted TIPS program of encouraging millions of Americans with access to others' homes to look for suspicious activities and become informers; use of data-mining to compile dossiers on citizens' commercial and other activities; controls on money laundering; the guilt-by-association implications of stretching conspiracy law to punish links to terrorist groups; proposals to ease the restrictions on the National Security Agency; and empowering the military to arrest suspected terrorists in the United States.

11. Mark Riebling, "Uncuff the FBI," *Wall Street Journal*, June 4, 2002, p. A20.

12. "In an age of anthrax, nuclear suitcases, and other easy-to-conceal weapons of mass destruction, the threat posed by al Qaeda and other terrorists might warrant trade-offs between liberty and security that are inconsistent with ordinary respect for civil liberties. . . .

"It is customary, and sensible, to fear that an overestimation of the current threat will lead us to abridge civil liberties in unjustifiable ways. But it is not senseless to fear as well that the gravitational pull of this trend might, in this or other circumstances, lead some to underestimate the threat we actually face." Jack L. Goldsmith and Cass Sunstein, "Military Tribunals and Legal Culture: What a Difference Sixty Years Makes," Public Law Research Paper 27 (University of Chicago, 2002), pp. 21–22, quotation on p. 21.

13. P. L. 107-56, 115 Stat. 272 (October 26, 2001).

14. See Charles Doyle, "The USA PATRIOT Act: A Sketch," Congressional Research Service, April 18, 2002.

15. See Neil A. Lewis, "Ashcroft Permits FBI to Monitor Internet and Public Activities," *New York Times*, May 31, 2002, p. A 20; and *The Attorney General's Guidelines on General Crimes, Racketeering Enterprise and Terrorism Enterprise Investigations*, May 30, 2002, Department of Justice.

16. See Tom Jackman and Dan Eggen, " 'Combatants' Lack Rights, U.S. Argues," *Washington Post*, June 20, 2002, p. A1.

17. *Hamdi* v. *Rumsfeld*, 316 F. 3d 450 (2003).

18. *Padilla* v. *Bush*, 233 F Supp.2d 564 (2002) (Michael B. Mukasey, J.) (recognizing statutory right to present facts through counsel, narrower than the Sixth Amendment right to counsel in criminal cases). The government has appealed.

19. *Youngstown Sheet & Tube*, 343 U.S. 646 (concurring opinion).

20. Richard A. Posner, "Security Versus Civil Liberties," *Atlantic Monthly*, December 2001, pp. 46–48.

21. John Mintz, "Report: U.S. Still Vulnerable," *Washington Post*, October 25, 2002, p. A1.

22. See, for example, George McGovern, "The Case for Liberalism," *Harper's*, December 2002, pp. 37–42; Neil K. Katyal and Laurence H. Tribe, "Waging War, Deciding Guilt: Trying the Military Tribunals," *Yale Law Journal*, vol. 111 (April 2002), pp. 1259–1310; and Fareed Zakaria, "Freedom vs. Security," *Newsweek*, July 8, 2002, pp. 26–31.

23. Terrorists could create something approaching anarchy if they succeeded in starting a smallpox epidemic or, especially, in obliterating with a nuclear explosion the nation's center of government in Washington or its economic hub in Manhattan.

24. See Neil A. Lewis, "Measure Backing Bush's Use of Force Is as Broad as a Declaration of War, Experts Say," *New York Times*, September 18, 2001, p. B7.

25. Linda Greenhouse, "In New York Visit, O'Connor Foresees Limits on Freedom," *New York Times*, September 29, 2001, p. B5.

26. See, for example, Stuart Taylor Jr., "A Nuclear Nightmare: It Could Happen Today," *National Journal*, November 10, 2001, pp. 3487–88, and "The Hawks Are Scary, the Doves More Dangerous," *National Journal*, October 5, 2002, pp. 2859–60.

27. For example, *Florida* v. *J.L.*, 529 U.S. 266 (2000); *Illinois* v. *Gates*, 462 U.S. 213 (1983); Foreign Intelligence Surveillance Act, 50 U.S.C. 1801, 1805 (probable cause to believe target is a foreign agent).

28. *Kyllo* v. *United States*, 533 U.S. 27 (2001)(agents may not aim thermal imaging device at home to detect heated marijuana garden inside without probable cause). The Geiger counter hypothetical is borrowed from the archives of a weblog shared by Professor Eugene Volokh of U.C.L.A. Law School (http://volokh.blogspot.com).

29. See *Edwards* v. *Arizona*, 451 U.S. 477 (1981) (police questioning must cease if arrested suspect requests counsel).

30. See, for example, *City of Indianapolis* v. *Edmund*, 531 U.S. 32 (2000); and Stuart Taylor Jr., "How Flawed Laws Help Terrorists and Serial Killers," *National Journal*, October 19, 2002, pp. 3035–36.

31. See Stuart Taylor Jr., "Politically Incorrect Profiling: A Matter of Life and Death," *National Journal*, vol. 33, no. 44 (November 3, 2001), pp. 3406–07; and see, for example,

Mark Murray, "Let the Blame Game Begin," *National Journal,* vol. 34, no. 31 (August 3, 2002), pp. 2316–2317 (as of July 9, 2002, only 215 of the 1,100 explosive-detention systems and 273 of the needed 6,000 smaller explosive-trace machines needed to scan all bags were in use).

32. Laurence H. Tribe, "Trial by Fury: Why Congress Must Curb Bush's Military Courts," *New Republic,* December 10, 2001, p.18.

33. Molly Ivins, "No Patriot Can Be Safer by Being Less Free," *Times Union,* August 10, 2002, p. A7.

34. *United States* v. *United States District Court,* 407 US 297 (1972).

35. 50 U.S.C. 1801. Although the FISA court has approved almost all of the Justice Department's more than 14,000 warrant applications since 1978, leading many to dismiss it as a meaningless rubber stamp, recent revelations suggest that the government's batting average may instead reflect a policy of seeking informal guidance first and filing formal applications only when approval seems assured. See Stuart Taylor Jr., "Spying by the Government Can Save Your Life," *National Journal,* vol. 34, no. 47 (November 23, 2002), pp. 3463–64. The FISA court excoriated the Justice Department and blighted at least one official's career for filing some seventy-five misleading warrant applications, mostly during the Clinton administration, in a decision unanimously rejecting the Bush administration's view that the USA Patriot Act dismantled the "wall" between foreign intelligence officials and criminal investigators. But the government persuaded a special appellate court to reverse that decision. See *In re Sealed Case,* Foreign Intelligence Court of Review, No. 02-001, November 18, 2002.

36. See, for example, David G. Savage, "Courts Likely to Endorse FBI Policy, Experts Say," *Los Angeles Times,* May 31, 2002, p. A22. Attorney General John Ashcroft issued completely rewritten, much less restrictive guidelines in May 2002. See also Louis Freeh, *Counterterrorism Efforts and the Events Surrounding the Terrorist Attacks of September 11, 2001,* testimony before Senate Select Committee on Intelligence and House Permanent Select Committee on Intelligence Joint Inquiry into the Terrorist Attacks of September 11, 2001, 107 Cong. 2 sess., October 8, 2002 ("FBI agents were statutorily barred from obtaining portions of credit reports on certain national security subjects which used car dealers could order and read.").

37. See Stewart Baker, "Civil Liberties in Wartime," *Slate,* posted September 18, 2001 ("Defending civil liberties is at the heart of the baby-boomer self-image, a self-image that's been packaged and sold to adolescents ever since. However powerful and rich and snobbish we ex-teen-agers become, we still see ourselves as rebels fighting a lonely battle against overweening authority. To make that myth work, we need an overweening authority to battle— preferably one that can't fight back. Intelligence agencies are perfect for that role"); Goldsmith and Sunstein, "Military Tribunals and Legal Culture," p. 22.

38. *Miranda* v. *Arizona,* 384 U.S. 436 (1966).

39. *Edwards* v. *Arizona,* 451 U.S. 477 (1981).

40. "Interrogations of detained enemy combatants . . . have helped to thwart an estimated 100 or more attacks against the United States or its interests after September 11, 2001." Respondents' [Government's] Motion for Reconsideration in Part, *Padilla* v. *Bush,* No. 02 Civ. 4445, S.D. N.Y., pp. 5–6.

41. *Olmstead* v. *United States,* 277 U.S. 438 (1928).

42. *Katz* v. *United States,* 389 U.S. 347 (1967).

43. *Warden* v. *Hayden*, 387 U.S. 294 (1967), overruling *Boyd* v. *United States*, 116 U.S. 616 (1886).

44. Benjamin Franklin in Daniel B. Baker, ed., *Political Quotations* (Detroit: Gale Research, 1991), p. 73. (Emphasis added.)

45. Robert O'Harrow Jr., "Six Weeks in Autumn," *Washington Post Magazine*, October 27, 2002, p.W6 (quoting Jim Dempsey of the Center for Democracy and Technology).

46. For example, Greg Miller, "Why U.S. Intelligence Stumbled: Hearings Portray Overwhelmed Agencies and Suggest 9/11 Could have Been Prevented," *Los Angeles Times*, October 19, 2002, part 1, p. 1.

47. See Stewart Baker, "Dangerous Secrets: Don't Give Up Security for a False Sense of Liberty," opinionjournal.com, October 5, 2001; and R. James Woolsey, "Blood Baath: The Iraq Connection," *New Republic*, September 24, 2001, p. 20 (After the first World Trade Center bombing, in 1993, "No one other than the prosecutors, the Clinton Justice Department, and the FBI had access to the materials surrounding that case until they were presented in court, because they were virtually all obtained by a federal grand jury and hence kept not only from the public but from the rest of the government under the extreme secrecy requirements of Rule 6(e) of the Federal Rules of Criminal Procedure.").

48. *In re Sealed Case*; and see Taylor, "Spying by the Government Can Save Your Life."

49. See David Johnston and Don Van Natta Jr., "Wary of Risk, Slow to Adapt, FBI Stumbles in Terror War," *New York Times*, June 2, 2002, sec. 1, p. 1.

50. See Nicholas D. Kristof, "Liberal Reality Check," *New York Times*, May 31, 2002, sec. A, p. 23 ("As we gather around FBI headquarters sharpening our machetes and watching the buzzards circle overhead, let's be frank: There's a whiff of hypocrisy in the air. One reason aggressive agents were restrained as they tried to go after Zacarias Moussaoui is that liberals like myself—and the news media caldron in which I toil and trouble—have regularly excoriated law enforcement authorities for taking shortcuts and engaging in racial profiling. As long as we're pointing fingers, we should peer into the mirror.").

51. See *Terminello* v. *Chicago*, 337 U.S. 1, 37 (1949) (Jackson, J, dissenting) ("There is danger that, if the Court does not temper its doctrinaire logic with a little practical wisdom, it will convert the constitutional Bill of Rights into a suicide pact.").

52. See, for example, Stuart Taylor Jr., "Let's Not Allow a Fiat to Undermine the Bill of Rights," *National Journal*, vol. 34, no. 29 (July 20, 2002), pp. 2143–44, "Congress Should Investigate Ashcroft's Detentions," vol. 34, no. 21 (May 25, 2002), p. 1536–37, "Don't Treat Innocent People Like Criminals," vol. 33, no. 49 (December 8, 2001), pp. 3729–30, and "Ashcroft's 'Trust-Us' Routine Is Getting a Little Stale," vol. 33, no. 46-47 (November 17, 2001), pp. 3569–70.

53. See Stuart Taylor Jr., "Military Tribunals Need Not Be Kangaroo Courts," *National Journal*, December 2, 2001. More than four months after the president's November 13 order, the Pentagon mollified some critics by publishing detailed procedural rules to ensure fair trials. See Katharine Q. Seelye, "Government Sets Rules for Military on War Tribunals," *New York Times*, March 21, 2002, sec. A, p. 1.

54. For example, Katharine Q. Seelye, "Bush Reconsiders Stand on Treating Captives of War," *New York Times*, January 29, 2002, sec. A, p. 1.

55. See Tom Jackman and Don Eggen, " 'Combatants' Lack Legal Rights, U.S. Argues," *Washington Post*, June 20, 2002, p. A1.

56. "To those who scare peace-loving people with phantoms of lost liberty, my message is this: Your tactics only aid terrorists, for they erode our national unity and diminish our resolve. They give ammunition to America's enemies, and pause to America's friends." Ashcroft testimony before Senate Judiciary Committee, December 6, 2001, excerpted in *New York Times*, December 7, 2001, p. B6.

57. See Baker, "Civil Liberties."

58. Goldsmith and Sunstein, "Military Tribunals and Legal Culture," p. 21 ("Compared to past wars led by Lincoln, Wilson, and Roosevelt, the Bush administration has, thus far, diminished relatively few civil liberties.").

59. See Christopher Edley Jr., "A U.S. Watchdog for Civil Liberties," *Washington Post*, July 14, 2002, p. B7.

60. See, for example, Alison Mitchell, "The Perilous Search for Security at Home," *New York Times*, July 28, 2002, sec. 4, p. 1.

61. See, for example, Siobhan Gorman, "Power to the Government," *National Journal*," vol. 34, no. 30 (July 27, 2002), pp. 2242–43 ("Figuring out the administration's ground rules for shifting more power to the government—and determining whether the administration is even abiding by its own rules—are incredibly difficult because the Justice Department balks at clearly defining crucial terms," such as "enemy combatant.").

62. See *In re Sealed Case.*

63. For example, Congress unthinkingly rushed into the statute books some questionable new powers for use in cases having nothing to do with terrorism, such as a provision authorizing more clandestine "sneak and peek" searches in routine criminal cases. See Schulhofer, *The Enemy Within*, pp. 42–43.

64. Title III of the Omnibus Crime Control and Safe Streets Act of 1968, 18 USC 2518; and Stephen J. Schulhofer, "At War with Liberty," *American Prospect* (Spring 2003), p. A5.

65. Moussaoui had been arrested for overstaying his visa on August 16, 2001, after an official at the Minnesota flight school called the FBI's Minneapolis office to warn that he had behaved oddly and might be planning a hijacking. He had received large wire transfers from overseas, which he used to pay $6,800 in cash for lessons on how to fly Boeing 747 jetliners despite meager experience. He had been unusually curious about whether doors could be opened during flight. French intelligence had said he was a fundamentalist with extremist political beliefs who had attended a radical mosque in London, had been to Pakistan and perhaps Afghanistan, and had recruited young jihadists to fight in Chechnya. He had expressed approval of Islamic terrorism to a traveling companion. After his arrest, he had refused to cooperate with investigators or consent to a search of his computer or other possessions. See, for example, Jim Yardley, "Student Tied to Terror Suspect Gave FBI Disturbing Portrait," *New York Times*, May 24, 2002, sec. A, p. 1.

66. Testimony of Eleanor Hill, staff director, before the Joint Select Intelligence Inquiry into the Terrorist Attacks of September 11, 2001, 107 Cong. 2 sess., September 24, 2002.

67. Riebling, "Uncuff the FBI."

68. 50 U.S.C. 1805 (a)(3)(A) and 1801 (a)(4), 1801 (b)(2)(c).

69. Rowley letter (www.time.com/time/covers/1101020603/memo.html). For example, see statements by Rep. Doug Bereuter (R-Neb.) and Senator Richard C. Shelby (R-Ala.) in testimony before the Joint Select Intelligence Committee, October 17, 2002;

and Philip Shenon, "Senate Report on Pre-9/11 Failures Tells of Bungling at FBI," *New York Times*, August 28, 2002, p. A14.

70. A French official has claimed anonymously that French intelligence told American authorities in late August 2001 that Moussaoui was a member of al Qaeda. FBI officials have denied this assertion. Raymond Bonner and Douglas Frantz, "French Suspect Moussaoui in Post-9/11 Plot," *New York Times*, July 28, 2002, sec. 1, p. 22.

71. See David Johnston and others, "FBI Inaction Blurred Picture before Sept. 11," *New York Times*, May 27, 2002, p. A1; and *In re Sealed Case*, p. 51, n. 29.

72. See Richard Lowry, "A Better Bureau," *National Review*, July 1, 2002, pp. 28–30.

73. On May 8, 2003, the Senate passed by 90 to 4 a Bush administration–endorsed proposal by Senators Jon Kyl (R-Ariz.) and Charles E. Schumer (D-N.Y.) to authorize FISA warrants even if the suspected international terrorist is a "lone wolf" unconnected to any group.

74. See Jeffrey Rosen, "Security Check," *New Republic,* December 16, 2002, p. 11 ("The better way to balance privacy and security in a world of integrated databases is to limit the use of evidence discovered in general data searches to the prosecution of terrorism and to prohibit the government from using it to prosecute low-level crimes.").

75. *Camara* v. *Municipal Court,* 387 U.S. 523, 534-39 (1967); See Akhil Reed Amar, *The Bill of Rights* (Yale University Press, 1998), pp. 68–73, and Amar, "Fourth Amendment First Principles," *Harvard Law Rev*iew, vol. 107 (February1994), pp. 757, 761–72.

76. *Skinner* v. *Railway Labor Executives' Association,* 489 U.S. 602 (1989) and cases cited there; and *Treasury Employees* v. *Von Raab,* 489 U.S. 656 (1989). For example, *Vernonia School District* v. *Acton,* 515 U.S. 646, 653 (1995). See also *In re Sealed Case,* p. 55 ("The nature of the 'emergency,' which is simply another word for threat, takes the matter out of the realm of ordinary crime control.").

77. George Orwell, *1984*, Signet classic (Penguin, 1981), p. 6.

78. See *Berger* v. *New York,* 388 U.S. 41, 65 (1967) (Douglas, J., concurring) ("A discreet selective wiretap or electronic 'bugging' is . . . the greatest of all invasions of privacy. It places a government agent in the bedroom, in the business conference, in the social hour, in the lawyer's office.").

79. See Neil A. Lewis, "Ashcroft Permits FBI to Monitor Internet and Public Activities," *New York Times*, May 31, 2002, p. A20; and Editorial, "An Erosion of Civil Liberties," *New York Times*, May 31, 2002, p. A22; see also Benjamin Weiser, "Rules Eased for Surveillance of New York Groups," *New York Times*, February 12, 2003, p. A17 (easing similar restrictions on police department). But see Schulhofer, *The Enemy Within*, pp. 55–63 (Ashcroft expanded investigative powers not only in counterterrorism investigations but also— indeed, primarily—in ordinary criminal cases, ignoring the lessons of FBI abuses under J. Edgar Hoover).

80. Sarah Downey and Michael Hirsh, "A Safe Haven?" *Newsweek*, September 30, 2002, pp. 30–33.

81. Michael Isikoff, "Touchy New Targeting," *Newsweek*, February 3, 2003, p. 6; and Eric Lichtblau, "FBI Tells Offices to Count Local Muslims and Mosques," *New York Times*, January 28, 2003, p. A13.

82. David Burnham, *The Rise of the Computer State* (Random House, 1983), p. 47.

83. See Rowley letter.

84. Freeh, *Counterterrorism Efforts,* testimony before Senate Select Committee on Intelligence and House Permanent Select Committee on Intelligence, October 8, 2002.

85. By April 2003, the Justice Department had shifted its theory on Moussaoui, arguing that he had planned to help hijack a fifth plane and crash it into the White House. Philip Shenon, "The Terror Suspect," *New York Times,* April 15, 2003, p. B10.

86. See *New York* v. *Quarles,* 467 U.S. 649, 686 (1984) (Marshall, J., joined by Brennan and Stevens, JJ. dissenting) ("If a bomb is about to explode or the public is otherwise imminently imperiled, the police are free to interrogate suspects without advising them of their constitutional rights. . . . All the Fifth Amendment forbids is the introduction of coerced statements at trial."). See Kevin Johnson and Richard Willing, "Ex-CIA Chief Revitalizes 'Truth Serum' Debate," *USA Today,* April 26, 2002; and Alan M. Dershowitz, *Why Terrorism Works: Understanding the Threat, Responding to the Challenge* (Yale University Press, 2002), pp. 247–48, note 6. In what lower courts found to be a coercive interrogation, a police officer named Ben Chavez insistently questioned Oliverio Martinez, without any *Miranda* warnings, as he struggled for his life at a hospital, suffering from several police-inflicted gunshot wounds. Martinez brought a civil suit against the police, including Chavez. One argument for dismissing the claim against Chavez was that he had done nothing illegal because the self-incrimination clause could be violated only by use of evidence at a criminal trial. A federal appeals court ruled that "Chavez's coercive, custodial questioning violated [Martinez's] . . . right[s]" under the self-incrimination clause. *Martinez* v. *City of Oxnard,* 270 F.3d 852 (9th Cir. 2001). In petitioning for review, Chavez argued that this decision flouted binding Supreme Court precedents.

87. See Dershowitz, *Why Terrorism Works,* p. 135; and Akhil Reed Amar and Renee B. Lettow, "Fifth Amendment First Principles: The Self-Incrimination Clause," *Michigan Law Review,* vol. 93 (March 1995), p. 857.

88. See Steve Fainaru, "Lawyer Challenges Al-Muhajir's Detention," *Washington Post,* June 12, 2002, p. A13 (quoting Defense Secretary Donald Rumsfeld: "We are not interested in trying him at the moment or punishing him [also known as Jose Padilla] at the moment. We are interested in finding out what he knows. He is an individual who unambiguously was interested in radiation weapons and terrorist activity, and was in league with al Qaeda.").

89. *United States* v. *Verdugo-Urquidez,* 494 U.S. 259, 264 (1990).

90. *Kastigar* v. *United States,* 406 U.S. 441, 453 (1972).

91. *Mahoney* v. *Kesery,* 976 F.2d 1054, 1061-62 (7th Cir. 1992).

92. It might still be able to hold in preventive or in military detention suspected terrorists who cannot be prosecuted.

93. *New York* v. *Quarles,* 467 U.S. 649 (1984).

94. *Oversight on Counterterrorism Efforts by the FBI,* testimony before Senate Judiciary Committee, June 6, 2002, 107 Cong. 2 sess, reported in Federal News Service online archive.

95. Rowley letter. ("Apparently no government attorney believes there is a 'public safety' exception in a situation like this?!")

96. See *Dickerson* v. *United States,* 530 U.S. 428 (2000) (striking down a 1968 act of Congress that sought to overrule *Miranda*).

97. Consider the polygraph-assisted FBI interrogation that drove Abdallah Higazy, an innocent Egyptian student detained after September 11, to make a confession that later

proved untrue. He later told reporters that after several hours, "I hyperventilated. I couldn't breathe. I felt I was going to faint. I wanted out of that room in any possible way." Benjamin Weiser, "Judge Considers an Inquiry on Radio Case Confession," *New York Times*, June 29, 2002, p. B3.

98. See *Rochin v. California*, 342 U.S. 165, 174 (1952); and *Leon v. Wainwright*, 734 F. 2d 770, 772–73 (11th Cir. 1984).

99. See Charles Lane, "Justices Ponder the Reach of Miranda Rights Ruling," *Washington Post*, December 5, 2002, p. A3.

100. See Dershowitz, *Why Terrorism Works*, pp. 131–63; and Jonathan Alter, "Time to Think about Torture," *Newsweek*, November 5, 2001, p. 45.

101. In 1995, for example, Philippine intelligence agents caught an al Qaeda member named Abdul Hakim Murad in a Manila bomb factory. Murad initially refused to tell Philippine investigators anything and was defiant through sixty-seven days of savage torture, including beatings that broke most of his ribs and lighted cigarettes crushed into his private parts. He finally cracked when agents disguised as Mossad agents threatened to take him to Israel. And what he revealed was a plot to assassinate Pope John Paul II, crash eleven U.S. airliners carrying some 4,000 people into the Pacific Ocean, and fly a private Cessna loaded with explosives into the CIA's headquarters. Philippine authorities finally turned him over to the United States. Matthew Brzezinski, "Bust and Boom," *Washington Post*, December 30, 2001, p. W9; and Steven Chapman, "No Tortured Dilemma," *Washington Times*, November 5, 2001, p. A18. See Dershowitz, *Why Terrorism Works*, pp. 136–38 (citing other examples in which torture may have saved lives).

102. Carlotta Gall, "U.S. Military Investigating Death of Afghan in Custody," *New York Times*, March 4, 2003, p. A14; Dana Priest and Barron Gellman, "U.S. Decries Abuse but Defends Interrogations," *Washington Post*, December 26, 2002, p. A1; and Rajiv Chandrasekaran and Peter Finn, "U.S. Behind Secret Transfer of Terror Suspects," *Washington Post*, March 11, 2002, p. A1.

103. See Michael J. Glennon, "Terrorism and the Limits of Law," *Wilson Quarterly* (Spring 2002), pp. 12–19; and see "Convention Against Torture and Other Cruel, Inhuman or Degrading Treatment or Punishment," adopted by U.N. General Assembly, December 10, 1984.

104. Glennon, "Terrorism and the Limits of Law."

105. See *County of Sacramento v. Lewis*, 523 U.S. 833, 849 (1998) ("conduct intended to injure in some way *unjustifiable by any government interest* is the sort of official action most likely to rise to the conscience-shocking level"). (Emphasis added.)

106. The Supreme Court of Israel, in a 1999 decision barring torture and violent shaking of suspected terrorists, noted the possibility of an "emergency conditions" defense for a member of the security service who honestly believed that rough interrogation was the only way to save lives in imminent danger. See Deborah Sontag, "Israel Court Bans Most Use of Force in Interrogations," *New York Times*, September 7, 1999, p. 1.

107. "If I assume that defendants are disposed to commit every opportune disloyal act helpful to Communist countries, it is still difficult to reconcile with traditional American law the jailing of persons by the courts because of anticipated but as yet uncommitted crimes. Imprisonment to protect society from predicted but unconsummated offenses is . . . unprecedented in this country and . . . fraught with danger of excesses and injustice." *Williamson v. United States*, 184 F. 2d 280 (1950) (Jackson, J., opinion in chambers) (foot-

note omitted). Steven Spielberg's movie *Minority Report*, released in 2002, in which a "Department of Pre-Crime" arrests Americans who might become criminals, dramatized where preventive detention could lead if carried to the limits of its logic.

108. See Timothy Carney and Mansoor Ijaz, "Intelligence Failure? Let's Go Back to Sudan," *Washington Post*, June 20, 2002, p. B4; and Samuel R. Berger, "Skeptical about Sudan," *Washington Post*, July 13, 2002, p. A19.

109. Congress has already authorized criminal prosecution for providing "material support" to a foreign terrorist group, including the defendant's own services as an agent of the group. See 18 U.S.C. 2339A and 2339B; and Stuart Taylor Jr., "Is There Freedom to Associate with Terrorists?" *National Journal*, vol. 34, no. 43 (October 26, 2002), pp. 3117–18. But this would not reach suspects who cannot be proved beyond a reasonable doubt to have provided "material support."

110. Alan M. Dershowitz, *Shouting Fire: Civil Liberties in a Turbulent Age* (Little, Brown, and Company, 2002), p. 432.

111. *Korematsu* v. *United States*, 323 U.S. 214, 241 (1944) (Murphy, J., dissenting).

112. *U.S.* v. *Salerno*, 481 U.S. 739 (1987).

113. *Addington* v. *Texas*, 441 U.S. 418 (1979); see *Kansas* v. *Hendricks*, 521 U.S. 346 (1997) (upholding Kansas's Sexually Violent Predator Act).

114. *Ex parte Quirin*, 317 U.S. 1, 31 (1942), *limiting Ex parte Milligan*, 71 U.S. (4 Wall.) 2 (1866); see *U.S.* v. *Salerno*, 481 U.S. 739, 748 (1987); and *Moyer* v. *Peabody*, 212 U.S. 78, 84 (1909).

115. *Hamdi* v. *Rumsfeld*; and *Padilla* v. *Bush*.

116. *Hamdi* v. *Rumsfeld*. While asserting that "we are not placing our imprimatur upon a new day of executive detentions," the appeals court upheld the detention of Hamdi without allowing him access to counsel or to any judge, based on the military's claim that he was "allied with enemy forces" (the Taliban) when captured in Afghanistan by the Northern Alliance.

117. *Padilla* v. *Bush*, 233 F. Supp. 2d, pp. 569, 604, 605 (S.D.N.Y. December 4, 2002) (rejecting the government's position that alleged enemy combatant has no right to counsel; dismissing as "gossamer speculation" the government's argument that he might use counsel as intermediary to pass messages to undetained terrorist cohorts; and holding that government must present "some evidence" to justify detaining alleged enemy combatant); *Padilla* v. *Rumsfeld*, 2003 U.S. Dist. LEXIS 3471 (S.D.N.Y. March 11, 2003) (rejecting government's motion for reconsideration on grounds that its prediction that any contact between Padilla and counsel would destroy interrogation was "speculative" and that Padilla has a right to respond to the government's allegations and needs a lawyer "to vindicate that right") (the government is appealing); see *American Bar Association Task Force on Treatment of Enemy Combatants: Preliminary Report* (Washington, August 8, 2002); and Henry Weinstein, "ABA Opposes Bush 'Enemy Combatants' Policy," *Los Angeles Times*, February 11, 2003, p. A7.

118. See Dan Eggen, "U.S. Holds 6 of 765 Detained in 9/11 Swoop," *Washington Post*, December 12, 2002, p. A20.

119. See Steve Fainaru and Margot Williams, "Material Witness Law Has Many in Limbo," *Washington Post*, November 24, 2002, p. A1; *U.S.* v. *Awadallah*, 202 F. Supp. 2d 55, 77 n. 28 (April 30, 2002) (Shira A. Scheindlin, J.) ("Relying on the material witness statute to detain people who are presumed innocent under our Constitution in order to prevent potential crimes is an illegitimate use of the statute.").

120. David Cole, "Enemy Aliens and American Freedoms," *Nation,* vol. 275, no. 9 (September 23, 2002), pp. 20–23.

121. "The Justice Department says every detainee [has] had access to counsel. Yet immigration lawyers contend that many detainees have had little or no access to legal counsel. It's impossible to know which side is correct, because the Justice Department has released virtually no information about the detainees." Gorman, "Power to the Government, " p. 2244.

122. See Eggen, "U.S. Holds 6 of 765 Detained."

123. See Fainaru and Williams, "Material Witness Law Has Many in Limbo."

124. For example, Taylor, "Don't Treat Innocent People Like Criminals."

125. See Matthew Brzezinski, "Hady Hassan Omar's Detention," *New York Times Magazine,* October 27, 2002, p. 50; and see also Stuart Taylor Jr., "Falsely Accused 'Enemies' Deserve Due Process," *National Journal,* vol. 35, no. 11, (March 15, 2003), pp. 785–86.

126. Geneva Convention relative to the Treatment of Prisoners of War, adopted August 12, 1949, art. 5. See *Al Odah* v. *United States,* 320 F. 3d 1134, 1137 (D.C. Cir. March 11, 2003) ("aliens detained outside the sovereign territory of the United States" are unprotected by the Constitution and outside jurisdiction of U.S. courts).

127. Public safety exception to *Miranda.*

128. See *Padilla* v. *Bush,* 233 F. Supp 2d, p. 608 (judicial review should examine "whether there is some evidence to support [the President's] conclusion that Padilla was . . . engaged in a mission against the United States on behalf of an enemy with whom the United States is at war.").

129. Unlike the McCarthy-era prosecutions and other measures against members of the U.S. Communist Party, which the Supreme Court curbed as imposing guilt by association, the proposed statute would reach only suspects whose release might lead to or facilitate life-threatening acts of terrorism. See Taylor, "Is There Freedom to Associate with Terrorists?"

130. This proposal is taken from Christopher Edley Jr., "A U.S. Watchdog for Civil Liberties," *Washington Post,* July 14, 2002, p. B7.

131. Eric Lichtblau and Josh Meyer, "Terrorist Signs Were Missed, FBI Chief Says," *Los Angeles Times,* May 30, 2002, part 1, p. 1.

132. David Johnston and Don Van Natta, Jr., "Wary of Risk, Slow to Adapt, FBI Stumbles in Terror War," *New York Times,* June 2, 2002, sec. 1, p. 1. FBI Director Robert Mueller told the Senate Judiciary Committee that investigating the 20,000 students attending American flight schools would have been "a monumental undertaking without any specificity as to particular persons." David Johnston, "FBI Says Pre-Sept. 11 Call for Inquiry Got Little Notice," *New York Times,* May 9, 2002, p. A34. But an investigation of the far smaller number of Arabs in flight schools would have been feasible. See also Barton Gellman, "Struggles Inside the Government Defined Campaign," *Washington Post,* December 20, 2001, p. A1 ("FBI investigators . . . were prevented from opening criminal or national security cases [investigating terrorist fund-raising] for fear that they would be seen as 'profiling' Islamic charities.").

133. Representative Mark Foley (R-Fla.), quoted in Dave Boyer, "Profiling Worries Called Hindrance in Terrorism Fight," *Washington Times,* June 4, 2002, p. A1.

134. Gabriel Schoenfeld, "How Inept Is the FBI?" *Commentary,* vol. 113, no. 5 (May 1, 2002), pp. 53–59. However, the Phoenix agent's suspicions and the arrest of Moussaoui *did* involve national-origin (if not racial) profiling: no FBI agent would have seen anything suspicious about a bunch of blonde Norwegians at flight schools.

135. See, for example, Jeff Gerth and Don Van Natta Jr., "U.S. Traces Path of Hijacker to Other Attacks," *New York Times*, October 6, 2001, p. A1.

136. Bill Dedman, "FAA Looking to Expand System," *Boston Globe*, October 12, 2001, p. A27.

137. So while CAPPS reportedly flagged nine of the nineteen hijackers for extra scrutiny, that was presumably limited to searching the checked bags of those who did check bags. David Stout, "9 Hijackers Drew Scrutiny on Sept. 11, Officials Say," *New York Times*, March 3, 2002, sec. 1, p. 20.

138. The CAPPS rules used on September 11 took shape after President Bill Clinton reacted to the 1996 crash of TWA Flight 800 (initially thought to be the work of terrorists) by putting Vice President Al Gore in charge of a White House commission to recommend improvements in airline security. From the start, Arab American and civil liberties groups pushed for a ban on any form of profiling that took note of ethnicity, national origin, or religion. The Gore Commission obliged. So did the Federal Aviation Administration, which developed the detailed rules, and the Justice Department's Civil Rights Division, which vetted them, reporting in 1997 that CAPPS gave no consideration to "race, color, national/ethnic origin, religion, or gender"; that it "is not connected to any law enforcement or intelligence databases"; and that "the additional security measures applied to CAPPS selectees . . . will concern their checked luggage only," not carry-on bags. All that was left for CAPPS to do was "screen passengers by analyzing passenger information relating only to the current travel of each passenger." See www.usccr.gov/pubs/misac2/app.htm. The agencies also stressed that the FAA would monitor and penalize any slippage into the forbidden types of profiling. Airlines and their security officials were on notice that if they searched a lot of Muslim-world passengers, there would be complaints and perhaps penalties. *Report by the Department of Justice to the Department of Transportation on the Department's Civil Rights Review of the Federal Aviation Administration's Proposed Automated Passenger Screening System*, October 1, 1997. See Dedman, "FAA Looking to Expand System"; David Armstrong and Joseph Periera, "Flight Risks: Nation's Airlines Adopt Aggressive Measures for Passenger Profiling," *Wall Street Journal*, October 23, 2001, p. A1 ("'Manual screening'—subjecting certain passengers to personal searches and questioning—'has been criticized by persons who perceived it as discriminating against citizens on the basis of race, color, national or ethnic origin and gender,' the FAA said in 1999 when it issued its proposed rules. . . . The system could avoid any perception of bias by doing baggage checks, which could be done without passengers' knowledge.").

139. According to "While Clinton Fiddled," a February 5 op-ed by former Clinton adviser Dick Morris in the *Wall Street Journal*: "When Mr. Clinton was advised to pass a law requiring that drivers' licenses for visas expire when their visas do (so that a routine traffic stop could trigger the deportation process), Deputy Chief of Staff Harold Ickes and White House adviser George Stephanopoulos worked hard to kill the idea. They derided the proposal, which called for the interface of FBI and Immigration and Naturalization Service data about illegal aliens, visa expirations and terrorist watch lists with state motor vehicle records, as racial profiling and warned it might alienate Mr. Clinton's political base. Had the idea been adopted, suicide bomber Mohammed Atta would have been subject to deportation when he was stopped for driving without a license, three months before Sept. 11, 2001."

140. Complaints plunged from seventy-eight in 1997 to eleven in 1998, thirteen in 1999, and fifteen in 2000, according to Department of Transportation data.

141. It is only in the past five years or so that profiling based on race, ethnicity, or national origin has become a civil rights cause celebre. The phrase "racial profiling" appeared in *New York Times* only three times in 1990, twice in 1991, and twice as recently as 1997, according to a search of the Nexis database. The same phrase appeared 270 times in 2000 and 384 times in 2001. What seems relatively new is not the practice, or the phrase, but rather the idea that racial profiling ranks high on the scale of encroachments on civil rights and civil liberties. Most people would rather be stopped and asked to consent to a search than denied a job, promotion, apartment, admission to college, or the right to sit at the front of the bus.

During campaign 2000, George W. Bush had promised Arab American groups—a critical constituency in Michigan—to "do something" to protect Arab Americans from being "profiled." Thomas J. Bray, "Gore's Arab-American Problem: How the 'Profiling' Issue Might Help Bush Win Michigan," *OpinionJournal.com,* October 17, 2000.

142. ABC News, "This Week," September 16, 2001. Later the same day Ashcroft gave himself rhetorical wiggle room by saying that he opposed profiling based "solely" on race. But he has never clarified whether this meant that—contrary to his initial statement—ethnicity could be used as one of several components of a security screening profile. At his January 2001 confirmation hearing, Ashcroft had said: "There should be no loopholes or safe harbors for racial profiling. Official discrimination of this sort is wrong and unconstitutional no matter what the context." See Samuel R. Gross and Debra Livingston, "Racial Profiling under Attack," *Columbia Law Review,* vol. 102 (June 2002), pp. 1413–14.

143. See *United States* v. *Martinez-Fuerte,* 428 U.S. 543, 563-64 (1976) ("We further believe that it is constitutional to refer motorists selectively to the secondary inspection area at the San Clemente checkpoint on the basis of criteria that would not sustain a roving-patrol stop. Thus, even if it be assumed that such referrals are made largely on the basis of apparent Mexican ancestry, we perceive no constitutional violation. . . . As the intrusion here is sufficiently minimal that no particularized reason need exist to justify it, we think it follows that the Border Patrol officers must have wide discretion in selecting the motorists to be diverted for the brief questioning involved.").

144. See Dave Boyer, "Despite Profiling Fears, FBI Won't Do It," *Washington Times,* June 7, 2002, p. A1.

145. See Daniel Pipes, "Don't Call It a Witch-Hunt," *Jerusalem Post,* February 5, 2003, p. 7.

146. Nurith C. Aizenman, "A Register of Immigrants' Fears," *Washington Post,* January 20, 2003, p. A1 (showing how the registration program puts a subset of the many foreigners who are in the United States illegally at risk of deportation); "More Foreign Men Told to Register," *New York Times,* November 23, 2002, p. A9; and Mary Beth Sheridan, "U.S. Wants Prints of Muslim Visitors," *Washington Post,* November 7, 2002, p. A3.

147. See Steven Brill, "The FBI Gets Religion," *Newsweek,* vol. 139, no. 4 (January 28, 2002), pp. 32–33; and Gorman, "Power to the Government."

148. Bay Fang, "Under Scrutiny, Always," *U.S. News and World Report,* January 6, 2003, pp. 26–30.

149. See Gross and Livingston, "Racial Profiling under Attack," pp. 1413–14 ("By our definition, it is not ethnic profiling for officers to focus their attention on people of a given

ethnicity because the police have information that the specific crime they are investigating [such as the 9/11 attacks] was committed by someone of that ethnic group. . . . Granted, the concept of a 'specific crime' grows somewhat hazy when the crime at issue is an ongoing conspiracy of indeterminate size—and one that potentially involves not just Middle Eastern men, but also others, from different racial or ethnic groups.").

150. CBS News, "60 Minutes," December 2, 2001.

151. Sharon Waxman, "Standing Watch: Airport Security Is Tighter than Ever. Does That Make Flying Safe Again?" *Washington Post*, July 20, 2002, p. C1. Administration officials who request anonymity suggest that despite Mineta's announced policy, the classified instructions given by his subordinates to airlines and security screeners subject to special scrutiny the bags of passengers known to be from certain listed Muslim countries. See also Zakaria, "Freedom vs. Security, " p. 30 ("As a swarthy young man with an exotic name, trust me, we're being checked.").

152. To be sure, the arrest in mid-2002 of more than ten U.S.-born Muslims on terrorism-related charges does call into question whether we can safely assume that future al Qaeda hijackers and bombers will be from overseas.

153. But see *Korematsu v. United States*, 323 U.S. 214 (1944) (Jackson, J., dissenting) ("Now the principle of racial discrimination is pushed from support of mild measures to very harsh ones, and from temporary deprivations to indeterminate ones. . . . Because we said that these citizens could be made to stay in their homes during the hours of dark, it is said we must require them to leave home entirely; and if that, we are told they may also be taken into custody for deportation; and if that, it is argued they may also be held for some undetermined time in detention camps. How far the principle of this case would be extended before plausible reasons would play out, I do not know.").

154. By contrast, the presence of large numbers of witnesses at airline security checkpoints provides a built-in deterrent to harassment of those who fit the profile.

155. Whether stopping cars based on a racial profile is an effective way to find drugs is much disputed. See David A. Harris, "Race Wars," *Weekly Standard*, February 4, 2002, p. 6 (arguing it is ineffective); and David A. Harris, *Profiles in Injustice: Why Racial Profiling Cannot Work* (New Press, 2002). But some of the same studies that have found dramatically higher stop rates for black and Hispanic drivers than for whites have also found that the percentage of drivers caught with drugs (the "hit rate") was no lower (and sometimes higher) for black and Hispanic drivers. These hit-rate data tend to confirm the efficiency of this kind of racial profiling as a drug-finding technique. For example, John Knowles, Nicola Persico, and Petra Todd, "Racial Bias in Motor Vehicle Searches: Theory and Evidence," *Journal of Political Economy*, vol. 109 (February 2001), pp. 203–28.

"Black men are six to eight times more likely to commit violent crimes than are white men," according to a January 10, 2002, op-ed in the *Wall Street Journal* by James Q. Wilson and Heather R. Higgins, p. A12. See also Gross and Livingston, "Racial Profiling under Attack," p. 1422. Black and Hispanic men also commit a disproportionate percentage of drug-trafficking crimes (although not of drug use). And a recent much-disputed study found that black drivers speed on the New Jersey turnpike at much higher rates than others. David Kocieniewski, "Study Suggests Racial Gap in Speeding in New Jersey," *New York Times*, March 21, 2002, p. B1. If so, then it would not be racial profiling at all for police to stop black drivers for speeding in disproportionate numbers.

156. "I have probably been through more ethnic profiling at airports than anyone who

has protested the practice on television. . . . Despite the inconvenience to me, I believe this scrutiny is a defensible tactic for picking out potential problem passengers. . . . The airline security procedures I ran into also protect me from terrorism. . . . Does anyone really want a security official to hesitate before stopping a suspicious passenger out of fear of an accusation of bias?" Fedwa Malti-Douglas, "Let Them Profile Me," *New York Times*, February 6, 2002, p. A21. See also Zakaria, "Freedom vs. Security" ("If the pool of suspects is overwhelmingly of a particular ethnic/racial/religious group, then it only makes sense to pay greater attention to people of that background"); Dennis Niemiec and Shawn Windsor, "Arab-Americans Believe Profiling Has Risen Since Sept. 11, Poll Shows," *Detroit Free Press*, October 1, 2001 ("Most Arab-Americans in metro Detroit believe that profiling, or extra scrutiny of people with Middle Eastern features or accents by law enforcement officials, has escalated since the Sept. 11 terrorist attacks. And that's OK with them: 61 percent said such extra questioning or inspections are justified, according to a *Detroit Free Press*-/EPIC-MRA poll conducted last week. Twenty-eight percent disagreed; 11 percent were undecided"). Even Hussein Ibish, spokesman for the American-Arab Anti-Discrimination Committee—who warns eloquently of the dangers of group-based profiling—"concedes that for everyone's safety, a little ethnic profiling is not, perhaps, such a bad thing. As long as the government doesn't say it is doing so [and] 'there's a stigma attached to essentially behaving in a racist way.'" Sharon Waxman, "Standing Watch," *Washington Post*, July 20, 2002, p. C1.

157. For example, Harris, "Race Wars"; Frank H. Wu, "A Practice That Tears at the Civic Fabric," *Christian Science Monitor*, February 21, 2002, Books section, p. 19.

158. See Paul Zielbauer, "Boston Airport, Sept. 11 to Live Down, Aspires to Big Changes," *New York Times*, June 20, 2002, p. A21. (Rafi Ron, former security director at Ben-Gurion International Airport in Israel and now a consultant on security at Boston's Logan Airpport, says: "Issues of nationality should be considered.") Armstrong and Periera, "Flight Risks." (Ray Kelly, an airline security expert who is former New York City police commissioner, says that national origin should be a factor in airline security profiles.)

159. Greg Schneider and Sarah Kehaulani Goo, "Twin Missions Overwhelmed TSA," *Washington Post*, September 3, 2002, p. A1.

160. The metal detectors and X-ray scanners that screen passengers and their carry-ons are not effective at detecting explosives and can miss small knives. The high-tech bomb-detection equipment that the government claims is now used to screen all checked bags is of uncertain reliability. And the government's rule requiring removal of the checked bags of any passengers who do not board their flights would be of no use against suicide bombers and could be circumvented by bombs timed to explode and connecting flights.

161. Michael Isikoff and Daniel Klaidman, "The Hijackers We Let Escape," *Newsweek*, vol. 139, no. 23 (June 10, 2002), pp. 20–28, quotation on p. 24 ("FBI officials have now prepared a detailed chart showing how agents could have uncovered the terrorist plot if they had learned [what the CIA knew] about Almihdhar and Alhazmi sooner, given their frequent contact with at least five of the other hijackers, 'There's no question we could have tied all 19 hijackers together,' the official said.").

162. "Hill Probers Upgrade Evidence Gathered from Moussaoui," *Washington Post*, June 6, 2002, p. A18 ("The evidence . . . included a computer disk containing information related to crop-dusting; the phone numbers in Germany of Ramzi Binalshibh, an al Qaeda fugitive [and former Atta roommate] who allegedly helped finance the plot; and flight deck

videos from an Ohio store where two of the hijackers, Mohammed Atta and Nawaf Alhazmi, had purchased the same equipment."").

163. Rowley letter.

164. The two on the watch list had shared addresses with three of the other hijackers, including Mohammed Atta. His phone numbers could have led to another five. An eleventh had used the same frequent flier number as one of first two. Checks on attendance at flights schools, expired visas, and other data might have led to the rest. See Stuart Taylor Jr., "Big Brother and Another Overblown Privacy Scare," *National Journal*, vol. 34, no. 49 (December 7, 2002), pp. 3541–42.

165. "How Did Hijackers Get Past Airport Security?" *Los Angeles Times*, September 23, 2001, p. A1. ("The FAA's weapon guidelines did not specifically mention razor-sharp box cutters—among the instruments said to be wielded by the hijackers. Some security screeners said they prohibited them; others said they permitted them as being within the 4-inch knife standard.")

PIETRO S. NIVOLA 14

Can the Government
Be Serious?

ON NOVEMBER 19, 1998, the following exchange drew chuckles from the audience during the House Judiciary Committee's hearings on the impending impeachment of President Clinton:

Mr. Delahunt. I am not idle. Will we take a supper break?
Mr. Hyde. No, we won't take a supper break. We will go straight through. We will keep the jury locked up without food and water. Right? You may send out for pizza.
Mr. Frank. Can we have a walk around the Mall?
Mr. Hyde. If you are walking around the Mall, I would want two police officers.
It is now a—well, a mixed—pleasure to ask . . . one of our valuable members, whom we will miss, Charles Schumer, to interrogate—question—our witness. Mr. Schumer, for five minutes.
Mr. Schumer. Thank you, Mr. Chairman. . . . Today, Mr. Starr, today after nearly five years of investigation, we conduct today's

The author is grateful for the advice and comments of Henry Aaron, Sarah Binder, Martha Derthick, Thomas Edsall, Carol Graham, Charles O. Jones, James Lindsay, Stephen Hess, Thomas Mann, Norman Ornstein, Jonathan Rauch, and A. James Reichley. Special thanks also are owed to Larissa Davis for her research assistance.

impeachment hearing having just received boxes of new documents from your office. . . . Mr. Chairman, I would say this to all of us on this committee: Maybe we should hang a sign outside the Judiciary Committee that says, "Out to lunch, gone fishing."[1]

In retrospect, that interlude of levity, amid the otherwise somber and sanctimonious proceedings, was not entirely a laughing matter. For in more respects than were recognized at the time, "out to lunch" and "gone fishing" were apt characterizations. From the early 1990s, when special prosecutors began probing an obscure land deal in Arkansas, to the last year of the decade, when the Senate finally closed the curtain on the long-running Clinton and Lewinsky spectacle, the White House and Congress dedicated something less than their undivided attention to the nation's greater needs. Washington at the end of the second millennium, like Rome at the start of the first, was consumed with palace intrigue, scandals, and arcane legal inquests.

Out to Lunch, Gone Fishing

A revealing gauge of the capital's fixation with these pastimes was the news media's choice of stories to report. On Christmas day in 1994 an aborted hijacking of an Air France jetliner, commandeered by Islamic extremists intending to fill the plane with fuel and crash it into the Eiffel Tower, made the first page of the *New York Times*. But this incident, portending similar events to come, was quickly forgotten. Stories about, say, the Whitewater investigation, which also occupied front-page space that month, continued to do so for many more. After controversies had run their course, the press often seemed at a loss for important news to recount. On September 10, 2001, three-quarters of the front page of the *Washington Post* was devoted to four stories: the tale of a foster girl who died in the custody of the District of Columbia's child protection agency, an opinion poll on a sales tax increase in Northern Virginia, Barry Bonds's sixty-three home runs and, biggest of all, how the Redskins dropped their opening game.

This provincial political climate prevailed at a time when the nation should have been mounting a sustained response to the growing worldwide scourge of terrorism. Fanatics with ties to Osama bin Laden bombed the World Trade Center in February 1993. In June 1996 they blew up the Dhahran barracks in Saudi Arabia, killing nearly a score of American servicemen. The attacks went unanswered. After truck bombs caused thousands of casualties at the American embassies in Dar es Salaam and Nairobi in August 1998, the president finally ordered a retaliation of sorts. Cruise missiles were lobbed at a pharmaceutical plant in the Sudan and ineffectually at an al Qaeda training camp in Afghanistan. Mr. bin Laden escaped, and the brief military action to stop him was not followed up. Bill Clinton's many political enemies suspected the missile strike to be a ploy, intended to divert attention from the real headline grabber: his grand jury testimony about his relationship with Monica Lewinksy.

The fascination with domestic scandals and investigations had become but one manifestation of a larger change in American public life: the descent to low politics. During the late decades of the twentieth century the national government increasingly digressed into concerns that carried it far afield from its core responsibilities.

The descent, I emphasize, did not occur because Congress and the president were gridlocked and unproductive. Quite the contrary: A divided government proved as adept as ever at cranking out legislation—and piling plenty of new assignments on the federal government. A number of the laws enacted between 1993 and 1997 were major feats.[2] A free trade zone with Canada and Mexico was approved. The delivery of public assistance was overhauled. The federal behemoth finally managed to balance its budget (albeit with the aid of a booming economy). For all of the government's accomplishments, however, its deficiencies were at least as remarkable. Among the momentous matters that were not being addressed forcefully enough was the urgent question of what to do about rogue states developing diabolical weapons and mass murderers eager to use the most lethal ones against the United States.[3]

In 1991 the Senate reached much more consensus on measures like a bill to help women find "nontraditional" jobs than on a resolution authorizing the use of force to repel Iraq's invasion of Kuwait. When the votes were finally counted, the Gulf resolution passed, but a tendency to delve into esoteric domestic issues while global problems were pressing recurred throughout the decade. And the sorts of domestic projects that interested policymakers were often notable for the extent to which they arrogated traditional competences of local governments. Federal micromanagement of local tasks expanded in many of the period's ambitious enactments—statutes like the Omnibus Crime Bill of 1994 and Safe Drinking Water Act of 1996—as well as through lesser measures.

A profusion of new commitments in this vein, however gratifying to a multitude of special interest groups, took up room that should have been reserved for the federal government's first obligations—controlling the nation's borders, thwarting the country's sworn enemies, and shoring up its homeland security. Bureaus responsible for some of these bedrock requirements were uncoordinated, poorly overseen, and sometimes inadequately supported. Faced with the burgeoning assortment of boutique programs it was expected to administer, much of the federal establishment strained to recruit the talent needed to staff its new layers of bureaucracy.[4] Not the least of the added frustrations in this process were the inordinate ordeals of vetting appointees. Often their tribulations were emblematic of some of the Beltway's most petulant politics.

The rest of this chapter inspects these developments more closely. It examines the deepening immersion of national public policy in the technicalities of relatively mundane domestic functions, including many that used to be left to the discretion of local authorities. It explores how transformations in partisan politics, legislative behavior, and the news media encouraged not only that phenomenon but also frequent engagement in tactical political vendettas and "gotcha" games. The chapter also assays some of the damage that was done to the capacity of the executive branch to brace for the onslaught of terrorism.

September 11 undoubtedly jolted the system. In its immediate aftermath the calamity was thought to have precipitated a fundamental transfiguration that would last for years to come. "America has changed," proclaimed the world's best weekly news magazine.[5] Prominent historians agreed. The devastation in lower Manhattan and the Pentagon, wrote one, "forced a reconsideration, not only of where we are as a nation and where we may be going, but also of where we've been, even who we are."[6]

That the impact was not quite so far-reaching, however, became apparent as the dust settled. As a subsequent portion of this chapter shows, although America's governing institutions were sobered, how durably remains to be seen. Preexisting political patterns were not wholly upended. Thus I contend that forces quite unrelated to those that rocked the nation in 2001 probably are needed to sustain a basic correction over the long run. Some of the correctives are sketched in the chapter's concluding section.

The Age of Low Politics

When John F. Kennedy became president in 1961, his inaugural address contained few words about domestic imperatives. (One sentence in his speech, about tyranny abroad, ended with a pledge to be "unwilling to witness or permit the slow undoing of those human rights to which this nation had always been committed, and to which we are committed *at home and round the world.*")[7] Foreign policy greatly preoccupied presidents, and was no sideshow for congressional leaders either, for most of the second half of the twentieth century. Politicians were never oblivious to the details of domestic policy, of course, but these did not overrun the national agenda.

By the time President Clinton delivered his state of the union address in February 1997, however, the emphasis was heavily on the home front. Clinton ruminated on such subjects as the enforcement of truancy laws, the advantage of school uniforms, the math tests of eighth graders, the need to connect hospitalized children to the Internet, the marshaling of work-study students as reading tutors, the importance "for parents to begin talking, singing, even reading to their infants," the urgency of a $1,500 college tuition tax credit, the ability of medical insurance to cover annual mammograms, the appropriate hospital stay for women after a mastectomy, the utility of flextime for employees, the revitalization of community waterfronts, the uses of community development banks, the record of Burger King and other businesses in creating jobs for welfare recipients, and so forth.[8]

This taste for appropriating the routine work of governors, mayors, hospital administrators, or school boards was strong during the Clinton years, but it had been building before. As East-West tensions subsided through the 1980s, and the outside world was perceived (or, rather, misperceived) to be far less threatening, Washington was tempted to retreat from entanglements overseas and instead take up internal particulars, many of which seemed decidedly diminutive by comparison. Players from both political parties and at both ends of Pennsylvania Avenue succumbed.

Federalizing Just About Everything

On Ronald Reagan's watch and that of his immediate successor, the federal government effectively got into the business of determining the minimum drinking age for motorists, setting the licensing standards for bus and truck drivers, overseeing spillages from thousands of city storm sewers, requiring asbestos inspections in classrooms, enforcing child support payments, establishing quality standards for nursing homes, replacing water coolers in local school buildings, ordering sidewalk ramps on city streets, purifying municipal water supplies, regulating where passengers should stand when riding city buses, mandating special education programs for preschoolers, and much more.[9]

To be sure, a great deal of this to-do list was drawn up by Democratic legislators, who pursued it more enthusiastically than did members of the other party. But after the Republicans won control of both the House and Senate in 1994, GOP lawmakers, too, frequently savored the opportunity to meddle in the management of local services rather than stick to matters more befitting, as Abraham Lincoln might have put it, "the majesty of the nation."[10]

During the 1990s Congress intruded in so many aspects of community law enforcement, for instance, that dozens of new offenses were swept into the grip of the U.S. penal code. Caught in the federal dragnet were small-time drug dealers and carjackers. (Deadly foreign saboteurs and subversives, as it turned out, slipped through.) Democrats denounced some of this usurpation of local criminal justice: "We federalize everything that walks, talks, and moves," complained Senator Joseph Biden of Delaware.[11] But when the conversation turned to hate crimes, "gender" crimes, or spousal abuse, the Democrats' reservations about "federalizing everything" seemed to vanish just as quickly.

These were often novel forms of federal domesticity. A great many home improvements that were once deemed strictly local responsibilities were promoted at the national level in earlier epochs as well. The Great Society years brimmed with such policies. The federal footprint was not negligible in the 1950s either. Then the cold war provided a national security pretext for sponsoring certain local public works—underwriting the building of bridges and roads, for instance, through the National System of Interstate and Defense Highways (as the massive federal road program was formally titled in 1956). But the major domestic initiatives of those periods could claim to be meeting authentic national requirements in fields where state policies indisputably fell short—constructing an indispensable nationwide infrastructure, addressing woeful race relations across the land, and providing medical insurance for the elderly and the indigent. The imperatives of domestic policy, moreover, did not displace those of international relations; they coexisted. National politicians did not yet regularly contemplate the many micro-themes that cluttered Clinton's speeches and the legislative hoppers of recent congresses. Such retail items were deemed the domain of state and municipal functionaries or of private firms and households.

Puttering at Home

The inward impulse of national politics may have seemed especially conspicuous during the Clinton presidency, marked most notably during its first term by detachment from troubles overseas. Following a brief and shallow recession, the Clintonites came to town in 1993 convinced that large parts of the U.S. economy needed radical surgery. While that operation was going on, unsettling events abroad were put on hold.

The attitude toward a festering crisis in the Balkans was illustrative (at least until the magnitude of Serbian atrocities belatedly stirred the North Atlantic Treaty Organization to intervene). A late-twentieth-century reprise of ethnic cleansing and national dismemberment on the doorstep of Europe was relegated to the margins of the administration's concerns during its first two years. As the bloodbath unfolded in the former Yugoslavia in 1993, the president remarked, "I felt really badly because I don't want to have to spend more time on [Bosnia] than is absolutely necessary because what I got elected to do was to get America to look at our own problems."[12]

The disengaged attitude seemed out of step with America's customary leadership across the Atlantic and eventually proved unsustainable. While it lasted, though, Clinton's stance was not altogether at odds with that of his predecessor. The Balkan disaster had been brewing for years. George H. W. Bush had marginalized it as well.

In fact, in the years bracketing the end of the Gulf war in 1991 to the onset of the war against terrorism in 2001, it could not be said that Republican administrations, presidential candidates, or congressional leaders were busier than their Democratic rivals fathoming America's global challenges. Some voices on the hard right were making louder isolationist noises; others seemed more vocal about symbols than substance in U.S. international relations—our dues assessment at the United Nations, the admissibility of family planning in foreign aid programs, and the like. At least in its second term the Clinton administration began to face more squarely the realities that demanded attention from the world's only superpower. Officials grew alarmed at the rising number of terrorist incidents. American warplanes hit Belgrade hard when Slobodan Milosevic unleashed his ethnic cleansers on Kosovo. Clinton also strove to broker a comprehensive settlement of the Israeli-Palestinian conflict.[13]

But if the holiday from foreign affairs was ending, it was not quite over. During the 2000 presidential campaign, Vice President Al Gore scarcely mentioned that America and the world were imperiled by terrorists, and neither did George W. Bush. In their book *The Age of Sacred Terror*, Daniel Benjamin and Steven Simon describe the bureaucratic inertia that hobbled U.S. efforts to mobilize against al Qaeda during the Clinton years.[14] The trouble continued well into the summer of 2001. Prescient warnings of

possible terrorist operations on American soil were generated at lower ech-
elons of the Federal Bureau of Investigation (FBI) and the Central Intelligence Agency (CIA) but then languished in administrative and legalistic
labyrinths.[15] On the morning of September 11 word reached President
Bush that a commercial airliner had slammed into the World Trade Center while he was sitting in on a second-grade classroom at the Emma E.
Booker Elementary School in Sarasota, Florida.

Nine years earlier, when Bush Sr. was nearing the end of his tenure, his
calendar, too, was filled with what might be called odd jobs. Here is an
example:

> On November 30, 1992, two cabinet secretaries charged with over-
> seeing the nation's food policies requested an urgent meeting with
> President George H. W. Bush. Louis W. Sullivan, secretary of health
> and human services, and Edward Madigan, secretary of agriculture,
> asked the president to decide issues so difficult that months of staff
> meetings, their own negotiations, and intervention by the Office of
> Management and Budget had failed to resolve them.
>
> The controversy they brought to the president was not about a
> giant recall of contaminated food or the future of genetic engineer-
> ing, however. It was about what the public should be told about fat.
> They could not agree on how to show high or low amounts on pack-
> ages of processed foods, whether recommended daily levels should be
> based on a 2,000-calorie-a-day diet or a 2,500-calorie-a-day diet, and
> what the term *light* on labels should mean.[16]

One can imagine Mr. Bush impatiently checking his watch during this
type of household chore (perhaps even wishing he could have vacated the
White House ahead of schedule). Most state governments, after all, were
already toiling over the tedious specifics of policies such as nutritional disclosures. That the forty-first president of the United States had to pass his
final days in office labeling soup cans, cereal boxes, and candy bars was
weird, but it was a sign of the times.

The Toll of Trivial Pursuits

A government so absorbed, even at the highest levels, in the minutiae of
myriad domestic undertakings might have difficulty organizing itself to
discharge other basic duties—including a timely and judicious allocation
of resources to combat international terrorism.

After Timothy McVeigh massacred 166 people in Oklahoma City in 1995, Congress passed the Antiterrorism and Effective Death Penalty Act. Expenditures for antiterrorism increased to almost $10 billion by 2001. The spending, however, was spread chaotically across a bewildering maze of agencies and programs, often reflecting a series of uncoordinated legislative earmarks.[17] Tossing funds hither and yon with no coherent strategy meant that dollars would hit or miss vital aspects of "preparedness." The Department of Justice, for example, wound up with a budget of just $15 million to train local personnel such as police officers, firefighters, and rescue workers who would be the first to respond in an emergency. It is not surprising that in three years the department managed to train only a miniscule fraction of these first responders.

Meanwhile, the FBI needed a computer system that would enhance the ability of its field offices to share information collected by agents. Congress did not get around to paying for that essentiality until the end of 2000—too late to be of much help a few months later.[18] Similarly, before September 11 the Immigration and Naturalization Service was unable to buy and install computers to keep track of foreign visitors on student visas. This necessary instrument did not become operational until 2003.[19] The U.S. Coast Guard, whose aging boats had to run after everything from marijuana smugglers to distressed private yachts, scrambled to protect the nation's most vulnerable places—its seaports.[20] Examples of neglect or disarray abounded. Whatever the many plausible explanations, one of them was simply that, amid all their diversions, policymakers could not readily "focus like a laser" on the central task at hand.

Some of the political activities that diverted energy in the wrong directions, moreover, not only dissipated money; they left various agencies shorthanded. In part the staffing problems inevitably derived from what Paul C. Light calls a thickening of the federal bureaucracy: The more things it was asked to do, the more slots it needed to fill—so many, in fact, that some remained unfilled.[21] In addition, nominees for appointed positions faced an increasingly grueling review process. Until the mid-1980s the majority of senior-level appointees were sworn in quickly, within two months or less. Afterward about 85 percent took considerably longer to clear the entry barrier—if it was cleared at all. Recent administrations have had to spend their first year with vacancy rates of more than 50 percent in posts that require Senate confirmation and to tolerate as much as 30 percent thereafter.

By the late 1980s many a capable citizen was likely to think twice before pursuing almost any high-ranking government job. For many the path to public service was now too politicized and hazardous. Various judicial nominees (most famously Robert Bork in 1987 and Clarence Thomas in 1991) were subjected to the most torturous proceedings, but appointments in the executive branch, too, could be put through the wringer or slowed to a crawl thanks to the increasingly common Senate practice of placing "holds" on nominations.[22] And for those who managed to traverse this minefield, further liabilities beset day-to-day work at the office. More than a few officials found themselves in the crosshairs of independent counsels, ever on the prowl for traces of impropriety.

In 1971 the number of public officials indicted for wrongdoing in the United States stood at approximately one hundred. Twenty years later the volume of indictments exceeded 1,400.[23] It strains credulity to suppose that the nation's public servants were fourteen times more malfeasant in 1991 than they were in 1971. No matter: The purge, often hyping relatively minor misdeeds, maintained a feverish pitch through most of the 1990s. Charges of improper conduct were leveled at four cabinet secretaries in the Clinton administration. Nearly forty other members of the administration, not charged with the commission of any crime, incurred big legal bills as a result of being called to testify before federal grand juries and congressional investigators.[24] In at least one of the inquisitions (the investigation of Henry Cisneros, then secretary of the Department of Housing and Urban Development), the incriminating allegations sprang from a matter so personal that if they had been pressed against, say, Alexander Hamilton, he also might have been driven from office.

So it was that in the 1990s the homeland's safety would be entrusted to a distracted government, spreading itself thin while often failing to replenish its ranks expeditiously. The Clinton administration's Justice Department did not just lack enough FBI officials who were fluent in Arabic; at the outset, it even had trouble finding an attorney general.[25]

Peace Dividend?

What accounted for the introspective politics of the 1990s? The end of the cold war was a contributing factor. With the collapse of the Soviet Union, gone was the great external threat that had compelled and defined U.S. internationalism for nearly half a century and that had simplified priorities accordingly. Now presumably relieved from policing the world, Americans could afford to fuss over internal imperfections (real or exaggerated). Among the outcomes of this self-examination were intensified efforts to keep public figures on the straight and narrow.

Yet the notion that the nation was finally at peace, and now could indulge in political luxuries that it had long deferred, should not be overstated. The post–cold war world, as any responsible decisionmaker in Washington knew, was not benign. China, an emerging industrial powerhouse, showed few signs of relaxing its repressive regime. Trouble-making tyrants ruled Iraq, Iran, Libya, North Korea, and Syria. Russia retained a huge and insecure stockpile of nuclear weapons. India and Pakistan were headed for a nuclear arms race. The Middle East remained a tinderbox. Millions died in Africa's tribal massacres. A genocidal Balkan war had by mid-1995 shredded the credibility of the United Nations. And there was more.

America declared war on terrorism in the fall of 2001, but terrorists had gone to war against America long before that. They murdered U.S. ambassadors to Afghanistan, Lebanon, and Sudan in the 1970s.[26] In 1979 fifty-two U.S. citizens were taken hostage at the American embassy in Tehran and held captive for 444 days. That year Islamic radicals also rioted in Pakistan and set fire to the U.S. embassy in Islamabad. In 1983 the American embassy in Beirut was blasted by a suicide car bombing that killed sixty-three people, including seventeen Americans. Six months after that, terrorists drove a van filled with explosives into the U.S. military barracks at the Beirut airport and killed 241 marines. In 1985 the passengers of a hijacked TWA jetliner were held hostage in Lebanon, and a disabled American citizen on board the cruise ship *Achille Lauro* was thrown into the Mediterranean Sea by Palestinian "freedom fighters." One month later, simultaneous suicide attacks were carried out against the check-in desks of Israeli and American airlines at the international airports of Rome and Vienna. In 1986 the bombing of a Berlin discotheque, in which forty-four Americans were wounded and one killed, was linked to Muammar Qaddafi's operatives. In retaliation President Reagan ordered U.S. Air Force F-111s to bomb Libyan installations. The Libyans then conspired to bring down Pan Am Flight 103 over Scotland in 1988.

More action loomed in the 1990s, with Americans very much in the line of fire—first at an Air Force base in Saudi Arabia in 1996, next at the embassies in Kenya and Tanzania, and then in October 2000 on the *USS Cole* in Yemen. Needless to say, it could have been worse. There could have been more U.S. casualties in the Gulf war. More New Yorkers might have died in the first attack on the World Trade Center. A plot to bomb the

Holland and Lincoln tunnels in 1993 was foiled. So were plans to bring down eleven American airliners in Asia two years later and to wreck the Los Angeles International Airport at around the time of the millennium celebration. Still, the overall course of events was worrisome. Well into his second term President Clinton spoke of placing "the fight against terrorism at the top of our agenda."[27]

The "top of our agenda," however, was a crowded place. A lot of other issues, no matter how picayune, jockeyed for position there. Thus episodes of terror (and close calls) came and went, and soon afterward the political process detoured to the domestic topic du jour—which could span from everybody's "right" to optimal medical services, a minimum-wage increase, and relief from the "backbreaking" cost of gasoline to Paula Jones's lawsuit or a flap about Interior Secretary Bruce Babbitt.[28] This propensity did not take hold just because Americans were out of danger as the cold war receded. It persisted while danger grew.

The Public

Up to a point the sorts of stories that captivated U.S. politics in the late twentieth century comported with the public's frame of mind. Ordinarily public opinion pays less heed to world affairs than to events closer to home. For all the visible signs of new perils abroad, people's perception of them surely was not so keen as to outweigh more proximate cares.[29] Hence in the early 1990s pocketbook worries, health care concerns, and anxiety about crime gained salience.

Nonetheless, the way some domestic issues were blown out of proportion often bore no close connection to public preferences. Polls signaled considerable unease with the state of the economy in 1992, but even by the most permissive standards of political oratory the Clinton campaign's depiction of U.S. economic frailty that year went overboard: The country was described as suffering its "worst economic performance since the Great Depression," even inviting comparisons with "Sri Lanka."[30] The notion that the nation's health care system needed a complete overhaul also was flogged further than the public was comfortable with. Some polls circa 1992 purported to find that most Americans favored reforming the entire system, but much larger majorities expressed satisfaction with the status quo.[31] By the spring of 1994, almost a third of the public regarded violent crime as the main predicament facing the country.[32] The extent to which this opinion translated into support for the wholesale federalization of crimes and penalties legislated that year, however, was far from obvious.

Home-based considerations such as "the economy," health care, and the problem of crime booked up political space for several years once the Gulf war had faded from memory. But whereas elements of these initial debates (particularly the ones on health policy and criminal justice) were not silly and had a basis in popular sentiment, various other disputes that unfolded during the rest of the decade were less pertinent from the general public's perspective. Yet they came to dominate the national conversation anyway.

A case in point was the growing political preoccupation with official misconduct—culminating with the dogged attempt to remove Clinton from office. In December 1998 the House of Representatives voted to impeach the president, with 98 percent of the Republican members concluding that Clinton's prevarications during the course of the year-long sex scandal rose to the level of high crime. This verdict of "the people's house" did not square with the views of the people. From the eruption of the scandal in January 1998 through the end of the Senate trial in February 1999 every national poll showed the public opposed to impeachment and conviction, typically by margins of two to one.[33]

Partisan Polemics

Intensifying the force of inside-the-Beltway feuds, including ones that most ordinary voters found overblown, was the heightened contentiousness of partisan politics. As James Q. Wilson observes in this volume, differences between the parties had widened. Party solidarity and distinctiveness increased as the Republicans gradually captured from the Democrats their conservative southern base and as districts for the House of Representatives were redrawn to minimize geographic comingling of the parties' respective constituencies. Also, although fewer incumbents in Congress were ousted in general elections, more members now worried about the possibility of having to defend their seats in primary elections. The upshot was a marked decline in the percentage of centrists—that is, members who were comfortable crossing party lines on selective issues (see figure 14-1).

Clowns to the Left, Jokers to the Right

The polarizing effect of redistricting has been profound. In the first fifteen House elections following World War II one party or the other gained an

Figure 14-1. *The Declining Political Center, 1984–98*

Percentage of moderate members

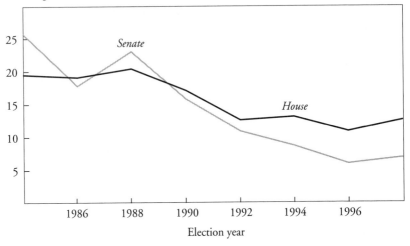

Election year

Source: Sarah A. Binder, *Stalemate: Causes and Consequences of Legislative Stalemate* (Brookings, 2003). See also Keith T. Poole and Howard Rosenthal, "Patterns of Congressional Voting," *American Journal of Political Science,* vol. 35 (February 1991), pp. 228–78. Ideological scores are calculated by Keith T. Poole and Howard Rosenthal, in *Congress: A Political-Economic History of Roll Call Voting* (Cambridge University Press, 1997). Scores for 1994 are based on roll call votes through December 1995.

average of twenty-nine seats. In the past fourteen elections the average switch was thirteen seats. Increasingly sophisticated computer software, especially in the past dozen years, permitted political cartographers to map accurately the spatial distribution of registered voters according to their partisan voting preferences. With more precision than ever, districts were gerrymandered to tilt reliably to one party or the other. Marginal districts, where candidates had to appeal to voters from both parties, became relatively scarce.

How primaries have polarized the parties warrants a little more explanation. In a simple two-party electoral system the natural tendency of candidates competing for single-member districts is to gravitate toward the center of the political spectrum. Primaries, however, do not encourage this convergence. The electorates in these contests tend to be small and unrepresentative of mainstream voters. Hence candidates are often forced to protect their flanks by moving *away* from the center—positioning themselves further to the left or right of the general public on issues that small but active factions regard as "litmus tests."[34]

The number of Democratic Party primaries for House elections was about the same in 1994 as in 1964. But on the Republican side, the number of primaries increased almost 75 percent over those thirty years. The threat of actual or potential primary challenges from the right may well be among the decisive forms of leverage that the GOP's base exercised to harden the party line on questions such as the Lewinsky affair. Among the Democrats similar pressure was at work, although emanating from the opposite extreme, and probably explains their own nearly unanimous stance on symbols of significance to that party's activists—like opposing impeachment, for example, or raising the minimum wage.

The latter, in fact, became almost as much an idée fixe for the Democrats as prosecuting Clinton was for the Republicans. It illustrates the lengths to which the left would go to prevail on a matter of less-than-earthshaking importance. Never mind that the wages of low-end workers were already keeping pace with the rise of average wages amid the tight labor market of the second half of the 1990s; in 1996 the White House began campaigning for a higher minimum wage, knowing full well that the idea was anathema to conservatives in the Republican-controlled Congress.[35] The Democrats' strategy was to exploit Senate rules, which permit the introduction of unrelated amendments, by offering the minimum-wage increase as an amendment to every piece of legislation that the majority leader, Robert Dole, brought to the floor. Lacking the votes to kill the wage proposal or impose cloture on legislation he wanted to pass, Dole pulled bill after bill off the floor, fueling news stories of congressional gridlock.[36] Eventually, in the heat of an election year, the Republicans had to capitulate.

Squabbles like this appear related to increased party polarization, but the extent or direction of causality (if any) is not self-evident. Parties cleaving to their extremes may engage more frequently in petty wrangles, but the wrangling may also drive the partisans further apart. Moreover, polarity and pettiness do not always go together. At times in American history the deeper the philosophical rift between the political parties, and the greater their disciplined fidelity to principles, the more likely they were to debate serious national questions rather than narrow, expendable, or phony ones. That certainly was the situation in the mid-nineteenth century when the nation was divided by the epic struggle over slavery. More recently, it would be an oversimplification to say that Republican politicians are tethered to a parochial agenda because their most active constituents—notably the religious right, which is thought to control as much as two-thirds of the GOP's state organizations—care only about domestic esoterica such as school prayer, sexual abstinence instruction, and the like.[37] Of the various constituencies at the core of the contemporary Republican Party, the evangelical movement has developed considerable appreciation of profoundly consequential social questions (bioethics, for instance) and *offshore* issues, including U.S. relations with China and North Korea, U.S. support for Israel, and U.S. assistance to fight the AIDS pandemic in Africa.

The Razor's Edge

When Washington wallowed in "low politics," more than polarized parties were involved. As the 1990s wore on, the Democrats and Republicans contended closely for supremacy. As good an indicator as any of the extraordinarily tight duel was the narrowing margin between the parties in the House of Representatives (see figure 14-2). The margin went from a comfortable cushion of seventy-one seats for the Democrats in 1984 to a mere twelve seats for the Republicans by 2000. In a competition where even the slightest political gain could tip the scales, neither side would pass up any opportunity to score points for partisan advantage by whatever means available. Obstructionism was one, the aim being to deprive an opponent of perceptible successes, unless credit for them could be usurped or shared. Thwarting or retarding the other side's policy initiatives (with veto threats, filibusters, and poison-pill amendments) became routine during some years, as did holding up its appointments to executive and judicial offices.[38] "Going public" with political posturing on policy debates became common. By stylizing issues in black-and-white terms, this behavior flung the gauntlet at the opposition and interfered with the quiet negotiations that are often necessary to bridge differences on complex problems.[39] Routing out the presumed official miscreants (especially of the opposing party) was also among the tactics. And so was continual trawling for potentially pivotal supporters and campaign contributors to energize.

In practice, much of this political niche marketing was to vocal factions and advocacy groups whose influence had been rising steadily over the past thirty years and who frequently regarded the laying on of federal hands, so to speak, as the answer to almost any community problem.[40] Whatever the challenges facing particular places in postmodern American society— stolen cars, teenage smoking, cable television access, domestic violence, drunken driving, impurities in local drinking water—lobbies or movements

Figure 14-2. *Majority Margins in the House of Representatives*

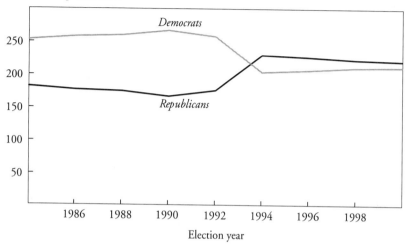

Source: Norman J. Ornstein, Thomas E. Mann, and Michael J. Malbin, *Vital Statistics on Congress,* 1984–85 through 1999–2000 (AEI Press, 1984–2000).

existed to amplify the cause and make it the national government's responsibility to follow up.[41] The evenly divided partisan environment of the 1990s, and its relentless pressure to fill campaign coffers, made pandering to many of these claimants more tempting. The circumstances probably helped to shed light on acts of Congress that, for example, displaced or duplicated state criminal codes in cases concerning car theft or violence against women and that advanced new federal standards for everything from local cable television rates to the blood-alcohol content of motorists who committed local traffic violations.

To be sure, control of Congress was closely contested at other junctures in the past half-century. The Democrats lost enough seats in both houses in the election of 1950 to cut their lead over the Republicans to thirty-five in the House and a mere one seat in the Senate. The balance in both chambers tipped, by razor-thin margins, to the Republicans two years later and then narrowly back to the Democrats in 1954. Yet the style of politics then was nothing like it is now.

Consider campaign spending. The total spent to elect the eighty-third Congress in 1952 was $36.4 million (in inflation-adjusted dollars).[42] By the time the 2000 election rolled around congressional candidates and their political parties were disbursing a total of $1.4 *billion* (not including large sums of independent spending, called "issue advocacy," by outside groups).[43] In the 1952 congressional elections, one of the most expensive campaigns was for a Senate seat in New Jersey, where the opposing candidates spent a combined total of almost $410,000 (again, adjusted for inflation). In 2000 the Democratic candidate *alone* shelled out more than 150 times that much to win the same seat.

Contemporary campaigning has become perpetual electioneering—or more accurately, in Hugh Heclo's words, a permanent "immense industry for studying, manufacturing, organizing, and manipulating public voices in support of candidates and causes."[44] The industry's lavish finances reflect the development of increasingly elaborate techniques of political salesmanship—televised advertising, continual polling, focus group probing, direct mail operations, "media buys," opposition research, and other devices designed to mold, massage, and mobilize possible sympathizers.[45] The business of elections, it is not too much to say, has come to resemble other multi-billion-dollar businesses. Like corporations adept at tailoring finely differentiated household products to segmented markets, now more than ever office seekers (or their legions of professional managers) have the capacity to customize a sales pitch for every carefully targeted group or subgroup of presumptive clients.

And like the vending of a vast selection of detergents or deodorants on today's supermarket shelves, the new norms of the political marketplace mean that politicians' policy portfolios are filled with narrowly gauged favors and frivolities, not just essentialities. The picture fifty years ago seemed quite different. With the notable exception of Senator Estes Kefauver's hearings on organized crime, the eighty-second Congress devoted more time to controversies in the international arena and considerably less to domestic affairs.[46] As a result legislation literally looked different. The less detailed was the domestic agenda, the shorter was the average length of the bills that passed. Public bills of the eighty-second Congress averaged less than three pages long—less than a fifth the average length of statutes enacted in the 105th Congress.

The Media Environment

No account of the modern political taste for turning government into a kind of overstocked domestic issues mart would be complete without mention of the news media. They filled the air with the equivalent of metro-section stories about localized misfortunes that supposedly merited extensive national scrutiny. Coverage of world events dwindled. By the mid-1990s the American press had downsized its overseas bureaus, and the major television networks were spending an average of six minutes a day on any news outside the United States.[47]

Politics and the Tube

For decades television journalism had been informing mass opinion and often framing the terms of public discourse. The 1952 Kefauver hearings were televised. By the closing years of the century, however, television had become *the* principal source of information for most Americans—and the subjects of its imagery typically trumped all others. So many examples of this displacement could be cited, it is hard to know where to begin. Here is but one. In June 1994, the United States seemed headed for a showdown with North Korea over its refusal to open its nuclear plants to international inspection. The North Korea story did not manage to stay on the upside of the issue-attention cycle for long. Among the happenings that promptly knocked it away were the scenes of O. J. Simpson's white Bronco being chased by local police cruisers in Los Angeles. At the expense of various other worthy topics, the network news programs proceeded to devote phenomenal amounts of airtime to the O. J. Simpson trial during the first nine months of 1995.[48]

The world as depicted on television news programs in the 1990s, observed James Fallows in his brilliant book on media politics, consisted of "a strange equivalence of spectacles" where no one event was necessarily more important than another.[49] The picture you watched, at least before September 11, might be about a U.S. warning on North Korean nukes. It could be the sight of the U.S. attorney general journeying to Miami to negotiate with the relatives of Elián Gonzales. It could be the smoldering hull of the USS *Cole*. It could be the arraignment of Tonya Harding. It could be a clip regarding Clinton's health care plan or, just as easily, "Troopergate" (one of several reported scandals and "missteps" that coincided with the health reform debate in 1993 and that probably helped to muddle it). With day-to-day coverage of events large and small qualifying interchangeably for primetime, it became harder for many people to distinguish worthwhile objects of public affairs from secondary or transitory ones.

Television images also often seemed to distort public perceptions of domestic policy problems, blowing them out of scale. For example, in the second half of 1992, figures on the U.S. economy showed inflation and interest rates to be low and unemployment to be rising moderately by historical standards.[50] But this mixed statistical reality was no match for the evening news segments, which zeroed in on plant closings, worker layoffs, mortgage foreclosures, and so on. With the "human face" of economic distress so graphically displayed, public confidence in the economy lagged well behind the recovery that was under way in the run-up to the presidential election. This enabled Clinton and Gore to campaign successfully against George Bush on "the economy, stupid," even as "the economy" was turning up.

Setting the Agenda

More than ever media hype seemed to highlight which perceived domestic predicaments would receive maximum recognition not only in electoral campaigns but also in congressional inquiries and even in the work of the government's bureaucracies. Greg Easterbrook recounts this unsettling case:

> Just a few months before the September 11 terrorist attacks, the Transportation Committee of the U.S. House of Representatives held a hearing on a grave threat to airline travel. As CNN cameras looked on, Transportation Secretary Norman Mineta, the star witness, was interrogated by committee members who chastised him about the lack of federal action regarding delays experienced by passengers at the nation's airport gates. Passenger inconvenience was reaching "crisis proportions," the committee declared. One out of every four flights in the United States was being delayed for twenty minutes or longer! Constituents were complaining! Members of Congress demanded that the government get more people into the air faster. Didn't the Department of Transportation understand that the slightest airline delay was a crisis?[51]

In hindsight it might seem ironical that the airline "crisis" Congress chose to probe in the first half of 2001 was "passenger inconvenience." That choice, though, was very much in line with frenzied journalistic accounts, including a *Newsweek* cover story, about congestion and tardy flights at a few busy airports (principally in Chicago, Los Angeles, and New York).[52]

Even the most serious and respectable news outlets portrayed local tragedies as nationwide faults requiring national oversight. Illustrative was what the *New York Times* decided to call in the spring of 2001 "Patterns of Police Violence." After covering a handful of rights abuses by city police departments, the nation's leading newspaper not only began perceiving "patterns" but also editorializing that "brutality aimed disproportionately at minorities has become *a national problem.*"[53] Never mind how sparse was the systematic evidence of such *patterns* of police brutality. Indeed, in all probability the contemporary behavior of most municipal police forces was less abusive toward communities of minorities than it had been in years past. The received wisdom now was that a new "problem" existed, that it was "national," and, by implication, that it needed the attention of federal officials. Little wonder that law enforcement agencies at all levels, from local police forces to the FBI, became hypersensitive to possible accusations of "profiling" or other controversial "patterns of practice."[54]

Last but not necessarily least, unconventional sources of news and commentary blossomed in the 1990s. Stories that the mainstream media declined to play up could still make headway through so-called "new media" sources such as radio talk shows and a proliferation of Internet "newsgroup" discussion forums. In 1993, for instance, the House of Representatives' "check kiting" scandal managed to join the decade's long litany of introspections on Capitol Hill largely because Rush Limbaugh and his counterparts in local markets pored over it at great length.[55]

Getting Real

Toward the end of 1998 the drift of political contestation in Washington reached a point where, as one perplexed member of Congress moaned, "We are now rapidly descending into a politics where life imitates farce." (The prophetic words were those of House minority leader Richard A. Gephardt. He expressed an impression that may have been on the minds of most Americans late that year as the floor debate on how to punish Bill Clinton took increasingly bizarre twists.)[56] The political culture of the capital post–September 11 has not exhibited (so far) anything comparable to the tragic-comic nadirs of the preceding years.

The presidency of George W. Bush started out with another round of lopsided emphasis on domestic initiatives—a tax adjustment, a proposal to deepen federal involvement in local public education, a plan to increase energy supplies, a scheme to support community services provided by local churches, and so on. After September 11 these ventures were not forgotten, but they were overshadowed by the president's concerted campaign against international terrorism and the outlaw states that could magnify the threat. Midway through his second term President Clinton pledged to battle terror in the twenty-first century "with the same rigor and determination we applied to the toughest security challenges of the [twentieth] century."[57] Perforce, following the carnage in New York, Pennsylvania, and Washington, Bush put Clinton's words into action.

For the first time al Qaeda's redoubts in Afghanistan felt the full force of U.S. military might. And America's muscular role on the world stage was not likely to stop there. The United States declared that it would strike, preemptively when necessary, at terrorist enemies and the regimes that backed them anywhere and that it would actively promote "free and open societies on every continent."[58] A president whose grasp of foreign affairs had appeared limited during the 2000 election proved to be an assertive internationalist. With refreshing clarity and determination, he challenged the international community to turn back the tide of terrorism but also to cease appeasing the ever-treacherous regime in Iraq. But that was not all. His administration soon signed with Russia a pact for steep cuts in nuclear arms, set sensible conditions for the creation of a viable Palestinian state, favored impressive increases in U.S. foreign aid, and proposed to spend large sums of money on the global AIDS crisis.

The administration's counterterrorism efforts informed its budgetary priorities and eventually led to a reasonably comprehensive proposal for a new cabinet-level Department of Homeland Security. For its part, Congress was more constructive than contrarious, at least at some important junctures—passing major legislation to secure the airports, renewing at long last the president's authority to negotiate international trade treaties, approving a resolution to force the disarmament of Iraq, and finally exercising more vigorous oversight over the federal government's faltering intelligence and law enforcement agencies.

Popular attitudes, and linked to them the behavior of the news media, also appeared to shift perceptibly. For years surveys had recorded a dismal level of public confidence in the federal government. In the weeks following September 11 the level improved dramatically. It sagged again by the spring of 2002—but hardly all the way back to the lows of, say, mid-2001.[59] Any appreciable overall rise in public trust of the government could grant policymakers more latitude to focus on antiterrorism, maybe even permitting them to shelve (for raisons d'état) a few unrelated policy demands.

The capacity to advance a coherent U.S. policy against global terror—one that takes a relatively consistent stand against a lot of messianic criminals, be they those of al Qaeda, Baghdad, or the Al Aqsa Martyrs Brigades—

may have been buttressed over the past year by somewhat greater public attentiveness to international events. The percentage of people who reported following international news in the spring of 2002 was up from where it had been in 1998. Indeed, more than 60 percent followed important developments abroad.[60] Recently, many more Americans (48 percent) were able to identify Yasser Arafat as the presumptive leader of the Palestinians than were able to identify key U.S. cabinet secretaries (Donald Rumsfeld, for instance, whom 29 percent recognize).[61] And polls last fall found that voters, for a change, were not assigning "the economy and jobs" a higher priority than "terrorism and national security."[62]

In part these subtle but noticeable conditions reflected changes in news coverage. The pre–September 11 world in the evening newscasts and front pages of newspapers was dense with domestic sagas. You were told more than you ever wanted to hear about California's electricity "crisis," the tribulations of health maintenance organization subscribers, the exclusion of homosexuals from the Boy Scouts, or Congressman Gary Condit's relationship with Chandra Levy. After September 11 foreign relations and military matters upstaged such stories. In fact, excluding segments about homeland security, domestic issues underwent a two-thirds decline in coverage on evening news programs between the middle of 2001 and early 2002.[63] Press reporting—principally by the *New York Times*, the *Wall Street Journal*, and the *Washington Post*—on the Afghan war, the al Qaeda network, and the government's lapses leading up to the day of reckoning became so formidably broad and deep it is hard to recall another time when the major American newspapers imparted to readers more significant knowledge and insights.

The political landscape post–September 11 also has had its share of scandals and investigations—but with a difference. This time the latest scandalous story did not revolve around curiosities like the past love affairs of cabinet officers or their determinations about Indian casino licenses. Rather, the sensational news has been about business fraud (Enron, WorldCom) on a scale so grand it has damaged U.S. financial markets and maybe even the rest of the economy. Whereas special prosecutors often seemed to rush at the tempests in the political teapots of the 1990s, the response to today's malfeasance has been rather different. Corrupt corporate executives have come under scrutiny, while public officials have been spared. The Independent Counsel Act of 1978 has finally been allowed to lapse, so criminal investigations once again are lodged where they should be: under the direct auspices of the Justice Department. Congressional oversight has not merely pondered human interest angles (such as the fate of Enron employees' pensions) but deliberated thoughtfully about market failures that require structural correction. And however flawed, historic campaign finance legislation to try to diminish the influence-peddling role of money, much of it from corporate sources, has been enacted.

Politics as Usual?

Differences in the dynamics of our politics before and after September 11 are discernible. Whether the changes are profound enough to place an enduring restraint on the pursuit of narrow political expediency and its trivializing effect on the federal government's purpose is another matter.

Here They Go Again

For all the redirection that President Bush has given the ship of state since Americans began taking the barbarities of terrorism seriously, his style has not always paralleled that of, let us say, Franklin D. Roosevelt after Pearl Harbor. When FDR described the state of the union on January 6, 1942, not a single domestic policy aside made its way into his address.[64] The nation was at war. "War costs money," the president explained. "That means taxes and bonds and bonds and taxes. It means cutting luxuries and other non-essentials." When George W. Bush addressed the nation on January 29, 2002, his account of the state of the union began with the accomplishments and challenges of another war, but later changed the subject.[65] Six paragraphs of his speech opened by stressing the goal of "good jobs"— how they "begin with good schools," how they rest on "affordable energy," how they depend on "tax relief" such as "doubling the child credit," and so forth. In a fashion that recalled Clinton's rhetoric, Bush would not only "grow the economy" and help to ensure "a steady paycheck" but also push a "patients' bill of rights," "coverage for prescription drugs," "broader homeownership," services by "faith-based groups," "early childhood development" programs, "new safeguards for 401(K) and pension plans." The shopping list seemed long; scant reference was made to sacrifice.

The mixture of guns and butter was but one exhibition of domestic politicking seemingly unfazed by September 11. The administration acquiesced to a farm bill that would boost agricultural subsidies to $180 billion over the next decade.[66] Amid the unavoidable logrolling that distorts energy bills, much of the administration's proposed legislation predictably degenerated into an assortment of subventions for influential interest groups such as the ethanol lobby. Budget legislation wending its way through the congressional sausage-maker hardly was bound by the president's security objectives; in slipped many additional millions of dollars of irrelevant spending for highways, schools, nursing homes, museums, fishing boats, and countless other earmarked blandishments.[67]

The consummate political calibration of federal expenditures and regulations was sometimes all too reminiscent of years past. Bush slapped a 30 percent tariff increase on imported steel, for instance. Although he later effectively nullified parts of this particular bailout, it was followed by another round of punitive tariffs on Canadian lumber. Sensitive to domestic economic considerations and resistance from various business and labor interests, the administration did not bring to an environmental conundrum of possibly incalculable importance—global warming—the policy leadership it deserved.

Some Explanations

New trade restrictions, protectionist crop supports, and defaults on climate-change policy may have seemed like myopic moves at a time when America's allies were being asked to stand behind our struggle against terrorists and ruthless despots worldwide. What explains the persistence of such parochial payoffs, some of which could further complicate an already distended federal agenda? "Shortsighted" vision—the stock answer of pundits and polemicists—will not do. For surges of small-time politics are inevitable in a democracy, and some no doubt will continue in ours, especially given a configuration of political inducements that the 2002 election modified but did not eliminate.

For one thing, although no problem outranked terrorism in the minds of most Americans during 2002, pollsters again divined that voters wanted the president and Congress to devote more time to difficulties at home.[68] How pronounced, or meaningful, these purported feelings actually were was, in a way, beside the point.[69] The constant electoral campaigns waged at the White House and the Capitol continued to interpret polling results as best approximations of the real world. Thus six months past September 11 the president was advised to keep traveling around the country, burnishing his reputation as a "compassionate conservative" who would put Washington to work on local schools, health care, and other "Mommy issues."[70] As for the congressional Democrats, their tack was to stress their customary prowess on such issues and put them at the center of the midterm election strategy.[71]

These reflexes have much to do with the fact that the battle for primacy between the political parties continues to be as pitched as ever. For the first time in half a century, the Republicans have attained (albeit tenuously) unified party control of the government. Yet few predicted this outcome; in the weeks, days, and even hours leading up to last fall's election, most observers regarded the congressional election as a toss-up. With control of the Senate hinging on the shift of a single seat, and with more than two-thirds of Senate elections in 2002 centered in the South and Midwest, it is not entirely surprising that opportunistic farm legislation was enacted last spring. With half a dozen seats separating majority from minority status in the House during the 107th Congress, it is not surprising that the White House tried to preempt the steel-import issue, thereby perhaps influencing a race or two last November.[72] Notwithstanding Bush's high approval ratings to date, events between now and 2004 could easily conspire to produce another fiercely fought presidential election in less than two-years' time.

Maneuvers like those on agricultural subsidies and steel protection could make Republicans sound a little like the antediluvian GOP whose motto in the nineteenth century was "vote yourself a farm, vote yourself a tariff." If that seemed faintly anachronistic, however, the stakes in the autumn of 2002 had seldom been higher: The reins of the U.S. government were up for grabs. The circumstances did not favor unflinching adherence to high principle by either party.

Further, last year's renewed effort to restrain the nonstop money chase in national politics did not lessen the fund-raising pressure for elective officeholders. Sharp party competition keeps up the pressure. And so does the endogenously induced expense of self-perpetuating campaign organizations, rolling along, as they do, with their throngs of professionals on big retainers, overhangs of debt, and generally bloated overhead.[73] In 2002 the combination of extraordinarily tight electoral rivalry in a handful of swing states and the permanent campaign's voracious financial appetite meant that American politicians, from the president on down, had to dedicate large amounts of time to prospecting for votes and dollars in places like Florida. Bush made no fewer than ten trips to that state during his first year and a half in office, answering locally popular concerns and passing the hat. In the two weeks before the election, the president set off on a dozen days of barnstorming in pivotal states and districts, even as he prepared for a possible war with Iraq.

September 11 subdued some of the worst partisan posturing that in the past had sought to taunt the opposition (for instance, humiliating its executive or judicial nominees or even running them out of town) and also produced a preponderance of policies designed for the near-term enjoyment of preferred clienteles rather than long-term service to the public interest. Because the parties frequently remain more responsive to their respective bases than to the general electorate, however, traces of these habits still resurface from time to time. In line with their favored advocacy groups, liberals in the 107th Congress resumed delaying various court appointments. Homeland security legislation bogged down in the Democratically controlled Senate where the Democrats and the White House locked horns for months over an old-fashioned labor issue—protection for civil servants in the new department. Appealing to its own traditional constituency, the Bush administration proposed further tax cuts regardless of the tepid public support for this canon of Republican orthodoxy or whether fiscal realities on the horizon warranted persevering with it.[74] Partisan base running like this seems likely to recur unless the root causes of political polarization, discussed earlier in this essay, abate markedly.

Conclusions and Suggestions

America was caught off guard on the morning of September 11, 2001. Maybe nothing could have prevented the debacle. It was not, after all, the first successful surprise attack on the United States and almost certainly would not be the last. However stretched or disconnected were key federal agencies, officials at various levels were not oblivious to the rise of terrorism, nor had recent congresses starved the overall budget that was required to confront the problem. Certainly the U.S. armed forces proved prepared for the battle when it was finally joined.

Still, the nation could have become more vigilant over the preceding years if its politics had not aggravated in government a kind of attention deficit disorder. Too often Washington appeared more engrossed in rarified internal quarrels, and in parsing legal fine points of public probity, than alert to world events that were putting Americans in mortal danger. And even if it had never gone off on these tangents, the government was overextended. The federal bureaucracy was frequently pressed to perform functions that were, if not unnecessary, ancillary to its primary public obligations and that mostly could have been relegated to state and local entities. It would have been helpful in the summer of 2001 if the FBI, for instance, had aimed more of its assets at cracking foreign terrorist cells as they plotted to devastate targets in New York and the capital. But the bureau was also assigned other duties—everything from painstaking field investigations for minor appointive posts to chasing common criminals.[75]

No doubt matters are not quite the same today. Much as the prospect of being hanged (as Samuel Johnson said) concentrates the mind, the body politic has taken notice of what September 11 signified. The mood of much of the American electorate, on edge but gritty, has strengthened the hand of President Bush and his ascendant Republican Party. Deliberations about how to harden the country's defense of its citizens' lives and property are certainly less desultory and more focused now than they were during the self-indulging politics of the 1990s. Al Qaeda's sanctuaries in Afghanistan have been smashed. And soon the dangerous dictatorships in Iraq and North Korea may no longer be permitted to pursue their sinister ambitions with impunity. For the better part of a decade, world leaders had temporized over how to disable Saddam Hussein as he flouted a stack of United Nations Chapter 7 resolutions regarding "threats to the peace, breaches of the peace, or acts of aggression." Today an American president has met this menace head-on.

All this implies that our political process has turned a corner. Yet time will tell whether the heartening reorientation will hold up over the long haul. Digressive compulsions have diminished but not vanished. What would it take to mute them further? Here, I suggest, are five admittedly rough answers.

Less Party Parity

In theory the presence of equally competitive political parties is good for any democracy. The tighter the competition, the greater the incentives for both sides to heed the preferences of the electorate at large and remain accountable to it. But in a political system where only about half of the general electorate votes in presidential elections, and where a far smaller share than that participates in the off-year contests and in the system's often decisive primaries, partisan parity in practice does not necessarily move office seekers closer to mainstream voters; all it may do is intensify the quest for support from fringe groups whose backing often has to be bought through specialized or localized appeals that most citizens, if asked, might deem eccentric or irrelevant.

Under the present circumstances, therefore, the nation might be better served if one party or the other were to succeed in widening its base and regaining a more conclusive advantage in congressional or presidential politics or, perhaps better still, both at once. Put another way, if his party had gained firm command of the House and Senate in 2000 and if he had won the presidency by more than a whisker, President Bush probably would not have had to divide quite so much of his time among fighting a complicated war while attending fund-raisers on behalf of Republican candidates from coast to coast and servicing the presumed local needs or wants.[76]

It is conceivable that what happened on November 5, 2002, was a breakthrough—perhaps the opening phase of a lasting era of Republican dominance. No doubt, the victory was historic. Only once before in the last century (in 1934) did a mid-term election yield gains for the president's party in both houses of Congress. The gains were made despite a weak economy and while the president performed something of a miracle—campaigning with the foreign policy problems of terrorism and Iraq deliberately in high profile. Moreover, this time the Republicans made significant inroads among groups of voters (women, for instance) who previously had tilted toward the Democrats.[77] The success of Republican candidates was aided, in part, by an edge in campaign cash. And that advantage is likely to widen as recent legislation dries up a major source of Democratic funding (soft money, or large donations from unions and wealthy individuals) while leaving intact a prime source of the GOP's resources (hard money, in the form of smaller contributions).[78]

But neither should the recent election be overinterpreted. Long-term Republican preeminence is far from certain. Helpful to the GOP in 2002 was that the presidential party had fewer seats in play than normal. If a mere 22,000 of the total votes cast had gone differently, the Senate could have remained in Democratic hands. If the new majorities in the 108th Congress drive an immoderate social agenda too hard, the same fluid voters who rallied behind the president last fall may slip away in 2004. Both parties will continue to share critical vulnerabilities. That Ralph Nader's Green Party cost the Democrats the presidency in 2000 is well known, for instance, but less understood is that third-party candidacies have decided the fate of Republican office seekers, too, from time to time. Last November, the fleeting campaign of a local Libertarian candidate drew off enough votes from John Thune, the Republican candidate for senator from South Dakota, to account for his narrow defeat. In the Senate, working control often requires super-majorities, not merely fifty-one seats.[79] That already distant prospect was rendered even more remote by losses like Thune's.

How to solidify an emergent governing majority—especially a stable one that will be more representative of centrist voters, not just larger collections of single-issue zealots—is a complex, perhaps intractable, dilemma. A starting point could be any appreciable increase in voter participation rates.[80] Exactly what would raise those rates, however, is itself a big puzzle.

A Break from Ceaseless Campaigning

Even a modest party realignment, if it had some staying power, could gradually give officeholders relief from the continual electioneering that strews too many political promises to domestic petitioners across the land—and ultimately overloads national policymakers with secondary and tertiary tasks. Moderating the political money supply (if that were possible) would help, too, especially since fund-raising is what the endless campaigning and promising are mostly about.

Alas, the body of law that attempts to govern campaign finance has typically run afoul of a more powerful law: namely, the one of unintended consequences. The latest reforms will prove to be no exception; constraining reliance on large donors, for instance, might only increase the amount of time candidates have to spend assembling a pot of money from smaller donors. Nonetheless, certain systemic revisions seem long overdue.[81] For example, enabling candidates and parties to obtain some "free" time on commercial television would ease their burden of raising millions for the single most expensive item in contemporary politics: television.[82] An arrangement along these lines would put the United States in step with other mature democracies, none of which expects their elected officials to cover all of the exorbitant costs of airtime. The alternative is unseemly: a lot of politicians incessantly tending to private contributors in order to defray an otherwise unaffordable campaign expense.

Parting from the Polls

Our politicians might also require less money—and get less sidetracked by ephemeral "popular" fancies—if they could somehow shed the habit of relying too readily on opinion polling, if not to set priorities, then to draw the contours of public policies.[83] American political leaders seem to attach inordinate credence to the findings of pollsters. Like the information supplied by Wall Street's supposedly masterful securities analysts, the services of pollsters are often oversold.

A major flaw of poll-driven governance is that it often seems biased by overestimation of the public's craving for an ever-expanding nanny state. The distortion happens in part because surveys tend to elicit opinions on proposed policies without adequately presenting respondents with the costs of the policies or with alternatives to them. Consider a recent example: the question of more federal aid to reduce school class size. Do most people support an increase in such federal aid? Naturally. But if, say, the question also mentions that such a program might not always confer more benefits than costs, large percentages of supporters jump ship.[84]

Further, polls on domestic policies often seem to *presuppose* a federal role rather than contemplate it as one of several possibilities. A poll that asks, for example, "Should the federal government spend more to improve education?" will inevitably yield a resounding yes. But why imply, as this typical query does, that *only* more federal spending is the secret to improving local education? A more balanced survey would ask, "How do you think education could be improved?" and then offer additional federal spending (along with additional federal taxes) as but one item on a wider menu of options.

In sum, the irony of a political process that turns on opinion polls (at least in their conventional and often inherently tendentious form) is that it is not necessarily more attuned to stable public desires. It does remain, however, more prone to increasing the size of government and spreading its labors in additional directions, whether most people prefer this dispersion intensely or not. Thus either better polling or simply less polling would probably enhance government circumspection and seriousness.

Good Enough for Government Work

If national policymaking were less about doing a little of everything, and more about doing a few important things well, among other things the sheer number of appointments in the executive branch could be decreased. Reducing the backlog of prospective personnel to be vetted might accelerate the clearance of appointees and enable them, literally, to get to their desks on time. Bush's FBI chief, Robert S. Mueller III, was sworn in a week before September 11. Although Mueller's was hardly an exceptionally long review, having him at the helm a little faster might have been useful.

To get on with the job of running the government, gains could be had by streamlining the disclosures of financial and background information that now bog down even middle-tier appointments. How badly does the nation need to know about the last fifteen years of foreign travel of its assistant secretary for public affairs at the Department of Housing and Urban Development?[85] Exactly what can feasibly be done to simplify the enlistment of talent eager to work for the government is a complicated question beyond the scope of these pages. Suffice it to say that this much seems clear: A more alluring process, less fraught with legalistic fussbudgeting not only in the recruitment stage but also on the job, is needed. A small but promising step, indirectly bearing on that goal, has been the abatement of the Independent Counsel Act—the well-intended ethics law of the 1970s that gradually became, as a former Reagan administration official later described it, "a loaded gun pointed at the executive branch."[86]

A Return to Federalism

Finally, there is the matter of federalism. Policymakers in Washington would be less encumbered if they could somehow desist from dabbling paternalistically in the quotidian administration of public education, municipal staffing practices, sanitation standards, routine criminal justice, and countless other areas normally in the orbit of local governments. Figuring out a sensible disengagement, however, implies reopening a large and unsettled debate: What are the proper spheres of national and local authority?

Jurists and theorists of the federal system have wrestled with that dilemma for ages. At the height of the cold war when American cities were thought to be in imminent danger of nuclear attack, the Eisenhower administration commissioned scholarly studies, not only to prepare for the worst but also to delineate an efficient division of labor among levels of government. The results were prosaic: A 1955 report titled *Civil Defense and Urban Vulnerability* concluded that "intergovernmental responsibilities" were "inappropriately defined and assigned" and then wound up recommending solutions such as more "national financial assistance to states and cities."[87]

During an earlier era—the last third of the nineteenth century and first third of the twentieth—the Supreme Court strove repeatedly to parse activities that Congress could constitutionally regulate and activities that would remain under the aegis of the states and local communities. The upshot was a welter of seemingly arbitrary distinctions: Federal laws governing the movement of lottery tickets, liquor, prostitutes, and harmful foods and drugs were upheld, while other basic functions—including manufacturing, insurance, and farming—were classified as *intra*state commerce, hence left to state regulators. By the 1940s, the court had all but given up trying to sustain such differentiations.

Some persisted, however. For example, according to the high court, the Commerce Clause duly empowered Congress to tell the city of San Antonio how to pay its transit system operators, but somehow the same clause did not give Congress the power to direct local police to perform background checks on prospective gun purchasers. In the age of terrorism, these sorts of juxtapositions seem especially peculiar.

A clean and stable demarcation between federal and local roles has proven impossible to draw over time—and I do not pretend to offer one here. Nonetheless, there ought to be some middle ground between either persevering stubbornly with futile theories of dual sovereignty or throwing up one's hands and accepting the proposition that national intervention is suitable for the garden-variety problems of local jurisdictions. The more indiscriminately the federal government distributes its exertions, the less adroit it will be in meeting world-class challenges when they arise.

The governmental institution that has come closest to pondering this trade-off has been the Supreme Court. The current court's federalism jurisprudence has sought to limit the scope of federal infringement on the traditional ambits of state and local polities. Although the majority's rationales have not always been persuasive, its critics have often been too dismissive. They should note, for instance, that some of the unwarranted expansion of federal jurisdiction over ordinary criminal cases during the past decade eventually drew the court's censure. "The pressure in Congress to appear responsive to every highly publicized societal ill or sensational crime" troubled Chief Justice William H. Rehnquist.[88] Writing in 1998, he urged Congress to ask itself "whether we want most of our legal relationships decided at the national rather than local level." The implications of such misgivings are all the more relevant now. Busting medicinal marijuana users, unwitting wetlands trespassers, car thieves, deadbeat dads, and bordellos in New Orleans may remain an appropriate component of law enforcement in this country. It no longer seems, however, like the best way for *federal* agents to spend their time.

In today's world these are just a few of the many pursuits a serious central government would do well to reconsider.

Notes

1. House Committee on the Judiciary, *Impeachment Inquiry: William Jefferson Clinton, President of the United States,* hearing before the House Committee on the Judiciary, 105 Cong. 2 sess. (Government Printing Office, 1998), p. 94.

2. Charles O. Jones stresses that the Clinton years, a time of acrimonious divided government after 1994, ironically produced plenty of "significant" legislation. The second session of the 104th Congress, in particular, was the third most productive single session of Congress in the postwar era. See Charles O. Jones, *Clinton and Congress: Risk, Restoration, and Reelection* (University of Oklahoma Press, 1999), pp. 167–70. Much of this legislative

activity continued to enlarge the scope of the federal government's already enormous policy portfolio. And an inspection, not only of legislative "productivity" but also of precisely
what was produced, suggests that much of the era's legislation (including, in important
respects, such achievements as welfare reform) immersed the federal government more
deeply in fields that were ordinarily the province of local authorities. This increased nation-
alization of local affairs was, to borrow a phrase originally coined by Charles de Gaulle, a
form of "low politics."

3. To say that such threats were not addressed forcefully enough is by no means to say
that they were mostly overlooked. A number of steps were taken, ranging from bombing
raids on Iraq in 1998 to more consequential measures such as a U.S.-Russian partnership
to prevent the defection of nuclear, chemical, and biological researchers to rogue states.

4. Staffing shortages were critical in key agencies such as the Immigration and Naturalization Service. See, for instance, William K. Rashbaum, "I.N.S. Agents Say Staffing
Hurts Anti-Terrorism Effort," *New York Times,* May 20, 2002, p. A20.

5. "Six Months On," *Economist,* March 9, 2001, p. 11.

6. John Lewis Gaddis, "And Now This: Lessons from the Old Era for the New One,"
in Strobe Talbott and Nayan Chanda, eds., *The Age of Terror: America and the World after
September 11* (Basic Books, 2001), p. 4.

7. John F. Kennedy, "Inaugural Address, January 20, 1961," in *Public Papers of the Presidents of the United States* (GPO, 1962), p. 1; italics added.

8. William J. Clinton, "Address before a Joint Session of the Congress on the State of
the Union, February 4, 1997," in *Public Papers of the Presidents of the United States* (GPO,
1998), pp. 109–17.

9. For a comprehensive account of the federalization phenomenon, see Pietro S.
Nivola, *Tense Commandments: Federal Prescriptions and City Problems* (Brookings, 2002).

10. Abraham Lincoln, "Address at Poughkeepsie, New York, February 19, 1861," in
John G. Nicolay and John Hay, eds., *Abraham Lincoln: Complete Works* (New York: Century
Company, 1920), p. 685.

11. Quoted in Edwin Meese III, "The Dangerous Federalization of Crime," *Wall Street
Journal,* February 22, 1999, p. A19.

12. Quoted in John B. Judis, "The Foreign Unpolicy," *New Republic,* July 12, 1993,
p. 18. See more generally, Pietro S. Nivola, "Commercializing Foreign Affairs?" in Randall
B. Ripley and James M. Lindsay, eds., *U.S. Foreign Policy after the Cold War* (University of
Pittsburgh Press, 1997), chap. 10.

13. However, the Camp David effort, which came at the very end of Clinton's tenure,
was a fiasco. The administration gambled that it could, in effect, shoot the moon with the
duplicitous Yasser Arafat in the summer of 2000.

14. Daniel Benjamin and Steven Simon, *The Age of Sacred Terror* (Random House,
2002).

15. David Johnston, Neil A. Lewis, and Don Van Natta Jr., "F.B.I. Inaction Blurred Picture before Sept. 11," *New York Times,* May 27, 2002, p. A1.

16. Mary Graham, *Democracy by Disclosure: The Rise of Technopopulism* (Brookings,
2002), pp. 62–63.

17. On this and the following points, see Joseph S. Nye Jr., "Government's Challenge:
Getting Serious about Terrorism," in James F. Hoge Jr. and Gideon Rose, eds., *How Did
This Happen? Terrorism and the New War* (New York: PublicAffairs, 2001).

18. Judith Miller, "Planning for Terror but Failing to Act," *New York Times*, December 30, 2001, p. B5. In the summer of 2001, the Bush administration rejected an FBI request for $58 million to hire an additional 149 counterterrorism field agents, 200 additional intelligence analysts, and 54 additional translators. David Johnston and Don Van Natta Jr., "Wary of Risk, Slow to Adapt, F.B.I. Stumbles in Terror War," *New York Times*, June 2, 2002, pp. 1, 24.

19. The delay proved to be a great boon to the September 11 hijackers. At least one of them, Hani Hanjour, entered the United States on a student visa, failed to show up for school, and remained in the country illegally. Kate Zernike and Christopher Drew, "Efforts to Track Foreign Students Are Said to Lag," *New York Times*, January 28, 2002, p. A1.

20. See Ronald Smothers, "Coast Guard Says Extra Tasks Stretch Harbor Safety Thin," *New York Times*, March 27, 2002, p. 12.

21. Paul C. Light, *Thickening Government: Federal Hierarchy and the Diffusion of Accountability* (Brookings, 1995). The Clinton administration invented as many new appointed positions in its eight years as the administrations of Kennedy, Johnson, Nixon, Ford, Carter, Reagan, and Bush Sr. had added in the previous thirty-two years. "Among the Clinton administration's innovations," writes Light, were "the soon-to-be-classic deputy to the deputy secretary, principal assistant deputy undersecretary, and associate principal deputy assistant secretary." See Paul C. Light, " Our Tottering Confirmation Process," *Public Interest*, vol. 147 (Spring 2002), pp. 64–65, 73.

22. Judge Bork's opponents abandoned all restraint. "When Bork's confirmation hearings before the Senate Judiciary Committee began on September 15, 1987, a parade of witnesses appeared to challenge the nomination. There was little testimony to suggest that Bork lacked the intelligence or experience to serve on the high court. . . . Every available tactic was used to attack and discredit the nominee: television and newspaper ads, direct-mail campaigns, petitions, polling, and fund-raising. Reporters even dug up copies of Judge Bork's video rental records." G. Calvin Mackenzie, "The State of the Presidential Appointments Process," in G. Calvin Mackenzie, ed., *Innocent until Nominated: The Breakdown of the Presidential Appointments Process* (Brookings, 2001), p. 23. Similar bloodletting attended the nomination of Justice Thomas. This time the process featured the testimony of a surprise witness, Anita Hill, who was persuaded to air salacious accusations on national television. Although appointees to cabinet posts have not been dragged through quite the same high-profile mire, several—John Tower in 1989 and Zoë Baird in 1993, among others—endured humiliating experiences. Subordinate positions have been littered with casualties, some even amid unified party control of the White House and the Senate. In 2001 Senator Jesse Helms placed holds on four Treasury Department nominees as a way of protesting the impact of textile imports on North Carolina's textile industry.

23. Benjamin Ginsberg and Martin Shefter, *Politics by Other Means: Politicians, Prosecutors, and the Press from Watergate to Whitewater* (W. W. Norton, 1999), p. 27.

24. Ginsberg and Shefter, *Politics by Other Means*, p. 183.

25. The FBI's (and CIA's) recruitment deficiencies were significant. For example, in unraveling a key element of al Qaeda's operations in the 1990s—the organization's financial flows—the U.S. government reportedly was hobbled by the insufficient number of intelligence officials in the FBI and CIA who understood the global banking system and, more basically, were fluent in Arabic. Miller, "Planning for Terror," p. B5. Serial "nanny"

scandals derailed nominations for attorney general. Both Zoë Baird and Judge Kimba Wood fell prey to charges involving the employment of their housekeepers or babysitters.

26. See the interesting essay by Charles Hill, "A Herculean Task: The Myth and Reality of Arab Terrorism," in Talbott and Chanda, eds., *The Age of Terror,* especially pp. 84–88.

27. William J. Clinton, "Remarks to the 53d Session of the United Nation's General Assembly in New York City, September 21, 1998," in *Public Papers of the Presidents of the United States, 1998* (GPO, 2000), pp. 1630, 1632.

28. "Instead of a backbreaking federal gas tax, we should try conservation," reasoned Bill Clinton and Al Gore during their 1992 campaign. The federal gasoline tax in 1992 amounted to 14 cents a gallon. Bill Clinton and Al Gore, *Putting People First: How We Can All Change America* (Times Books, 1992), p. 91. In 1996 the White House attached great importance to raising the minimum wage to $5.15 per hour. Beginning in the fall of 1997, Interior Secretary Bruce Babbitt underwent an eighteen-month investigation that centered on his department's decision to deny a license to a particular Indian casino. (The burning question was whether the administration had been swayed by pressure from competing tribes that had made significant campaign contributions to the Democratic National Committee.)

29. See James M. Lindsay, "The New Apathy: How an Uninterested Public Is Reshaping Foreign Policy," *Foreign Affairs,* vol. 79, no. 5 (September–October 2000), pp. 2–8. Although opinion polls indicated a rising level of concern about terrorism after the truck bombs killed six people in the World Trade Center in 1993 and 166 people in Oklahoma City two years later, overall attention paid to the outside world by the American public continued to sag. In a January 2000 Gallup poll respondents relegated world affairs to twentieth place in ranking the importance of issues for the presidential campaign. Nye Jr., "Government's Challenge," p. 200. That said, commentators and policymakers may well have perceived the American public as even more insular and disengaged than it actually was. See Steven Kull and I. M. Destler, *Misreading the Public: The Myth of a New Isolationism* (Brookings, 1999).

30. Quoted in Fred Barnes, "What It Takes," *New Republic,* October 19, 1992, and "In Their Own Words: Transcript of Speech by Clinton Accepting Democratic Nomination," *New York Times,* July 17, 1992. In January 1992, 43 percent of the public considered "the economy" to be "the most important problem facing the country," but "unemployment" and "lack of jobs" drew a much lower percentage. It seems implausible that these circumstances warranted evoking "the Great Depression." See Pew Research Center for the People and the Press, "News Release," February 22, 2001, p. 23.

31. During the relevant period, roughly 75 to 80 percent of Americans in various surveys reported being satisfied with the medical care they and their families received. Daniel Yankelovich, "The Debate That Wasn't: The Public and the Clinton Health Care Plan," in Henry Aaron, ed., *The Problem That Won't Go Away: Reforming U.S. Health Care Financing* (Brookings, 1996), p. 76.

32. Pew Research Center for the People and the Press, "News Release," p. 23.

33. See Gary C. Jacobson, "Party Polarization in National Politics: The Electoral Connection," in Jon R. Bond and Richard Fleisher, eds., *Polarized Politics: Congress and the President in a Partisan Era* (Washington: CQ Press, 2000), p. 10.

34. See David Brady and Morris Fiorina, "Congress in the Era of the Permanent Campaign," in Norman Ornstein and Thomas Mann, eds., *The Permanent Campaign and Its Future* (Washington: American Enterprise Institute Press, 2000), p. 135.

35. The minimum-wage issue made its initial appearance amid discussion of expanded work-study programs, community policing, V-chips for television sets, right-to-know provisions for local pollution control, and numerous other items in President Clinton's 1996 State of the Union Address. William J. Clinton, "Address before a Joint Session of the Congress on the State of the Union, January 23, 1996," in *Public Papers of the Presidents of the United States* (GPO, 1996), p. 82. On the steep rise in the wages of workers in the lowest percentiles after 1995, see Gary Burtless, "Comments on 'Are Less Skilled Women Crowding out Labor Market Participation among Less Skilled Men,' by Rebecca M. Blank and Jonah Gelbach," unpublished manuscript (Brookings Institution, 2000), especially chart 1.

36. For an account of this classic incident of partisan gaming, see Barbara Sinclair, "Hostile Partners: The President, Congress, and Lawmaking in the Partisan 1990s," in Bond and Fleisher, eds., *Polarized Politics,* p. 147.

37. On the organizational influence of the religious right, see Morris P. Fiorina, "Extreme Voices: A Dark Side of Civic Engagement," in Theda Skocpol and Morris P. Fiorina, eds., *Civic Engagement in American Democracy* (Brookings and Russell Sage, 1999), p. 409. I owe the subheading "Clowns to the Left, Jokers to the Right" to Fiorina's inspired essay.

38. President Clinton threatened to veto 69 percent of the major measures considered by the 105th Congress, and fully half of those measures encountered some filibuster-related problem. Sinclair, "Hostile Partners, "p. 145. The filibuster, which had been considered a parliamentary weapon of last resort, was trivialized in the 1990s. The minority now wielded it routinely against the majority's legislative agenda. Sarah A. Binder and Steven S. Smith, *Politics or Principle? Filibustering in the United States Senate* (Brookings, 1997), p. 16.

39. Samuel Kernell, *Going Public: New Strategies of Presidential Leadership,* 3d ed. (Washington: CQ Press, 1997), pp. 253–54.

40. For a definitive examination of the rising influence of citizen lobbying groups with an interest in "postmaterialist" issues (civic quality-of-life concerns), see Jeffrey M. Berry, *The New Liberalism: The Rising Power of Citizen Groups* (Brookings, 1999). Berry's study stresses the power of groups with liberal orientations, but conservative lobbies were also gaining clout, albeit through the use of somewhat different political resources and outlets.

41. One of many examples: In 1994 the home schooling movement managed to blitz the House of Representatives with half a million communications, tying up Capitol Hill switchboards and fax machines for several days. Morris P. Fiorina and Paul E. Peterson, *The New American Democracy,* 2d. ed. (New York: Longman, 2001), p. 190.

42. The figure is in year-2000 dollars.

43. See Norman J. Ornstein, Thomas E. Mann, and Michael J. Malbin, *Vital Statistics on Congress, 2001–2002* (Washington: American Enterprise Institute Press, 2002), p. 25.

44. Hugh Heclo, "Campaigning and Governing: A Conspectus," in Ornstein and Mann, eds., *The Permanent Campaign,* p. 23.

45. For two good volumes giving a ground-level view of the campaign industry at work, see James A. Thurber and Candice J. Nelson, eds., *Campaign Warriors: Political Consultants in Elections* (Brookings, 2000), and James A. Thurber, ed., *The Battle for Congress: Consultants, Candidates, and Voters* (Brookings, 2001).

46. Ornstein, Mann, and Malbin, *Vital Statistics on Congress,* p. 7.

47. James Fallows, *Breaking the News: How the Media Undermine American Democracy* (Pantheon Books, 1996), p. 199. By contrast, ten years earlier international news claimed a significantly larger allocation of the typical evening broadcast.

48. Fallows, *Breaking the News*, p. 244.

49. Fallows, *Breaking the News*, pp. 52–53, 219.

50. C. Eugene Steuerle, Edward M. Gramlich, Hugh Heclo, and Demetra Smith Nightingale, *The Government We Deserve: Responsive Democracy and Changing Expectations* (Washington: Urban Institute Press, 1998), p. 99.

51. Greg Easterbrook, "The All-Too-Friendly Skies: Security as an Afterthought," in Hoge Jr. and Rose, eds., *How Did This Happen?* p. 163.

52. The title on the cover of *Newsweek*, April 23, 2002, cried, "Air Hell: 7 Ways to Fix Flying." Real "air hell," however, arrived five months later.

53. "Patterns of Police Violence," *New York Times*, April 18, 2001, p. A22; italics added.

54. See Walter Pincus, "FBI Wary of Investigating Extremist Muslim Leaders," *Washington Post*, October 29, 2001, p. A4. Why was the now-famous July 2001 memorandum from an FBI agent in Phoenix rejected by headquarters? (The memo urged a broad survey of Middle Eastern men attending aviation schools.) Among the reasons, reportedly, was that some officials worried that the memo's recommendations might be criticized in Congress as racial profiling. Johnston and Van Natta Jr., "Wary of Risk," p. 24.

55. Fallows, *Breaking the News*, p. 70.

56. The comment followed the spectacle of Representative Bob Livingston's confession of sin and decision to resign. See *Congressional Quarterly Almanac, 1998* (Washington: CQ Press, 1998), p. 12.

57. Clinton's words were in an address to the U.S. Naval Academy on May 22, 1998. Nye Jr., "Government's Challenge," p. 201.

58. "Remarks by the President at the 2002 Graduation Exercise of the U.S. Military Academy, West Point," New York, June 1, 2002.

59. Asked, "How much of the time can you trust the government in Washington to do what is right?" 57 percent of respondents replied, "always/mostly" in October 2001. But by May 2002 the percentage had dropped back to 40 percent. Commentators made much of this sharp retreat. See "Here They Go Again," *Economist*, June 8, 2002, p. 27. Nevertheless, 40 percent was still appreciably better than 30 percent, the figure in July 2001.

60. Polltakers seemed oddly unimpressed with this remarkably high figure, because it reflected attentiveness "only" when "major" developments occurred. Why a rational majority of people should be expected to pay close attention to anything *less* than "major" events abroad or at home is a mystery. See Pew Center for People and the Press, "Public's News Habits Little Changed by September 11," June 9, 2002, p. 1.

61. Pew Center for People and the Press, "Public's News Habits," p. 21.

62. *New York Times*/CBS News poll, October 3–5, 2002.

63. Project for Excellence in Journalism, *The New War on Terrorism: The Not So New Television News Landscape* (Washington, May 23, 2002), p. 4.

64. Franklin D. Roosevelt, "Address to the Congress on the State of the Union, January 6, 1942," in *The Public Papers and Addresses of Franklin D. Roosevelt, 1942 Volume* (New York: Harper and Brother, 1950), pp. 32–42.

65. George W. Bush, "Address before a Joint Session of the Congress on the State of the Union, January 29, 2002," in *Weekly Compilation of Presidential Documents: George W. Bush, 2002* (GPO, 2002), pp. 133–39.

66. What connection wasting more money on farm subsidies could conceivably have to post–September 11 exigencies was a puzzlement, although President Bush tried to give the

idea this spin: "It's in our national security interests that we be able to feed ourselves," he told the National Cattlemen's Beef Association in February 2002. Mike Allen, "Bush Calls Farm Subsidies a National Security Issue," *Washington Post*, February 9, 2002, p. A4.

67. John Lancaster, "Writing a Budget to Win By: Lawmakers in Tight Races to Bring Spending Home," *Washington Post*, March 29, 2002, pp. A1, A14.

68. See Adam Nagourney and Janet Elder, "Public Says Bush Needs to Pay Heed to Weak Economy," *New York Times*, October 7, 2002, p. A1.

69. How strongly the public insists that its elected officials attend to domestic issues at the expense of international ones, including the war on terrorism, is not crystal clear. On the one hand, when asked, "Which is more important to you in deciding how to vote for Congress: domestic issues (like taxes, health care, and education) or international ones (like terrorism and the Middle East)?" almost 80 percent say domestic issues. On the other hand, when asked what Congress's top priorities should be, people put antiterrorism and national security first. *Economist,* June 8, 2002, p. 27. One wonders how respondents would answer a question suggesting that there might be a trade-off, even an inconsistency, between combating terrorism as a first priority and simultaneously concentrating on domestic issues, also as a first priority.

70. Elisabeth Bumiller, "Looking to Elections, Bush Plays up Domestic Issues," *New York Times,* May 10, 2002, p. A1.

71. Alison Mitchell, "Facing Wartime President, Democrats Focus on Home Front," *New York Times,* April 22, 2002, p. A23.

72. "'I hate to say it,' a Democratic consultant said, 'but I think he's taken this issue off the table.'" Mike Allen, "Politics a Key Force in Forging Policy," *Washington Post,* March 6, 2002, p. E4.

73. "It turns out that most of what political marketing does resolves into spending money on itself," writes Hugh Heclo, "Campaigning and Governing," p. 26. See also Anthony Corrado, "Running Backward: The Congressional Money Chase," in Ornstein and Mann, eds., *The Permanent Campaign.*

74. Public enthusiasm for additional tax reductions in 2002 was underwhelming. Only 41 percent agreed that Congress should "stimulate the economy" with "new tax cuts," according to a Gallup poll in January 2002. And when matters were worded in a manner that suggested potential benefits from *not* cutting taxes, even Bush's original round of tax reductions appeared to receive a negative reception. Among respondents to a Zogby poll conducted at the end of January and beginning of February 2002, 63 percent favored *rolling back* last year's tax cut when asked, "Tell me if you favor or oppose rolling back the tax cut if it means deficits would decrease?"

75. See, for example, "House of the Rising Farce," *Economist,* June 15, 2001, p. 30, about the FBI's six-month operation in 2001 to shut down a house of ill repute in New Orleans. Evidently, the complete background checks required for Senate-confirmable nominees require some thirty face-to-face interviews conducted by FBI agents. "The same full field investigation is undertaken for the 53 members of the U.S. Holocaust Memorial Council—part-time unpaid advisory posts—as for the head of the CIA or the secretary of defense," writes Norman Ornstein, "The Overstretched FBI," *Washington Post,* June 4, 2002, p. A17.

76. Loss of the governorship in Florida, for instance, could have affected Republican chances in the 2004 national election. Florida was the ultimate battleground state in 2000

and was likely to be one again. Also, adverse redistricting there could cost the GOP control of the House. Thus the president visited the state frequently, taking positions that aligned with local interests—the Cuban community's hard line on Castro, the retirees' fear of reforming the social security system, the environmentalists' opposition to offshore oil drilling, and so forth.

77. On this point, and for an insightful assessment of the 2002 election results in general, see Thomas B. Edsall, "The Sum of Its Parts No Longer Works for the Democratic Party," *Washington Post*, November 24, 2002, p. B4. In 2002 considerably more voters across the board seemed to perceive the Democratic Party as lacking a "clear plan for the country" (49 percent) than perceived such a lack in the Republican Party (39 percent). Adam Nagourney and Janet Elder, "In Poll, Americans Say Both Parties Lack Clear Vision," *New York Times*, November 2, 2002, p. 1.

78. Thomas B. Edsall, "Republicans' Big Cash Edge," *Washington Post*, November 7, 2002, p. A27.

79. As is well known, Senate rules permit many opportunities for obstruction by the minority. Sixty votes—the number needed for cloture on filibusters—is often the majority effectively needed to govern the chamber.

80. Overall voter turnout in 2002 (39.3 percent) was slightly higher than it was in the 1998 mid-term election (37.6 percent).

81. Campaign finance "reforms" have a way of becoming cures worse than the disease. Yet, worse or not, the status quo is troublesome. Disease may not be the right metaphor for it, but as Frank Sorauf has suggested, an arms race probably is. For like arms races among nations, the dynamics of contemporary political financing risk "destabilization of the system, the result of which is a lack of confidence in all limits, a declining sense of how much is enough, an escalating insecurity, and a consequent scrambling for more weapons." What follows, Sorauf continues, "is overkill, the raising and spending of money out of all proportion to a reality-based assessment of need." Frank J. Sorauf, "What *Buckley* Wrought," in E. Joshua Rosenkranz, ed., *If Buckley Fell: A First Amendment Blueprint for Regulating Money in Politics* (New York: Century Foundation Press, 1999), p. 50.

82. Notice that support for suggestions along these lines reaches beyond liberal reformers and includes proponents with conservative persuasions. See, for instance, A. James Reichley, *The Life of the Parties: A History of American Political Parties* (Lanham, Md.: Rowman and Littlefield, 2000), p. 345.

83. An illustration: "During the White House's budget battles with Republicans in late 1995 and 1996," write Lawrence Jacobs and Robert Shapiro, "opinion surveys were at times conducted and analyzed by Richard Morris, Mark Penn, and Douglas Schoen nearly every night." Lawrence R. Jacobs and Robert Y. Shapiro, "The Politicization of Public Opinion: The Fight for the Pulpit," in Margaret Weir, ed., *The Social Divide: Political Parties and the Future of Activist Government* (Brookings, 1998), pp. 96, 106. Although Jacobs and Shapiro argue that neither the White House nor the congressional leadership in the 1990s reduced policymaking to mere pandering to apparent public preferences, polling had become a much-exploited technique for "test marketing" and crafting policy presentations.

84. One study found that support for federal aid to reduce class size dropped some 35 percent when questionnaires noted that this program might be successful only "occasionally." See, in general, Robert Weissberg, "The Problem of Polling," *Public Interest*, vol. 148

(Summer 2002), especially pp. 41–43. For a general treatment of complexities and paradoxes of public attitudes as measured in the polls, see Albert H. Cantril and Susan Davis Cantril, *Reading Mixed Signals: Ambivalence in American Public Opinion about Government* (Woodrow Wilson Center Press and Johns Hopkins University Press, 1999).

85. I take the liberty of paraphrasing Paul C. Light's excellent essay, "Our Tottering Confirmation Process," p. 74.

86. Terry Eastland, quoted in Ginsberg and Shefter, *Politics by Other Means*, p. 33.

87. Commission on Intergovernmental Relations, *Civil Defense and Urban Vulnerability* (GPO, June 1995), pp. 1–4.

88. William H. Rehnquist, "The 1998 Year-End Report of the Federal Judiciary," *The Third Branch: Newsletter of the Federal Courts*, vol. 31, no. 1 (January 1999), p. 3.

JAMES Q. WILSON 15

Reflections on the Political Context

THIRTY-SIX YEARS have elapsed since the Brookings Institution published its first edition of *Agenda for the Nation*. During those years our national government has changed; the change, however, is not easily measured. The number of rules issued by the federal bureaucracy increases in some years and falls in others; the number of bills passed by Congress goes up and down; some presidents are popular and others are not. And, until September 11, 2001, many Americans were concerned about retaining a budget surplus, but after the terrorist attacks on that day, hardly anyone was worried about budgetary balances, at least for the time being. These and similar changes reflect swings in the political mood, in the dispositions of presidents, and in public reactions to the circumstances of the moment. They do not necessarily indicate deeper shifts in the nation's politics.

The deeper changes are revealed not in polls of opinion or even in demands for policy but in the federal government's responses to opinions and demands. Look at policymaking a half century ago. In 1956 Congress passed, and President Eisenhower signed, the Federal-Aid Highway Act. In a mere twenty-eight pages, that bill authorized a new interstate highway system and the taxes to pay for it. It imposed only a few constraints: highway contractors had to pay prevailing wages, the Bureau of Public Roads had to consult with state highway departments, and public hearings had to be held. This short law created an American monument: a highway system that linked every state capital and every large city (and many small ones as well), and that made it possible to drive nonstop (except at rush hour in a few places) from virtually any point in the country to another.

More than three decades later, in a law that was more than ten times longer than its predecessor, Congress reauthorized the highway program in the Intermodal Surface Transportation Efficiency Act of 1991 (ISTEA). ISTEA contained a vast number of new rules, duties, and constraints. The secretary of transportation (a post that had been created in 1966) was directed to relieve congestion, improve air quality, preserve historic sites, encourage the use of seat belts and motorcycle helmets, control erosion and storm-water runoff, reduce drunk driving, require environmental impact studies, restrict outdoor advertising, require metropolitan-area planning, set aside 10 percent of highway construction funds for small businesses owned by people classified as disadvantaged, buy iron and steel from U.S. suppliers, and give preferential treatment to Native Americans when a highway is built near their reservations. And this is just a partial list of what the secretary was—somehow—supposed to do.[1]

What had happened? Congress's commitment to highways had not diminished, although the 1991 bill did add support for mass transit to the 1956 law. Authorized spending reached new highs in ISTEA, but there was nothing unusual about that. The important change was that the secretary of transportation (and, by implication, the entire federal government) was now held responsible for a great deal more than building roads. Arguments over the essence of federalism—that is, over the proper allocation of tasks between the states and the national government—had apparently ended. There was no longer much debate about what Washington was expected to do.

When Dwight Eisenhower was president, hardly anybody thought that Washington should make policies about crime, guns, education, abortion, medical care (except for veterans), the environment, automobile safety, local advertising, the economically disadvantaged, or minorities' access to jobs and schooling. Today people assume that Washington will have policies on all these matters and more—and the Supreme Court has decided that most of them are constitutional.

During the eight years of the Eisenhower administration, the most important pieces of domestic legislation passed by Congress created the interstate highway system, gave the states the right to drill offshore for oil, granted statehood to Alaska and Hawaii, and provided (mild) guarantees of civil rights. Three decades later, during the first four years of the Clinton administration, Congress considered bills about (among countless other items) endangered species, dolphin-safe tuna, abortion, local education, the homeless, family leave, gun control, carjackers, same-sex marriages, hate crimes, gender equity in schools, smoking on federal property, and the addition of 100,000 new officers to city police departments.

Barriers on what the national government could or could not legitimately undertake had changed. For one thing, a legislator defending states' rights rarely could protect the states against federal incursions. In fact, states' rights as barriers to federal legislation had pretty much ended with the passage of civil rights laws in the early 1960s. Of course, the legitimacy barrier, as I have called it, persisted longer in some realms of public policy than others.[2] But even where old constraints seemed strong, they seldom endured. No sooner had knowledgeable observers concluded that the national political process would remain at an impasse over gun-control and family-leave legislation, for example, than Congress passed laws about gun control and family leave.[3]

But it is not entirely accurate to say that the legitimacy barrier has "collapsed," especially since the Supreme Court has been trying, of late, to restore portions of it. The Constitution still requires that Congress often act indirectly—by, for example, mandating that the states perform certain tasks without federal financial support (collecting most of our federal personal income taxes, for instance) or compelling businesses to supply certain benefits without financial compensation (furnishing special accommodations for disabled people).

As the federal government's policy agenda has widened, the range of groups interested in influencing policy has expanded. Between the early 1960s and the early 1980s, the number of registered lobbyists increased more than sixtyfold and the number of lawyers, journalists, and trade associations more than threefold.[4] There was nothing sinister about this sharp rise in the number of activists who were trying to shape policy: our constitutional system, more than almost any other, is designed so that it (properly) supplies policymakers with information about what groups want and how citizens think. The bigger the agenda, the more people will strive to determine how it is managed. Naturally, this increase in activism led to an increase in private spending on elections, setting a course that can scarcely be stopped by efforts to regulate campaign finance.

Moreover, the style of American national politics has changed in ways that do not obviously follow from the broadening of the national agenda.

Not only has the scope of its activities expanded, but many of those activities have proven divisive.

Polarization

At a time of increasing public aversion to partisanship, polarization in Congress was more acute in the past decade than at any time since the debate over civil rights in the early 1960s. Party votes in Congress—that is, votes in which a majority of one party opposed a majority of the other—have become more common. In 1970 only about one-third of all House and Senate votes were party votes; by 1998, over half were.[5] As Pietro Nivola recounts in chapter 14, when the House voted on the impeachment of President Clinton, 98 percent of the Republicans voted for at least one of the four impeachment articles and 98 percent of the Democrats voted against all four—and this sharp division occurred despite the fact that the public opposed both impeachment and conviction. Moreover, Nivola could have added that the Republicans' strict party-line voting did not even reflect the sentiments of voters in many districts represented by Republicans. On the basis of public opinion polls taken in 1998 and 1999, Gary Jacobson concluded that voters in many such districts opposed impeachment—a circumstance that did not stop the Republican members, with scarcely any exceptions, from voting for impeachment.[6]

Party unity on roll calls offers further examples of increasing polarization. Party unity is defined as the percentage of each party's members in the House and Senate who vote with other members of their party when at least half of that party is opposed by at least half of the other party. Around 1970 about 70 percent of all members voted with their party colleagues; by 1998, the proportion had arisen to about 90 percent.[7] Of course, some of these recent votes were on rather minor matters, but even on big questions party unity tends to prevail. When President Clinton's tax-increase bill was sent to Congress in 1993, not a single House or Senate Republican voted for it. But every House Democrat (save eleven) and every Senate Democrat (save two) voted for the bill.

The changing character of the Senate has been nicely captured in a recent essay by Barbara Sinclair. In the 1950s policies were typically made behind closed doors—often by a courtly older senator, probably a conservative southern Democrat. In the 1970s policy tended to be made after sharp floor debate—often led by an entrepreneurial lawmaker, liberal or conservative. By the 1990s the lawmaker was more likely to come across as a partisan warrior, dueling with his rivals and relying heavily on public relations and the threat of filibusters.

The combined effect of greater partisanship and novel parliamentary procedures brought about these changes in political style. Filibusters once required a senator to continue to hold forth while his colleagues slept on cots, waiting for the orator to tire. In more recent years, "double tracking" became common: a bill that is the object of a filibuster gets shelved temporarily so that debate can continue on other matters; thus, any senator can now threaten a filibuster without having to make a long speech. In the 1950s there was one filibuster for each Congress; by the 1990s, there were at least twenty-eight for each Congress.

A filibuster can, of course, be ended by the vote of at least sixty senators. By the 1990s there were more than forty-eight cloture votes per Congress— meaning, in practical terms, that it takes a supermajority of at least sixty senators to pass any controversial legislation. And the need for supermajorities, in turn, has meant that almost all important Senate business has to be done under unanimous consent agreements that any senator can easily block. To prevent such obstruction, the majority and minority leaders must confer extensively to be certain that no aggrieved senator will place a "hold" on Senate action. All these arrangements help account for the increase in the power of individual senators—and for the burden that their individualism can place on party leadership.[8]

I have said that members of Congress are both more individualistic and more partisan. How can both statements be true? An autonomous individual is beholden to no institution, but a political party is an institution. The answer, I think, is that most members of Congress take positions, advance ideas, and seek reelection as people who are relatively independent of congressional leaders. At the same time, most members now have a stronger ideological commitment to a party view of how the world should work, and take positions that conform to their party's politics. Because members value personal ideology and ties to constituents more than party loyalty, lining up votes is a challenge for today's party whips. Nevertheless, they do whip members into line, in part because contemporary American political parties have acquired more ideological coherence and are no longer merely machines distributing material favors to their followers. (This is not to say, of course, that none of the traditional incentive systems under the parties' control continue to play a role. The parties still control cherished committee assignments, for instance, and procedural rules in the House as set down by the Rules Committee.)

Between the end of the Second World War and the late 1960s, the ideological gap between Democrats and the Republicans in Congress narrowed; after around 1970, it widened substantially. When George Wallace said, in the late 1960s, that there was not a dime's worth of difference between the Democrats and the Republicans, he was exaggerating a bit, but he was right to think that the differences between the parties had lessened. But by the late 1990s that statement would have been utterly wrong.

Part of this change has an obvious explanation: the collapse of the Democratic Party in many parts of the South. In the early 1960s, scarcely any Republicans from the Deep South held seats in Congress, but by the mid-1990s the Republicans had become the majority party in that region. This change led to the near collapse of the old conservative coalition, the alliance between Republicans and conservative Southern Democrats that for decades had often cast the deciding votes in both the House and the Senate. For liberal politicians to control Congress, they had to elect extraordinary majorities of northern Democrats—which they did, in 1964, on the coattails of Lyndon Johnson's victory, but not on many other occasions.

Today the conservative coalition is now part of one party: conservative Southerners tend to vote for Republicans. At the same time, the rapid growth in the number of African American voters since the 1965 voting rights laws began to be enforced, coupled with redistricting plans that consolidated many black voters into predominately black districts, produced a number of liberal members representing the South. Taken together, these transformations have created a Congress in which Democrats (including Democrats in parts of the South) are overwhelmingly liberal and Republicans are largely conservative. Among the Democratic members of Congress who were least likely to support President Clinton's legislative agenda in the 1990s, about half came, not from the South, but from states such as Montana, Illinois, and Minnesota. Every one of the most liberal legislators at present is a Democrat; every one of the most conservative members is a Republican.

But on many issues Americans today are less likely to describe themselves as staunchly liberal or conservative than they were decades ago. Consider abortion. The public's views have scarcely changed since 1973: some people want all women to have unfettered access to abortion, some want a flat ban on abortion, but most want to authorize abortion under certain circumstances (for example, if the mother has been the victim of rape or incest.)[9] But in Congress, scarcely any Democrats fail to support access to abortion, and very few Republicans fail to oppose it. On this issue, public opinion is unimodal: that is, most people are in the middle. In Congress, opinion is bimodal: that is, members are either fully in favor of or fully opposed to abortion rights.

But perhaps Congress is more divided because, as Gary Jacobson has argued, the voters are in some ways more divided. Using data drawn from voter surveys, Jacobson found that voters are now more likely to say that there are important differences between Democrats and Republicans, to describe themselves as liberals or conservatives, and to favor parties with which they have an ideological affinity. These findings imply that the connection between a voter's party identification and his or her position on political issues, especially social issues, has grown stronger.

For example, Jacobson found that in 1980 only 30 percent of voters who opposed abortion under all circumstances identified themselves as Republicans; by 1998, 71 percent did so. Jacobson contends that, contrary to what many people have assumed, Congress has become more polarized because the voters have become more polarized.[10] Many people may be fed up with politics and either do not vote or vote for third parties, but the voting minority is more ideologically distinct today than it was in the 1970s.

Larry Bartels has shown that since the 1980s partisan loyalties have rebounded among voters in both presidential and congressional elections. The proportion of voters who strongly identify with one of the two major parties has increased, while the share of those who describe themselves as independents has shrunk somewhat. As a result, partisan voting has become more common, not only within but outside the South, among both young and old, and among well-educated and less well educated voters alike.[11] Building on these findings, Marc J. Hetherington found that voters have become more partisan in part because the parties in Congress have drawn apart. As members of Congress retreated further into their partisan camps, voters (particularly more educated voters) began to more strongly differentiate between the parties as well.[12]

Taking a different view, Melissa P. Collie and John Lyman Mason suggest that ideological changes among voters have been "marginal at best."[13] They support this conclusion with evidence drawn from an analysis of public opinion in two kinds of congressional districts: Democrats voting in districts held by Democratic representatives and Republicans voting in districts held by Republican representatives. What Collie and Lyman found is that, as measured by a polling scale, the professed ideological positions of such voters changed little during the years from 1972 through 1994.[14] Such change as did occur was limited to Republicans' having become a bit more conservative. The same results held when Collie and Mason limited the analysis to "strong Democrats" (as opposed to "weak Democrats" and "independents who lean Democratic") and "strong Republicans." Once again, the political distance between voters in Democratic and Republican districts remained fairly constant over two decades.[15]

The differences in the findings of Jacobson, Bartels, and Hetherington on the one hand and Collie and Mason on the other may be worth further investigation, but I suspect that, for several reasons, they cannot be resolved. First, we have no data that will allow us to link what voters in each congressional district think to how their representatives behave. To obtain such data would mean polling perhaps five hundred voters in each district, several years apart. Happily, no one thinks it is worth spending money to interview over twenty thousand voters at different times just to resolve an academic puzzle. Second, none of the analyses focuses on the voters who are likely to make a big difference in how Congress behaves. The most consequential participants are the activists: people who give campaign money, go to candidates' meetings, write press reports and conduct talk shows, and join or lead interest groups that lobby politicians. These are also the players who are likely to have a large role in contested primary elections, where they often make up a disproportionate share of all voters.

To be sure, Jacobson does hint at what activists may think. For example, he examined opinion data on Clinton's impeachment from several congressional districts and found that the voters in each district opposed impeachment. But when he looked at the views of Republican voters who lived in districts where the representatives were Republican, he found that they strongly favored impeachment even though they were outnumbered by impeachment opponents. By the same token, Democratic voters who lived in districts with Democratic representatives opposed impeachment even more strongly than did their districts as a whole.[16]

Other research has shown that voters who participate in primaries often have views on abortion that differ from those of the much larger group of voters who participate in general elections. Liberals tend to dominate Democratic primaries and conservatives to dominate Republican ones. This pattern poses an especially vexing problem for Republicans. In Senate races, for example, Republican primary voters are likely to be against abortion, which puts primary winners in a difficult position: they must now face a general election in which the state's voters are, overall, much more moderate on the abortion issue. Taking a firm enough position on abortion to win the primaries—and then backtracking enough to successfully contest a general election—makes for a tense balancing act for Republican office seekers.[17] The same problem affects some Democrats. To win primary elections they may have to endorse gun control, while to win the general elections they may have to denounce gun control. After the dramatic election of 1994, when the GOP won control of the House for the first time in forty years, the change in party control increased the tension. When Newt Gingrich became Speaker of the House, senior members were often passed over for junior ones when it came time to select committee chairs. Chairs were limited to six-year terms, but they were given the power to choose their own subcommittee chairs. In addition, proxy voting was banned, public funding for caucuses was eliminated, committee staffs were cut in size, and more open debate rules were promised.

For a while it seemed as if the House was being converted into an American version of the British House of Commons, with strong party leadership and central policy direction. Party power trumped committee power, and many bills were reported to the House floor without even receiving a committee hearing. Many of the new members had pledged to support a party platform, the Contract with America, that promised important legislative changes. The Republican Conference became a principal agent and was pressing for action on the Contract with America.

But it could not last. The Constitution does not allow for parliamentary government—a constraint that became evident when the Senate failed to act on many bills that had been passed in the House, and the president ignored most of the Republicans' demands. (The Senate defeated these measures largely through "holds" and threatened filibusters, of the sort described earlier.) After the 1996 and 1998 elections reduced the Republican majority, Newt Gingrich resigned as Speaker and as a House member. It was a fitting parliamentary gesture, perhaps, but it also signaled the end of the brief experiment in parliamentary-style rule of the House. Even without Speaker Gingrich, however, the party divisions in Congress remained intense.

It would be helpful if we could learn more about the role of activist Republicans and Democrats to determine whether their heightened partisanship affects the behavior of Congress. That is no easy task, however. Jacobson, on the basis of some polling data, argues that the parties' "most politically active supporters—the source of money and other kinds of help, and the pool from which House candidates themselves are drawn—have diverged" over the last several decades.[18]

This thesis, if true, may help explain the abortion puzzle. In a nutshell, the problem is as follows: since *Roe* v. *Wade* was decided in 1973, American voters have not substantially changed their views on abortion, but opinions in Congress have changed dramatically, driving Democrats and Republicans far apart. Why should Congress have become so polarized on this issue when the public at large was not? Offering one possible answer, Greg D. Adams suggests that Congress became increasingly divided because abortion became a litmus test for people seeking nomination for office: in the tight political world of primary nominations, to get on the Democratic ticket you had to be pro-choice, and to get on the Republican ticket you had to be anti-abortion. In 1976 there was a difference, though not a vast one, between how Senate Democrats and Republicans voted on abortion. But by 1986 the gap had widened greatly, and the House followed much the same pattern. In the course of a decade or so, Democrats became vastly more pro-choice and Republicans vastly more anti-abortion, even though public opinion on the subject remained essentially unchanged.

There were exceptions, of course, but fewer and fewer. Moreover, the dispute over abortion changed the *distribution* of opposing views among voters: for several years after *Roe* was decided, Republican voters were *more* pro-choice than Democratic ones. But as abortion became a powerful ideological tool and as party activists made it a litmus test for candidate nominations, the Republicans became more anti-abortion and the Democrats more pro-choice.[19]

The abortion issue demonstrates the complexity of the relationship between events, mass opinion, and the behavior of elites. An event (the Supreme Court decision) precipitated a public disagreement. But once activist groups managed to gain influence over the nomination process for office seekers, the impact of the disagreement had an increasingly strong impact on Congress—and positions taken by office seekers began, in turn, to alter and intensify the attitudes of partisan voters.

Abortion is not the only issue that has set off escalating political conflict. When I wrote for *Agenda for the Nation* in 1967, a civil rights bill had just been passed but Washington was not much interested in the environment, gun control, or campaign finance; affirmative action was barely on the horizon, and AIDS was unknown. Now political careers are made and broken on the basis of debates about these issues.

The debates have at least one feature in common: they all concern social problems that arouse deep passions and defy easy compromises. To a visitor from Mars, this statement might seem absurd. Of course, one can negotiate about the environment by bargaining over clean-air tolerances, about gun control by adjusting the budget devoted to law enforcement, and about campaign finance by choosing acceptable private funding levels. But none of these approaches reflects how real-world political and media actors treat these matters. To the editorial writers in many big-city newspapers and national magazines, and to other power brokers who influence government's decisions to intervene in a widening range of perceived problems, striking the "correct" stance—and, often, drawing a line in the sand—is regarded as a test of personal integrity and public-spiritedness, if not human decency.

This is not an easy claim to prove, but the editorial pages of the *New York Times* and media advertisements for opposing candidates offer plentiful evidence. Political slogans no longer focus on whether Candidate A is for "the rich" or on whether Candidate B is for "the working people"; instead, they tout the candidates' positions on "hot" issues: Candidate A voted "against gun control" and "in favor of cutbacks in environmental protection" while accepting money from "special interests"; Candidate B "favors people over guns," "cherishes the environment," and refuses to accept money from political action committees.

It is not entirely clear to me why certain issues remain political symbols while others cease to be. At one time, Social Security was supposedly the "third rail" in American politics: touch it and you die. Now candidates can at least discuss different ways of sustaining the national commitment to support elderly Americans, including perhaps some form of private retirement accounts as part of the total package. At another time, a vote to give the Panama Canal to Panama was a death knell for quite a few politicians, but the canal was given away and nobody thinks much about it anymore. Twenty years ago people chose sides according to how they felt about busing as a means of integrating the public schools, but busing—and the associated controversy—is now largely a thing of the past, in part because it failed to actually integrate the schools. In time, other hot buttons of the day may cool off, too, so that public officials will be able to discuss guns, the environment, campaign spending, abortion, and affirmative action more or less dispassionately. But right now we are a long way from that day.

The trouble is not that these issues exist. It is that Washington is expected to have a policy for almost any issue. Though the central government here is less burdensome and intrusive than it is in European democracies (at least with respect to commercial or economic matters), its scope has expanded dramatically over the past half-century—even though the Supreme Court has tried of late to reestablish some old limits. Without such limits, governmental activism in itself generates new issues, some of which will turn into symbols (as have abortion, gun control, affirmative action, and the environment) that will be used to ensure or deny candidates access to elective office. The upshot will be continued polarized majorities in Congress.

The Decline of Competitive Districts

The continued decline of House districts with competitive elections has wrought far-reaching changes in the relationship between voters and their congressional delegates. Redistricting that occurred after the 2000 federal census accentuated this trend, but it is not new. Between 1952 and 2000, 93 percent of the House incumbents who sought reelection won.[20] During the first thirty years of this period, the reelection rate was 92 percent; during the last ten it was 94 percent.

Of course, the frequency with which incumbents get reelected is somewhat misleading because incumbents who fear defeat often choose not to seek reelection. But even allowing for self-selection, it is clear that state legislatures have worked steadily to make seats safe for incumbents. Charlie Cook predicted that in 2002 there would not be a single competitive House seat in California, Illinois, Massachusetts, Michigan, Pennsylvania, or Wisconsin.[21] He was right. No incumbent lost, most won more than 60 percent of the vote, and in Massachusetts six of its ten house seats were uncontested.

With virtually no interparty competition in most House districts, the main electoral tussles are limited to party primaries in which Democrats argue over who is most liberal and Republicans over who is most conservative. And with few House seats changing hands, party conferences in the House have become less moderate, as the Democratic caucus leans more to the left and the Republican conference more to the right.

Regardless of whether the arguments of Jacobson and other scholars about other sources of political polarization are right or wrong, redistricting alone appears to have polarized opinion in Congress more than the average voter might wish. In any event, what we have today is a legislative body that differs sharply from the days when very few primary elections empowered groups of activists, and when a narrower national agenda gave fewer such groups an interest in being empowered.

The Courts

The courts have also contributed to political polarization. America is by most measures the most classically liberal (in the original sense of the term) nation in the world. We tax less—and, as Gary Burtless and Christopher Jencks show in chapter 3, our system of income distribution is less egalitarian than those of most other Western democracies. Few (if any) of our laws, however, are more unusual than those that govern abortion. In England, Israel, Greece, Germany, and Switzerland, as in various other democratic nations, a woman seeking an abortion during the third trimester must seek two qualified medical opinions and get the approval of a committee of experts. Even in Sweden, a democracy as different from America's as one can imagine, abortions are not available after the eighteenth week of pregnancy.[22]

Our position on abortion is an outlier because it is based on a judicial edict, not a legislative decision. A court creates (or acknowledges) rights; a legislature makes negotiated law. In America, through *Roe* v. *Wade*, the Supreme Court created an enforceable right; in England, Israel, Greece, Germany, Sweden, and Switzerland, parliaments created complex rules to govern abortion. The source of the decision makes a great difference in the politics of abortion. In the United States, people who favor access to abortion call it a constitutional right; people who oppose it call it an affront to morality or religion. Congress has been able to do virtually nothing to affect the *Roe* ruling, and even the Supreme Court has been able to modify it only slightly.

Granted, some people feel quite comfortable with this arrangement because they believe that access to abortion—the "right to choose"—is indeed a fundamental right, albeit one mentioned nowhere in the Constitution and one that presupposes that a fetus is not a person no matter how close to birth it may be. But my aim is not to argue that *Roe* was wrongly decided; it is only to illustrate the difference between a policy that is based on a court-decreed right and one that reflects a political choice.

Unlike abortion, civil rights are in fact protected by the Constitution; and they have the advantage, to my mind, of being quite securely founded on explicit constitutional language and reflecting a universal principle of moral equality that is almost impossible to deny. As a consequence, civil rights have become so broadly accepted that virtually no one tries to enter politics by suggesting that we deny rights to blacks or women. Civil rights (apart from affirmative action) is no longer a polarizing issue because, for almost everyone now, there is only one "right" side.

The courts, especially federal ones, occupy a distinctive place in the American constitutional system because their powers are great and their members are not elected. Moreover, judicial rules and federal laws offer a wide variety of incentives to use courts. For example, because federal judges can issue injunctions—and thereby block the implementation of any act of Congress or state legislature for months or years—savvy interest groups have learned where to turn in the judicial system to obtain the injunction they want. In the case of civil rights suits, federal law requires the award of attorneys' fees to plaintiffs who undertake successful suits against federal, state, or local government agencies. To avoid the risk of paying a potentially large fee, many defendants capitulate, whatever the merits of the case. Moreover, if a government agency loses a civil rights suit, judges often issue "structural injunctions" or appoint special masters authorized to manage the most minute details of the agency's operations.[23] These and similar actions can confer real benefits on society, but they can also impose great costs by removing political judgment from the conduct of public affairs.

To those who support the trend, courts that make policy are "doing good when politicians have failed us"; to critics of the trend, court-made policies are inherently bad because they are made by unelected decision-makers. A more dispassionate label has been supplied by Robert Kagan: "adversarial legalism." Americans are much more likely than people in other democratic nations to take matters to court—with results that are more punitive, more expensive, and more unpredictable.[24]

Consider the new system of "regulation by litigation" (the phrase is Robert Reich's).[25] In the 1970s and 1980s, Congress deregulated market entry and price-setting in such industries as transportation, financial services, and telecommunications.[26] At the same time, Congress sharply increased governmental regulation of many nonprice aspects of the economy, including occupational health, auto safety, water and air quality, and consumer products. In earlier eras, the administration of new regulations would ordinarily have enjoyed judicial deference. Bureaucrats would have been allowed to act within the framework of their statutory authority, with minimum oversight from the courts. Certainly the courts would not have intervened to create new policies on matters Congress had not addressed.

That was the old system. Under the new system, the courts now often tell administrators what to do—and, if statutes are silent on a subject, invent new policies. The reach of the Clean Air Act of 1970, for instance, has been powerfully shaped by court decisions that told the Environmental Protection Agency (EPA) to prevent the "significant deterioration" of air quality in areas that already met federal air standards, to devise transportation-control plans for cities with high levels of smog, to create new control programs for various chemicals, and to refrain from considering economic and technological feasibility in setting standards.[27]

Judges, to be sure, do not bound into the fray on their own; litigants set the courts in motion. And certain forms of litigation have especially far-reaching implications. Class-action suits, for example, affect what products may be sold under which conditions. Class actions were brought to remove asbestos from buildings, compensate women for the supposed ill effects of breast implants, impose new taxes on tobacco and regulate tobacco advertisements, ban the sale of exterior auto parts not made by the car's manufacturer, and hold gun manufacturers responsible for distributing their products in ways that made them more available to criminals.[28]

The courts obviously have an important role to play in curbing bureaucratic misrule and enforcing civil rights and liberties. But few can deny that, over the past forty years, judges at all levels of government in this country have increasingly assumed new responsibilities in the realms of making policy and managing public administration. Sometimes the new activities of federal and state courts help the plaintiffs—but sometimes, to the plaintiff's surprise, they render their interests harder to serve; and sometimes the legal outcomes simply transfer wealth from one group (say, cigarette manufacturers) to others (state governments and trial lawyers).

The Master Settlement Agreement (MSA) that, in 1998, ended a legal struggle between tobacco companies and state attorneys general reveals how different a court-imposed solution is from a legislatively designed one. Instead of restricting tobacco sales, the MSA required tobacco companies to pay well over $200 billion to the states—money that would have to come from further sales of tobacco. (A cartoon by Jeff McNelly makes the implications clear: Beside a roadway sign saying, "Caution: Highway Construction," there is another saying, "Thank You for Smoking.") Instead of allowing new firms to enter the industry, the MSA went a long way toward transforming the four largest firms into a permanent cartel. Instead of allowing tobacco firms to lobby the government, it disbanded the industry's chief lobbying organization and barred lobbying, even by the firms themselves, in state and local legislative venues. It did little to restrict the sale of cigarettes to minors. And it allowed private attorneys to collect immense fees for having helped to draft the settlement.

As Martha Derthick has shown, federal legislation would have had a different focus: the bills that had been debated before the MSA was agreed to would have restricted sales to youth, authorized the Food and Drug Administration to regulate tobacco products, and would not have sent billions of dollars to a few tort lawyers. The bills did not pass, however, in large measure because they had insufficient public support. So the anti-tobacco crusade moved on to a different set of institutions, the plaintiffs' bar and the courts, where public opinion counts for much less.[29]

I do not wish to argue the merits of these new court-fashioned responsibilities, only to highlight how much they have changed how we are governed. More and more of our policymaking has been shifted to democratically unaccountable bodies. Legislatures often make mistakes or act too slowly, but they have three virtues: they gather facts from a wide variety of sources, make laws prospectively rather than retrospectively, and are constrained by the public's sentiments. Courts often act wisely and humanely, but they also have three defects: they gather facts narrowly, often only from the parties to a suit; they often act retrospectively, punishing behavior that was legal at the time it occurred; and they are less accountable to the public than elected bodies.[30]

Moreover, the rise in class-action suits has greatly enhanced the financial prospects of both plaintiffs and their lawyers, and many in the legal profession value not just the public interest they think they are serving but the money to be made from their service. Although class actions were traditionally tried in federal courts under carefully formulated rules and precedents, many such suits have, of late, been brought in state courts, where there are few rules or precedents. In 2001 Microsoft faced 118 class-action suits; in that same year, State Farm Insurance faced 139, only 9 of which were brought in federal court.

A recent study recounted the growth of national class-action litigation in three counties, two of which are so small, and include such tiny cities, that were it not for the extraordinary amount of legal wrangling going on, no one would notice them. Madison County, Illinois (population about 250,000), in a recent year had more class actions each year than any U.S. county save Cook County, Illinois, and Los Angeles County, California. In 2000, thirty-nine class action suits were filed in Madison County; two years earlier, the judges there had handled only two. The great majority were filed on behalf of national classes, even though none of the defendant companies and few of the plaintiff's law firms were based in that jurisdiction. The same five firms filed nearly half the cases.[31]

Of course, class-action suits often admirably serve the interests of seriously aggrieved clients who have similar problems. The beginning of the end of de jure racial segregation in the schools was a class-action case, *Brown v. Board of Education*. When such cases begin in state courts, however, forum-shopping often seems to be the motivating factor. In the case of Madison County, the abrupt increase in class-action suits did not come about because the area is populous, because large corporations are headquartered there, or because it is the locale of especially grievous injuries. Rather, it occurred because Madison County judges are known to be friendly to trial lawyers. Shifting such suits to federal court, moreover, would not be a cost-free reform; it would further encumber the already overtaxed national judiciary. But whatever the pros and cons of such a shift, Congress has considered it so far with little effect.[32] Any significant change in the current rules of the game will not be made easily, as long as trial lawyers remain a major source of campaign donations to members of Congress.

Of late the Supreme Court has been limiting, to some extent, congressional encroachment on the sovereignty of state governments. This development stems from a keen interest, at least among five justices on the high court, in restoring what they see as an appropriate division of labor between the federal government and the states. In one case, the Court said that Congress could not prohibit guns from being carried near schools, in another that Congress could not require local law enforcement agencies to conduct background checks on gun purchasers, and in yet another that women could not bring suit in federal court against people who had committed violence against them. In all these cases, the view of the majority on the Court was that the Constitution did not give Congress the authority, under the interstate commerce clause, to enact laws that were designed to address truly local matters.[33]

The Supreme Court has also placed some new limits on the freewheeling practices of American civil litigation, in part by limiting the kinds of "scientific" evidence that can be introduced in civil suits. According to a 1923 decision by a federal appellate court, a person could qualify as an expert if his or her expertise had survived the test of "general acceptance in the particular field in which it belongs."[34] This "rule," if that is what it could be called, allowed almost anyone with a college degree or a professional credential to be an expert—and, of course, the lawyers for both plaintiffs and defendants became skilled at hiring sympathetic experts. As a result, the application of questionable science in court proceedings proliferated. Moreover, until 1993, federal courts could weigh expert testimony if the experts (defined as anyone qualified by "knowledge, skill, experience, training, or education") were allowed to testify—which they were, if the judge believed that in some sense the experts' opinion would help the court reach a more informed verdict. This was too loose a standard.

In 1993, in an effort to constrain the use of expert testimony, the Supreme Court held that a judge could allow a person to testify as an expert only if his or her claims met genuine scientific standards. Had the claims withstood falsification? Did they have a low error rate? Had the underlying argument been published in a scientific journal?[35] The higher bar is an important improvement, but it still leaves the trial judge free to apply the criteria as he or she sees fit, subject only to appellate review.

And the new rules cover only cases that actually go to trial. The chief risk of a class-action suit is the cost of a trial and the defendant's uncertainty about the jury's verdict. Since, to forestall potentially heavy losses, many corporate defendants decide to reach a settlement rather than go to trial, tougher rules about expert testimony are only a small step forward.

Because, as noted earlier, court-made policies tend to be viewed as being based on rights, they become the basis for the kinds of broad social claims that, increasingly, lead people to choose sides. However meritorious in individual cases, "self-evident" claims about rights and principles can make political discourse and congressional politics more divisive. There are important exceptions, to be sure, but they tend to be those on which the nation has at long last reached consensus on just—as distinct from controversial—claims. For the most part, basic justice for African Americans, for example, has attained that consensual status.

Another consequence of our courts' heightened involvement in policy is that judicial nominations have become divisive events in themselves. With so much at stake in judicial decisions, who the judges are has assumed great importance. In 1967 Thurgood Marshall, certainly a controversial nominee to the Supreme Court, was questioned by the Senate Judiciary Committee for eleven hours, and only one representative of an interest group made an appearance. But in 1987 Robert Bork was subjected to thirty hours of questioning stretched over nearly a week; his hearings lasted twelve days and included eighty-seven hours of testimony from eighty-six representatives of interest groups.[36]

Amassing the Power to Govern

The expansion of government intervention within a constitutional system makes it difficult to enact a comprehensive and "rational" set of policies. It also makes politics more demanding. The more the government does, the greater the stakes of public office and the harder politicians have to work to stay on the job. Sidney Blumenthal, in a 1982 book, said that Washington politicians were involved in a "permanent campaign," an endless process of image-making and strategic calculation that "remakes government into an instrument designed to sustain an elected official's popularity."[37] During the administration of President Clinton (for which Blumenthal would later work), polls were taken almost daily to find out what the voters thought and to what appeals they would respond. This tactic neither began nor ended with Clinton, however. It first appeared in the mid-twentieth century, was put to more frequent use during the Nixon administration, and burgeoned dramatically during the Reagan and Clinton years. Almost everything that presidents or senators do is designed to secure their tenure, and hence is staged with an eye to public opinion.

Some of this, as Nivola argues in chapter 14, can be attributed to the skilled salesmanship of opinion pollsters, some to the weaknesses of party organizations among the voters, and some to the influence of television. But these contributing factors, though important, may be less fundamental than the sheer volume of issues with which government deals. With so many of them in play and so many interest groups mobilized on both sides of every question—yet without any assured, parliamentary-style governing majority in the legislature to readily dispatch decisions—political leaders must scramble each day to assemble the political resources they need to govern.

Creating those resources means getting voters, especially the attentive and activist ones, on your side. It means posing in newsworthy places, framing the right choices, choosing the right rhetoric, and finding the right sound bites to convey that you've got the matter under control. No one did this better than Ronald Reagan and Bill Clinton.[38] But because the most dependable voters are divided between liberals and conservatives, keeping one step ahead of the opposition isn't easy, even for such masters as Reagan and Clinton.

Needless to say, not all voters are Democratic or Republican partisans. Many have never acquired or have lost interest in politics, or have turned to third parties. Public trust in government seems to have declined precipitously since the late 1950s, especially among voters in the middle of the ideological spectrum.[39] Far fewer Americans today than half a century ago say that they can trust the government in Washington to do the right thing, avoid wasting money, and be in the hands of honest men and women, instead of a few special interests. There was a blip in public confidence in the federal government right after September 11, 2001, but that surge now seems to have been temporary.

Just why the loss of trust occurred is a matter of much debate, especially since it was not limited to government but affected many other institutions, including corporations, universities, the media, and labor unions.[40] And though people are less confident about the integrity of many organizations, they still like the country as a whole, the freedoms it protects, their local institutions (neighborhood schools and the companies for which they work), and the public officials closest to them (their own representatives in Congress, for instance).

Perhaps what really needs to be explained is why confidence was so high decades ago. If more people felt confident about our national authorities in Eisenhower's day, perhaps that feeling had something to do with the fact that the country had recently won a war against Nazi Germany and militaristic Japan, was standing up firmly to the threat of the Soviet Union, and possessed a currency that was the unchallenged standard of value in the world. Beyond that, the national government did less then to affect the ordinary lives of citizens than it does now. Our public officials may have been held in higher esteem simply because less was expected of them.

Whatever the reasons for the decline of trust, for a long time scholars could find no evidence that the change was of any practical consequence. The extent of political participation is by no means a simple function of trust, and in any case the lack of trust had no clear impact on who won elections. But today we have good reason to think that diminished trust does indeed make a difference, especially for the support garnered by third-party candidates. George Wallace in 1968 got a lot of his votes from the most distrustful portion of the electorate; Ross Perot in 1992 got his votes from the same source. Recent research has confirmed that when there are only two presidential candidates, distrustful voters choose whoever does not represent the incumbent party—and in a three-candidate race, tend to vote for the third-party candidate.[41]

Public Policies and the Constitution

Some will say that Americans distrust their central government because, under the restrictions imposed by an eighteenth-century constitution, the system cannot simultaneously respond to a wide range of demands and act in a rational and coordinated fashion. The Constitution, after all, requires a separation of power, prevents a governing majority from being easily formed, and thus frustrates clear leadership. If only the government could "act," the argument goes, it could regain public confidence—simply by putting an end to the complaint that elected officials do little but quarrel, "without getting anything done."

The argument has its flaws. In many countries with parliamentary regimes, not only in the United States with its presidential democracy, trust in public institutions has diminished.[42] The frequently divided U.S. government, moreover, manages to produce a lot of public policy: it is, in other words, often quite capable of action, though whether many of its actions have been timely enough, or worthwhile, are questions about which honest people may differ.

We have become less trusting for many reasons, most of which are not well understood. Among them are an increasing dislike of authority of almost any kind, exaggerated expectations about what government ought to (and can) do for society, and the mass media's propensity to dramatize daily the government's failure to do all that is expected of it.

Whether one likes our constitutional system or prefers a European model is very much a matter of personal conviction. I happen to be fond of what we have here, for it is an arrangement that largely avoids sudden, ill-considered changes; keeps the tax rate relatively low; and still encourages market and voluntary efforts to address most human needs. This is not to say that no refinements are warranted, though I leave it to other essays in this book to suggest what those might be. The main trouble with our system, in my view, is not that it acts slowly and after many compromises, but that it cannot readily cope with all that it is asked to act upon, and that it sometimes relies too much on politically unaccountable bodies, such as the courts, to make political decisions.

Still, in a serious crisis, the political process in this county can and does respond effectively. It did so in the days after the bombardment of Fort Sumter, the attack on Pearl Harbor, and the terrorist strikes on the World Trade Center and the Pentagon. Politics tends to be what happens between great crises. Although I prefer politics to crises, the crises remind us that the American system of government remains resilient.

Notes

1. I take this example from my essay "Can the Bureaucracy Be Deregulated?" in John J. DiIulio Jr., ed., *Deregulating the Public Service* (Brookings, 1994), pp. 42–44.

2. This was the phrase I coined in another essay, "New Politics, New Elites, Old

Publics," in Marc K. Landy and Martin A. Levin, eds., *The New Politics of Public Policy* (Johns Hopkins University Press, 1995), pp. 249–67.

3. Marc K. Landy and Martin A. Levin, "The New Politics of Public Policy," in Landy and Levin, *New Politics,* p. 294.

4. Hedrick Smith, *The Power Game: How Washington Works* (Ballantine, 1988), pp. 24, 29–30.

5. Harold W. Stanley and Richard G. Niemi, *Vital Statistics on American Politics 1999–2000* (Washington: CQ Press, 2000), p. 211.

6. Gary C. Jacobson, "The Electoral Basis of Partisan Polarization in Congress," paper presented at the annual meeting of the American Political Science Association, Washington, D.C., August 31–September 3, 2000, pp. 1–2.

7. Stanley and Niemi, *Vital Statistics,* p. 212.

8. Barbara Sinclair, "The New World of U.S. Senators," in Lawrence C. Dodd and Bruce I. Oppenheimer, eds., *Congress Reconsidered,* 7th ed. (Washington: CQ Press, 2001), pp. 1–19.

9. See, for example, Gallup Poll, March 30, 2000, and ABC News/Beliefnet Poll, June 20, 2001.

10. Jacobson, "Partisan Polarization," pp. 3–6.

11. Larry M. Bartels, "Partisanship and Voting Behavior, 1952–1996," *American Journal of Political Science,* vol. 44, no. 1 (2000), pp. 35–50.

12. Marc J. Hetherington, "Resurgent Mass Partisanship: The Role of Elite Polarization," *American Political Science Review,* vol. 95, no. 3 (2001), pp. 619–31.

13. Melissa P. Collie and John Lyman Mason, "The Electoral Connection between Party and Constituency Reconsidered: Evidence from the U.S. House of Representatives, 1972–1994," in David W. Brady, John F. Cogan, and Morris P. Fiorina, eds., *Continuity and Change in House Elections* (Palo Alto, Calif.: Stanford University, Hoover Institution, 2000), p. 233.

14. Ibid., p. 220.

15. Ibid., p. 223.

16. Jacobson, "Partisan Polarization," p. 2.

17. David Brady and Edward P. Schwartz, "Ideology and Interests in Congressional Voting: The Politics of Abortion in the U. S. Senate," *Public Choice,* vol. 84 (1995), pp. 25–48.

18. Jacobson, "Partisan Polarization," p. 4.

19. Greg D. Adams, "Abortion: Evidence of an Issue Evolution," *American Journal of Political Science,* vol. 41, no. 3 (1997), pp. 718–37; Brady and Schwartz, "Ideology and Interests."

20. Charlie Cook, "Safe Seats Stunting Skills of Lawmakers," *National Journal,* December 1, 2001, p. 3704.

21. Ibid.

22. For a review of these rules, see James Q. Wilson, "On Abortion," *Commentary,* January 1994; and Mary Ann Glendon, *Abortion and Divorce in Western Law* (Harvard University Press, 1987).

23. George Liebmann, "Curb Judges and Restore Politics," *American Enterprise,* (October/November 2001), pp. 48–49.

24. Robert A. Kagan, "The Consequences of Adversarial Legalism," in Robert A. Kagan and Lee Axelrad, eds., *Regulatory Encounters* (University of California Press, 2000), pp. 372–413.

25. Reich is quoted in Victor E. Schwartz and Leah Lorber, "*State Farm* v. *Avery:* State Court Regulation through Litigation Has Gone Too Far," *Connecticut Law Review*, vol. 13, no. 4 (2001), pp. 1215–37.

26. For a superb study of these changes, see Martha Derthick and Paul J. Quirk, *The Politics of Deregulation* (Brookings, 1985).

27. R. Shep Melnick, *Regulation and the Courts* (Brookings, 1983), especially pp. 1–2, 264.

28. Let me confess to a bias on this matter. I am a director of State Farm Insurance, which lost a class-action suit in Illinois and is now prohibited from allowing parts, other than those made by the original manufacturer, to be used to fix damaged bumpers, fenders, and hoods on cars—even though the nonoriginal parts are just as good and much cheaper. The company's position was also taken by certain groups aligned with Ralph Nader, so I don't feel that my views endorse capitalist exploitation.

29. See the splendid analysis in Martha A. Derthick, *Up in Smoke: From Legislation to Litigation in Tobacco Politics* (Washington: CQ Press, 2002).

30. Schwartz and Lorber, "*State Farm* v. *Avery.*"

31. John H. Beisner and Jessica Davidson Miller, "They're Making a Federal Case out of It . . . in State Court," *Civil Justice Report of the Manhattan Institute of New York City* (September 2001).

32. This is not simply a reactionary complaint; see the editorial in the liberal *Washington Post*, August 27, 2001, p. A14.

33. *United States* v. *Lopez*, 514 U.S. 549 (1995); *Printz* v. *United States*, 117 S. Ct. 2365 (1997); *United States* v. *Morrison*, 2000 Lexis 3422 (2000). See the discussion of some of these cases and others in Michael Greve, *Real Federalism* (Washington: American Enterprise Institute Press, 1999).

34. *Frye* v. *United States*, 293 F. 1013 (D.C. Cir. 1923), and Federal Rules of Evidence, sec. 702.

35. *Daubert* v. *Merrell Dow Pharmaceuticals*, 509 U.S. 579, 595 (1993). This decision overturned the old *Frye* rule.

36. Robert A. Katzmann, "Comments on the Judicial Connection," in Paul S. Herrnson, Ronald G. Shaiko, and Clyde Wilcox, eds., *The Interest Group Connection* (Chatham, N.J.: Chatham House, 1998), p. 322.

37. Sidney Blumenthal, *The Permanent Campaign* (Simon & Schuster, 1982), p. 23. For an insightful history of this idea, see Hugh Heclo, "Campaigning and Governing: A Conspectus," in Norman Ornstein and Thomas Mann, eds., *The Permanent Campaign and Its Future* (Washington: American Enterprise Institute Press, 2000), pp. 1–37.

38. With one difference. In my opinion Reagan said what he believed, whereas Clinton believed what he said.

39. David C. King, "The Polarization of American Parties and Mistrust of Government," in Joseph Nye, Philip D. Zelikow, and David C. King, eds., *Why People Don't Trust Government* (Harvard University Press, 1997), pp. 155–78.

40. On this and related matters, see Nye, Zelikow, and King, *Why People Don't Trust Government*, especially pp. 1–2.

41. Marc J. Hetherington, "The Effect of Political Trust on the Presidential Vote, 1968–1996," *American Political Science Review*, vol. 93, no. 2 (1999), pp. 311–26.

42. See Ronald Inglehart, "Postmaterialist Values and the Erosion of Institutional Authority," in Nye, Zelikow, and King, *Why People Don't Trust Government*, pp. 217–36.

Contributors

HENRY J. AARON
Brookings Institution

ALAN J. AUERBACH
University of California–Berkeley

LAEL BRAINARD
Brookings Institution

GARY BURTLESS
Brookings Institution

IVO H. DAALDER
Brookings Institution

J. BRADFORD DELONG
University of California–Berkeley

VICTOR R. FUCHS
National Bureau of Economic Research

WILLIAM G. GALE
Brookings Institution

ALAN M. GARBER
Stanford University

CLAUDIA GOLDIN
Harvard University

HOWARD GRUENSPECHT
Department of Energy

CHRISTOPHER JENCKS
Harvard University

LAWRENCE F. KATZ
Harvard University

JAMES M. LINDSAY
Brookings Institution

ROBERT LITAN
Brookings Institution

PIETRO S. NIVOLA
Brookings Institution

MICHAEL O'HANLON
Brookings Institution

PETER R. ORSZAG
Brookings Institution

PAUL R. PORTNEY
Resources for the Future

SAMARA R. POTTER
University of Michigan

STEVEN SIMON
RAND

AUDREY SINGER
Brookings Institution

STUART TAYLOR
National Journal

JAMES Q. WILSON
University of California–Los Angeles

Index

Taiwan: international trade, 355; relations with U.S., 291; U.S. defense of, 382, 388–89; U.S. aid to, 330

Taxation: alternative minimum tax, 118, 120; early withdrawals from pension or tax-sheltered plans, 186–87; effect of cuts on economic growth, 44, 111–12, 130; effect of different rates on investments, 43; effect of high rates on labor utilization, 82–83; equipment investment credit, 43; expiration dates for certain provisions, 118–19, 132–33; and income inequality, 73; increase needed to cover federal spending, 111; international comparison, 78; Joint Committee on Taxation scores for legislation, 136–37; R&D subsidies, 46; saving incentives, 42, 192

Tax-preferred savings for retirement. *See* Pensions and tax-preferred savings

Tax Reform Act of *1986*, 43

Technology: demand for educated work force, 27; demand for highly skilled workers, 71; and immigration screening, 417; investment in, 44–46; military technology, 390–92

Television: campaign use, 514; journalism, 503–04

Temple Mount: proposed attack on, 405

Tenet, George, 419

Terrorism, 12–13, 403–30; civilian targets, 416; events before September *11*, 486–87, 495; and international trade, 347; and Israeli-Palestinian conflict, 421–22; and jihad, 407–08, 413; Middle

East terrorists, 410; religious motivation, 12, 403–06; rogue regimes, 321, 487; Salafi clerics' influence, 413; weapons of, 297. *See also* Al Qaeda; Counterterrorism; September *11* attacks; Weapons of mass destruction

Terrorism Prevention Act, 459–561

Textiles and apparel trade, 316, 350, 352

Thaler, Richard, 202

Theory of Justice, A (Rawls), 99

Third party: effect in U.S. politics, 513, 546

Thune, John, 513

Tobacco litigation: Master Settlement Agreement (MSA), 541–42

Torture: use in questioning detainees, 453–54

Trade, international, 9–10, 345–57; African-produced clothing, 316, 350; agriculture, 350–51; bilateral agreements, 346, 352–55; Caribbean Basin rollback, 348; and counterterrorism, 347; domestic adjustment to, 356–57; free-trade agreements, 353–55; free-trade policies, 318; and globalization, 296; history, 345–46; liberalization benefits, 349–50; presidential trade promotion authority, 347; protectionist measures of Bush administration, 316, 348, 509, 510; recession and, 347; trade adjustment assistance, 356; and wage inequality, 71; and weapons of mass destruction, 417. *See also* World Trade Organization

Training. *See* Education and training

Transportation, Department of, 7, 262, 265, 528

Treasury Department, 7, 262